GUIDE TO BISHOPS' REGISTERS OF ENGLAND AND WALES

A Survey from the Middle Ages to the Abolition of Episcopacy in 1646

DAVID M. SMITH

Director, Borthwick Institute,
University of York

LONDON
OFFICES OF THE ROYAL HISTORICAL SOCIETY
UNIVERSITY COLLEGE LONDON, GOWER STREET
LONDON WC1E 6BT
1981

To C. A. J. R.

ISBN 0 901050 72 5

Printed in Great Britain by Butler & Tanner Ltd
Frome and London

CONTENTS

ACKNOWLEDGEMENTS

On the last folio of a vast register of a late thirteenth-century bishop of Lincoln a clerk of the sixteenth century, no doubt at the completion of a time-consuming search of the volume for a particular piece of information, has written *Finit liber faeliciter!* A similar sentiment is in my own mind as I write this prefatory note. It was in the autumn of 1973 that Mrs Norah Gurney, my predecessor as Director of the Borthwick Institute at York, suggested that I might like to undertake this guide. She had intended to compile a guide herself and had in fact been invited to do so by the Royal Historical Society, but sadly ill-health prevented her starting the work and upon her tragically early death in February 1974 the Society asked if I would be willing to carry out her original intention. In the six or so years it has taken to complete the guide, I have accumulated many obligations to the archivists and librarians throughout the country who have, without exception, helpfully and courteously assisted my researches and answered my many questions. Many friends, strategically placed at or near diocesan centres, have generously provided me with hospitality on my travels. Obviously in the time permitted I have not been able to study each register in the same detail as someone who is working on a single volume for publication or a research degree and clearly there will be many errors and omissions. New information and amendments will always be gratefully received. Already I owe a great debt of gratitude to many scholars, notably Miss Melanie Barber, Dr Janet Burton, Professor C. R. Cheney, Mrs Jayne Cook, Miss Judith Cripps, Professor R. B. Dobson, Dr R Dunning, Mrs Audrey Erskine, Professor Joan Greatrex, Mr G. M. Griffiths, Dr C. Harper-Bill, Mrs Joyce Horn, Dr C. Kitching, Miss Kathleen Major, Mrs Dorothy Owen, Mr M. Snape, Mrs Joan Varley, and Canon D. Walker, who have kindly answered specific enquiries or assisted with information. I am also very grateful to my colleague, Dr W. J. Sheils, who has read and commented on many sections of the text. Finally, thanks must be expressed to those friends from whom I have received welcome encouragement at times when the task seemed never-ending and who have been content to hear about bishops' registers to a degree far beyond the calls of friendship.

DAVID M. SMITH

PREFACE

When R. C. Fowler published his pamphlet on *Episcopal Registers of England and Wales* in 1918, he could state with justification that the number of scholars and historians who had systematically studied the registers of English bishops was not very great. It can scarcely be claimed that this state of affairs still exists. Thanks to the efforts of the Canterbury and York Society and certain county record societies, the number of available editions of bishops' registers has been considerably increased since the time Fowler was writing—indeed the only medieval diocese still not represented in print is Norwich—and in addition a few studies on more general aspects of episcopal registration have been published.[1] The aim of the present guide is to describe all existing bishops' registers in the ecclesiastical provinces of Canterbury and York from the beginnings of registration in the early thirteenth century up to the abolition of episcopacy in 1646. As certain bishops continued to administer their dioceses after 1646, the final volume described in each diocesan series will often include acts after this date and may even on occasion contain a record of business from after the Restoration of 1660.

The keeping of bishops' registers is very much a phenomenon of the thirteenth century. The available evidence indicates that by the last decade of that century all English dioceses save one had begun formal registration of ecclesiastical business.[2] Apart from the sees of Lincoln and York, where registration of acts is found from *c.* 1214 × 1217 and 1225 respectively, all evidence for the keeping of registers in other bishoprics dates from the second half of the century[3]—Coventry and Lichfield, Exeter and Rochester in the 1250s, Bath and Wells, Norwich, Winchester and Worcester in the 1260s, Canterbury, Hereford and Salisbury in the 1270s and Carlisle, Chichester, Durham and London in the 1280s. Of the four Welsh dioceses, the earliest registers survive from the late fourteenth century, and the general evidence for formal registration is more difficult to come by, since the surviving records are so meagre and fragmentary.

Although the total number of episcopal registers still in existence cannot fail to be impressive, there have of course been serious losses throughout the entire period under consideration. Careless storage, political and religious strife, and natural disasters have all been contributive factors. It is perhaps salutary to note that as far as we can discover at present, the earliest known registers of at least twelve dioceses have all disappeared.[4] References to these lost registers are often to be found in later volumes of the same diocese, or among the compilations of antiquaries such as Matthew Hutton, Thomas Baker, Andrew Ducarel, Christopher

[1] See C. R. Cheney, *English Bishops' Chanceries 1100–1250* (Manchester, 1950), especially pp. 100–10; M. T. Clanchy, *From Memory to Written Record: England 1066–1307* (London, 1979), pp. 53–5; D. M. Owen, *The Records of the Established Church in England, excluding parochial records* (British Records Association, Archives and the User 1, London, 1970), pp. 15–17; and also an article by C. Jenkins, 'Some thirteenth-century registers', *Church Quarterly Review* xcix (1924), 69–115. Articles and studies of individual registers are noted under the appropriate diocese in the guide. For an article on a specific aspect of registers see H. S. Bennett, 'Medieval Ordination Lists in the English Episcopal Registers', *Studies presented to Sir Hilary Jenkinson*, ed. J. Conway Davies (Oxford, 1957), pp. 20–34. For lists of Dominicans ordained by English bishops, see *A Survey of Dominicans in England, based on the ordination lists in episcopal registers (1268 to 1538)*, ed. A. B. Emden (Rome, 1967). The late Dr Emden's lists of some other ordinands etc. taken from bishops' registers are now deposited in the Bodleian Library, Oxford. C. J. Offer, *The Bishop's Register* (London, 1929) prints translations of selected entries from medieval registers. Bibliographical lists of printed registers have been compiled by L. A. Haselmayer, *Medieval English Episcopal Registers* (Church Historical Society, London, 1938), and A. D. Frankforter, 'The Episcopal Registers of Medieval England: an inventory', *British Studies Monitor* vi (1976), 3–22.

[2] The exception is Ely, where no evidence has so far been found of a register earlier than John Hotham's (1316–37), but of course this need not signify that earlier registers could not have been kept.

[3] For details of these registers see under the relevant diocesan section in the guide. Where the earliest evidence of registration is a reference to a lost register, the beginning of the particular bishop's episcopate has been taken as the starting point of registration.

[4] For a list of lost registers see C. R. Cheney, *op. cit.* app. ii, pp. 147–9. This list has occasionally been supplemented by new evidence, particularly from the royal writs of *cerciorari* (see below). Lost registers are recorded in the bibliographical note in each diocesan section. For the attitude of bishops' executors to the registers (perhaps another contributive factor) see *English Bishops' Chanceries*, p. 147; *Register of Henry Chichele* iii, pp. 427–31.

Hunter, Edward Yardley and James Torre, whose abstracts occasionally remain the only evidence for the existence of a particular register. It is indeed fortunate that later bishops often had occasion to inspect the registers of predecessors in the case of a dispute or to verify rights or claims, but another useful source for tracing the existence of registers which have long since disappeared is the series of royal writs of *cerciorari* (ecclesiastical) and their returns among the Chancery files (Tower and Rolls Chapel) in the Public Record Office (C269). These writs (many of which concern cases involving patronage rights in parochial benefices) are chiefly addressed to bishops and often require the recipient to inspect and certify entries in his own or his predecessors' registers. In these ways it is possible to gain a clearer idea of some of the losses which have occurred.

I have already briefly referred to the enrolments of Hugh of Wells, bishop of Lincoln (1209–35) and Walter de Gray, archbishop of York (1215–55): whether they were the first as well as the earliest extant attempts at formal episcopal registration is obviously impossible to determine. Certainly we should not expect episcopal registration much earlier, considering that registration in the royal and papal chanceries was only just beginning in the late twelfth and early thirteenth centuries. Taking into account the prevailing circumstances and the precedent of royal registration, Professor Cheney has argued that they probably were,[5] and I have no reason to disagree with his judgement. Both Bishop Hugh and Archbishop Walter had held high office in King John's chancery and were familiar with the registrational innovations of Archbishop Hubert Walter when chancellor. It was understandable that they should draw upon their previous administrative experience after they were raised to the ranks of the episcopate. At the same time it must be remembered that any new development is not entirely isolated and it is feasible (although there is no evidence) that other bishops may have experimented with a system of record-keeping shortly before the formal registration of acts occurred at Lincoln and York. We already know that some bishops kept a *matricula* or *scrutinium*, that is to say, a systematic survey of churches in the diocese providing information on incumbents, patrons, values and so on. References exist to such records being kept at Lincoln, London, Norwich, Salisbury and Worcester, the earliest being from the twelfth century.[6] Unfortunately, the episcopal scribes used the word *matricula* as a very general term for any formal record, as I have shown elsewhere,[7] and any attempt to trace the early history of ecclesiastical registration is bedevilled by the imprecision of terminology. Examples of its usage have been found in the thirteenth-century Lincoln records, merely denoting the institution rolls of successive bishops. Another, more intriguing, example of its use is to be found in the institution register of Bishop John Dalderby of Lincoln (1300–20).[8] In the specific entry, Dalderby inspects four documents, *examinatis matriculis predecessorum nostrorum episcoporum Lincolniensium que in ecclesia nostra Lincolniensi ad perpetuam rerum gestarum memoriam reponuntur*. The documents in question are two letters of presentation by the prior and convent of Spalding to the Lincolnshire church of Surfleet and the two corresponding letters of institution issued by Dalderby's predecessors, William of Blois (1203–6) and Hugh of Wells (1209–35). What the *matricule* are in this case is puzzling. They cannot be *matricule* in the technical sense, since these surveys contain brief details of benefices, not transcripts of entire documents. The wording also rules out original documents (in any case original letters of institution would not have survived among the episcopal archives). On the other hand, it is unusual, although not actually impossible (Salisbury and Carlisle provide examples), that letters of presentation as well as letters of institution were entered in a formal register. If the Hugh of Wells' entries had survived in isolation, it might have been presumed that they were taken from his Lincoln archdeaconry charter roll, which the bishop is known to have kept but which is now lost. Yet, the mention of Hugh's predecessor raises the question as to whether this can be the case. To admit the former is also to imply registration in the time of William of Blois. Like any isolated piece of evidence referring to material recorded a century before, it is tantalising

[5] Cheney, *op. cit.*, pp. 106–8.
[6] *ibid.*, pp. 110–19.
[7] 'The Rolls of Hugh of Wells, Bishop of Lincoln 1209–35', *Bulletin of the Institute of Historical Research* xlv (1972), 176–7.
[8] Lincolnshire Archives Office, Episcopal Register II, fos. 27*v*–28*r*.

and totally inconclusive as a proof of formal registration in the later accepted sense. It serves only to indicate how precarious our knowledge is of early episcopal administration.

I have tried to indicate in the bibliographical notes prefacing each diocesan section the main features of the series of registers and any significant registrational changes adopted in the course of time. Some dioceses evolved a particular arrangement and adhered to it fairly consistently, others made conscious changes or modifications which seem to be influenced by practices elsewhere, an understandable situation considering the number of bishops translated from one see to another. Certain general trends can perhaps be discerned in all these registers: firstly, a period of experimentation and the gradual evolution of an acceptable system of registration which usually attained its final form in the course of the fourteenth century; and latterly, following the Reformation changes (and as a consequence the disappearance of a vast amount of previously registered business concerning the papacy, religious houses, chantries and oratories, indulgences, dispensations and so forth) a simplification in arrangement often tending towards a single, chronologically arranged, general register, with perhaps ordinations still kept separately. But this is mere generalisation and like all generalisations is hedged in with many caveats. Individual circumstances often played an important part: at York, for instance, in the sixteenth century, the registrar and his clerks got so far behind in entering acts in the episcopal registers that the contemporaneous 'rough' notebooks in which they briefly noted diocesan business before formal registration gradually grew into a separate series of diocesan institution act books and in the end superseded the registers.[9] An additional factor which must also be taken into account was the growing departmentalism in matters of church government leading to the creation of additional series of registers to deal with specific business—court books, visitation books, probate registers and act books, licence books, institution books, ordination registers and so on—and removing the relevant material from the once 'omnibus' general register.

The bishop's register is a deliberately created working record of certain administrative acts of the bishop or his officials and also containing copies of some incoming business. It is a composite record, usually made up of several different sections. As such, it is particularly difficult to define. If pressed, one could with justification claim that the main distinctive feature of an episcopal register—indeed one might call it the 'staple diet'—is the record of institutions of clergy to benefices and related material—the appointment of parish clergy to rectories and vicarages, of chaplains to chantries and hospitals and of higher clergy to dignities and canonries in cathedral and collegiate churches.[10] Coupled with these entries are the exchanges of livings; resignations and occasionally deprivations of incumbents; appointments of coadjutors; inquiries conducted into the causes of vacancies and rights of patronage; and a host of similar business relating to benefices and the parochial clergy. All other categories of business—the ordination of clergy to the three major orders of subdeacon, deacon and priest, the confirmation of the elections of heads of religious houses, the noting of business relating to church fabric and property, visitations, royal and papal letters, indulgences, commissions, licences, dispensations and other memoranda, the records of financial and estate administration and so on—are all found in episcopal registers but not invariably so. It is really only business closely related to the appointment of clergy that is guaranteed a place in these volumes, and it is not hard to see why this should be. The diocesan bishop needed up-to-date information readily available on the incumbents of the parish churches, the patronage of the livings, the duties and responsibilities of the clergy and patrons, the pensions payable, the division of tithes, the provision of services and so forth. The register could provide him with this information.

In format, Bishop Hugh of Lincoln and Archbishop Walter of York followed royal precedents and kept their records in the form of rolls. By 1266 at York and 1290 at Lincoln

[9] D. M. Smith, 'The York institution act books: diocesan registration in the sixteenth century', *Archives* 13 (1977–8), 171–9.

[10] For lists of dignitaries and prebendaries of cathedral churches, see the volumes produced by the Institute of Historical Research, London University in their revision of John Le Neve, *Fasti Ecclesiae Anglicanae*. The period 1300–1541 has been completed (12 vols., 1962–7); three volumes have so far appeared for the 1066–1300 period, and five volumes for the 1541–1857 period. The individual volumes are not cited in the bibliographical notes in the guide.

this method of enrolment had been abandoned in favour of the quire for the general register, although it must be added in qualification that rolls continued to be used by the diocesan clerks for various types of records long after the thirteenth century.[11] While the early enrolments had allowed a certain amount of subdivision—the bishops of Lincoln had institution rolls, charter rolls, vicarage rolls, memoranda rolls etc., all arranged by archdeaconry, and York used the face of the roll for spiritual business and the dorse for temporal matters, they could not have been very easy to consult and the adoption of the book permitted a greater degree of sophistication in sectional arrangement. When the quires were kept separate (and the volume was not usually bound up until the end of the bishop's pontificate), it was a simple matter to create, for ease of reference, a great number of sections, using territorial or category subdivisions: among such might be institutions and collations (in some larger dioceses often arranged by archdeaconry), royal writs, ordinations, archiepiscopal mandates, papal letters, monastic elections and confirmations, visitations, letters dimissory, licences, commissions, testamentary business, inquisitions and general memoranda (sometimes described as *liber memorandorum*, *diverse littere*, *facta diversa*, *littere communes*, *varie littere* and so on). The present guide will indicate the variety of subdivisions that could be employed by the episcopal registrar and his clerks and indeed it is to be expected that there was considerable variation in the keeping of registers. Even allowing for the inevitable losses it is clear that certain diocese registered a great deal more business than others. The episcopal clerks of the large dioceses of Norwich, for instance, were apparently content to keep full records of institutions and ordinations but as for more general memoranda restricted themselves for the most part to selected appropriation deeds, ordinations of vicarages and chantries, unions of benefices, compositions and other material. However, the memoranda sections of registers from some other large dioceses like Lincoln, Exeter and York are much more extensive in scope, and obviously the size of the diocese had little to do with the amount of business registered. In addition, from the fourteenth century onwards, the evolution of the permanent office of vicar-general as the bishop's general administrative deputy and the employment of titular or Irish bishops as suffragans, led to the creation of a separate register of acts of the vicar-general, and a register of acts performed by the bishop when he was outside his diocese (the register *extra diocesim*). Both were normally bound up with the main register. Because of the uncertainty of the length of the bishop's absence or the term of office of the vicar-general (he was appointed during pleasure) no attempt is usually made, apart from ordinations, to divide up the registered business into categories. These two types of registers are almost invariably arranged as one chronological sequence of acts. As for the actual entries in the registers, from the very beginnings of registration in the thirteenth century both full transcripts of documents and precise and comprehensive summaries of acts are found. Again, there seems to have been no hard and fast rule about which form was used for entries: obviously business considered important for various administrative and legal reasons is likely to be transcribed *in extenso*, and routine business such as institutions, grants of licences etc. is more likeley to be summarised by the clerks.

I have so far been referring to registers of diocesan bishops. Of course the archbishops of Canterbury and York, as well as being diocesan bishops, exercised provincial jurisdiction over the suffragan sees in their provinces, and this activity is reflected in their registers—they have sections containing such matters as the confirmation and consecration of bishops, letters to the suffragans, visitation records, and business connected with meetings of Convocation of the Clergy and the raising of ecclesiastical subsidies and taxes, but even more prominent are the records noting the administration of vacant bishoprics by the archiepiscopal officials. In most cases in the middle ages the exercise of jurisdiction in vacant dioceses was regulated

[11] For example, at York, the 1311 Durham visitation rolls of Archbishop Greenfield (1306–15) still survive and references have been found to a roll of ordinations of Archbishop Melton (1317–40) and a visitation roll of Archbishop Neville (1374–88), *Borthwick Institute Bulletin* 1 (1975–8), 34–5. Rolls recording visitations of York Minister *c.* 1509 and Southwell collegiate church in the early fifteenth century also survive among the archives at the Borthwick Institute, York (D/C. VP; MD. 26). As M. T. Clanchy, *op. cit.*, p. 54 has pointed out, the English bishops began by imitating the English royal chancery (rolls) and only later brought their records into line with papal and European episcopal practice (books).

by formal agreements and compositions.[12] In general the archbishops of the respective provinces exercised this right of vacancy administration and a careful record was kept of all acts performed during the vacancies. These registers are frequently duplicated—a 'fair' copy being made of the 'working' quires—and are found in both the archiepiscopal archives and among the records of the appropriate see. Such duplication is of course understandable since the information was required by both parties—by the archbishop for the record of his official's administration on his behalf, by the new bishop for information on what had happened during the vacancy.

It has also been claimed that bishops' registers were at times kept in duplicate, and it is certainly true that occasional duplicates are found—Archbishop Wickwane's York register, for instance—but I believe it would be a misconception to think that these duplicates were kept simultaneously. I would incline to the view, on the evidence I have located, that one was copied (often involving rearrangement of the material) after the first had been completed: in other words there was a 'working' register and a later 'fair' copy.[13]

Finally, having looked at the sort of material likely to be found entered in the registers, it remains to consider what can be found out about methods of registration. How were the registers compiled? From what sources were they registered? How frequently was the selected material entered up? As is to be expected, the registers have revealed no startlingly new information on this subject, but merely have confirmed previous assumptions that there was no hard and fast rule and that while some original documents were probably on occasion copied before despatch, by far the greatest bulk of material was registered from drafts or brief notes of the essential details of each act, or at a later date possibly from 'rough' books.[14] The common form of a great number of administrative entries would be suitable for the employment of such methods, and indeed the ink changes and the often quite wide chronological disorder in the registers would further support the conclusion that registration was periodic rather than immediate.

ARRANGEMENT OF THE GUIDE

The guide is arranged by ecclesiastical province, the archiepiscopal see being placed first and the suffragan dioceses thereafter in alphabetical order. Each diocesan section includes the following:

Repositories: a list of record repositories in which the registers and related material are deposited, with the abbreviations used to denote the individual repositories in the appended descriptive list.

Area: a brief note about the area of the diocese in the period under consideration and its territorial divisions, with references to any published maps and to any changes in boundaries effected before 1646. Obviously it has not proved feasible to go into very precise details over the diocesan boundaries but, where possible, reference is made to published works which provide more detailed information.

Bibliographical Note: a section which includes references to any printed archival guides or handlists and any articles on registration or an individual register, as well as comments upon any significant features or developments in matters of registration. The earliest evidence of episcopal registration in the diocese is noted, as are references to registers which are now no longer extant. Attention is also drawn to any diocesan registry finding-aids, antiquarian compilations, lists and indexes of selected information (e.g. wills, parochial fasti), and to any published works which have made extensive use of the registers.

[12] For vacancy compositions and agreements see I. J. Churchill, *Canterbury Administration* (2 vols, London, 1933), i. pp. 161–240; ii, pp. 41–118; R. Brentano, 'Late medieval changes in the administration of vacant suffragan dioceses: province of York', *Yorkshire Archaeological Journal* 38 (1952–5), 496–503.

[13] In addition to the York evidence (see under York below), see also *Registrum Simonis de Gandavo, diocesis Saresbiriensis A.D. 1297–1315* i, ed. C. T. Flower and M. C. B. Dawes (Canterbury and York Society 40, 1934), p. lv.

[14] See Cheney, *op. cit.*, pp. 103–4; *The Registers of Roger Martival, Bishop of Salisbury, 1315–1330* iv, ed. K. Edwards and D. M. Owen (Canterbury and York Society 68, 1975), pp. xxiii–xxv.

Description of the Registers: The appended lists include both details of the diocesan series of bishops' registers and of the records of *sede vacante* administration taken from the archiepiscopal or capitular registers. Records of archiepiscopal visitations of sees within the province are not noted, but later separate institution books and ordination registers are recorded at the end of the sequence. The arrangement of these handlists is chronological, although there are on occasion inevitable lapses from the correct sequence, dictated by the nature of certain composite volumes. Subsidiary act books (institution books or ordination registers) are generally added at the end of the main series, if their contents extend in date over several episcopates.

The spelling of bishops' names is in accordance with the second edition of the *Handbook of British Chronology* (Royal Historical Society, 1961). At times there may appear to be a discrepancy between the acknowledged dates of a bishop's episcopate or of a vacancy, and the actual duration of the episcopate or vacancy as indicated by the covering dates of the register's contents. In the first instance this usually occurs when a bishop is translated to another see. The provision or nomination did not normally become effective until the restitution of the temporalities of the new see, so that in practice the bishop could continue to administer his old diocese long after being formally translated to another bishopric. The apparent extension of a vacancy into the pontificate of a new bishop can also be explained by the fact that certain post-vacancy acts, such as the acquittance of the custodians of the spiritualities after they had rendered an account, are often entered at the end of the vacancy register.

Each entry gives the name of the repository in which the register is to be found, with the archival location reference (if any), and a brief description of the manuscript—the material, measurements, foliation, and nature of the binding. If the volume has been heavily damaged by damp or rodents or has been extensively repaired, this is noted in the description. The medial size of the folio is approximate to the nearest $\frac{1}{4}''$, but clearly there can be considerable variations within a single volume of ostensibly uniform size and the measurements given should merely be taken as a useful indicator. If the irregularity in size is considerable, this is noted and either an average measurement supplied or else the extreme variants recorded. In cases where the size of constituent quires or gatherings varies considerably this information is noted in the description of the manuscript, together with the number of folios involved. When describing the composition of the volumes, Roman numerals are used to denote end-papers and insertions. Understandably, many of the registers reveal evidence of several numbering sequences over the centuries. While these series can often be useful indications of losses or rearrangement, in all instances the most recent foliation or pagination has been adopted in these lists. Square brackets are occasionally employed in the foliation for the sake of convenience, either distinguishing folios given the same number by the scribe in error (hence the use of [A], [B], etc.), or else indicating that certain folios are not numbered in the original manuscript, but require numbers for the purposes of description. In the case of unpublished registers, blank folios are also noted.

In those instances where the register has already been published, there follows a brief note on the arrangement of the volume and any significant points in matters of registration. When the register has not been edited for publication, the handlist includes an analytical description, indicating, where appropriate, the subdivisions of the register, with the covering dates of each section. Dates have been given in the modern style allowing of course for the pre-1752 practice of starting the new year on March 25 instead of January 1. It should be noted in passing that the covering dates given are of the earliest and latest entries found, *not* the first and last in the section, which is by no means the same thing considering that the arrangement of the registers can often be confused. The entries in any register are never in precise chronological order and even in the best kept registers one should expect occasional discrepancies. Likewise space does not permit a very detailed analysis of each constituent section of a register. Hence, an institutions section could also contain cognate benefice material (collations, resignations, inductions etc.) and there can obviously be discrepancies between the scope and contents of memoranda sections.

Where appropriate, the description concludes with a note drawing attention to the existence of any select indexes, calendars, or transcripts in record repositories or local history libraries, or any significant extracts in print (not every published extract can of course be recorded), or any unpublished editions completed for university theses. Only completed theses are noted and readers should refer to the annual *Historical Research for University Degrees in the United Kingdom: Theses in Progress*, and future *These Completed*, published by the Institute of Historical Research of London University for current work. No attempt has been made to list those monographs and studies of individual bishops or diocesan administration, which although making extensive and general use of the registers do not publish substantial extracts from them.

PRINCIPAL ABBREVIATIONS

A.A.S.R.	*Associated Architectural Societies' Reports and Papers*
Canterbury Administration	I. J. Churchill, *Canterbury Administration* (2 vols., London, 1933)
cent.	century
Davis	G. R. C. Davis, *Medieval Cartularies of Great Britain: a short catalogue* (London, 1958)
English Bishops' Chanceries	C. R. Cheney, *English Bishops' Chanceries 1100–1250* (Manchester, 1950)
Lambeth Institutions	A. Hamilton Thompson, 'Lambeth institutions to benefices, being a calendar of institutions to benefices in the old diocese of Lincoln during vacancies of the episcopal see and during the visitations by the Archbishops of Canterbury as metropolitans, with collations of benefices made by the Archbishops jure devoluto, from the archiepiscopal registers in the Library of Lambeth Palace 1279–1532', *A.A.S.R.* 40 (1930–1), 33–110
n.d.	no date
opp.	opposite
pa.	parish (of)
prob.	probate
Register of Henry Chichele	*The Register of Henry Chichele, Archbishop of Canterbury, 1414–1443*, ed. E. F. Jacob and H. C. Johnson (4 vols., Canterbury and York Society 42, 45–7, 1938–47)
Register of John Pecham	*The Register of John Pecham, Archbishop of Canterbury, 1279–1292*, ed. F. N. Davis and D. L. Douie (2 vols., Canterbury and York Society 64–5, 1908–69)
Registrum Johannis Peckham	*Registrum Epistolarum Fratris Johannis Peckham, Archiepiscopi Cantuariensis*, ed. C. T. Martin (3 vols., Rolls ser., 1882–5)
Registrum Matthei Parker	*Registrum Matthei Parker diocesis Cantuariensis A.D. 1559–1575*, transcribed by E. M. Thompson and ed. W. H. Frere (3 vols., Canterbury and York Society 35–6, 39, 1928–33)
Registrum Roberti Winchelsey	*Registrum Roberti Winchelsey Cantuariensis Archiepiscopi*, ed. R. Graham (2 vols., Canterbury and York Society 51–2, 1952–6)
Registrum Simonis Langham	*Registrum Simonis Langham, Cantuariensis Archiepiscopi*, ed. A. C. Wood (Canterbury and York Society 53, 1956)
Registrum Thome Bourgchier	*Registrum Thome Bourgchier, Cantuariensis Archiepiscopi, A.D. 1454–1486*, ed. F. R. H. Du Boulay (Canterbury and York Society 54, 1957)
Sede Vacante Institutions	*Calendar of Institutions by the Chapter of Canterbury Sede Vacante*, ed. C. Eveleigh Woodruff and I. J. Churchill (Kent Archaeological Society Records Branch 8, 1924)
ser.	series
T.R.H.S.	*Transactions of the Royal Historical Society*
VCH	*Victoria County History*
Wilkins, *Concilia*	D. Wilkins, *Concilia Magnae Britanniae et Hiberniae A.D. 446–1718* (4 vols., London, 1737)

Worcester Sede Vacante Register	*The Register of the diocese of Worcester during the vacancy of the see, usually called registrum sede vacante, 1301–1435*, ed. J. W. Willis Bund (Worcestershire Historical Society 8, 1897)

CANTERBURY

Repositories

1. Lambeth Palace Library, London SE1 7JU (LPL).
2. Canterbury Cathedral Archives and Library, The Precincts, Canterbury CT1 2EG (CAL).
3. University Library, West Road, Cambridge CB3 9DR (CUL).
4. Public Record Office, Chancery Lane, London WC2A 1LR (PRO).
5. Bodleian Library, Department of Western Manuscripts, Oxford OX1 3BG (Bodl.).
6. Kent County Archives Office, County Hall, Maidstone ME14 1XH (KAO).

Area

The diocese of Canterbury consisted of a single archdeaconry and basically comprised that part of Kent to the east of the river Medway. In addition, the archbishop had eight deaneries of immediate jurisdiction outside his diocese: the Arches (in the London diocese), Bocking (London and Norwich), Croydon (Winchester and London), Risborough (Lincoln), Shoreham (Rochester), South Malling, Pagham and Tarring (all Chichester).[1]

Bibliographical Note

There is a detailed handlist to the registers of the archbishops of Canterbury from John Pecham (1279–92) to Randall Davidson (1903–28) issued as a National Register of Archives duplicated list in 1960.[2] The registers are also the subject of a survey by Miss Irene Churchill in the Lambeth Lectures for the same year[3] and a comparative study of the Canterbury and York registers has been made by Professor E. F. Jacob.[4]

It has often been claimed that Archbishop Robert Kilwardby (1273–8) had a register which fell into the hands of the papal chamberlain, but the evidence is not sufficient to confirm the existence of a formal register such as existed from the time of Pecham onwards.[5] There are losses at a later date: no registers survive for the period 1328–49, nor for the brief pontificate of Roger Walden (1397–9), if indeed he ever kept one,[6] and in the early sixteenth century only part of Archbishop Deane's register has come down to us, and no ordinations survive from the time of Cranmer onwards.

The format and subdivisions of the registers will become apparent from a consultation of the appended descriptive list. After an initial period of development and some flexibility in matters of registration, the archiepiscopal clerks began to adhere to fairly strict category sections for registered business: the appointment and confirmations of bishops in the southern province; a record of vacancy administration of suffragan sees; general memoranda (sometimes known as *diverse littere*, *facta diversa*, or *commissiones diverse*); institutions and

[1] *VCH Kent* ii (1926), pp. 110–11, and map facing p. 112; I. J. Churchill, *Canterbury Administration* i (London, 1933), pp. 40, 62–81, in particular p. 63, n. 6. For further maps of the diocese see the frontispiece to R. C. Jenkins, *Diocesan Histories: Canterbury* (London, 1880); B. L. Woodcock, *Medieval Ecclesiastical Courts in the Diocese of Canterbury* (Oxford, 1952), facing p. 1; Ordnance Survey, *Map of Monastic Britain: (south sheet)* (2nd edn., 1954).

[2] D. M. Owen and others, *Handlist of the registers, act books and institution act books of the archbishops of Canterbury* (typescript, 1960); also noted in H. J. Todd, *A Catalogue of the Archiepiscopal Manuscripts in the Library at Lambeth Palace* (London, 1812), pp. 266–7.

[3] I. J. Churchill, 'The Archbishops' Registers' in *Mediaeval Records of the Archbishops of Canterbury* (Lambeth Lectures for 1960, London, 1962), pp. 11–20.

[4] *The medieval registers of Canterbury and York* (St Anthony's Hall publication 4, York, 1953).

[5] C. R. Cheney, *English Bishops' Chanceries*, p. 147.

[6] Miss Churchill, *Canterbury Administration* (2 vols., London, 1933) i, p. 570, suggests that Walden may not have exercised spiritual administration. For a reference to Stratford's register (1333–48), now lost, see Public Record Office, C269/8/7.

collations in the Canterbury diocese and archiepiscopal peculiars (often including *sede vacante* and other provincial business *iure devoluto*); visitations of the diocese and province; ordinations of clergy. In addition to these regular subdivisions others are found from time to time covering such categories as testamentary business; royal writs (sometimes separated from the general memoranda section); papal bulls; Convocation business; registers of vicars-general; and occasional business such as the proceedings against heretics in Courtenay's register, or the section in Warham's register containing earlier papal bulls, archiepiscopal and episcopal *acta* and other charters relating to churches appropriated to religious corporations (presumably inspected at time of visitation).

During a vacancy of the archbishopric, the prior and convent (later the dean and chapter) of Canterbury cathedral exercised jurisdiction, and the records of their *sede vacante* administration are either entered in the capitular registers or at a later date are bound up with the archbishop's register. For some of the fourteenth-century vacancies, the records exist in more than one source, but they are by no means duplicates, as is sometimes found in the York *sede vacante* registers.

While several of the medieval archiepiscopal registers have now been printed by the Canterbury and York Society, much still remains to be studied in the original. Indexes to the registers from Pecham to Thomas Herring (1747–57), compiled by Dr Andrew Ducarel (1713–85), are contained in 67 manuscript volumes in Lambeth Palace Library. The indexes are arranged by place with a summary of the act (institutions etc.) and a highly selective subject index. There is also a Ducarel index for the 1558–9 vacancy and in the last century J. B. Sheppard compiled indexes of the Canterbury capitular registers for *sede vacante* business. Copies of the latter are both at Lambeth Palace Library and Canterbury Cathedral Library. They have in fact been superseded as far as vacancy institutions and wills are concerned by the publications of C. Eveleigh Woodruff and Miss I. J. Churchill.[7] Wills and administrations entered in the archiepiscopal registers to the beginning of the seventeenth century have been indexed by J. Challenor Smith.[8] Registers of wills proved in the Prerogative Court of Canterbury begin in 1383[9] and these of course have not been noted in the descriptive list. Similarly *sede vacante* will registers of the Canterbury cathedral chapter (e.g. CAL, register F, fos. i*v*–109*v* (for 1500–1) and fos. 165*r*–263*v* (for 1503)) have not been included.

Whenever there is a separate section of the register for archiepiscopal visitations, the dioceses visited are noted in the description. This is not done in the case of the section devoted to vacancy administration of suffragan sees, since the individual vacancies are noted under the appropriate diocese.

While a large number of archiepiscopal registers remain unpublished, this is not to deny that very many extracts from them have already appeared in print. To attempt to give an exhaustive list of such publications is an impossible task but it is feasible to indicate some of the chief works which have made considerable use of these registers. Notable among these are Thomas Rymer's *Foedera* (20 vols., London, 1704–35); David Wilkins, *Concilia Magnae Britanniae et Hiberniae A.D. 446–1718* (4 vols., London, 1737); Edmund Gibson, *Codex juris ecclesiastici Anglicani* (2 vols., London, 1713); Irene Churchill, *Canterbury Administration: the administrative machinery of the Archbishopric of Canterbury illustrated from original records* (2 vols., London, 1933), *Visitation Articles and Injunctions of the period of the Reformation*, ed. W. H. Frere and W. M. Kennedy (Alcuin Club 14–16, 1910) includes material from other dioceses), and of course works on the Reformation period by such writers as John Foxe and John Strype.

[7] *Calendar of Institutions by the Chapter of Canterbury Sede Vacante*, ed. C. Eveleigh Woodruff and I. J. Churchill (Kent Archaeological Society Records Branch 8, 1924); C. Eveleigh Woodruff, *Sede Vacante Wills: a calendar of wills proved before the commissary of the Prior and Chapter of Christ Church, Canterbury, during vacancies of the see* (Kent Archaeological Society Records Branch 3, 1914). The bulk of the latter wills deal with the 1500–1 and 1503 vacancies, referred to below.

[8] *Index to Wills recorded in the Archiepiscopal Registers at Lambeth Palace* (London, 1919), reprinted from *The Genealogist*, new ser. 34, 53–64, 149–66, 219–34 and 35, 45–51, 102–26; administrations are indexed in *The Genealogist* 7, 204–12, 271–84, and new ser., 1, 80–2.

[9] See J. M. Hoare, *The Records of the Prerogative Court of Canterbury: a provisional guide* (Public Record Office, 1976).

JOHN PECHAM (1279–1292)

LPL, no class reference. Parchment register; average 13½″ × 8¾″; fos. i + 248, foliated 1–213, 215–249; stamped leather binding on wooden boards, re-spined.

The arrangement of the register is described in both the Rolls Series and the Canterbury and York Society editions and also in D. L. Douie, 'Archbishop Pecham's register', *Studies in Church History* 1 (1964), 173–5. There are sections for the temporalities, letters to the pope and cardinals, letters to the king, and letters to bishops, collations and institutions, proxies and commissions, sequestrations, injunctions for religious houses, and general sections described as *facta diversa* and *littere communes*, in both of which are found records of ordinations of clergy. There is also a section of documents connected with the archbishop's negotiations with the Welsh. As bound at present, the arrangement is somewhat confused and it is probable that several sections are missing, as there is relatively little for the later years of Pecham's pontificate.

Printed, *Registrum Epistolarum Fratris Johannis Peckham, Archiepiscopi Cantuariensis*, ed. C. T. Martin (3 vols., Rolls Series, 1882–5). Martin published selected entries from the register and omitted what he considered to be 'formal documents'. The printed entries were rearranged in a single, chronological order. All the entries omitted in this edition are printed in *The Register of John Pecham, Archbishop of Canterbury, 1279–1292*, ed. F. N. Davis and others (vol. 1), and D. L. Douie (vol. 2) (2 vols., Canterbury and York Society 64, 65, 1908–69).

VACANCY 1292–1294

1. CAL, register Q. Parchment register; 10″ × 7½″; fos. iii + 238 + vii (paper, 8″ × 6¼″) + i (paper, 9¾″ × 7″) + iii, foliated 1–242 (including inserts); blank: fos. 1*v*–2*v*, 9*r*–10*v*, 19*v*, 23*v* 26*v*, 51*r*–52*v*, 53*v*–56*v*, 57*v*–59*r*, 69*v*–72*v*, 79*r*–80*v*, 94*r*, 135*v*–137*v*, 158*v*–159*v*, 169*v*, 177*r*–*v*, 190*r*, 202*v*, 231*v*–232*v*, 241*v*–242*v*; modern binding.

11*r*–44*v*, 60*r*–67*r*	Canterbury vacancy business Dec. 1292–Feb. 1295 (includes record of the election of Archbishop Winchelsey, occasional Llandaff *sede vacante* institutions, but also many later entries)

2. CUL, MS. Ee.5.31 (register of Henry of Eastry, prior of Christ Church, Canterbury), fos. 35*r*–64*r*. Parchment register; average 10¾″ × 7½″.

35*r*–64*r*	Canterbury vacancy business Dec. 1292–Nov. 1294

A facsimile of this document is available at Lambeth Palace Library, MS. Facsimiles I. Institutions in both these registers are calendared (by place) in *Sede Vacante Institutions*.

ROBERT WINCHELSEY (1294–1313)

LPL, no class reference. Parchment register, guarded; 12¼″ × 9¼″; fos. ii (paper) + i + vii (paper, 8¾″ × 7″, Ducarel's synopsis of the register) + i (limp parchment cover) + 340 + i + ii (paper), foliated 1–29, 31–70, 72–115, 115*, 116–160, 162–200, 202–343; modern binding.

Winchelsey's register differs slightly in arrangement from his predecessor's. There are still sections for letters to Rome, to the king and to bishops (the two last-mentioned now combined), for business relating to the temporalities, ordinations of clergy, collations and institutions (entered separately), visitation injunctions and *diverse littere et communes* (sometimes called *varie littere*), but in addition sections are found dealing primarily with court business (chiefly citations and mandates), and judgements and compositions. There are also a few folios devoted to the Church's grievances against the king and his officials (*gravamina*), business relating to church councils and the Templars, the taxation of Nicholas IV, and other miscellaneous memoranda. The register is by no means complete: there are no admissions to benefices before 1308, and no ordinations after 1306.

Printed, *Registrum Roberti Winchelsey Cantuariensis Archiepiscopi*, ed. R. Graham (2 vols., Canterbury and York Society 51, 52, 1952–6).

SUSPENSION OF ARCHBISHOP WINCHELSEY 1306–1308[10]

CUL, MS. Ee.5.31, fos. 104*r*–108*r* (for description see 1292–4 vacancy).

Canterbury business during the suspension July 1306–Nov. 1307

A facsimile of this document is available at Lambeth Palace Library, MS. Facsimiles I. Institutions are calendared (by place) in *Sede Vacante Institutions*.

VACANCY 1313

1. CAL, register Q, fos. 73*r*–119*r* (for description see 1292–4 vacancy).

   Canterbury vacancy business (in some confusion, including later entries and some precedents) May–Dec. 1313.

2. CUL, MS. Ee.5.31, fos. 121*r*–140*r* (for description see 1292–4 vacancy).

   Canterbury vacancy business May–Dec. 1313

A facsimile of this document is available at Lambeth Palace Library, MS. Facsimiles I. Institutions in both these registers are calendared (by place) in *Sede Vacante Institutions*.

WALTER REYNOLDS (1313–1327)

LPL, no class reference. Parchment register, guarded; average 13¼″ × 8¾″, except for fos. 52–63, 12¼″ × 8¼″; fos. 114–25, 12¼″ × 9″; fos. 286–95, 12″ × 8″; fos. ii (paper) + ii (folded papal bull of Martin V, July 1425, re-translating Richard Fleming from York to Lincoln) + 316 + i + ii (paper), foliated [i–ii], 1–316, [317]; blank: fos. [i*r*, ii*v*], 40*v*–43*v*, 50*r*, 51*v*, 74*r*, 82*r*–83*v*, 86*r*, 92*v*–95*v*, 103*v*, 110*r*, 160*r*–163*v*, 168*r*–169*v*, 187*v*–192*v*, 201*r*–205*v*, 208*v*–210*v*, 242*r*–248*r*, 266*v*–270*v*, 273*r*, 294*v*–295*v*, 313*v*–315*r*, [317*v*]; modern binding.

As can be seen from the attempted analysis below, this register is somewhat confused in arrangement as far as the recording of general memoranda is concerned. The headings *commissiones* and *diverse littere deprecatorie* are found, apparently distinguishing the sections, but in the case of the former the entries are in general by no means confined to commissions and contain all types of administrative memoranda (letters, mandates, licences, dispensations, proxies etc.).

1*r*–4*r*	register of Walter Reynolds before he received the pallium Oct. 1313–Feb. 1314
4*r*–14*r*	general register (institutions, memoranda, ordinations, etc.) Jan. 1314–Feb. 1315
14*v*–32*v*	institutions and collations (including provincial business *iure devoluto*) Feb. 1315–Feb. 1323
33*r*–40*r*	general memoranda (mostly legal business) Apr. 1313–May 1316
44*r*–49*v*	papal bulls, followed by dispensations (some entries repeat those in the preceding section) Apr. 1313–Sept. 1316
50*v*–51*r*	papal bulls, dispensations and absolutions Jan. 1317–Mar. 1318
52*r*–53*v*	general memoranda Feb.–Mar. 1315 (Apr. ?1315)
54*r*–70*v*	general memoranda June 1314–June 1316
70*v*–71*v*	general memoranda Aug. 1321
72*r*–79*r*	general memoranda (mostly royal and papal letters) Feb. 1316–Oct. 1317
79*v*–80*r*	list of archiepiscopal properties, and valuation for a clerical tenth n.d.
80*v*–81*v*	visitation of Christ Church, Canterbury Jan.–Feb. 1324

[10] Archbishop Winchelsey was suspended by Pope Clement V from administration of the diocese and province of Canterbury on 12 February 1306, and the suspension was not removed until 22 January 1308.

84*r*–89*v*	commissions and general memoranda Apr. 1315–Jan. 1320 (fo. 89*v* has the contemporary heading *commissiones*)
90*r*–92*r*	commissions July 1315–June 1318 (with 1 additional entry Nov. 1322)
96*r*–103*r*	general memoranda (including several appropriation deeds and ordinations of vicarages) Apr. 1320–Feb. 1324
104*r*–113*v*	general memoranda Apr. 1314–Mar. 1316 (with a few additional entries to Sept. 1321)
114*r*–126*v*	*diverse littere deprecatorie* (in somewhat confused order; the bulk of the material is undated) Mar. 1315–Feb. 1317
127*r*–155*v*	commissions and general memoranda (continues on from fo. 89*v*) Jan. 1320–July 1327
156*r*–157*v*	Exeter vacancy business Oct. 1326–Jan. 1327
157*v*	list of cardinals; note of archbishop's visit to Rome, Jan. 1327; and memorandum of letter sent to the bishop and dean of Lincoln about the archbishop of York bearing his cross in the southern province, Aug. 1327
158*r*–159*v*	commissions and general memoranda July–Nov. 1327 (with 1 *sede vacante* entry Dec. 1327 at the end)
164*r*–167*v*	bonds, acquittances and dispensations (not always in strict chronological order) Mar. 1323–Sept. 1327
171*r*–187*r*	ordinations May 1315–May 1326
193*r*–199*v*	general memoranda (including papal bulls; not always in chronological order) May 1326–Sept. 1327
200*r*–*v*	licences for non-residence Dec. 1326–Oct. 1327
206*r*–208*r*	general memoranda Sept.–Oct. 1327
211*r*–241*v*	papal bulls and related business (at times in considerable confusion) Dec. 1313–Apr. 1325
248*v*	list of cardinals; note of those persons licensed as confessors and preachers in the Canterbury diocese Dec. 1323–Oct. 1327
249*r*–266*r*	institutions and collations (including *sede vacante* and other provincial business) Apr. 1323–Nov. 1327
271*r*–277*v*	general memoranda (in some confusion; this section includes Norwich *sede vacante* material) Jan. 1325–Oct. 1326
278*r*–285*v*	bonds and acquittances (in confusion) Oct. 1314–Aug. 1322
286*r*–290*v*	letters dimissory and licences for non-residence July 1322–Mar. 1327
291*r*–294*v*	significations for excommunication (the heading also notes licences for non-residence, but I can find none in this section) July 1321–Aug. 1327
296*r*–313*r*	royal writs Nov. 1317–Dec. 1326
315*v*–inside back cover	table of select contents

Lambeth Palace Library, Ducarel index 4 covers this register. A study based on this register by Dr J. R. Wright, *The Church and the English Crown 1305–1334: a study based on the register of Archbishop Walter Reynolds* was published by the Pontifical Institute of Mediaeval Studies at Toronto in 1980. Dr Wright also has an edition of this register in progress.

VACANCY 1327–1328

CAL, register Q, fos. 121*r*–176*v* (for description see 1292–4 vacancy).

Canterbury vacancy business (confused arrangement at the beginning) Nov. 1327–July 1328

Institutions are calendared (by place) in *Sede Vacante Institutions*. Ordination lists Mar.–May 1328 (CAL, Bunce II, p. 17) are printed *ibid.*, app. B, pp. 147–54.

VACANCY 1333

1. CAL, register Q, fos. 178*r*–203*r* (for description see 1292–4 vacancy).

    Canterbury vacancy business Oct. 1333–Jan. 1334

2. CAL, register G. Parchment register; fos. iv+ii (paper, 12½″ × 8¾″)+24 (10½″ × 8″)+1 (11¾″ × 6¾″)+23 (10¼″ × 7″)+1 (11¾″ × 7″)+266 (average 11½″ × 8¾″, except for fos. 80–119, average 11¼″ × 8″)+ii (paper, 12½″ × 8¾″)+iv, foliated 1–24, xxv–xlix, 25–290; blank: fos. xlix*r*–*v*, 43*v*, 48*v*, 51*v*, 59*v*, 60*r*, 63*v*, 134*r*–135*v*, 139*v*, 154*v*, 160*v*, 220*v*, 229*v*, 284*v*; modern binding.

    xxvi*r*–xlviii*v* Canterbury vacancy business Oct. 1333–Feb. 1334

Institutions in both these registers are calendared (by place) in *Sede Vacante Institutions.*

VACANCY 1348

1. CAL, register G, fos. 25*r*–48*r* (for description see 1333 vacancy).

    Canterbury vacancy business Aug.–Dec. 1348

2. CAL, *ibid.*, fos. 80*r*–105*r*.

    Canterbury vacancy business Aug.–Nov. 1348

3. CAL, register Q, fos. 203*v*–239*v* (for description see 1292–4 vacancy).

    Canterbury vacancy business (in part a duplicate of the above) Aug.–Dec. 1348

Institutions in these registers are calendared (by place) in *Sede Vacante Institutions.*

FIRST VACANCY 1349

1. CAL, register G, fos. 49*r*–63*r* (for description see 1333 vacancy).

    Canterbury vacancy business May–Aug. 1349

2. CAL, *ibid.*, fos. 114*r*–119*v*.

    Canterbury vacancy business June–July 1349

Institutions in both these sections are calendared (by place) in *Sede Vacante Institutions.*

SECOND VACANCY 1349

CAL, register G, fos. 64*r*–79*v* (for description see 1333 vacancy).

Canterbury vacancy business Aug.–Dec. 1349.

Institutions are calendared (by place) in *Sede Vacante Institutions.*

SIMON ISLIP (1349–1366)

LPL, no class reference. Parchment register (partially eaten by rodents at lower edge); 15″ × 10″; fos. 347+i, foliated 1–72, 72[A], 73–197, 199–347, [348]; blank: fos. 216*r*–217*v*, 229*v*, 232*v*, 234*r*–235*r*, 236*v*, 241*v*, 247*v*–249*r*, 264*r*, 329*r*–332*v*; stamped leather binding on wooden boards, re-spined.

1*r*–4*v*	register heading and bulls of provision, with material relating to Islip's appointment and consecration Oct.–Dec. 1349
4*v*–215*v*	general memoranda Dec. 1349–Mar. 1366 (This large section is much confused in places, particularly in the early 1350s, and not apparently due to misbinding. What seems to have happened is that in addition to the general series of memoranda which continues in approximate chronological order throughout the whole section, the clerks have disrupted this main sequence from time to time by grouping together specific categories

of business covering a period of years. Most notable are the following: fos. 15*v*–16*r*, archiepiscopal nomination of nuns to convents in the southern province Mar. 1350–July 1351; leases Sept. 1350–Mar. 1352 (16*v*); dispensations for illegitimacy Nov. 1350–Aug. 1357 (32*v*–33*r*); homages and fealties Sept. 1352–Feb. 1361 (60*r*); further dispensations Aug. 1352–Oct. 1361 (62*v*); visitations of Canterbury (72*r*–*v*) and Rochester (74*v*–76*v*) dioceses Sept.–Oct. 1350; and a rental of the temporalities of the vacant see of Rochester Oct. 1352–Feb. 1353 (77*r*–*v*). Whether these entries have been made later wherever there were blank spaces, or whether it is indicative of registration long after the acts they record is not at all certain. The result is in some way an unsatisfactory compromise between the more numerous subdivisions of the earlier Canterbury registers and the one sequence of general memoranda to be found from the time of Islip's successor, Simon Langham.)

218*r*–247*r*	record of appointment of bishops and vacancy administration of suffragan sees July 1357–Feb. 1366
249*v*	acquittance of the executors of the will of John de Vere, earl of Oxford May 1364
250*r*–307*v*	institutions and collations in the diocese of Canterbury and archiepiscopal peculiars (including some *sede vacante* institutions and other provincial business) Dec. 1349–Mar. 1366
308*r*–326*v*	ordinations Feb. 1350–Feb. 1366
327*r*–328*v*	composition over vacancy jurisdiction in the Norwich diocese Aug. 1330 (16th-cent. copy)
333*r*–342*r*	record of the vacancy administration of the Norwich diocese Jan.–Apr. 1355
342*r*	note of letters sent to the Officials *sede vacante* of St Asaph and Bangor Oct. 1357–Feb. 1358
342*v*	commissions to the Official *sede vacante* of St Asaph Feb. 1357, with a note of similar commissions sent to the Official of Bangor Apr. 1357
343*r*–346*v*	royal writs July 1359–May 1365
347*r*–[348*v*]	later table of contents

Lambeth Palace Library, Ducarel indexes 5–6 cover this register. Fos. 327*r*–328*v* are printed in *Canterbury Administration* ii, pp. 64–9, using old foliation.

VACANCY 1366

CAL, register G, fos. 120*r*–160*r* (for description see 1333 vacancy).

Canterbury vacancy business Apr.–Oct. 1366

Institutions are calendared (by place) in *Sede Vacante Institutions*.

SIMON LANGHAM (1366–1368)

LPL, no class reference. Parchment register; 14¼″ × 10″; fos. i (paper) + 145 + i (paper), foliated 1–3, 3[A], 4–100, 102–144, [145]; stamped leather binding on wooden boards, re-spined.

The register begins with a return of pluralists in 1366 in response to a constitution of Pope Urban V. There are also sections of general memoranda; institutions and collations; archiepiscopal visitations; testamentary business; a record of vacancy administration of suffragan sees; royal writs; licences for non-residence; and ordinations.

Printed, *Registrum Simonis Langham, Cantuariensis Archiepiscopi*, ed. A. C. Wood (Canterbury and York Society 53, 1956).

VACANCY 1368

CAL, register G, fos. 161*r*–169*v* (for description see under 1333 vacancy).

Canterbury vacancy business Dec. 1368–Jan. 1369

Institutions are calendared (by place) in *Sede Vacante Institutions*.

WILLIAM WHITTLESEY (1368–1374)

LPL, no class reference. Parchment register; 14½″ × 10″, except for fos. 152–9, 12″ × 9¼″; fos. i + 172, foliated 1–172; blank: fos. 68*v*, 96*v*–97*v*, 131*r*–*v*, 171*r*; stamped leather binding on wooden boards, re-spined.

1*r*–68*r*	register heading and general memoranda Oct. 1368–June 1374
69*r*–96*r*	institutions and collations in the diocese of Canterbury and archiepiscopal peculiars (including some vacancy institutions and other provincial business) Jan. 1369–May 1374
98*r*–130*v*	wills prob. Apr. 1369–June 1374
132*r*–159*v*	record of vacancy administration of suffragan sees and the confirmation of bishops Jan. 1369–Mar. 1374
160*r*–164*v*	royal writs Apr. 1369–Apr. 1374
165*r*–170*v*	ordinations June 1369–Apr. 1374
171*v*–172*r*	taxation of dioceses in the southern province for a tenth (1375) and for legatine procurations
172*v*–inside back cover	later table of contents

Lambeth Palace Library, Ducarel index 8 covers this register.

VACANCY 1374–1375

CAL, register G, fos. 170*r*–209*r* (for description see 1333 vacancy).

Canterbury vacancy business June 1374–May 1375

Institutions are calendared (by place) in *Sede Vacante Institutions*.

SIMON SUDBURY (1375–1381)

LPL, no class reference. Parchment register; 14″ × 10″; fos. i + 150 + i, foliated 1–150, [151]; blank: fos. 77*v*, 110*r*–*v*, 112*v*, 135*v*–136*v*; stamped leather binding on wooden boards, re-spined.

1*r*–77*r*	register heading and general memoranda (including acts by the vicar-general during Sudbury's absence in Bruges) May 1375–May 1381
78*r*–109*v*	testamentary business July 1375–May 1381
111*r*–112*r*	institutions by the vicar-general during Sudbury's absence in Bruges Nov. 1375–Mar. 1376
113*r*–135*r*	institutions and collations in the diocese of Canterbury and archiepiscopal peculiars (including some vacancy acts and other provincial business) June 1375–June 1381
137*r*–142*r*	ordinations June 1375–Dec. 1377
142*v*–144*v*	royal writs May 1376–June 1379
145*r*–150*v*	ordinations (cont.) Mar. 1378–June 1381
151*v*–inside back cover	later table of contents

Lambeth Palace Library, Ducarel index 9 covers this register.

VACANCY 1381

1. Bodl., MS. Ashmole 794, fos. 248r–253v. Parchment; 12″ × 8″; fos. 6; blank: none.

Canterbury vacancy business June–Dec. 1381

A facsimile of this document is available at Lambeth Palace Library, MS. Facsimiles I.

2. CAL, register G, fos. 221r–232v (for description see 1333 vacancy).

Canterbury vacancy business June–Dec. 1381

Institutions in both these registers are calendared (by place) in *Sede Vacante Institutions*.

WILLIAM COURTENAY (1381–1396)

1. LPL, no class reference. Parchment register; 14¾″ × 10″; fos. ii+353+ii, foliated 1–126, 126A, 127–140, 142–289, [289A], 290, 300–361, [362]; blank: fos. 46r, 56v, 67v, 126Av, 128r, 131v, 145v, 166v, 172v, 241v, 284v, [289Ar–v], 312v, 339v; stamped leather binding on wooden boards, re-spined.

1r–10r	bulls of provision etc. and acts of Courtenay as *electus confirmatus*, receipt of pallium Sept. 1381–Jan. 1382
10r–16v	general memoranda (not always in chronological order) Apr.–July 1382
17r–v	nomination of nuns to convents in the southern province May 1382–May 1383
18r–v	dispensations for study and licences for non-residence May–Dec. 1382
18v–24v	general memoranda (continuation of above) July–Dec. 1382
25r–35r	proceedings against heretics May–Nov. 1382
35r–72v	general memoranda (continuation of above, occasionally in considerable confusion) Jan. 1383–Sept. 1387
73r–77v	Convocation business Feb. 1388–April. 1391
78r–85v	Convocation business Dec. 1383–Mar. 1388
86r–159v	record of metropolitical visitations of the dioceses of Exeter, Bath and Wells, Worcester, Chichester, Rochester, Lincoln, and Salisbury Jan. 1384–July 1390
160r–167v	record of vacancy administration of suffragan sees June 1385–Apr. 1390
168r–172r	general memoranda (continuation of above) Sept. 1387– [ ] 1390
173r–v	accounts of the custodians of the spiritualities of the diocese of St Asaph Dec. 1389–Apr. 1390
174r–182v	general memoranda Feb. 1388–Feb. 1391
183r–187v	papal letters of grace and indults Dec. 1383–Apr. 1386
188r–241v	testamentary business Jan. 1383–Aug. 1391
242r–282v	institutions and collations in the diocese of Canterbury and archiepiscopal peculiars (including vacancy institutions and other provincial business; the last entry is incomplete) Jan. 1382–July 1391
283r–289v	general memoranda Nov. 1388–Mar. 1391
290r–304v	compositions and appropriations of churches (including copies of earlier documents) 13th cent.–Aug. 1386
305r–312r	ordinations May 1382–Mar. 1391
313r–326r	record of vacancy administration of suffragan sees Apr. 1382–Feb. 1390
327r–331v	royal writs *et alie littere secrete tam latine quam gallice* Apr. 1382–Dec. 1389
332r–339r	general memoranda Feb. 1390–May 1391

340*r*–345*v* register of vicar-general during archiepiscopal absences Feb. 1384–Dec. 1389
346*r*–361*v* record of vacancy administration of suffragan sees Apr. 1385–Dec. 1389
[362*r*] later table of contents
[362*v*] contemporary text of bishop's oath

Lambeth Palace Library, Ducarel indexes 10–11 cover this register. Fos. 86*r*–159*v* are printed in J. H. Dahmus, *The Metropolitical Visitations of William Courteney, Archbishop of Canterbury, 1381–1396* (Urbana, 1950), pp. 71–202; fo. 289*r*–*v* *ibid.*, pp. 208–9; the proceedings against heretics (fos. 25*r*–35*r*) are mostly printed in Wilkins, *Concilia* iii, pp. 157–73, as are several extracts from this register relating to Convocation matters.

2. LPL, bound with register of Archbishop John Morton, volume II, fos. 181*r*–228*r* (for description see under Morton).

181*r*–186*v* ordinations Dec. 1392–Apr. 1396
187*r*–190*v* commissions and dispensations July 1392–June 1396
191*r*–194*v* record of visitation of the Canterbury diocese July 1393
195*r*–197*r* Convocation business Aug. 1394–May 1395
199*r*–223*v* institutions and collations in the diocese of Canterbury and archiepiscopal peculiars (including vacancy acts and other provincial business) Sept. 1391–Dec. 1395
224*r*–228*r* general memoranda Mar. 1392–Sept. 1395

Fos. 191*r*–194*v* are printed in J. H. Dahmus, *op. cit.*, pp. 202–8.

3. PRO, Prob. 11/1 (Prerogative Court of Canterbury probate register 'Rous'), fos. 37*r*–39*v*. Parchment quire (last folio excised); $15\frac{3}{4}'' \times 11\frac{1}{4}''$; fos. 3; blank: fos. 38*v*–39*v*.

37*r*–38*r* a quire from Courtenay's register dealing with appointments of bishops (first entry incomplete) Feb. 1396

Calendared by J. C. C. Smith, *Index of Wills proved in the Prerogative Court of Canterbury 1383–1558*, i (British Record Society, Index Library 10, 1893), pp. x–xi.

VACANCY 1396

CAL, register G, fos. 235*r*–276*v* (for description see 1333 vacancy).

Canterbury vacancy business Aug. 1396–Jan. 1397

Institutions are calendared (by place) in *Sede Vacante Institutions.*

THOMAS ARUNDEL (1396–1397; 1399–1414)

1. LPL, volume I. Parchment register; $14\frac{3}{4}'' \times 11''$, except for fos. 455–62, $14\frac{3}{4}'' \times 9\frac{3}{4}''$; fos. i + 556 + ii, foliated 1–47, 50–201, 203–288, 290–294, 296–323, 323[A], 324–418, 418[A], 419–438, 438[A], 439–497, 499–518, 521–561, [562–564]; blank: fos. 43*r*–*v*, 50*r*–*v*, 62*r*, 69*v*–70*v*, 74*v*–75*v*, 91*v*–92*v*, 140*v*, 141*v*–144*v*, 151*v*–152*v*, 161*v*–162*v*, 167*v*, 187*v*, 257*v*, 261*v*, 309*v*, 317*v*, 323*v*–323[A]*v*, 344*r*–346*v*, 352*v*, 402*v*, 418[A]*r*–419*v*, 453*v*–454*v*, 459*r*–462*v*, 465*r*, 468*r*, 470*r*–*v*, 475*v*, 490*r*–*v*, 497*v*–513*v*, 518*v*, 539*v*; stamped leather binding on wooden boards, re-spined.

1*r*–*v* monition to the citizens of London regarding tithing customs in the city Aug. 1397
2*r*–5*v* bulls of translation of Arundel etc., acts as *electus confirmatus* and receipt of pallium Sept. 1396–Feb. 1397
5*v*–9*v* commissions and general memoranda Feb.–Apr. 1397
10*r*–42*v* papal bulls, appointments of bishops and general memoranda (including earlier documents) Mar. 1397–Aug. 1408
(There is some chronological confusion. The bulk of the section contain bulls and other records relating to the appointment and

	confirmation of bishops, but there is also much administrative miscellanea. Fo. 32*r* is annotated in a contemporary hand *primus quaternus bullarum*, but it is certainly not the first quire of the section.)
44*r*–74*r*	Convocation business Feb. 1397–Aug. 1408 (fo. 51*r* contains the register heading after Arundel's restoration 1399)
76*r*–80*v*	proposals for the healing of the Papal Schism presented to Henry IV by Cardinal Ugguccione of Bordeaux Oct. 1408
81*r*–91*r*	record of the election of Pope Gregory XII and cognate material relating to the Schism and the General Council (not in strict chronological order) Nov. 1406–Oct. 1408
93*r*–150*r*	commissions (in some confusion) Oct. 1399–Nov. 1408
150*v*–151*r*	royal writs July 1406–Apr. 1408
153*r*–257*r*	testamentary business Jan. 1397–Oct. 1408
258*r*–259*r*	list of benefices in the archbishop's collation
259*v*	list of benefices in the collation of Canterbury cathedral priory in the deanery of Arches
260*r*–323*r*	institutions and collations in the diocese of Canterbury and archiepiscopal peculiars (including vacancy acts and other provincial business) Oct.–Nov. 1397, Oct. 1399–Dec. 1408
324*r*–343*v*	ordinations Mar.–Apr. 1397, Dec. 1399–Dec. 1408
347*r*	list of cardinals created by Pope Innocent VII in 1405, and 3 letters nominating scholars to Canterbury College, Oxford Sept. 1405–Oct. 1409
347*r*–352*r*	commissions and general memoranda (in chronological confusion) June 1401–Oct. 1405
353*r*–418*v*	general memoranda Oct. 1399–Apr. 1409 (in considerable confusion. Fo. 403*r* bears the contemporary heading *quaternus de diversis litteris*. A lot of documents are undated. One entry on fo. 382*r* is dated at Canterbury, Apr. 1398, but this is clearly an error as Roger Walden was archbishop by this time.)
420*r*–430*v*	*querele* and other legal business Oct. 1399–Nov. 1406
431*r*–*v*, 442*r*–*v*	documents concerning a visitation of the chapter of Hereford cathedral July 1404 (16th-cent. copy)
432*r*–441*v*, 443*r*–453*r*	general memoranda (in considerable disorder. Fo. 443*r* is headed in a contemporary hand *primus quaternus litterarum*) Mar. 1401–Nov. 1408
455*r*–468*v*	record of vacancy administration of suffragan sees Aug. 1397–Jan. 1406 (on fo. 465*v* is a stray document about the election of the prioress of Davington Mar. 1402)
469*r*–497*r*	record of visitations of the dioceses of Canterbury, Chichester, Coventry and Lichfield, and Ely Mar. 1397–Dec. 1405
499*r*–549*v*	record of vacancy administration of suffragan sees Oct. 1404–Oct. 1407
550*r*–561*r*	royal writs Oct. 1399–July 1406
561*v*	note on the summoning of clergy to parliament
[562*r*–564*r*]	later table of select contents

Fo. 1*r*–*v* is printed in Wilkins, *Concilia* iii, pp. 231–2; fos. 81*r*–91*r* *ibid.*, pp. 286–302; and the bulk of the Convocation business on fos. 44*r*–74*r* is also printed by Wilkins. Fos. 76*r*–80*v* are printed in *The St Albans Chronicle 1406–1420*, ed. V. H. Galbraith (Oxford, 1937), app. ii, pp. 136–52. The Ely visitation material is printed in *Camden Miscellany XVII*, ed. S. J. A. Evans (Camden Third Series, 64, 1940), pp. 44–56.

2. LPL, volume II. Parchment register; 14¾″ × 11″; fos. 203 + ii, foliated 1–180, 182–204, [205]; blank: fos. 1*r*, 19*v*–21*v*, 26*r*, 34*r*–35*v*, 94*v*, 102*r*–*v*, 146*r*–*v*, 176*v*–177*v*, 199*r*–200*v*; stamped leather binding on wooden boards, re-spined.

1*r*–27*v*	Convocation business (last entry incomplete) Jan. 1401–Dec. 1411
28*r*–33*v*	Convocation business *temp.* Archbishop John Stafford Oct. 1444–July 1445
36*r*–51*v*	testamentary business (last entry incomplete) Nov. 1408–June 1410
52*r*–69*v*	institutions and collations in the diocese of Canterbury and archiepiscopal peculiars (including vacancy acts and other provincial business) Jan. 1409–Jan. 1414
70*r*–73*r*	record of visitation of Glastonbury abbey Sept. 1408–Nov. 1409
73*v*–77*r*	record of vacancy administration of the Salisbury diocese July–Sept. 1407
77*v*–94*r*	record of metropolitical visitations of the dioceses of Norwich and Lincoln Mar. 1411–Apr. 1412 (with extraneous material to Sept. 1413)
95*r*–101*v*	ordinations Mar. 1409–Dec. 1413
103*r*–110*v*	testamentary business Feb.–Oct. 1409
111*r*–132*v*	general memoranda (in considerable confusion. The clerks described this section either as *facta diversa* or as *littere communes*; the last entry is incomplete) Sept. 1407–Mar. 1412
133*r*–142*r*	commissions Feb. 1410–Nov. 1413
142*v*–145*v*	letter to the bishop of London about Oldcastle and the Lollards
147*r*–176*r*	testamentary business Nov. 1411–Jan. 1414
178*r*–186*v*	Convocation business Jan.–Apr. 1401
187*r*–198*v*	record of vacancy administration of the Norwich diocese May–Oct. 1413
201*r*–204*v*	register of wills of the prior and convent of Canterbury cathedral *sede vacante* Feb.–May 1414
[205*r*–*v*]	later table of select contents

Fos. 142*v*–145*v* are printed in Wilkins, *Concilia* iii, pp. 353–7; and for Convocation business 1401 (178*r*–186*v*) see *ibid.*, pp. 254–63; fos. 70*r*–73*r* are printed in *Register of Thomas Bekynton, Bishop of Bath and Wells, 1443–1465*, ii (Somerset Record Society 50, 1935), pp. 550–7.
Lambeth Palace Library, Ducarel indexes 12–15 cover these registers.

VACANCY 1414

CAL, register G, fos. 277*r*–290*v* (badly damaged) (for description see 1333 vacancy).

Canterbury vacancy business Feb.–May 1414

Institutions are calendared (by place) in *Sede Vacante Institutions.*

HENRY CHICHELE (1414–1443)

1. LPL, volume I. Parchment register; 15″ × 11″; fos. i + 497 + i, foliated [i–viii], 1–233, 236–317, 319–356, 356 [A], 358–465, 467–483, 483 [A], 484–489, 489 [A], 490; stamped leather binding on wooden boards, re-spined.
2. LPL, volume II. Parchment register; $14\frac{3}{4}$″ × 11″; fos. i + 403, foliated 1–191, 193–246, 246[A], 247–267, 267[A], 268–309, 320–411, [412]; stamped leather binding on wooden boards, re-spined.

The first volume of this impressive register contains three sections: the record of appointments of bishops and confirmations of the elections of heads of religious houses in the Canterbury diocese and in vacant sees; institutions and collations in the diocese of Canterbury and archiepiscopal peculiars (including vacancy institutions and those *ratione visitationis*); and testamentary business. The second volume includes Convocation business; a record of vacancy administration in suffragan sees; archiepiscopal visitations; general memoranda (commissions, letters, royal writs etc.); and ordinations (including a few *sede vacante* or *ratione visitationis*). A detailed description of the registers and a note of losses are to be found on pp. lx–lxi of the first volume of the printed edition.

Printed, *The Register of Henry Chichele, Archbishop of Canterbury, 1414–1443, vol. I*, ed. E. F. Jacob (Canterbury and York Society 45, 1943), containing the first two sections of the first volume of the register; *vol. II*, ed. E. F. Jacob and H. C. Johnson (Canterbury and York Society 42, 1938), containing the testamentary business; *vol. III*, ed. E. F. Jacob (Canterbury and York Society 46, 1945), containing Convocation business, records of vacancy administration and visitations; *vol. IV*, ed. E. F. Jacob (Canterbury and York Society 47, 1947), containing general memoranda and ordinations.

JOHN STAFFORD (1443–1452)
JOHN KEMPE (1452–1454)

LPL, no class reference. Parchment register; 14½" × 10½"; fos. i (paper) + 348 + i (paper), foliated [i], 1–72, 74–116, 117A, 117B, 118–347; blank: fos. 39*r*–40*v*, 54*r*–56*v*, 110*r*–*v*, 194*v*, 207*v*–209*v*, 213*v*, 217*v*–218*v*, 228*v*, 233*v*, 241*r*–*v*, 247*v*, 250*v*, 252*v*–253*v*, 256*r*–*v*, 320*v*, 327*r*, 328*r*–*v*, 340*r*–*v*; stamped leather binding on wooden boards, re-spined.

1*r*–207*r* register of Archbishop John Stafford

- 1*r*–38*v* bulls of translation etc., followed by general memoranda (in confusion at the end) May 1443–Aug. 1450
- 41*r*–42*v* record of visitation of the Canterbury diocese Mar.–Aug. 1444
- 43*r*–45*r* Rochester vacancy business (including the appointment of the new bishop) Feb.–June 1444 (*recte*)
- 45*r*–49*r* business relating to the tenth for the crusade against the Turks (record of events to Dec. 1446)
- 49*r*–*v* royal confirmation of Edward III's *inspeximus* of charters of Richard I and John relating to the archbishop's rights in the Canterbury mint
- 49*v*–53*v* memoranda, mostly papal dispensations Feb. 1448–Mar. 1452
- 57*r*–72*v* record of vacancy administration of the Norwich diocese Dec. 1445–Mar. 1446
- 74*r*–109*v* institutions and collations in the diocese of Canterbury and archiepiscopal peculiars (including vacancy acts and other provincial business) May 1443–May 1452
- 111*r*–194*r* testamentary business Sept. 1443–Nov. 1451 (this section is misbound; it should begin on fo. 118*r*)
- 196*r*–207*r* ordinations Dec. 1443–Apr. 1452

210*r*–347*v* register of Archbishop John Kempe

- 210*r*–213*r* bulls of translation of Kempe etc. July–Dec. 1452
- 214*r*–217*r* record of the provision and appointment of bishops Aug. 1452–Apr. 1453
- 219*r*–232*r* Convocation business Dec. 1452–Sept. 1453
- 232*v*–233*r* planned itinerary for the visitation of the Canterbury diocese Sept.–Oct. 1453
- 234*r*–244*v* general memoranda (in some confusion) Sept. 1452–Mar. 1454
- 245*r*–246*r* indulgences Dec. 1453–Feb. 1454
- 246*v* nominations of nuns to convents in the southern province Oct. 1452–June 1453
- 246*v*–247*r* grants of oratories and portable altars Oct. 1452–Jan. 1454
- 248*r* licences to preach Oct. 1452–Jan. 1454
- 248*v* grants of corrodies July–Sept. 1453
- 249*r*–*v* nominations of scholars and officials to All Souls College, Oxford Apr.–Oct. 1453
- 250*r* marriage licences Jan.–Feb. 1454 (*recte*)

251*r*–252*r*	list of benefices in the archbishop's collation, with values; and list of churches in the collation of Canterbury cathedral priory in the deanery of Arches
254*r*–255*v*	ordinations Sept. 1452–Sept. 1453
257*r*–320*r*	testamentary business (in occasional confusion) Sept. 1452–Mar. 1454
321*r*–326*v*	institutions and collations in the diocese of Canterbury and archiepiscopal peculiars (including vacancy and other provincial business) Sept. 1452–Feb. 1454
327*v*	certificate of inquiry into the patronage of Harrietsham church, co. Kent (incomplete—archbishop's commission Aug. 1453)
329*r*–339*v*	record of vacancy administration of the diocese of Coventry and Lichfield [?July] 1452, and Nov. 1452–Apr. 1453
341*r*–347*v*	record of visitation of the collegiate church of South Malling Aug.–Dec. 1453
347*v*–inside back cover	later table of select contents

Lambeth Palace Library, Ducarel indexes 23–25 cover this register. Fos. 45*r*–49*r* are discussed by E. F. Jacob, 'Archbishop John Stafford', *T.R.H.S.*, 5th series, 12 (1962), 17–22; reprinted in *Essays in Later Medieval History* (Manchester, 1968), pp. 52–7. The text is printed in Wilkins, *Concilia* iii, 547–52; fo. 49*r*–*v* is printed *ibid.*, 552–4.

THOMAS BOURGCHIER (1454–1486)

1. LPL, no class reference. Parchment register; 16½″ × 12¼″; fos. i + 160, foliated 1–55, 58–161, [162]; stamped leather binding on wooden boards, re-spined.
   Bourgchier's register is incomplete, and only the record of clerical ordinations has not suffered losses. In arrangement, the register follows the pattern of Stafford's—general memoranda (bulls, commissions, letters, licences etc.); institutions and collations (including some vacancy and other provincial business); Convocation business; testamentary business; a record of vacancy administration (only the register for the Exeter diocese has survived); and ordinations.
2. LPL, register of Archbishop John Morton, volume II, fos. 173*r*–179*r* (for description see under Morton).

   a quire of general memoranda 1479–1485 which was not bound up with the main register.
3. KAO, MS. Book PRC 17.9, a bifolium used to cover a volume of wills proved in the archdeacon's court at Canterbury 1503–1509, and containing notes of some of Bourgchier's secular appointments 1459–1486.

   Printed, *Registrum Thome Bourgchier, Cantuariensis Archiepiscopi, A.D. 1454–1486*, ed. F. R. H. Du Boulay (Canterbury and York Society 54, 1957).

VACANCY 1486

CAL, register R. Parchment register; average 13″ × 9½″; fos. iii + 189 + vi (paper, 12½″ × 7¾″) + iii, foliated 1–105, 105A, 106–188; blank: fos. 21*v*, 35*v*, 39*r*–v, 65*r*–*v*, 99*v*–100*v*, 106*v*–107*v*, 159*v*–160*v*, 180*v*–182*r*; modern binding.

1*r*–38*r*	Canterbury vacancy business Mar.–Aug. 1486

Institutions are calendared (by place) in *Sede Vacante Institutions*.

JOHN MORTON (1486–1500)

1. LPL, volume I. Parchment register; 15½″ × 12″; fos. i (paper) + 250, foliated 1–36, 40–63, 65–142, 144–187, 190–256, [257]; blank: fos. 3*v*, 36*v*, 40*r*–*v*, 77*r*–*v*, 92*v*–93*v*, 98*v*–101*v*, 107*v*–109*v*, 138*v*, 140*r*–141*v*, 157*v*–158*v*, 163*r*–166*v*, 174*v*, 181*r*–183*v*, 185*v*, 187*v*, 190*r*–*v*, 197*v*–198*v*, 215*r*–*v*, 226*v*, [257*v*]; stamped leather binding on wooden boards, re-spined.

1*r*–3*r*	bulls of translation etc. Oct.–Dec. 1486
4*r*–32*v*	papal bulls and general memoranda (not in chronological order) Apr. 1486–Oct. 1493
33*r*–54*v*	Convocation business and taxation of the clergy Feb. 1487–Mar. 1491
55*r*–197*r*	record of vacancy administration of suffragan sees Nov. 1490–Mar. 1500
199*r*–202*r*	foundation statutes of Ellis Davy's almshouses, Croydon Apr. 1447
202*r*–206*v*	business relating to the translation of the relics of St Swithin, and the projected canonisation of King Henry VI Apr. 1476–Nov. 1498
207*r*–214*v*	dispute between the archbishop and the bishop of London over testamentary jurisdiction Mar. 1494–Feb. 1496
216*r*–226*r*	papal bulls (not in chronological order) Mar. 1491–July 1499
227*r*–250*v*	dispute between the archbishop and Winchester cathedral priory over the spiritual revenues of the churches of East Meon and Hambledon during the vacancy of the see (with extracts from earlier documents) May 1494–Nov. 1497
251*r*–256*v*	grants of administration Jan. 1487–Oct. 1490 (an entry on fo. 255*v* dated May 1499 should in all probability read 1489)
[257*r*]	later table of select contents

2. LPL, volume II. Parchment register (composite volume); fos. i (paper)+xiv (paper, 16th-cent. index, 12½" × 8")+166 (16" × 13")+4 (16" × 13½")+8 (16" × 12¼")+48 (16" × 11½")+i (paper), foliated 2–128, 130–228; blank: fos. 7*r*, 47*r*–50*r*, 61*v*–62*v*, 122*r*–123*r*, 127*v*, 171*v*–172*v*, 179*v*–180*v*, 197*v*–198*v*, 228*v*; stamped leather binding on wooden boards, re-spined.

2*r*–121*v*	record of vacancy administration of the Norwich diocese Feb.–July 1499
123*v*–127*r*	*inspeximus* by Archbishop Chichele's chancellor of documents relating to the foundation and statutes of Holy Trinity College, Bredgar Oct. 1430
128*r*–136*v*	institutions and collations in the diocese of Canterbury and archiepiscopal peculiars (including vacancy and other provincial business) Jan. 1487–Mar. 1489
137*r*–144*v*	ordinations (last entry incomplete) Mar. 1488–Mar. 1499
145*r*–168*v*	institutions and collations (cont.) Nov. 1489–Sept. 1500
169*r*–171*r*	acts of Archbishop Henry Deane (see below)
173*r*–179*r*	acts of Archbishop Thomas Bourgchier (see above)
181*r*–228*r*	acts of Archbishop William Courtenay (see above)

Both of Morton's registers have been edited by C. Harper-Bill, 'An edition of the register of John Morton, archbishop of Canterbury, 1486–1500' (London University Ph.D., 1977). Lambeth Palace Library, Ducarel indexes 28–30 cover these registers. A general description of the registers by C. Jenkins, 'Cardinal Morton's register' is printed in *Tudor Studies presented by the Board of Studies in History in the University of London to Albert Frederick Pollard*, ed. R. W. Setson-Watson (London, 1924), pp. 26–74. Fos. 207*r*–214*v* are discussed by C. Harper-Bill, 'Bishop Richard Hill and the Court of Canterbury, 1494–96', *Guildhall Studies in London History* 3 (1977), 1–12. For an article on the 1499 Norwich vacancy see under Norwich.

VACANCY 1500–1501

CAL, register R, fos. 40*r*–171*v* (for description see 1486 vacancy).

Canterbury vacancy business Sept. 1500–July 1501 (including Ely and Winchester vacancy business)

Institutions are calendared (by place) in *Sede Vacante Institutions*.

HENRY DEANE (1501–1503)

1. LPL, bound with register of Archbishop John Morton, volume II, fos: 169*r*–171*r* (for description see under Morton).

institutions and collations in the diocese of Canterbury and archiepiscopal peculiars July 1501–Dec. 1502

For the Ducarel index see under Morton.

2. PRO, Prob. 11/13 (Prerogative Court of Canterbury probate register 'Blamyr'), fos. 1*r*–16*r*. Parchment; 15½″ × 13½″; fos. 16; blank: fos. 1*v*, 6*v*–8*v*, 16*v*. Two quires from Archbishop Deane's register.

1*r*	register heading
2*r*–16*r*	bulls of translation etc., commissions and appointments, vacancy accounts, etc. (including a few copies of earlier documents) May 1501–Oct. 1502

Calendared by J. C. C. Smith, *Index of Wills proved in the Prerogative Court of Canterbury 1383–1558*, i (British Record Society, Index Library 10, 1893), pp. xvi–xix.

VACANCY 1503

CAL, register R, fos. 172*r*–180*r* (for description see 1486 vacancy).

Canterbury vacancy business Feb.–July 1503

Institutions are calendared (by place) in *Sede Vacante Institutions*.

WILLIAM WARHAM (1503–1532)

1. LPL, volume I. Parchment register; 17″ × 13¼″; fos. iv (paper) + 216 + iv (paper), foliated 1–53, 53*, 54–114, 114*, 115–122, 123*, 123–157, 158*, 158–167, 167*, 168–188, 190–201, 203–213; blank: fos. 27*r*–34*v*, 83*v*, 86*v*, 142*r*–143*v*, 176*r*–*v*, 179*r*–181*v*, 187*r*–190*v*, 200*v*, 213*r*–*v*; modern binding.

2. LPL, volume II. Parchment register; 17″ × 13¼″; fos. iv (paper) + 209 + iv (paper), foliated 214–255, 260–286, 286*, 287, 288, 290–426; blank: fos. 237*v*–239*v*, 261*v*, 265*r*, 267*r*–*v*, 283*r*, 286**r*–*v*, 307*v*, 316*v*, 318*v*–319*v*, 320*v*, 400*v*, 419*r*–*v*, 426*v*; modern binding.

Volume I

1*r*–26*v*	bulls of translation of Warham etc., followed by general memoranda, papal letters etc. (there is some chronological confusion. The bulk of this section approximates to the section recording appointments of bishops to be found in other registers, but there is also much administrative memoranda and also miscellanea, such as business relating to the peace treaty 1510) Nov. 1503–Nov. 1525
35*r*–89*v*	record of visitation of the diocese of Canterbury and the immediate jurisdictions, with a list of procurations of religious houses etc. Apr. 1511–July 1512
90*r*–158*v*	copies of earlier papal bulls, archiepiscopal and episcopal *acta* and other charters concerning churches appropriated to religious houses, colleges, chantries etc. (arranged by religious house etc.)
159*r*–175*v*	proceedings against heretics, abjurations etc. (in some confusion) Apr. 1511–June 1512
177*r*–178*v*	*Quod Registrum Cantu*[*a*]*r' faciat fidem* (extracts from Aretinus)
182*r*–186*v*	list of 'many great errours and pestilent heresies' May 1530
191*r*–212*v*	record of vacancy administration of suffragan sees Jan.–Dec. 1504

Volume II

214*r*–254*v*	record of vacancy administration of suffragan sees Feb. 1504–July 1509
255*r*	account of the commissary-general of Calais and the Marches 1509
259*v*	accounts of the dean of Pagham and Tarring Sept. 1508–Sept. 1510
260*r*–*v*	accounts of the dean of Shoreham, Croydon, Bocking and Risborough Jan. 1509–Jan. 1511
261*r*	account of monies paid to the archbishop by his receiver for collations and institutions Dec. 1505–Jan. 1511
262*r*–266*v*	ordinations Mar. 1505–Dec. 1509, Apr. 1511–Mar. 1513
268*r*–316*r*	record of vacancy administration of suffragan sees Feb. 1513–July 1530
317*r*–318*r*	archiepiscopal confirmation of a composition between the vicar of Darenth and the inhabitants of the chapelry of St Margaret, Hilles, co. Kent Jan. 1523
320*r*–397*v*	institutions and collations in the diocese of Canterbury and archiepiscopal peculiars (including vacancy and other provincial business) Sept. 1504–July 1529
398*r*–399*v*	foundation deed of chantry at Pagham 1382
400*r*	will of Robert Warham, prob. Apr. 1529
401*r*–405*v*	institutions and collations (cont.) July 1529–Dec. 1531
406*r*–407*v*	foundation deed of chantry at Chiddingstone Oct. 1517
408*r*–411*v*	foundation deed and related documents of chantry at St Pancras church, London Dec. 1522–Dec. 1524
412*r*–413*v*	ordination of the vicarage of Shoreham and chapel of Otford July 1531
414*r*–416*v*	institutions and collations (cont.) Sept. 1531–July 1532
417*r*–418*v*	composition between Southwark priory and the vicar of Nutley July 1531
420*r*–425*v*	*processus pro clericis convictis infra gaolam de Maydeston' . . . existentibus purgandis et a carceralibus vinculis liberandis* Aug. 1507–Oct. 1511
426*r*	later select index

Lambeth Palace Library, Ducarel indexes 31–33 cover these registers. The 1511 visitation (fos. 35*r*–89*v*) is discussed by M. Bateson, 'Archbishop Warham's visitation of monasteries, 1511', *English Historical Review* 6 (1891), 18–35; see also S. R. Maitland, 'Archbishop Warham's visitation in the year 1511', *British Magazine* xxix–xxxii (1846–7). An English paraphrase of fos. 182*r*–186*v* is printed by P. Hughes, *The Reformation in England ii, Religio Depopulata* (London, 1961), pp. 331–46; the full text is printed in Wilkins, *Concilia* iii, pp. 727–37.

THOMAS CRANMER (1533–1553)

LPL, no class reference. Parchment register; 16½″ × 13″; fos. 439, foliated 1–75, 78–276, 278–338, 338[A], 339–405, 405[A], 406–421, 421[A], 422–431, 431[A], 432, 433, 433[A], 434, 435, [436, 437]; blank: fos. 6*r*–8*v*, 14*v*, 37*v*–38*v*, 46*v*, 52*r*–*v*, 66*v*, 79*v*, 80*v*, 88*r*–*v*, 140*v*, 147*r*–148*v*, 163*v*–164*v*, 192*v*, 200*v*, 213*r*–*v*, 225*v*–228*v*, 336*v*–338[A]*v*, 433[A]*v*–[437*v*]; stamped leather binding on wooden boards, re-spined.

1*r*–5*v*	papal provision of Cranmer, consecration, and grant of pallium Mar. 1533
9*r*–14*r*	royal writs for Convocation Mar. 1539–Aug. 1553
15*r*–80*r*	*commissiones diverse* (licences, commissions, grants, mandates, royal letters, visitation business etc., in some chronological confusion) Dec. 1532–June 1553
81*r*–87*v*	confirmation of the bishop of Ely Apr. 1534
89*r*–137*v*	record of vacancy administration of suffragan sees May 1538–Aug. 1553

137*v*–140*r* record of visitation of the Norwich diocese July 1534
141*r*–146*v* divorce of Anne of Cleves and Henry VIII 1540
149*r*–336*r* record of the confirmation and consecration of bishops Apr. 1534–May 1553
(fos. 215*r*–216*v* contain commissions and a letter regarding Henry VIII's injunctions 1538)
339*r*–424*r* institutions and collations in the diocese of Canterbury and archiepiscopal peculiars (including vacancy and other provincial business) Apr. 1533–Sept. 1553
424*v*–426*v* lists of benefices in the archbishop's collation and their value, benefices once belonging to the archbishop, and *sacerdotia* belonging to the archbishop by reason of the exchanges with Henry VIII and Edward VI
427*r*–429*v* *acta* in the trial of William Curtney *alias* Curtnall, convicted clerk Oct. 1543
430*r*–433*r* *acta* concerning the purgation of George Gower and others Nov. 1548–June 1551
433*v*–433[A]*r* indenture over exchange of advowsons of Monks Risborough, Bucks., and Midley, Kent Apr. 1548

Institutions to benefices *sede vacante* (fos. 89*r*–137*v*) are calendared in A. J. Edwards, 'The *sede vacante* administration of Archbishop Thomas Cranmer, 1533–53' (London University M. Phil., 1968). Lambeth Palace Library, Ducarel indexes 34–36 cover this register. The letter about Henry VIII's injunctions (fos. 215*v*–216*v*) is printed by H. Gee and W. J. Hardy, *Documents illustrative of English church history* (*A.D. 314–1700*) (London, 1896), pp. 275–81.

VACANCY 1553–1556

1. CAL, register N. Paper register; fos. iii+291+iii, fos. 1–170 $11\frac{3}{4}'' \times 8''$, from fo. 171 $11\frac{3}{4}'' \times 8\frac{1}{2}''$, foliated [i], 1–134, 134A, 135–187, 187A, 188–212, 212A, 213–274; blank: fos. [i*v*], 39*v*–54*v*, 100*r*–*v*, 123*v*, 134*r*–*v*, 135*r*–138*v*, 170*r*–171*v*, 200*v*, 201*r*, 212*v*, 212A*v*, 236*v*, 237*r*, 256*v*, 259*r*–260*v* (and several unnumbered folios); modern binding.

5 fos. (unnumbered at beginning)
index to first part of volume
[i*r*] vacancy register heading
1*r*–169*v* Canterbury vacancy register
1*r*–32*v* commissions Dec. 1553–Feb. 1556
33*r*–39*r* consecrations of bishops Oct. 1554–Sept. 1555
55*r*–99*v* institutions in the diocese of Canterbury and archiepiscopal peculiars (including some vacancy institutions in other sees) Dec. 1553–Jan. 1556
101*r*–134A*r* record of vacancy administration of suffragan sees Jan. 1554–Mar. 1556
139*r*–169*v* proceedings against married clergy in the dioceses of Canterbury and Rochester Mar. 1554–Mar. 1556
172*r*–273*v* 15th-cent. Canterbury priory register (this is the second part of the composite volume)

2. CAL, register V1. Paper register (damaged by fire and extensively repaired); average $15\frac{1}{2}'' \times 10\frac{1}{4}''$; fos. ii+82+ii, foliated 1–82; blank: fo. 7*r*; modern parchment-covered boards.

This is a miscellaneous register containing both *sede vacante* and capitular material, somewhat confused. It is clear that many entries were registered a considerable time after the events they describe. *Sede vacante* material after Cranmer's suspension and deprivation occurs on fos. 1, 5–7, 9–13, 16–20, 22–28, 32, 37, 45–49, [ ] 1553–Jan. 1556.

Institutions in both these volumes are calendared (by place) in *Sede Vacante Institutions*.

REGINALD POLE (1556–1558)

LPL, no class reference. Parchment register; 16½″ × 13½″; fos. ii (paper)+84+iii (paper), foliated [i–ii], 1–82; blank: fos. [ir–v, iiv], 14v, 64v–66v, 82v; stamped leather binding on wooden boards, re-spined.

[iir]	coat of arms of Pole
1r–v	register heading
1v–6v	papal provision and consecration of Pole Dec. 1555–Mar. 1556
7v–13v	record of provision and consecration of bishops Mar.–Dec. 1557
13v–14r	royal grant of advowsons to Pole Nov. 1558
15r–31v	*commissiones diverse* Mar. 1556–Nov. 1558
32r–36v	record of visitation of the diocese of Canterbury, the deanery of Arches, and commissions for the visitations of All Souls College, Oxford Apr. 1556–Oct. 1558
37r–64r	record of vacancy administration of suffragan sees Mar. 1556–Nov. 1558
67r–82r	institutions and collations in the diocese of Canterbury (including vacancy and other provincial business) Apr. 1556–Nov. 1558

Lambeth Palace Library, Ducarel index 37 covers this register.

VACANCY 1558–1559

1. CAL, register V1, fos. 34–35, 50–52 (for description see 1553–6 vacancy).

   Canterbury vacancy business Nov.–Dec. 1558

2. CAL, register U2. Paper register; 15″ × 10½″; fos. i+106, foliated 1–30, 32–75, 78–109; blank: fo. 109v; leather binding, embossed.

1r–6v	commissions Nov. 1558–July 1559
7r–13v	testamentary business Jan.–Nov. 1559
14r–19r	institutions in the diocese of Canterbury and archiepiscopal peculiars Dec. 1558–July 1559
19r–20r	testamentary business July–Nov. 1559
20v–106v	record of vacancy administration of suffragan sees Dec. 1558–Dec. 1559
107r–108v	lease and confirmation of the rectory of Cleeve, Glos. Mar. 1559
109r	miscellaneous document May 1571

Lambeth Palace Library, Ducarel index for this vacancy (another copy at Canterbury Cathedral Archives and Library). Institutions in both these registers are calendared (by place) in *Sede Vacante Institutions*.

MATTHEW PARKER (1559–1575)
VACANCY 1575–1576

1. LPL, volume I. Parchment register; 17″ × 14″; fos. i+413, foliated [i], 1–149, 149[A], 150–212, 212[A], 213–226, 228–264, 266–309, 309[A], 310–352, 354–413; stamped leather binding on wooden boards, re-spined.

   This register follows the familiar pattern: after the record of Parker's consecration, there are sections containing records of the confirmation and consecration of bishops, 1559–72; the vacancy administration of suffragan sees, 1559–71; *commissiones diverse*, 1559–71 (including a record of ordinations celebrated under commission); the record of the archbishop's visitations, 1560–9; and finally, institutions and collations in the diocese of Canterbury and archiepiscopal peculiars, 1559–71.

2. LPL, volume II. Parchment register; 16″ × 13″; fos. i (paper)+135+i (paper), foliated [i–ii], 1–133; stamped leather binding on wooden boards, re-spined.
   This continuation of the first register follows the same arrangement. The 1575–6 vacancy register,

which occupies fos. 108–132, is subdivided into *commissiones diverse*, institutions in the Canterbury diocese, and a record of vacancy administration in suffragan sees.

Printed, *Registrum Matthei Parker diocesis Cantuariensis, A.D. 1559–1575*, transcribed by E. M. Thompson and ed. W. H. Frere (3 vols., Canterbury and York Society 35, 36, 39, 1928–33).

EDMUND GRINDAL (1576–1583)
VACANCY 1583

1. LPL, volume I. Parchment register; 16½″ × 13¼″; fos. iv (paper) + 291 + iv (paper), foliated i–ii, 1–23, 23A, 24–143, 144A, 144B, 145–286; blank: fos. i*v*, ii*v*, 23*v*, 83*r*–86*v*, 285*v*–286*v*; modern binding.

i*r*	coat of arms of Grindal
ii*r*	register heading, and note of Grindal's death
1*r*–10*v*	record of the election and confirmation of Grindal Feb. 1576
10*v*–77*v*	record of the confirmation and consecration of bishops Apr. 1576–Dec. 1582
78*r*–83*r*	record of visitation of the Canterbury diocese Apr. 1576–June 1577
87*r*–143*v*	record of metropolitical visitations of the dioceses of St David's, Llandaff, Bath and Wells, Bristol, Chichester, Winchester, Salisbury, Oxford, St Asaph, Exeter, Hereford, Gloucester, Bangor, Peterborough, Norwich, and Coventry and Lichfield (in some chronological confusion) June 1576–June 1583
144A*r*–284*v*	*commissiones diverse* Feb. 1576–June 1583
285*r*	memorandum of Grindal's executors about the defacing of the archiepiscopal seals July 1583

2. LPL, volume II. Parchment register; 16½″ × 13¼″; fos. iv (paper) + 328 + iv (paper), foliated 287–317, 319–415, 415[A], 416–587, 589–600, 2nd series 591–604, [605]; blank: fos. 378*v*–380*v*, 458*r*–459*v*, 490*v*–491*v*, 508*v*–509*v*, 573*v*, 574*v*, 590*v*, 599*v*–600*v*, 2nd series 599*v*, 600*v*–604*v*; modern binding.

287*r*–508*r*	record of vacancy administration of suffragan sees (not in strict chronological order) Mar. 1576–June 1583	
510*r*–571*r*	institutions and collations in the diocese of Canterbury and archiepiscopal peculiars (including some provincial business *iure devoluto*) Feb. 1576–July 1583	
571*r*–573*r*	list of benefices in the archbishop's collation, arranged alphabetically	
574*r*–590*r*	Canterbury vacancy register	
	574*r*	register heading
	575*r*–579*r*	*commissiones diverse* July–Sept. 1583
	579*r*–580*r*	visitation of the diocese of Canterbury July 1583
	580*r*–587*v*	record of vacancy administration of suffragan sees July–Sept. 1583
	589*r*–590*r*	institutions in the diocese of Canterbury July–Aug. 1583
591*r*–599*r*	articles, citation etc. in a cause concerning the warden and fellows of Merton College, Oxford Nov. 1581–Dec. 1582	
(*2nd series*)		
591*r*–599*r*	contemporary table of contents and index	
600*r*	names of advocates and proctors *temp.* Grindal	

Lambeth Palace Library, Ducarel indexes 42–44 cover these registers.

JOHN WHITGIFT (1583–1604)
VACANCY 1604

1. LPL, volume I. Parchment register; $16\frac{1}{2}'' \times 13''$; fos. i (paper) + 495, foliated [i], 1–63, [63A], 64–87, 89–100, 102–267, 269–496; blank: fos. [i*r*–*v*], 84*v*, 220*v*, 247*v*, 295*v*, 369*v*, 387*v*, 419*v*; stamped leather binding on wooden boards, re-spined.

1*r*–8*v*	record of the election and confirmation of Whitgift Sept. 1583
9*r*–84*r*	record of the confirmation and consecration of bishops Mar. 1584–Dec. 1591
85*r*–206*v*	*commissiones diverse* Oct. 1583–June 1593
207*r*–261*v*	record of visitations of the dioceses of Bangor, Coventry and Lichfield, Hereford, Llandaff, Salisbury, Gloucester, St Asaph, Exeter, St David's, Norwich, Peterborough, Bath and Wells, Canterbury, and Rochester Feb. 1584–Feb. 1590
262*r*–275*r*	wills proved during the visitation of Canterbury and Rochester dioceses June 1589–July 1590
275*v*–276*v*	visitation of the Bocking deanery and wills proved there *ratione visitationis* Aug. 1590
277*r*–448*v*	record of vacancy administration of suffragan sees Oct. 1583–June 1592
449*r*–496*v*	institutions and collations in the diocese of Canterbury and archiepiscopal peculiars (including some provincial business *iure devoluto*) Oct. 1583–Jan. 1592

2. LPL, volume II. Parchment register; $17\frac{1}{4}'' \times 13''$; fos. i (paper) + 356 + i (paper), foliated [i], 1–355; blank: fos. [i*r*–*v*], 103*v*–104*v*, 163*v*–164*v*, 187*r*–*v*, 223*r*–224*v*, 274*r*–*v*, 305*r*–306*v*, 311*r*–312*v*, 354*v*–355*v*; stamped leather binding on wooden boards, re-spined.

1*r*–103*r*	record of the confirmation and consecration of bishops Nov. 1592–Oct. 1597
105*r*–163*r*	*commissiones diverse* June 1593–Dec. 1597
165*r*–310*v*	record of vacancy administration of suffragan sees May 1592–Dec. 1597
313*r*–350*r*	institutions and collations in the diocese of Canterbury and archiepiscopal peculiars (including some provincial business *iure devoluto*) Feb. 1592–Dec. 1597 (with 1 entry Nov. 1589)
351*r*–*v*	contemporary table of contents
351*v*–354*r*	contemporary place index of institutions

3. LPL, volume III. Parchment register; $17'' \times 13''$; fos. i (paper) + 294 + i (paper), foliated [i], 1–287, [288–293]; blank: fos. [i*r*–*v*], 85*r*–*v*, 156*v*–157*v*, 165*v*, 180*r*–181*v*, 240*v*–245*v*, 287*v*, [290*r*–293*v*]; stamped leather binding on wooden boards, re-spined.

1*r*–84*v*	record of the confirmation and consecration of bishops July 1598–Feb. 1604
86*r*–156*r*	*commissiones diverse* (the last few entries date from the vacancy of the archbishopric) Dec. 1597–July 1604
158*r*–240*r*	record of vacancy administration of suffragan sees June 1597–Feb. 1604
246*r*–278*v*	institutions and collations in the diocese of Canterbury and archiepiscopal peculiars (including some provincial business *iure devoluto*) Dec. 1597–Feb. 1604
279*r*–287*r*	Canterbury vacancy register Mar.–Dec. 1604
[288*r*–*v*]	contemporary table of contents
[289*r*–*v*]	contemporary place index of institutions

Lambeth Palace Library, Ducarel indexes 45–51 cover these registers.

RICHARD BANCROFT (1604–1610)
VACANCY 1610–1611

LPL, no class reference. Parchment register; 17″ × 13½″; fos. ii (paper) + 313 + i (paper), foliated [i], 1–310, [311, 312]; blank: fos. [i*r*–*v*], 122*v*–123*v*, 177*r*–*v*, [312*v*]; stamped leather binding on wooden boards, re-spined.

1*r*–9*r*	record of the election and confirmation of Bancroft Dec. 1604
9*r*–116*v*	record of the confirmation and consecration of bishops Dec. 1604–Oct. 1610
116*v*–122*r*	record of the confirmation and consecration of the bishop of Coventry and Lichfield *sede vacante* Dec. 1610
124*r*–176*v*	*commissiones diverse* Jan. 1605–Oct. 1610
178*r*–233*v*	record of visitations of the dioceses of Bath and Wells, Bristol, St David's, Worcester, Exeter, Norwich, Llandaff, Coventry and Lichfield, Hereford, Chichester, Salisbury, Winchester, Ely, Oxford, Peterborough, Rochester, Bangor, St Asaph, Canterbury, and Gloucester Mar. 1605–Feb. 1610
234*r*–265*v*	record of vacancy administration of suffragan sees (including a few entries for Coventry and Lichfield and Gloucester *sede vacante*, 1610) Jan. 1605–Dec. 1610
266*r*–303*v*	institutions and collations in the diocese of Canterbury and archiepiscopal peculiars (including some provincial business *iure devoluto*) Dec. 1604–Aug. 1610
303*v*–309*v*	Canterbury vacancy register Nov. 1610–Apr. 1611
309*v*–310*r*	record of vacancy administration of the Rochester diocese by the dean and chapter of Canterbury *sede vacante* Jan.–Mar. 1611
310*v*–[311*r*]	contemporary table of contents
[311*v*–312*r*]	contemporary index of institutions

Lambeth Palace Library, Ducarel index 52 covers this register.

GEORGE ABBOT (1611–1633)
VACANCY 1633

1. LPL, volume I. Parchment register; 16½″ × 13¾″; fos. i (paper) + 440 + i (paper), foliated [i], 1–100, 102–437, [438–440]; blank: fos. [i*r*–*v*], 151*v*, 220*v*–223*v*, 292*v*–295*v*, 327*v*, 386*v*–387*v*, [440*v*]; stamped leather binding on wooden boards, re-spined.

1*r*–9*v*	record of the election and confirmation of Abbot Mar.–Apr. 1611
9*v*–151*r*	record of the confirmation and consecration of bishops June 1611–Mar. 1619
152*r*–220*r*	*commissiones diverse* Apr. 1611–Mar. 1619
224*r*–292*r*	record of visitations of the dioceses of Exeter, Bristol, Gloucester, Salisbury, Bath and Wells, Norwich, Peterborough, Oxford, Hereford, Bangor, St Asaph, Worcester, St David's, Llandaff, Ely, Chichester, Rochester, Canterbury, Winchester, and Coventry and Lichfield Mar. 1612–Oct. 1616
296*r*–386*r*	record of vacancy administration of suffragan sees Apr. 1611–Apr. 1619
388*r*–437*v*	institutions and collations in the diocese of Canterbury and archiepiscopal peculiars (including some provincial business *iure devoluto*) June 1611–Mar. 1619
437*v*–[438*v*]	contemporary table of contents
[439*r*–440*r*]	contemporary place index of institutions

2. LPL, volume II. Parchment register; 17″ × 14″; fos. i (paper) + 364 + i (paper), foliated [i], 1–360, [361–363]; blank: fos. [i*r*–*v*], 175*r*–176*v*, 309*r*–310*v*, [363*v*]; stamped leather binding on wooden boards, re-spined.

1*r*–174*v*	record of the confirmation and consecration of bishops May 1619–Feb. 1629
177*r*–240*v*	*commissiones diverse* Mar. 1619–May 1629
241*r*–308*v*	record of vacancy administration of suffragan sees May 1619–Feb. 1629
311*r*–360*v*	institutions and collations in the diocese of Canterbury and archiepiscopal peculiars (including some provincial business *iure devoluto*, and occasional licences for curates and preachers) Mar. 1619–Feb. 1629
360*v*–[361*v*]	contemporary table of contents
[362*r*–363*r*]	contemporary place index of institutions

3. LPL, volume III. Parchment register; 17¼″ × 14″; fos. i (paper) + 206 + i (paper), foliated 1–204, [205, 206]; blank: fos. 96*r*–*v*, 144*v*, [206*r*–*v*]; stamped leather binding on wooden boards, re-spined.

1*r*–90*v*	record of the confirmation and consecration of bishops Sept. 1629–Mar. 1633
91*v*–95*v*	record of the visitation of the diocese of Canterbury, Dulwich College, and the deaneries of South Malling, Pagham and Tarring Feb. 1630–Oct. 1632
97*r*–144*r*	*commissiones diverse* May 1629–July 1633
145*r*–182*v*	record of vacancy administration of suffragan sees Aug. 1629–June 1633
183*r*–202*v*	institutions and collations in the diocese of Canterbury and archiepiscopal peculiars (including some provincial business *iure devoluto*) Apr. 1629–Aug. 1633
202*v*–204*v*	Canterbury vacancy register Aug. 1633
204*v*–[205*r*]	contemporary table of contents
[205*r*–*v*]	contemporary place index of institutions

Lambeth Palace Library, Ducarel indexes 53–55 cover these registers.

WILLIAM LAUD (1633–1645)

1. LPL, volume I. Parchment register; 18″ × 14¼″; fos. i (paper) + 330 + i (paper), foliated [i–iii], 1–323, [324–327]; blank: fos. [i*r*–*v*, ii*v*–iii*v*], 74*r*–76*v*, 90*r*–92*v*, 186*r*–188*v*, 291*v*, 307*v*, [326*v*–327*v*]; stamped leather binding on wooden boards, re-spined.

[ii*r*]	coat of arms of Laud
1*r*–12*r*	record of the election and confirmation of Laud Sept. 1633
12*r*–73*v*	record of the confirmation and consecration of bishops Oct. 1633–Jan. 1638
77*r*–185*v*	record of visitations of the dioceses of Canterbury, Rochester, Salisbury, Exeter, Bath and Wells, Bristol, Lincoln, Norwich, Winchester, Coventry and Lichfield, Worcester, Gloucester, Chichester, Peterborough, London, Hereford, St David's, Llandaff, Bangor, and St Asaph Nov. 1633–Aug. 1637
189*r*–291*r*	*commissiones diverse* Oct. 1633–Feb. 1638
292*r*–307*r*	record of vacancy administration of suffragan sees Sept. 1633–Mar. 1638 (1 collation, Nov. 1638, added at the end in a later hand)
308*r*–323*v*	institutions and collations in the diocese of Canterbury and archiepiscopal peculiars (including some provincial business *iure devoluto*) Nov. 1633–Mar. 1638

323*v*–[324*r*] contemporary table of contents
[324*r*–326*r*] contemporary place index of institutions

2. LPL, volume II. Parchment register; 18″ × 13¾″; fos. 104, foliated 1–104; blank: fos. 23*r*–24*v*, 35*r*–36*v*, 64*v*, 102*v*–104*v*; stamped leather binding on wooden boards, re-spined.

1*r*–22*v* record of vacancy administration of the see of Lincoln by reason of the suspension of Bishop John Williams July 1637–Aug. 1638
25*r*–102*r* record of the confirmation and consecration of bishops Aug. 1637–June 1642

3. LPL, VX.IIA/I/IA. Paper register (repaired); 12″ × 8″; fos. vi (paper) + 49 + vi (paper), foliated 1–49; blank: fos. 4*r*, 13*v*, 24*v*, 27*v*, 49*v*; modern binding.

1*r*–49*r* record of vacancy administration of the see of Lincoln as above July 1637–Aug. 1638

This is clearly a draft register, of which a 'final' version was entered in the second volume of the archbishop's register above.

4. LPL, VB.2/1. Paper register (repaired); the size of the folios varies considerably: 1–4, 7–11, 14–26, 31–34 12¼″ × 8″; 5–6, 27–30 12¾″ × 8″; 12–13 11¼″ × 7¼″; 35–40, 12″ × 8″; 41 11¾″ × 7¾″; fos. vi + 44 + vi, foliated 1–44; blank: fos. 13*r*–*v*, 24*v*, 39*v*–40*v*, 42*v*–44*v*; modern binding.

1*r*–42*r* institutions and other acts Nov. 1633–Mar. 1639

This is a draft register and many of the entries have been entered in the first volume of the archbishop's register above.

Lambeth Palace Library, Ducarel indexes 56–57 cover these registers.

BANGOR

Repositories

1. National Library of Wales, Aberystwyth, Dyfed SY23 3BU (NLW).
2. Lambeth Palace Library, London SE1 7JU (LPL).
3. Canterbury Cathedral Archives and Library, The Precincts, Canterbury CT1 2EG (CAL).

Area

The diocese of Bangor extended over Anglesey, Carnarvonshire and western Merionethshire and in addition included two detached districts: the deanery of Dyffryn Clwyd in Denbighshire, containing Ruthin and neighbouring parishes and entirely surrounded by the diocese of St Asaph; and the deanery of Arwystli in Montgomeryshire situated between the dioceses of St Asaph and St David's.[1] These boundaries were not altered until the nineteenth century. The diocese was divided into the two archdeaconries of Anglesey and Merioneth.

Bibliographical Note

In common with the other Welsh dioceses, Bangor has suffered its fair share of losses as far as episcopal registers are concerned, and all the pre-1646 registers of its bishops are now contained in two composite volumes, together with the register of the vicar-general of Bishop John Salcot (1534–9), bound up in a miscellaneous volume.[2] The earliest is the register of Bishop Benedict Nicolls (1408–18), the sole medieval survivor, but almost a century elapses before a fragment of another register survives. The second volume comprises the registers of bishops from Arthur Bulkeley (1543–52) to Edmund Griffith (1634–7): the records of these bishops take the form of a general, chronological register, including ordinations in the main sequence. Nicolls' register has been printed, as have abstracts of institutions and ordinations in the sixteenth- and seventeenth-century volumes.

VACANCY 1357

1. LPL, register of Archbishop Simon Islip, fo. 220*r–v*.[3]

   Bangor vacancy business (financial) Jan.–Oct. 1358

2. *ibid.*, fo. 342*v*.

   note of Bangor vacancy commissions Apr. 1357
   (a further note about a letter sent in Feb. 1358 is on fo. 342*r*)

VACANCY 1366

1. LPL, register of Archbishop Simon Islip, fos. 245*v*–247*r*.

   Bangor vacancy business Jan.–Feb. 1366

[1] A. Hamilton Thompson, 'The Welsh Medieval Dioceses', *Journal of the Historical Society of the Church in Wales* 1 (1947), 90–111, especially 94; A. I. Pryce, *The Diocese of Bangor during three centuries* (Cardiff, 1929), pp. lxxxvii–lxxxviii; for Arwystli see J. E. Lloyd, *A History of Wales from the earliest times to the Edwardian Conquest* (2 vols., 2nd edn., London, 1911), i, pp. 249–50. For a map of the diocese see Ordnance Survey, *Map of Monastic Britain: (south sheet)* (2nd edn., 1954); W. Rees, *An Historical Atlas of Wales from early to modern times* (2nd edn., London, 1972), plate 33.

[2] For a description of the contents of the extant registers see A. I. Pryce, 'The Reformation in the diocese of Bangor, as illustrated by the records', *Transactions of the Anglesey Antiquarian Society and Field Club* (1939), 43–60.

[3] See under Canterbury for a description of this and subsequent archiepiscopal and capitular registers.

2. CAL, register G, fos. 125*r*–143*v* *passim.*

Bangor vacancy business May–Sept. 1366, among the general section of Canterbury institutions

VACANCY 1375–1376

LPL, register of Archbishop Simon Sudbury, fo. 117*r–v*.

Bangor vacancy business Apr.–May 1376, among the general section of Canterbury institutions

VACANCY 1404–1408

LPL, register of Archbishop Thomas Arundel, volume I, fos. 304*v*–319*r* *passim.*

Bangor vacancy business Sept. 1405–Mar. 1408, among the general section of Canterbury institutions

BENEDICT NICOLLS (1408–1418)
THOMAS SKEVINGTON (1509–1533)

NLW, B/BR/1. Composite register; $11\frac{3}{4}'' \times 8\frac{3}{4}''$ (Nicolls), $11\frac{3}{4}'' \times 8\frac{3}{4}''$ (Skevington); fos. iv (paper) + 7 (parchment) + 18 (paper) + iv (paper), foliated 1–25; blank: fos. 19*v*, 21*v*, 24*r*–25*r*; modern binding.

1*r*–7*v* register of Bishop Benedict Nicolls [Apr. 1408]–Dec. 1417
8*r*–25*v* fragment of the register of Bishop Thomas Skevington June 1512–Aug. 1525

There is a 16th-cent. copy of Bishop Benedict's register in NLW, B/Misc. Vol./27, pp. 155–85 and a partial copy in the same volume (pp. 45–50), and yet another fragmentary copy, *ibid.*, B/Misc./272. These partial copies were also made in the 16th century.

Fos. 1*r*–7*v* are printed by A. I. Pryce, 'The register of Benedict, bishop of Bangor, 1408–1417', in *Archaeologia Cambrensis* 77 (1920), 80–107. The institutions between fos. 8*r*–25*v* are calendared by A. I. Pryce, *The Diocese of Bangor in the Sixteenth Century, being a digest of the registers of the bishops A.D. 1512–1646* (Bangor, 1923), pp. 1–6.

VACANCY 1423–1425

LPL, register of Archbishop Henry Chichele, volume I, fos. 158*r*–160*v* *passim.*

Bangor vacancy business Oct. 1425–Mar. 1426, among the general section of Canterbury institutions

Printed, *Register of Henry Chichele* i, pp. 228–32 *passim.*

VACANCY 1435–1436

LPL, register of Archbishop Henry Chichele, volume I, fos. 209*v*–213*r* *passim.*

Bangor vacancy business Feb.–Oct. 1436, among the general section of Canterbury institutions

Printed, *Register of Henry Chichele* i, pp. 290–4 *passim.*

VACANCY 1504–1505

1. LPL, register of Archbishop William Warham, volume II, fos. 214*r*–221*v*.

Bangor vacancy business Aug.–Nov. 1504

The clergy lists on fos. 216*r*–217*v* are calendared in A. I. Pryce, *The Diocese of Bangor in the Sixteenth Century*, app. A, pp. 81–4.

2. *ibid.*, fos. 322*v*–325*r passim.*

Bangor vacancy business Jan.–Sept. 1505, among the general section of Canterbury institutions

VACANCY 1508–1509

1. LPL, register of Archbishop William Warham, volume II, fos. 252*r*–253*v*.

Bangor vacancy business Jan.–June 1509

2. *ibid.*, fo. 335*r*.

Bangor vacancy act May 1509 (1 entry), among the general section of Canterbury institutions

JOHN SALCOT (1534–1539)

NLW, B/Misc. Vol./27 ('Acta 3'), pp. 195–214. Paper register (bound in composite volume); $11\frac{3}{4}'' \times 8''$; fos. 10; blank: pp. 207, 214.

195–213 register of master William Capon, vicar-general of Bishop Salcot May 1534–Jan. 1538.

Institutions are calendared in A. I. Pryce, *The Diocese of Bangor in the Sixteenth Century*, pp. 7–8.

VACANCY 1541–1542

LPL, register of Archbishop Thomas Cranmer, fos. 382*v*–383*r*.

Bangor vacancy business Sept. 1541

Calendared in A. J. Edwards, 'The *sede vacante* administration of Archbishop Thomas Cranmer, 1533–53' (London University M.Phil., 1968).

ARTHUR BULKELEY (1542–1553)
VACANCY 1553–1555
WILLIAM GLYNN (1555–1558)
VACANCY 1558–1559
ROWLAND MEYRICK (1559–1566)
VACANCY 1566
NICHOLAS ROBINSON (1566–1585)
VACANCY 1585–1586
HUGH BELLOTT (1586–1595)
RICHARD VAUGHAN (1596–1597)
HENRY ROWLANDS (1598–1616)
LEWIS BAYLY (1616–1631)
VACANCY 1631–1632
DAVID DOLBEN (1632–1633)

VACANCY 1633–1634
EDMUND GRIFFITH (1634–1637)

NLW, B/BR/2.[4] Parchment register; $12\frac{1}{2}'' \times 8\frac{1}{4}''$; fos. iv (modern paper) + i (paper) + 147 + iv (modern paper), foliated [i–ii], 1–114, 124–154; blank: fos. [*ir*–*iiv*], 114*v*, 134*v*, 154*v*; modern binding.

1*r*–13*r*	register of Bishop Arthur Bulkeley Mar. 1542–Mar. 1553
13*r*–15*v*	*sede vacante* register Apr. 1554–July 1555 (see also below)
16*r*–20*v*	register of Bishop William Glynn May 1556–May 1558
20*v*–21*r*	*sede vacante* register July–Dec. 1558 (see also below)
21*r*–26*r*	register of Bishop Rowland Meyrick Apr. 1560–Jan. 1566
26*v*	*sede vacante* register June–July 1566
27*r*–51*v*	register of Bishop Nicholas Robinson May 1567–Feb. 1585
51*v*	*sede vacante* register Mar.–Apr. 1585 (see also below)
52*r*–63*v*	register of Bishop Hugh Bellott Mar. 1586–Sept. 1595
64*r*–*v*	register of Bishop Richard Vaughan Jan. 1596–July 1597
64*v*–102*v*	register of Bishop Henry Rowlands Jan. 1599–July 1616
103*r*–137*r*	register of Bishop Lewis Bayly Jan. 1617–Oct. 1631
137*r*–138*r*	*sede vacante* register Oct. 1631–Feb. 1632 (see also below)
138*r*–142*r*	register of Bishop David Dolben Apr. 1632–Nov. 1633
142*v*–143*v*	*sede vacante* register Nov. 1633 (see also below)
144*r*–154*r*	register of Bishop Edmund Griffith Apr. 1634–Mar. 1637

Institutions and ordinations are calendared in A. I. Pryce, *The Diocese of Bangor in the Sixteenth Century*, pp. 9–80. On pp. 46–7 Pryce includes acts of Bishop William Roberts (1637–65) for the years 1637–46, ostensibly as though they were contained in this volume. This is certainly no longer the case and I have been unable to trace the source of Pryce's information.

VACANCY 1553–1555

1. LPL, register of Archbishop Thomas Cranmer, fos. 136*r*–137*v*.

   Bangor vacancy business Mar.–May 1553

   Institutions are calendared in A. J. Edwards, 'The *sede vacante* administration of Archbishop Thomas Cranmer, 1533–53' (London University M.Phil., 1968).

2. CAL, register N, fos. 113*r*–115*v*.

   Bangor vacancy business Jan. 1554–July 1555

   Institutions are calendared (by place) in *Sede Vacante Institutions*; they are also listed in A. I. Pryce, *The Diocese of Bangor in the Sixteenth Century*, app. B, p. 85.

VACANCY 1558–1559

1. LPL, register of Archbishop Reginald Pole, fos. 62*r*–63*v*.

   Bangor vacancy business June–Oct. 1558

2. CAL, register U2, fos. 28*r*–29*v*.

   Bangor vacancy business Dec. 1558–May 1559

   Institutions are calendared (by place) in *Sede Vacante Institutions*.

[4] The flyleaf records that the volume was put together and bound at the expense of Bishop Warren in 1793.

3. LPL, register of Archbishop Matthew Parker, volume I, fo. 148*r*.

Bangor vacancy business Oct.–Dec. 1559

Printed, *Registrum Matthei Parker* i, pp. 168–9.

VACANCY 1566

LPL, register of Archbishop Matthew Parker, volume I, fos. 180*v*–185*r*.

Bangor vacancy business Jan.–May. 1566

Printed, *Registrum Matthei Parker* i, pp. 230–45.

VACANCY 1585–1586

LPL, register of Archbishop John Whitgift, volume I, fos. 381*r*–384*v*.

Bangor vacancy business Feb.–Dec. 1585

VACANCY 1595–1596

LPL, register of Archbishop John Whitgift, volume II, fos. 299*r*–300*v*.

Bangor vacancy business Sept.–Nov. 1595

VACANCY 1597–1598

LPL, register of Archbishop John Whitgift, volume III, fos. 195*r*–197*r*.

Bangor vacancy business July 1597–Oct. 1598

VACANCY 1616

LPL, register of Archbishop George Abbot, volume I, fos. 334*v*–337*v*.

Bangor vacancy business July–Nov. 1616

VACANCY 1631–1632

LPL, register of Archbishop George Abbot, volume III, fos. 150*v*–153*r*.

Bangor vacancy business Oct. 1631–Feb. 1632 (with additional entry Sept. 1632)

VACANCY 1633–1634

LPL, register of Archbishop William Laud, volume I, fos. 298*r*–300*r*.

Bangor vacancy business Nov. 1633–Feb. 1634

VACANCY 1637

LPL, register of Archbishop William Laud, volume I, fos. 304*v*–305*r*.

Bangor vacancy business May–June 1637

BATH AND WELLS

Repositories

1. Somerset Record Office, Obridge Road, Taunton TA2 7PU (SRO).
2. Lambeth Palace Library, London SE1 7JU (LPL).
3. Canterbury Cathedral Archives and Library, The Precincts, Canterbury CT1 2EG (CAL).
4. Borthwick Institute, University of York, St Anthony's Hall, York YO1 2PW (BI).

Area

The diocese of Bath and Wells was coterminous with the county of Somerset until 1542 when three chapelries of the parish of Bedminster were transferred to the newly created bishopric of Bristol.[1] The diocese was divided into the three archdeaconries of Bath, Wells and Taunton.

Bibliographical Note

The Bath and Wells episcopal registers have been briefly listed in the First Report of the Historical Manuscripts Commission.[2] Giffard's is the earliest known register of this diocese, but there have been losses between his brief tenure of the see (1265–6) and the episcopate of John Droxford (1309–29), whose register is the next to survive. In 1311 the registers of William of March (1293–1302) and Walter Haselshaw (1302–8) were in the hands of their respective executors and Bishop Droxford was attempting to recover possession of them.[3] Records of ordinations were certainly kept by Droxford and his successor Ralph of Shrewsbury (see below) but have not survived, and the late fourteenth-century bishops' registers have likewise disappeared. The first two extant registers are more diverse in their registrational arrangement than their later counterparts. From the time of Nicholas Bubwith (1408–24), the registers follow a threefold division: a general, chronological register of institutions and memoranda; a register of ordinations; and, until the Reformation, a register of elections, chiefly monastic. A separate ordinations register exists for the pontificate of Gilbert Bourne (1554–9) and in view of the fact that the later sixteenth-century registers contain no record of ordinations it is a strong possibility that there were later ordinations books which are now missing. From the time of Bishop Godwin (1584–90), a separate act book of institutions survives, which links with, and supplements, the entries in the contemporary registers.

The 1874 Historical Manuscripts Report referred to above includes in the list the register of Bishop Walter Curle (1629–32). This volume is not now among the diocesan records in the Somerset Record Office and recent enquiries (Jan. 1980) at the Diocesan Registry in Wells have failed to locate it.

Calendars of all the episcopal registers from 1265 to 1559 (excepting certain ordinations lists) have been published by the Somerset Record Society. A place index to the bishops' registers 1309–1727 (including references to the now lost Curle register) is to be found among the diocesan archives at the Somerset Record Office (D/D/B. Reg. 30). Somerset wills 1363–1491 entered in the Canterbury archiepiscopal registers are also published in the Somerset

[1] *VCH Somerset* ii (1911), app. ii, p. 67 and map facing. For a map of the diocese see the frontispiece to W. Hunt, *Diocesan Histories: Bath and Wells* (London, 1885); Ordnance Survey, *Map of Monastic Britain: (south sheet)* (2nd edn., 1954).

[2] *Historical Manuscripts Commission: First Report* (1874), pp. 92–3.

[3] C. R. Cheney, *English Bishops' Chanceries*, p. 147, citing *Register of Drokensford*, p. 38. Sir Henry Maxwell-Lyte (in *Proceedings of the Somersetshire Archaeological and Natural History Society* 78 (1932), 45, refers to two authenticated extracts from the lost register of Bishop John Harewell (1367–86) printed in J. Batten, *Historical and Topographical Collections relating to the early history of parts of South Somerset* (Yeovil, 1894), pp. 17, 20, 23.

Record Society series,[4] and lists of incumbents from the thirteenth to eighteenth centuries have been compiled by F. W. Weaver using as his basis the notes of Archdeacon Edmund Archer in the British Library.[5]

A word is in order here about the present foliation of the Bath and Wells registers. They are now numbered in pencil by the opening (i.e. the verso of one folio and the recto of the succeeding one have the same number). This method of numbering has proved somewhat confusing for an analytical description, and in the following descriptive list the number on the recto has been taken to indicate both the recto and verso of that particular leaf, ignoring the opening in the numeration.

WALTER GIFFARD (1265–1266)

BI, Reg. 2, fos. 64*r*–66*r*, 70*r*–71*v*, 79*r*–*v*, 83*r*–*v* (for description, see under York).

This fragment of the earliest extant Bath and Wells register is now bound up with Giffard's register as archbishop of York. It covers the period Aug. 1264 to Nov. 1266, that is to say, including acts of Giffard as bishop-elect. It is clear that the clerks used territorial and jurisdictional subdivisions for the register, sectional headings still surviving for the archdeaconries of Bath, Taunton, and Wells, and for the jurisdiction of the dean of Wells and abbot of Glastonbury. A photocopy of this register is available at the Somerset Record Office.

Printed, *The Registers of Walter Giffard, Bishop of Bath and Wells, 1265–6, and of Henry Bowett, Bishop of Bath and Wells, 1401–7*, ed. T. S. Holmes (Somerset Record Society 13, 1899), pp. 1–11.

VACANCY 1308–1309

LPL, register of Archbishop Robert Winchelsey, fos. 27*r*, 52*r*.[6]

Bath and Wells vacancy business Mar.–Apr. 1309

Printed, *Registrum Roberti Winchelsey* ii, pp. 1107–8, 1219.

JOHN DROXFORD (1309–1329)

SRO, D/D/B. Reg. 1. Parchment register; average $13\frac{1}{2}'' \times 8\frac{1}{2}''$, except for the section of Shrewsbury's register, fos.276–289, $12\frac{1}{2}'' \times 9\frac{1}{4}''$; fos. ii+276+14+9+ii, foliated 1–195, 195A, 196–291, 291A, 292–297; hide-covered pasteboards.

Droxford's is a very disorganised register and there is evidence of some losses, since records of ordinations are known to have been kept.[7] There are certain sections devoted to particular business, e.g. royal writs, *ballive episcopatus . . . et intrinseca camere*, *registrum pro institucionibus et inducccionibus*, *dispensacionibus et licenciis studendi*, *littere patentes*, *transcripta diversarum litterarum*, but unfortunately these divisions are by no means adhered to all the time and at a later date they tend to merge into one chronological register, although even then a section for royal writs is still found.

Printed, *Calendar of the Register of John de Drokensford, Bishop of Bath and Wells* (*A.D. 1309–1329*), ed. E. Hobhouse (Somerset Record Society 1, 1887), using old foliation. For the section of Shrewsbury's register see below.

[4] *Somerset medieval wills: second series 1501–1530, with some Somerset wills proved at Lambeth* (Somerset Record Society 19, 1903).

[5] *Somerset Incumbents* (*13th–18th cents.*) (Bristol, 1889). See also H. C. Maxwell-Lyte, 'Somerset Incumbents, A.D. 1354–1401', *Proceedings of the Somersetshire Archaeological and Natural History Society* 78 (1932), 44–108, 175–88. M. F. Stieg, 'The Parochial Clergy in the diocese of Bath and Wells 1625–1685' (Berkeley, California, Ph.D., 1970) lists the clergy of the diocese in this period, with benefices and covering dates (appendix iii, pp. 262–90). There is a copy of this thesis in the Somerset Record Office.

[6] See under Canterbury for a description of this and subsequent archiepiscopal and capitular registers.

[7] *Register of Drokensford*, p. 162.

RALPH OF SHREWSBURY (1329–1363)

1. SRO, D/D/B. Reg. 2. Parchment register; average $13\frac{3}{4}'' \times 8\frac{3}{4}''$; fos. iii +435+iii, foliated 1–83, 83A, 84–102, 104–209, 209[A], 210–367, 367[A], 368–407, 407[A], 408–432; stamped leather-covered wooden boards.
2. SRO, D/D/B. Reg. 1, fos. 276–289 (for description see above under Droxford).

Unlike its immediate predecessor, Shrewsbury's register takes the form of a general chronological register, except in so far as some, but not all, royal writs are collected together in sections (fos. 107–26, 214–47), and inserted between gatherings of the general register. The large volume is incomplete, ending in 1354, and the small section bound up with Droxford's register covers acts for the period 1362–3. Shrewsbury also refers to his ordination register, now lost.[8]

Printed, *The Register of Ralph of Shrewsbury, Bishop of Bath and Wells, 1329–1363*, ed. T. S. Holmes (2 vols., Somerset Record Society 9, 10, 1896).

VACANCY 1363–1364

LPL, register of Archbishop Simon Islip, fos. 242*r*–244*v*.

Bath and Wells vacancy business Sept. 1363–Apr. 1364

VACANCY 1386

LPL, register of Archbishop William Courtenay, fos. 263*r*–264*r passim.*

Bath and Wells vacancy business July–Oct. 1386, among the general section of Canterbury institutions

VACANCY 1400–1401

LPL, register of Archbishop Thomas Arundel, volume I, fos. 268*r*–279*r passim.*

Bath and Wells vacancy business Apr. 1400–Sept. 1401, among the general section of Canterbury institutions

HENRY BOWET (1401–1407)

SRO, D/D/B. Reg. 3. Parchment register; fos. 1–24, $12'' \times 10''$; fos. 26–58, $13'' \times 10''$; fos. i (paper)+57+ i (paper), foliated 1–24, 26–58; limp parchment covers.

This register is basically a general record of acts in chronological order, entries from fo. 26 concerning acts of Bowet's vicar-general. From fo. 48*v* to the end of the volume are entered acts of the time of Bowet's successor, Nicholas Bubwith.

Printed, *The Register of Walter Giffard, Bishop of Bath and Wells, 1265–6, and of Henry Bowett, Bishop of Bath and Wells, 1401–7*, ed. T. S. Holmes (Somerset Record Society 13, 1899), pp. 14–96.

NICHOLAS BUBWITH (1408–1424)

SRO, D/D/B. Reg. 4. Parchment register; $13\frac{1}{4}'' \times 10''$; fos. 259 (252–9 are loose), foliated 1–259; limp parchment covers.

As stated above, the last ten folios of Bishop Bowet's register contain acts of Bubwith's vicar-general, most of which are re-entered in the Bubwith register. The latter is a little confused at the beginning. It starts with acts of 1410 and 1411, but on fo. 8*r* there is a formal register heading and the entries begin in Dec. 1407. In general arrangement, the volume follows the subsequently common pattern: a general register, including acts of the vicar-general (fos. 1–212); a register of elections (fos. 213–235); and a register of ordinations (fos. 236–255). At the end of the register (fos. 256–259) is a copy of the *regule cancellarie* of Pope John XXIII.

Printed, *The Register of Nicholas Bubwith, Bishop of Bath and Wells, 1407–1424*, ed. T. S. Holmes (2 vols., Somerset Record Society 29, 30, 1914), using the old foliation.

[8] *Register of Shrewsbury* ii, p. 723.

VACANCY 1424–1425

LPL, register of Archbishop Henry Chichele, volume I, fos. 152*r*–161*v passim.*

Bath and Wells vacancy business Nov. 1424–May 1425, among the general section of Canterbury institutions

Printed, *Register of Henry Chichele* i, pp. 220–33 *passim.*

JOHN STAFFORD (1425–1443)

SRO, D/D/B. Reg. 5. Parchment register; 15″ × 10¾″; fos. i (paper) + 246 + i (paper), foliated 1–130, 130A, 131–244, [245, 246]; parchment-covered pasteboards.

This register is also divided into three constituent sections: a general, chronological register (fos. 1–195), including acts of the bishop's vicars-general together with a record of ordinations celebrated on vicarial authority; a register of elections (fos. 196–198); and a register of ordinations (fos. 199–244).

Printed, *The Register of John Stafford, Bishop of Bath and Wells, 1425–1443*, ed. T. S. Holmes (2 vols., Somerset Record Society 31, 32, 1915–16), using the old foliation. Corrections by I. FitzRoy Jones are printed in *Notes and Queries for Somerset and Dorset* 23 (1942), 117, 126–9.

VACANCY 1443

LPL, register of Archbishop John Stafford, fos. 74*r*–75*r passim.*

Bath and Wells vacancy business May–Oct. 1443, among the general section of Canterbury institutions

THOMAS BECKINGTON (1443–1465)

SRO, D/D/B. Reg. 6. Parchment register; 14½″ × 10½″; fos. i (paper) + 411 + i (paper), foliated 1–411; parchment-covered pasteboards.

Beckington's register follows the usual pattern: a general, chronological register (fos. 1–310); a section on elections (fos. 311–359); and an ordinations register (fos. 360–406). At the end of the volume are two vernacular letters to dukes of Somerset (fo. 407) and a record of the visitation of Glastonbury abbey in 1408 by Archbishop Arundel of Canterbury (fos. 408–411).

Printed, *The Register of Thomas Bekynton, Bishop of Bath and Wells, 1443–1465*, ed. H. C. Maxwell-Lyte and M. C. B. Dawes (2 vols., Somerset Record Society 49, 50, 1934–5).

VACANCY 1465–1466

SRO, D/D/B. Reg. 29. Paper register (composite volume); fos. ii + i (parchment cover) + 27 (12¼″ × 8½″) + 4 (12″ × 8½″) + i (parchment cover) + 15 (11½″ × 8¼″) + i (parchment cover) + ii, foliated [i], 1–25, [26, 27], 1–3, 1, 1–15; modern binding.

This volume contains the record of vacancy administration 1465–6, 1495–6 and 1503–4. The 1465–6 vacancy register occupies fos. 1–15 of the final series of foliation. It is a general register, with ordinations included in the main sequence.

Printed, except for the ordinations, *The Registers of Robert Stillington, Bishop of Bath and Wells, 1466–1491, and Richard Fox, Bishop of Bath and Wells, 1492–1494*, ed. H. C. Maxwell-Lyte (Somerset Record Society 52, 1937), pp. xxi-xxviii.

ROBERT STILLINGTON (1466–1491)

SRO, D/D/B. Reg. 7. Parchment register; 14½″ × 11″; fos. ii + 257 + i, foliated 1–90, 90A, 91–254 (there are 2 blank, unnumbered folios between 107 and 108); stamped leather-covered wooden boards.

The general register is divided between acts of the vicars-general (fos. 1–78, 108–169) and of the bishop for the brief period 1471–9 (fos. 79–107). There are also the customary registers of elections (fos. 240–253) and ordinations (fos. 170–239).

Printed, except for the ordinations, *The Registers of Stillington and Fox*, pp. 1–173.

VACANCY 1491–1492

1. LPL, register of Archbishop John Morton, volume I, fos. 63*r*–76*v*.

 Bath and Wells vacancy business July 1491–Apr. 1492

2. *ibid*., volume II, fo. 149*v*.

 Bath and Wells vacancy act July 1491 (1 entry), among the general section of Canterbury institutions

 Both sections are calendared in C. Harper-Bill, 'An edition of the register of John Morton, archbishop of Canterbury, 1486–1500' (London University Ph.D., 1977).

RICHARD FOX (1492–1494)

SRO, D/D/B. Reg. 8. Parchment register; $14\frac{3}{4}'' \times 11\frac{1}{4}''$; fos. 50 + i, foliated [i], 1–50; stamped leather-covered wooden boards.

Fox's register has the usual three sections: a general register (fos. [i]–37), the acts chiefly emanating from the vicar-general; a register of ordinations (fos. 38–44); and a register of elections (fos. 45–49). The first section is not always entered up in chronological order.

Printed, *The Register of Richard Fox, while Bishop of Bath and Wells, A.D. MCCCCXCII–MCCCCXCIV*, ed. E. Chisholm Batten (privately printed, 1889); also calendared in *The Registers of Stillington and Fox*, pp. 174–200. The latter volume omits the ordinations.

VACANCY 1494–1496

1. SRO, D/D/B. Reg. 29, 2nd series, fos. 1*r*–3*r*, 3rd series, fo. 1*r*–*v* (for description, see 1465–6 vacancy).

 The record of this vacancy administration comprises a general register (2nd series, fos. 1–3) and an ordinations section (3rd series, fo. 1).

 Printed, except for the ordinations, *The Registers of Oliver King, Bishop of Bath and Wells, 1496–1503, and Hadrian de Castello, Bishop of Bath and Wells, 1503–1518*, ed. H. Maxwell-Lyte (Somerset Record Society 54, 1939), pp. xxi-xxiii.

2. LPL, register of Archbishop John Morton, volume I, fos. 135*r*–139*v*.

 Bath and Wells vacancy business Dec. 1494–Dec. 1495

3. *ibid*., volume II, fo. 158*r*.

 Bath and Wells vacancy act May 1495 (1 entry), among the general section of Canterbury institutions

 Items 2 and 3 are calendared in C. Harper-Bill, 'An edition of the register of John Morton, archbishop of Canterbury, 1486–1500' (London University Ph.D., 1977).

OLIVER KING (1496–1503)

SRO, D/D/B. Reg. 9. Parchment register; $14'' \times 10\frac{3}{4}''$; fos. i (paper) + 141 + i (paper), foliated 1–45, [45A], 46–87, [87], 88–139; limp parchment covers.

King's register is likewise divided into three sections: a general register (fos. 1–107), including acts of the vicar-general; a register of ordinations from Sept. 1497 (fos. 108–124); and a register of elections (fos. 125–139). Ordinations Dec. 1496–May 1497 are entered in the general register.

Printed, *The Registers of King and Castello*, pp. 1–88, using the old foliation. The ordinations are not included in this edition.

VACANCY 1503–1504

1. SRO, D/D/B. Reg. 29, 1st series, fos. 1*r*–27*v* (for description, see 1465–6 vacancy).

   This general register (including ordinations in the main sequence) covers the vacancy administration of the officials first deputed by the prior and convent of Canterbury *sede vacante* and then by the new archbishop, William Warham.

   Printed, except for the ordinations, *The Registers of King and Castello*, pp. 89–101.

2. CAL, register F, fos. 278*r*–283*v*.

   Bath and Wells vacancy business Sept.–Nov. 1503

   Institutions are calendared (by place) in *Sede Vacante Institutions*. This register begins earlier than the Bath and Wells copy (see above).

3. LPL, register of Archbishop William Warham, volume I, fos. 191*r*–200*r*.

   Bath and Wells vacancy business Jan.–Oct. 1504

ADRIAN DE CASTELLO (1504–1518)

SRO, D/D/B. Reg. 10. Parchment register; 15″ × 12″; fos. v (paper)+168+i (paper), foliated [i–ii], 1–160, [160A], 161–165; parchment-covered pasteboards.

Castello's register follows the arrangement of its predecessors: a general register (fos. 1–138), chiefly containing acts of his vicar-general; a register of ordinations (fos. 139–159); and a register of elections (fos. 160–165). There is some misbinding: fos. 105–10 should in fact follow fo. 114.

Printed, except for the ordinations, *The Registers of King and Castello*, pp. 102–91.

THOMAS WOLSEY (1518–1523)

SRO, D/D/B. Reg. 11. Parchment register; 15″ × 12″; fos. i (paper)+33+i (paper), foliated [i], 0–30, [31]; limp parchment covers.

This slim volume contains the general register of Wolsey's vicar-general (fos. 0–22) and the register of ordinations (fos. 23–30).

Printed, except for the ordinations, *The Registers of Thomas Wolsey, Bishop of Bath and Wells, 1518–1523, John Clerke, Bishop of Bath and Wells, 1523–1541, William Knyght, Bishop of Bath and Wells, 1541–1547, and Gilbert Bourne, Bishop of Bath and Wells, 1554–1559*, ed. H. Maxwell-Lyte (Somerset Record Society 55, 1940), pp. 1–26. This edition uses the old foliation.

JOHN CLERK (1523–1541)

SRO, D/D/B. Reg. 12. Parchment register; 14¾″ × 11″; fos. ii (paper)+121+ii (paper), foliated [i], 1–48, 50–121; limp parchment covers.

Clerk's register is incomplete. It is divided into four sections: a general register (fos. [i]–55), ending in June 1534; a register containing purgations of criminous clerks (fos. 56–61, *registrum de purgacionibus convictorum clericorum*), which includes at the end additional material not concerned with purgations; a register of elections (fos. 63–88), ending in Dec. 1525, and a register of ordinations (fos. 89–121), ending in May 1526.

Printed, except for the ordinations, *The Registers of Wolsey, Clerke, Knyght, and Bourne*, pp. 27–89.

WILLIAM KNIGHT (1541–1547)

SRO, D/D/B. Reg. 13. Parchment register; 14¾″ × 11½″; fos. i (paper)+39+i (paper), foliated [i], 1–38; limp parchment covers.

This volume is a single, general register of acts of Knight's vicar-general. There are no ordinations extant.

Printed, *The Registers of Wolsey, Clerke, Knyght, and Bourne*, pp. 90–119.

VACANCY 1547–1548

LPL, register of Archbishop Thomas Cranmer, fo. 409*v*.

Bath and Wells vacancy business Nov. 1547–Jan. 1548, among the general section of Canterbury institutions

Institutions are calendared in A. J. Edwards, 'The *sede vacante* administration of Archbishop Thomas Cranmer, 1533–53' (London University M.Phil., 1968).

VACANCY 1553–1554

CAL, register N, fo. 101*r*–*v*.

Bath and Wells vacancy business Jan.–Mar. 1554

Institutions are calendared (by place) in *Sede Vacante Institutions*.

GILBERT BOURNE (1554–1559)

1. SRO, D/D/B. Reg. 14. Parchment register; 15¼″ × 12¾″; fos. i (paper) + 40 + i (paper), foliated [i–ii], 1–38; parchment-covered pasteboards.

   This volume is a general register in chronological order, and ordinations were recorded in a separate volume (see below).

   Printed, *The Registers of Wolsey, Clerke, Knyght, and Bourne*, pp. 120–57.

2. SRO, D/D/Vc. 70. Paper register, unbound (in a very fragile condition); 12½″ × 8¼″; fos. 35, not foliated.

   Draft of Bishop Bourne's register, covering entries nos. 692–815 (1554–6) in the printed edition.

3. SRO, D/D/Vc. 53. Paper register, folios loose (in a very fragile condition); 12″ × 8¼″; fos. 21, not foliated [1–21 given to them for purposes of this description, although there may be losses. The fragile state of the document prevents close examination]; blank: fos. [21*r*–*v*]; bifolium of a medieval manuscript serves as a cover.

   [1*r*–20*v*] ordinations Dec. 1554 (earliest legible date, fo. 2*r*)–June 1559

VACANCY 1559–1560

LPL, register of Archbishop Matthew Parker, volume I, fos. 150*v*–151*r*.

Bath and Wells vacancy business Feb. 1560

Printed, *Registrum Matthei Parker* i, pp. 176–7.

GILBERT BERKELEY (1560–1581)

SRO, D/D/B. Reg. 15. Parchment register; 19″ × 13¼″; fos. 62, foliated 1–61, [62]; blank: fo. [62*r*–*v*]; limp parchment covers.

1*r* register heading, and later note of the bishop's death
1*v*–61*v* general register (no ordinations) Apr. 1560–Oct. 1581

VACANCY 1581–1584

1. LPL, register of Archbishop Edmund Grindal, volume II, fos. 466*v*–490r.

   Bath and Wells vacancy business Nov. 1581–June 1583

2. *ibid.*, register of the dean and chapter of Canterbury *sede vacante* (part of Grindal II), fos. 583*v*–586*r*.

   Bath and Wells vacancy business July–Sept. 1583

3. *ibid.*, register of Archbishop John Whitgift, volume I, fos. 332*r*–345*r*.

   Bath and Wells vacancy business Oct. 1583–Aug. 1584

THOMAS GODWIN (1584–1590)

1. SRO, D/D/B. Reg. 16. Parchment quire; $17'' \times 11\frac{3}{4}''$; fos. 8, foliated [i], 1–7; blank: fo. [i*v*]; the first folio acts as the cover and bears the bishop's name and coat of arms.

1*r* register heading
1*v*–2*r* vicar-general's commission and confirmation by the cathedral chapter Apr.–May 1587
2*v*–7*r* institutions and collations Sept. 1584–Jan. 1587
7*v* later registry title (bishop's name and covering dates)

2. SRO, D/D/B. Reg. 17. Paper register; $13\frac{1}{2}'' \times 8\frac{1}{2}''$; fos. ii+28+ii, foliated 1–24, [25–28]; blank: fos. [25*r*–28*v*]; modern binding.

1*r*–24*v* general register (grants, licences, annual returns of admissions to the Barons of the Exchequer, dispensations, royal writs, letters of orders) Jan. 1587–Sept. 1590

See also the Institution Book 1584–1625 below.

VACANCY 1590–1593

1. LPL, register of Archbishop John Whitgift, volume I, fos. 425*v*–448*v*.

Bath and Wells vacancy business Nov. 1590–June 1592

2. *ibid.*, volume II, fos. 217*r*–222*v*.

Bath and Wells vacancy business July 1592–Feb. 1593

JOHN STILL (1593–1608)

SRO, D/D/B. Reg. 18. Parchment register; $18\frac{1}{4}'' \times 12\frac{1}{4}''$; fos. i (paper)+23+i (paper), foliated [i–ii], 1–18, [19–21]; blank: fos. [i*v*, ii*v*], 6*r*, 18*v*–[21*v*]; parchment-covered pasteboards.[9]

[i*r*] later registry title (bishop's name and covering dates)
[ii*r*] coat of arms of bishop and register heading
1*r*–18*r* institutions and collations (occasional misplaced entries) Feb. 1593–Mar. 1603
(see also Institution Book 1584–1625 below)

VACANCY 1608

LPL, register of Archbishop Richard Bancroft, fos. 240*r*–242*r*.

Bath and Wells vacancy business Feb.–Apr. 1608

JAMES MONTAGUE (1608–1616)

See the Institution Book 1584–1625 below.

VACANCY 1616

LPL, register of Archbishop George Abbot, volume I, fos. 337*v*–339*v*.

Bath and Wells vacancy business Oct.–Nov. 1616

ARTHUR LAKE (1616–1626)

SRO, D/D/B. Reg. 19. Parchment register; $18\frac{1}{4}'' \times 12\frac{1}{4}''$; fos. i (paper)+16+i (paper), foliated [i], 1–16; blank: fos. [i*v*], 16*v*; limp parchment covers.

[9] There is evidence of misbinding: fo. 1 should in fact follow fo. 5 and the earliest entries begin on fo. 2.

[i*r*]	coat of arms of bishop
1*r*–15*v*	institutions, collations and cognate material (inquisitions, resignations) Jan. 1617–Dec. 1620
16*r*	18th-cent. note that there are a further 117 institutions of Lake's time in the paper book of institutions (see below, Institution Book 1584–1625)

VACANCY 1626

LPL, register of Archbishop George Abbot, volume II, fos. 247*r*–277*r*.

Bath and Wells vacancy business May–Sept. 1626

VACANCY 1628

LPL, register of Archbishop George Abbot, volume II, fos. 304*v*–306*v*.

Bath and Wells vacancy business July–Sept. 1628

VACANCY 1629

LPL, register of Archbishop George Abbot, volume III, fos. 146*v*–148*v*.

Bath and Wells vacancy business Sept.–Nov. 1629

VACANCY 1632

LPL, register of Archbishop George Abbot, volume III, fos. 174*v*–176*v*.

Bath and Wells vacancy business Nov. 1632

WILLIAM PIERS (1632–1670)

SRO, D/D/B. Reg. 20. Parchment and paper register; $11\frac{3}{4}'' \times 9''$; fos. ii (paper)+35 (parchment)+71 (paper)+vi (paper), paginated [i–vi], 1–66, then foliated 66–132, [133–136]; blank: pp. [i–ii, iv–vi], fo. [136*r*–*v*]; parchment-covered pasteboards.

At the front of the volume are 6 loose paper folios, table of contents, late 17th/early 18th cent.

[iii]	register heading
1–66	institutions, collations and ordinations Dec. 1632–Aug. 1640
66*r*–78*v*	institutions and collations Oct. 1641–Dec. 1645
79*r*	note about the lack of institutions 1649–60
79*v*–131*v*	institutions and collations June 1660–Mar. 1670
132*r*–[135*v*]	ordinations Dec. 1662–Sept. 1669

INSTITUTION BOOK

THOMAS GODWIN (1584–1590)
JOHN STILL (1593–1608)
JAMES MONTAGUE (1608–1616)
ARTHUR LAKE (1616–1626)

SRO, D/D/B. Reg. 31. Paper register; $12\frac{1}{4}'' \times 7\frac{3}{4}''$; fos. 47, foliated [i–v], 1–40, [41–42]; blank: fos. [i*v*, v*v*], 16*v*, 25*r*–*v*, [41*r*–42*v*]; limp parchment covers.

[i*r*]	miscellaneous administrative notes
[ii*r*–v*r*]	place index

1*r*–10*r*	institutions and collations *temp*. Godwin Sept. 1584–May 1590 (with a few later entries Feb. 1593–June 1594 at end)
10*v*	institution Nov. 1599 (1 entry)
11*r*–16*r*	institutions and collations *temp*. Still Apr. 1603–Feb. 1608 (with a few additional entries at end)
17*r*–28*v*	institutions and collations *temp*. Montague May 1608–Sept. 1616
28*v*–40*v*	institutions and collations *temp*. Lake Jan. 1617–Sept. 1625 (marginal place headings have been added for the 1626 entries but the entries themselves are not registered)

The next institution book dates from 1661 (SRO, D/D/Vc. 54).

BRISTOL

Repositories

1. Lambeth Palace Library, London SE1 7JU (LPL).
2. Gloucestershire Record Office, Worcester Street, Gloucester GL1 3DW (GRO).
3. Canterbury Cathedral Archives and Library, The Precincts, Canterbury CT1 2EG (CAL).

Area

Until 1541 Bristol was situated in the diocese of Worcester and in that year was part of the area removed to form the new bishopric of Gloucester. A year later, on 4 June 1542, the diocese of Bristol was created, comprising the city of Bristol, a few Gloucestershire parishes within the rural deanery of Bristol, three chapelries of the parish of Bedminster in Somerset (formerly in the Bath and Wells diocese) and the county of Dorset, which had been transferred from the diocese of Salisbury. There were no further changes in the boundaries of the Bristol diocese until 1836 when it was united with the bishopric of Gloucester, to be reconstituted as a separate diocese in 1897.[1]

Bibliographical Note

The diocese of Bristol has the dubious distinction, shared only, within the provinces of Canterbury and York, by the sees of Llandaff and Sodor and Man, of having no extant episcopal registers for the period under consideration. The archives of the diocese and cathedral chapter have suffered their fair share of disasters and this may possibly account for the loss of the earlier registers.[2] Whatever the cause, the episcopal act books and registers of institutions only survive from 1762,[3] two earlier tabulated institution books being extant for the period 1714–61.[4]

It is of course possible to reconstruct something from the files of administrative papers which are now deposited in the Bristol Archives Office (Council House, Bristol BS1 5TR) and, in addition, the records of *sede vacante* administration are to be found in the archiepiscopal registers at Lambeth Palace Library and among the Canterbury capitular archives. Perhaps fortunately, the see was left vacant for two long periods during Elizabeth I's reign and was held *in commendam* by two successive bishops of Gloucester, Richard Cheyney (from 1562 to 1579) and John Bullingham (from 1581 to 1589). It has become apparent, however, that during these two periods, the archbishop and his officials by no means left the administration of the diocese exclusively to these commendatory bishops. The Canterbury registers contain far more entries about the Bristol diocese than the episcopal act book of Gloucester and there seems to have been no very clear-cut division of administrative responsibilities, material of a similar routine nature being found in both sources.

Lists of incumbents for the archdeaconry of Dorset during this period have been compiled from various sources, including the archiepiscopal registers, by G. D. Squibb[5] and the Hockaday collections at the Gloucestershire Record Office and Gloucester City Library (Brunswick Road, Gloucester GL1 1HT) include material for the Bristol diocese.[6]

[1] For a description of the diocesan boundaries, see I. M. Kirby, *Diocese of Bristol: a catalogue of the records of the bishop and archdeacons and of the dean and chapter* (Bristol, 1970), pp. ix, xvi–xix.

[2] For a brief account of the disasters, see I. M. Kirby, *Bristol Catalogue*, p. ix.

[3] Bristol Archives Office, Ep/A/1/1–6. One stray institution for 1546 survives in the first cause book, *ibid.*, Ep/J/1/1. The record of an ordination held by the bishop of Bristol in Exeter cathedral in Oct. 1645 is in Devon Record Office, Exeter diocesan records, Chanter catalogue 50, fo. 83*r*.

[4] *ibid.*, Ep/A/5/1–2.

[5] 'Dorset incumbents, 1542–1731' in *Proceedings of the Dorset Natural History and Archaeological Society* 70 (1948), 99–117; 71 (1949), 110–32; 72 (1950), 111–28; 73 (1951), 141–62; 74 (1952), 60–78; 75 (1953), 115–32; also published separately in one volume.

[6] See I. M. Kirby, *Bristol Catalogue*, app. ii, pp. 158–9.

VACANCY 1554

CAL, register N, fos. 104*r*–106*r*.[7]

Bristol vacancy business June–Sept. 1554

Institutions are calendared (by place) in *Sede Vacante Institutions.*

VACANCY 1558–1589

(held *in commendam* by the bishop of Gloucester 1562–1579, 1581–1589)

1. CAL, register U2, fos. 36*r*–39*r*.

Bristol vacancy business Dec. 1558–July 1559

Institutions are calendared (by place) in *Sede Vacante Institutions.*

2. LPL, register of Archbishop Matthew Parker, volume II, fos. 26*r*–45*v*.

Bristol vacancy business Jan. 1560–May 1575

Printed, *Registrum Matthei Parker* iii, pp. 946–84.

3. *ibid.*, register of the dean and chapter of Canterbury *sede vacante* (part of Parker II), fos. 122*v*–128*r*.

Bristol vacancy business May–Nov. 1575

Printed, *ibid.*, iii, pp. 1168–85.

4. *ibid*, register of Archbishop Edmund Grindal, volume II, fos. 290*v*–344*v*.

Bristol vacancy business Mar. 1576–June 1583

5. *ibid.*, register of the dean and chapter of Canterbury *sede vacante* (part of Grindal II), fos. 580*r*–581*r*.

Bristol vacancy business Aug. 1583

6. *ibid.*, register of Archbishop John Whitgift, volume I, fos. 277*r*–295*r*.

Bristol vacancy business Oct. 1583–July 1589

7. GRO, GDR.27A, act book of the bishops of Gloucester 1570–1630.

This act book contains *passim* institutions to benefices etc. in the Bristol diocese performed by the bishops of Gloucester. They cover the periods Feb. 1571, June–Oct. 1577, July 1582–Dec. 1588. As far as can be seen, these entries are not duplicated in the Lambeth registers.

GRO, Hockaday Index 30 is an index of personal names in the volume. Additional information on the administration of the Bristol diocese by the commendatory bishops of Gloucester is provided by an 18th-century index to Gloucester diocesan records which lists presentation deeds, bonds, induction mandates, resignation deeds and other benefice papers relating to the Bristol diocese in the period 1571–1588 (GRO, GDR.1B, pp. 151–53).

VACANCY 1593–1603

1. LPL, register of Archbishop John Whitgift, volume II, fos. 201*r*–213*v*.

Bristol vacancy business Feb. 1593–Dec. 1597

2. *ibid.*, register of Archbishop John Whitgift, volume III, fos. 182*r*–189*v*.

Bristol vacancy business June 1597–Apr. 1601

VACANCY 1617

LPL, register of Archbishop George Abbot, volume I, fos. 342*r*–346*r*.

Bristol vacancy business Feb.–Aug. 1617

[7] See under Canterbury for a description of this and subsequent capitular and archiepiscopal registers.

VACANCY 1619

LPL, register of Archbishop George Abbot, volume I, fos. 385*r*–386*r*.

Bristol vacancy business Mar.–Apr. 1619

VACANCY 1622–1623

LPL, register of Archbishop George Abbot, volume II, fos. 269*r*–271*v*.

Bristol vacancy business Oct. 1622–Feb. 1623

VACANCY 1632

LPL, register of Archbishop George Abbot, volume III, fos. 179*r*–180*v*.

Bristol vacancy business Nov.–Dec. 1632

VACANCY 1636–1637

LPL, register of Archbishop William Laud, volume I, fos. 303*v*–304*v*.

Bristol vacancy business July–Sept. 1636.

CHICHESTER

Repositories

1. West Sussex Record Office, West Street, Chichester PO19 1RN (WSRO).
2. Lambeth Palace Library, London SE1 7JU (LPL).
3. Canterbury Cathedral Archives and Library, The Precincts, Canterbury CT1 2EG (CAL).
4. Bodleian Library, Department of Western Manuscripts, Oxford OX1 3BG (Bodl.).

Area

Peculiar jurisdictions excepted, the diocese of Chichester was coterminous with the county of Sussex. A description of the ecclesiastical divisions of the county is given in *VCH Sussex* ii (1907), pp. 42–4. A map of the diocese is *ibid.*, facing p. 42. A more recent description is contained in F. W. Steer and I. M. Kirby, *Diocese of Chichester: a catalogue of the records of the bishop, archdeacons, and former exempt jurisdictions* (Chichester, 1966), pp. xxii–xxiii.

Bibliographical Note

A detailed handlist of the Chichester episcopal registers is to be found in the guide to the diocesan archives compiled by F. W. Steer and I. M. Kirby, and a brief list of the registers 1397–1596 is also printed in the Historical Manuscripts Commission report on the muniments of the bishop.[1] The earliest extant Chichester register dates from 1397 but there are considerable gaps in the series in the fifteenth century, and some in the early seventeenth century. It is also apparent that many earlier registers have disappeared. In answer to a royal writ of 28 Oct. 1441 concerning the rectory of Rotherfield, Bishop Praty caused a search to be made of the episcopal registers and the return to this writ provides evidence for the existence of registers of Gilbert of St Leofard (1288–1305), John Langton (1305–37), Robert Stratford (1337–62), William Reade (1369–85), and John Rickingale (1426–29), all now lost.[2] Praty reported that he had no registers in his keeping earlier than Gilbert of St Leofard's. There is also a possible reference to the register of Bishop Richard Mitford (1390–5) but this is not definitely proved.[3] In addition, it has been claimed that a bifolium in Robert Reade's register is in fact part of Mitford's register.[4]

From the mid-fifteenth century to the mid-sixteenth century the registers are usually subdivided into several category sections but from then onwards, this arrangement gives way in most cases to a general, chronological register, with only a separate ordinations section being retained.

Two eighteenth-century antiquaries, Andrew Ducarel and William Clarke, made extensive use of these episcopal registers,[5] as did James Bennett Freeland, deputy diocesan registrar, in the mid-nineteenth century. Indexes and abstracts of material in the bishops' registers survive among his local antiquarian collections.[6] Later in the century, the Rev. M. E. C. Walcott published a brief description of the registers[7] and listed the marginal headings of the registers

[1] *A Catalogue of the Records of the Bishop, Archdeacons and Former Exempt Jurisdictions* (Chichester, 1966), pp. 1–5; *Historical Manuscripts Commission, Reports on Manuscripts in Various Collections* i (1901), pp. 177–8.

[2] WSRO, Ep. I/1/2, fos. 57*r*–58*r*, abstracted in *Miscellaneous Records* (Sussex Record Society 4, 1905), pp. 206–8. *Historical Manuscripts Commission, Various Collections* i, p. 177 also lists references to lost registers, mainly taken from the cartulary, Liber E (now WSRO, VI/1/4). For other references, St Leofard to William Reade, see Public Record Office, C269/3/7, C269/5/35, C269/6/1, C269/8/14.

[3] W. D. Peckham, 'Bishop Mitford's register' in *Sussex Notes and Queries* 13 (1950–3), 40.

[4] *The Episcopal Register of Robert Rede* ii (Sussex Record Society 10, 1910), p. 373.

[5] See Steer and Kirby, *Catalogue*, p. 5 (Ep. I/2).

[6] *ibid.*, pp. 79–80 (Ep. I/52).

[7] 'Kalendar of the Episcopal Registers of Chichester', *Transactions of the Royal Society of Literature of the United Kingdom*, 2nd series, ix (1870), 245–55.

from Robert Reade to Robert Sherborne.[8] The registers were also used by George Hennessy in his *Chichester Diocesan Clergy Lists: or, The Clergy Succession from the earliest time to the year 1900* (London, 1900) and *Supplement* (1901). This compilation has serious limitations and annotated and corrected copies are to be found at the West Sussex Record Office in Chichester and in the Library of the Sussex Archaeological Society at Lewes.[9] The author's own annotated copy is now in the Gurney Library of the Borthwick Institute, York. Since Hennessy's time, Mr W. D. Peckham has calendared and indexed the institutions and collations in the Chichester episcopal registers and *sede vacante* admissions in the Canterbury archiepiscopal and capitular registers. His 'Chichester Diocese Institutions' comprise several volumes in the West Sussex Record Office, the relevant ones for the present study being MP.1094 (covering the years 1279–1502), MP.1095 (1503–59), MP.1096 (1560–1658) and MP.1099 (peculiar jurisdictions 1279–1845). The institutions are calendared in chronological sequence and there is a place index to each volume. Moreover, an extensive card index of Chichester diocesan institutions and collations from the middle ages to the present century can be consulted at the Library of the Sussex Archaeological Society, Lewes. It contains material from the Chichester and Canterbury registers and other printed and manuscript sources, and is arranged both by place and clergy surname.

The binding pastedowns of the earlier registers (WSRO, Ep. I/1/1a–Ep. I/1/6a) have been described by Dr Neil Ker (Ep. I/88/29). Microfilms of the episcopal registers can be consulted in the East Sussex Record Office, Pelham House, St Andrew's Lane, Lewes BN7 1UN.

VACANCY 1287–1288

LPL, register of Archbishop John Pecham, fos. 36*r*–37*r passim*, 128*r*, 129*v*–130*r*.[10]

Chichester vacancy business Oct. 1287–Apr. 1288

Printed, *Register of John Pecham* i, pp. 67–73 *passim*, 248–53; *Registrum Johannis Peckham* iii, pp. 951–2.

VACANCY 1362

LPL, register of Archbishop Simon Islip, fos. 237*v*–238*v*, 241*r*.

Chichester vacancy business Apr.–Oct. 1362

Institutions are calendared in WSRO, MP.1094.

VACANCY 1385–1386

LPL, register of Archbishop William Courtenay, fos. 257*v*–261*r passim*.

Chichester vacancy business Sept. 1385–Mar. 1386, among the general section of Canterbury institutions

Institutions are calendared in WSRO, MP.1094.

VACANCY 1389–1390

LPL, register of Archbishop William Courtenay, fos. 160*r*–164*v*.

Chichester vacancy business July 1389–Feb. 1390

Business for this vacancy June 1389–Feb. 1390 is also to be found *ibid.*, fo. 274*r*–*v*, among the general section of Canterbury institutions. All institutions are calendared in WSRO, MP.1094.

[8] 'The Medieval Registers of the Bishops of Chichester', *ibid.*, 215–44.
[9] See also W. D. Peckham, 'Hennessy's Clergy List' in *Sussex Notes and Queries* 8 (1940–1), 170–2.
[10] See under Canterbury for a description of this and subsequent archiepiscopal and capitular registers.

ROBERT READE (1396–1415)

WSRO, Ep. I/1/1. Parchment register; $12\frac{1}{2}'' \times 9\frac{1}{4}''$; fos. iii ($13'' \times 10''$)+i (leaf from illuminated manuscript, $12\frac{3}{4}'' \times 9\frac{1}{2}''$)+177+viii (paper, 17th-cent. table of contents, $12\frac{1}{2}'' \times 8\frac{1}{2}''$)+i (paper, typescript copy (inaccurate) of 2 documents)+iii ($13'' \times 10''$), foliated [i], 1–186 (includes insert); modern binding, incorporating some of the original calf on the front cover (old binding pastedowns separately guarded, Ep. I/1/1a).

This register is basically divided between a section of general memoranda, on the one hand, and a section of institutions, ordinations, and monastic confirmations, on the other. However, a careful division between these two sections is not always preserved and several commissions, indulgences and the like are to be found among the institutions. At the end of the volume a considerable amount of miscellaneous material, mostly memoranda, has been added, including what is claimed to be a fragment of Richard Mitford's register.

Printed, *The Episcopal Register of Robert Rede, ordinis predicatorum, lord bishop of Chichester, 1397–1415*, ed. C. Deedes, (2 vols., Sussex Record Society 8, 10, 1908–10), vol. i containing the memoranda section (fos. 1–63), vol. ii the remainder of the register. The marginal headings of the register were previously printed by M. E. C. Walcott. 'The Medieval Registers of the Bishops of Chichester', in *Transactions of the Royal Society of Literature of the United Kingdom*, 2nd series, ix (1870), 216–24.

VACANCY 1415–1418

1. LPL, register of Archbishop Henry Chichele, volume I, fos. 18*r*–20*r*, 64*v*–96*r* *passim*.

Chichester vacancy business July 1415–May 1418, among the general section of Canterbury institutions and the section concerning appointments of bishops etc.

Printed, *Register of Henry Chichele* i, pp. 44–9, 136–68 *passim*.

2. *ibid.*, volume II, fos. 188*r*–217*v*.

Chichester vacancy business June 1415–May 1418

Printed, *Register of Henry Chichele* iii, pp. 431–67.

VACANCY 1420–1421

LPL, register of Archbishop Henry Chichele, volume I, fos. 120*r*–124*v* *passim*.

Chichester vacancy business Oct. 1420–Apr. 1421, among the general section of Canterbury institutions

Printed, *Register of Henry Chichele* i, pp. 194–9 *passim*.

VACANCY 1421–1422

LPL, register of Archbishop Henry Chichele, volume I, fo. 133*v*.

Chichester vacancy act June 1422 (1 entry), among the general section of Canterbury institutions

Printed, *Register of Henry Chichele* i, p. 205.

VACANCY 1429–1431

1. LPL, register of Archbishop Henry Chichele, volume I, fos. 176*r*–187*v* *passim*.

Chichester vacancy business July 1429–Jan. 1431, among the general section of Canterbury institutions

Printed, *Register of Henry Chichele* i, pp. 255–69 *passim*.

2. *ibid.*, volume II, fos. 241*r*–246*r*.

Chichester vacancy business July 1429–Feb. 1431

Printed, *Register of Henry Chichele* iii, pp. 485–90.

VACANCY 1438

LPL, register of Archbishop Henry Chichele, volume I, fos. 218*v*–221*r* *passim*.

Chichester vacancy business Feb.–July 1438, among the general section of Canterbury institutions

Printed, *Register of Henry Chichele* i, pp. 298–300 *passim*.

RICHARD PRATY (1438–1445)

WSRO, Ep. I/1/2. Parchment register; $14'' \times 9\frac{3}{4}''$; fos. ii $(14\frac{1}{2}'' \times 9\frac{3}{4}'')$ + ii (leaves from a medieval manuscript, $13\frac{3}{4}'' \times 8\frac{3}{4}''$) + 115 + viii (paper, $12\frac{1}{4}'' \times 8''$) + i (leaf from a medieval manuscript) + ii $(14\frac{1}{4}'' \times 9\frac{3}{4}'')$, foliated [i–ii], 1–42, 43A, 43B, 44–124; blank: fos. 43A*v*, 118*r*–123*v*; modern binding, incorporating portions of original parchment covers (old binding pastedowns separately guarded, Ep. I/1/2a).

1*r*	17th-cent. index of memoranda
1*v*	15th-cent. note of the divisions of the register
2*r*–43A*r*	institutions and collations Aug. 1438–Aug. 1445
43B*r*–60*v*	*mandata superiorum* (in confused order) May 1439–Aug. 1444
61*r*–70*v*	elections and confirmations of heads of religious houses Oct. 1438–Jan. 1445
71*r*–*v*	copy of petition of Michael Poynings, Lord of Poynings, and the inhabitants of Crawley Oct. 1350.
72*r*–83*v*	visitation business Sept. [?1441]–Sept. 1442 (at the end is included a later copy of a benefice augmentation Apr. 1424)
84*r*–106*v*	memoranda and *acta maiora memorie commendanda* (unions of churches, augmentations, grants of pensions, copies of earlier charters, in confused order) July 1438–July 1445
107*r*–115*r*	ordinations Sept. 1438–Mar. 1445
115*v*	later memoranda *temp.* Bishops Moleyns and Arundel
116*r*–117*v*	17th–18th-cent. place index of institutions
124*r*–*v*	leaf of medieval illuminated manuscript

The marginal headings of the register are printed by M. E. C. Walcott, 'The Medieval Registers of the Bishops of Chichester', in *Transactions of the Royal Society of Literature of the United Kingdom*, 2nd series, ix (1870), 224–30. Fos. 2*r*–43A*r* are calendared by C. Deedes, 'Extracts from the episcopal register of Richard Praty, S.T.P., Lord Bishop of Chichester, 1438–1445', in *Miscellaneous Records* (Sussex Record Society 4, 1905), pp. 110–37; fos. 61*r*–70*v* are printed in full (with translations), *ibid.*, pp. 142–86; fos. 107*r*–115*r* are calendared, *ibid.*, pp. 188–97.

VACANCY 1445–1446

LPL, register of Archbishop John Stafford, fos. 84*v*–86*v* *passim*.

Chichester vacancy business Sept.–Nov. 1445, among the general section of Canterbury institutions

Institutions are calendared in WSRO, MP.1094.

VACANCY 1450

LPL, register of Archbishop John Stafford, fos. 103*v*–104*v* *passim*.

Chichester vacancy business Feb.–Apr. 1450, among the general section of Canterbury institutions

Institutions are calendared in WSRO, MP.1094.

EDWARD STORY (1478–1503)
RICHARD FITZJAMES (1503–1506)
ROBERT SHERBORNE (1508–1536)

1. WSRO, Ep. I/1/3. Parchment register; 13″ × 10½″; fos. i (13¼″ × 10¾″) + 199 + vi (paper, 12¼″ × 8″), foliated 1–177, 179–206; blank: fos. 12*v*, 96*v*, 152*r*, 159*r*, 201*v*–206*v*; modern binding, incorporating portions of original parchment covers (old binding pastedowns separately guarded, Ep. I/1/3a).

1*r*–2*r*	register heading and record of the bishop's installation June 1478.
2*r*–33*r*	primary visitation business May–July 1478
33*r*–96*r*	general register (institutions, collations, ordinations 1478–81, commissions, dispensations, royal writs, Convocation business, monastic confirmations and other memoranda. There is some confusion in the arrangement. There are no institutions and collations after 1481) Aug. 1478–Mar. 1502
97*r*–158*v*	[*mandata superiorum*] Dec. 1483–Sept. 1502
159*v*–162*v*	foundation documents and statutes of Holy Trinity hospital, Arundel, n.d., and accounts 32–34 Henry VI
163*r*–166*v*	arbitration and compositions between Lewes priory and the rectors of Westmeston (June 1497) and Rodmell (Aug. 1500)
167*r*–173*r*	appropriation of Findon church June-July 1502
173*v*–176*r*	grant of pension from Rye vicarage 1502
176*v*	2 manumissions Jan. 1503
177*r*–199*v*	ordinations Mar. 1484–Dec. 1502
200*r*	17th-cent. note of compositions, ordinations, contained in the register
200*v*	note of admission by Bishop Edward (Story) Aug. 1506 (*sic*)
201*r*	17th-cent. select index

2. WSRO, Ep. I/1/4. Parchment register; fos. i (16″ × 12½″) + 24 (13″ × 10½″) + 12 (13¾″ × 11″) + 75 (15″ × 12″) + i (16″ × 12½″), foliated 1–111; blank: fos. 45*v*, 64*v*; modern parchment binding, incorporating some original binding (old binding pastedowns separately guarded, Ep. I/1/4a).

1*r*–36*v*	institutions *temp.* Bishop Story Jan. 1481–Nov. 1486, Jan.–Oct. 1491, June 1499–Feb. 1503	
37*r*–44*v*	institutions etc. (including monastic elections) *temp.* Bishop FitzJames Feb. 1504–Jan. 1506	
45*r*–111*v*	register of Bishop Sherborne	
	45*r*	17th-cent. note about Sherborne's register
	46*r*–64*r*	institutions Apr. 1523–Mar. 1536
	65*r*–74*v*	collations Apr. 1523–Jan. 1536
	75*r*–78*v*	grants of pensions Dec. 1523–Aug. 1529
	79*r*–89*v*	augmentations and ordinations of vicarages, unions of benefices [ ] 1524–Sept. 1534
	90*r*–102*v*	visitation business May 1524–July 1527
	103*r*–111*v*	*mandata superiorum* Jan. 1522–Jan. 1536
	111*v*	16th-cent. *repertorium* (selective)

Institutions *temp.* Bishop Story in both these registers are calendared in WSRO, MP.1094; institutions *temp.* Bishops FitzJames and Sherborne are calendared *ibid.*, MP.1095. Another calendar of FitzJames' register (Ep. I/1/4, fos. 37–44) by W. D. Peckham is WSRO, Ep. I/88/11 (1927, indexed). Copies of this calendar are deposited in the British Library and the Sussex Archaeological Society, Lewes.

VACANCY 1503

CAL, register F, fos. 264*r*–277*v*.

Chichester vacancy business Apr.–Nov. 1503.

Institutions are calendared (by place) in *Sede Vacante Institutions.*

VACANCY 1506–1508

1. LPL, register of Archbishop William Warham, volume II, fos. 245*v*–251*v*.

   Chichester vacancy business Aug. 1506–Nov. 1508

2. *ibid.*, fos. 329*r*–333*r passim.*

   Chichester vacancy business Nov. 1506–Apr. 1508, among the general section of Canterbury institutions

Institutions in both these sections are calendared in WSRO, MP.1095. Some of the vacancy entries in the first section are calendared in WSRO, Ep. I/88/11 (copies also at the British Library and Sussex Archaeological Society, Lewes).

ROBERT SHERBORNE (1508–1536)

WSRO, Ep. I/1/5. Parchment register; $13\frac{3}{4}'' \times 11\frac{1}{2}''$; fos. ii (fragments of documents from the original binding) + 145 + x (paper, $12\frac{1}{4}'' \times 8''$), foliated [i–ii], 1–9, 9B, 10–108, 108A, 109–153; blank: fos. 34*v*, 51*v*, 108A*v*, 130*v*, 145*r*–152*v*; modern binding, incorporating some of the original binding and wooden boards.

3*r*–8*r*, 10*r*–22*v*	register heading, and institutions Jan. 1509–Mar. 1523
9*r*–*v*	note of arrangement and subdivision of the register
23*r*–34*r*	collations Dec. 1508–Feb. 1523
35*r*–51*r*	elections and confirmations of monastic heads etc., and grants of pensions (in confused order) June 1516–Mar. 1522
52*r*–84*v*	appropriations of churches (including many copies of earlier documents) 12th cent.–Apr. 1522
85*r*–107*v*	visitation business Apr.–Sept. 1521
108*r*–108A*r*	purgation of criminous clerks June 1509
109*r*–114*v*	testamentary business Mar. 1518–July 1520
115*r*–132*v*	[*mandata superiorum*] (including miscellaneous grants and commissions) Nov. 1509–Nov. 1535
133*r*–*v*	manumissions Feb. 1523–July 1536
134*r*–*v*	royal licences May 1518–Oct. 1526 (with 1 additional entry July 1543)
135*r*–136*v*	compositions and awards Dec. 1511–July 1514
137*r*–140*v*	copy of statutes of Holy Trinity hospital, Arundel Dec. 1387
141*r*–142*r*	monastic injunctions July 1518
142*v*	list of wills in the *testamenta* section (fos. 109–14)
143*r*–144*v*	17th-cent. place index of institutions
153*r*	rough notes of contents

Fos. 3*r*–22*v*, 35*r*–51*r* have been calendared by W. D. Peckham, Ep. I/88/11 (copies also at the British Library and the Sussex Archaeological Society, Lewes). Fos. 141*r*–142*r* have been published in translation by W. Turner, 'Injunctions given to the prior and convent of Boxgrave, A.D. 1518', in *Sussex Archaeological Collections* 8 (1857), 61–6. The 12th-century episcopal charters occurring in the *appropriaciones beneficiorum* section (fos. 52–84) are printed in *The Acta of the Bishops of Chichester, 1075–1207*, ed. H. Mayr-Harting (Canterbury and York Society 56, 1964), nos. 5, 13, 59, 111, 114, 118, 129.

RICHARD SAMPSON (1536–1543)
GEORGE DAY (1543–1551; 1553–1556)
JOHN SCORY (1552–1553)

WSRO, Ep. I/1/6. Parchment register; 14½″ × 10″; fos. (5 documents from binding) + i (paper) + 117, foliated [i], 1–117; blank: fos. 9*r*–*v*, 115*v*, 116*v*–117*v*; modern parchment binding (old binding pastedowns separately guarded, Ep. I/1/6a). A section of this manuscript originally contained part of a copy of Bishop Sherborne's Donation which was scraped and re-used (see Steer and Kirby, *Catalogue*, p. 3).

1*r*–8*v*	register of Bishop Sampson (contains a record of the bishop's installation, grants of advowsons, unions of churches and memoranda. Fo. 7*r* bears the heading *mandata superiorum* but the section, which is incomplete, gives the impression of being more of a general memoranda register) Aug. 1536–Apr. 1539
10*r*–83*v*	register of Bishop Day (contains institutions and collations, with more general material—licences, mandates, royal writs, commissions, Convocation business and general memoranda) May 1543–Jan. 1552
84*r*–87*v*	register of Bishop Scory general register (as Day's) July 1552–July 1553
87*v*–114*v*	register of Bishop Day (restored) general register Aug. 1553–Aug. 1556
115*r*	augmentation of Henfield vicarage 1576
116*r*	selective contents list (incomplete)

VACANCY 1543

LPL, register of Archbishop Thomas Cranmer, fos. 388*r*–391*v*.

Chichester vacancy business Apr. 1543, among the general section of Canterbury institutions

Institutions are calendared in A. J. Edwards, 'The *sede vacante* administration of Archbishop Thomas Cranmer, 1533–53' (London University M.Phil., 1968).

VACANCY 1551–1552

LPL, register of Archbishop Thomas Cranmer, fos. 129*v*–132*r*.

Chichester vacancy business Oct. 1551–Apr. 1552

Institutions are calendared in A. J. Edwards, *op. cit.*

VACANCY 1556–1557

1. LPL, register of Archbishop Reginald Pole, fos. 54*r*–56*v*.

   Chichester vacancy business Aug. 1556–Nov. 1557

   Another Chichester vacancy act, July 1557, is to be found *ibid.*, fo. 73*r*, among the general section of Canterbury institutions.

2. WSRO, Ep. I/10/10. Paper register (damaged); 12″ × 8¾″; fos. 49, foliated 1–49; no covers.

   Instance book, Chichester consistory court, containing *passim* vacancy institutions etc. Aug. 1556–Nov. 1557

The institutions in both these documents are calendared in WSRO, MP.1095.

JOHN CHRISTOPHERSON (1557–1558)
VACANCY 1558–1559

WILLIAM BARLOW (1559–1568)
RICHARD CURTIS (1570–1582)
THOMAS BICKLEY (1586–1596)

WSRO, Ep. I/1/7. Parchment register; $13\frac{1}{4}'' \times 10\frac{1}{2}''$; fos. i+88+viii (paper, $12\frac{1}{4}'' \times 8''$)+i, foliated [i], 1–20, 20A, 21–63, 68–77, 81–103; blank: fos. 13*v*, 39*r*, 43*v*, 57*v*–63*v*, 68*r*–77*v*, 83*r*–*v*, 85*v*, 87*v*–88*v*, 90*r*–*v*, 91*v*, 95*r*–103*v*; modern binding.

1*r*–12*r*	general register of Bishop Christopherson Nov. 1557–Dec. 1558	
12*r*–13*r*	*sede vacante* register Jan.–Apr. 1559 (see also below for earlier vacancy business)	
14*r*–30*v*	general register of Bishop Barlow Jan. 1560–July 1568	
31*r*–43*r*	register of Bishop Curtis	
	31*r*–37*v*	installation of bishop, and institutions and collations May 1570–Jan. 1572
	38*r*–*v*	union of benefices Nov. 1572
	39*v*–43*r*	institutions and collations Mar. 1578–July 1582
44*r*–89*v*	register of Bishop Bickley	
	44*r*–56*v*	institutions and collations June 1586–Apr. 1596
	86*r*	document of Elizabeth I concerning a subsidy May 1587
	86*v*–87*r*	ordinances of the archbishop of Canterbury Mar. 1587
	89*r*–*v*	ordinations June 1586–Apr. 1587
56*v*–57*r*	miscellaneous business Nov. 1638	
81*r*–82*v*	miscellaneous business July–Sept. 1666	
84*r*–85*r*	miscellaneous business July 1664	
91*r*	ordinations *temp*. Bishop Barlow Sept. 1567–June 1568	
92*r*–94*v*	ordinations *temp*. Bishop Barlow Apr. 1560–Apr. 1567	

The institutions are calendared in WSRO, MP.1095–6. To cover the gaps in the register of Richard Curtis, W. D. Peckham has compiled a list of institutions etc. 1571–1580 from the composition books in the Public Record Office (WSRO, MP.966).

VACANCY 1558–1559

1. CAL, register U2, fos. 41*v*–55*r*.

   Chichester vacancy business Jan.–Dec. 1559

   Institutions are calendared (by place) in *Sede Vacante Institutions*.

2. LPL, register of Archbishop Matthew Parker, volume I, fo. 147*r*–*v*.

   Chichester vacancy business Dec. 1559

   Printed, *Registrum Matthei Parker* i, pp. 166–8.

VACANCY 1568–1570

LPL, register of Archbishop Matthew Parker, volume I, fos. 191*r*–200*v*.

Chichester vacancy business Aug. 1568–Apr. 1570

Printed, *Registrum Matthei Parker* i, pp. 260–87.

VACANCY 1582–1586

1. LPL, register of Archbishop Edmund Grindal, volume II, fos. 502*r*–508*r*.

   Chichester vacancy business Sept. 1582–Apr. 1583

2. *ibid*., register of dean and chapter of Canterbury *sede vacante* (part of Grindal II), fos. 586*r*–587*v*.

   Chichester vacancy business July–Aug. 1583.

3. LPL, register of Archbishop John Whitgift, volume I, fos. 345*v*–365*v*.

Chichester vacancy business Oct. 1583–Nov. 1585

All institutions are calendared in WSRO, MP.1096.

VACANCY 1596

LPL, register of Archbishop John Whitgift, volume II, fos. 300*v*–302*r*.

Chichester vacancy business May–Aug. 1596

Institutions are calendared in WSRO, MP.1096.

ANTHONY WATSON (1596–1605)
LANCELOT ANDREWES (1605–1609)
SAMUEL HARSNETT (1609–1619)
PETER GUNNING (1670–1675)

1. WSRO, Ep. I/1/8. Paper register; fos. iii + 33 ($12\frac{3}{4}$″ × $8\frac{1}{4}$″) + 25 ($12\frac{1}{2}$″ × 8″) + 19 ($11\frac{3}{4}$″ × $7\frac{3}{4}$″) + 25 ($11\frac{3}{4}$″ × $7\frac{1}{2}$″) + 4 ($12\frac{1}{2}$″ × 8″) + iii, foliated 1–32, 33A, 33B, 34–105; blank: fos. 27*v*, 33A*r*, 45*r*–*v*, 51*r*, 52*r*–*v*, 74*v*–78*v*, 99*r*–101*v*, 104*v*–105*v*; modern parchment covers, enclosing original parchment covers.

1*r*–33A*v*	register of Bishop Watson	
	1*r*–27*r*	institutions and collations Sept. 1596–Mar. 1605
	28*r*–29*v*	ordinations Mar. 1600–Oct. 1603
	30*r*–33A*v*	proceedings on admissions to benefices (not in strict chronological order) Feb. 1597–June 1599
33B*v*–57*v*	register of Bishop Andrewes	
	33B*v*	register heading
	34*r*–44*v*	institutions and collations Feb. 1606–Oct. 1609
	46*r*–50*v*	resignation proceedings Mar. 1606–Oct. 1609
	51*v*	licences to preach Feb. 1606–Sept. 1609, and licences for curates Mar. 1608–Oct. 1609
	53*r*–*v*	certificates to the Exchequer noting recusants who conformed July 1606–Aug. 1609
	54*r*	ordinations Oct. 1607–Sept. 1609
	56*v*–57*v*	indexes of institutions, various licences, and letters dimissory
54*v*–55*v*	list of institutions during the archbishop's visitation Apr.–Oct. 1605	
56*r*	names of preaching ministers deprived at East Grinstead Apr. 1605	
58*r*–73*v*	institutions and collations *temp.* Bishop Harsnett Dec. 1609–Aug. 1619	
74*r*	institutions (2 entries) Apr. 1624, Jan. 1640	
79*r*–98*v*	register of Bishop Gunning Nov. 1670–Feb. 1675	
102*r*–104*r*	18th-cent. place index, arranged under category headings (institutions, resignations, licences etc.)	

2. WSRO, Ep. I/1/8a. Paper register; $12\frac{3}{4}$″ × 8″; fos. 56, foliated 1–30, 49–74; blank: fos. 28*v*–29*v*, 30*v*, 73*r*–74*v*; modern parchment covers. This volume is in the nature of a rough book and, with minor exceptions, fos. 1–28, 30, 49–61 are a precise copy of the relevant sections of Ep. I/1/8. Fos. 62*r*–66*r* contain an undated clerical subsidy list and fos. 66*v*–72*v* a visitation exhibit book for the 1630s (cf. Ep. I/19/10).

1*r*–28*r*	register of Bishop Watson	
	1*r*–27*r*	institutions and collations Sept. 1596–Mar. 1605
	27*v*	ordinations Mar. 1600–Oct. 1603
	28*r*	proceedings on admissions to benefices Feb.–Aug. 1597

30*r*–60*v* register of Bishop Andrewes
- 30*r* register heading
- 49*r*–59*v* institutions and collations Feb. 1606–Oct. 1609
- 59*v*–60*r* resignation proceedings Mar.–June 1606
- 60*r* licences to preach Feb. 1606–Sept. 1609, and licences for curates Mar. 1608–Oct. 1609
- 60*v* certificates to the Exchequer noting recusants who conformed July 1606–Aug. 1609, and ordinations Oct. 1607–Sept. 1609

61*r–v* list of institutions during the archbishop's visitation Apr.–Oct. 1605

All institutions are calendared in WSRO, MP.1096, except for those of the time of Bishop Peter Gunning (in MP.1097).

VACANCY 1605

LPL, register of Archbishop Richard Bancroft, fos. 205*r*–207*r*.

record of the archiepiscopal visitation of the diocese *sede vacante* (including institutions) Sept.–Oct. 1605

Fos. 202*r*–205*r* of Bancroft's register contains a record of the archiepiscopal visitation *sede plena*, Mar.–Sept. 1605. See also above, for a list of institutions performed *ratione visitationis*. Institutions are calendared in WSRO, MP.1096.

VACANCY 1609

LPL, register of Archbishop Richard Bancroft, fo. 257*r*.

'Nihil actum fuit quoad jurisdictionem ecclesiasticam diocesis Cicestrensis predicte durante vacatione predicta.'

VACANCY 1628

LPL, register of Archbishop George Abbot, volume II, fos. 301*v*–303*v*

Chichester vacancy business May–Aug. 1628

Institutions are calendared in WSRO, MP.1096.

RICHARD MONTAGUE (1628–1638)

1. WSRO, Ep I/1/9. Paper register; 11¾″ × 7¾″; fos. 12, foliated 1–14 (including original covers); blank: fos. 1*v*–2*v*, 4*r*–14*v*; modern parchment binding, enclosing original parchment covers.
   - 1*r* register heading (original front cover)
   - 3*r–v* institutions and collations Oct.–Dec. 1628
2. Bodl., Ashmole 1144, pp. 365–92. Paper; 11¼″ × 7¼″; fos. 14; blank: pp. 365–6.
   - 367–392 institutions and collations Mar. 1629–Apr. 1634

Both registers are printed by W. D. Peckham, 'The Acts of Bishop Montague' in *Sussex Archaeological Collections* 86 (1947), 141–54.

COVENTRY AND LICHFIELD

Repositories

1. Lichfield Joint Record Office, Public Library, Bird Street, Lichfield WS13 6PN (LRO).
2. Lambeth Palace Library, London SE1 7JU (LPL).
3. Canterbury Cathedral Archives and Library, The Precincts, Canterbury CT1 2EG (CAL).

Area

The medieval diocese of Coventry and Lichfield comprised five archdeaconries—Chester, Coventry, Derby, Salop and Stafford—and extended over the counties of Stafford, Chester and Derby, the southern part of Lancashire, the northern part of Shropshire, northern and eastern Warwickshire, a few parishes in Flintshire and a single parish in Denbighshire. The archdeaconry of Chester, together with the Welsh parishes, were removed in 1541 to form part of the new diocese of Chester, but there were no further changes in the diocesan boundaries until the nineteenth century.[1]

Bibliographical Note

The Lichfield registers have been described in considerable detail by Dr David Robinson in a National Register of Archives handlist ('The registers of the bishops of Lichfield', 46 pp., typescript, 1968) and in his subsequent guide, *Staffordshire Record Office Cumulative Hand List, part 1: Lichfield Joint Record Office, Diocesan, Probate and Church Commissioners' Records* (Staffordshire County Council, 1970), pp. 2–7. The earliest surviving register dates from the episcopate of Walter Langton (1296–1321) but until the late fourteenth century at least the register of his predecessor, Roger Meuland or Longespée (1258–95) was still extant.[2] The medieval registers divide most commonly into three main sections—institutions, general memoranda (diverse letters) and ordinations. A separate section for licences and letters dimissory is found until the time of Bishop Burghill (1398–1414) and in the registers of Walter Langton and Geoffrey Blyth (1503–31) the collations of prebends are recorded separately. Indeed, the earliest register contains several category subdivisions not found in later volumes. In common with other extensive English dioceses the registry clerks of the bishops of Coventry and Lichfield adopted a geographical division by archdeaconry to cope with the bulk of institutions and related business. However, the registers of the vicars-general were, with a single exception, simply chronological in arrangement. There are no records of ordinations between 1531 and 1623 and from the middle of the sixteenth century the registers tend to contain only records of institutions and collations and occasional miscellaneous business.

There is in the Lichfield Diocesan Registry an incomplete seventeenth-century index ('Repertory') of the episcopal registers, arranged by place within each archdeaconry division. Upon cursory examination, most entries noted in fact seem to be taken from the first two registers. A photocopy of this index is available in the Lichfield Joint Record Office. The sixteenth- and seventeenth-century registers have been used to compile lists of Staffordshire

[1] A detailed description of the diocesan boundaries is given in *Staffordshire Record Office, Cumulative Hand List, part 1: Lichfield Joint Record Office* (Stafford, 1970), pp. 1–2, but see also *VCH Derbyshire* ii (1907), p. 40 (with map opposite); *VCH Lancashire* ii (1908), pp. 99–101 (with folding map between pp. 98–9); *VCH Shropshire* ii (1973), pp. 1–8; *VCH Staffordshire* iii (1970), pp. 92–8; *VCH Warwickshire* ii (1908), p. 50 (with map opposite); P. Heath, 'The medieval archdeaconry and Tudor bishopric of Chester', *Journal of Ecclesiastical History* 20 (1969), 243–52. There is also a map of the diocese as a frontispiece to W. Beresford, *Diocesan Histories: Lichfield* (London, 1883).

[2] Cheney, *English Bishops' Chanceries*, p. 148. The evidence cited would seem to suggest that Meuland's was the first Lichfield register. It is interesting to note that on fo. 204*v* of John Burghill's register is a note about the ordination of Cheadle church by Bishop Meuland in 1260 taken 'de uno rotulorum domini Rogeri Meuland' quondam episcopi Co. et Lich.' Is this a possible indication of the format of the lost Meuland register?

parochial clergy by W. N. Landor in *Staffordshire Incumbents and Parochial Records* (*1530–1680*) (William Salt Archaeological Society, 3rd ser., 1915).

VACANCY 1295–1296

LPL, register of Archbishop Robert Winchelsey, fos. 177*v*–193*r* *passim.*[3]

Coventry and Lichfield vacancy business Jan.–June 1296

Printed, *Registrum Roberti Winchelsey* i, pp. 60–112 *passim.*

WALTER LANGTON (1296–1321)

LRO, B/A/1/1. Parchment register; $11\frac{1}{2}'' \times 8\frac{1}{4}''$, except for fos. 123–42, $11\frac{1}{4}'' \times 7\frac{1}{2}''$; fos. i + iii (paper) + 216 + iii (paper) + i, foliated [i], 1–216, 216A, 217, 218; blank: fos. 30*v*, 77*v*, 80*v*, 81*v*, 84*v*, 99*r*, 142*r*; modern binding.

[i*v*] brief note of select contents, 16th–17th cent.

1*r*–4*r* institutions, collations, grants of custody of benefices, licences and other memoranda Sept. 1298–Dec. 1299
(the institution entries have archdeaconry names beside them in the margin, and have been subsequently entered in the separate archdeaconry sections (see below))

5*r*–7*v* Coventry archdeaconry (including acts of the vicar-general) Feb. 1298–Jan. 1307

7*v* 16th-cent. copy of charter of Bishop Alexander Stavensby appropriating High Ercall church to Shrewsbury abbey, Oct. 1228, and confirmation by Coventry cathedral priory

8*r*–11*r* Chester archdeaconry (including acts of the vicar-general) Mar. 1298–Feb. 1307

11*v* 16th-cent. copy of charter of Bishop Hugh Nonant granting Baschurch church to Shrewsbury abbey, n.d., and confirmation by Coventry cathedral priory, Feb. 1224; confirmation by Bishop Roger to Shrewsbury abbey of certain named tithes, n.d.

12*r*–14*v* Derby archdeaconry [June] 1298–Nov. 1306

14*v* 16th-cent. copy of charter of Bishop Alexander Stavensby granting certain tithes of Wellington church to Shrewsbury abbey, 1232; and confirmation by Coventry cathedral priory, n.d.

15*r*–16*v* Stafford archdeaconry Jan. 1299–Apr. 1307

16*v*–17*r* 16th-cent. copy of ordination of Lapley vicarage by Bishop Roger Meuland, Mar. 1266

17*v* 16th-cent. copy of charter of Abbot N. of Lilleshall inspecting Bishop Roger Meuland's ordination of Lilleshall vicarage, dated Mar. 1286, Aug. 1315

18*r*–19*v* Salop archdeaconry Mar. 1298–Feb. 1307

20*r*–*v* *negocia forinseca que non contingunt iurisdictionem episcopi* (mostly financial business) Dec. 1298–Nov. 1304

21*r*–*v*, 26*r* collations of prebends Feb. 1297–Feb. 1306

22*r*–24*v* grants of custody of churches in all archdeaconries Dec. 1299–Dec. 1306

24*v*–25*r* copies of 2 bulls of Pope Boniface VIII in connection with a lawsuit over the church of Pagham, dioc. Chichester Feb. 1302

25*r* letter of Bishop Langton concerning certain monks of Haughmond Jan. 1305

25*v* licence for oratory, note about sealing of charters, and ordination of vicarage Feb. 1301–Apr. 1302

[3] See under Canterbury for a description of this and subsequent archiepiscopal and capitular registers.

26*v*	16th-cent. copy of Bishop Langton's ratification of the appropriation of Kingstone church to Rocester abbey by Bishop Roger, Aug. 1305; and royal licence to hold the church notwithstanding mortmain statute, Mar. 1280
27*r*–30*r*	register of vicar-general Oct. 1307–Nov. 1308
31*r*–33*r*	register of vicar-general
	31*r–v* Derby archdeaconry May 1312–July 1313
	32*r* Salop archdeaconry May 1312–Jan 1313
	32*v* Chester archdeaconry Oct. 1312–May 1313
	32*v* Stafford archdeaconry June 1312–May 1313
	33*r* Coventry archdeaconry June 1312–May 1313
33*r–v*	16th-cent. copy of composition between Dieulacres abbey and the rectors of Pulford and Eccleston, Jan. 1316
34*r*–40*v*	Coventry archdeaconry May 1307–May 1317
41*r*–48*v*	Stafford archdeaconry June 1307–Jan. 1317
49*r*–55*v*	*Feoffamenta facta per episcopum in episcopatu de vastis et escaetis et alia forinseca* (grants of land, financial business, with occasional dispensations etc.) Aug. 1307–Oct. 1316
56*r*–63*v*	Chester archdeaconry Aug. 1307–May 1317
64*r*–69*v*	Salop archdeaconry June 1307–Feb. 1321
70*r*–77*r*	Derby archdeaconry May 1307–Aug. 1318
78*r*–80*r*	Coventry archdeaconry Mar. 1317–Oct. 1321
81*r*	Salop archdeaconry May–Oct. 1321
82*r*–84*r*	Derby archdeaconry Mar. 1318–Sept. 1321
85*r*–88*r*	Chester archdeaconry May 1317–Oct. 1321
88*v*	16th-cent. copy of ordination of the prebendal vicarage of Alrewas and chapelries, May 1324
89*r*–91*v*	Stafford archdeaconry Feb. 1317–Sept. 1321 (at the end an ordination of a vicarage Mar. 1311)
92*r*–141*v*	ordinations June 1300–Apr. 1321 (fo. 99*v* contains copies of grants by Bishop Langton to Selby abbey of land in, and the advowson of, Adlingfleet, n.d.)
142*v*	extract from a letter of Pope Boniface VIII allowing friars to be ordained by any Catholic bishop
143*r*–216*v*	ordination register of Bishop Roger Northburgh (see below)

For 19th-century extracts from Langton's register, see SMS.229 in the William Salt Library, Stafford.

VACANCY 1321–1322

LPL, register of Archbishop Walter Reynolds, fo. 29*v*.

Coventry and Lichfield vacancy business Dec. 1321–Jan. 1322, among the general section of Canterbury institutions

VACANCY 1321–1322
ROGER NORTHBURGH (1322–1358)

1. LRO, B/A/1/1, fos. 143*r*–216*v* (for description see under Langton).

   ordination register Sept. 1322–Sept. 1358

2. LRO, B/A/1/2. Parchment register; 13″ × 9½″; fos. i + iii (paper) + 16 (11½″ × 7¼″) + 217 + ii (paper) + i, foliated A–D, 1–233; blank: fos. A*v*–B*v*, C*v*, 16*r–v*, 85*v*, 97*v*, 135*v*, 182*v*, 188*v*, 207*v*, 233*v*; modern binding.

D*v*	brief note of select contents
1*r*–2*r*	*sede vacante* register Nov. 1321–Apr. 1322

2*v*	form of oath of apparitor, and 2 appointments of apparitors Nov. 1350, Sept. 1355
3*r*–4*r*	register of vicar-general of bishop-elect May–June 1322
4*v*–6*v*	licences Aug. 1322–Nov. 1331
7*r*–8*v*	licences, letters dimissory July 1322–Sept. 1334
9*r*–15*v*	licences (for study), letters dimissory Mar. 1329–May 1358 (these three preceding sections all contain similar material but overlap in date)
17*r*–62*v*	Coventry archdeaconry June 1322–Sept. 1358
63*r*–97*r*	Derby archdeaconry Apr. 1322–May 1358
98*r*–135*r*	Chester archdeaconry June 1322–May 1358
136*r*–201*v*	Stafford archdeaconry May 1322–Oct. 1358
202*r*–233*r*	Salop archdeaconry July 1322–Oct. 1358

3. LRO, B/A/1/3. Parchment register; $13\frac{1}{2}'' \times 9\frac{1}{4}''$, except for fos. 48–51, $10\frac{3}{4}'' \times 7\frac{1}{2}''$; fos. i+i (paper)+151+ii (paper)+i, foliated 1–151; blank: fos. 92*v*, 150*r*; modern binding.

1*r*–149*v*	*registrum ... de commissionibus et aliis litteris emanentibus* (general memoranda, in approximate chronological order, with occasional lapses) Apr. 1322–Nov. 1358
150*v*	note of appropriations of churches mentioned in the register
151*r*	3 documents relating to financial business, Feb. 1333 and 2 undated

In this register, some material of a similar nature, e.g. appropriations of churches, ordinations of vicarages and chantries, is sometimes found grouped together.

The marginal headings of this register have been printed by E. Hobhouse, 'The Register of Roger de Norbury, Bishop of Lichfield and Coventry from A.D. 1322 to A.D. 1358: an abstract of contents and remarks', in *Collections for a history of Staffordshire* (William Salt Archaeological Society, old series 1, 1880), pp. 241–88.

VACANCY 1358–1360

LPL, register of Archbishop Simon Islip, fos. 220*v*–222*r*.

Coventry and Lichfield vacancy business Nov. 1358–Sept. 1360

VACANCY 1358–1360
ROBERT STRETTON (1360–1385)

1. LRO, B/A/1/4. Parchment register; $15\frac{1}{4}'' \times 11''$; fos. i+i (paper)+i+7 ($12'' \times 8\frac{1}{2}''$)+106+i, foliated A, 1–113; modern binding.

This volume contains the *sede vacante* register from Nov. 1358 to Sept. 1360, and the five archdeaconry sections of Stretton's register.

Printed, *The registers or act books of the bishops of Coventry and Lichfield. Book 4, being the register of the guardians of the spiritualities during the vacancy of the see, and the first register of Bishop Robert de Stretton, 1358–1385: an abstract of the contents*, ed. R. A. Wilson (William Salt Archaeological Society, new series 10, part 2, 1907).

2. LRO, B/A/1/5i. Parchment register; $11'' \times 7\frac{1}{4}''$; fos. i+39+i, foliated 1–39; modern binding.

This section contains the register of the vicars-general 1360, licences and a record of friars admitted according to the constitution *super cathedram*.

3. LRO, B/A/1/5ii. Parchment register; $13\frac{1}{2}'' \times 10''$; fos. i+92+i, foliated 40–131; modern binding.

This final section of Stretton's register contains the memoranda register (*registrum commissionum et aliarum diversarum execucionum*) and the register of ordinations.

These two registers are printed, *The registers or act books of the bishops of Coventry and Lichfield. Book 5, being the second register of Bishop Robert de Stretton, A.D. 1360–1385: an abstract of the contents*, ed. R. A. Wilson (William Salt Archaeological Society, new series 8, 1905).

VACANCY 1385–1386

1. LPL, register of Archbishop William Courtenay, fos. 165*r*–166*r*.

Coventry and Lichfield vacancy business June 1385–July 1386

2 Lichfield vacancy acts are also to be found *ibid.*, fo. 258*r*, among the general section of Canterbury institutions.

2. *ibid.*, fos. 346*r*–353*v*.

Coventry and Lichfield vacancy business Apr. 1385–Jan. 1386

WALTER SKIRLAW (1386)
RICHARD SCROPE (1386–1398)

LRO, B/A/1/6. Parchment register; $14\frac{1}{4}'' \times 10\frac{1}{4}''$; fos. i+i (limp parchment cover)+159+i (limp parchment cover)+iii (paper)+i, foliated 1–159; blank: fos. 14*v*, 51*v*, 62*v*, 121*v*, 139*v*, 159*r*; modern binding.

1*r*–*v*	Coventry archdeaconry (Skirlaw) Jan.–Sept. 1386
1*v*–14*r*	Coventry archdeaconry (Scrope) Oct. 1386–Feb. 1398
15*r*–*v*	Derby archdeaconry (Skirlaw) Feb.–Sept. 1386
15*v*–29*v*	Derby archdeaconry (Scrope) Dec. 1386–Apr. 1398
30*r*–51*r*	Stafford archdeaconry (Scrope) Nov. 1386–May 1398
52*r*–*v*	Chester archdeaconry (Skirlaw) Jan.–Aug. 1386
52*v*–62*r*	Chester archdeaconry (Scrope) Jan. 1387–Oct. 1397
63*r*	Salop archdeaconry (Skirlaw) Feb.–June 1386
63*r*–74*r*	Salop archdeaconry (Scrope) Jan. 1387–May 1398
74*v*	pleas *de quo warranto* before the itinerant justices in Warwickshire 13 Edward I (2 documents relating to Bishop Roger Meuland)
75*r*–121*r*	general memoranda (Scrope) Dec. 1386–Jan. 1398 (the first section, fos. 75–113, contains material Mar. 1390–Jan. 1398; the second section, fos. 114–21, material Dec. 1386–June 1397, most of it earlier in the period. It is clear, however, that it is not simply a case of misbinding.)
122*r*	licences etc., granted by Skirlaw's vicar-general Jan.–July 1386
122*v*–137*r*	licences etc., granted by Scrope and his vicar-general Dec. 1386–Apr. 1398
137*r*–139*r*	union of the manor or priory of Wolston with the Charterhouse of St Anne, Coventry June–July 1397
140*r*–141*r*	ordinations (Skirlaw) Mar.–Sept. 1386
141*r*–158*v*	ordinations (Scrope) Dec. 1386–Apr. 1398
159*v*	copy of writ of Edward IV to Bishop Hales Sept. 1481

It is evident that the Lichfield clerks continued the register begun for Bishop Skirlaw after his brief episcopate. Entries for Bishop Scrope continue straight on after Skirlaw entries, with only a new register heading at the appropriate point.

VACANCY 1398
JOHN BURGHILL (1398–1414)

LRO, B/A/1/7. Parchment register; $15'' \times 10\frac{1}{2}''$; fos. i+i (paper)+i+238+i+i, foliated A, 1–238, 238A; blank: fos. 48*v*, 75*v*, 104*v*, 119*v*, 127*v*, 233*v*, 237*r*–238*r*; modern binding.

A*v*	16th-cent. selective list of contents
	2 *sede vacante* entries May–June 1398
1*r*–3*v*	*sede vacante* register Apr.–Sept. 1398
4*r*–34*v*	Coventry archdeaconry Oct. 1398–Mar. 1414
35*r*–48*r*	Derby archdeaconry Apr. 1405–Apr. 1414
49*r*–75*r*	Stafford archdeaconry Sept. 1398–Mar. 1414
76*r*–85*v*	Derby archdeaconry Sept. 1398–Sept. 1404
86*r*–104*r*	Chester archdeaconry Oct. 1398–Feb. 1414
105*r*–119*r*	Salop archdeaconry Oct. 1398–Feb. 1414
120*r*–123*v*	miscellaneous entries (institutions, collations, letters questory, dispensations, delivery of imprisoned clerk etc.) Sept. 1398–Apr. 1399
124*r*–127*r*	licences and letters dimissory Sept. 1398–Dec. 1399
128*r*–139*v*	register of the process between the rector of Mancetter and the Augustinian friars of Atherstone 1375
140*r*–211*v*	general memoranda Sept. 1398–Oct. 1413
	(this register in effect comprises two main sections: licences etc. (fos. 140–59, 195–204) and dispensations and other memoranda (fos. 160–94, 205–11). There is some grouping together of material of a similar nature)
212*r*–236*v*	ordinations Sept. 1398–Apr. 1414

VACANCY 1414–1415

1. CAL, register G, fos. 289*r*–290*v* (badly damaged).

   Coventry and Lichfield vacancy business May 1414

2. LPL, register of Archbishop Henry Chichele, volume I, fos. 61*r*–64*v* *passim*.

   Coventry and Lichfield vacancy business Sept. 1414–June 1415, among the general section of Canterbury institutions

   Printed, *Register of Henry Chichele* i, pp. 132–5 *passim*

3. *ibid.*, volume II, fos. 117*r*–148*r*.

   Coventry and Lichfield vacancy business June 1414–May 1415

   Printed, *Register of Henry Chichele* iii, pp. 291–347.

JOHN CATTERICK (1415–1419)

LRO, B/A/1/8. Parchment register; $14\frac{3}{4}'' \times 11\frac{3}{4}''$; fos. i+44+i, foliated 1–17, 19–45; blank: fos. 17*v*, 22*r*, 33*v*–34*v*, 45*r*; modern binding (prior to 1972 this volume was bound up with B/A/1/7).

This volume is the register of the bishop's vicar-general.

1*r*	vicar-general's commission June 1415
1*r*–8*v*	Coventry archdeaconry (confused arrangement, obviously written up much later) June 1415–Nov. 1419
9*r*–12*v*	Derby archdeaconry (same confused arrangement; the terminal date is somewhat uncertain because of the confusion) July 1415–(?) May 1419
13*r*–14*v*	Stafford archdeaconry Feb. 1416–Oct. 1419
15*r*–17*r*	Salop archdeaconry Sept. 1416–Aug. 1419
19*r*–21*v*	Chester archdeaconry Apr. 1416–Sept. 1419
22*v*	dispensation for marriage Aug. 1415
23*r*–33*r*	general memoranda (confused arrangement) Sept. 1415–Sept. 1419
35*r*–44*v*	ordinations Sept. 1415–Dec. 1419
44*v*	note of dispensation for marriage Aug. 1481

45v grant of next presentation June 1480, and letter of institution to chantry Mar. 1443

VACANCY 1419–1420

LPL, register of Archbishop Henry Chichele, volume I, fos. 106*r*–109*v* *passim.*

Coventry and Lichfield vacancy business Feb.–Apr. 1420, among the general section of Canterbury institutions

Printed, *Register of Henry Chichele* i, pp. 177–81 *passim.*

WILLIAM HEYWORTH (1420–1447)

LRO, B/A/1/9. Parchment register; 14½″ × 11½″; fos. i+i+243+i (paper)+i, foliated [i], 1–244; blank: fos. 45*v*, 72*v*, 100*v*, 128*v*, 142*r*, 180*r*, 204*v*, 244*v*; modern binding.

[i*v*] 16th–18th-cents. notes of select documents, and administrative jottings
1*r*–5*v* register of vicars-general Dec. 1420–June 1421
5*v*–45*r* Coventry archdeaconry May 1421–Dec. 1446
46*r*–72*r* Stafford archdeaconry Apr. 1421–Mar. 1447
73*r*–94*v* Derby archdeaconry July 1421–Feb. 1447
95*r*–108*v* Salop archdeaconry Sept. 1421–Sept. 1446
109*r*–110*v* royal grant of Lapley priory to the college of St Bartholomew, Tong, and confirmation by Bishop William, on papal authority
111*r*–128*r* Chester archdeaconry May 1421–Sept. 1446
129*r*–204*r* general memoranda (occasionally confused arrangement, and some additional material has been entered at the end of the section. The section includes visitation business, foundation statutes etc. The terminal date may possibly be amended, as the section is very chronologically confused) Feb. 1421–Mar. 1444
205*r*–243*v* ordinations Dec. 1420–Mar. 1444

VACANCY 1447

LPL, register of Archbishop John Stafford, fo. 93*r*–*v* *passim.*

Coventry and Lichfield vacancy business Apr.–May 1447, among the general section of Canterbury institutions

VACANCY 1447
WILLIAM BOOTH (1447–1452)

LRO, B/A/1/10. Parchment register; 13″ × 9½″; fos. i+iii (paper)+i+114+i+iii (paper)+i, foliated A–D, 1–74, 76–119; blank: fos. A*v*–D*r*, 1*v*, 3*v*, 4*v*, 5*r*, 27*v*, 55*v*, 60*v*, 74*v*, 85*v*, 115*v*–119*r*; modern binding.

1*r*–5*v* *sede vacante* register
- 1*r* commission to custodians Mar. 1447
- 1*r* Coventry archdeaconry June 1447
- 2*r*–*v* Derby archdeaconry Apr.–May 1447
- 3*r* Stafford archdeaconry May 1447
- 4*r* Salop archdeaconry Apr. 1447
- 5*v* ordinations June 1447

6*r*–13*v* Coventry archdeaconry Aug. 1447–Aug. 1452
14*r*–20*v* Stafford archdeaconry Sept. 1447–Aug. 1452
21*r*–23*v* Derby archdeaconry Jan. 1448–May 1452
24*r*–27*r* Salop archdeaconry Jan. 1448–July 1452

28*r*–32*v*	Chester archdeaconry July 1447–Aug. 1452
33*r*–104*v*	general memoranda (not always in chronological sequence. Some material of a similar nature is grouped together, e.g. appropriations of churches, ordinations of vicarages) Sept. 1447–June 1452
105*r*–115*r*	ordinations (including suffragan commission) Aug. 1447–June 1452

VACANCY 1452

LPL, register of Archbishop John Kempe, fo. 321*r–v*

Coventry and Lichfield vacancy act Sept. 1452 (1 entry), among the general section of Canterbury institutions

VACANCY 1452

VACANCY 1452–1453

REGINALD BOULERS (1453–1459)

LRO, B/A/1/11. Parchment register; $13\frac{1}{2}'' \times 9\frac{3}{4}''$; fos. i+7 ($13'' \times 9\frac{1}{2}''$)+110+i, foliated 1–117; blank: fos. 7*v*, 96*v*; modern binding.

1*r–v*	*sede vacante* register Sept.–Oct. 1452 (see also above)
2*r*–7*r*	*sede vacante* register Nov. 1452–Apr. 1453 (see also below)
8*r–v*	register of vicars-general Apr.–Oct. 1453
9*r*–11*v*	register of vicar-general Nov. 1453–June 1455
12*r*–13*r*	register of vicar-general July–Aug. 1455
13*v*	register of vicar-general Feb.–Mar. 1456
14*r*–15*v*, 61*r*–64*v*, 16*r*–17*v*	Stafford archdeaconry Apr. 1453–Jan. 1459
18*r*–19*v*	register heading, with bull of translation of Boulers, and commissions appointing officials, suffragan etc. Feb.–July 1453
20*r*–27*v*	Coventry archdeaconry June 1453–Jan. 1459
28*r*–33*v*	Derby archdeaconry June 1453–Oct. 1458
34*r*–35*v*	Salop archdeaconry Sept. 1453–Dec. 1458
36*r*–43*v*	Chester archdeaconry Aug. 1453–Nov. 1458
44*r*–60*v*, 65*r*–96*r*	general memoranda May 1453–Oct. 1458
97*r*–117*v*	ordinations May 1453–Mar. 1459

Calendared by P. Hosker, 'An edition of the register of Bishop Reginald Boulers, bishop of Lichfield, 1453–9' (Liverpool University Ph.D., 1978).

VACANCY 1452–1453

1. LPL, register of Archbishop John Kempe, fos. 329*r*–339*v*.

Coventry and Lichfield vacancy business Nov. 1452–Apr. 1453

2. *ibid*., fos. 321*v*–324*r passim*.

Coventry and Lichfield vacancy business Nov. 1452–Mar. 1453, among the general section of Canterbury institutions

VACANCY 1459

JOHN HALES (1459–1490)

LRO, B/A/1/12. Parchment register; $13'' \times 10''$; fos. i+iv (paper)+i (cover)+i+8 ($13'' \times 9''$)+282+i, foliated A–B, Bi, Bii, C–D, 1–177, 177A, 178–291 (177 is an inserted letter); blank: fos. A*v*, B*v*–Bii*v*, D*r*, 4*v*, 6*v*, 62*v*, 95*v*, 123*v*, 177*v*, 231*v*; modern binding.

1*r*–6*r*	*sede vacante* register May–Oct. 1459 (with additional entry, Dec. 1478, at the end)
7*r*–*v*	will and probate act Nov. 1472
8*r*	dispensation for marriage Sept. 1479
8*v*	extract from pipe roll 16 Edward IV (1476–7)
9*r*–*v*	register heading and commissions for vicar-general and suffragan Dec. 1459–Feb. 1460
10*r*–39*v*	Coventry archdeaconry Dec. 1459–Aug. 1490
40*r*–62*r*	Stafford archdeaconry Dec. 1459–Sept. 1490
63*r*–80*v*	Derby archdeaconry Dec. 1459–Sept. 1490
81*r*–95*r*	Salop archdeaconry Dec. 1459–June 1490
96*r*–*v*	subsidy granted in Convocation Mar.–Apr. 1481
97*r*–123*r*	Chester archdeaconry Dec. 1459–Oct. 1489/1490 (?) (it is not really clear which year is intended in the terminal entry. The bishop was dead by Oct. 1490, so probably 1489 is the correct date, in which case the last-recorded date in this section would be Mar. 1490)
124*r*–177*r*	general memoranda (*registrum . . . de diversis litteris*, etc.) Dec. 1459–July 1490 (not always in chronological order; includes copies of earlier documents)
177A*r*	confirmation of marriage, Aug. 1480, and a copy of extract from pipe roll 2 Richard III (1484–5)
177A*v*	documents relating to a clerical tenth, n.d.
178*r*–291*r*	ordinations Mar. 1460–Sept. 1490 (this section is misbound and the correct order, chronologically, should be as follows: 178–209, 246–91, 210–23, 232–45, 224–31)
291*v*	later note of select contents

VACANCY 1490–1493

1. LPL, register of Archbishop John Morton, volume I, fos. 55*r*–62*v*.

   Coventry and Lichfield vacancy business Nov. 1490–Dec. 1491

2. *ibid.*, volume II, fos. 150*r*–153*v passim*.

   Coventry and Lichfield vacancy business Oct. 1491–Aug. 1492, among the general section of Canterbury institutions

Calendared in C. Harper-Bill. 'An edition of the register of John Morton, archbishop of Canterbury, 1486–1500' (London University Ph.D., 1977). See also below for further vacancy material.

VACANCY 1490–1493
WILLIAM SMITH (1493–1496)
VACANCY 1496
JOHN ARUNDEL (1496–1502)

LRO, B/A/1/13. Parchment register; $13\frac{1}{4}'' \times 10''$; fos. ii+176+i, foliated 119–161, 164–221, 223–297 (fos. 162–3 missing; the foliation continues from B/A/1/11); blank: fos. 147*v*, 156*v*, 201*v*; modern binding.

119*r*–123*v*	*sede vacante* register Oct. 1490–May 1491 (with additional entry, Feb. 1492)
124*r*–133*r*	*sede vacante* register May 1491–May 1492 (with additional entry, Aug. 1493)
133*v*–138*r*	*sede vacante* register May–Dec. 1492 (The division of this vacancy register as indicated is due to the changes of custodians of the spiritualities)

Register of Bishop William Smith

138*r*–*v*	register of the commissaries of Bishop-elect Smith Jan. 1493
139*r*–*v*	register heading, with commissions for officials etc. n.d.
140*r*–142*v*	Coventry archdeaconry Mar. 1493–Jan. 1496
143*r*–147*r*	Stafford archdeaconry Feb. 1493–Jan. 1496
148*r*–151*v*	statutes and ordinances of St John's hospital, Lichfield Nov. 1495
152*r*–154*v*	Derby archdeaconry Mar. 1493–Jan. 1496
155*r*–156*r*	Salop archdeaconry Mar. 1493–Jan. 1496
157*r*–158*v*	Chester archdeaconry Feb. 1493–Dec. 1495
159*r*–170*v*	general memoranda (including earlier material) Mar. 1493–Jan. 1496
171*r*–191*v*	ordinations Mar. 1493–Dec. 1495
192*r*–199*v*	*sede vacante* register Jan.–June 1496

Register of Bishop John Arundel

200*r*–201*r*	register heading, with commissions for officials etc. Nov.–Dec. 1496
202*r*–206*v*	Coventry archdeaconry Mar. 1497–Oct. 1501
207*r*–215*r*	Stafford archdeaconry Mar. 1497–June 1501
215*v*	administrative note about oath Aug. 1533
216*r*–221*r*	Derby archdeaconry Dec. 1496–Oct. 1501
221*v*	1 collation, Mar. 1502, and royal inspeximus of 1291 taxation of clergy relating to the value of 2 benefices in the Stafford archdeaconry Oct. 10 Henry VIII (1518)
222*r*–229*v*	Salop archdeaconry Nov. 1496–Mar. 1502
230*r*–234*v*	Chester archdeaconry Nov. 1496–Sept. 1501
235*r*–*v*	ordinations May 1502
236*r*–257*v*	general memoranda (last entry incomplete) July 1497–June 1502
258*r*–297*v*	ordinations Dec. 1496–Sept. 1501

VACANCY 1496

LPL, register of Archbishop John Morton, volume I, fos. 142*r*–157*r*.

Coventry and Lichfield vacancy business Jan.–Nov. 1496

Calendared in C. Harper-Bill, 'An edition of the register of John Morton, archbishop of Canterbury, 1486–1500' (London University Ph.D., 1977).

VACANCY 1502–1503

CAL, register F, fos. 284*r*–288*v*.

Coventry and Lichfield vacancy business Mar.–Aug. 1503

Institutions are calendared (by place) in *Sede Vacante Institutions*.

GEOFFREY BLYTH (1503–1531)

1. LRO, B/A/1/14i. Parchment register; 16″ × 12½″; fos. i + ii (paper) + 116 + i, foliated 1–45, 45*, 46–110, 110*, 111–115 (110* is an insert); blank: fos. 2*v*, 49*v*, 110**v*; modern binding.

1*r*–2*r*	register heading, with commissions for officials etc. Sept. 1503
2*r*	monition for visitation Apr. 1527
3*r*–18*r*	Coventry archdeaconry (including some dispensations not normally in the archdeaconry sections) Oct. 1503–Nov. 1531
18*v*	caveat June 1533
19*r*–24*v*	Stafford archdeaconry Oct. 1503–Mar. 1528 (there is a gap in the entries between Jan. 1520 and Sept. 1526, and see also below)

25*r*–28*v*	collations Mar. 1504–Mar. 1531 (including on fos. 27*v*–28*r* Stafford archdeaconry institutions, July 1528–Feb. 1531)
29*r*–30*v*	foundation of Vernon chantry in the college of St Bartholomew, Tong Apr. 13 Henry VIII, and caveat Apr. 1505
31*r*	Stafford archdeaconry Apr.–Dec. 1531
31*v*	caveat Mar. 1536
32*r*–43*v*	Derby archdeaconry Jan. 1504–Sept. 1531
44*r*–52*v*	Salop archdeaconry Apr. 1503 (*sic*)–Sept. 1531 (the first date, if correct, is before Bishop Blyth's provision and consecration)
53*r*–68*v*	Chester archdeaconry Oct. 1503–Dec. 1531
69*r*–115*v*	general memoranda (including copies of earlier documents. In chaotic order, but includes much interesting material relating to heresy trials, Convocation material, and the treason trial of Bishop Blyth. The earliest Blyth material I have located is Aug. 1504 and the latest document is an addition of May 1536)

2. LRO, B/A/1/14ii. Parchment register; 13¼″ × 9″; fos. 220, unfoliated (but numbered [1–220] for purposes of this description); blank: fos. [8*v*, 219*v*–220*v*]; limp parchment covers.

[1*r*–219*r*]	ordinations Sept. 1503–June 1531

VACANCY 1531–1534

ROWLAND LEE (1534–1543)

LRO, B/A/1/14iii. Parchment register; 15″ × 11″; fos. ii (paper) + i + 39, foliated A, 1–39; blank: fos. A*v*, 39*v*; modern binding.

1*r*–5*v*	*sede vacante* register	
	1*r*–*v*	commission of vicar-general and official Jan. 1532
	2*r*	Coventry archdeaconry Mar.–July 1532
	2*v*	Stafford archdeaconry Feb.–July 1532
	2*v*–3*r*	Derby archdeaconry Feb.–July 1532
	3*r*	Salop archdeaconry Apr. 1532
	3*r*	Chester archdeaconry May 1532
	3*v*–5*v*	ordinations Feb.–May 1532
	(see also below, fos. 6*r*–8*r*)	
5*v*	2 documents relating to Warrington church Oct. 1537, July 1540	
6*r*–8*r*	general memoranda Feb. 1533	
8*r*–9*v*	caveats (in disordered arrangement) Aug. 1517–May 1554	
10*r*–11*v*	register heading, with commissions and other miscellaneous business Apr. 1534–Sept. 1538	
12*r*–18*v*	Coventry archdeaconry May 1534–Dec. 1542	
19*r*–23*v*	Stafford archdeaconry Apr. 1534–Jan. 1543	
23*v*	caveats 23 Henry VIII (1531–2)–Dec. 1537, and 2 n.d.	
24*r*–*v*	indenture relating to the tithes of Winwick Mar. 1539	
24*v*	caveats Dec. 1537–Nov. 1552, and 3 n.d.	
25*r*–29*r*	Derby archdeaconry Apr. 1534–Jan. 1543	
29*r*–30*v*	caveats Apr. 1520–Apr. 1555	
31*r*–33*v*	Salop archdeaconry Apr. 1534–Jan. 1543	
33*v*	caveats Dec. 1535–27 Henry VIII (1545–6), some n.d.	
34*r*–38*v*	Chester archdeaconry May 1534–Jan. 1543	
38*v*–39*r*	caveats May 1542–1 Mary (1553–4)	

VACANCY 1543

LPL, register of Archbishop Thomas Cranmer, fo. 387*r*.

Coventry and Lichfield vacancy act Feb. 1543 (1 entry), among the general section of Canterbury institutions

Calendared in A. J. Edwards, 'The *sede vacante* administration of Archbishop Thomas Cranmer, 1533–53' (London University M.Phil., 1968).

RICHARD SAMPSON (1543–1554)
VACANCY 1554
RALPH BAYNES (1554–1559)
VACANCY 1559–1560
THOMAS BENTHAM (1560–1579)
VACANCY 1579–1580
WILLIAM OVERTON (1580–1609)

1. LRO, B/A/1/14iv. Paper register; 15¼″ × 11″; fos. i+21+i, foliated 40–60 (continues on from B/A/1/14iii); blank: fos. 40*r*, 50*v*, 51*r*, 52*v*, 59*r*; modern binding.

Register of Bishop Richard Sampson

40*v*–44*v*	Coventry archdeaconry May 1543–Mar. 1553
45*r*–50*r*	Stafford archdeaconry Mar. 1543–Mar. 1553
51*v*–52*r*	composition relating to Codsall church Sept. 1554
53*r*–56*v*	Derby archdeaconry Mar. 1543–Feb. 1553
57*r*–58*v*	Salop archdeaconry Mar. 1543–June 1552
59*v*	2 collations to St John's collegiate church, Chester Apr.–May 1543
59*v*–60*r*	caveats Dec. 1535–May 1542

2. LRO, B/A/1/15. Parchment register; 16″ × 11″; fos. i+i (paper)+i+70+i, foliated A, 1–21, 23–25, 29–50, 57–59, 62–70, 80–91; blank: fos. A*v*, 23*r*, 25*r*, 34*v*, 59*v*, 62*r*, 70*v*, 80*r*, 86*r*, 89*r*; modern binding.

Register of Bishop Sampson

1*r*–2*r*	Coventry archdeaconry Nov. 1553–Sept. 1554
2*v*–4*v*	Stafford archdeaconry Apr. 1553–Mar. 1555
5*r*–6*r*	Derby archdeaconry May 1553–Aug. 1554
6*r*–7*r*	Salop archdeaconry Apr. 1553–Sept. 1554.

Vacancy register 1554

7*v*–8*r*	appointment of custodians of the spiritualities Sept. 1554
8*r*–*v*	Coventry archdeaconry Oct.–Nov. 1554

Register of Bishop Ralph Baynes and Vacancy register 1559–60

9*r*–12*v*	Coventry archdeaconry May 1555–Apr. 1559
12*v*	Coventry archdeaconry *sede vacante* Mar. 1560 (1 entry)
13*r*–16*v*	Stafford archdeaconry Apr. 1555–May 1559
17*r*–19*v*	Derby archdeaconry Apr. 1555–Apr. 1559
20*r*–21*v*	Salop archdeaconry Apr. 1555/Feb. 1556–June (?1559, possibly 1558) (It is not always clear from the entries which year is intended)
23*v*–24*r*	union of the churches of Sutton and Duckmanton Feb. 1559
24*v*	royal letter to Bishop Bentham Feb. 1565
25*v*	royal letter to the bishop about the leasing of episcopal lands June 1634

Registers of Bishops Thomas Bentham and William Overton and Vacancy register 1579–80

29*v*–30*v*	Coventry archdeaconry May 1560–Feb. 1562

30*v*	institutions performed by the archbishop of Canterbury during his visitation of the diocese Oct. 1560
31*r*	Stafford archdeaconry Mar.–Sept. 1561
31*v*–32*r*	Coventry archdeaconry Apr. 1562–Mar. 1563
32*v*–33*v*	Stafford archdeaconry Mar. 1561–Nov. 1562
33*v*	collations Feb.–Nov. 1562
33*v*–34*r*	Stafford archdeaconry June 1563–Nov. 1564
35*r*–36*r*	Coventry archdeaconry May 1563–Dec. 1564
36*v*–37*r*	Stafford archdeaconry June 1563–Nov. 1564 (this is a duplicate of entries on fos. 33*v*–34*r*)
37*v*–39*v*	Derby archdeaconry Apr. 1560–Feb. 1565
40*r*–41*v*	Salop archdeaconry June 1560–Oct. 1563
42*r*–48*r*	Coventry archdeaconry Apr. 1565–Dec. 1578
48*r*	Coventry archdeaconry *sede vacante* Oct. 1579 (1 entry)
48*r*–49*r*	Coventry archdeaconry Apr. 1581–Aug. 1582
49*v*–50*r*	2 royal letters over a tithe suit Mar. 1634, Feb. 1636
50*v*	mandate to the inhabitants of Redfern to attend Kenilworth church June 1637
57*r*–58*r*	copies of documents relating to Colwich church Apr. 1317, Apr. 1368
58*r*–59*r*	copy of the union of Alvaston chapel and the church of St Michael, Derby Dec. 1440
62*v*–69*r*	Stafford archdeaconry Aug. 1565–Feb. 1579
69*r*	Stafford archdeaconry *sede vacante* Sept.–Oct. 1579
69*v*–70*r*	Stafford archdeaconry Mar. 1581–July 1584
80*v*–84*v*	Derby archdeaconry Oct. 1565–May 1578
85*r*–*v* (*reversed*)	union of the churches of Church Lawford and King's Newnham Feb. 1596
86*v*–87*v* (*reversed*)	lease of the rectory of Wem Dec. 1584
88*r*–*v* (*reversed*)	appointment of custodians of the spiritualities *sede vacante* Feb. 1579
89*v*–91*r*	document concerning the customary dues paid by parishioners of Leigh, Staffs. Dec. 1572
91*r*–*v*	appointment by the vicar-general of a substitute to exercise his office July 1584

See below for further vacancy material for 1559–60 and 1579–80.

VACANCY 1559–1560

1. CAL, register U2, fos. 103*v*–104*r*.

Coventry and Lichfield vacancy business June–Nov. 1559

Institutions are calendared (by place) in *Sede Vacante Institutions*.

2. LPL, register of Archbishop Matthew Parker, volume I, fos. 175*v*–178*r*.

Coventry and Lichfield vacancy business Dec. 1559–Mar. 1560

Printed, *Registrum Matthei Parker* i, pp. 219–25.

VACANCY 1579–1580

LPL, register of Archbishop Edmund Grindal, volume II, fos. 426*v*–442*r*.

Coventry and Lichfield vacancy business Feb. 1579–Sept. 1580

VACANCY 1609

LPL, register of Archbishop Richard Bancroft, fos. 249*r*–256*r*.

Coventry and Lichfield vacancy business Apr.–Nov. 1609

VACANCY 1610

LPL, register of Archbishop Richard Bancroft, fos. 259*v*–263*r*.

Coventry and Lichfield vacancy business Feb.–Dec. 1610 (the last few entries date from the vacancy of the see of Canterbury)

VACANCY 1614

LPL, register of Archbishop George Abbot, volume I, fos. 328*r*–329*r*.

Coventry and Lichfield vacancy business Feb.–Mar. 1614

VACANCY 1618–1619

LPL, register of Archbishop George Abbot, volume I, fos. 383*r*–384*v*.

Coventry and Lichfield vacancy business Oct. 1618–Jan. 1619

THOMAS MORTON (1619–1632)

LRO, B/A/1/16. Paper register; 13½″ × 8½″; fos. 101 (including 7 loose sheets at the end), numbered pp. 2–7, 10–15, fos. 1–88, pp. 1–16 (some leaves missing at the beginning); blank: pp. 3–7, 12–14, fos. 87*r*–*v*, 2nd series pp. 5–6; hide binding (covers detached).

pp. 10–11	later place index, letters M–W only
fos. 1*r*–86*v*	general acts (chronological arrangement, mostly institutions and collations; the last entry is incomplete) Mar. 1619–Jan. 1632
(*2nd series*)	
pp. 1–16	ordinations [ ] 1623–June 1631 (last entry incomplete)

VACANCY 1632

LPL, register of Archbishop George Abbot, volume III, fos. 163*v*–174*v*.

Coventry and Lichfield vacancy business July–Nov. 1632

DRAFT REGISTER

LRO, B/A/2ii/1. Paper register (repaired); 12″ × 8¼″; fos. i + 24 + v, paginated 1–48; blank: pp. 1, 2, 37, 42–48; modern binding.

3–41 brief record of institutions, Coventry archdeaconry Dec. 1537–Feb. 1603

ELY

Repositories

1. Ely Diocesan Records, University Library, West Road, Cambridge CB3 9DR (CUL).
2. Lambeth Palace Library, London SE1 7JU (LPL).
3. Canterbury Cathedral Archives and Library, The Precincts, Canterbury CT1 2EG (CAL).

Area

The bishopric of Ely was established by King Henry I in 1109, removing from the diocese of Lincoln the Isle of Ely and all the county of Cambridge, except for a few parishes in the rural deanery of Fordham which were in the diocese of Norwich.[1]

Bibliographical Note

The Ely registers are described in detail in Mrs D. M. Owen's guide to the diocesan archives.[2] As can be seen from the following analytical list, the arrangement of these volumes varies considerably from the detailed subdivisions of the earliest extant register, that of Simon Montacute, to the three sections (general acts, memoranda and ordinations) of Bishop Alcock. Montacute's was not the first register, for there is evidence for a register kept in the time of Bishop John Hotham (1316–37), which is now lost. In 1344 a search of Bishop Hotham's register was ordered in connection with the record of a divorce and five years later an institution was checked in the same register.[3] There have also been later losses. Virtually all the seventeenth-century records have disappeared; only that of Bishop Martin Heton (1600–9) survives in the original, but fortunately there is a transcript of the lost register of Bishop Lancelot Andrewes (1609–19) among the Baker Manuscripts in Cambridge University Library. A separate ordinations register exists for the second half of the sixteenth century but ordinations were again entered in the register in the time of Bishop Andrewes.

A brief calendar of the registers from Simon Montacute to Richard Cox has been printed by J. H. Crosby in the *Ely Diocesan Remembrancer* between 1889 and 1914. A copy of these Crosby abstracts, with addenda and an index by W. M. Palmer, is available in the Rare Books Reading Room of Cambridge University Library, Adv. c. 116.1. Lists of incumbents for the diocese have also been compiled by Crosby and are in Cambridge University Library, Add. MSS. 6380–1. They are arranged by benefice. Abstracts from the registers (including from seventeenth-century volumes now lost) are among the Cole and Baker Manuscripts in the British Library and Cambridge University Library.[4]

VACANCY 1286

LPL, register of Archbishop John Pecham, fos. 121*v*–122*r*.[5]

Ely vacancy business July 1286

Printed, *Registrum Johannis Peckham* iii, pp. 925–7.

[1] See D. M. Owen, *A Catalogue of the Records of the Bishop and Archdeacon of Ely* (Cambridge, 1971), p. vii, hereafter *Ely Records*; E. Miller, *The Abbey and Bishopric of Ely* (Cambridge, 1951), p. 75. For a map of the deaneries and parish churches of the medieval diocese, see M. Aston, *Thomas Arundel: a study of church life in the reign of Richard II* (Oxford, 1967), opp. p. 132.

[2] *Ely Records*, pp. 1–6. This list supersedes those in *Historical Manuscripts Commission: Twelfth Report*, part 9, pp. 382–5; and A. Gibbons, *Ely Episcopal Records: a calendar and concise view of the episcopal records preserved in the muniment room of the Palace at Ely* (Lincoln, 1891), pp. 142–7, 392–420. See also D. M. Owen, 'Ely Diocesan Records', *Studies in Church History* 1 (1964), 176–83.

[3] C. R. Cheney, *English Bishops' Chanceries*, p. 148, citing the calendar of Lisle's register in *Ely Diocesan Remembrancer*. See also Public Record Office, C269/3/32 for a further reference.

[4] Cited in *Ely Records*, p. 1, and see also *Studies in Church History* 1 (1964), 181.

[5] See under Canterbury for a description of this and subsequent archiepiscopal and capitular registers.

VACANCY 1298–1299

LPL, register of Archbishop Robert Winchelsey, fos. 244*v*–265*r* *passim.*[6]

Ely vacancy business June 1298–Mar. 1299

Printed, *Registrum Roberti Winchelsey* i, pp. 258–331 *passim.*

VACANCY 1302–1303

LPL, register of Archbishop Robert Winchelsey, fos. 285*v*–288*r* *passim.*[6]

Ely vacancy business Mar.–Oct. 1302

Printed, *Registrum Roberti Winchelsey* i, pp. 432–46 *passim.*

VACANCY 1310

LPL, register of Archbishop Robert Winchelsey, fos. 17*v*–18*r*.

Ely vacancy act [ ] 1310 (1 entry)

Printed, *Registrum Roberti Winchelsey* ii, pp. 1071–3.

SIMON MONTACUTE (1337–1345)
VACANCY 1345
THOMAS DE LISLE (1345–1361)

CUL, EDR, G/1/1. Parchment register; average 13¼″ × 8¾″; fos. i (paper) + 218 + iv (parchment covers, including a papal bull) + i (paper), foliated 1–64, 69–94, 120, 96–108, 108 [A], 109–119, 121–125, 1–30, 35–101; blank: fos. 37*r*–*v*, 45*v*, 46*r*, 56*r*, 62*v*–63*v*, 104*v*, 125*r*; 2nd series, 53*v*, 83*r*–*v*, 87*r*, 89*v*, 90*v*; pasteboard covers (with fragment of hide attached).

Register of Bishop Simon Montacute

1*r*–36*v*	general register Mar. 1337–May 1345 (the entries are not always in strict chronological order and an attempt has sometimes been made to gather together related material e.g. licences 1340–5 on fos. 15*r*–16*v*)
38*r*–64*v*	*quaternus de emanentibus* Sept. 1337–May 1343
69*r*–94*v*	royal writs Aug. 1337–Mar. 1345
120*r*	admission of friars according to the constitution *super cathedram* Sept. 1337–Apr. 1343 (see also fo. 90*r* of Lisle's register)
120*v*	appointment of penitentiaries Sept. 1337–Jan. 1341 (continued below)
96*r*–97*r*	letters dimissory Sept. 1337–Jan. 1345
97*r*–119*v*	ordinations Mar. 1338–May 1345
121*r*–*v*	appointment of penitentiaries July 1341–Nov. 1344 (see above for earlier entries)
122*r*–124*v*	ordinations to first tonsure June 1340–May 1345
125*v*	list of cardinals

Register of Bishop Thomas de Lisle and 1345 vacancy business

1*r*–46*v*, 74*r*–*v*	general register Sept. 1345–Jan. 1356
47*r*–*v*	visitation business *sede vacante* July–Aug. 1345
48*r*–53*r*	visitation business, appointments of heads of religious houses etc. Nov. 1346–July 1352

[6] See also R. Graham, 'The administration of the diocese of Ely during the vacancies of the see, 1298–9 and 1302–3', *T.R.H.S.*, 4th ser., 12 (1929), 49–74.

54*r*–66*v*	*quaternus de emanentibus* Sept. 1345–Mar. 1352
67*r*–73*v*, 75*r*–82*v*	royal writs Sept. 1345–Feb. 1355 (in some chronological confusion)
84*r*–*v*	ordinations to first tonsure Apr. 1346–Oct. 1355
85*r*–86*v*	letters dimissory Dec. 1345–Dec. 1355
87*v*–88*v*	appointment of penitentiaries Nov. 1345–Sept. 1352
89*r*	admission of friars according to the constitution *super cathedram* Apr. 1346–Feb. 1352
90*r*	admission of friars as above, *temp*. Bishop Montacute Oct.–Nov. 1344
91*r*–101*v*	ordinations Apr. 1346–Sept. 1356

Montacute's register is calendared briefly in *Ely Diocesan Remembrancer* 54 (Nov. 1889)–85 (June/July 1892); Lisle's register is calendared *ibid*., 86 (July/Aug. 1892)–113 (Oct./Nov. 1894).

VACANCY 1361–1362

LPL, register of Archbishop Simon Islip, fos. 235*v*–236*r*.

Ely vacancy business July 1361–Feb. 1362

An exchange of benefices in Ely and Canterbury dioceses, Aug. 1361, is recorded on fo. 289*r*.

THOMAS ARUNDEL (1374–1388)

CUL, EDR, G/1/2. Parchment register; $15\frac{1}{4}'' \times 11\frac{3}{4}''$; fos. i (paper) + i (limp parchment cover) + 117 + i (limp parchment cover) + i (paper), foliated 1–8, 8[A], 9–62, 74–89, 100–137; blank: fo. 78*v*; paper-covered pasteboards.

1*r*–62*r*	general register Aug. 1373–Aug. 1388
62*v*	17th-cent. copies of charters of 13th-cent. bishops of Ely to Ely cathedral
74*r*–78*r*	proceedings in the Court of Canterbury concerning the obedience of the Chancellor of Cambridge University 1374
79*r*–114*v*	royal writs and mandates from archbishops etc. Sept. 1376–June 1388
115*r*–126*r*	ordinations May 1374–May 1388
126*v*	17th-cent. copies of charters of 13th-cent. bishops of Ely to Ely cathedral

Calendared in *Ely Diocesan Remembrancer* 113 (Oct./Nov. 1894)–142 (Mar./Apr. 1897).

VACANCY 1388

LPL, register of Archbishop William Courtenay, fos. 269*v*–270*r*.

Ely vacancy business Sept. 1388, among the general section of Canterbury institutions

JOHN FORDHAM (1388–1425)

CUL, EDR, G/1/3. Parchment register; $14'' \times 10\frac{1}{4}''$; fos. i (limp parchment cover) + 250 + i + i (limp parchment cover), foliated 1–149, 160–172, 174–222, 224–249, 260–272; blank: none; hide-covered pasteboards.

1*r*–12*v*, 174*r*–207*v*	memoranda Apr. 1388–Oct. 1408
13*r*–107*v*	institutions Oct. 1388–Oct. 1408
107*v*–110*v*	ordinations (incomplete) Dec. 1420–Sept. 1422 (see also below)
111*r*–172*v*	royal writs and mandates Jan. 1391–Jan. 1411

208*r*–219*r*	copies of appropriation deeds, ordinations of vicarages etc. 13th–15th cents.
219*v*	contents list of the following section
220*r*–229*v*	statutes, compositions and agreements Nov. 1401–July 1402
230*r*–249*v*	ordinations Dec. 1388–June 1411
260*r*	admission of friars to hear confessions May 1411–Nov. 1419
260*r*	admission of friars according to the constitution *super cathedram* Sept. 1411–Aug. 1415
260*v*	16th-cent. copy of a charter of Bishop Eustace (1198–1215) to Ely cathedral
261*r*–272*v*	ordinations Apr. 1412–Sept. 1419

Calendared in *Ely Diocesan Remembrancer* 143 (Apr./May 1897)–204 (May/June 1902).

VACANCY 1425–1426

LPL, register of Archbishop Henry Chichele, volume I, fos. 43*v*–45*r*.

Ely vacancy business Mar. 1426, among the section concerning appointments of bishops etc.

Printed, *Register of Henry Chichele* i, pp. 96–102.

VACANCY 1435–1436

LPL, register of Archbishop Henry Chichele, volume I, fo. 209*r*.

Ely vacancy act Oct. 1435 (1 entry), among the general section of Canterbury institutions

Printed, *Register of Henry Chichele* i, p. 289.

THOMAS BOURGCHIER (1443–1454)

CUL, EDR, G/1/4. Parchment register; $14\frac{1}{2}'' \times 10\frac{1}{4}''$; fos. ii (paper)+68+i (limp parchment cover)+ii (paper), foliated 1–45, 45[A], 46–67; blank: fos. 15*v*, 28*v*, 44*v*, 48*v*, 49*v* 52*v*, 67*v*; parchment-covered pasteboards.

1*r*–43*v*	general register Dec. 1443–July 1454
44*r*–48*r*	ordinations Mar. 1444–June 1454 (some entries are out of order; see also below)
49*r*	presentation deed Aug. 1454
50*r*–52*r*	statutes for the chantry of St Mary, Newton n.d. (*temp.* Bourgchier)
53*r*–60*v*	institutions etc. by the vicar-general Feb. 1444–Dec. 1445
61*r*–64*v*	election of a prioress, Convocation mandates Aug.–Oct. 1444
65*v*–66*v*	ordinations Mar.–Sept. 1445 (see also above)
67*v*	grant of office of keeper of Somersham July 1534

Calendared in *Ely Diocesan Remembrancer* 205 (June/July 1902)–227 (Apr./May 1904).

WILLIAM GREY (1454–1478)

CUL, EDR, G/1/5. Parchment register; $14'' \times 10\frac{1}{4}''$; fos. i (paper)+226+i (limp leather cover)+i (paper), foliated 1–226; blank: fos. 99*v*–100*v*, 128*v*, 154*v*, 160*v*, 162*v*, 189*v*, 196*v*, 218*v*, 219*r*; paper-covered pasteboards (leather fragments remaining on spine).

1*r*–99*r*	general register July 1454–July 1478
101*r*–128*r*	memoranda (writs, mandates, Convocation business, taxation, appropriations, endowments etc.) Oct. 1457–Mar. 1477

129*r*–160*r*	augmentation of vicarages, appointments of heads of religious houses, proceedings against Lollards June 1454–Mar. 1475
161*v*–174*v*	archiepiscopal mandates July 1470–Mar. 1475 (see also below)
175*r*–179*v*	bull of Pius II against the Turks Mar. 1464
180*r*–189*v*	royal writs, taxation business, appointments of heads of religious houses, purgations etc. Nov. 1463–Aug. 1466
190*r*–194*v*	archiepiscopal mandates Mar.–Dec. 1468 (see also above)
195*r*–196*r*	Sawston composition Jan. 1472
197*r*–200*v*	Stoke Quy chantry foundation Sept. 1455
201*r*–217*v*	ordinations Sept. 1454–Sept. 1476 (some lacunae, and incomplete at the end)
218*r*	installation of a prior [Jan. 1462]
220*r*–223*v*	taxation of Nicholas IV, 1291, for the diocese
224*r*–226*r*	names of patrons of churches in the diocese, arranged by rural deanery

Calendared in *Ely Diocesan Remembrancer* 228 (May/June 1904)–276 (new series 29, May 1908).

JOHN ALCOCK (1486–1500)

CUL, EDR, G/1/6. Parchment register; 13¾″ × 10″; fos. ii (paper) + i + 140 + v (paper), paginated 1–220, foliated 223–252; blank: p. 220, fo. 252*v*; hide-covered pasteboards.

1–138	general register Oct. 1486–Aug. 1500
139–219	memoranda (mandates, royal writs, Convocation business, acts of court etc.) Jan. 1487–Aug. 1495
223*r*–252*r*	ordinations Dec. 1486–May 1500 (fo. 231 is loose and duplicates entries on fos. 232*r*–233*r*)

Calendared in *Ely Diocesan Remembrancer* 277 (new series 30, June 1908)–304 (new series 57, Sept. 1910).

VACANCY 1500–1501

CAL, register R, fos. 66*r*–106*r*.

record of the visitation of the diocese *sede vacante* Oct. 1500–July 1501

VACANCY 1505–1506

LPL, register of Archbishop William Warham, volume II, fos. 240*r*–245*r*.

Ely vacancy business Aug. 1505–July 1506

VACANCY 1515

LPL, register of Archbishop William Warham, volume II, fos. 276*r*–281*r*.

Ely vacancy business Mar.–Aug. 1515

Visitation business, Apr. 1515 on fo. 277*r* is printed in *Camden Miscellany XVII* (Camden Third Series, 64, 1940), pp. 65–7.

NICHOLAS WEST (1515–1533)
THOMAS GOODRICH (1534–1554)
THOMAS THIRLBY (1555–1559)
RICHARD COX (1559–1581)
VACANCY 1581–1600

1. CUL, EDR, G/1/7. Parchment register; fos. viii (paper) + 176 (14½″ × 11″) + 90 (paper, 14½″ × 11½″) + iii (paper), foliated [i–viii], 1–65, 67–90, 100–112, 117–238, 241–254, 254[A], 255–283 (including in-

serts); blank: fos. [ir, iir–vv, viiir–v], 54r–v, 73v, 209v, 216v, 222v, 227v, 229v, 233v–234v, 235v, 253v, 254v, 257v, 259r–283r; paper-covered pasteboards (originally parchment covers, now inserted loose at the front of the register).

[vir–viiv] 17th-cent. select table of contents

Register of Bishop Nicholas West

1r–44v general register (*registrum ... de et super litteris patentibus et aliis munimentis et scripturis quibuscumque per eundem reverendum patrem concessis*) Oct. 1515–Feb. 1529

45r–73r commissions, appointments of heads of religious houses, appropriations, compositions, grants of pensions Oct. 1515–Oct. 1524 (including an earlier document 1512)

74r–79v wills June 1516–Feb. 1527

80r–87v ordinations Feb. 1516–Apr. 1520

Register of Bishop Thomas Goodrich, part 1 (once had separate foliation)

88r–190v general register Mar. 1534–May 1554 (some considerable chronological confusion; includes copies of many earlier documents)

191r–258v miscellanea (compositions, appropriation deeds, elections of bishops, will of Bishop Wren, royal letters, consecration of college chapels etc.) Mar. 1565–Mar. 1881

283v miscellaneous notes and references to selected documents in the register

West's register is calendared in *Ely Diocesan Remembrancer* 305 (new series 58, Oct. 1910)–319 (new series 72, Dec. 1911); Goodrich's register is calendared *ibid.*, 319 (new series 72, Dec. 1911)–336 (new series 89, May 1913).

2. CUL, EDR, G/1/8. Paper register; $15\frac{1}{4}'' \times 9\frac{3}{4}''$; fos. ii + 128 + i, foliated 1–27, 30–38, 43–65, 67–69, 73–78, 81–88, 141–184, 317–318, 320–324, [325]; blank: fos. 8r, 11r, 12r, 43r–45v, 58v–78v, 88v, 141v, 142v, 143v, 144v, 145v, 146v, 147v, 149v, 183v, 184v, 317r, 318v, 320r, 324v; parchment-covered pasteboards.

Register of Bishop Thomas Goodrich, part 2

1r–10v acts in office cases Aug. 1540–May 1543

11v–12r royal proclamation May 1541 (printed), and related memoranda

13r–14v copies of chantry foundations, augmentations of vicarages etc. exhibited at visitation Aug. 1543

15r–16r acts in office case Jan. 1542

17r collation Jan. 1554

17v relaxation of inhibition Oct. 1547

18r–22v institutions, licences etc. (some institutions are also recorded above, G/1/7) Jan. 1550–May 1554

Register of Bishop Thomas Thirlby

23r–42v institutions etc. July 1554–June 1559

46r–50v archiepiscopal mandates, Convocation business etc. Feb. 1554–Oct. 1557

Register of Bishop Richard Cox

51r–58r royal and archiepiscopal mandates, letters, writs etc. May 1560–May 1581 (and occasional later material)

81r–84r acts in office case Oct. 1555

84v–88r miscellaneous acts relating to the union and consolidation of benefices Aug.–Nov. 1561

141r–180r institutions Oct. 1562–July 1581

180r–v 2 acts of John (Long), archbishop of Armagh Aug. 1584–Dec. 1585

Vacancy Register

180*v*–184*r*	acts in cases, resignations etc. Mar. 1583–Nov. 1601
317*v*–318*r*	'orders for the better encrease of learninge in the inferiour Ministers and for more diligent preachinge and catechisinge sent downe by my lorde grace of Canterburie' Aug. 1587
320*v*	list of annual pensions due to Bishop Cox and his successors
321*r*	index of appropriations
321*v*–324*r*	16th-cent. list of procurations due to the bishop at his visitation (arranged by rural deanery)
[325*r*]	suspension for contumacy *temp.* Bishop Goodrich

Calendared in *Ely Diocesan Remembrancer* 336 (new series 89, May 1913)–355 (new series 108, Dec. 1914). Fos. 81*r*–84*r* are printed, *Acts and Monuments of John Foxe*, ed. J. Pratt (London, 1877), vii, pp. 402–6. See also below for 1581–1600 vacancy.

VACANCY 1554

CAL, register N, fos. 106*v*–111*v*.

Ely vacancy business May–Sept. 1554

Institutions are calendared (by place) in *Sede Vacante Institutions.*

VACANCY 1559

1. CAL, register U2, fos. 101*v*–102*r*.

   Ely vacancy business Nov. 1559

   Institutions are calendared (by place) in *Sede Vacante Institutions.*

2. LPL, register of Archbishop Matthew Parker, volume I, fo. 146*v*.

   Ely vacancy business Dec. 1559

   Printed, *Registrum Matthei Parker* i, pp. 164–5.

VACANCY 1581–1600

1. LPL, register of Archbishop Edmund Grindal, volume II, fos. 460*r*–465*v*.

   Ely vacancy business July 1581–May 1583

2. LPL, register of the dean and chapter of Canterbury *sede vacante* (part of Grindal II), fo. 583*r*–v.

   Ely vacancy business July 1583

3. LPL, register of Archbishop John Whitgift, volume I, fos. 309*r*–331*v*.

   Ely vacancy business Oct. 1583–June 1592

4. LPL, register of Archbishop John Whitgift, volume II, fos. 165*r*–176*v*.

   Ely vacancy business July 1592–Nov. 1597

5. LPL, register of Archbishop John Whitgift, volume III, fos. 158*r*–165*r*.

   Ely vacancy business Feb. 1598–Feb. 1600

   Items 1–5 are calendared in A. Gibbons, *Ely Episcopal Records*, pp. 435–60.

MARTIN HETON (1600–1609)

CUL, EDR, G/1/9. Paper register; $11\frac{1}{2}'' \times 9\frac{3}{4}''$; fos. vi+105+iv, foliated [i–iv], 1–82, [83–104]; blank: fos. [i*v*, iv*r*], 82*v*–[83*v*, 84*v*, 89*r*–99*r*, 100*r*, 101*r*–104*r*]; hide-covered pasteboards (both covers detached).

[i*r*]	administrative memoranda
[ii*r*–iii*v*]	place and name index (arranged under category divisions, e.g. leases, licences, advowsons etc.)
[iv*v*]	register heading
1*r*–82*r*	general register June 1600–June 1609
[84*r*–88*v*]	copy of the *liber feodarius* of the bishop made in the time of Robert Furnes, feodary of Bishop Goodrich, Oct. 1535
[99*v*]	list of fellows of Peterhouse 'at my comming to be Bp. of Elie'
[100*v*]	list of fellows of Jesus College 'at my comming to be Bp. of Elie'

VACANCY 1609

LPL, register of Archbishop Richard Bancroft, fos. 256*v*–257*r*.

Ely vacancy business July–Nov. 1609

LANCELOT ANDREWES (1609–1619)

The register of Bishop Andrewes is now missing but a transcript survives among the Baker manuscripts, CUL, Mm.1.39, pp. 128–47 (modern foliation 66*r*–75*v*).

128–145 (66*r*–74*v*)	institutions Mar. 1610–Feb. 1619
146–147 (75*r*–*v*)	ordinations Sept. 1611–Oct. 1618

VACANCY 1619

LPL, register of Archbishop George Abbot, volume I, fo. 385*r*.

Ely vacancy act Feb. 1619 (1 entry)

VACANCY 1626–1628

LPL, register of Archbishop George Abbot, volume II, fos. 296*v*–301*r*.

Ely vacancy business Oct. 1626–June 1628

VACANCY 1631

LPL, register of Archbishop George Abbot, volume III, fos. 148*v*–150*v*.

Ely vacancy business May–Oct. 1631

VACANCY 1638

LPL, register of Archbishop William Laud, volume I, fos. 306*v*–307*r*.

Ely vacancy business Feb.–Mar. 1638

ORDINATIONS REGISTER

CUL, EDR, A/5/1. Paper register; 12″ × 8″; fos. 90 (some now loose and others trimmed), foliated 1–30, 30B, 31–45, 45B, 46–74, 74A, 75–87; blank: fos. 1*r*–*v*, 5*v*, 38*r*, 45B*v*, 46*v*–47*v*, 50*v*, 51*v*, 69*v*, 72*r*, 74A*v*, 80*v*; 15th-cent. parchment leaf used as a cover.

2*r*–37*v*	examinations of candidates Dec. 1574–Dec. 1580 (includes ordination list Apr. 1575)

38*v*–51*r*	subscriptions and ordinations Dec. 1574–Mar. 1581 (not in strict chronological order)
52*r*–54*v*	ordinations July 1560–Mar. 1562
55*r*–66*v*	examinations of candidates Apr. 1568–Dec. 1569
67*v*–74*v*	examinations of candidates July 1560–June 1561
74A*r*	list of 11 questions administered to candidates for ordination
75*r*–80*r*	examinations of candidates Mar. 1582
81*r*–87*v*	ordinations Dec. 1563–Sept. 1570

Fo. 74A*r* is printed in A. Gibbons, *Ely Episcopal Records: a calendar and concise view of the episcopal records preserved in the muniment room of the Palace at Ely* (Lincoln, 1891), p. 4. A summary analysis of this ordination book is printed in R. O'Day, *The English Clergy: the emergence and consolidation of a profession 1558–1642* (Leicester, 1979), pp. 58–65.

EXETER

Repositories

1. Devon Record Office, Castle Street, Exeter EX4 3PQ (DRO).
2. Lambeth Palace Library, London SE1 7JU (LPL).
3. Canterbury Cathedral Archives and Library, The Precincts, Canterbury CT1 2EG (CAL).

Area

Peculiars excepted, the diocese of Exeter consisted of the counties of Devon and Cornwall, and was divided into the four archdeaconries of Exeter, Barnstaple, Totnes, and Cornwall. There were no changes in the diocesan boundaries until the nineteenth century.[1]

Bibliographical Note

The Exeter episcopal registers are listed in the typescript guide by J. F. Chanter, 'A Catalogue of the Records and Documents of the Bishops of Exeter' (1920), available in the Devon Record Office: they are also briefly listed in the printed *Devon Record Office, Brief Guide: part 1, Official and Ecclesiastical* (Exeter, 1968), pp. 41–2, and in H. Reynolds, *A short history of the ancient diocese of Exeter* (Exeter, 1895), app. B, pp. iii–v. No reference has been found to any registers before 1258.

In arrangement, the registers undergo considerable modification during the period under consideration, even accounting for occasional losses of individual sections. The earliest volumes—those of Bronescombe and Quivil—are basically in the form of a single, general register. The next register—that of Walter Stapledon (1308–26)—includes sections for royal writs and ordinations, as well as the general register. The episcopate of his successor, John Grandisson (1327–69), witnesses further developments in arrangement. His register, now bound into three volumes, has the most subdivisions of any Exeter register; in addition to sections for institutions and collations, and for general memoranda (*registrum commune*), there are further subdivisions for royal writs; papal letters; *littere private*; appropriations; commissions; pensions, bonds and acquittances; and dispensations and letters dimissory. From the late fourteenth century, the registrational arrangement is relatively stable with sections for institutions; *registrum commune*; royal writs; and ordinations, with slight variations from time to time. Commissions are entered up separately until the pontificate of Edmund Stafford (1395–1419), and a section for homages and fealties is found in Stafford's register and in that of his predecessor, Thomas Brantingham. Also in the time of Bishop Stafford there is a section for wills and testamentary business and this is found under Lacy and Neville; similarly for the period 1456–1501 each register contains a section for inquisitions. In the fifteenth century, too, registers of vicars-general are bound up with the bishops' registers. From Bishop Arundel (1502–4) to Bishop Alley (1560–70) there is a threefold division of the registers: institutions; *registrum commune*; and ordinations. A change occurs at the beginning of the episcopate of William Bradbridge (1571–8) with the creation of a separate series of ordination registers, and from then on the bishop's register in effect becomes an institutions register. From 1568 there are separate volumes known as 'act books', containing licences for curates and preachers, marriage licences, and miscellaneous business,[2] and in 1628 a further series, the 'patent books', begins. These volumes contain patents of office, faculties, consecrations, orders etc.[3]

[1] For a map of the diocese see Ordnance Survey, *Map of Monastic Britain: (south sheet)* (2nd edn., 1954).

[2] DRO, Chanter catalogue 41 onwards. 41 covers the years 1568–99; the last section, 1598–9 is described by Chanter as a *registrum commune*, but it is not.

[3] DRO, Chanter catalogue 57 onwards. 57 covers the years 1628–1733.

The registers from 1258 to 1419 and the institutions register of Bishop Lacy (1420–55) have been printed by the Rev. F. C. Hingeston-Randolph between 1886 and 1909, chiefly in index form. In consequence it is not always possible to gain an idea of the register's format and the result is often unsatisfactory to would-be users. To echo Dom David Knowles' words about Hingeston-Randolph, 'his name is kept in memory, if not in benediction, by students of the Exeter episcopal registers'.[4] The remainder of Edmund Lacy's register has recently been edited by Professor G. R. Dunstan.

Among the diocesan archives are the customary registry finding-aids: two late sixteenth- or early seventeenth-century volumes of place indexes of compositions, appropriations etc. (DRO, Chanter catalogue 40), and of institutions from Bronescombe to Veysey (Chanter catalogue 40c); and a late eighteenth-century place index of the registers 1258–1783 (Chanter catalogue 39). J. F. Chanter also compiled a calendar of Exeter institutions and other acts entered in the Canterbury archiepiscopal and capitular registers *sede vacante* or *ratione visitationis* ('Chanter's Register of Institutions').[5] This volume is available in the Devon Record Office.

The Hope revision of G. L. Hennessy's 'Institutions of incumbents to Devon benefices: extracts from the manuscript registers of the bishops of Exeter, 1456–1894' (1898) is available for consultation in the West Country Studies Library in the City Library, Castle Street, Exeter. It is divided into four manuscript volumes: 1. Devon incumbents: parishes, chantries, priories (by place); 2. Devon and Cornwall incumbents: index of institutions (by incumbent); 3. Devon incumbents: patrons, officers, prebendaries (by place); 4. Cornwall incumbents and patrons: parishes, chantries etc. (by place).

WALTER BRONESCOMBE (1258–1280)
PETER QUINEL or QUIVEL (1280–1291)

DRO, Exeter diocesan records, Chanter catalogue 1. Parchment register, composite volume; fos. i (paper)+106 ($10\frac{1}{2}'' \times 6\frac{3}{4}''$), except for fo. 109. ($8'' \times 6''$)+23 ($9\frac{1}{2}'' \times 6''$)+7 ($10\frac{1}{4}'' \times 6''$)+22 ($8\frac{1}{4}'' \times 5\frac{3}{4}''$)+iv (paper), foliated [i–iv], 1–62, 62[A], 63–102, 109–137, [138–162], with many documents inserted; blank: fos. [138*r*–*v*, 139*v*–140*r*, 141*v*]; rough hide-covered wooden boards.

[i*v*, ii*v*–iv*v*]	later notes of select contents
[ii*r*]	late 14th-cent. lists of documents handed over to Bishop T(homas Brantingham) by Nicholas Braybrok
1*r*	note about cancellations in the register

Register of Bishop Walter Bronescombe

2*r*–98*v*	general register Feb. 1258–July 1280
98*v*–99*r*	3 16th-cent. copies of medieval charters relating to St Nicholas priory, Exeter
99*v*–102*r*	copies of royal charters (Ethelred, Cnut, Edward the Confessor, John)

Register of Bishop Peter Quinel or Quivel

102*r*, 110*v*	acts of Bishop Peter, Feb. 1281, entered at the end of Bronescombe's register
109*r*	final concord *temp.* John and copy of charter of Bishop J(ohn) of Exeter
109*v*	16th-cent. copy of a charter relating to St Nicholas priory, Exeter
110*r*–*v*	copy of bull of Pope Gregory the Great to Augustine
110*v*	16th-cent. copy of composition relating to St Nicholas priory, Exeter

[4] M. D. Knowles, 'Great historical enterprises. IV, The Rolls Series', *T.R.H.S.*, 5th ser., 11 (1961), 146; reprinted in *Great Historical Enterprises and Problems in Monastic History* (London, 1962), p. 114.

[5] 'A register of institutions and some other events relating to the diocese of Exeter recorded in the registers of the Archbishops and the Dean and Chapter of Canterbury mainly during the periods of *sede vacante* at Exeter and the archiepiscopal visitations, with notes from the Lateran registers of the Popes and various other documents' (typescript, 1924).

111*r*–133*v*	general register (incomplete) July 1281–Dec. 1288
134*r*	memoranda
134*v*–137*v*	list of documents in the treasury of Exeter *temp.* Bishop Bronescombe
[142*r*–162*v*]	taxation of Pope Nicholas IV, 1291 (section relating to the Exeter diocese)

Printed, *The Registers of Walter Bronescombe (A.D. 1257–1280), and Peter Quivil (A.D. 1280–1291), Bishops of Exeter, with some records of the episcopate of Bishop Thomas de Bytton (A.D. 1292–1307); also the Taxation of Pope Nicholas IV, A.D. 1291 (Diocese of Exeter)*, ed. F. C. Hingeston-Randolph (London and Exeter, 1889).

WALTER STAPLEDON (1308–1326)

DRO, Exeter diocesan records, Chanter catalogue 2. Parchment register; $11\frac{3}{4}'' \times 8''$; fos. iii (paper) + 236 + ii(paper), foliated [i–iv], 1–5, 9–23, 25–89, 100–177, 180–244, [245–248], with inserts; blank: fos. [iii*v*–iv*v*], 12*r*, 13*v*, 23*v*, 70*v*, 105*v*, [246*r*–247*r*, 248*r*]; buckram-covered boards, with hide-covered spine.

[i*r*–iii*r*]	later heading, followed by select contents notes
1*r*–2*v*	miscellaneous documents 1324–5
3*r*–5*v*	*registrum ... de litteris clausis factis et receptis* as bishop-elect Mar.–Oct. 1308
9*r*–11*v*	list of rents of the bishopric
11*v*	document relating to Paignton manor 1309
12*v*–23*r*	documents relating to Bosham
25*r*–28*v*	visitation of the royal free chapel of Bosham Jan. 1310
28*v*	list of royal free chapels in England
29*r*–184*v*	general register as bishop-elect and then as bishop Mar. 1308–June 1325
185*r*–216*v*	royal writs Mar. 1308–Feb. 1322
217*r*–244*v*	ordinations (first tonsure lists are arranged by archdeaconry and peculiar jurisdiction) Dec. 1308–Dec. 1321

Printed, *The Register of Walter de Stapeldon, Bishop of Exeter (A.D. 1307–1326)*, ed. F. C. Hingeston-Randolph (London and Exeter, 1892).

VACANCY 1326–1327

LPL, register of Archbishop Walter Reynolds, fos. 156*v*–157*v*.[6]

Exeter vacancy business Oct. 1326–Jan. 1327

The institutions are calendared in DRO, Chanter's 'Register of Institutions'.

JOHN GRANDISSON (1327–1369)

1. DRO, Exeter diocesan records, Chanter catalogue 3. Parchment register; $12'' \times 9''$; fos. iii (paper) + 233 + i (paper), foliated [i], 1–42, [42A], 43–51, [51A], 52–88, [88A–C], 89–93, [93A], 94, [94A], 95–130, [130A], 131–221, [222–224], excluding inserts; blank: fos. [i*r*–*v*], 34*v*–35*r*, 42*v*, 51*v*–[51A*v*], [88A*r*–88C*v*], 93*v*–[93A*v*, 94A*r*–*v*], 107*v*, 109*v*, 115*v*, [130A*r*–*v*], 195*v*, [223*r*–*v*]; buckram-covered boards, with hide-covered spine.

1*r*–34*r*	royal writs Mar. 1328–June 1363
35*v*–42*r*	papal letters Apr. 1327–May 1353
[42A*r*–*v*]	select contents list
43*r*–48*v*	documents relating to the foundation of the collegiate church at Ottery St Mary June 1342–July 1343
49*r*–51*r*	visitation of the royal free chapel of Bosham May 1363

[6] See under Canterbury for a description of this and subsequent archiepiscopal and capitular registers.

52*r*–88*v*	*littere private* Aug. 1327–[ ]1349
89*r*–109*r*	miscellaneous documents (papal privileges, visitation of the cathedral etc.) Dec. 1331–July 1368
110*r*–221*r*	*registrum commune* May 1342–Mar. 1362 (for previous section see below)
221*v*–[224*v*]	later list of select contents

2. DRO, Exeter diocesan records, Chanter catalogue 4. Parchment register; 12″ × 9″; fos. v (paper) + ii (limp parchment covers) + 230 + ii + v (paper), foliated 1–14, [14A], 15–20, [20A], 21–27, [27A], 28–80, 100–206, 208–242, [243–248]; blank: fos. 22*v*, [27A*r*–*v*], 38*v*, [247*v*–248*v*]; hide covered wooden boards, re-covered in buckram.

1*r*–14*r*	appropriations of churches and ordinations of chantries June 1329–June 1338
15*r*–20*r*	commissions Feb. 1328–July 1334
20*v*–[20A*v*]	select contents list
21*r*	mandate for excommunication June[?1328]
21*v*–22*r*	visitation decrees for Exeter cathedral n.d.
23*r*–27*v*	*pensiones, obligaciones et acquietancie* Apr. 1329–Feb. 1340
28*r*–37*v*	dispensations and letters dimissory Oct. 1329–Oct. 1335
38*r*	petition to the king about the maintenance of the rights and privileges of the church in Cornwall n.d.
39*r*–242*v*	*registrum commune* Aug. 1327–May 1342 (includes copies of earlier documents; for continuation see above)
[243*r*–247*r*]	later list of select contents

3. DRO, Exeter diocesan records, Chanter catalogue 5. Parchment register; 11¼″ × 8½″; fos. v (paper) + 164 + v (paper), foliated 1–164; blank: fo. 163*r*–*v*; hide-covered wooden boards, recovered with buckram.

1*r*–156*r*	institutions Mar. 1328–Nov. 1368
156*v*–158*v*	taxation of churches in the diocese (? Pope Nicholas IV, 1291)
159*r*–162*r*	memoranda concerning the collection of first fruits Oct. 1329–Sept. 1333
162*v*, 164*v*	later list of select contents
164*r*	acquittances given for first fruits from churches Apr. 1331–June 1333

Printed, *The Register of John de Grandisson, Bishop of Exeter (A.D. 1327–1369): part I, 1327–1330, with some account of the episcopate of James de Berkeley (A.D. 1327)*, ed. F. C. Hingeston-Randolph (London and Exeter, 1894); *part II, 1331–1360* (London and Exeter, 1897); *part III, 1360–1369, together with the register of institutions* (London and Exeter, 1899).

VACANCY 1369–1370

LPL, register of Archbishop William Whittlesey, fos. 75*r*–77*v* *passim*.

Exeter vacancy business Jan.–Mar. 1370, among the general section of Canterbury institutions

The institutions are calendared in DRO, Chanter's 'Register of Institutions'.

THOMAS BRANTINGHAM (1370–1394)

1. DRO, Exeter diocesan records, Chanter catalogue 6. Parchment register, part of edge damaged by damp; 13″ × 9″; fos. iii (paper) + 130 + ii (paper, 12¼″ × 8″, later select contents list) + i + iii (paper), foliated 1–68, 70–131; blank: fo. 174*r*; buckram-covered boards, with hide-covered spine.

1*r*–131*v*	*registrum commune* (last entry incomplete) May 1370–May 1392

2. DRO, Exeter diocesan records, Chanter catalogue 7. Parchment register, part of edge damaged by damp; $12\frac{3}{4}'' \times 9''$; fos. v (paper) + 203 + 18 original receipts etc. + 70 + v (paper), foliated [i], 1–28, 30–34, 36–103, 105–110, 112–115, 119–154, [155], 2nd series 4–7, 10–56, [57–59], 3rd series 1–18, 4th series [1–3], 5th series 1–67; blank: fos. 100*r*, 112*r*–*v*, 119*r*–*v*, 2nd series [58*r*–59*v*], 4th series [1*v*–2*r*, 3*r*], 5th series 29*v*, 37*v*; buckram-covered boards, with hide-covered spine.

1*r*–6*v* — *registrum commune* Mar.–May 1370 (this should precede fo. 1 of the volume above. Some later material to Aug. 1372 is inserted)
7*r*–154*r* — institutions May 1370–Nov. 1394

(*2nd series*)
4*r*–7*v* — miscellaneous memoranda (incomplete: also entered in the *registrum commune*) Apr.–Oct. 1372
10*r*–56*v* — commissions May 1370–Jan. 1388
[57*r*–*v*] — later select contents notes

(*3rd series*)
1–18 — visitation expenses, receipts and other financial business (originals and drafts) Aug. 1382–Apr. 1384

(*4th series*)
[1*r*, 2*v*, 3*v*] — administrative memoranda May 1376–Dec. 1387

(*5th series*)
1*r*–12*v*, 15*r*–22*v* — royal writs July 1370–Oct. 1383
13*r*–14*r* — homages and fealties Dec. 1370–Aug. 1380
14*v* — administrative memoranda (3 entries) July 1372 (2 undated)
23*r*–67*r* — ordinations June 1370–Sept. 1392 (some memoranda is inserted on fos. 26*v*–29*r*, 36*v*–37*r*)
67*v* — later select contents notes

Printed, *The Register of Thomas de Brantyngham, Bishop of Exeter* (*A.D. 1370–1394*), *part I*, ed. F. C. Hingeston-Randolph (London and Exeter, 1901); *part II* (London and Exeter, 1906).

VACANCY 1394–1395

LPL, register of Archbishop John Morton, volume II (Courtenay section), fo. 220*r*–*v*.

Exeter vacancy business Feb.–Apr. 1395, among the general section of Canterbury institutions

Printed, *Register of Thomas de Brantyngham, part I*, p. 138.

EDMUND STAFFORD (1395–1419)

1. DRO, Exeter diocesan records, Chanter catalogue 8. Parchment register, part of edge damaged by damp; $13\frac{3}{4}'' \times 9\frac{3}{4}''$; fos. iii (paper) + 326 + iv (paper), foliated 1–149, 160–334, [335, 336]; blank: fos. 248*v*, 299*v*, [336*v*]; buckram-covered boards, with calf-covered spine.

1*r*–248*r* — *registrum commune* Jan. 1395–Sept. 1419
249*r*–299*r* — ordinations Sept. 1395–June 1419
300*r*–334*r* — testamentary business May 1397–Aug. 1419
334*v*–[335*v*] — later select contents notes

2. DRO, Exeter diocesan records, Chanter catalogue 9. Parchment register; $13\frac{3}{4}'' \times 9\frac{1}{2}''$, except for fos. 224–30, $11\frac{1}{4}'' \times 7\frac{1}{4}''$; fos. v (paper) + 354 + v (paper), foliated 1–205, 209–268, 271–296, 303–330, 332–364, [365, 366]; blank: fos. 26*v*, 66*v*, 205*v*, 296*v*, 312*r*, [366*v*]; buckram-covered boards, with calf-covered spine.

1*r*–15*r* vicar-general's register July 1395–Mar. 1400
15*v*–26*r* vicar-general's register Sept. 1400–Mar. 1403
27*r*–205*r* institutions July 1395–Sept. 1419
209*r*–268*v* commissions June 1395–Aug. 1419
271*r*–274*v* statutes of the royal free chapel of Bosham June 1399–Jan. 1401
275*r*–296*r* miscellaneous ordinations, appropriations etc. Mar. 1401–Aug. 1417
303*r*–309*v* royal writs June 1395–Sept. 1399
309*v* fees of the archdeacon of Canterbury for enthroning bishops of the province
310*r*–311*v* homages and fealties Jan. 1396–July 1419
312*r*–318*r* royal writs Oct. 1400–Mar. 1405
318*r*–321*v* Archbishop Arundel's provincial constitutions against the Lollards and royal commissions to the bishop about the Lollards Mar.–Aug. 1400
322*r*–323*v* royal statute against the Lollards
324*r*–330*v* 'Sensuent les estatuz faiz en parlement tenu a Leycestre le darrein iour davril lan seconde du regne del Roi Henry V'
332*r*–364*r* royal writs Dec. 1409–July 1419
364*v*–[366*r*] later select contents notes

Printed, *The Register of Edmund Stafford* (*A.D. 1395–1419*)*: an index and abstract of its contents*, ed. F. C. Hingeston-Randolph (London and Exeter, 1886).

VACANCY 1419–1420

LPL, register of Archbishop Henry Chichele, volume I, fos. 105*r*–120*r* *passim*.

Exeter vacancy business Jan.–Oct. 1420, among the general section of Canterbury institutions

Printed, *Register of Henry Chichele* i, pp. 176–94 *passim*.

EDMUND LACY (1420–1455)

1. DRO, Exeter diocesan records, Chanter catalogue 10. Parchment register, some edges damaged by damp; $13\frac{1}{2}'' \times 10\frac{1}{2}''$, except for fos. 26–34, $13\frac{1}{4}'' \times 9\frac{1}{4}''$; fos. iii (paper) + 293 + iii (paper), foliated 1–292, [293]; blank: fos. 16*v*, 24*r*–*v*, 37*v*, [293*r*–*v*]; buckram-covered boards, with hide-covered spine.

1*r*–23*v* miscellaneous memoranda (not in any order, and including copy of earlier document) May 1427–July 1443
25*r*–34*v* vicar-general's register Nov. 1420–June 1421 (with additional entries 1429)
35*r*–37*r* commissary-general's register Dec. 1425–July 1429
38*r*–43*v* commissary-general's register July 1422–Aug. 1428
44*r*–*v* commissary-general's register Oct. 1428–Apr. 1429
45*r*–292*r* institutions Nov. 1420–Sept. 1455
292*v* later select contents notes

Printed, *The Register of Edmund Lacy, Bishop of Exeter* (*A.D. 1420–1455*)*: part I, the register of institutions, with some account of the episcopate of John Catrik* (*A.D. 1419*), ed. F. C. Hingeston-Randolph (London and Exeter, 1909). Fos. 1*r*–23*v* are printed in *The Register of Edmund Lacy, Bishop of Exeter, 1420–1455: Registrum Commune* iv, ed. G. R. Dunstan (Canterbury and York Society 63, 1971), appendix, pp. 260–318. Addenda and corrigenda to the Hingeston-Randolph edition are printed *ibid.* v (Canterbury and York Society 66, 1972), p. xxv.

2. DRO, Exeter diocesan records, Chanter catalogue 11. Parchment register, part of edge damaged by damp; $13\frac{1}{4}'' \times 9\frac{3}{4}/11\frac{1}{2}''$ (great variation in width); fos. i (paper) + 579 + vi (paper), foliated 1–332, 332 [A], 334–416, 418–464, 466–580, [581]; buckram-covered boards, with hide-covered spine.

This large volume comprises five main sections, the *registrum commune*, both of the vicar-general (fos. 1–19) and of the bishop himself (fos. 20–416), a miscellaneous section containing a record of processes, compositions, injunctions and indentures (fos. 418–495), a register of wills (fos. 498–517), and a register of ordinations (fos. 519–580). The arrangement and compilation of this volume and its companion register have been discussed in detail by Professor Dunstan in *The Register of Edmund Lacy* v, pp. xi–xx, and in 'Some aspects of the register of Edmund Lacy, Bishop of Exeter, 1420–1455', *Journal of Ecclesiastical History* 6 (1955), 37–47.

Printed, *The Register of Edmund Lacy, Bishop of Exeter, 1420–1455: Registrum Commune*, ed. G. R. Dunstan (5 vols., Canterbury and York Society 60–3, 66, 1963–72). Fos. 1–234 were first printed in *The Register of Edmund Lacy, Bishop of Exeter (A.D. 1420–1455): part II, the Registrum Commune*, ed. C. G. Browne and O. J. Reichel (Devon and Cornwall Record Society, 1915), but the stocks of this volume were destroyed during the Second World War.

VACANCY 1455–1456

LPL, register of Archbishop Thomas Bourgchier, fos. 31*r*–34*v*.

Exeter vacancy business Sept. 1455–Apr. 1456

Printed, *Registrum Thome Bourgchier*, pp. 151–62.

GEORGE NEVILLE (1456–1465)

DRO, Exeter diocesan records, Chanter catalogue 12, part 1. Parchment register, damaged at edge by damp; 14¼″ × 10½″; fos. ii (paper) + 144 + ii (paper), foliated 1–23, 28, 29, 32–113, 118–155; blank: none; buckram-covered boards, with hide-covered spine.

1*r*–29*v* institutions Apr. 1456–June 1465
32*r*–69*v* *registrum commune* Apr. 1456–Feb. 1466
70*r*–137*v* inquisitions (includes occasional dispensations, mandates, election of head of religious house etc.) Dec. 1456–June 1465
137*v*–141*v* testamentary business Oct. 1463–Apr. 1465 (last entry incomplete)
142*r*–155*v* ordinations May 1456–June 1465

JOHN BOOTH (1465–1478)
PETER COURTENAY (1478–1487)
RICHARD FOX (1487–1492)
OLIVER KING (1493–1495)
RICHARD REDMAN (1496–1501)
JOHN ARUNDEL (1502–1504)

DRO, Exeter diocesan records, Chanter catalogue 12, part 2. Parchment register; fos. ii (paper) + 174 (14″ × 11″) + 43 (14½″ × 11¼″) + 14 (14½″ × 11¾″) + ii (paper), foliated [i], 1–33, 46, 47, 37–45, 48, 34–36, 50–141, 141A, 142–173, 2nd series 1–43, 3rd series 1–14; blank: fos. [i*r*–*v*], 48*v*, 52*v*, 77*v*, 82*v*, 83*v*, 96*v*, 118*v*, 125*v*, 127*v*, 160*v*, 162*v*, 170*v*, 172*v*, 2nd series 37*v*, 3rd series 2*v*, 14*v*; buckram-covered boards, with hide-covered spine.

Register of Bishop John Booth
1*r*–36*v* institutions June 1465–Apr. 1478 (there is some chronological confusion at times)
50*r*–52*r* wills Apr. 1466–Oct. 1467
53*r*–71*v* inquisitions Aug. 1465–June 1473 (last entry incomplete)
72*r*–77*r* memoranda (dispensations, appointments of penitentiaries etc. not in chronological order) Mar. 1468–Oct. 1474

Register of Bishop Peter Courtenay
78*r*–82*r* inquisitions Jan.–Nov. 1479
83*r*–90*v* institutions Sept. 1478–Sept. 1480

91*r*–94*v*	ordinations Dec. 1478–May 1480
95*r*–96*r*	dispensations, and award between the vicar of Loddiswell and the inhabitants of Buckland-Tout-Saints chapelry Apr. 1471–Mar. 1480

Register of Bishop Richard Fox

97*r*–118*r*	institutions (by both bishop and vicar-general) May 1487–Apr. 1492
119*r*–125*r*	institutions (by bishop) Mar. 1488–Apr. 1492
126*r*–127*r*	wills *temp.* Courtenay June 1478–Mar. 1480
128*r*–150*v*	inquisitions May 1487–Aug. 1491 (not in order, some misbinding)
151*r*–160*r*	ordinations June 1487–Apr. 1492
161*r*	later select contents notes

Register of Bishop Oliver King

161*v*–162*r*	vicar-general's register (commission and memoranda) Feb. 1493
163*r*–164*v*	inquisitions Feb. 1493–Sept. 1495
165*r*–172*r*	institutions Mar. 1493–Nov. 1495
173*r*–*v*	ordinations (incomplete) June 1493–Mar. 1494

Register of Bishop Richard Redman
(2nd series)

1*r*–23*r*	institutions and inquisitions Nov. 1497–Oct. 1501
24*r*–36*v*	inquisitions (includes wills, dispensations etc.) Mar. 1498–Aug. 1501
37*r*	papal dispensations Jan. 1486–Sept. 1494
38*r*–43*r*	ordinations Dec. 1497–Mar. 1501
43*v*	later select contents notes

Register of Bishop John Arundel
(3rd series)

1*r*–5*v*	*registrum commune* Sept. 1502–Mar. 1504
6*r*–12*v*	institutions July 1502–Mar. 1504
13*r*–14*r*	ordinations Mar.–Dec. 1503

VACANCY 1492–1493

1. LPL, register of Archbishop John Morton, volume I, fos. 118*r*–134*v*.

   Exeter vacancy business May 1492–Feb. 1493

2. *ibid.*, volume II, fos. 152*v*–153*r*.

   Exeter vacancy act July 1492 (1 entry), among the general section of Canterbury institutions

The institutions are calendared in DRO, Chanter's 'Register of Institutions'; both items are also calendared in C. Harper-Bill, 'An edition of the register of John Morton, archbishop of Canterbury, 1486–1500' (London University Ph.D., 1977).

VACANCY 1504–1505

LPL, register of Archbishop William Warham, volume I, fos. 201*r*–212*v*.

Exeter vacancy business Mar.–Dec. 1504

A clergy list for the diocese, probably compiled for a visitation during this vacancy, is to be found in LPL, Carte Miscellanee XVIII/13. The institutions are calendared in DRO, Chanter's 'Register of Institutions'.

HUGH OLDHAM (1505–1519)

DRO, Exeter diocesan records, Chanter catalogue 13. Parchment register; 14″ × 10¾″, except for fos. 184–96, 13¼″ × 10½″; fos. iv (paper) + 183 + 13 + iii (paper), foliated [i], 1–93, 95–195, [196]; blank: fos. [i*v*], 81*v*, [196*r*–*v*]; buckram-covered boards, with hide-covered spine.

[i*r*]	later select contents notes
1*r*–81*r*	institutions Jan. 1505–June 1519
82*r*–130*v*	ordinations Jan. 1505–Sept. 1518 (the last entry is incomplete)
131*r*–183*r*	*registrum commune* Nov. 1504–July 1517 (not always in chronological order)
183*v*	later select contents notes
184*r*–195*v*	cathedral statutes

VACANCY 1519

1. LPL, register of Archbishop William Warham, volume II, fos. 272*v*–275*v*.

   Exeter vacancy business June–Nov. 1519

2. *ibid.*, fo. 369*r*.

   Exeter vacancy act Oct. 1519 (1 entry), among the general section of Canterbury institutions

The institutions are calendared in DRO, Chanter's 'Register of Institutions'.

JOHN VEYSEY (1519–1551; 1553–1554)
MILES COVERDALE (1551–1553)
VACANCY 1554–1555

1. DRO, Exeter diocesan records, Chanter catalogue 14. Parchment register; 14″ × 10¾″; fos. v (paper) + 190 + vii (paper), foliated 1–88, 90–141, [142–191]; blank: fo. [142*r*]; buckram-covered boards, with hide-covered spine.

1*r*–141*v*	institutions Nov. 1519–Aug. 1551
[142*v*–191*v*]	ordinations Dec. 1519–Mar. 1544

2. DRO, Exeter diocesan records, Chanter catalogue 15. Parchment register; 13¼″ × 9¼″; fos. v (paper) + 123 + i (limp parchment cover) + v (paper), foliated 1–24, [24A], 25–122, [123]; blank: fos. 26*v*, 100*r*, [123*v*]; buckram-covered boards, with hide-covered spine.

1*r*–85*v*	*registrum commune* Dec. 1519–Jan. 1542
86*r*–99*v*	copy of the *Valor Ecclesiasticus* for the Exeter diocese
100*v*–121*v*	*registrum commune* June 1541–July 1551 (there is some chronological confusion in this section)
122*r*–[123*r*]	later select contents notes

3. DRO, Exeter diocesan records, Chanter catalogue 16. Parchment register; 11¾″ × 9″; fos. i (mounted parchment cover) + 44 + i (mounted parchment cover), foliated [i], 1–43, [44]; blank: fos. 12*r*, 13*v*, 33*v*, 35*r*; stamped leather binding.

Register of Bishop Miles Coverdale

1*r*–11*v*	institutions Sept. 1551–Sept. 1553
12*v*–13*r*	ordinations Dec. 1551–May 1553

Register of Bishop John Veysey (restored)

14*r*–31*v*	institutions Nov. 1553–Oct. 1554
31*v*	vacancy institution Nov. 1554 (1 entry) (this entry is repeated in the vacancy register below)
32*r*–33*r*	ordinations Feb.–Sept. 1554

34*r*–*v* copy of royal dispensation Aug. 1535
35*r*–[44*r*] caveats for admission to benefices (includes 1 institution and copy of an earlier grant of next presentation) Apr. 1553–Oct. 1558

4. DRO, Exeter diocesan records, Chanter catalogue 17. Parchment register; 11½″ × 8¾″; fos. i (paper)+i+31+i, unfoliated, for purposes of this description, numbered [i, 1–31]; blank: fos. [iv, 25*r*]; stamped leather binding.

[1*r*] note that the caveats *temp.* Bishop Alley are entered in this register
[1*v*] heading of Bishop Coverdale's *registrum commune*
[2*r*–12*r*] articles of religion, with Coverdale's subscription 1553
[12*v*–14*v*] caveats for admission to benefices July 1569–June 1570
[15*r*–18*v*] *registrum commune* of Bishop Coverdale Sept. 1551–June 1552 (with additional entry, Nov. 1586)
[19*r*] caveats Mar. 1588
[19*v*–22*r*] caveats Jan. 1571–Oct. 1574
[22*r*–23*r*] caveats Apr.–Oct. 1587
[23*v*–24*r*] *registrum commune* of Bishop Coverdale Jan.–Feb. 1553
[24*v*] caveats June–Aug. 1587
[25*v*–31*r*] *registrum commune* of Bishop Veysey (restored) Nov. 1553–Apr. 1554
[31*v*] later select contents notes

VACANCY 1554–1555

CAL, register N, fos. 116*r*–120*r*.

Exeter vacancy business Nov. 1554–July 1555

Institutions are calendared (by place) in *Sede Vacante Institutions* and in DRO, Chanter's 'Register of Institutions'.

JAMES TURBERVILLE (1555–1559)
VACANCY 1559–1560
WILLIAM ALLEY (1560–1570)

1. DRO, Exeter diocesan records, Chanter catalogue 18. Parchment register; 11½″ × 8½″; fos. i (mounted parchment cover)+i+102+i (mounted parchment endpaper), foliated [i], 1–93, [94–101]; blank: fos. 47*r*–*v*, 52*r*–53*v*; stamped leather binding.

Register of Bishop James Turberville
1*r*–46*v* institutions (includes letters, licences, commissions and other occasional memoranda) Oct. 1555–May 1559

Sede Vacante register (see also below)
46*v* institution Feb. 1560 (1 entry, and notes of 3 later acts Dec. 1560–Dec. 1562)
48*r*–51*v* union of the rectory and vicarage of Brent May 1559 (*temp.* Turberville)
54*r*–61*r* vacancy business Jan.–June 1560

Register of Bishop William Alley
61*v*–85*v* election of bishop, and institutions May 1560–Aug. 1564

Register of Bishop Turberville (*continued*)
86*r*–87*v* ordinations Mar. 1557–Sept. 1558

Register of Bishop Alley (*continued*)
88*r*–93*r* ordinations Oct. 1560–Dec. 1564
93*v*–[101*v*] caveats Feb. 1558–Mar. 1564

2. DRO, Exeter diocesan records, Chanter catalogue 19. Parchment register; 11″ × 9¼″; fos. i (mounted parchment cover) + 47 + i (mounted parchment cover), foliated [i], 1–38, then paginated 39–53, [54]; blank: fos. [i*v*], 9*v*; stamped leather binding.

i*r*	note that institutions and collations *temp.* Bishop Alley are contained in the register
1*r*–6*v*	*registrum commune* of Bishop Turberville (includes copies of earlier documents) Nov. 1555–Feb. 1556
7*r*–*v*	copy of dispensation issued by Archbishop Cranmer and confirmed by Henry VIII Nov. 1537
8*r*–33*r*	institutions *temp.* Bishop Alley (includes occasional grants, indentures, confirmations) Aug. 1563–Mar. 1570
33*v*–36*v*	caveats Dec. 1584–Apr. 1587
37*r*–p. [54]	ordinations *temp.* Bishop Alley Sept. 1565–Mar. 1570
[54]	later select contents note

VACANCY 1559–1560

1. CAL, register U2, fo. 106*r*–*v*.

Exeter vacancy business Nov.–Dec. 1559

Institutions are calendared (by place) in *Sede Vacante Institutions* and in Chanter's 'Register of Institutions'.

2. LPL, register of Archbishop Matthew Parker, volume I, fos. 171*v*–175*r*.

Exeter vacancy business Jan.–June 1560

Printed, *Registrum Matthei Parker* i, pp. 214–19.

See also vacancy material above.

VACANCY 1570–1571

LPL, register of Archbishop Matthew Parker, volume I, fos. 206*r*–213*v*.

Exeter vacancy business Apr. 1570–Mar. 1571

Printed, *Registrum Matthei Parker* i, pp. 309–28.

WILLIAM BRADBRIDGE (1571–1578)
JOHN WOOLTON (1579–1594)

DRO, Exeter diocesan records, Chanter catalogue 20. Parchment register; 12¼″ × 8¾″; fos. ii (paper) + 73 + i (paper, contents list) + iv (paper), foliated [i–ii], 1–71; blank: fos. [i*v*, ii*v*]; modern binding.

[i*r*]	heading of Bradbridge's register
[ii*r*]	similar heading
1*r*–44*v*	institutions *temp.* Bishop William Bradbridge Apr. 1571–June 1578
44*v*–71*r*	institutions *temp.* Bishop John Woolton Oct. 1579–Aug. 1582
71*v*	later select contents notes

VACANCY 1578–1579

LPL, register of Archbishop Edmund Grindal, volume II, fos. 381*r*–401*v*.

Exeter vacancy business July 1578–July 1579

The institutions are calendared in DRO, Chanter's 'Register of Institutions'.

VACANCY 1594–1595

LPL, register of Archbishop John Whitgift, volume II, fos. 233*r*–240*v*.

Exeter vacancy business Mar. 1594–Feb. 1595

The institutions are calendared in DRO, Chanter's 'Register of Institutions'.

JOHN WOOLTON (1579–1594)
GERVASE BABINGTON (1594–1597)
WILLIAM COTTON (1598–1621)
VALENTINE CAREY (1621–1626)

DRO, Exeter diocesan records, Chanter catalogue 21. Parchment register; $14\frac{3}{4}'' \times 11''$; fos. ii (paper)+122+ii (paper), foliated 1–28, 30–123; blank: fo. 123*v*; buckram-covered boards, with hide-covered spine.

1*r*–56*v*	institutions *temp.* Bishop John Woolton Sept. 1582–Mar. 1594
56*v*–63*v*	institutions *temp.* Bishop Gervase Babington Mar. 1595–Sept. 1597
64*r*–115*v*	institutions *temp.* Bishop William Cotton (includes occasional indentures) Nov. 1598–Aug. 1621
116*r*–123*r*	institutions *temp.* Bishop Valentine Carey Nov. 1621–May 1626

A place index of institutions is in DRO, Chanter catalogue 40d.

VACANCY 1597–1598

1. LPL, register of Archbishop John Whitgift, volume II, fos. 213*v*–216*v*.

   Exeter vacancy business Oct.–Dec. 1597

2. *ibid.*, fos. 307*r*–310*v*.

   Exeter vacancy business Oct.–Dec. 1597

3. *ibid.*, volume III, fos. 197*v*–205*r*.

   Exeter vacancy business Oct. 1597–Nov. 1598

All the institutions are calendared in DRO, Chanter's 'Register of Institutions'. Sections 1 and 2 are identical.

VACANCY 1621

LPL, register of Archbishop George Abbot, volume II, fos. 266*r*–268*v*.

Exeter vacancy business Aug.–Nov. 1621

The institutions are calendared in DRO, Chanter's 'Register of Institutions'.

VACANCY 1626–1627

LPL, register of Archbishop George Abbot, volume II, fos. 277*r*–286*r*.

Exeter vacancy business June 1626–Oct. 1627.

The institutions are calendared in DRO, Chanter's 'Register of Institutions'.

JOSEPH HALL (1627–1641)
RALPH BROWNRIGG (1642–1659)

1. DRO, Exeter diocesan records, Chanter catalogue 22. Parchment register; $11\frac{1}{2}'' \times 9''$; fos. v (paper)+50+v (paper). foliated 1–27, 27*, 28–49; blank: fo. 49*r*–*v*; buckram-covered boards, with hide-covered spine.

1*r*–48*v*	institutions (includes some inquisitions) *temp.* Bishop Joseph Hall Dec. 1627–Nov. 1637.

2. DRO, Exeter diocesan records, Chanter catalogue 23. Parchment register; 12″ × 9″; fos. ii (paper) + 38 + ii (paper), paginated 1–64, [65–76]; blank: pp. [66–69]; rough hide binding.

1–34	institutions *temp.* Bishop Hall Dec. 1637–Nov. 1641
35–64	institutions *temp.* Bishop Ralph Brownrigg June 1642–June 1646
[65]	modern notes of institutions 1646–1663
[70–76]	modern place index of institutions

ORDINATIONS REGISTER

DRO, Exeter diocesan records, Chanter catalogue 50. Parchment register; 11½″ × 8¼″; fos. i + 97 + 6 (paper, rough sheets bound in, average 11¼″ × 7½″) + i, unfoliated (for purposes of this description numbered 1–103); blank: fos. [1*v*, 79*v*, 98*v*, 99*v*, 100*v*, 101*v*, 102*v*, 103*v*]; leather binding.

[1*r*]	heading of Bradbridge's ordination register
[2*r*–30*v*]	ordinations *temp.* Bishop William Bradbridge Mar. 1572–June 1578
[30*v*–52*r*]	ordinations *temp.* Bishop John Woolton Sept. 1579–Jan. 1594
[52*v*–56*v*]	ordinations *temp.* Bishop Gervase Babington Aug. 1595–Sept. 1597
[57*r*–81*v*]	ordinations *temp.* Bishop William Cotton July 1599–May 1621
[81*v*–83*r*]	ordinations *temp.* Bishop Valentine Carey Sept. 1622–Sept. 1624
[83*r*]	ordinations held by Thomas, Bishop of Bristol, in Exeter cathedral Oct. 1645
[83*v*–91*r*]	ordinations *temp.* Bishop Joseph Hall Sept. 1628–July 1636 (see also below)
[91*v*–93*r*]	ordinations *temp.* Bishop John Gauden Jan. 1661–Feb. 1662
[93*r*–97*v*]	ordinations *temp.* Bishop Seth Ward Sept. 1662–June 1667
[98*r*–101*r*]	ordinations *temp.* Bishop Hall Sept. 1636–Sept. 1641
[102*r*]	ordinations *temp.* Bishop Ralph Brownrigg Oct. 1645
[103*r*]	ordinations *temp.* Bishop Ward Mar. 1664

GLOUCESTER

Repositories

1. Gloucestershire Record Office, Worcester Street, Gloucester GL1 3DW (GRO).
2. Lambeth Palace Library, London SE1 7JU (LPL).
3. Hereford and Worcester Record Office, St Helen's, Fish Street, Worcester WR1 2HN (HWRO).
4. Canterbury Cathedral Archives and Library, The Precincts, Canterbury CT1 2EG (CAL).

Area

In 1541 the diocese of Gloucester was created out of the dioceses of Worcester and Hereford. The area of the new diocese was coterminous with the county of Gloucester, although the deanery of the Forest, west of the river Severn, while being in the new diocese, remained under the jurisdiction of the archdeacon of Hereford until 1836. In 1542 most of the rural deanery of Bristol was formed into the bishopric of Bristol. Only ten parishes from the old deanery remained in the Gloucester diocese and constituted a separate rural deanery of Bristol.[1] After this immediate change in boundaries, there were no further alterations in the area of the diocese until the nineteenth century.

Bibliographical Note

A detailed handlist of the Gloucester bishops' act books is to be found in I. M. Kirby, *Diocese of Gloucester: a catalogue of the records of the bishop and archdeacons* (Gloucester, 1968), among the 'GDR volumes' originally listed by F. S. Hockaday (pp. 1–33).[2] The act books are basically records of institutions in approximate date order, although part of the first volume is in some chronological confusion. During the time in the late sixteenth century when the see of Bristol was held *in commendam* by Bishops Cheyney and Bullingham, entries relating to the Bristol diocese are to be found in these act books. With the exception of the 1554 vacancy, when the dean and chapter of Gloucester apparently exercised jurisdiction, a record of *sede vacante* administration is to be found in the Canterbury archiepiscopal registers.

The historians of Gloucestershire, such as Furney, Bigland and Fosbrooke, have by no means neglected these act books as a source of information on incumbents[3] but the most exhaustive work on these records was carried out in the early years of this present century by F. S. Hockaday.[4] The Hockaday Indexes, now in the Gloucestershire Record Office, include indexes of persons recorded in the bishops' act books, together with a note of their benefices, and these indexes are supplemented by the Hockaday Abstracts (arranged by parish) and the Hockaday Collections (transcripts, lists, notes etc.), both in Gloucester City Library, Brunswick Road, Gloucester GL1 1HT.[5] Gaps in the act books can be filled in from

[1] For a description of the diocesan boundaries, see *VCH Gloucestershire* ii (1907), pp. 48–51 and map facing p. 48; I. M. Kirby, *Diocese of Gloucester: a catalogue of the records of the bishop and archdeacons* (Gloucester, 1968), pp. xvi–xix; I. Gray and E. Ralph, *Guide to the Parish Records of the City of Bristol and the County of Gloucester* (Bristol and Gloucestershire Archaeological Society Records Section 5, 1963), pp. xiv–xv; See also 'Benefices in the dioceses of Gloucester and Bristol with the deaneries in which they were placed in 1541 and in 1912 and for the period 1836–97', Gloucester City Library, Hockaday Collection 5(1).

[2] Some of these volumes have been described in *Historical Manuscripts Commission, Reports on Manuscripts in Various Collections* vii (1914), pp. 68–9.

[3] For the local historians of Gloucestershire, see E. A. L. Moir, 'The Historians of Gloucestershire: Retrospect and Prospect', in H. P. R. Finberg ed., *Gloucestershire Studies* (Leicester, 1957), pp. 267–90.

[4] For F. S. Hockaday, see the obituary by Roland Austin in *Transactions of the Bristol and Gloucestershire Archaeological Society* 46 (1924), 379–83.

[5] His compilations are described in I. M. Kirby, *Gloucester Catalogue*, app. i, pp. 127–30.

Hockaday's list, 'Bishops' certificates, dioceses of Gloucester and Bristol, 1559–1564, 1575–1645 and 1665–1836, extracted from the Public Record Office' (Hockaday Collection 7(3)).

JOHN WAKEMAN (1541–1549)
JOHN HOOPER (1551–1554)
VACANCY 1554
JAMES BROOKS (1554–1559)
RICHARD CHEYNEY (1562–1579)

GRO, GDR.2A. Paper register (repaired, damaged at edges); 11½″ × 8″; fos. x + 3 (inserted 18th-cent. index, 11½″ × 3″) + 108 + x, paginated (by Hockaday) i–v, 1–216, [217–222], later foliated (after repair) 1–114 (fos. 23, 27–28 are insertions); blank: fos. 3*v*, 23*v*, 27*v*–28*v*, 31*r*–*v*, 33*v*, 49*r*–*v*, 63*r*–64*r*, 65*v*, 67*v*, 72*v*, 78*v*, 79*v*–84*r*, 92*v*, 101*v*–107*v*, 110*v*, 111*v*–114*v*; modern binding.

1*r*–3*r*	18th-cent. table of contents (place names only)	
4*r*–13*v*	a confused section of the register, beginning with institutions in 1551 but containing copies of many earlier dispensations (earliest entry, Apr. 1537) and an occasional letter of institution, diocese of Worcester (earliest entry, Oct. 1521), before the Gloucester diocese was formed. Some of these dispensations are linked with later institutions etc. being exhibited on that occasion. Whether all are of this type is doubtful. An early institution, Dec. 1542, is also recorded and the last 'current' act business is dated Apr. 1555	
14*r*–65*r*	institutions and other acts before the diocesan chancellor, his substitutes, and occasionally the bishop himself	
	14*r*–26*v*, 29*r*	Sept. 1547–Sept. 1549
	27*r*, 29*r*–39*v*	Mar. 1551–Mar. 1554
	39*v*	*sede vacante* acts by the dean and chapter of Gloucester Mar.–Apr. 1554
	40*r*–62*v*	May 1554–Apr. 1555
	64*v*–65*r*	Aug. 1555, May–July 1556 (continued in GDR.11)
66*r*–67*r*	documents relating to a grant of next presentation to Minchinhampton Jan. 1551, Aug. 1558	
68*r*–*v*	abstract of contents (by place)	
69*r*	table of contents (by place) of fos. 84*v*–86*v*	
69*v*	admission of the dean of Gloucester Feb. 1566	
70*r*–78*r*	miscellaneous benefice, probate and court material, and administrative jottings Aug. 1559–Oct. 1568	
79*r*	caveat Mar. 1572	
84*v*–86*v*	institutions Mar. 1564–Apr. 1565	
87*r*–92*r*	list of autograph subscriptions of clergy admitted to benefices (many entries undated, the 15th entry being the earliest dated one) June 1573–Apr. 1579	
93*r*–100*v*, 111*r*	list of autograph subscriptions of those ordained by the bishop of Gloucester 'synce the laste parliament' (no dates)	
101*r*	list of autograph subscriptions of preachers (no dates)	
108*r*–110*r*	list of autograph subscriptions of 'preistes or ministers made by other forme than was appointed in the tyme of Kynge Edwarde the sixt or in this tyme of our soveraigne Ladie quene Elizabeth' (no dates)	

GRO, Hockaday Index 4, index of personal names in the volume. Hooper was bishop of Worcester and Gloucester 1552–4 and some Gloucestershire entries are to be found in Hooper's Worcester register (HWRO, b 716.093–BA.2648/9(iv), fos. 39–43 (June 1552–June 1553)).

VACANCY 1549–1551

LPL, register of Archbishop Thomas Cranmer, fos. 105*r*–107*v*.[6]

Gloucester vacancy business Dec. 1549–Mar. 1551

The institutions are calendared in A. J. Edwards, 'The *sede vacante* administration of Archbishop Thomas Cranmer, 1533–53' (London University M.Phil., 1968).

JAMES BROOKS (1554–1558)[7]

GRO, GDR.11. Paper register; $11\frac{3}{4}'' \times 8''$; fos. 141, paginated 1–280; limp parchment covers.

252–253 institutions by the diocesan chancellor July–Oct. 1556

These entries follow straight on entries on fo. 65*r* of GDR.2A. The rest of GDR.11 is a court book, including some copies of depositions. An index of persons is available in the GRO, Hockaday Index 13.

VACANCY 1558–1562

1. GRO, GDR.14. Paper register (repaired); $11\frac{3}{4}'' \times 8''$; fos. 44, paginated 1–88; modern binding.

   1–7 institutions (first 2 entries lost) Sept. 1558–July 1559

   The rest of GDR.14 is a court book and a probate act book. The second of the first two lost entries can be supplied from GDR.15 below.

2. GRO, GDR.15. Paper register (repaired); $12'' \times 8''$; fos. 158, paginated 1–316; modern binding.

   3–7 institutions Sept. 1558–July 1559

   This volume is badly damaged and many entries are lost. At least one folio is missing between the present pages 6 and 7, containing entries between Jan.–July 1559. The entries, if complete, would probably constitute a duplicate of pp. 1–7 of GDR.14 above. The rest of GDR.15 is a court book with sections containing copies of depositions, notes of caveats and a record of probate and administration acts. An index of persons to GDR.14–15 is available at GRO, Hockaday Indexes 16–17.

3. LPL, register of Archbishop Reginald Pole, fos. 63*v*–64*r*.

   Gloucester vacancy business Sept.–Nov. 1558

4. CAL, register U2, fos. 26*r*–27*v*.

   Gloucester vacancy business Dec. 1558–Nov. 1559

   Institutions are calendared (by place) in *Sede Vacante Institutions*.

5. LPL, register of Archbishop Matthew Parker, volume I, fos. 155*v*–160*r*.

   Gloucester vacancy business Feb. 1560–Apr. 1562

   Printed, *Registrum Matthei Parker* i, pp. 188–97. At least three vacancy institutions were entered in the Gloucester court books, GRO, GDR.17, pp. 242 (Nov. 1561), 276 (Feb. 1562); GDR.10, p. 107 (Mar. 1562).

[6] See under Canterbury for a description of this and subsequent archiepiscopal and capitular registers.

[7] Although the *Handbook of British Chronology* states that Brooks was deprived in 1559 and died in Feb. 1560, Archbishop Reginald Pole's register records that the 1558 vacancy was caused 'per obitum bone memorie domini Jacobi Brokes ultimi episcopi ...' (fo. 63*v*).

RICHARD CHEYNEY (1562–1579)
JOHN BULLINGHAM (1581–1598)
GODFREY GOLDSBOROUGH (1598–1604)
THOMAS RAVIS (1605–1607)
HENRY PARRY (1607–1610)
GILES THOMPSON (1611–1612)
MILES SMITH (1612–1624)
GODFREY GOODMAN (1625–1656)

GRO, GDR.27A. Paper register; 12″ × 8″; fos. i + 13 + 5 (inserted 18th-cent. index) + 238 + i, paginated i–xxxviii, 1–482 (including inserts); blank: pp. i–vi, viii, x, xii, xiv, xvi, xviii, xx, xxii, xxiv, xxvi, xxviii, xxxviii, 111–12, 156, 231–2, 252–4, 289, 291–2, 310, 344–6, 360–2, 381–2, 385–6, 396, 416–17, 471–5, 481–2; limp parchment covers.

vii–xxxvii (odd numbers only)		18th-cent. place index
1–2		forms of oath and institution, and administrative jottings
3		register heading
3–465		general register Sept. 1570–Mar. 1620
	3–108	acts of Bishop Richard Cheyney Sept. 1570–Apr. 1579 (p. 106 includes 2 later entries of Jan.–Feb. 1582)
	108–229	acts of Bishop John Bullingham Sept. 1581–Mar. 1598
	229–230	additional entry July 1599
	233–286	acts of Bishop Godfrey Goldsborough Aug. 1598–May 1604
	287–288	congé d'élire and election of Bishop Ravis Oct.–Dec. 1604
	290	memoranda May–June 1605 and letter of presentation June 1603
	293–321	acts of Bishop Thomas Ravis May 1605–May 1607
	322–338	acts of Bishop Henry Parry Oct. 1607–Oct. 1610
	338–353	acts of Bishop Giles Thompson Mar. 1611–June 1612
	353–465	acts of Bishop Miles Smith July 1612–Mar. 1620
466–469		documents relating to the rectory of Kemerton Feb. 1627–Nov. 1628
470		entry relating to the rectory of North Cerney Nov. 1630
476–480		list of ordinands (also entered in the general register) and administrative memoranda Dec. 1605–Dec. 1618

GRO, Hockaday Index 30, index of personal names in the volume. The volume also includes certain institutions to benefices in the diocese of Bristol and cognate material (see under Bristol).

VACANCY 1579–1581

LPL, register of Archbishop Edmund Grindal, volume II, fos. 442*r*–457*v*.

Gloucester vacancy business Apr. 1579–Aug. 1581

VACANCY 1598

LPL, register of Archbishop John Whitgift, volume III, fos. 205*v*–207*v*.

Gloucester vacancy business June–Nov. 1598

VACANCY 1604–1605

1. LPL, register of the dean and chapter of Canterbury *sede vacante* (part of Whitgift III), fos. 284*r*–286*r*.
   Gloucester vacancy business June–Dec. 1604
2. LPL, register of Archbishop Richard Bancroft, fos. 234*r*–235*r*.
   Gloucester vacancy business Jan.–Feb. 1605

VACANCY 1607

LPL, register of Archbishop Richard Bancroft, fos. 239*v*–240*r*.
Gloucester vacancy business May 1607

VACANCY 1610–1611

1. LPL, register of Archbishop Richard Bancroft, fos. 264*v*–265*v*.
   Gloucester vacancy business Oct.–Nov. 1610
   The last 2 entries date from the vacancy of the see of Canterbury, but there do not appear additional *sede vacante* entries relating to Gloucester.
2. LPL, register of Archbishop George Abbot, volume I, fos. 300*r*–302*r*.
   Gloucester vacancy business Apr.–May 1611

VACANCY 1612

LPL, register of Archbishop George Abbot, volume I, fos. 302*v*–304*r*.
Gloucester vacancy business June–Sept. 1612

MILES SMITH (1612–1624)
GODFREY GOODMAN (1625–1656)
VACANCY 1660–1661
WILLIAM NICOLSON (1661–1672)
VACANCY 1672
JOHN PRITCHETT (1672–1681)

GRO, GDR.142A. Paper register; 12″ × 8″; fos. 102, paginated 1–155, [155A–B], 156–202; blank: pp. 2–6, 38, 40, 46, 52–60, 67–80, 86–98, 101–10, [155B], 170–2, 179, 193–202; limp parchment covers.

7–43	institutions, ordinations etc. June 1620–Dec. 1630, Sept. 1632–Mar. 1636, Sept. 1640–June 1642 (the earlier entries of the 1620s are in some chronological confusion)
43–45	institution and subscription *sede vacante* Oct. 1660
47–51	documents relating to the rectory of Yate May 1659–Oct. 1662
61–66	installations of the archdeacon and prebendaries of Gloucester cathedral and election of Bishop Nicolson Aug.–Nov. 1660
81–85	institutions Jan.–May 1661
99–100	caveats Aug. 1637–Oct. 1638 and 1 institution Oct. 1637
111–112	appointment of rural deans Mar. 1639
113–120	institutions and subscriptions Oct. 1641–Sept. 1642
121	caveats Jan. 1661
122–160	institutions Feb. 1664–Dec. 1671
160–161	institutions *sede vacante* Mar.–May 1672

162–178 election of Bishop Pritchett and institutions Sept. 1672–Dec. 1673
180–192 18th-cent. place index, citing obsolete folio references (includes a very selective number of personal names)

GRO, Hockaday Index 36, index of personal names in the volume.

VACANCY 1624–1625

LPL, register of Archbishop George Abbot, volume II, fos. 273*v*–274*r*.

Gloucester vacancy business Oct. 1624–Feb. 1625

HEREFORD

Repositories

1. Hereford Diocesan Registry, 5 St Peter Street, Hereford (HDR) (appointments are necessary).
2. Lambeth Palace Library, London SE1 7JU (LPL).
3. Canterbury Cathedral Archives and Library, The Precincts, Canterbury CT1 2EG (CAL).

Area

The medieval diocese of Hereford comprised Herefordshire, except for eight parishes in the south-west of the county in the diocese of St David's, the south-western half of Shropshire, the town of Monmouth and neighbouring parishes, Gloucestershire west of the river Severn (the deanery of the Forest), a few parishes in western Worcestershire, which formed part of the Burford rural deanery in the archdeaconry of Shropshire, six parishes in the east of Radnorshire, and a few parishes on the eastern edge of Montgomeryshire.[1] It was divided into the two archdeaconries of Hereford and Shropshire. The deanery of the Forest was transferred to the newly created bishopric of Gloucester in 1541, although it remained under the jurisdiction of the archdeacon of Hereford until 1836.

Bibliographical Note

The earliest surviving Hereford register, that of St Thomas Cantilupe, is probably the first that existed in the diocese—certainly in 1347 it was the earliest extent register,[2] although Bishop Booth (1516–35) mentions the name of John le Breton (1269–75) in a later list of episcopal registers.[3] No other references have been found to registers of Cantilupe's immediate predecessors and it is doubtful how much reliance can be placed upon the Booth evidence.

While the medieval series of registers is remarkably complete,[4] there have been a few later losses—the register of Edmund Audley (1492–1502) was still in existence in 1527[5] but a seventeenth-century index to the registers, to be found in the Hereford Diocesan Registry, records that it disappeared in the Civil War, along with the registers of Adrian de Castello (1502–4) and Herbert Westfaling (1586–1602). This same source notes the disappearance of the composite volume containing the registers of Booth, Fox (1535–8) and Bonner (1538–9), but a later note indicates that this volume was eventually recovered by Bishop Bisse (1713–21), the bishop having found it in the library of the Bishop of Ely.

Apart from some increased registrational subdivisions in the fourteenth-century registers, the Hereford volumes generally take the form of a single chronological register, with a separate section for ordinations, and occasionally registers of vicars-general. In the first half of the seventeenth century, the system of diocesan registration seems to have broken down and all that survives for the episcopates of Robert Bennett and his immediate successors is more in the nature of rough act books or else volumes devoted to specific business, such as caveats. In 1687 a registry clerk significantly wrote: 'Note that the Registers of the 6 last precedeing Bishopps are soe intermixt in this and other Books that they cannot be reduced to any good

[1] For a map of the medieval diocese see the frontispiece to H. W. Phillott, *Diocesan Histories: Hereford* (London, 1888); Ordnance Survey, *Map of Monastic Britain: (south sheet)* (2nd edn., 1954).

[2] *Registrum Johannis Trillek*. i, p. 317.

[3] *Registrum Johannis Gilbert*, p. 127. Bishop Booth, indeed, seems to have been responsible for the collecting up and binding of the earlier Hereford registers, if his autograph note in Gilbert's register is to be credited.

[4] For a general description of the registers, see D. Walker, 'The Bishops' Registers of the Diocese of Hereford, 1275–1539', *Transactions of the Woolhope Naturalists' Field Club* 36 (1958–60), 291–7, and also S. H. Martin, 'The Bishops' Registers of the Diocese of Hereford', *ibid.* 31 (1942–5), xxxiv–xliii.

[5] *Registrum Caroli Bothe*, p. 197, see also pp. 75–6, 160–1.

order or method but all that can be found entred in the said Books are collected into Tables for every Bishopps Time out of this and 3 other Books marked with Lib: 1 : 2 : 3 : which are all that are now remaining in the Bishopps Registry where in the Acts of the said Bishopps were entred concerning matters of moment.'[6]

All the registers from 1275 to 1539 have been published by the Cantilupe Society and the Canterbury and York Society, often, it must be said, in very abbreviated and unsatisfactory form, and a composite index of contents and parishes has been the subject of a separate publication.[7] In addition, the institutions and collations to be found in the registers from 1539 to 1900 have been abstracted and printed by Canon Bannister.[8] There are also five indexes of the late seventeenth and early eighteenth centuries in the Diocesan Registry, providing lists of places and some contents mentioned in the episcopal registers.

THOMAS CANTILUPE (1275–1282)

HDR, no reference. Parchment register; 11½″ × 6¾″; fos. i+ii+73+ii+i, foliated 1–49, 51–74 (excluding inserts); hide-covered wooden boards.

The first folio of the register is headed *Registrum de spiritualibus*. The register is approximately chronological in arrangement and ordinations are included in the main sequence.

Printed, *The register of Thomas de Cantilupe, bishop of Hereford* (*A.D. 1275–1282*), transcribed by R. G. Griffiths and introd. by W. W. Capes (Cantilupe Society, 1906, and Canterbury and York Society 2, 1907).

VACANCY 1282–1283

LPL, register of Archbishop John Pecham, fo. 190*r*.[9]

Hereford vacancy act Oct. 1282 (1 entry)

Printed, *Register of John Pecham* ii, p. 177.

RICHARD SWINFIELD (1283–1317)

HDR, no reference. Parchment register; 10¾″ × 7¼″; fos. i+204+i, foliated 1–97, 98A, 98B, 99–109, 110A, 110B, 111–209 (including inserts); modern leather re-covered wooden boards.

A general chronological register, beginning with Swinfield's acts as bishop-elect and continuing straight on after his consecration. Institutions and collations etc., calendared in an appendix in the printed edition, are included in the main sequence of the register. No record of ordinations survives for this episcopate.

Printed, *Registrum Ricardi de Swinfield, episcopi Herefordensis, A.D. MCCLXXXIII–MCCCXVII*, ed. W. W. Capes (Cantilupe Society, and Canterbury and York Society 6, 1909).

VACANCY 1317

LPL, register of Archbishop Walter Reynolds, fos. 20*r*–21*r passim*.

Hereford vacancy business May–July 1317, among the general section of Canterbury institutions.

ADAM ORLETON (1317–1327)

HDR, no reference. Parchment register; 11¼″ × 7½″, except for fos. 80–91A, 95–101 (11″ × 6½″), 91B–94 (9¾″ × 6¾″); fos. i+108+i, foliated 1–90, 91A, 91B, 92–107; modern leather re-covered wooden boards.

[6] 1634–1678 volume, fo. 177*r*.

[7] E. N. Dew, *Index to the Registers of the Diocese of Hereford 1275–1535* (Hereford, 1925).

[8] A. T. Bannister, *Diocese of Hereford: Institutions etc.* (*A.D. 1539–1900*) (Hereford, 1923). J. Duncomb, *Collections towards the history and antiquities of the county of Hereford*, 3 vols. (Hereford, 1804–82) and continuations (1886–1915) list parochial incumbents.

[9] See under Canterbury for a description of this and subsequent archiepiscopal and capitular registers.

A general, chronological register like its predecessor, the only notable difference being that the headings to the entries are not placed in the margin, as is usual, but across the folio. Again, there is no record of ordinations.

Printed, *Registrum Ade de Orleton episcopi Herefordensis, A.D. MCCCXVII–MCCCXXVII*, ed. A. T. Bannister (Cantilupe Society, 1907, and Canterbury and York Society 5, 1908).

THOMAS CHARLTON (1327–1344)

HDR, no reference. Parchment register, a composite volume containing the registers of Charlton, Courtenay, Polton, Spofford (part 2), and Beauchamp; 12½″ × 9¼″ (Charlton); 12½″ × 9″ (Courtenay, Polton); 12½″ × 8¾″ (Spofford); and 12¾″ × 8½″ (Beauchamp); fos. ii (paper) + 202 + i (paper), foliated i–iii, 1–56, 1–41, 1–18, 1–12, i, 1–14, i, 1–40, i, 1–12, 14–16; leather-covered wooden boards.

Charlton's register (fos. i–iii, 1–56, 1–41 of this composite volume) is the first Hereford register to be subdivided into category sections, firstly a section (without a heading) chiefly devoted to commissions (1st series, fos. 1*r*–11*v*), followed by sections containing royal writs (fos. 12*r*–23*r*), institutions, collations, dispensations, licences etc. (*quaternus de institucionibus et dispensacionibus*, fos. 24*r*–31*v*, 35*r*–56*v*), letters dimissory (fos. 32*r*–34*r*), and ordinations (2nd series, fos. 1*r*–41*v*). The institutions section includes acts of Charlton's vicars-general.

Printed, *Registrum Thome Charlton, episcopi Herefordensis, A.D. MCCCXXVII–MCCCXLIV*, ed. W. W. Capes (Cantilupe Society, 1912, and Canterbury and York Society 9, 1913).

JOHN TRILLEK (1344–1360)

HDR, no reference. Parchment register; 13¾″ × 9″; fos. ii (paper) + 267 + ii (paper), foliated 1–3, 3A, 4–12, 1–61, 65–257; parchment covers, mounted on pasteboard.

Trillek's register begins when he was bishop-elect (fos. 1*r*–5*v*) and is followed by the register of his acts after consecration (fos. 6*r*–257*v*). The latter is subdivided into four sections: institutions, dispensations, licences etc. (*quaternus de ecclesiarum et aliorum beneficiorum collacionibus, institucionibus et inducccionibus eorundem, dispensacionibus eciam eleccionibus et licenciis studii vel obsequii*, fos. 6*r*–64*v*); diverse letters (*quaternus de bullis et litteris apostolicis, commissionibus eciam et diversorum execucionibus mandatorum* . . ., fos. 65*r*–128*v*); royal writs (fos. 129*r*–175*r*); letters dimissory and ordinations (fos. 178*r*–257*v*).

Printed, *Registrum Johannis de Trillek, episcopi Herefordensis, A.D. MCCCXLIV–MCCCLXI*, ed. J. H. Parry (Cantilupe Society, 1910, and Canterbury and York Society 8, 1912).

VACANCY 1360–1361

LPL, register of Archbishop Simon Islip, fos. 230*r*–231*v*.

Hereford vacancy business Jan.–Dec. 1361 (with acquittances to Mar. 1362)

LEWIS CHARLTON (1361–1369)
VACANCY 1369

HDR, no reference. Parchment register, a composite volume containing the registers of Charlton, the 1369 vacancy, Gilbert, and Mascall; 14¼″ × 9¾″ (Charlton, Gilbert, Mascall), and 11″ × 8½″ (1369 vacancy); fos. i (paper) + ii (medieval pastedowns) + 229 + i (paper), foliated i–ii, 1–31, 33–42, i, 1–3, i–iii, 1–74, 76–97, i–iv, 1–79; leather-covered wooden boards.

Until early 1363, the entries of the register (fos. 1*r*–31*v*) are continuous but divided between *instituciones, littere dimissorie et licencie*, and ordinations (implying registration at the end of a year, rather than more regularly). From then on, there is a single, general register in approximate chronological order and encompassing the two earlier sections. A separate register of ordinations (fos. 33*r*–42*v*) is kept from 1363 (it is now misbound). The *sede vacante* register (2nd series, fos. i*r*–3*r*) is chronological in arrangement. There are no ordinations.

Printed, *Registrum Ludowici de Charltone, episcopi Herefordensis, A.D. MCCCLXI–MCCCLXX*, ed. J. H. Parry (Cantilupe Society, 1913, and Canterbury and York Society 14, 1914).

WILLIAM COURTENAY (1370–1375)

HDR, no reference. Parchment register, a composite volume containing the registers of Thomas Charlton, Courtenay, Polton, Spofford (part 2), and Beauchamp (for description, see under Charlton).

Courtenay's is a general, chronological register (3rd series, fos. 1*r*–18*v*), with a separate section of ordinations (4th series, fos. 1*r*–12*r*).

Printed, *Registrum Willelmi de Courtenay, episcopi Herefordensis, A.D. MCCCLXX–MCCCLXXV*, ed. W. W. Capes (Cantilupe Society, 1913, and Canterbury and York Society 15, 1914).

JOHN GILBERT (1375–1389)

HDR, no reference. Parchment register, a composite volume containing the registers of Lewis Charlton, the 1369 vacancy, Gilbert, and Mascall (for description, see under Charlton).

Gilbert has a general register (2nd series, fos. 1*r*–75*v*) and a register of ordinations (fos. 77*r*–97*r*). The former bears the heading (fo. 10*r*), *quaternus de ecclesiarum et aliorum beneficiorum collacionibus, institucionibus et inducionibus eorundem, dispensacionibus et eleccionibus et licenciis studii vel obsequii ac eciam dimissoriis et aliis litteris diversis*. Sometimes the chronological order is a little confused. One noticeable registrational feature relating to admissions to benefices is the registering, in many instances, of the presentation deed as well as a record of the act of institution.

Printed, *Registrum Johannis Gilbert, episcopi Herefordensis, A.D. MCCCLXXV–MCCCLXXXIX*, ed. J. H. Parry (Cantilupe Society, 1913, and Canterbury and York Society 18, 1915).

JOHN TREFNANT (1389–1404)

HDR, no reference. Parchment register; $14\frac{3}{4}'' \times 9\frac{3}{4}''$; fos. ii (paper) + 145 + ii (paper) (parchment endpaper pasted to one of the paper sheets at each end of the volume), foliated 1–94, 97–147; leather-covered pasteboard.

Trefnant's register contains a general, chronological register of acts (fos. 1*r*–56*r*), the register of his vicar-general (fos. 57*r*–59*r*), a register of ordinations and letters dimissory (fos. 133*r*–146*r*) and sections devoted to royal charters of privileges and the various disputes between the bishop and his cathedral chapter, and a record of other disputes and agreements (fos. 64*r*–132*v*). A substantial part of this miscellaneous section is devoted to the trial of heretics (fos. 97*r*–131*r*).

Printed, *Registrum Johannis Trefnant, episcopi Herefordensis, A.D. MCCCLXXXIX–MCCCCIV*, ed. W. W. Capes (Cantilupe Society, 1914, and Canterbury and York Society 20, 1916).

VACANCY 1404

LPL, register of Archbishop Thomas Arundel, volume I, fo. 295*v*.

Hereford vacancy act Apr. 1404 (1 entry), among the general section of Canterbury institutions

ROBERT MASCALL (1404–1416)

HDR, no reference. Parchment register, a composite volume containing the registers of Lewis Charlton, the 1369 vacancy, Gilbert, and Mascall (for description, see under Charlton).

Mascall's own register (3rd series, fos. 1*r*–20*v*, 25*r*–65*v*) is for the most part chronological (there is occasional confusion) and general in arrangement, except for a section (fos. 57*r*–65*v*) devoted to litigation, subsidies and correspondence with the king and archbishop. There also survives a register of the bishop's vicar-general (fos. 21*r*–24*v*) and a register of ordinations (fos. 66*r*–79*v*, the last folio being misplaced).

Printed, *Registrum Roberti Mascall, episcopi Herefordensis, A.D. MCCCCIV–MCCCCXVI*, ed. J. H. Parry and introd. by C. Johnson (Cantilupe Society, 1916, and Canterbury and York Society 21, 1917).

VACANCY 1417

LPL, register of Archbishop Henry Chichele, volume II, fos. 185*r*–186*r*.

Hereford vacancy act Jan. 1417 (1 entry)

Printed, *Register of Henry Chichele* iii, pp. 427–31.

EDMUND LACY (1417–1420)

HDR, no reference. Parchment register; 14½″ × 11″, except for 2nd series, fos. i, 1–17 (12¾″ × 8½″); fos. ii (paper) + 62 + ii (paper), foliated i–iv, 1–34, 36–41, i, 1–17; rough hide binding.

The register is in three sections: Lacy's own general register (fos. iv*r*–34*r*), the register of ordinations (fos. 36*r*–41*v*), and the register of the bishop's vicar-general (2nd series, fos. 1*r*–16*r*).

Printed, *Registrum Edmundi Lacy, episcopi Herefordensis, A.D. MCCCCXVII–MCCCCXX*, transcribed by J. H. Parry and ed. A. T. Bannister (Cantilupe Society, 1917, and Canterbury and York Society 22, 1918).

THOMAS POLTON (1420–1421)

HDR, no reference. Parchment register, a composite volume containing the registers of Thomas Charlton, Courtenay, Polton, Spofford (part 2), and Beauchamp (for description, see under Charlton).

Polton's is a general, chronological register (5th series, fos. 1*r*–12*v*), with a separate section of ordinations (fos. 13*r*–14*r*).

Printed, *Registrum Thome Poltone, episcopi Herefordensis, A.D. MCCCCXX–MCCCCXXII*, ed. W. W. Capes (Cantilupe Society, 1916, and Canterbury and York Society 22, 1918).

THOMAS SPOFFORD (1422–1448)

1. HDR, no reference. Parchment register; 13¼″ × 9″; fos. 315, foliated i–viii, 1–179, 179A, 180–252, 1–54; limp leather covers.

   This volume contains the bishop's general register (fos. 1*r*–252*v*), the register of his vicars-general (2nd series, fos. 1*r*–5*r*) and the register of ordinations (fos. 7*r*–52*r*), all to 1442.

2. HDR, no reference. Parchment register, a composite volume containing the registers of Thomas Charlton, Courtenay, Polton, Spofford (part 2), and Beauchamp (for description, see under Charlton).

   This composite volume contains the general register (6th series, fos. 1*r*–32*v*) and the ordinations register (fos. 33*r*–40*v*) for the years 1443–8.

   Printed, *Registrum Thome Spofford, episcopi Herefordensis, A.D. MCCCCXXII–MCCCCXLVIII*, ed. A. T. Bannister (Cantilupe Society, 1917, and Canterbury and York Society 23, 1919).

VACANCY 1448–1449

LPL, register of Archbishop John Stafford, fo. 99*r*.

Hereford vacancy act Jan. 1449 (1 entry), among the general section of Canterbury institutions

RICHARD BEAUCHAMP (1449–1450)

HDR, no reference. Parchment register, a composite volume containing the registers of Thomas Charlton, Courtenay, Polton, Spofford (part 2), and Beauchamp (for description, see under Charlton).

The register is divided into the register of Beauchamp's vicar-general (7th series, fos. 1*r*–*v*), the bishop's general register (fos. 2*r*–12*v*), and the register of ordinations (fos. 15*v*–16*v*).

Printed, *Registrum Ricardi Beauchamp, episcopi Herefordensis, A.D. MCCCCXLIX–MCCCCL*, ed. A. T. Bannister (Cantilupe Society, 1917, and Canterbury and York Society 25, 1919).

VACANCY 1450–1451

LPL, register of Archbishop John Stafford, fo. 107*r*.

Hereford vacancy act Dec. 1450 (1 entry), among the general section of Canterbury institutions

REGINALD BOULERS (1451–1453)

HDR, no reference. Parchment register; $14\frac{3}{4}'' \times 10''$; fos. ii (paper)+13+ii (paper), foliated 1–13; parchment covers (mounted on pasteboard).

The register is divided into two sections: general acts (fos. 1*r*–10*v*), and ordinations (fos. 11*r*–12*v*).

Printed, *Registrum Reginaldi Boulers, episcopi Herefordensis, A.D. MCCCCL–MCCCCLIII*, ed. A. T. Bannister (Cantilupe Society, 1917, and Canterbury and York Society 25, 1919).

JOHN STANBURY (1453–1474)

HDR, no reference. Parchment register, a composite volume containing the registers of Stanbury and Milling and the 1492 vacancy register; $13\frac{1}{4}'' \times 9''$, except for the register of Milling's vicar-general (3rd series, fos. 1–11, $12\frac{1}{4}'' \times 8\frac{1}{2}''$) and the vacancy register (4th series, fos. 1–4, $13\frac{1}{2}'' \times 11\frac{1}{4}''$); fos. ii (paper)+239+ii (paper), foliated 2–100, 111–134, 3–93, 1–11, 1–4; leather-covered wooden boards.

Stanbury's is a general, chronological register (fos. 2*r*–95*v*), with a separate vicar-general's register (fos. 96*r*–100*v*), and a register of ordinations (fos. 111*r*–134*r*). It is probable that at least a section of Stanbury's register is missing, since an inspected entry in Milling's register (*Registrum* ... *Millyng*, p. 18) cannot be located in the present register.

Printed, *Registrum Johannis Stanbury, episcopi Herefordensis, A.D. MCCCCLIII–MCCCCLXXIV*, ed. J. H. Parry and A. T. Bannister (Cantilupe Society, 1918, and Canterbury and York Society 25, 1919).

THOMAS MILLING (1474–1492)
VACANCY 1492

HDR, no reference. Parchment register, a composite volume (for description, see above).

Milling has a general, chronological register (2nd series, fos. 3*r*–74*v*), but with a gap between Aug. 1480 and July 1481 (there is a new heading for the register in 1481 on fo. 43*r*). There is also an ordinations register (fos. 75*r*–93*r*) and a register of the vicar-general (3rd series, fos. 1*r*–3*r*), which contains ordinations celebrated by his authority. The vacancy register (4th series, fos. 1*r*–4*v*) is, as usual, chronological in arrangement.

Printed, *Registrum Thome Millyng, episcopi Herefordensis, A.D. MCCCCLXXIV–MCCCCXCII*, ed. A. T. Bannister (Cantilupe Society, 1919, and Canterbury and York Society 26, 1920).

VACANCY 1492

LPL, register of Archbishop John Morton, volume II, fo. 151*v*.

Hereford vacancy act Feb. 1492 (1 entry), among the general section of Canterbury institutions

Calendared in C. Harper-Bill, 'An edition of the register of John Morton, archbishop of Canterbury, 1486–1500' (London University Ph.D., 1977).

VACANCY 1504

LPL, register of Archbishop William Warham, volume II, fos. 236*r*–237*r*.

Hereford vacancy business Aug. 1504 (commission and accounts only)

RICHARD MAYEW (1504–1516)

VACANCY 1516

HDR, no reference. Parchment register; 14″ × 10½″; fos. ii (paper) + 142 + ii (paper, 11″ × 7¾″) + ii (paper), foliated i–v, 1–132, 132A, 133–138; rough hide binding.

Following the common pattern, Mayew's register contains the general, chronological register of the bishop and his vicars-general (fos. 1*r*–105*v*), and a register of ordinations (fos. 106*r*–133*v*). The *sede vacante* register (fos. 134*r*–136*v*) is also chronological in arrangement.

Printed, *Registrum Ricardi Mayew, episcopi Herefordensis, A.D. MDIV–MDXVI*, ed. A. T. Bannister (Cantilupe Society, and Canterbury and York Society 27, 1919).

VACANCY 1516

1. LPL, register of Archbishop William Warham, volume II, fos. 270*v*–272*r*.

   Hereford vacancy business Apr.–Nov. 1516 (commission and accounts only)

2. *ibid.*, fo. 362*r*.

   Hereford vacancy act Nov. 1516 (1 entry), among the general section of Canterbury institutions

CHARLES BOOTH (1516–1535)

EDWARD FOX (1535–1538)

VACANCY 1538–1539

[EDMUND BONNER (1538–1539)]

HDR, no reference. Parchment register; 14¼″ × 11″; fos. ii (paper) + 13 (18th-cent. paper index, 14¼″ × 10¼″) + 2 (18th-cent. paper index, fragmentary, 10″ × 7″) + 307 + ii (paper), foliated A–H, 1–238, i, 1–11; parchment-covered boards.

Booth and Fox each have a general, chronological register of acts (fos. 1*r*–209*v*; 2nd series, fos. 1*r*–34*r* respectively), and a separate register of ordinations (fos. 210*r*–238*v*; 2nd series, fos. 35*r*–38*r*). The vacancy register (3rd series, fos. 1*r*–11*v*) and the register of Bonner before his translation to London (4th series, fos. 1*r*–11*v*) are both chronological in arrangement, but neither contains any record of ordinations.

Printed, *Registrum Caroli Bothe, episcopi Herefordensis, A.D. MDXVI–MDXXXV*, ed. A. T. Bannister (Cantilupe Society, and Canterbury and York Society 28, 1921). This volume includes abstracts of the registers of Fox and Bonner, but the ordinations *temp.* Fox are not printed.

VACANCY 1538–1539

1. LPL, register of Archbishop Thomas Cranmer, fos. 89*r*–104*v*.

   Hereford vacancy business May 1538–Jan. 1539

   Institutions are calendared in A. J. Edwards, 'The *sede vacante* administration of Archbishop Thomas Cranmer, 1533–53' (London University M.Phil., 1968).

2. *ibid.*, fo. 365*v*.

   Hereford vacancy act Aug. 1538 (1 entry), among the general section of Canterbury institutions

   See also the vacancy register described above, under Booth.

JOHN SKIP (1539–1552)

HDR, no reference. Parchment register; 14½″ × 11¼″; fos. ii (paper) + 90 + ii (paper), foliated 1–90; blank: none; rough hide binding.

1*r*–88*v*	general register Nov. 1539–Mar. 1552
89*r*–90*v*	ordinations Sept. 1540–Mar. 1548

A modern transcript of this register by P. G. S. Baylis is deposited in Hereford Cathedral Library. Institutions and collations are calendared in *Hereford Institutions 1539–1900*, pp. 1–8.

VACANCY 1552–1553

LPL, register of Archbishop Thomas Cranmer, fos. 132*r*–134*r*.

Hereford vacancy business Apr. 1552–May 1553

Institutions are calendared in A. J. Edwards, 'The *sede vacante* administration of Archbishop Thomas Cranmer, 1533–53' (London University M.Phil., 1968).

JOHN HARLEY (1553–1554)
ROBERT WHARTON (1554–1557)
JOHN SCORY (1559–1585)

HDR, no reference. Parchment register; 13½″ × 11½″ (Harley and Wharton), 15″ × 11½″ (Scory); fos. ii (paper) + 69 + ii (paper), foliated 1, 1–15, i, 1–51; blank: fo. i*v* and one unnumbered sheet between fos. 6 and 7; rough hide binding.

Register of Bishop John Harley

1*r*–*v*	general register June–July 1553 (no ordinations)
1*v*	table of contents

Register of Bishop Robert Wharton

1*r*–14*v*	general register Apr. 1554–Sept. 1557 (includes ordinations in the main sequence)
14*v*–15*v*	place index

Register of Bishop John Scory

i*r*	register heading
1*r*–49*v*	general register Jan. 1560–Oct. 1580 (includes ordinations in the main sequence, except for below)
50*r*–51*v*	ordinations Mar. 1561–Sept. 1562

Institutions and collations in this volume are calendared in *Hereford Institutions 1539–1900*, pp. 8–26.

VACANCY 1554

CAL, register N, fo. 103*r*–*v*.

Hereford vacancy business Mar. 1554

Institutions are calendared (by place) in *Sede Vacante Institutions*.

VACANCY 1557–1559

1. LPL, register of Archbishop Reginald Pole, fos. 57*r*–61*r*.

Hereford vacancy business Oct. 1557–Sept. 1558

2. CAL, register U2, fos. 30*r*–35*v*.

Hereford vacancy business Dec. 1558–Dec. 1559

Institutions are calendared (by place) in *Sede Vacante Institutions*.

VACANCY 1585–1586

LPL, register of Archbishop John Whitgift, volume I, fos. 384*v*–387*r*.

Hereford vacancy business June 1585–Jan. 1586 (includes at the end 1 visitation entry, Mar. 1585)

VACANCY 1602–1603

LPL, register of Archbishop John Whitgift, volume III, fos. 224*v*–231*r*.

Hereford vacancy business Mar. 1602–Feb. 1603

ROBERT BENNETT (1603–1617)
VACANCY 1617
FRANCIS GODWIN (1617–1633)
VACANCY 1633–1634
AUGUSTINE LINDSELL (1634)
VACANCY 1634–1635
MATTHEW WREN (1635)
THEOPHILUS FIELD (1635–1636)
GEORGE COKE (1636–1646)
NICHOLAS MONK (1661)
HERBERT CROFT (1662–1691)

1. HDR, no reference. Paper register; 10¼″ × 6½″ (fos. 1–145), 9¾″ × 7″ (pp. 1–548); fos. ii + 428 + ii, foliated i–v, 1–145, then paginated 1–475, 474[A], 475[A], 476–554; blank: fos. i*v*, ii*v*–iii*v*, iv*v*, v*v*, 35*v*, 79*v*–80*r*, 81*v*, 83*r*–*v*, 103*v*, 107*v*–108*r*, 113*v*–114*r*, 118*v*, pp. 32, 54–6, 128, 142, 205, 220, 224, 254, 260, 298, 416–17, 456–7, 497; hide-covered binding.

fos. 1*r*–145*v*	'Bennett, book I' caveats and other administrative business (commissions, muster rates, accounts, indentures, licences, collations, returns to the Barons of the Exchequer etc.) Feb. 1610–July 1617
pp. 1–91	'Bennett, book II' administrative memoranda (faculties, indentures, muster rates, commissions, returns to Barons of the Exchequer, institutions etc., not in chronological order) June 1612–Sept. 1617
pp. 92–548	administrative acts of Bishop Francis Godwin Mar. 1618–Mar. 1627 (better organised than Bennett's, in effect a rough book)

2. HDR, no reference. Paper register; 10¼″ × 6½″; fos. ii + 136 + ii, foliated i, 1–135; blank: fos. i*v*, 1*v*–2*r*, 9*v*, 27*v*, 39*v*–40*r*, 45*v*–46*r*, 52*v*–54*v*; hide-covered binding.

1*r*	'Bennett, book III' administrative acts July–Sept. 1617
2*r*	vacancy business Nov. 1617
3*r*–52*r*	administrative acts of Bishop Godwin (mostly court material, acts of court) Dec. 1617–Mar. 1626
55*r*–135*v*	caveats June 1617–June 1635

3. HDR, no reference. Paper register; 11½″ × 7½″; fos. ii + 313 + 12 (index, 10¼″ × 7½″) + ii, foliated 1–51, 56–115, 117–223, 223A, 224–227, 227A–D, 228–277; blank: fos. 45*r*, 48*v*, 56*r*–70*v*, 94*v*, 106*v*, 114*v*–115*v*, 117*r*–*v*, 134*v*–135*v*, 157*r*–*v*, 162*v*, 172*v*–173*r*, 194*v*, 227D*r*, 238*v* + 36 unnumbered blank folios at the end of the volume; hide-covered binding.

1*r*–176*r*	administrative acts Aug. 1634–July 1641 (institutions, visitation material, wills, indentures, commissions,

	muster rates, citations, acts of court, writs, consecration deeds, copies of earlier documents etc.—in considerable confusion)
176*v*	list of bishops 1603–62
177*r*	heading of Bishop Monk's register, and note about registers 1687 (see above, bibliographical note)
177*v*–184*v*	letters of orders, endowments etc. (including earlier material) Oct. 1660–Sept. 1661
184*v*–277*v*	register of Bishop Herbert Croft Feb. 1662–Apr. 1678 (in occasional disorder)

Pre-1646 institutions and collations in these volumes are calendared in *Hereford Institutions 1539–1900*, pp. 26–31.

VACANCY 1617

LPL, register of Archbishop George Abbot, volume I, fos. 357*r*–358*v*.

Hereford vacancy business Oct.–Nov. 1617

VACANCY 1633–1634

1. LPL, register of Archbishop George Abbot, volume III, fos. 180*v*–182*v*.

Hereford vacancy business Apr.–June 1633

2. LPL, register of Archbishop William Laud, volume I, fos. 295*v*–298*r*.

Hereford vacancy business Sept. 1633–Mar. 1634

VACANCY 1634–1635

LPL, register of Archbishop William Laud, volume I, fos. 301*v*–302*v*.

Hereford vacancy business Nov. 1634–Feb. 1635

VACANCY 1635

LPL, register of Archbishop William Laud, volume I, fos. 302*v*–303*v*.

Hereford vacancy business Dec. 1635

VACANCY 1636

LPL, register of Archbishop William Laud, volume I, fos. 175*r*–177*r*.

record of the visitation of the diocese *sede vacante* June–Sept. 1636

LINCOLN

Repositories

1. Lincolnshire Archives Office, The Castle, Lincoln LN1 3AB (LAO).
2. Lambeth Palace Library, London SE1 7JU (LPL).
3. Canterbury Cathedral Archives and Library, The Precincts, Canterbury CT1 2EG (CAL).

Area

The medieval diocese of Lincoln was divided into eight archdeaconries: those of Leicester, Bedford, Oxford and Buckingham followed in extent the civil divisions of the respective counties; Northampton archdeaconry comprised the counties of Northampton and Rutland; Huntingdon encompassed the county of Huntingdon and the northern portion of Hertfordshire; and in the north of the bishopric the limits of the extensive archdeaconry of Lincoln coincided with the boundaries of Lincolnshire, except for the West Riding of Lindsey which formed the small archdeaconry of Stow.[1] The archdeaconry of Northampton was removed from the diocese in 1541 with the creation of the bishopric of Peterborough, and in the following year the Oxford archdeaconry was constituted a separate bishopric. There were no further changes in the diocesan boundaries until the nineteenth century.

Bibliographical Note

The Lincoln episcopal registers have been described in great detail by Miss Kathleen Major in her valuable guide to the Lincoln diocesan muniments,[2] and they have been the subject of a general survey by Canon C. W. Foster in his address to the Canterbury and York Society.[3] To Lincoln belongs the distinction of having the earliest extant episcopal registers, and in all probability the rolls of Hugh of Wells (1209–35), beginning about 1214–15, may indeed represent the first attempts at diocesan registration in England. The changes and developments in registration at Lincoln have been discussed elsewhere and will in any case become obvious from the analytical descriptions set out below. Basically, the roll was in use until the end of the thirteenth century, and in 1290 the registrar of Bishop Oliver Sutton (1280–99) began what became the first volume of the magnificent series of Lincoln registers. The registers were subdivided into several regular sections: institutions (arranged by archdeaconry); collations of dignities and prebends; memoranda; royal writs; and ordinations, to which, particularly in the fourteenth century, could be added further category sections dealing with such matters as dispensations; various licences; letters dimissory; testamentary business; and occasional visitation injunctions and related material. There is some confusion in arrangement and

[1] *VCH Lincolnshire* ii (1906), map between pp. 78–9; *VCH Rutland* i (1908), p. 158, and map facing p. 159; *VCH Northamptonshire* ii (1906), pp. 75–8, and map between pp. 78–9; *VCH Leicestershire* i (1907), pp. 398–401; *VCH Huntingdonshire* i (1926), pp. 375–6, with map; *VCH Bedfordshire* i (1904), app. i, pp. 346–7, and map facing p. 346; *VCH Buckinghamshire* i (1905), pp. 344–5, and map facing p. 346; *VCH Hertfordshire* iv (1914), pp. 362–4, and map facing p. 365; *VCH Oxfordshire* ii (1907), pp. 58–63, and map between pp. 58–9; *The Registrum Antiquissimum of the Cathedral Church of Lincoln*, ed. K. Major, ix (Lincoln Record Society 62, 1968), pp. 255–62. For a map of the diocese see the frontispiece to E. Venables and G. G. Perry, *Diocesan Histories: Lincoln* (London, 1897); and Ordnance Survey, *Map of Monastic Britain: (south sheet)* (2nd edn., 1954).

[2] *A Handlist of the Records of the Bishop of Lincoln and of the Archdeacons of Lincoln and Stow* (Oxford, 1953).

[3] 'The Lincoln Episcopal Registers', *A.A.S.R.* 41 (1932–3), 155–68b, and see also K. Major, 'The Lincoln Diocesan Records', *T.R.H.S.* 4th ser., 22 (1940), 39–66. For the evolution of enrolment at Lincoln in the thirteenth century see D. M. Smith, 'The Rolls of Hugh of Wells, Bishop of Lincoln 1209–35', *Bulletin of the Institute of Historical Research* 45 (1972), 155–95. For the *sede vacante* records of the diocese see D. M. Williamson, '*Sede vacante* records of the diocese of Lincoln', *Bulletin of the Society of Local Archivists* 12 (1953), 13–20; and also C. W. Foster, 'Institutions to benefices in the diocese of Lincoln', *A.A.S.R.* 39 (1928–9), 179–216.

certainly some losses in the sixteenth century and the volumes for the later part of the century tend to adopt the form of a general register.

The thirteenth-century rolls from Hugh of Wells to Richard Gravesend (1258–79) have been published jointly by the Lincoln Record Society and the Canterbury and York Society, and the edition of the rolls and register of Bishop Oliver Sutton is now nearing completion. *Sede vacante* institutions to benefices[4] and visitation business, and sixteenth-century institutions and cognate material have been printed by those indefatigable historians of the church of Lincoln, Professor A. Hamilton Thompson and Canon C. W. Foster. In the Lincolnshire Archives Office are the indexes of institutions and collations in the registers from the early thirteenth century to 1663 compiled by Canon Foster and arranged by parish within archdeaconry divisions, and by cathedral dignities and prebends. In addition there are several publications and manuscript compilations which list incumbents for a particular archdeaconry or county in the ancient diocese.[5] An index of wills in the bishops' registers from 1320 to 1547 has been published,[6] and lists and abstracts of some of these wills are also in A. Gibbons, *Early Lincoln Wills 1280–1547* (Lincoln, 1888). Several vernacular documents in the late medieval registers have been printed by Andrew Clark.[7] In addition to modern finding-aids and published work, there are two manuscript *repertoria* of the Lincoln diocesan registry which on occasion can prove to be very useful—the *Vetus Repertorium*, compiled in the early fourteenth century and now in Cambridge University Library, MS. Dd.10.28,[8] and the *Repertorium* of Robert Toneys, the registrar, compiled in 1507–8 and now Add. Reg. 5 among the diocesan archives in the Lincolnshire Archives Office.

HUGH OF WELLS (1209–1235)

LAO, no class reference. Fourteen parchment rolls, and a small parchment register (item 15 below).

1. *Roll I*; roll of 5 membranes, known as the *rotulus curtus et grossus*, 125½″ × 5¾″, to which two other *rotuli inclusi* have been sewn at the base of mem. 5, the first one of 2 membranes (51¼″ × 6″), the second of a single membrane (21¼″ × 5¾″). This is the Lincoln archdeaconry vicarages roll (with institutions).
2. *Roll IA*; roll of 12 membranes, 277¾″ × 8″, being the Lincoln archdeaconry institution roll from the eleventh to the twenty-fifth pontifical year (Dec. 1219–Dec. 1234).
3. *Roll II*; roll of 9 membranes, 197½″ × 8″, being the Northampton archdeaconry institution roll from the eleventh to the twenty-sixth pontifical year (Dec. 1219–Feb. 1235).

[4] A. Hamilton Thompson, 'Lambeth institutions to benefices, being a calendar of institutions to benefices in the old diocese of Lincoln during vacancies of the episcopal see and during the visitations by the Archbishops of Canterbury as metropolitans, with collations of benefices made by the Archbishops jure devoluto, from the archiepiscopal registers in the Library of Lambeth Palace 1279–1532', *A.A.S.R.* 40 (1930–1), 33–110.

[5] Among these are several works by Canon Foster in *A.A.S.R.* 30 (1909–10), 47–118, 379–90 (for Lincolnshire 1587–1660); 37 (1923–5), 144–76, 322–36 (for Leicestershire 1535–1660); *Bedfordshire Historical Record Society* 8 (1924), pp. 133–64 (for Bedfordshire 1535–1660); 'MS. Fasti Ecclesiae Bedfordensis: lists of incumbents of the benefices up to the early nineteenth century', by F. A. Blaydes (Page-Turner), with index, deposited in the Bedfordshire Record Office; W. M. Noble, 'Incumbents of the county of Huntingdon', *Transactions of the Cambridgeshire and Huntingdonshire Archaeological Society*, ii (1904–7), 157–64, 181–204; iii (1908–14), 50–6, 97–104, 117–40, 157–72, 189–204, 251–66, 271–86, 327–38. Several county histories also provide lists of incumbents, e.g. G. Baker, *The history and antiquities of the county of Northampton* (2 vols, London, 1822–41); J. E. Cussans, *History of Hertfordshire* (3 vols, London, 1870–81); T. Blore, *The history and antiquities of the county of Rutland* (1 vol., all published, Stamford, 1811). This list is by no means exhaustive. See also under Peterborough and Oxford dioceses.

[6] *Calendars of Lincoln Wills 1320–1600*, ed. C. W. Foster (British Record Society, Index Library 28, 1902), pp. 1–17.

[7] *Lincoln Diocese Documents 1400–1544* (Early English Text Society, original ser., 149, 1914).

[8] D. M. Owen, 'A Lincoln diocesan book in the Cambridge University Library', *Lincolnshire Architectural and Archaeological Society Reports and Papers* 10 (1963–4), 138–47; and the same writer in 'Vetus Repertorium, an early memorandum book of the diocese of Lincoln', *Transactions of the Cambridge Bibliographical Society* 7 (1965), 100–6. A photocopy of the *Vetus Repertorium* is available for consultation at the Lincolnshire Archives Office. The *Repertorium* is a composite volume but the relevant portion is of the early fourteenth century.

4. *Roll III*; roll of 7 membranes, 137¼″ × 7¾″, being the Oxford archdeaconry institution roll from the eleventh to the twenty-sixth pontifical year (Dec. 1219–Feb. 1235).
5. *Roll IV*; roll of 5 membranes, 96¼″ × 7½″/8¼″ (fragmentary at end of roll), being the Stow archdeaconry institution roll from the eleventh to the twenty-fifth pontifical year (Dec. 1219–Dec. 1234).
6. *Roll V*; roll of 6 membranes, numbered 2–7, 142″ × 7¾″, being the Leicester archdeaconry institution roll from the eleventh to the twenty-sixth pontifical year (Dec. 1219–Feb. 1235). The loose membrane, once numbered as 1 of this roll, is now kept with roll XI, to which it actually belongs.
7. *Roll VB*; roll of 5 membranes, 119¼″ × 7¾″, being the Leicester archdeaconry '*matricula*'.
8. *Roll VI*; roll of 5 membranes, 111¼″ × 7¾″, being the Bedford archdeaconry institution roll from the eleventh to the twenty-fifth pontifical year (Dec. 1219–Dec. 1234).
9. *Roll VII*; roll of 6 membranes, 134½″ × 7¾″, being the Buckingham archdeaconry institution roll from the eleventh to the twenty-fifth pontifical year (Dec. 1219–Dec. 1234).
10. *Roll VIII*; roll of 3 membranes (fragment), 69″ × 7½″, being the Huntingdon archdeaconry institution roll from the eleventh to the nineteenth pontifical year (Dec. 1219–Dec. 1227).
11. *Roll IX*; roll of 9 membranes, 201¼″ × 7¾″/8″, being the Northampton archdeaconry charter roll, Jan. 1220–Jan. 1235.
12. *Roll X*; roll of 13 membranes, 181″ × 6″/8¼″, being the institution roll for all archdeaconries *c.* 1214 × Dec. 1218.
13. *Roll XI*; known as the *quinque rotuli simul*, comprising one loose membrane (17¼″ × 7½″, fragmentary, Leicester archdeaconry) and four small rolls, sewn at the head, (1. 20½″ × 7½″; 2. 13″ × 7¼″; 3. 21¾″ × 6½″; 4. 21″ × 6¾″), being the vicarage rolls for the archdeaconries of Bedford, Buckingham, Huntingdon, Leicester, Northampton, Oxford and Stow.
14. *Roll XII*; roll of 5 membranes, 182½″ × 7¼″, being the institution roll for all archdeaconries for the tenth pontifical year (Dec. 1218–Dec. 1219).
15. Add. Reg. 6. Parchment register; 9¾″ × 8¼″; fos. i+iv (paper)+34+vi (paper)+i, foliated i–ii, 1–34; hide-covered pasteboards.
 Liber Antiquus, a register of vicarages and copies of appropriation deeds etc.

Items 1–14 are printed in *Rotuli Hugonis de Welles, episcopi Lincolniensis, A.D. MCCIX–MCCXXXV*, vol. I, ed. W. P. W. Phillimore (Canterbury and York Society 1, 1909 and Lincoln Record Society 3, 1912), vol. II, ed. W. P. W. Phillimore and others (Canterbury and York Society 3, 1907, and Lincoln Record Society 6, 1913); vol. III, ed. F. N. Davis (Canterbury and York Society 4, 1908, and Lincoln Record Society 9, 1914). Item 15 is printed in *Liber Antiquus de Ordinationibus Vicariarum tempore Hugonis Wells, Lincolniensis episcopi, 1209–1235*, ed. A. Gibbons (Lincoln, 1888). For a discussion of these enrolments see D. M. Smith, 'The rolls of Hugh of Wells, bishop of Lincoln 1209–35' in *Bulletin of the Institute of Historical Research* 45 (1972), 155–95.

ROBERT GROSSETESTE (1235–1253)

LAO, no class reference. Eight parchment rolls.

1. *Roll I*; roll of 16 membranes, 361″ × 8¾″, being the Lincoln archdeaconry institution roll.
2. *Roll II*; roll of 11 membranes, 257¼″ × 8¼″/8¾″, being the Northampton archdeaconry institution roll.
3. *Roll III*; roll of 8 membranes, 186½″ × 8¼″, being the Oxford archdeaconry institution roll.
4. *Roll IV*; roll of 6 membranes, 121¼″ × 7¾″/8½″, being the Stow archdeaconry institution roll.
5. *Roll V*; roll of 8 membranes, 173″ × 8½″, being the Leicester archdeaconry institution roll
6. *Roll VI*; roll of 7 membranes, 143½″ × 8½″, being the Bedford archdeaconry institution roll.
7. *Roll VII*; roll of 8 membranes, 159¾″ × 8¼″, being the Buckingham archdeaconry institution roll.
8. *Roll VIII*; roll of 7 membranes, 149½″ × 7½″/8½″, being the Huntingdon archdeaconry institution roll.

All the rolls, except for item 2, contain entries from 1235 to 1253; the second roll includes entries only up to the seventeenth pontifical year of the bishop (1252).

Printed, *Rotuli Roberti Grosseteste, episcopi Lincolniensis, A.D. MCCXXXV–MCCLIII*, ed. F. N. Davis (Canterbury and York Society 10, 1913, and Lincoln Record Society 11, 1914), pp. 1–502.

HENRY LEXINGTON (1254–1258)

LAO, no class reference. One parchment roll of 2 membranes, 45½″ × 9″, being the Huntingdon archdeaconry institution roll 1254–8.

Printed, *Rotuli Roberti Grosseteste*, pp. 508–14.

RICHARD GRAVESEND (1258–1279)

LAO, no class reference. Nine parchment rolls.

1. *Roll I*; roll of 33 membranes, 715″ × 8½″/9¾″, being the Lincoln archdeaconry institution roll.
2. *Roll II*; roll of 19 membranes, 397¾″ × 8½″/9½″, being the Northampton archdeaconry institution roll.
3. *Roll III*; roll of 7 membranes, 127¼″ × 9″, being the Stow archdeaconry institution roll.
4. *Roll IV*; roll of 15 membranes, 270″ × 9¼″, being the Leicester archdeaconry institution roll.
5. *Roll V*; roll of 11 membranes, 218″ × 9″/9½″, being the Bedford archdeaconry institution roll.
6. *Roll VI*; roll of 13 membranes, 260″ × 9¼″, being the Oxford archdeaconry institution roll.
7. *Roll VII*; roll of 12 membranes, 214″ × 9″/9¾″, being the Huntingdon archdeaconry institution roll.
8. *Roll VIII*; roll of 13 membranes, 255¾″ × 8¾″/9¾″, being the Buckingham archdeaconry institution roll.
9. *Roll IX*; roll of 1 membrane (damaged), 21″ × 5½″ (formerly Lincoln Dean and Chapter muniment Dj/35/3), being, on the face, a roll of induction mandates addressed to the archdeacon of Stow (not in chronological order) and, on the dorse, a survey of benefices in the rural deanery of Manlake and Corringham (Stow archdeaconry).

Rolls I–VIII all contain entries from 1258 to 1279.

Printed, *Rotuli Ricardi Gravesend, diocesis Lincolniensis*, ed. F. N. Davis with additions by C. W. Foster and A. Hamilton Thompson (Canterbury and York Society 31, and Lincoln Record Society 20, 1925).

VACANCY 1279–1280

LPL, register of Archbishop John Pecham, fo. 22*v*.[9]

Lincoln vacancy act Jan. 1280 (1 entry)

Printed, *Registrum Johannis Peckham* i, p. 90. See also below for further *sede vacante* business.

VACANCY 1279–1280
OLIVER SUTTON (1280–1299)
VACANCY 1299–1300

1. LAO, no class reference. Six parchment rolls. Sutton was consecrated on 19 May 1280 and certain of the institution rolls contain *sede vacante* institutions 1280.
   1. *Roll I*; roll of 22 membranes, 549½″ × 9½″/10¼″, being the Lincoln archdeaconry institution roll Jan. 1280–May 1290
   2. *Roll II*; roll of 13 membranes, 338¼″ × 9¾″, being the Northampton archdeaconry institution roll Jan. 1280–Apr. 1290

[9] See under Canterbury for a description of this and subsequent archiepiscopal and capitular registers.

3. *Roll III*; roll of 5 membranes, 113¾″ × 9¼″/10″, being the Stow archdeaconry institution roll May 1280–Mar. 1290
4. *Roll IV*; roll of 4 membranes (fragment, lacking the beginning of the roll), 90½″ × 9¾″, being the Leicester archdeaconry institution roll Aug. 1286–May 1290
5. *Roll V*; roll of 5 membranes, 122″ × 10″, being the Bedford archdeaconry institution roll Apr. 1280–Feb. 1290
6. *Roll VI*; roll of 3 membranes (fragment, lacking the beginning of the roll), 51¼″ × 9½″, being the custody roll for the whole diocese May 1298–Nov. 1299

2. LAO, Episcopal Register I. Parchment register; 12″ × 8″; fos. i (paper) + 208 + i (paper) + 205, foliated [i], 1–414; blank: fos. 209*r*–*v*, 210*v*, 244*r*–245*v*, 254*v*–255*v*, 279*v*, 292*r*–293*v*, 303*v*, 314*r*–315*v*, 333*v*–334*v*, 350*r*–352*v*, 366*v*, 414*r*–*v*; leather binding.

1*r*–208*v* memoranda May 1290–Sept. 1299
211*r*–243*v* institutions, Lincoln archdeaconry May 1290–Oct. 1299
246*r*–254*r* institutions, Stow archdeaconry July 1290–Nov. 1299
256*r*–279*r* institutions, Northampton archdeaconry May 1290–Oct. 1299
280*r*–291*v* institutions, Leicester archdeaconry May 1290–Nov. 1299
294*r*–303*r* institutions, Huntingdon archdeaconry May 1290–Sept. 1299
304*r*–313*v* institutions, Bedford archdeaconry May 1290–Aug. 1299
316*r*–333*r* institutions, Buckingham archdeaconry May 1290–Nov. 1299
335*r*–349*v* institutions, Oxford archdeaconry June 1290–Nov. 1299
353*r*–362*v* collations of dignities and prebends Aug. 1290–Oct. 1299
363*r*–364*r* dispensations Mar.–Oct. 1299
364*v*–366*r* *sede vacante* register (institutions) Dec. 1299–Mar. 1300 (with a later document added on fo. 366*r*) (see also below)
367*r*–413*v* ordinations May 1290–Sept. 1299

Printed, *The Rolls and Register of Bishop Oliver Sutton, 1280–1299*, ed. R. M. T. Hill, vol. I (Lincoln Record Society 39, 1948), containing Roll I and fos. 211*r*–243*v* of the register; vol. II (Lincoln Record Society 43, 1950), containing Roll II and fos. 256*r*–279*r* of the register; vols. III–VI (Lincoln Record Society 48, 52, 60, 64, 1954–69), containing the memoranda section of the register (fos. 1*r*–208*v*); vol. VII (Lincoln Record Society 69, 1975), containing the ordinations (fos. 367*r*–413*v*). Two more volumes are required to complete the edition, and there is a typescript of the Oxford, Buckingham and Huntingdon archdeaconries institutions (fos. 335*r*–349*v*, 316*r*–333*r*, 294*r*–303*r*) already in the possession of the Lincoln Record Society. The rolls and register are described in detail on pp. xiii–xvii of the first printed volume.

VACANCY 1299–1300

1. LAO, Lincoln Dean and Chapter muniment A/4/7/2. Parchment roll of 4 membranes; 53¾″ × 9½″.

royal writs relating to cases involving clerks, land in frankalmoign, and to collectors of the subsidy Nov. 1299–Feb. 1300

2. LPL, register of Archbishop Robert Winchelsey, fo. 274*r*.

Lincoln vacancy business Jan. 1300

Printed, *Registrum Roberti Winchelsey* i, p. 371.

See above for further vacancy material.

JOHN DALDERBY (1300–1320)
VACANCY 1320

1. LAO, Episcopal Register II. Parchment register; 12¼″ × 9″; fos. i (paper) + 364, numbered [i], 1–366 (38 and 89 are inserts); blank: fos. 101*v*, 141*r*–*v*, 194*r*–*v*, 229*v*, 274*v*, 303*r*–304*v*, 329*r*–*v*, 339*r*–*v*, 345*v*–348*v*, 360*r*–*v*; leather binding.

1*r*–82*v*	institutions, Lincoln archdeaconry Apr. 1300–Jan. 1320
83*r*–101*r*	institutions, Stow archdeaconry Aug. 1300–Nov. 1319
102*r*–140*v*	institutions, Northampton archdeaconry Mar. 1300–Dec. 1319
142*r*–173*v*	institutions, Oxford archdeaconry Apr. 1300–Dec. 1319
174*r*–193*v*	institutions, Buckingham archdeaconry Aug. 1300–Jan. 1320
195*r*–221*v*	institutions, Leicester archdeaconry (with later additional entries) Apr. 1300–Dec. 1319
222*r*–229*r*	copies of charters relating to the chapel of Noseley, Leics. and the Martival family late 13th–early 14th cents.
230*r*–254*v*	institutions, Huntingdon archdeaconry May 1300–Nov. 1319
255*r*–274*r*	institutions, Bedford archdeaconry June 1300–Nov. 1319
275*r*–302*v*	collations of dignities and prebends July 1300–Sept. 1319
305*r*–328*v*	dispensations for study *iuxta formam constitucionis novelle* (i.e. *Cum ex eo*) Mar. 1300–Dec. 1319
330*r*–338*r*	commendations of churches Mar. 1301–Apr. 1318 (the heading contains a note that earlier commendations are to be found in the respective archdeaconry institutions sections)
340*r*–345*r*	documents relating to the college at Kirby Bellars, Leics. Aug.–Oct. 1319
349*r*–366*v*	*sede vacante* register
	349*r*–355*v* institutions Jan.–Aug. 1320
	356*r*–*v* *registrum causarum* Mar.–May 1320
	357*r*–366*v* memoranda Jan.–Aug. 1320
	(fos. 361–6 are misbound and should come before 357–9)

Other copies of charters on fos. 222*r*–229*r* and related Noseley documents are printed in *A.A.S.R.* 25 (1900), 431–58; 26 (1901), 276–320.

2. LAO, Maddison 2/1. Parchment bifolium; 12″ × 9″; formerly used as a cover for a correction book (bears title *Correctiones 1602*).

fragment of an ordination register (dated entry May 1309)

3. LAO, Episcopal Register III. Parchment register; 12″ × 9″; fos. iii (paper, now loose) + 419 + iii (paper), foliated [i–iii], 1–433 (including inserts); blank: fos. 187*v*, 432*v*–433*v* (and the dorses of inserts); hide-covered binding (front cover loose).

1*r*–432*r* memoranda Mar. 1300–Jan. 1320

A modern typescript calendar in six volumes by Dr C. Clubley is available at the Lincolnshire Archives Office. Fragments of a roll of royal writs 1308–9 are among the muniments of the Dean and Chapter of Lincoln (LAO, A/4/7/2a–c).

HENRY BURGHERSH (1320–1340)
VACANCY 1340–1342

1. LAO, Episcopal Register IV. Parchment register; 12″ × 9¼″; fos. iii (paper) + i (1585 will) + 414 + iii (paper), foliated [i–iv], 1–415 (including 1 insert); blank: fos. 96*v*, 110*v*, 160*v*, 244*v*, 258*r*, 290*v*, 321*v*, 324*v*, 395*v*–396*v*, 414*v*–415*v*; hide-covered binding.

1*r*–90*v*	institutions, Lincoln archdeaconry Sept. 1320–Nov. 1340 (fo. 85 should follow directly on fo. 80; fos. 81–84 are an interpolated section relating to Beckingham chantry)
91*r*–96*v*	institutions *sede vacante*, Lincoln archdeaconry Dec. 1340–May 1342
97*r*–109*v*	institutions, Stow archdeaconry Dec. 1320–Nov. 1340
110*r*	institutions *sede vacante*, Stow archdeaconry Apr. 1341–July 1342
111*r*–156*v*	institutions, Leicester archdeaconry Oct. 1320–Nov. 1340
157*r*–160*r*	institutions *sede vacante*, Leicester archdeaconry Jan. 1341–Sept. 1342

161*r*–238*v*	institutions, Northampton archdeaconry Sept. 1320–Dec. 1340
239*r*–244*r*	institutions, *sede vacante*, Northampton archdeaconry Jan. 1341–May 1342
245*r*–287*r*	institutions, Oxford archdeaconry Sept. 1320–Dec. 1340
287*v*–290*r*	institutions *sede vacante*, Oxford archdeaconry Feb. 1341–July 1342
291*r*–321*r*	institutions, Bedford archdeaconry Sept. 1320–Dec. 1340
322*r*–324*r*	institutions *sede vacante*, Bedford archdeaconry Feb. 1341–Aug. 1342
325*r*–358*r*	institutions, Buckingham archdeaconry July 1320–Nov. 1340
358*v*–360*v*	institutions *sede vacante*, Buckingham archdeaconry Jan. 1341–July 1342
361*r*–392*v*	institutions, Huntingdon archdeaconry Sept. 1320–Nov. 1340
393*r*–395*r*	institutions *sede vacante*, Huntingdon archdeaconry Dec. 1340–Apr. 1342
397*r*–414*r*	collations of dignities and prebends Oct. 1320–May 1340

2. LAO, Episcopal Register V. Parchment register; 12″ × 9¼″; fos. iii (paper) + 255 + ii (paper) + 232 + ii (paper), foliated [i–iii], 1–589; blank: fos. 59*v*, 83*r*–*v*, 159*v*, 178*v*, 255*v*–257*v*, 588*v*–589*v*; hide-covered binding.

1*r*–33*v*	dispensations *cum ex eo* Sept. 1320–Dec. 1340
34*r*–59*r*	licences (to visit Rome, *standi in obsequiis*, and for non-residence) Oct. 1323–Dec. 1340
60*r*–82*v*	testamentary business Sept. 1320–Oct. 1340
84*r*–147*v*	letters dimissory Oct. 1323–Mar. 1340
148*r*–155*v*	appointment of penitentiaries Oct. 1337–June 1340
156*r*–159*r*	letters dimissory (cont.) Mar.–Dec. 1340
160*r*–178*r*	licences to celebrate in oratories Oct. 1323–Dec. 1340
179*r*–201*v*	licences to study and to let churches to farm Oct. 1323–Dec. 1340
202*r*–255*v*	*commissiones in causis ecclesiarum* (commissions for institutions, exchanges of benefices) Sept. 1323–Dec. 1340
258*r*–361*v*, 368*r*–588*r*	memoranda Sept. 1320–Dec. 1340
362*r*–367*v*	letters questory and indulgences Oct. 1323–Dec. 1329 (includes other memoranda)

At least four quires of this register, numbered XVII (between fos. 387 and 388), XXI (fos. 411–12), XXVIII (fos. 463–4) and XXXI (fos. 487–8), are missing. There are also two quires numbered XIV but no quire XV, and probably there is no quire XV missing.

3. LAO, Episcopal Register VB. Parchment register; 12½″ × 9½″; fos. i (fragment of parchment cover) + iii (paper) + 214 + iii, foliated [i–iii], 1–212, [213, 214]; blank: fos. [213*v*–214*v*]; hide-covered binding.

1*r*–[213*r*]	royal writs May 1321–July 1340

Fos. 1–93 have been calendared by Miss J. Cripps (LAO, MCD. 997).

THOMAS BEK (1342–1347)

VACANCY 1347

1. LAO, Episcopal Register VI. Parchment register; 12″ × 9¼″; fos. ii (paper) + i (16th cent. will) + 150 + i (16th cent. will) + ii (paper), foliated 1–151 (including 1 insert); blank: fos. 28*v*, 47*v*, 79*v*, 123*v*; hide-covered binding (front cover loose).

1*r*–26*r*	institutions, Lincoln archdeaconry Sept. 1342–Feb. 1347
26*v*–28*r*	institutions *sede vacante*, Lincoln archdeaconry Feb.–May 1347
29*r*–30*r*	institutions, Stow archdeaconry Feb. 1343–Jan 1347

30*v*	institutions *sede vacante*, Stow archdeaconry Apr.–May 1347 (unfinished)
31*r*–46*r*	institutions, Leicester archdeaconry Sept. 1342–Feb. 1347
46*v*–47*r*	institutions *sede vacante*, Leicester archdeaconry Mar.–June 1347
48*r*–77*v*	institutions, Northampton archdeaconry Oct. 1342–Feb. 1347
78*r*–79*r*	institutions *sede vacante*, Northampton archdeaconry Mar.–June 1347
80*r*–87*v*	institutions, Oxford archdeaconry Sept. 1342–Sept. 1346 (penultimate entry; last entry is too faded for date to be legible)
88*r*–*v*	institutions *sede vacante*, Oxford archdeaconry Mar.–Apr. 1347
89*r*–95*v*	institutions, Bedford archdeaconry Dec. 1342–Jan. 1347 (unfinished)
96*r*–103*r*	institutions, Buckingham archdeaconry Oct. 1342–Jan. 1347
103*r*–*v*	institutions *sede vacante*, Buckingham archdeaconry Feb.–May 1347
104*r*–114*r*	institutions, Huntingdon archdeaconry Sept. 1342–Jan. 1347
114*r*–*v*	institutions *sede vacante*, Huntingdon archdeaconry Mar.–May 1347
115*r*–123*r*	collations of dignities and prebends Jan. 1343–Dec. 1346
124*r*–151*v*	*ordinationes cantariarum* Dec. 1328–Feb. 1347

2. LAO, Episcopal Register VII. Parchment register; 12½″ × 9½″; fos. iii (paper) + 113 + ii (paper) + 106 + iii (paper), foliated [i–iii], 1–221; blank: fos. 92*v*, 106*r*–*v*, 114*r*–115*v*, 122*r*–123*v*, 129*r*–130*v*, 139*v*–140*v*, 158*v*–159*v*, 178*v*, 221*r*–*v*; hide-covered binding.

1*r*–89*r*	memoranda Aug. 1342–Jan. 1347
89*r*–92*r*	memoranda *sede vacante* Mar.–June 1347
93*r*–99*r*	appointment of penitentiaries (including commissions to absolve) Oct. 1342–Feb. 1347
99*r*–100*v*	appointment of penitentiaries *sede vacante* Mar.–June 1347
101*r*–105*v*	bonds and acquittances Oct. 1342–Jan. 1347
105*v*	bonds and acquittances *sede vacante* Apr.–May 1347
107*r*–112*v*	*liber incarceratorum* (commissions to receive convicted clerks, gaol delivery, judgments) Oct. 1342–May 1346
112*v*–113*r*	as above (but headed *commissiones et processus pro incarceratis et incarcerandis*) *sede vacante* Mar.–Apr. 1347 (with earlier entries, May 1345, added at the end)
116*r*–121*v*	dispensations *cum ex eo* Oct. 1342–Feb. 1347
121*v*	similar dispensations, *sede vacante* Apr.–May 1347
124*r*–128*v*	licences for study and to let churches to farm Oct. 1342–Feb. 1347
128*v*	similar licences *sede vacante* Mar.–June 1347
131*r*–138*v*	licences *standi in obsequiis* Sept. 1342–Feb. 1347
139*r*	similar licences *sede vacante* Mar.–June 1347
141*r*–158*r*	letters dimissory Oct. 1342–Feb. 1347
158*r*	letters dimissory *sede vacante* Mar.–May 1347
160*r*–177*v*	licences to celebrate in oratories Oct. 1342–Feb. 1347
177*v*–178*r*	similar licences *sede vacante* Feb.–June 1347
179*r*–205*v*	*commissiones in causis ecclesiarum* (commissions for institutions, exchanges of benefices, to receive resignations, to hold inquiries, confirm elections etc.) Oct. 1342–Feb. 1347
205*v*–208*v*	similar commissions *sede vacante* Feb.–June 1347
209*r*–219*r*	testamentary business Dec. 1342–Feb. 1347
219*r*–220*v*	testamentary business *sede vacante* Mar.–June 1347

A modern typescript calendar of fos. 131*r*–139*r* is available at the Lincolnshire Archives Office, and at the Borthwick Institute, York (Add. MS. 126).

3. LAO, Episcopal Register VIIB. Parchment register; $12\frac{3}{4}'' \times 9\frac{1}{2}''$; fos. 84, foliated 2–85 (begins in the middle of an ordination list and it is probable that at least one gathering is missing); blanks: none; limp parchment covers.

2*r*–10*r*	ordinations (including notes of letters dimissory) Dec. 1345–Feb. 1347
10*v*–16*v*	ordinations *sede vacante* Feb.–May 1347
17*r*–67*r*	royal writs Nov. 1342–Jan. 1347
67*r*–*v*	royal writs *sede vacante* Feb.–Mar. 1347
68*r*–85*r*	visitation injunctions to religious houses and *dimissiones* Feb. 1343–July 1346
85*r*–*v*	injunctions and *dimissiones*, *sede vacante* Apr.–May 1347

JOHN GYNWELL (1347–1362)
VACANCY 1362–1363

1. LAO, Episcopal Register VIII. Parchment register; $13\frac{1}{2}'' \times 9\frac{1}{2}''$; fos. iv (paper) + 189 + iii (paper), foliated [i–iv], 1–189; blank: fos. 17*v*, 49*v*, 69*v*, 166*v*; hide-covered binding.

1*r*–187*r*	memoranda (there has been some misbinding, so that certain pontifical years are out of sequence. There are also occasional interpolations, e.g. 1352 cathedral visitation, fos. 167*r*–177*v*) Oct. 1350–July 1362
187*v*–189*v*	medieval subject index

2. LAO, Episcopal Register IX. Parchment register; $13\frac{3}{4}'' \times 9''$; fos. 41 + iii (paper) + i (will 1571) + 388, foliated 1–49, 58–446 (including inserts); blank: fos. 6*v*, 32*v*, 41*v*, 44*v*, 46*r*–48*v*, 75*v*, 87*v*, 97*v*, 157*v*, 158*v*, 161*v*, 168*r*, 233*v*, 279*v*, 318*v*, 345*v*, 351*v*, 379*v*, 386*v*–387*v*, 394*r*–*v*, 414*v*, 415*v*; leather building.

1*r*–6*r*	*commissiones ecclesiarum* June 1347–Dec. 1349
7*r*–14*v*	*commissiones officiariorum* (appointment of officials etc., *ad hoc* commissions) June 1347–Jan. 1349
15*r*–17*v*	*commissiones ad instanciam* (commissions to hear causes, hold inquiries etc.) June 1347–Apr. 1349
18*r*–19*v*	memoranda Sept. 1348–Apr. 1349
20*r*–23*v*	*commissiones diverse* Dec. 1348–May 1349
24*r*–v	archiepiscopal mandates July–Sept. 1347
25*r*–30*r*	foundations of chantries Dec. 1347–Sept. 1348
30*v*, 32*r*	injunctions for Lincoln cathedral Feb. 1348
33*r*	*liber incarceratorum* (as in Bek's register) [ ] 1347–Aug. 1348
35*r*–44*r*	commissions and memoranda (in chronological confusion) Apr. 1348–July 1350
58*r*–153*v*	institutions, Lincoln archdeaconry (8 folios of memoranda at the beginning) Apr. 1349–July 1362
154*r*–173*v*	institutions, Stow archdeaconry Sept. 1347–July 1362
174*r*–239*v*	institutions, Northampton archdeaconry June 1347–July 1362
240*r*–279*r*	institutions, Oxford archdeaconry Sept. 1347–July 1362
280*r*–322*v*	institutions, Buckingham archdeaconry June 1347–July 1362
323*r*–338*v*	documents relating to the foundation of Newarke College, Leicester
339*r*–379*r*	institutions, Leicester archdeaconry June 1347–July 1362
380*r*–414*r*	institutions, Huntingdon archdeaconry July 1347–June 1362
415*r*	register of Bishop Gynwell as vicar-general of the archdeacon of Richmond July–Sept. 1348
416*r*–442*v*	institutions, Bedford archdeaconry Oct. 1347–July 1362
443*r*–446*v*	collations of dignities and prebends Mar. 1349 (*recte*)–Feb. 1362

The institutions in the Black Death period are studied by A. Hamilton Thompson, 'The Registers of John Gynewell, Bishop of Lincoln, for the years 1349–1350' in *Archaeological Journal* 68 (1911), 301–60. For Newarke College (fos. 323–38) see A. Hamilton Thompson, *The History of the Hospital and the New College of the Annunciation of St. Mary in the Newarke, Leicester* (Leicester, 1937), also *A.A.S.R.* 32 (1913–14), 245–92, 515–68; 33 (1915–16), 178–215, 412–72. The contents of fo. 415*r* are noted in *Yorkshire Archaeological Journal* 25 (1920), 163.

3. LAO, Episcopal Register IXB. Parchment register: 14″ × 9″; fos. 66 + 10 (paper) + 28, foliated 1–104; blank: fo. 68*v*; limp parchment covers.

1*r*–104*v*	royal writs June 1347–May 1362

4. LAO, Episcopal Register IXC. Parchment register; 13½″ × 9″; fos. 33, paginated 1–66; blank: pp. 36, 38, 48, 66; limp parchment covers (loose).

1–4	licences for study and to farm churches June 1347–Apr. 1350
5–12	licences *standi in obsequiis* and for absences June 1347–Apr. 1350
13–20	licences to celebrate in oratories June 1347–June 1348
21–32	royal writs *temp.* Bishop Buckingham Nov. 1371–June 1374 (pp. 21–4 should come between pp. 28 and 29, but have been misbound)
33–37	dispensations *cum ex eo* June 1347–Nov. 1350
39–47	licences to choose confessors and penitentiaries June 1347–Mar. 1350
49–58	licences to celebrate in oratories (cont.) July 1348–Sept. 1350
59–65	dispensations for illegitimacy Jan. 1348–Mar. 1350

Inside the back cover is a contemporary note of commissions for receiving criminous clerks; inside the front cover is a similar note about rights of penitentiaries and what they may deal with. The cover contains the title *Liber dispensationum*.

5. LAO, Episcopal Register IXD. Parchment register, unbound and unsewn; 13½″ × 9¼″; fos. 114, foliated 1–114; blank: fos. 4*v*, 11*v*–12*r*, 28*v*, 36*v*, 46*v*, 50*v*, 52*v*, 61*v*, 106*v*, 114*v*; limp parchment covers (loose).

There is at least one folio lost at the beginning, as the present first folio begins half-way through an ordination list.

1*r*–106*r*	ordinations Mar. 1348 (first datable entry)–June 1362
107*r*–114*r*	ordinations *sede vacante* Sept. 1362–May 1363

For further 1362–3 vacancy acts see below.

VACANCY 1362–1363

LPL, register of Archbishop Simon Islip, fos. 227*r*–229*r*.

Lincoln vacancy business Aug. 1362–June 1363 (with acquittances to Apr. 1365)

Institutions are calendared (by archdeaconry and place) in *Lambeth Institutions*.

JOHN BUCKINGHAM (1363–1398)

1. LAO, Episcopal Register X. Parchment register: 14″ × 10½″; fos. 462, foliated 1–462; blank: fo. 155*v*; leather binding.

1*r*–126*v*	institutions, Lincoln archdeaconry July 1362–Sept. 1383
127*r*–152*v*	institutions, Stow archdeaconry Jan. 1364–Dec. 1384
153*r*–155*r*	collations of dignities and prebends June–Nov. 1363
156*r*–230*v*	institutions, Northampton archdeaconry June 1363–Aug. 1383
231*r*–282*v*	institutions, Leicester archdeaconry July 1363–Nov. 1383
283*r*–334*v*	institutions, Huntingdon archdeaconry June 1363–Sept. 1383

335*r*–378*v*	institutions, Oxford archdeaconry June 1363–Aug. 1382
379*r*–406*v*	institutions, Bedford archdeaconry June 1363–Feb. 1386
407*r*–462*v*	institutions, Buckingham archdeaconry Aug. 1363–Jan. 1384

The last entries of the Stow and Buckingham archdeaconry sections are unfinished and reflect the later arbitrary binding of the sections. Fo. 462*v* should be followed immediately by fo. 376*r* of Episcopal Register XI. Although the Stow archdeaconry section of the latter register also begins in mid-entry (fo. 96*r*), it does not follow directly on fo. 152*v* above.

2. LAO, Episcopal Register XI. Parchment register; 13½″ × 10¾″; fos. 442, foliated [i], 1–94, 94A, 95–175, 178–239, 241–287, 289–340, 342–445; blank: fos. 62*r*, 121*v*, 292*r*, 340*v*, 342*r*–*v*, 373*v*–374*r*, 426*v*, 431*v*, 445*v*; hide-covered binding.

1*r*–93*v*	institutions, Lincoln archdeaconry Sept. 1383–Feb. 1398
94*r*–95*v*	16th-cent. place index (Lincoln)
96*r*–120*r*	institutions, Stow archdeaconry Jan. 1385–Apr. 1398
120*v*–121*r*	16th-cent. place index (Stow)
122*r*–191*v*	institutions, Northampton archdeaconry Aug. 1383–May 1398
192*r*–193*v*	16th-cent. place index (Northampton)
194*r*–238*r*	institutions, Leicester archdeaconry Dec. 1383–May 1398
238*v*–239*v*	16th-cent. place index (Leicester)
241*r*–290*r*	institutions, Huntingdon archdeaconry Sept. 1383–June 1398
290*v*–291*v*	16th-cent. place index (Huntingdon)
292*v*–293*v*	16th-cent. place index (Oxford)
294*r*–340*r*	institutions, Oxford archdeaconry Oct. 1382–June 1398
343*r*–*v*	16th-cent. place index (Bedford)
344*r*–373*r*	institutions, Bedford archdeaconry Jan. 1386–June 1398
374*v*–375*v*	16th-cent. place index (Buckingham)
376*r*–426*r*	institutions, Buckingham archdeaconry Feb. 1384–June 1398
427*r*–432*r*	commissions July 1389–Aug. 1394
432*r*–445*r*	collations of dignities and prebends Feb. 1390–Apr. 1398

3. LAO, Episcopal Register XII. Parchment register; 13¼″ × 10¼″; fos. iii (paper) + i + 482 + x (paper, index) + i, foliated [i–iv], 1–16, 18–23, 25–497 (including inserts); blank: fos. 373*v*, 469*r*–*v*, 487*v*, 497*v* and the dorses of the inserts; hide-covered binding.

1*r*–468*v*	memoranda June 1363–July 1398
470*r*–481*v*	visitation of Lincoln cathedral Jan. 1394–May 1395
482*r*–487*r*	documents relating to Bishop Buckingham's chantry June 1387–Nov. 1397
488*r*–499*r*	late 16th-cent. index of contents

For royal writs 1371–4 see above, Episcopal Register IXC, pp. 21–32.

HENRY BEAUFORT (1398–1404)

LAO, Episcopal Register XIII. Parchment register; 13¾″ × 11″; fos. iv (paper) + 67 + ii (paper) + 267 + iii (paper), foliated 1–339 (including inserts); blank: fos. 69*r*–70*v*, 184*v*, 206*v*, 245*v*, 261*v*, 314*v*, 339*v*; hide-covered binding.

1*r*–68*v*	memoranda (in chronological sequence, but with additional documents entered at the end of the section) Aug. 1398–Dec. 1404
71*r*–81*v*	royal writs Sept. 1398–Dec. 1404
82*r*–118*v*	ordinations Sept. 1398–Mar. 1405
119*r*–175*v*	institutions, Lincoln archdeaconry Aug. 1398–Mar. 1405
176*r*–184*r*	institutions, Stow archdeaconry July 1398–Mar. 1405
185*r*–206*r*	institutions, Leicester archdeaconry Apr. 1398–Feb. 1405
207*r*–245*r*	institutions, Northampton archdeaconry July 1398–Mar. 1405

246*r*–261*r*	institutions, Bedford archdeaconry July 1398–Feb. 1405
262*r*–284*v*	institutions, Huntingdon archdeaconry Sept. 1398–Mar. 1405
285*r*–314*r*	institutions, Buckingham archdeaconry Sept. 1398–Feb. 1405
315*r*–332*v*	institutions, Oxford archdeaconry July 1398–Jan. 1405
333*r*–339*r*	collations of dignities and prebends Mar. 1399–Feb. 1405

VACANCY 1405

LPL, register of Archbishop Thomas Arundel, volume I, fo. 468*v*.

Lincoln vacancy accounts (after the actual vacancy) Aug. 1405–Jan. 1406

PHILIP REPINGDON (1405–1419)
VACANCY 1419–1420

1. LAO, Episcopal Register XIV. Parchment register; 13½″ × 10¼″; fos. ii (modern endpapers) + iv (paper) + 495 + ii (paper) + iii (modern endpapers), foliated 1–205, 208–256, 256A, 257–270, 270A, 271–364, 364A, 365–373, 375, 378–497; blank: fos. 281*v*, 321*v*, 373*v*; leather binding.

1*r*–103*r*	institutions, Lincoln archdeaconry Apr. 1405–Feb. 1420
103*v*–104*v*	institutions *sede vacante*, Lincoln archdeaconry Feb.–May 1420
105*r*–137*v*	institutions, Stow archdeaconry June 1405–Jan. 1420
138*r*–204*v*	institutions, Leicester archdeaconry May 1405–Jan. 1420
205*r*–*v*	institutions *sede vacante*, Leicester archdeaconry Feb.–May 1420
208*r*–280*r*	institutions, Northampton archdeaconry Apr. 1405–Jan. 1420
280*v*–281*r*	institutions *sede vacante*, Northampton archdeaconry Feb.–May 1420
282*r*–320*v*	institutions, Bedford archdeaconry Apr. 1405–Jan. 1420
320*v*–321*r*	institutions *sede vacante*, Bedford archdeaconry Mar.–May 1420
322*r*–372*r*	institutions, Huntingdon archdeaconry Apr. 1405–Jan. 1420
372*v*–373*r*	institutions *sede vacante*, Huntingdon archdeaconry Feb.–Apr. 1420
375*r*–424*r*	institutions, Oxford archdeaconry Apr. 1405–Jan. 1420
424*r*–*v*	institutions *sede vacante*, Oxford archdeaconry Mar.–May 1420
425*r*–473*r*	institutions, Buckingham archdeaconry Apr. 1405–Jan. 1420
473*v*	institutions *sede vacante*, Buckingham archdeaconry Apr. 1420
474*r*–497*r*	collations of dignities and prebends Mar. 1405–Jan. 1420
497*v*	institutions to prebends *sede vacante* Apr. 1420

2. LAO, Episcopal Register XV. Parchment register; 14″ × 11¼″; fos. iv (paper) + 80 + 15 (12¼″ × 8½″) + 112, foliated 1–207; blank: fos. 81*v*, 95*v*; hide-covered binding.

1*r*–207*v*	memoranda May 1405–Nov. 1419

Fos. 1*r*–100*v* are printed in *The Register of Bishop Philip Repingdon, 1405–1419*, ed. M. Archer (2 vols, Lincoln Record Society 57, 58, 1963). The two final volumes of this edition are expected to be published in the early 1980s.

3. LAO, Episcopal Register XVB. Parchment register; 13½″ × 10½″; fos. 12 (loose quires), paginated [A–D], 1–20; no binding.

[A–D], 1–20	royal writs (not in strictly chronological order. The three quires constituting this register do not follow on continuously) Mar. 1405–Jan. 1416

[A–D], formerly in the miscellaneous rolls section of the diocesan archives, was transferred here when identified.

VACANCY 1419–1420

LPL, register of Archbishop Henry Chichele, volume I, fos. 105*v*–110*r* *passim*.

Lincoln vacancy business Jan.–May 1420, among the general section of Canterbury institutions.

Printed, *Register of Henry Chichele* i, pp. 177–82 *passim*.

VACANCY 1419–1420
RICHARD FLEMING (1420–1424; 1425–1431)[10]
VACANCY 1424–1425

LAO, Episcopal Register XVI. Parchment register; 14″ × 11″; fos. iii (paper) + 223 + iv (paper), foliated 1–5, 9–35, 41–43, 49–85, 88–117, 120–123, 123A, 124–128, 131–145, 147–159, 163–165, 169–204, 208–251; blank: fos. 5*r*, 29*v*, 35*v*, 72*v*, 85*v*, 145*v*, 159*v*, 182*r*, 200*r*, 204*v*, 239*v*; hide-covered binding.

1*r*–4*v*	*sede vacante* register (commissions and wills) Dec. 1419–Apr. 1421
5*v*	royal writs June–July 1420
9*r*–25*v*	institutions, Lincoln archdeaconry June 1420–May 1424
26*r*–28*r*	institutions, Lincoln archdeaconry, by Archbishop of Canterbury's Official *ratione visitationis* Feb.–June 1425
28*v*–29*r*	institutions *sede vacante*, Lincoln archdeaconry July–Oct. 1425
30*r*–35*r*	institutions, Lincoln archdeaconry June 1427–Jan. 1431
41*r*–43*v*	institutions, Stow archdeaconry June 1420–Feb. 1424
49*r*–71*r*	institutions, Northampton archdeaconry July 1420–May 1424
71*v*–72*r*	institutions, Northampton archdeaconry, by the Archbishop's Official *ratione visitationis* Mar.–June 1425
73*r*–85*r*	institutions, Northampton archdeaconry June 1427–Dec. 1430
88*r*–102*v*	institutions, Leicester archdeaconry June 1420–May 1424
103*r*–*v*	institutions, Leicester archdeaconry, by the Archbishop's Official *ratione visitationis* Apr.–June 1425
104*r*–116*v*	institutions, Huntingdon archdeaconry July 1420–May 1424
117*r*–*v*	institutions, Huntingdon archdeaconry, by the Archbishop's Official *ratione visitationis* Mar.–June 1425
120*r*–128*v*	institutions, Bedford archdeaconry June 1420–May 1424
131*r*–144*v*	institutions, Oxford archdeaconry May 1420–Apr. 1424
145*r*	institutions, Oxford archdeaconry, by the Archbishop's Official *ratione visitationis* Mar.–Apr. 1425
147*r*–158*v*	institutions, Buckingham archdeaconry June 1420–May 1424
159*r*	institutions, Buckingham archdeaconry, by the Archbishop's Official *ratione visitationis* Mar.–Apr. 1425
163*r*–165*v*	collations of dignities and prebends July 1420–Feb. 1424
169*r*–187*r*	ordinations May 1420–Apr. 1424
187*r*–188*v*	ordinations by authority of the Archbishop of Canterbury *ratione visitationis* May 1424–Mar. 1425
189*r*–193*r*	acts of the Archbishop *ratione visitationis* (mainly institutions) Apr.–June 1425
193*v*–195*v*	ordinations *ratione visitationis* Mar.–June 1425
196*r*–198*v*	institutions *ratione visitationis* Mar.–Apr. 1425
199*r*–*v*	ordinations *sede vacante* June 1425 (with note about ordinations held in Oct. 1425)
200*v*–204*r*	ordinations Feb. 1426–Sept. 1427

[10] Richard Fleming was translated to the archbishopric of York in 1424 but, following objections, was re-translated to Lincoln in 1425. In the intervening vacancy period, an archiepiscopal visitation of the diocese was undertaken.

208*r*–237*v*, memoranda Mar. 1420–Mar. 1424 (*recte*)
240*r*–247*v* (It is likely there is some misbinding. It seems probable that fos. 240–247 should come between fos. 215 and 216. There is in any case some slight chronological confusion)
238*r*–239*r* memoranda *sede vacante* July–Sept. 1425
248*r*–251*v* royal writs June 1420–Oct. 1423 (see also above fo. 5*v*)

Various monastic visitation injunctions and related documents, taken chiefly from the memoranda section of this volume, are printed in *Visitations of Religious Houses in the diocese of Lincoln, vol. I: injunctions and other documents from the Registers of Richard Flemyng and William Gray, Bishops of Lincoln, A.D. MCCCCXX–MCCCCXXXVI*, ed. A. Hamilton Thompson (Lincoln Record Society 7, 1914, and Canterbury and York Society 17, 1915). Archbishop Chichele's register also contains a section relating to acts in the Lincoln diocese *ratione visitationis* (see below). Fos. 208*r*–251*v* have been calendared by Mr N. Bennett (LAO, MCD. 1130).

VACANCY 1424–1425

1. LPL, register of Archbishop Henry Chichele, volume I, fo. 150*r*–*v*.

   Lincoln vacancy business May–June 1424, among the general section of Canterbury institutions

   Printed, *Register of Henry Chichele* i, pp. 218–19 *passim*.

2. LPL, *ibid.*, volume I, fos. 240*r*–263*v*.

   institutions in the Lincoln diocese *ratione visitationis* June 1424–Jan. 1426

   Printed, *ibid.*, pp. 320–48.

3. LPL, *ibid.*, volume II, fos. 397*v*–400*v*.

   ordinations in the Lincoln diocese *ratione visitationis* June 1424–Sept. 1425

   Printed, *ibid.*, iv, pp. 360–7.

4. LPL, *ibid.*, volume II, fos. 401*v*–403*r*.

   ordinations *sede vacante* Sept. 1425

   Printed, *ibid.*, pp. 370–3.

VACANCY 1431

1. LPL, register of Archbishop Henry Chichele, volume I, fos. 187*v*–193*r* *passim*.

   Lincoln vacancy business Feb.–Nov. 1431, among the general section of Canterbury institutions

   Printed, *Register of Henry Chichele* i, pp. 269–74 *passim*.

2. LPL, *ibid.*, volume II, fos. 407*r*–408*r*.

   ordinations *sede vacante* May 1431

   Printed, *ibid.*, iv, pp. 380–3.

WILLIAM GRAY (1431–1436)

LAO, Episcopal Register XVII. Parchment register; $14\frac{1}{4}'' \times 11\frac{1}{4}''$; fos. iii (paper) + 199 + iv (paper), foliated 1–14, 16–18, 20–54, 56–65, 68–72, 75–86, 88, 89, 100–119, 121–125, 128–143, 145–221; blank: fos. 18*v*, 36*v*, 86*v*, 143*v*, 188*v*, 195*v*; hide-covered binding.

1*r*–14*v*	institutions, Lincoln archdeaconry Aug. 1431–Feb. 1436
16*r*–18*r*	institutions, Stow archdeaconry May 1432–Aug. 1435
20*r*–36*r*	institutions, Northampton archdeaconry Aug. 1431–Jan. 1436
37*r*–44*v*	institutions, Leicester archdeaconry Nov. 1431–Feb. 1436
45*r*–54*v*	institutions, Buckingham archdeaconry Sept. 1431–Jan. 1436
56*r*–65*v*	institutions, Oxford archdeaconry Aug. 1431–Jan. 1436
68*r*–72*v*	institutions, Bedford archdeaconry Sept. 1431–Jan. 1436
75*r*–81*v*	institutions, Huntingdon archdeaconry Sept. 1431–Jan. 1436
83*r*–86*r*	collations of dignities and prebends Oct. 1431–Nov. 1435
88*r*–119*v*, 145*r*–188*r*	memoranda (confused arrangement and there is some misbinding) Aug. 1431–Jan. 1436
121*r*–125*r*	visitation of Lincoln cathedral Apr.–Sept. 1432
128*r*–*v*	injunctions for Crowland abbey n.d.
129*r*–143*r*	proceedings against the dean and chapter of Lincoln Oct. 1433–May 1435
189*r*–195*r*	royal writs Sept. 1431–July 1435
196*r*–203*v*	injunctions to religious houses (last entry incomplete) n.d.
204*r*–221*v*	ordinations Sept. 1431–Jan. 1436

Fos. 121*r*–125*r*, 128*r*–*v*, 196*r*–203*v* are printed in *Visitations of Religious Houses, vol. I: 1420–1436.*

VACANCY 1436–1437

LPL, register of Archbishop Henry Chichele, volume I, fos. 50*v*, 209*v*–215*r passim.*

Lincoln vacancy business Feb. 1436–Feb. 1437, among the general section of Canterbury institutions, and the section concerning appointments of bishops etc.

Printed, *Register of Henry Chichele* i, pp. 116–17, 290–6 *passim.*

WILLIAM ALNWICK (1437–1449)

LAO, Episcopal Register XVIII. Parchment register; $13\frac{1}{2}'' \times 10\frac{3}{4}''$; fos. iii (paper) + 189 + iv (paper), foliated 1–25, 28–77, 80–111, 113–170, 172–195; blank: fos. 106*v*, 111*r*, 114*v*, 190*v*, 195*v*; hide-covered binding.

1*r*–77*v*	memoranda (incomplete and in considerable confusion) Feb. 1437–Feb. 1449
80*r*–106*r*	institutions, Lincoln archdeaconry Jan. 1438–Oct. 1449
107*r*–111*r*	collations of dignities and prebends July 1438–Oct. 1444
113*r*–114*r*	institutions, Stow archdeaconry Apr. 1439–May 1445
115*r*–144*v*	institutions Northampton archdeaconry (some additional entries at end) Apr. 1437–Nov. 1449
145*r*–163*v*	institutions, Leicester archdeaconry (the earliest entries are *temp.* Bishop Gray and the latest *temp.* Bishop Lumley) Mar. 1435–Feb. 1450
164*r*–170*v*	institutions, Huntingdon archdeaconry (the latest entries are *temp.* Bishop Lumley) Mar. 1439–Mar. 1450
172*v*–180*v*	institutions, Oxford archdeaconry (last entry incomplete) Apr. 1439–Nov. 1449
181*r*–190*r*	institutions, Bedford archdeaconry Sept. 1439–Mar. 1449
191*r*–195*r*	institutions, Buckingham archdeaconry Mar. 1438–Sept. 1449

VACANCY 1449–1450

LPL, register of Archbishop John Stafford, fos. 101*v*–104*r passim.*

Lincoln vacancy business Dec. 1449–Mar. 1450, among the general section of Canterbury institutions

Institutions are calendared (by archdeaconry and place) in *Lambeth Institutions.*

VACANCY 1449–1450
MARMADUKE LUMLEY (1450)
VACANCY 1450–1452

LAO, Episcopal Register XIX. Parchment register; $12\frac{3}{4}'' \times 10''$ (fos. 1–33), $12\frac{3}{4}'' \times 9\frac{1}{2}''$ (fos. 34–72), $13\frac{1}{2}'' \times 11''$ (fos. 73–83), $14'' \times 11\frac{1}{4}''$ (fos. 84–166); fos. iv (paper)+80+ii (paper)+81+iv (paper), foliated i, 1–26, 28–34, 37, 39–41, 43–55, 55A, 56–166; blank: fos. i*v*, 5*v*, 6*r*, 17*v*, 24*v*, 26*v*, 41*v*, 83*r*–85*v*, 86*v*–90*v*, 126*v*, 139*r*–*v*, 165*v*–166*v*; hide-covered binding.

i*r*	ordinations Apr. 1452 (begins in mid-entry)	
1*r*–9*v*	*sede vacante* register	
	1*r*	register heading
	1*v*–2*v*	institutions, Lincoln archdeaconry (in some confusion) Dec. 1449–Mar. 1450
	3*r*–*v*	institutions, Northampton archdeaconry Dec. 1449–Mar. 1450
	4*r*	institutions, Buckingham archdeaconry Jan.–Mar. 1450
	4*r*	institutions, Bedford archdeaconry Jan.–Feb. 1450
	4*v*–5*r*	union of chapels of Great and Little Newton dependent on Geddington Mar. 1450
	6*v*–9*v*	ordinations Dec. 1449–Feb. 1450
10*r*–26*v*	register of Bishop Marmaduke Lumley	
	10*r*–11*v*	ordinations Mar. 1450 (on fo. 11*v* a note of a vacancy ordination Apr. 1451)
	12*r*–14*v*	memoranda Mar.–Nov. 1450
	15*r*–17*r*	ordinations Apr.–Sept. 1450
	18*r*–20*v*	institutions, Lincoln archdeaconry Mar.–Oct. 1450
	20*v*–22*r*	institutions, Northampton archdeaconry Mar.–Nov. 1450
	22*v*–23*r*	institutions, Oxford archdeaconry Mar.–Oct. 1450
	23*r*–*v*	institutions, Huntingdon archdeaconry Sept.–Nov. 1450
	23*v*–24*r*	institutions, Buckingham archdeaconry May–Nov. 1450
	25*r*–26*r*	unions of benefices May 1450
28*r*–82*v*	*sede vacante* register	
	28*r*–37*v*	ordinations Dec. 1450–Apr. 1452 (fos. 34, 37 constitute a loose bifolium; fo. 34*r*–*v* is a copy of entries on fo. 33*v*; fo. 37*v* a partial copy of fo. i*r*)
	39*r*–50*v*	memoranda Dec. 1450–Mar. 1452 (includes 1 document of Aug. 1450)
	51*r*–53*v*	register heading, and institutions Dec. 1450–Feb. 1451
	54*r*–*v*	will Feb. 1451
	55*r*–59*v*	ordinations (copy of fos. 28*r*–32*r*) Dec. 1450–Apr. 1451
	59*v*–63*r*	institutions Mar.–July 1451
	63*v*	ordinations (copy of fo. 33*r*) June 1451
	64*r*–67*v*	institutions Aug.–Dec. 1451
	68*r*–*v*	ordinations (copy of fo. 32*v*) Sept. 1451
	69*r*–72*v*	institutions Dec. 1451–May 1452
	73*r*–82*v*	copy of the above, institutions only Dec. 1450–Mar. 1452

The remainder of this register (fos. 91*r*–164*v*) contains acts of Bishops Bullingham, Cooper and Wickham and the vacancy register of 1595 and is described below in the appropriate chronological sequence.

VACANCY 1450–1452

LPL, register of Archbishop John Stafford, fos. 107*r*–109*v* *passim.*

Lincoln vacancy business Dec. 1450–Mar. 1451, among the general section of Canterbury institutions

Institutions are calendared (by archdeaconry and place) in *Lambeth Institutions.*

JOHN CHEDWORTH (1452–1471)
VACANCY 1471–1472

LAO, Episcopal Register XX. Parchment register; $14\frac{1}{4}'' \times 11\frac{1}{2}''$; fos. iv (paper) + 112 + ii (paper) + 212 + iii (paper), foliated 1–324; blank: fos. 72*v*, 112*v*–114*v*, 199*v*–201*v*, 203*v*, 245*r*, 250*v*–251*r*, 322*v*, 323*v*–324*v*; hide-covered binding.

1*r*–112*r*	memoranda (including a few later documents added at the end) May 1452–Oct. 1471
115*r*–117*r*	place index (Lincoln)
117*r*–155*r*	institutions, Lincoln archdeaconry July 1452–Nov. 1471
155*v*–156*v*	institutions *sede vacante*, Lincoln archdeaconry Dec. 1471–Mar. 1472
156*v*	place index (Stow)
157*r*–162*v*	institutions, Stow archdeaconry Aug. 1452–Oct. 1471
163*r*–*v*	composition for the vicarage of Horncastle Oct. 1467 (copy of 1606)
164*r*–196*r*	institutions, Northampton archdeaconry July 1452–Nov. 1471
196*v*–197*r*	institutions *sede vacante*, Northampton archdeaconry Dec. 1471–Mar. 1472
197*v*–199*r*	place index (Northampton)
202*r*–203*r*	place index (Leicester)
204*r*–225*r*	institutions, Leicester archdeaconry June 1452–Oct. 1471
225*v*–226*r*	institutions *sede vacante*, Leicester archdeaconry Dec. 1471–Mar. 1472
226*v*–227*v*	place index (Oxford)
228*r*–249*v*	institutions, Oxford archdeaconry June 1452–Nov. 1471
249*v*–250*r*	institutions *sede vacante*, Oxford archdeaconry Dec. 1471–Jan. 1472
251*v*–252*v*	place index (Buckingham)
253*r*–275*v*	institutions, Buckingham archdeaconry June 1452–Nov. 1471
275*v*–276*v*	institutions *sede vacante*, Buckingham archdeaconry Dec. 1471–Mar. 1472
277*r*–295*r*	institutions, Bedford archdeaconry June 1452–Nov. 1471
295*r*–*v*	institutions *sede vacante*, Bedford archdeaconry Dec. 1471–Mar. 1472
296*r*–*v*	place index (Bedford)
297*r*–*v*	place index (Huntingdon)
298*r*–315*v*	institutions, Huntingdon archdeaconry June 1452–Oct. 1471
315*v*	institutions *sede vacante*, Huntingdon archdeaconry Jan. 1472
316*r*–322*r*	collations of dignities and prebends June 1452–Sept. 1471
323*r*	royal writs June 1452

THOMAS ROTHERHAM (1472–1480)

LAO, Episcopal Register XXI. Parchment register; $14'' \times 10\frac{3}{4}''$; fos. iv (paper) + 188 + iv (paper), foliated i–ii, 1–27, 30–35, 38–58, 62–90, 93–106, 109–123, 125–198; blank: fos. 30*r*, 58*v*, 77*v*, 90*v*, 106*v*, 123*v*, 125*v*, 172*r*, 180*r*–*v*, 183*v*, 192*v*–193*v*, 198*r*–*v*; hide-covered binding.

i*v*–ii*v*	place index (Lincoln)
1*r*–27*v*	institutions, Lincoln archdeaconry Mar. 1472–Aug. 1480
30*v*	place index (Stow)
31*r*–35*v*	institutions, Stow archdeaconry Oct. 1472–Aug. 1480
38*r*–*v*	place index (Northampton)
39*r*–58*r*	institutions, Northampton archdeaconry Apr. 1472–Sept. 1480
62*r*–*v*	place index (Leicester)
63*r*–77*r*	institutions, Leicester archdeaconry May 1472–Aug. 1480
78*r*–*v*	place index (Oxford)
79*r*–90*r*	institutions, Oxford archdeaconry Apr. 1472–July 1480
93*r*–*v*	place index (Buckingham)
94*r*–106*r*	institutions, Buckingham archdeaconry Apr. 1472–Sept. 1480
109*r*–*v*	place index (Huntingdon)
110*r*–123*r*	institutions, Huntingdon archdeaconry Apr. 1472–Sept. 1480
125*r*	place index (Bedford)
126*r*–133*v*	institutions, Bedford archdeaconry Apr. 1472–July 1480
134*r*–171*v*	ordinations Mar. 1472–May 1480
172*v*	contents table to memoranda
173*r*–197*v*	memoranda (in considerable confusion) Apr. 1472–Nov. (*sic*) 1480

JOHN RUSSELL (1480–1494)

LAO, Episcopal Register XXII. Parchment register; $14\frac{1}{2}'' \times 11\frac{1}{4}''$; fos. iv (paper) + 119 + ii (paper) + 163 + iv (paper), foliated 1–281; blank: fos. 92*v*, 119*v*–121*v*, 122*v*–123*r*, 161*r*–*v*, 168*v*–169*r*, 202*v*, 273*v*; hide-covered binding.

1*r*–54*v*	ordinations Sept. 1480–Sept. 1494
55*r*–118*v*	memoranda (in confused arrangement) Sept. 1480–Sept. 1494
118*v*–119*r*	contents table to memoranda
123*v*–124*v*	place index (Lincoln)
125*r*–160*v*	institutions, Lincoln archdeaconry Sept. 1480–Dec. 1494
161*r*	place index (Stow)
162*r*–168*r*	institutions, Stow archdeaconry Sept. 1480–Apr. 1494
169*v*–170*v*	place index (Northampton)
171*r*–201*r*	institutions, Northampton archdeaconry Oct. 1480–Nov. 1494
201*v*–202*r*	place index (Leicester)
203*r*–218*v*	institutions, Leicester archdeaconry Sept. 1480–Dec. 1494
219*r*–233*v*	institutions, Oxford archdeaconry Nov. 1480–Aug. 1494
233*v*–234*v*	place index (Oxford)
235*v*–249*v*	institutions, Buckingham archdeaconry Oct. 1480–Dec. 1494
250*r*–*v*	place index (Buckingham)
251*r*–263*v*	institutions, Huntingdon archdeaconry Sept. 1480–Nov. 1494
263*v*–264*v*	place index (Huntingdon)
265*r*–*v*	place index (Bedford)
266*r*–273*r*	institutions, Bedford archdeaconry Nov. 1480–Nov. 1494
274*r*–281*v*	collations of dignities and prebends Sept. 1480–Dec. 1494

VACANCY 1494–1496

1. LPL, register of Archbishop John Morton, volume I, fos. 94*r*–117*v*.

   Lincoln vacancy business Jan. 1495–Feb. 1496 (an entry on fo. 105*r* dated Oct. 1498 should presumably read Oct. 1495)

2. LPL, *ibid.*, volume II, fos. 157*v*–160*r passim.*

   Lincoln vacancy business Feb. 1495–Jan. 1496, among the general section of Canterbury institutions.

Calendared in C. Harper-Bill, 'An edition of the register of John Morton, archbishop of Canterbury, 1486–1500' (London University Ph.D., 1977). Institutions are calendared (by archdeaconry and place) in *Lambeth Institutions.*

VACANCY 1494–1496
WILLIAM SMITH (1495–1514)

1. LAO, Episcopal Register XXIII. Parchment register; $14\frac{1}{4}'' \times 11''$; fos. iv (paper)+ii (parchment covers)+409+iii (paper), foliated i, 1–103, 112–117, 104–111, 118–408; blank: fos. i*r*–*v*, 3*v*, 13*v*, 15*v*, 270*r*–*v*, 308*r*, 349*v*, 351*v*, 384*r*–*v*; hide-covered binding.

1*r*–15*r*	*sede vacante* register	
	1*r*–3*r*	general acts Jan. 1495
	4*r*–7*r*	institutions, Lincoln archdeaconry Jan. 1495–Jan. 1496 (with additional entry Feb. 1499 at end)
	7*v*	institutions, Stow archdeaconry Mar.–Dec. 1495
	8*r*–*v*	institutions, Northampton archdeaconry Mar.–Nov. 1495
	9*r*–*v*	institutions, Leicester archdeaconry Mar. 1495–Jan. 1496 (with additional entry Jan. 1499)
	10*r*–*v*	institutions, Oxford archdeaconry Mar.–July 1495 (with additional entry Oct. 1498)
	10*v*	institutions, Bedford archdeaconry July 1495
	11*r*–12*v*	institutions, Huntingdon archdeaconry Mar. 1495–Jan. 1496
	13*r*	institutions, Buckingham archdeaconry Mar.–Dec. 1495
	14*r*–15*r*	place index to institutions, arranged by archdeaconry
16*r*–408*v*	register of Bishop William Smith	
	16*r*–29*r*	collations of dignities and prebends Apr. 1496–Oct. 1513
	29*v*–31*v*	place index (Lincoln)
	32*r*–147*r*	institutions, Lincoln archdeaconry Feb. 1496–Dec. 1513
	147*r*–*v*	place index (Stow)
	148*r*–160*v*	institutions, Stow archdeaconry July 1496–Aug. 1513
	161*r*–162*v*	place index (Northampton)
	163*r*–225*r*	institutions, Northampton archdeaconry Feb. 1496–Dec. 1513
	225*v*–226*v*	place index (Leicester)
	227*r*–268*v*	institutions, Leicester archdeaconry Mar. 1496–Aug. 1513
	269*r*–270*r*	place index (Oxford)
	271*r*–307*v*	institutions, Oxford archdeaconry Mar. 1496–Dec. 1513
	308*v*–309*v*	place index (Buckingham)
	310*r*–349*r*	institutions, Buckingham archdeaconry Mar. 1496–Sept. 1513
	350*r*–351*r*	place index (Huntingdon)
	352*r*–382*v*	institutions, Huntingdon archdeaconry Apr. 1496–Aug. 1513
	383*r*–*v*	place index (Bedford)
	385*r*–408*v*	institutions, Bedford archdeaconry Mar. 1496–July 1513

2. LAO, Episcopal Register XXIV. Parchment register; 15″ × $10\frac{3}{4}$″; fos. iv (paper) + 335 + vi (paper, 12″ × 8″, later general contents table) + iii (paper), foliated 1–335; blank: fos. 94*v*, 131*v*–132*r*, 199*v*; hide-covered binding.

1*r*–94*r*	ordinations Feb. 1496–Dec. 1513
95*r*	settlement by Bishop John White of a dispute at Brasenose College, Oxford Jan. 1555
95*v*	record of the deprivation of Matthew Parker as dean of Lincoln Jan. 1555
96*r*–335*v*	memoranda (last entry incomplete) Nov. 1495–Jan. 1510

See also below, Episcopal Register XXV, fos. 102*r*–110*v* for further memoranda 1513.

VACANCY 1514

1. LPL, register of Archbishop William Warham, volume II, fos. 284*r*–286**r*.

Lincoln vacancy business Jan.–Mar. 1514

2. LPL, *ibid.*, fos. 352*v*–353*r passim*.

Lincoln vacancy business Jan.–Mar. 1514, among the general section of Canterbury institutions

Institutions are calendared (by archdeaconry and place) in *Lambeth Institutions*.

THOMAS WOLSEY (1514)
WILLIAM ATWATER (1514–1521)
VACANCY 1521

LAO, Episcopal Register XXV. Parchment register; $14\frac{1}{4}$″ × $11\frac{1}{4}$″; fos. 138 + vii (paper), foliated 1–138; blank: fos. 25*r*, 36*v*, 50*v*, 59*v*, 60*v*, 134*v*, 136*v*, 137*v*–138*v*; hide-covered binding.

1*r*–11*v*	register of Bishop Thomas Wolsey	
	1*r*	institutions, Stow archdeaconry June–Aug. 1514
	1*v*	place index (Northampton)
	2*r*–*v*	institutions, Northampton archdeaconry Apr.–Sept. 1514 (with 2 cancelled entries Oct. 1517)
	2*v*	place index (Leicester)
	3*r*–*v*	institutions, Leicester archdeaconry May–Aug. 1514 (with additional entry Mar. 1515)
	3*v*	place index (Bedford)
	4*r*	institutions, Bedford archdeaconry Apr.–Aug. 1514
	4*v*	place index (Buckingham)
	5*r*	institutions, Buckingham archdeaconry Mar.–June 1514
	5*v*	place index (Huntingdon)
	6*r*	institutions, Huntingdon archdeaconry Mar.–Oct. 1514
	6*v*	place index (Oxford)—*the institutions are missing*
	7*r*–11*v*	ordinations Mar.–Sept. 1514
12*r*–134*r*	register of Bishop William Atwater	
	12*r*–24*v*	institutions, Lincoln archdeaconry Dec. 1514–Jan. 1521
	25*v*	place index (Stow)
	26*r*–27*r*	institutions, Stow archdeaconry Nov. 1514–Jan. 1521
	27*r*–*v*	place index (Northampton)

	28*r*–35*v*	institutions, Northampton archdeaconry Jan. 1515–Nov. 1520
	36*r*	place index (Leicester)
	37*r*–42*v*	institutions, Leicester archdeaconry Dec. 1514–Jan. 1521 (fo. 42 should come between fos. 37 and 38)
	43*r*–*v*	place index (Oxford)
	44*r*–49*v*	institutions, Oxford archdeaconry Dec. 1514–Jan. 1521
	50*r*	place index (Buckingham)
	51*r*–55*r*	institutions, Buckingham archdeaconry Dec. 1514–Feb. 1521
	55*v*	place index (Huntingdon)
	56*r*–59*r*	institutions, Huntingdon archdeaconry Nov. 1514–Dec. 1520
	60*r*	place index (Bedford)
	61*r*–64*v*	institutions, Bedford archdeaconry May 1515–Nov. 1520
	65*r*–*v*	table of contents to memoranda
	66*r*–101*v*	memoranda (in considerable confusion, and including many copies of earlier documents) Jan. 1516–Nov. 1520
	102*r*–110*v*	memoranda *temp.* Bishop Smith July–Aug. 1513
	111*r*–134*r*	ordinations Dec. 1514–Dec. 1520
135*r*–137*r*	*sede vacante* register (see also below)	
	135*r*–136*r*	ordinations Feb.–Mar. 1521
	137*r*	institutions Feb.–Mar. 1521

VACANCY 1521

LPL, register of Archbishop William Warham, volume II, fos. 287*r*–291*v*.

Lincoln vacancy business Feb.–May 1521

Institutions are calendared (by archdeaconry and place) in *Lambeth Institutions*.

JOHN LONGLAND (1521–1547)
HENRY HOLBEACH (1547–1551)

1. LAO, Episcopal Register XXVI. Parchment register; $14\frac{1}{2}'' \times 11''$, except for fos. 47–50, $13\frac{1}{4}'' \times 9\frac{1}{2}''$; fos. iv (paper) + 310 + v (paper, index) + iv (paper), foliated 1–310; blank: fos. 16*v*, 55*r*, 67*r*–*v*, 149*v*, 290*v*; hide-covered binding.

1*r*–46*v*, 51*r*–66*v*	ordinations May 1521–Apr. 1547
47*r*–51*v*	injunctions for Newarke College, Leicester (after the 1525 visitation) n.d.
68*r*–310*v*	memoranda (in slight confusion at the end) May 1521–Nov. 1545

Fos. 47*r*–51*v* are printed in translation in A. Hamilton Thompson, *The History of the Hospital and the New College of the Annunciation of St. Mary in the Newarke, Leicester* (Leicester, 1937), pp. 183–96. Visitation injunctions for Elstow, Studley, Nun Cotham and Missenden (in the memoranda section) are printed by E. Peacock, 'Injunctions of John Longland, Bishop of Lincoln, to certain monasteries in his diocese', *Archaeologia* 47 (1882), 49–64.

2. LAO, Episcopal Register XXVII. Parchment register; $14\frac{1}{2}'' \times 11\frac{1}{4}''$; fos. iv (paper)+291+iv (paper), foliated 1–291; blank; fos. 90*v*, 98*r*–*v*, 102*v*, 105*v*–106*v*, 153*r*–*v*, 254*v*, 273*v*–274*r*, 276*v*, 279*v*, 282*v*, 283*v*, 284*v*, 291*r*–*v*; hide-covered binding.

1*r*–274*v*	register of Bishop John Longland	
	1*r*–19*v*	collations of dignities and prebends, and commissions of officials May 1521–Mar. 1547
	20*r*–*v*	place index (Lincoln, part 1)
	21*r*–89*r*	institutions, Lincoln archdeaconry May 1521–May 1547
	89*v*–90*r*	place index (Lincoln part 2)
	91*r*–102*r*	institutions, Stow archdeaconry Sept. 1521–Apr. 1547
	103*r*–*v*	place index (Stow)
	104*r*–105*r*	place index (Northampton)
	107*r*–144*v*	institutions, Northampton archdeaconry June 1521–Oct. 1541
	145*r*–*v*	place index (Leicester)
	146*r*–174*v*	institutions, Leicester archdeaconry June 1521–Mar. 1547
	175*r*–199*v*	institutions, Oxford archdeaconry May 1521–Oct. 1546
	200*r*–230*v*	institutions, Buckingham archdeaconry June 1521–Mar. 1547
	231*r*–254*r*	institutions, Huntingdon archdeaconry June 1521–Mar. 1547
	255*r*–273*r*	institutions, Bedford archdeaconry May 1521–Apr. 1547
	274*v*	composition relating to the vicarage of Carlton le Moorland *temp*. Bishop Richard Gravesend (1258–79)
275*r*–290*v*	register of Bishop Henry Holbeach	
	275*r*–276*r*	institutions, Bedford archdeaconry Nov. 1547–May 1551
	277*r*–279*r*	institutions, Huntingdon archdeaconry Sept. 1547–Nov. 1551
	280*r*–282*r*	institutions, Buckingham archdeaconry Nov. 1547–June 1551
	283*r*	business relating to Oxford colleges 154[ ]–June 1550
	284*r*	institutions, Stow archdeaconry Aug. 1549–June 1551
	285*r*–287*r*	institutions, Leicester archdeaconry Nov. 1547–June 1551
	287*v*–290*v*	place index

Fos. 275*r*–287*r* are calendared in C. W. Foster, 'Institutions to benefices in the diocese of Lincoln, 1547–1570: Calendar no. II', *A.A.S.R.* 25 (1899–1900), 506–19 (using old foliation).

VACANCY 1547

LPL, register of Archbishop Thomas Cranmer, fos. 405*r*–406*r*.

Lincoln vacancy business May–Aug. 1547

Institutions are calendared in A. J. Edwards, 'The *sede vacante* administration of Archbishop Thomas Cranmer, 1533–53' (London University M.Phil, 1968).

VACANCY 1551–1552

LPL, register of Archbishop Thomas Cranmer, fos. 121*v*–128*r*.

Lincoln vacancy business Aug. 1551–May 1552

Institutions are calendared in A. J. Edwards, *op. cit.*

JOHN LONGLAND (1521–1547)
HENRY HOLBEACH (1547–1551)
JOHN TAYLOR (1552–1554)
JOHN WHITE (1554–1556)
THOMAS WATSON (1557–1559)
NICHOLAS BULLINGHAM (1560–1571)
THOMAS COOPER (1571–1584)

LAO, Episcopal Register XXVIII. Paper register (composite volume); 12″ × 8″; fos. viii + 230 + vii, foliated 1, 3–96, 98–232 (including inserts); blank: fos. 31*r*–36*v*, 41*v*, 43*r*–50*v*, 62*v*, 74*v*, 96*v*, 151*r*–*v*, 160*r*–*v*, 165*r*–*v*, 167*v*, 174*v*, 191*v*–195*v*, 205*v*, 219*v*, 224*v*–232*v*; modern binding.

This is not a register in the usual sense, but comprises five separate sections discovered by Canon C. W. Foster and later bound together. These sections contain a record of institutions in the mid-16th century but are not chronologically arranged and must have been compiled from a variety of sources some time after the events they record. Only the first part is arranged by archdeaconry sections.

1*r*–96*r*	institutions in the diocese Feb. 1541–Sept. 1579	
	1*r*–28*v*	Lincoln archdeaconry Feb. 1541–Nov. 1570
	29*r*–30*v*	place index (Lincoln)
	37*r*–40*v*	Stow archdeaconry [ ] 1548–Nov. 1570
	41*r*	place index (Stow)
	42*r*–*v*	headships of Oxford and Cambridge colleges Apr. 1563–May 1570
	51*r*–61*r*	Leicester archdeaconry Nov. 1541–Sept. 1579
	61*v*–62*r*	place index (Leicester)
	63*r*–73*r*	Buckingham archdeaconry 1550/1–Dec. 1570
	73*v*–74*r*	place index (Buckingham)
	75*r*–84*v*	Bedford archdeaconry Apr. 1554–Dec. 1570
	85*r*–*v*	place index (Bedford)
	86*r*–95*r*	Huntingdon archdeaconry June 1542–Nov. 1570
	95*v*–96*r*	place index (Huntingdon)
98*r*–139*v*	institutions in the diocese Apr. 1554–May 1569	
140*r*–150*v*	institutions in the diocese Aug. 1557–Apr. 1559	
152*r*–181*v*	institutions in the diocese June 1554–July 1556	
182*r*–191*r*	place index	
196*r*–219*r*	institutions in the diocese Apr. 1561–Mar. 1563 (entries on fos. 196*r*–211*v* duplicate those in Episcopal Register XIX, fos. 117*v*–132*v* below)	
220*r*–224*r*	place index	

Fos. 1*r*–96*r* are printed by C. W. Foster, 'Institutions to benefices in the diocese of Lincoln, 1540–1570: Calendar no. I', *A.A.S.R.* 24 (1897–8), 1–32, 467–525 (using old foliation); fos. 98*r*–139*v* are printed by C. W. Foster, 'Institutions to benefices in the diocese of Lincoln in the sixteenth century', *Lincolnshire Notes and Queries* 5 (1896–8), 129–44, 164–81, 194–209, 227–43; 6 (1900–1), 3–11 (using old foliation); fos. 140*r*–150*v* are printed *ibid.*, 6, 11–19, 45–53, 78–83 (using old foliation); fos. 152*r*–181*v* are printed *ibid.*, 6, 83–5, 102–11, 142–7 (using old foliation); and fos. 196*r*–219*r* (additional entries) are printed by C. W. Foster, 'Institutions to benefices in the diocese of Lincoln, 1547–1570: Calendar no. II', *A.A.S.R.* 25 (1899–1900), 499–505. A bound volume of these printed institutions, annotated by Canon Foster, is available at the Lincolnshire Archives Office.

VACANCY 1554

CAL, register N, fos. 102*r*–103*r*.

Lincoln vacancy business Mar.–Apr. 1554 (1 entry erroneously dated 1555)

Institutions are calendared (by place) in *Sede Vacante Institutions*.

VACANCY 1556–1557

LPL, register of Archbishop Reginald Pole, fos. 42*v*–48*v*.

Lincoln vacancy business Sept. 1556–July 1557

THOMAS WATSON (1557–1559)
NICHOLAS BULLINGHAM (1560–1571)

LAO, Episcopal Register XXVIIIA. Paper register; $8\frac{1}{4}'' \times 6''$, except for fos. 23–26, 28–29, $12\frac{1}{4}'' \times 8\frac{1}{4}''$; fos. 60, foliated 1–62 (including inserts); blank: fos. 1*v*, 10*r*, 18*r*, 21*v*–22*v*, 25*r*–*v*, 32*r*–*v*, 33*v*, 34*v*–36*v*, 41*r*–42*v*, 43*v*–44*r*, 46*r*–48*v*, 50*r*–*v*, 52*r*–*v*, 55*r*–56*r*, 57*v*, 58*v*; limp parchment covers.

1*r*–62*v* ordinations (not in chronological order at the beginning) Sept. 1557–May 1569

VACANCY 1559–1560

1. CAL, register U2, fos. 94*v*–98*v*.

Lincoln vacancy business July–Dec. 1559

Institutions are calendared (by place) in *Sede Vacante Institutions*.

2. LPL, register of Archbishop Matthew Parker, volume I, fos. 149B*r*–150*r*.

Lincoln vacancy business Dec. 1559–Feb. 1560

Printed, *Registrum Matthei Parker* i, pp. 173–6.

NICHOLAS BULLINGHAM (1560–1571)
THOMAS COOPER (1571–1584)
VACANCY 1584
WILLIAM WICKHAM (1584–1595)
VACANCY 1595

LAO, Episcopal Register XIX, fos. 91–164 (for description see under vacancy 1449–50, Marmaduke Lumley (1450) and vacancy 1450–2).

91*r*–134*r*	register of Bishop Nicholas Bullingham	
	91*r*–132*v*	institutions Feb. 1560—June 1562
	133*r*–134*r*	indenture and confirmation Apr.–June 1569
134*r*–142*v*	register of Bishop Thomas Cooper	
	134*r*–138*v*	institutions July 1577–Dec. 1579
	140*r*–141*v*	place index of institutions (archdeaconry subdivisions)
	142*r*–*v*	institutions Sept. 1572–Oct. 1580
143*r*–146*r*	*sede vacante* register (institutions) May–Nov. 1584	
146*v*–162*r*	register of Bishop William Wickham	
	146*v*–152*v*	institutions Dec. 1584–Feb. 1586
	153*r*–162*r*	unions of benefices June 1562–June 1593
162*r*–163*v*	*sede vacante* register (institutions) Apr.–May 1595	
163*v*–164*r*	augmentation of North Kelsey vicarage Mar.–Sept. 1462 (copy)	
164*v*	institutions Feb. 1564–Nov. 1574	

Fos. 91*r*–132*v* are printed by C. W. Foster, 'Institutions to benefices in the diocese of Lincoln, 1547–1570: Calendar no. II', *A.A.S.R.* 25 (1899–1900), 460–98; fos. 164*v* is printed *ibid.*, 498–9. Fos. 134*r*–142*v* are printed, except for entries duplicated in Episcopal Register XXIX, in *Lincoln Episcopal Records*

in the time of Thomas Cooper, S.T.P., Bishop of Lincoln, A.D. 1571–A.D. 1584, ed. C. W. Foster (Lincoln Record Society 2, 1912, and Canterbury and York Society 11, 1913), pp. 103–47.

VACANCY 1571

LPL, register of Archbishop Matthew Parker, volume I, fos. 204*r*–206*r*.

Lincoln vacancy business Jan.–May 1571

Printed, *Registrum Matthei Parker* i, pp. 301–9; also printed in *Lincoln Episcopal Records 1571–1584*, pp. 305–7.

THOMAS COOPER (1571–1584)

LAO, Episcopal Register XXIX. Paper register; 16″ × 11″; fos. ii + 121 + ii, foliated [i–ii], 1–48, 50, 50A, 51–57, 60–65, 67, 67A, 68–113, 115–120, [121, 122]; modern binding.

A register of institutions to benefices, collations of dignities and prebends, and ordinations, the first mentioned being subdivided into archdeaconry sections. The volume is now incomplete, and records of institutions are extant only for the archdeaconries of Lincoln, Leicester, Buckingham, Bedford, and Huntingdon.

Printed, *Lincoln Episcopal Records 1571–1584*, pp. 1–101. This includes an attempted reconstruction from other sources of the missing institutions for the Stow archdeaconry.

THOMAS COOPER (1571–1584)
VACANCY 1584
WILLIAM WICKHAM (1584–1595)
VACANCY 1595
WILLIAM CHADERTON (1595–1608)
WILLIAM BARLOW (1608–1613)
RICHARD NEILE (1614–1617)
GEORGE MONTAIGNE (1617–1621)

LAO, Add. Reg. 1 ('The Brown Book'). Paper register; 12″ × 8″; fos. iv + 228 + v, foliated 2–7, 13–22, 22A, 23–83, 85–201, 203–229, 229A–C, 230–232; blank: fos. 54*v*, 77*r–v*, 78*v*, 79*v*, 80*v*–81*v*, 83*r–v*, 86*v*, 88*v*–89*v*, 90*v*, 91*v*, 92*v*, 93*v*, 136*r*, 140*v*, 157*v*, 158*v*, 211*v*, 212*v*, 214*v*, 221*r*, 229A*r*–229C*v*, 232*v*; hide-covered binding.

2*r*–18*v*	general register of Bishop Thomas Cooper (first entry incomplete; no institutions) May 1580–Sept. 1583
21*r*–39*r*	*sede vacante* register Apr.–Nov. 1584
39*v*–130*r*	general register of Bishop William Wickham (no institutions) Dec. 1584–Aug. 1594
130*v*–135*v*	*sede vacante* register Apr.–May 1595
136*v*–209*v*	general register of Bishop William Chaderton (no institutions) June 1595–Apr. 1607
210*r*–232*r*	miscellaneous acts, not entered in any order (visitation business, commissions, causes etc.) July 1608–Mar. 1619

A manuscript calendar by Canon R. E. G. Cole is available at the Lincolnshire Archives Office. Fos. 2*r*–18*v* are calendared in *Lincoln Episcopal Records 1571–1584*, pp. 149–56.

VACANCY 1584

LPL, register of Archbishop John Whitgift, volume I, fos. 370*r*–379*v*.

Lincoln vacancy business Mar.–Dec. 1584

See also above for further vacancy business.

VACANCY 1595

LPL, register of Archbishop John Whitgift, volume II, fos. 264*r*–268*v*.

Lincoln vacancy business Feb.–May 1595

See also above for further vacancy business.

WILLIAM CHADERTON (1595–1608)

LAO, Episcopal Register XXX. Paper register; 14″ × 9″; fos. v + 271 + v, foliated i–ii, 74–214, 218–272, 272A, 273–328, [329–344]; blank: fos. i*v*–ii*v*, 119*r*–120*r*, 121*v*–122*v*, 128*r*, 133*r*–134*r*, 136*v*–137*r*, 151*r*, 161*v*, 162*v*–163*r*, 187*v*–188*r*, 206*v*–219*v*, 233*r*, 322*v*; modern binding.

74*r*–328*v*	general register Aug. 1597–Apr. 1608
[329*r*–344*v*]	index (to letter P only)

VACANCY 1608

LPL, register of Archbishop Richard Bancroft, fos. 242*v*–247*r*.

Lincoln vacancy business Apr.–June 1608

WILLIAM BARLOW (1608–1613)
RICHARD NEILE (1614–1617)
VACANCY 1617
GEORGE MONTAIGNE (1617–1621)
VACANCY 1621
JOHN WILLIAMS (1621–1641)
THOMAS WINNIFFE (1642–1654)
and later bishops

LAO, Add. Reg. 3 ('the Red Book'). Paper register; 12″ × 7¾″; fos. vi + 353 + ii, foliated 1–100, 102–288, 288A, 289–298, 298A, 299, 300, 300A–B, 301, 302, 302A, 303–343, [344–349]; blank: fos. 115*v*, 129*v*, 199*v*, 202*v*, 214*v*, 216*v*, 218*r*–*v*, 222*v*, 223*v*–225*v*, 229*v*–230*v*, 236*v*, 255*v*, 261*r*, 273*r*–*v*, 278*v*, 283*r*, 288A*r*–*v*, 292*v*, 298A*r*–*v*, 300A*r*–300B*v*, 302A*r*–*v*, [349*v*]; modern binding.

1*r*–20*r*	acts of Bishop William Barlow (mostly visitations) Apr. 1611–July 1613
20*r*–31*r*	acts of Bishop Richard Neile (mostly visitations) Mar.–July 1614
31*v*–37*r*	commissions of appointment of officials of Bishop Barlow Mar.–Sept. 1609
37*r*–49*v*	acts of Bishop Neile (mostly visitations) Aug. 1615–July 1617
50*r*–72*r*	*sede vacante* register Oct.–Dec. 1617
72*v*–108*r*	acts of Bishop George Montaigne Feb. 1618–Jan. 1621
108*v*–109*r*	letter of Official *sede vacante* Sept. 1621
109*r*–129*r*	miscellaneous acts, in no chronological order Feb. 1622–Oct. 1632
130*r*–137*v*	*sede vacante* register Sept.–Dec. 1621
137*v*–154*v*	miscellaneous acts, chiefly of the vicar-general (in chronological confusion) May 1621–June 1634
155*r*–197*v*	visitation of the diocese by Archbishop Laud Mar.–Sept. 1634
198*r*–222*r*	acts of Bishop John Williams and his officials (including much probate material) May 1635–Aug. 1641
222*r*	sequestrations Aug. 1642

223*r*	faculty Mar. 1666 (1 entry)
226*r*–v	2 letters of Charles I Aug. 1642
227*r*–343*v*	miscellaneous acts, chiefly faculties Mar. 1662–Sept. 1693
[344*r*–348*v*]	index

A manuscript calendar by Canon R. E. G. Cole is available at the Lincolnshire Archives Office. Fos. 227*r*–343*v* are discussed and some faculties printed by R. E. G. Cole, 'Some Lincolnshire Faculties, A.D. 1663–1693', *A.A.S.R.* 30 (1909–10), 19–46.

VACANCY 1613–1614

LPL, register of Archbishop George Abbot, volume I, fos. 304*r*–327*r*.

Lincoln vacancy business Sept. 1613–May 1614 (includes accounts of procurations and synodals)

A certificate of acts performed during this vacancy is to be found in Lambeth Palace Library, Carte Miscellanee XIII/40.

VACANCY 1617

LPL, register of Archbishop George Abbot, volume I, fos. 346*v*–357*r*.

Lincoln vacancy business Oct.–Dec. 1617

See also above for 1617 vacancy acts.

VACANCY 1621

LPL, register of Archbishop George Abbot, volume II, fos. 264*r*–266*r*.

Lincoln vacancy business Aug.–Nov. 1621

See also above for 1621 vacancy acts.

JOHN WILLIAMS (1621–1641)
THOMAS WINNIFFE (1642–1654)
ROBERT SANDERSON (1660–1663)

LAO, Episcopal Registers XXXI and XXXII, bound together. Paper register; pp. 1–92, $11\frac{3}{4}'' \times 7\frac{3}{4}''$; pp. 91A–178, $11\frac{3}{4}'' \times 7\frac{3}{4}''$; Register XXXII, $12\frac{1}{4}'' \times 8''$; fos. v+i (parchment cover)+48+i (parchment cover)+44+39+v, paginated (Register XXXI) i–iv, 1–18, 17A, 18A, 19–46, 49–92, 91[A], 92[A], 93–178; foliated (Register XXXII) [i–iv], 1–17, 17[A], 18–26, [27–38]; blank: pp. ii–iv, 17A, 18A, 19, 20, 35, 36, 57–60, 66–70, 91, 92, 91[A], 92[A], 127, 128, 158–178 (Register XXXII), fos. [i*v*–iv*v*], 26*v*, [29*v*, 32*v*, 33*v*–38*v*]; modern binding.

Register XXXI

1–17	institutions and collations *temp.* Bishop John Williams Nov. 1640–Nov. 1641
17–18	institutions *temp.* Bishop Thomas Winniffe Feb.–Mar. 1642 (cancelled)
21–35	institutions and collations *temp.* Bishop Winniffe Feb. 1642–Oct. 1646
76	collations Nov. 1649
77–90	place index
93–125	ordinations Dec. 1640–Oct. 1646
129–157	ordinations Oct. 1660–Nov. 1662

Register XXXII

1*r*–26*r*	general register of Bishop Robert Sanderson Oct. 1660–Jan. 1663
[27*r*–29*r*]	index of institutions
[30*r*–32*r*]	index of ordinations
[33*r*]	index of appointments of officials, licences etc.

Pp. 129–57 have been printed by P. B. G. Binnall, 'Bishop Sanderson's Ordination Book', *Lincolnshire Architectural and Archaeological Society Reports and Papers* 9 (1961), 63–88.

SUSPENSION OF BISHOP WILLIAMS 1637–1638

LPL, register of Archbishop William Laud, volume II, fos. 1*r*–22*v*.

administration of the diocese of Lincoln by reason of the suspension of Bishop Williams July 1637–Aug. 1638

For a draft of this register see Lambeth Palace Library, VX.IIA/I/IA (noted under Canterbury).

ACT BOOK

LAO, Add. Reg. 2. Paper register, unbound; average 12″ × 8″; fos. 225, foliated 1–8, 9A, 9–28, 30–53, 62–87, 89–117, 117A, 118, 120–133, 133A, 134–233; blank: fos. 6*v*, 9*v*–10*v*, 11*v*, 12*v*, 13*v*, 16*r*–17*v*, 22*v*–23*v*, 24*v*, 25*v*, 27*v*–28*v*, 31*v*, 33*v*, 34*v*, 43*r*–*v*, 44*v*, 45*v*, 48*v*–49*v*, 53*r*–*v*, 63*v*, 64*v*, 68*v*–69*v*, 70*v*, 71*v*, 74*v*, 76*v*, 83*r*–*v*, 84*v*, 86*v*, 87*v*, 89*v*, 106*v*, 108*v*, 110*r*–*v*, 114*r*–*v*, 117*v*–118*v*, 120*v*, 122*r*–*v*, 124*v*, 126*v*, 128*v*, 130*v*, 132*v*, 135*r*–*v*, 194*r*–*v*, 211*r*–*v*, 225*r*–*v*, 230*v*.

1*r*–233*v*	general acts, not entered in chronological order (institutions, wills, indentures, lawsuits, accounts) Sept. 1559– [ ] 1626, with copies of earlier documents, 14th–16th cents., most of them exhibited in causes

A typescript brief calendar of contents is kept with the volume.

LLANDAFF

Repositories

1. Lambeth Palace Library, London SE1 7JU (LPL).
2. Canterbury Cathedral Archives and Library, The Precincts, Canterbury CT1 2EG (CAL).
3. University Library, West Road, Cambridge CB3 9DR (CUL).

Area

The boundaries of the diocese of Llandaff were the subject of much dispute in the middle ages. The Gower peninsula and its hinterland, the Ewyas district, and Ystradyw in Breconshire all came under the jurisdiction of the bishop of St David's, and the bishop of Hereford included the district of Erging (Archenfield), around Monmouth, in his diocese. The Llandaff diocese was in effect restricted to most of Glamorgan and Monmouthshire.[1]

Bibliographical Note

The earliest extant Llandaff episcopal register covers the years 1819–51,[2] but a draft register survives for 1817–19.[3] There are act books of an earlier date, the first of which, extending from 1660 to 1678, was printed in the first decade of this century,[4] but for the entire period under consideration in this present volume the only registered Llandaff material is to be found in the archiepiscopal and capitular registers of Canterbury.

VACANCY 1287–1297

1. LPL, register of Archbishop John Pecham, fos. 32*r*–41*v* *passim*.[5]

   Llandaff vacancy business June 1287–Feb. 1291

   Printed, *Register of John Pecham* i, 55–96 *passim*.

2. CAL, register Q, fos. 14*v*–15*r* *passim*.

   Llandaff vacancy business June–Aug. 1293

   Institutions are calendared (by place) in *Sede Vacante Institutions*.

3. CUL, MS. Ee.5.31, fos. 60*v*–63*v* *passim*.

   Llandaff vacancy business Apr.–Sept. 1294

   Institutions are calendared (by place) in *Sede Vacante Institutions*.

[1] A Hamilton Thompson, 'The Welsh Medieval Dioceses', *Journal of the Historical Society of the Church in Wales* 1 (1947), 90–111, especially 95–7; W. de G. Birch, *Memorials of the See and Cathedral of Llandaff* (Neath, 1912); F. G. Cowley, 'The emergence of the territorial diocese' in *Glamorgan County History, vol. III: The Middle Ages*, ed. T. B. Pugh (Cardiff, 1971), pp. 89–94. For the boundary disputes see J. Conway Davies, *Episcopal Acts and cognate documents relating to Welsh Dioceses 1066–1272* i (Historical Society of the Church in Wales 1, 1946), pp. 147–90. For a map of the diocese see the frontispiece to E. J. Newell, *Diocesan Histories: Llandaff* (London, 1902); Ordnance Survey, *Map of Monastic Britain: (south sheet)* (2nd edn., 1954); W. Rees, *An Historical Atlas of Wales from early to modern times* (2nd edn. London, 1972), plates 32–33.

[2] Cardiff Central Library, MS. 3.468; a facsimile is in the National Library of Wales, Aberystwyth, LL/BR/1.

[3] National Library of Wales, LL/BR/14.

[4] *Ibid.*, LL/SB/1, printed in *Acts of the Bishops of Llandaff, Book 1*, ed. J. A. Bradney (Llandaff Records 2, Cardiff, 1908).

[5] See under Canterbury for a description of this and subsequent archiepiscopal and capitular registers.

VACANCY 1361

LPL, register of Archbishop Simon Islip, fos. 239*v*–240*r*.

Llandaff vacancy business Oct. 1361–May 1362

Another acquittance after the vacancy, May 1362, is recorded on fo. 232*r*.

VACANCY 1385–1386

LPL, register of Archbishop William Courtenay, fo. 262*r*.

Llandaff vacancy act May 1386 (1 entry), among the general section of Canterbury institutions

VACANCY 1423–1425

LPL, register of Archbishop Henry Chichele, volume I, fos. 138*r*–156*r* *passim*.

Llandaff vacancy business Mar. 1423–July 1425, among the general section of Canterbury institutions

Printed, *Register of Henry Chichele* i, pp. 208–26 *passim*.

VACANCY 1517

LPL, register of Archbishop William Warham, volume II, fos. 281*v*–283*r*.

Llandaff vacancy business Jan.–Feb. 1517

VACANCY 1545

LPL, register of Archbishop Thomas Cranmer, fo. 394*v*.

Llandaff vacancy act Mar. 1545 (1 entry), among the general section of Canterbury institutions

Calendared in A. J. Edwards, 'The *sede vacante* administration of Archbishop Thomas Cranmer, 1533–53' (London University M.Phil., 1968).

VACANCY 1563–1566

LPL, register of Archbishop Matthew Parker, volume I, fos. 178*v*–180*v*.

Llandaff vacancy business Nov. 1563–Apr. 1566

Printed, *Registrum Matthei Parker* i, pp. 226–30.

VACANCY 1574–1575

LPL, register of Archbishop Matthew Parker, volume II, fos. 61*v*–62*r*.

Llandaff vacancy business Nov. 1574–Feb. 1575

Printed, *Registrum Matthei Parker* iii, p. 1016.

VACANCY 1590–1591

LPL, register of Archbishop John Whitgift, volume I, fos. 420*r*–424*v*, continued on fos. 219*r*–220*r*.

Llandaff vacancy business Oct. 1590–Aug. 1591

VACANCY 1595

LPL, register of Archbishop John Whitgift, volume II, fos. 268*v*–269*v*.
Llandaff vacancy business Mar.–July 1595

VACANCY 1601

LPL, register of Archbishop John Whitgift, volume III, fos. 223*r*–224*v*.
Llandaff vacancy act Sept. 1601 (1 entry)

VACANCY 1617–1618

LPL, register of Archbishop George Abbot, volume I, fos. 358*v*–359*r*.
Llandaff vacancy business Nov. 1617–May 1618

VACANCY 1627

LPL, register of Archbishop George Abbot, volume II, fo. 301*r*–*v*.
Llandaff vacancy business Sept.–Nov. 1627

LONDON

Repositories

1. Guildhall Library, Aldermanbury, London EC2P 2EJ (GL).
2. Lambeth Palace Library, London SE1 7JU (LPL).
3. Canterbury Cathedral Archives and Library, The Precincts, Canterbury CT1 2EG (CAL).

Area

The medieval diocese of London was divided into four archdeaconries: London, comprising the city of London and a few parishes in Middlesex; Middlesex, which included the rest of the county of Middlesex, the deanery of Braughing in Hertfordshire, and the three Essex deaneries of Dunmow, Harlow, and Hedingham; Essex, which consisted for the most part of those southern parts of the county nearest to London; and Colchester, which contained the north of Essex, except for the three deaneries already mentioned under the jurisdiction of the archdeacon of Middlesex. There were of course many peculiars and exempt jurisdictions in the diocese, the most notable perhaps being the archbishop of Canterbury's peculiars of Bocking (Essex) and the Arches (London). In 1540 Middlesex and Westminster were removed to form the new bishopric of Westminster but this was suppressed after ten years and jurisdiction was resumed by the bishop of London. In 1550 the archdeaconry of St Alban's was created, containing 26 parishes in Hertfordshire and Buckinghamshire which had once belonged to the abbey of St Alban's. In the nineteenth century there were further changes in the diocesan and archidiaconal boundaries.[1]

Bibliographical Note

A list of the episcopal registers of London to 1700 has been published by Richard Newcourt in the preface to his *Repertorium*.[2] No reference has been found to any bishop's register earlier than Richard Gravesend's (1280–1303), apart from mention of a *matricula* of Bishop Fulk Basset (1244–59).[3] The earliest extant registers are by no means complete, as the analytical description indicates, but later fourteenth- and fifteenth-century registers contain all or several of the following subsections: institutions and collations; memoranda; ordinations; royal writs; archiepiscopal mandates; elections of heads of religious houses; and testamentary business. The early sixteenth-century registers are generally restricted to a threefold division: institutions and collations; memoranda; and ordinations. Separate ordination registers are found from 1550 and from then on the episcopal registers basically become institutions registers with occasional memoranda.

In the Guildhall Library there is a nineteenth-century volume of indexes to bishops' registers 1306–1829 (MS. 18,318), being transcripts of indexes to be found in the registers arranged

[1] *VCH London* i (1909), app. i, pp. 400–4; *VCH Middlesex* i (1969), pp. 139–40; *VCH Essex* ii (1907), pp. 81–3, with map; R. Newcourt, *Repertorium Ecclesiasticum Parochiale Londinense* (2 vols, London, 1708–10), i, pp. 56–8, 65–9, 74–7, 83–6, 94; *J. Le Neve, Fasti Ecclesiae Anglicanae 1541–1857:* I *St Paul's, London*, ed. J. M. Horn (London, 1969), pp. xi, 14. For a map of the diocese see Ordnance Survey, *Map of Monastic Britain:* (*south sheet*) (2nd edn., 1954).

[2] R. Newcourt, *Repertorium* i, pp. iv–vii; also mentioned in *Historical Manuscripts Commission: Various Collections VII* (1914), pp. 1–2.

[3] Gravesend's register is now lost but there are references to it in the returns to the writs of *cerciorari* (Public Record Office, C269/3/3, C269/6/22, C269/8/25), as there are to the missing fourteenth-century registers of Ralph Stratford (1340–54) (C269/6/6, 22, C269/7/28, C269/8/25), Michael Northburgh (1355–61) (C269/4/18, C269/6/6, 22, C269/8/25) and William Courtenay (1375–81) (C269/8/25). For Fulk Basset's *matricula* see C. R. Cheney, *English Bishops' Chanceries*, pp. 113–14, and also references to it in the Public Record Office, C269/6/22, C269/7/5, 38). A copy of this *matricula* survives in the muniment book W.D.9 among the capitular archives of St Paul's cathedral.

in two sequences: an index of installations, consecrations, consolidations, letters patent, leases, etc.; and a place index of institutions and collations. There is also a typescript list of wills and administrations entered in the episcopal registers from 1313 to 1548, compiled by J. H. Bloom in 1927 (GL, MS. 10,024). Lists of incumbents for all the archdeaconries to 1700 have been compiled by Richard Newcourt in his *Repertorium* referred to above. A revision of the London archdeaconry section was published by G. Hennessy in 1898.[4]

RALPH BALDOCK (1304–1313)
GILBERT SEGRAVE (1313–1316)
RICHARD NEWPORT (1317–1318)
STEPHEN GRAVESEND (1319–1338)

GL, MS. 9531/1. Parchment register; $13'' \times 9''$ (fos. xi–xiii, $9\frac{3}{4}'' \times 7''$); fos. 106, foliated [a], i–v, v^2, vi–civ; hide-covered pasteboards (last quire, fos. lxxxxvii–civ loose). Also loose at the end of the volume, fos. 12, $11\frac{1}{4}'' \times 8''$, 16th-cent. index with later additions.

Fos. i–xlviii originally formed a separate volume—the register *de diversis litteris* of the four bishops—and from an earlier foliation (1–34, 47–58) it is evident that there are sections missing. Some time in the 14th century this volume was prefaced by a table briefly noting the contents for precedent purposes (entries relating to folios no longer extant are listed as appendix ii of the printed edition). It seems quite clear, however, that the editor was mistaken in describing this register *de diversis litteris* as a deliberately compiled formulary book. The manuscript gives every indication of being a working episcopal register (no doubt there were separate institution registers) which was later used to provide precedents for the registry clerks. Entries for Segrave's episcopate follow straight on those of Baldock, on the same folio (xxxv), with a marginal note to distinguish them. There is no contemporary heading for the short section covering Newport's pontificate, but Gravesend's has a separate heading (fo. xli). The later section of the composite volume (fos. xliv–civ) was also once kept as a separate volume, if the evidence of a second series of foliation can be relied upon. This volume contains a record of institutions and collations performed by Bishop Stephen Gravesend or his vicars-general from his third pontifical year (1321).

Printed, *Registrum Radulphi Baldock, Gilberti Segrave, Ricardi Newport, et Stephani Gravesend, episcoporum Londoniensium, A.D. MCCCIV–MCCCXXXVIII*, ed. R. C. Fowler (Canterbury and York Society 7, 1911).

VACANCY 1361–1362

LPL, register of Archbishop Simon Islip, fo. 237*r–v*.[5]

London vacancy business Sept. 1361–Apr. 1362

An exchange of benefices in London and Canterbury dioceses, Oct. 1361, is recorded *ibid.*, fo. 291*v*.

VACANCY 1361–1362
SIMON SUDBURY (1362–1375)

GL, MS. 9531/2. Parchment register; $12\frac{1}{4}'' \times 8\frac{3}{4}''$ (2 initial unnumbered fos., 1–3, ii–xvii, 4 following unnumbered fos.), $12'' \times 9''$ (98 unnumbered fos., xvii (1)–160; fos. 5+x (16th-cent. paper index, $11\frac{1}{2}'' \times 8''$)+203+ii (16th-cent. paper table of contents, $11\frac{1}{2}'' \times 7\frac{1}{2}''$)+74, foliated (2 unnumbered), 1–3, ii–xvi, (102 unnumbered), xvii(1)–cii(86), 87–160; modern binding.

Fos. ii–xvi and the following four unnumbered folios contain a record of the acts of the Official *sede vacante* 1361–2, and the ordinations celebrated during the vacancy. Sudbury's register is divided into

[4] G. Hennessy, *Novum Repertorium Ecclesiasticum Parochiale Londinense, or London Diocesan Clergy Succession from the earliest time to the year 1898* (London, 1898). A typescript list of addenda and corrigenda to the *Novum Repertorium* for the period 1560–1603, compiled by H. G. Owen, is available in the Library of the Institute of Historical Research, London University (appendix to 'London parish clergy in the reign of Elizabeth I', London University Ph.D., 1957).

[5] See under Canterbury for a description of this and subsequent archiepiscopal and capitular registers.

the following sections: institutions and collations; royal writs; ordinations; monastic elections (incomplete); mandates received from the archbishop of Canterbury. The institutions section is arranged chronologically but there is no territorial subdivision by archdeaconry. Within the section acts performed by the bishop or his vicars-general are so distinguished by appropriate headings.

Printed, *Registrum Simonis de Sudbiria diocesis Londoniensis, A.D. 1362–1375*, ed. R. C. Fowler and C. Jenkins (Canterbury and York Society 34, 38, 1927–38). The first volume contains all vacancy acts and Sudbury's register, except for ordinations *sede vacante* and *sede plena*, which constitute the second volume. See also C. Jenkins, 'Sudbury's London register' in *Church Quarterly Review* 107 (1928), 222–54.

WILLIAM COURTENAY (1375–1381)

It is not known when Courtenay's London register disappeared (it was still in existence in May 1395, Public Record Office, C269/8/25), but Dr A. K. McHardy has printed a collection of his *acta* issued while bishop of London in *The Church in London, 1375–1392* (London Record Society 13, 1977), nos. 547–652.

ROBERT BRAYBROOKE (1382–1404)

GL, MS. 9531/3. Parchment register; $12\frac{1}{2}'' \times 9\frac{3}{4}''$; fos. ii (paper) + ii + 494 (including 6 paper fos., fos. 459–64, and 3 paper fos., $11\frac{3}{4}'' \times 8\frac{1}{2}''$, fos. 465–7), foliated [i–ii], 1–228, 228A, 229–494 (including insert); blank: fos. [i*r*, ii*v*], 60*r*–*v*, 122*v*, 131*r*, 240*r*, 268*r*, 302*v*, 358*r*–360*v*, 397*v*, 463*r*–*v*, 467*v*, 480*v*–485*r*; modern binding.

[ii*v*]	register heading
1*r*–59*v*	ordinations Mar. 1382–Dec. 1401
61*r*–256*v*	institutions and collations (including vicar-general material) Jan. 1382–Dec. 1401
257*r*–267*v*	copies of appropriation deeds, ordinations of vicarages and chantries 13th–15th cents.
268*v*	selective list of churches and chantries occurring in the institutions section above
269*r*–305*v*	archiepiscopal mandates (occasional chronological confusion) May 1382–June 1401
306*r*–357*v*	elections and confirmations of heads of religious houses and hospitals Jan. 1382–Jan. 1402
361–392*r*	licences and letters dimissory (including vicar-general material; there is some gathering together of similar business) Feb. 1382–Nov. 1401
392*v*–394*v*	appropriation deed Mar.–Apr. 1389
395*r*	subsidy business Oct. 1395
395*v*–396*v*	foundation of chantry Oct. 1397
397*r*–423*v*	royal writs Jan. 1382–Apr. 1402
424*r*–458*v*	testamentary business Feb. 1382–Feb. 1402
459*r*–464*v*	late 15th/early 16th cent. selective table of contents (with later annotations)
465*r*–467*r*	16th cent. alphabetical arrangement of the preceding table (with later annotations)
468*r*–478*r*	alphabetical index of places
478*v*–480*r*	table of chantries and free chapels noted in the register
485*v*–494*v*	documents in the case between the bishop of London and the archbishop of Canterbury over the latter's pretended prerogative in respect of visitation and probate (incomplete at end) June 1397–May 1399

VACANCY 1404–1405

LPL, register of Archbishop Thomas Arundel, volume I, fo. 300*r*.

London vacancy act Dec. 1404 (1 entry), among the general section of Canterbury institutions

ROGER WALDEN (1405–1406)
NICHOLAS BUBWITH (1406–1407)
RICHARD CLIFFORD (1407–1421)
JOHN KEMPE (1422–1425)
ROBERT FITZHUGH (1431–1436)

GL, MS. 9531/4. Parchment register; 13″ × 9¾″; fos. xvi (paper, 13¼″ × 9¾″) + 17 + 2 (paper, table, 12½″ × 8″) + 78 + iv (paper, table, 12¼″ × 8½″) + 168 + 2 (11½″ × 7¾″) + xiv (paper, 13¼″ × 9¾″), foliated 1–274[6]; blank: fos. 1*r*–3*v*, 8*v*, 10*v*–11*v*, 15*r*–*v*, 18*r*–19*v*, 22*v*, 97*v*, 100*v*, 135*v*–136*v*, 184*v*, 209*r*–210*v*, 272*v*; modern binding.

4*r*–20*v*	register of Bishop Roger Walden	
	4*r*	register heading
	4*v*–5*v*	institutions July–Dec. 1405
	5*v*	collations Nov. 1405–Jan. 1406
	6*r*–8*r*	exchanges of benefices July–Dec. 1405
	9*r*–10*r*	late 15th-/early 16th-cent. table of contents
	12*r*–14*v*	archiepiscopal mandates July–Sept. 1405
	16*r*–17*v*	ordinations Sept.–Dec. 1405
	20*r*–*v*	royal writs July–Nov. 1405
21*r*–36*v*	register of Bishop Nicholas Bubwith	
	21*r*–22*r*	16th-cent. place index of institutions
	23*r*–29*r*	institutions Sept. 1406–Sept. 1407
	29*v*–30*v*	archiepiscopal mandates July 1407 and appointment of notary Oct. 1406
	31*r*–35*r*	ordinations Dec. 1406–May 1407
	35*r*–36*r*	royal writs Jan. 1406–July 1407
	36*v*	one will, prob. Jan. 1407 and two vows of chastity Apr.–June 1407
37*r*–191*v*	register of Bishop Richard Clifford	
	37*r*–97*r*	ordinations Dec. 1407–Mar. 1421
	98*r*–100*r*	16th-cent. copy of composition between Westminster abbey and the rector of Shepperton, and episcopal confirmation Sept.–Oct. 1410
	101*r*–*v*	16th-cent. table of appropriations, compositions, endowments, ordinations, unions etc. *temp.* Clifford, Kempe and FitzHugh
	102*r*–104*v*	16th-cent. place index of institutions *temp.* Clifford
	105*r*–135*r*	institutions and collations Nov. 1407–Dec. 1410
	137*r*–168*v*, 185*r*–188*v*	archiepiscopal mandates Oct. 1407–Sept. 1419
	169*r*–184*r*	appropriation deeds and ordination of vicarage Mar. 1410–Dec. 1411
	189*r*–190*v*	copy of composition between Colchester abbey and the rector of Stanway, Nov. 1364
	190*v*–191*v*	appropriation of Braintree church Aug. 1416
192*r*–213*v*	register of Bishop John Kempe	

[6] There are two series of modern pencil foliation, one starting at the first folio of Walden's register, the other including the three endpapers, so that the first folio of Walden is numbered 4. I have adopted the latter foliation.

	192*r*–198*r*	ordinations June 1422–Dec. 1424
	198*v*–199*v*	late 15th-/early 16th-cent. place index of institutions *temp*. Kempe
	200*r*–208*v*	institutions June 1422–May 1423
	211*r*–213*v*	statutes and provincial constitutions against the Lollards
214*r*–274*v*		register of Bishop Robert FitzHugh
	214*r*–216*v*	late 15th-/early 16th-cent. place index of institutions *temp*. FitzHugh
	217*r*–224*v*	ordinations Dec. 1431-Dec. 1435
	225*r*–265*r*	institutions etc. Aug. 1431–Jan. 1436
	265*r*–268*v*	visitation business May 1433–Apr. 1434
	269*r*–*v*	elections and confirmations of heads of religious houses Apr. 1432–Aug. 1434
	270*r*–272*r*	documents relating to the chantry of St. Petronella at Harlow church, 1305–Oct. 1424
	273*r*–274*v*	documents relating to a case about a chapelry in the parish of Great Tey Dec. 1433–Mar. 1434

The registers of Bishops Walden and Bubwith (fos. 4*r*–36*v*) have been edited by U. C. Hannam, 'The administration of the see of London under Bishops Roger Walden (1405–1406) and Nicholas Bubwith (1406–1407) with a transcript of their registers' (London University M.A., 1951). An earlier foliation has been used in this edition.

VACANCY 1421–1422

1. LPL, register of Archbishop Henry Chichele, volume I, fo. 130*r*–*v*.

   London vacancy act Oct. 1421 (1 entry), among the general section of Canterbury institutions

   Printed, *Register of Henry Chichele* i, pp. 202–3.

2. *ibid*., volume II, fos. 391*r*–392*v*.

   London ordinations *sede vacante* Dec. 1421

   Printed, *ibid*., iv, pp. 346–9.

WILLIAM GRAY (1426–1431)

GL, MS. 9531/5. Parchment register; $13'' \times 8\frac{3}{4}''$; fos. x (paper, $13\frac{1}{4}'' \times 9''$) + 62 + ii (paper, $11\frac{1}{2}'' \times 7\frac{3}{4}''$) + 6 + iv (paper, $12'' \times 8''$) + 26 + x (paper, $13\frac{1}{4}'' \times 9''$), foliated 1–50, 50A, 51–99; blank: fos. 1*r*–*v*, 14*v*–15*v*, 56*v*, 60*v*–61*v*, 62*v*–64*r*, 66*r*, 77*r*–79*v*, 92*v*–94*v*, 99*r*; modern binding.

2*r*–14*r*	ordinations Sept. 1426–Feb. 1431
16*r*–56*r*	institutions May 1426–Aug. 1431
57*r*–60*r*	late 15th-/early 16th-cent. place index of institutions
62*r*	16th-cent. table of appropriations, compositions, endowments, unions, injunctions, etc. (see below)
64*v*–69*v*, 74*r*–76*v*	memoranda (appropriation, ordination of vicarage, composition, unions of benefices, injunctions) Jan. 1428–June 1431
70*r*–73*v*	copy of foundation deed of the college or chantry of Halstead Nov. 1412
80*r*–92*r*	elections and confirmations of heads of religious houses Dec. 1426–Aug. 1430
95*r*–97*r*	testamentary business Jan. 1427–Mar. 1430

97*v*–98*v*	list of churches, arranged by deanery, with a note of procurations, synodals, Peter's Pence, etc.
99*v*	administrative memoranda and notes

ROBERT GILBERT (1436–1448)
VACANCY 1448–1450

GL, MS. 9531/6. Parchment register; 14½″ × 10½″; fos. x (paper, 15¼″ × 12¼″)+iii (paper, 15″ × 10¼″)+3 (14½″ × 10½″)+iv (paper, 12″ × 8½″)+iv (paper, 11¾″ × 8¾″)+viii (paper, 14½″ × 10½″)+215+x (paper, 15¼″ × 12¼″), foliated 1–212, 214, 215, 217–239; blank: fos. 1*v*–3*r*, 8*r*, 9*v*, 10*v*, 13*v*–14*v*, 22*v*, 130*v*, 151*r*–*v*, 187*v*–189*v*, 220*r*, 226*v*, 228*r*–229*r*, 230*r*, 239*v*; modern binding.

4*r*–6*v*	15th-cent, table of institutions and collations, arranged by folio (starts on 4*v* with heading, and 4*r* entries follow on 6*v*)
7*r*–10*r*	15th-cent. selective tables of contents
11*r*–13*r*	table of contents
15*r*–22*r*	place index of institutions (? 16th cent.)
23*r*–100*r*	institutions and collations etc. Oct. 1436–June 1448
100*v*	form of appointment of the Official of the court of Canterbury when the archbishopric is vacant June 1278
101*r*–122*v*	archiepiscopal mandates etc. Mar. 1437–June 1447
123*r*–125*v*	royal writs June 1437–May 1445
126*r*–130*r*	papal business, dispensations and cognate material May 1438–June 1441
131*r*–150*v*	elections and confirmations of heads of religious houses etc. (some entries are out of order) Apr. 1437–May 1445
152*r*–183*v*	ordinations Dec. 1436–May 1448
184*r*–187*r*	testamentary business Feb. 1437–June 1448
190*r*–230*v*	memoranda, including copies of many earlier documents 12th–15th cents.
231*r*–238*v*	*sede vacante* register July 1448–June 1449

THOMAS KEMPE (1450–1489)
VACANCY 1489

GL, MS. 9531/7. Parchment register; 15¼″/14½″ × 10¼″ (great variations); fos. iii (paper)+i (limp parchment cover)+221+8 (12¼″ × 8½″)+12+x (paper, 15¼″ × 10¼″)+16+9 (12¾″ × 9¼″)+7 (13¾″ × 9¼″)+16+i (limp parchment cover)+iii (paper), foliated 1–233, 1–32, 1–16; blank: fos. (1st series) 225*v*, 233*v* (some unnumbered fos. also blank); hide-covered wooden boards (spine broken).

(*1st series*)

1*r*–221*v*	institutions and collations Feb. 1450–Mar. 1489
between 221 and 222, 8 unnumbered fos.	appropriation of St Giles church, Maldon, to Beeleigh abbey Feb. 1482
222*r*–225*r*	*sede vacante* register Apr.–Oct. 1489
226*r*–227*r*	ordinations *sede vacante* Apr.–Sept. 1489
228*r*–233*r*	correspondence and valuation in respect of clerical subsidy Sept. 1489
10 unnumbered fos.	place index of institutions

(*2nd series*)

1*r*–16*v*	elections and confirmations of heads of religious houses etc. Nov. 1463–Nov. 1484
17*r*–23*v*	monastic election (Barking) Apr. 1499
24*r*–*v*	17th cent. copy of the explanation of the statutes concerning residentiary canons of St Paul's Mar. 1443

26*r*–32*r*	elections and confirmations of heads of religious houses and archiepiscopal mandates *sede vacante* May–Aug. 1489
32*v*	17th-cent. index of wills
(*3rd series*)	
1*r*–16*v*	testamentary business, prob. Mar. 1465–Jan. 1486

RICHARD HILL (1489–1496)
VACANCY 1496
THOMAS SAVAGE (1496–1501)
VACANCY 1501–1502
WILLIAM WARHAM (1502–1503)
VACANCY 1503–1504
WILLIAM BARONS (1504–1505)
VACANCY 1505–1506
RICHARD FITZJAMES (1506–1522)

GL, MS. 9531/8. Parchment register; $15\frac{3}{4}'' \times 12\frac{1}{4}''$, except for 2nd series, fos. 1–16, $15\frac{1}{4}'' \times 11\frac{1}{4}''$; fos. viii (modern paper)+i (paper)+113+viii (modern paper), foliated [i], 1–18, 1–16, 19–36, 1–16, 37–44, 1–24, 45, 47–57, [58]; blank: fos. 3rd series, 16*v*, 1st series (resumed) 36*v*, 45*v*, 48*v*; modern binding.

Register of Bishop Richard Hill

(*1st series*)	
1*r*–18*v*	institutions and collations Nov. 1489–Feb. 1496
(*2nd series*)	
1*r*–14*v*	ordinations Dec. 1489–Feb. 1496

Sede Vacante register 1496

15*r*–16*r*	ordinations Apr. 1496

Register of Bishop Thomas Savage

(*1st series resumed*)	
19*r*–20*v*	provision, installation etc. of bishop Aug.–Oct. 1496
21*r*–36*r*	institutions etc. Oct. 1496–Jan. 1500
(*3rd series*)	
1*r*–16*r*	ordinations Dec. 1497 (*recte* 1496)–Apr. 1501

Register of Bishop William Warham

(*1st series resumed*)	
37*r*–38*r*	provision and installation of bishop Oct. 1501–Oct. 1502
38*r*–44*v*	institutions etc. Oct. 1502–Jan. 1504

Sede Vacante register 1501–1502

(*4th series*)	
1*r*–3*r*	ordinations June–Dec. 1501

Register of Bishop Warham (cont.)

3*r*–7*v*	ordinations by authority of the bishop-elect Feb.–Sept. 1502
7*v*–11*r*	ordinations Dec. 1502–Dec. 1503

Sede Vacante register 1503–1504

11*r*–13*r*	ordinations Mar.–June 1504

Register of Bishop William Barons

13*r*–15*v*	ordinations Sept. 1504–Sept. 1505

Sede Vacante register 1505–1506

15*v*–18*v*	ordinations Dec. 1505–June 1506

Register of Bishop Richard FitzJames
18*v*–24*r* ordinations Dec. 1506–Mar. 1509 (includes note about later ordinations being entered in the following register)

24*v* list of annual payments to the archdeacon of London from churches

Sede Vacante register 1503–1504 (cont.)
(*1st series resumed*)
45*r* institutions Jan.–Mar. 1504

Register of Bishop Barons (cont.)
47*r*–48*r* provision and installation of bishop Aug.–Dec. 1504
49*r*–52*v* institutions etc. Sept. 1504–Oct. 1505

Sede Vacante register 1505–1506 (cont.)
53*r*–56*v* register Oct. 1505–Aug. 1506

56*v* institution Oct. 1506 (1 entry)
57*r*–[58*v*] index of places

RICHARD FITZJAMES (1506–1522)

GL, MS. 9531/9. Parchment register; average 15½″ × 12″, except for fos. 21–21D, 11½″ × 7¾″, and fos. 93–108, 12½″ × 9″; fos. x (paper) + 25 + 5 + 70 + 18 + 101 + iv (paper) + 1 + x (paper), foliated [i–iii], 1–20, 22, 23, 21, 21A–21D, 24–27, 29, 28, 30–97, 97[A], 98–115, 117–159, 161–165, 156–184, 1–15, [16–20] (clearly there is some misbinding); blank: fos. 21D*r*, 92*v*, 1 unnumbered fo. between 92 and 93, 108*v*, 144*v*, 147*v*, 156*v*, 184*v*, [3rd series, 20*v*]; modern binding.

[ii*v*] institution Nov. 1507 (1 entry)
[iii*r*] ordinations *temp*. FitzJames Dec.–Feb. (no year given)
1*r*–82*v* institutions etc. Mar. 1509–Dec. 1521
(initially this section resembles a general register since, besides institutions, collations and cognate material, there are also recorded some compositions, confirmations, injunctions, commissions, grants, papal bulls, dispensations, abjurations of heretics, elections of heads of religious houses etc. Gradually the section becomes more and more confined to institutions. Some of the documents are registered out of order)
83*r*–86*v* elections and confirmations of heads of religious houses Nov. 1510–Sept. 1512 (see also below)
87*r*–92*r* proceedings of the bishops of Winchester and Norwich touching residence at St Paul's in accordance with a bull of Pope Leo X, dated Aug. 1513
93*r*–108*r* inquisition over the rights of patronage of the church of St Michael, Cornhill, London, with copies of earlier documents Aug. 1515
109*r*–152*r*, 157*r*–165*v* elections and confirmations of heads of religious houses etc. (also includes royal writs, material relating to subsidies and tenths, and other administrative business. The entries are not in chronological order) Jan. 1511–Oct. 1521
152*r*–156*r* place of institutions
(*2nd series*)
156*r*–184*r* ordinations Mar. 1509–Jan. 1522
(for ordinations 1506–9 see the previous volume)
(*3rd series*)
1*r*–15*r* clerical wills (*registrum de testamentis presbiterorum*) Apr. 1508–Nov. 1517

15*v*	extracts from the statutes of appropriations 15 Richard II and 4 Henry IV
[16*r*–18*r*]	selective table of memoranda (alphabetical)
[18*v*–19*r*]	table of wills

On fo. 184*r* there are three references to copies of dispensations 'in libro papiri de ordinibus', a volume which has now disappeared.

VACANCY 1522

LPL, register of Archbishop William Warham, volume II, fos. 295*r*–307*r*.

London vacancy business Jan.–Aug. 1522

CUTHBERT TUNSTALL (1522–1530)
VACANCY 1530

GL, MS. 9531/10. Parchment register; $14\frac{1}{2}'' \times 11''$; fos. xiv (paper)+167+xiv (paper), foliated [i–iv], 1–69, 80–89, 100–131, 131A, 132–166, 1–12, 167, 168, [169, 170] (there is also a binding foliation 1–167); blank: fos. 102*v*, 125*v*, [170*v*]; modern binding.

[iii*r*]	list of suppressed religious houses in the diocese of London 1536–39
[iii*v*]	list of chantries in St Paul's cathedral with time permitted for presentation before the collation falls to the bishop by lapse
[iv*r*]	list of chantries (elsewhere) with patronage rights etc.
[iv*v*]	list of bishops of London
1*r*–31*r*	institutions etc. May 1522–Mar. 1530
31*v*	legatine institution Dec. 1526
32*r*–166*v*	general memoranda Aug. 1522–Nov. 1529 (the arrangement of this section is confused, and includes copies of earlier documents and a few additions of the 1530s. On fo. 258*v* is a table of contents as far as fo. 157).
(*2nd series*)	
1*r*–12*v*	ordinations Sept. 1522–Mar. 1530
(*1st series resumed*)	
167*r*–[168*r*]	*sede vacante* register Mar.–July 1530
[168*v*–169*v*]	place index of institutions

VACANCY 1530

LPL, register of Archbishop William Warham, volume II, fos. 311*r*–316*r*.

London vacancy business Mar.–July 1530 (see also above)

JOHN STOKESLEY (1530–1539)

GL, MS. 9531/11. Parchment register; $14\frac{3}{4}'' \times 11''$; fos. x (paper)+160+x (paper), foliated 1–160; blank: fos. 5*r*–*v*, 9*v*, 48*v*, 58*r*–*v*, 99*v*, 122*r*–*v*, 127*v*, 141*r*–*v*, 150*v*, 159*v*–160*v*; modern binding.

2*r*–3*v*	place index of institutions
3*v*–4*v*	table of contents of memoranda
6*r*–9*r*	provision and installation of bishop, commissions etc. Mar. 1530–Nov. 1532
10*r*–48*r*	institutions (including bull of provision and record of the bishop's consecration) Mar. 1530–Sept. 1539
49*r*–127*r*	general memoranda Feb. 1531–July 1538 (the arrangement of this section is chronologically chaotic, and

	some attempt has been made to group together similar material (not always successfully) e.g. elections of heads of religious houses, confirmations of leases etc.)
128*r*–131*v*, 136*v*	ordinations Mar. 1531–May 1539
132*r*–136*r*, 137*r*–159*r*	copies of documents 12th–16th cents. relating to benefices (appropriations, ordinations of vicarages, chantry foundations, grants of advowsons, unions, etc.)

EDMUND BONNER (1539–1549)
VACANCY 1549–1550

GL, MS. 9531/12, part 1. Parchment register; 15¾″ × 13″; fos. ii (paper)+i (medieval manuscript paste-down)+274+ii (paper), foliated 1–54, 56–97, 170–177, 98–105, 108–111, 106, 107, 112–169, 178–246, 248–257, 257[A], 258–275 (also a modern binding foliation 1–276, including inserts); blank: fos. 169*r*–*v*, 176*v*–177*v*, 275*v*; modern binding.

1*r*–97*v*, 98*r*–129*v*	general memoranda (not always in chronological sequence) Nov. 1539–Mar. 1549
170*r*–176*r*	ordinations Dec. 1540–Mar. 1549
130*r*–166*r*, 166*v*–167*r*	institutions Nov. 1539–Sept. 1549
166*r*–*v*	institutions during the royal visitation Nov.–Dec. 1547
167*v*–168*r*	institutions *sede vacante* Feb.–Mar. 1550
168*v*	Privy Council letter to the bishop about masses held in St Paul's cathedral, enjoining that communion should only be celebrated at the high altar; and bishop's letter to the dean June 1549
178*r*–217*v*	testamentary business prob. Feb. 1540–Mar. 1549
218*r*–241*v*	documents chiefly concerned with proceedings against Bishop Bonner and his subsequent deprivation June 1549–Feb. 1550
242*r*–275*r*	register of Bishop Thirlby of Westminster (1540–1550) (see under Westminster)

VACANCY 1550

LPL, register of Archbishop Thomas Cranmer, fos. 115*v*–119*r*.

London vacancy business Feb.–Mar. 1550 (see also above)

Institutions are calendared in A. J. Edwards, 'The *sede vacante* administration of Archbishop Thomas Cranmer, 1533–53' (London University M.Phil., 1968).

NICHOLAS RIDLEY (1550–1553)
EDMUND BONNER (restored 1553–1559)

GL, MS. 9531/12, part 2. Parchment register; 15¾″ × 13″; fos. ii (paper)+209+xxiii (paper, index)+i (paper)+ii (paper), foliated 275–483, [484–496]; blank: fos. 322*r*–*v*, 447*v*, [496*v*]; modern binding.

Register of Bishop Nicholas Ridley

275*r*	register heading
275*v*–278*r*	nomination and installation of bishop Apr. 1550
278*r*–306*v*	memoranda Apr. 1550–July 1553
307*r*–318*v*	institutions Apr. 1550–July 1553
319*r*–321*v*	ordinations June 1550–May 1553

Register of Bishop Edmund Bonner

323*r*	register heading

323*r*–447*r*	memoranda Sept. 1553–Mar. 1559
448*r*–482*r*	institutions Sept. 1553–Mar. 1559
482*v*–483*r*	institutions performed by the Queen's commissaries-general during the royal visitation July–Dec. 1559
[484*r*–496*r*]	table of contents (memoranda) and place index of institutions

VACANCY 1559

1. CAL, register U2, fos. 78*v*–90*r*.

London vacancy business June–Dec. 1559

Institutions are calendared (by place) in *Sede Vacante Institutions*

2. LPL, register of Archbishop Matthew Parker, volume I, fo. 146*r*.

London vacancy act Dec. 1559 (1 entry)

Printed, *Registrum Matthei Parker* i, p. 164.

EDMUND GRINDAL (1559–1570)
VACANCY 1570
EDWIN SANDYS (1570–1577)
JOHN AYLMER (1577–1594)

GL, MS. 9531/13, part 1. Parchment register; 17″ × 13¼″; fos. ii (paper) + 282 + ii (paper), foliated 1–282; blank: fos. 1*r*, 43*r*–*v*, 74*v*, 85*r*–86*v*, 93*v*, 108*r*–110*v*, 282*v*; modern binding.

1*v*–74*r*	installation of Grindal and memoranda (not in strict chronological order) Dec. 1559–Feb. 1570
75*r*–84*v*	memoranda of Bishop Sandys (in confusion) July 1570–Feb. 1577
87*r*–107*v*	memoranda of Bishop Aylmer Jan. 1579–Apr. 1589
111*r*–155*v*	institutions *temp.* Grindal Dec. 1559–May 1570
155*v*–156*r*	institutions *sede vacante* May–July 1570
156*r*–189*v*	institutions *temp.* Sandys Sept. 1570–Jan. 1577
189*v*–282*r*	institutions *temp.* Aylmer Apr. 1577–Mar. 1594

On fo. 189*v* is a note which states that there were no institutions in the vacancy between Sandys and Aylmer. For further vacancy business 1570 and 1577 and memoranda of Aylmer see below.

VACANCY 1570

LPL, register of Archbishop Matthew Parker, volume I, fos. 201*r*–203*r*.

London vacancy business May–June 1570

Printed, *Registrum Matthei Parker* i, pp. 287–98.

VACANCY 1577

LPL, register of Archbishop Edmund Grindal, volume II, fos. 288*v*–290*r*.

London vacancy business Mar. 1577

VACANCY 1594–1595

1. LPL, register of Archbishop John Whitgift, volume II, fos. 246*v*–260*r*.

London vacancy business June–Nov. 1594

2. GL, MS. 14279. Paper; 12″ × 8″; fos. 4, not foliated (the verso of the 3rd folio and the whole of the 4th folio are blank)

London vacancy business Aug.–Nov. 1594

JOHN AYLMER (1577–1594)
RICHARD BANCROFT (1597–1604)
RICHARD VAUGHAN (1604–1607)
THOMAS RAVIS (1607–1609)
GEORGE ABBOT (1610–1611)
JOHN KING (1611–1621)
VACANCY 1621
GEORGE MONTAIGNE (1621–1628)

GL, MS. 9531/13, part 2. Parchment register; 17″ × 13¾″; fos. ii (paper) + 150 + ii (paper), foliated 283–432; blank: fos. 338*r–v*, 341*r*–342*v*, 370*r–v*, 374*r–v*, 380*v*, 396*v*, 425*v*–427*v*, 429*v*–430*v*; modern binding.

283*r*–337*v*	institutions *temp.* Bancroft Apr. 1597–Feb. 1600
339*r*–340*v*	indenture and confirmations Nov. 1579–Apr. 1580
343*r*–372*r*, 375*r*–376*r*, 403*r–v*	memoranda *temp.* Bancroft (in very confused order, including copies of 13th-cent. compositions, letters patent of Henry VIII, Edward VI and Elizabeth I, orders regarding the exercise of ecclesiastical jurisdiction, a list of bishops of London, and a copy of returns 1597–8 to the archbishop of Canterbury about clergy instituted and ordained, and recusants excommunicated) Nov. 1597–Mar. 1603
372*v*–373*v*, 377*v*–380*r*, 383*r*–386*v*, 428*r*–429*r*	tables of church dues and fees for several London parish churches Feb. 1622–Nov. 1627
376*v*–377*v*, 397*r*–402*v*	memoranda *temp.* King (in disorder) June 1612–Nov. 1620
381*r*–383*r*	memoranda *temp.* Aylmer Feb. 1592–Dec. 1593
387*r*–390*r*	installation of Bishop Ravis and memoranda June 1607–Feb. 1609
390*v*–395*v*	installation of Bishop Abbot and memoranda Feb. 1610–Apr. 1611
396*r*	licence to build a chapel *sede vacante* June 1621
404*r*–406*r*	installation of Bishop Vaughan Dec. 1604
406*r*–416*v*	miscellaneous memoranda (including consecrations of chapels and churchyards) *temp.* Vaughan, Abbot and King May 1605–Dec. 1620
417*r*–420*v*	index of contents (memoranda) of parts 1 and 2
421*r*–425*r*	index of places (institutions) of parts 1 and 2
431*r*–432*v*	commission about a will and depositions of witnesses Jan.–Feb. 1533

VACANCY 1596–1597

LPL, register of Archbishop John Whitgift, volume II, fos. 275*r*–284*r*.

London vacancy business June 1596–May 1597

RICHARD BANCROFT (1597–1604)
RICHARD VAUGHAN (1604–1607)

THOMAS RAVIS (1607–1609)
GEORGE ABBOT (1610–1611)
JOHN KING (1611–1621)
GEORGE MONTAIGNE (1621–1628)
VACANCY 1628
WILLIAM LAUD (1628–1633)

GL, MS. 9531/14. Paper register; $13\frac{3}{4}'' \times 8\frac{1}{2}''$, except for fos. 258–70, $12'' \times 7\frac{3}{4}''$; fos. x–257 + 14 + 37 + x, foliated 1–260, 260A, 261–270 (followed by 20 blank unnumbered folios), 1–14, 14A, 15–17; blank: fos. 1*v*, 2*v*–11*v*, 83*v*–85*v*, 90*v*–91*v*, 102*v*–103*v*, 169*r*–173*v*, 191*v*, 203*r*–*v*, 260A*r*–*v*, 264*r*–*v*, (2nd series), 13*r*–*v*, 14*v*, 14A*r*–17*v*; modern binding.

12*r*–68*v*, 86*r*–88*r*	institutions *temp.* Bancroft Apr. 1600–Dec. 1604	
69*r*–83*r*, 88*r*–90*r*	institutions *temp.* Vaughan (in confusion) Jan. 1605–Feb. 1606	
92*r*–102*r*	institutions *temp.* Vaughan Mar. 1606–Mar. 1607	
104*r*–147*r*	institutions *temp.* Ravis May 1607–Nov. 1609	
147*r*–168*v*	institutions *temp.* Abbot Feb. 1610–Apr. 1611	
174*r*–256*v*	institutions *temp.* King Sept. 1611–Mar. 1621	
257*r*–*v*	institutions *temp.* Montaigne 1626 (no month given)–Oct. 1628	
258*r*–270*v*	copies of returns of institutions to the Barons of the Exchequer	
	258*r*–260*v*	return Apr. 1627–Apr. 1628
	261*r*–263*v*	return Apr. 1629–Apr. 1630
	265*r*–267*v*	return Apr.–Dec. 1630
	268*r*–270*v*	return Dec. 1630–Jan. 1632
(*2nd series*)		
1*r*–12*v*	index of places	
14*r*	collation Feb. 1626 (1 entry)	

VACANCY 1604

LPL, register of Archbishop Richard Bancroft, fo. 234*r*. 'Nihil omnino expeditum fuit in eadem diocesi dicta vacatione durante'.

VACANCY 1607

LPL, register of Archbishop Richard Bancroft, fos. 236*r*–239*r*.

London vacancy business Apr. 1607

VACANCY 1609–1610

LPL, register of Archbishop Richard Bancroft, fos. 257*v*–259*v*.

London vacancy business Dec. 1609–Jan. 1610

VACANCY 1611

LPL, register of Archbishop George Abbot, volume I, fos. 296*r*–300*r*.

London vacancy business Apr.–Aug. 1611

VACANCY 1621

LPL, register of Archbishop George Abbot, volume II, fos. 251*v*–260*r*.

London vacancy business Mar.–July 1621

VACANCY 1628

LPL, register of Archbishop George Abbot, volume II, fos. 303*v*–304*v*.

London vacancy business July 1628

WILLIAM LAUD (1628–1633)
WILLIAM JUXON (1633–1660)

GL, MS. 9531/15. Parchment register; 17″ × 11½″; fos. x (modern paper) + ii (paper) + 158 + i (paper) + x (modern paper), foliated A–D, 1–43, 43A, 44–154; blank: fos. 9*v*–10*v*, 16*r*–17*v*, 41*r*–*v*, 118*r*–124*r*, 134*r*–135*v*, 138*r*–149*v*, 154*v* + 1 unnumbered folio between fos. 74 and 75; modern binding.

A*r*–D*v*	election of Laud as bishop July 1628
1*r*–9*r*, 18*r*–40*r*	installation of Laud and memoranda, including court business (in some disorder) July 1628–Mar. 1633
11*r*–15*v*	memoranda *temp.* Juxon Aug. 1634–Nov. 1641
42*r*–74*v*	institutions *temp.* Laud Aug. 1628–Sept. 1633
75*r*–117*v*	installation of Juxon and institutions Nov. 1633–Oct. 1646
124*v*–133*v*	institutions after Juxon's restoration July–Sept. 1660
136*r*–137*v*	copy of an Act for making the precinct of Covent Garden parochial 12 Charles II
150*r*–152*v*	index of places (institutions)
153*r*–*v*	index of contents (memoranda)
154*r*	similar index of contents (later)

VACANCY 1633

LPL, register of Archbishop William Laud, volume I, fos. 292*r*–295*v*.

London vacancy business Sept.–Oct. 1633

ORDINATIONS REGISTERS

1. GL, MS. 9535/1. Paper register; 11½″ × 7¾″; fos. 168 (+4 loose sheets), foliated [i–ii], 1–94, 96–165, [166–171]; blank: fos. [i*r*–ii*v*], 81*v*, 161*v*, [166*r*–171*v*]; limp parchment covers.

1*r*–161*v*	ordinations (with examinations and copies of letters of orders) June 1550–Mar. 1578
162*r*–165*v*	drafts, ordinations Sept.–Dec. 1577

2. GL, MS. 9535/2. Paper register; 13¾″ × 8½″; fos. ii + 242 + ii, foliated [i–iii], 1–239; blank: fos. [i*v*–iii*v*], 84*r*–86*v*, 133*r*–*v*, 146*v*–147*v*, 165*r*–*v*, 176*v*–177*v*, 180*r*–*v*, 187*r*, 188*v*, 191*r*–*v*, 225*v*, 237*r*–239*v*; modern binding.

1*r*–236*v*	ordinations (with examinations and copies of letters of orders) Mar. 1578–June 1628

Both these ordinations registers are indexed in GL, MS. 9535A (An alphabetical index to ordinations 1550–1842, compiled by R. M. Glencross, 1940).

NORWICH

Repositories

1. Norfolk and Norwich Record Office, Central Library, Norwich NR2 1NJ (NNRO).
2. Lambeth Palace Library, London SE1 7JU (LPL).
3. Canterbury Cathedral Archives and Library, The Precincts, Canterbury CT1 2EG (CAL).

Area

The diocese of Norwich comprised the counties of Norfolk and Suffolk and was subdivided into the four archdeaconries of Norfolk, Norwich, Suffolk, and Sudbury. In addition, a few parishes in Cambridgeshire, adjacent to Newmarket, were also in the Norwich diocese and formed part of the Suffolk rural deanery of Fordham.[1] There were no changes in the diocesan boundaries until the nineteenth century.

Bibliographical Note

The Norwich registers from 1299 to 1618 are briefly described in the First Report of the Historical Manuscripts Commission.[2] References have been found to the registers of Roger Skerning (1266–78) and Ralph Walpole (1289–99), both now lost.[3] That the registers are often referred to as 'institution books' is perhaps indicative of the restricted nature of the volumes, although in fairness it must be pointed out that there is some variation in the arrangement over the centuries. Bishop Salmon's register, covering the years 1299–1325, is a chronological register of institutions and collations, with occasional appointments of rural deans and confirmations of heads of religious houses. Later fourteenth- and fifteenth-century registers almost invariably include in addition a memoranda section, containing in particular copies of appropriation deeds, compositions, and ordinations of vicarages. Registers *extra diocesim* occur in the fifteenth century and ordinations are recorded only from 1413.[4] There are separate ordination books from 1532 to 1619, but from 1624 these entries are once more recorded in the registers. The basic pattern of a single, chronological register resumes in the sixteenth century after the episcopate of Richard Nykke (1501–35) when, except for a few years, formal registration appears to have fallen into desuetude.

Not a single Norwich register has yet been edited, but Blomefield (for Norfolk parishes) and Suckling and Gage (for Suffolk) have used the registers to compile lists of parochial incumbents.[5] *Sede vacante* institutions 1288–1559 among the Canterbury registers have been calendared by Bishop M. N. Trollope[6] and a considerable amount of material has been

[1] See *VCH Norfolk* ii (1906), app. iii, pp. 311–14, with map facing p. 314; *VCH Suffolk* ii (1907), pp. 12–14, 51–2, with map facing p. 51. There is also a map of the medieval diocese as a frontispiece to A. Jessop, *Diocesan Histories: Norwich* (London, 1884); and Ordnance Survey, *Map of Monastic Britain: (south sheet)* (2nd edn., 1954).

[2] *Historical Manuscripts Commission: First Report* (1874), pp. 86–7.

[3] Public Record Office, C269/3/20 (Walpole), C269/5/12 (Skerning and Walpole). The former is the return to a writ of 1346; the latter to one of 1371.

[4] See J. F. Williams, 'Ordination in the Norwich diocese in the fifteenth century', *Norfolk Archaeology* 31 (1956), 347–58, which discusses the ordination lists 1413–86.

[5] F. Blomefield, *An essay towards a topographical history of the county of Norfolk* (11 vols., London, 1805–10), and see also J. N. Chadwick, *Index nominum: being an index of Christian and surnames (with arms) mentioned in Blomefield's History of Norfolk* . . . (King's Lynn, 1862); W. B. Gerish, *Index of places in An essay towards a topographical history of the county of Norfolk* (manuscript, 1919, at Yarmouth Public Library, photocopy at Norwich City Library). J. Gage, *The history and antiquities of Suffolk, Thingoe Hundred* (London, 1838); A. Suckling, *The history and antiquities of the county of Suffolk* (2 vols., London, 1846–8). See also C. Morley, 'Catalogue of Beneficed Clergy of Suffolk, 1086–1550', *Proceedings of the Suffolk Institute of Archaeology* 22 (1934–6), 29–85; R. F. Bullen, 'Catalogue of Beneficed Clergy of Suffolk, 1551–1631 (with a few of earlier date)', *ibid.*, 294–320. Both are indexed by parish *ibid.*, 321–33.

[6] NNRO, MC. 16/61, compiled in 1914.

abstracted and indexed by Rev. J. F. Williams (1878–1971) and others, details of which are noted in the analytical list. Indexes of the episcopal registers from 1299 to the early eighteenth century have been compiled by Bishop Thomas Tanner (1674–1735) and are deposited in the Norfolk Record Office among the diocesan muniments (Reg. 30/1, Reg. 31/2). They comprise two volumes arranged by archdeaconry and rural deanery with details of incumbents etc. set out under the individual parish headings. The first volume covers the archdeaconry of Norwich and part of the Norfolk archdeaconry (Brooke to Hingham deaneries); the second contains the remainder of the Norfolk archdeaconry (Humbleyard to Waxton deaneries) and the archdeaconries of Suffolk and Sudbury.

VACANCY 1288–1289

LPL, register of Archbishop John Pecham, fos. 37*v*–39*r* *passim.*[7]

Norwich vacancy business Sept. 1288–Jan. 1289

Printed, *Register of John Pecham* i, pp. 75–83 *passim.*

JOHN SALMON (1299–1325)

NNRO, Reg/1/1. Parchment register; $11\frac{3}{4}'' \times 8''$; fos. 122+v (paper), foliated 1–6, 6[A], 7–67, 69–112, 112[A], 113–121; blank: fos. 120*r*–121*v*; hide-covered boards.

1*r*–119*v*	institutions (including vicarial acts, collations, appointments of rural deans and heads of religious houses) Oct. 1299–July 1325

VACANCY 1325

1. LPL, register of Archbishop Walter Reynolds, fos. 255*v*–257*v* *passim.*

Norwich vacancy business July 1325–Mar. 1326, among the general section of Canterbury institutions

2. *ibid.*, fos. 274*v*–277*v*.

Norwich vacancy business Apr.–Aug. 1325

3. *ibid.*, fo. 143*r*–*v*.

Norwich vacancy business Oct. 1325, among the general memoranda section

Institutions are calendared by Bishop M. N. Trollope (1914) in NNRO, MC. 16/61.

[ROBERT BALDOCK (1325)]
WILLIAM AYERMINE (1325–1336)

NNRO, Reg/1/2. Parchment register; $12'' \times 8\frac{1}{2}''/12\frac{1}{4}'' \times 9''$ (variation); fos. ii (paper)+108+79 (Bek's register)+ii (paper), foliated [i–ii], 1–95, 95[A], 96–104, [105], 1–78, [79]; blank: fos. 77*v*–78*v*, 97*v*–98*v*; Bek: 75*v*, 77*v*–[79*v*]; hide-covered boards (bound with Reg/1/3).

Register of Bishop-elect Robert Baldock

1*r*–*v*	commission and institutions etc. Aug.–Sept. 1325

Register of Bishop William Ayermine

2*r*–77*r*	institutions (including acts of the vicar-general) Sept. 1325–Mar. 1336
79*r*–86*v*	memoranda (commissions, proxies, licences, appropriations, ordinations of chantries and vicarages etc.) Dec. 1325–Sept. 1329 (incomplete at the end)

[7] See under Canterbury for a description of this and subsequent archiepiscopal and capitular registers.

87*r*–97*r*	dispensations and licences for non-residence Nov. 1325–Mar. 1336
99*r*–104*r*	letters dimissory Nov. 1325–Mar. 1336
104*v*	16th-cent. note of an exemplification of Ayermine's register made by Bishop Percy in 1365

Fos. 94–95 (dispensations and licences 1329–32) and 99–104 are calendared and indexed by J. F. Williams (NNRO, MC. 16/4).

ANTONY BEK (1337–1343)

NNRO, Reg/1/3. For description see above; bound up with Reg/1/2.

1*r*–73*v*	institutions Apr. 1337–Dec. 1343
73*v*–74*v*	appointment of notary Apr. 1343
74*v*–77*r*	appropriation deeds and an ordination of a vicarage Aug. 1338–May 1339

WILLIAM BATEMAN (1344–1355)

NNRO, Reg/2/4. Parchment register; average 13″ × 10″; fos. ii (paper) + 156 + ii (paper), foliated 1–89, 91–156, [157]; blank: fo. [157*r*–*v*]; hide-covered boards.

1*r*–40*v*	appropriation deeds, compositions, ordinations of vicarages and cognate documents (not in chronological order, and the last entry is incomplete) Feb. 1347–Nov. 1354
41*r*–156*r*	institutions etc. Jan. 1344–Jan. 1355
156*v*	16th-cent. copy of 1277 document about a chapel, pa. Lodden

A calendar of fos. 41*r*–156*r*, with a place index, by E. D. Stone (1932) is in NNRO, MC. 16/49; a calendar of fos. 72*r*–120*v* (Black Death institutions) is *ibid.*, MS. 21509/60.

VACANCY 1355–1356

LPL, register of Archbishop Simon Islip, fos. 333*r*–342*r*.

Norwich vacancy business Jan.–Apr. 1355

Institutions are calendared by Bishop M. N. Trollope (1914) in NNRO, MC. 16/61.

THOMAS PERCY (1356–1369)

NNRO, Reg/2/5. Parchment register; 14″ × 9¾″; fos. x (paper) + 93 + i (paper), foliated 1–93; blank: fos. 8*v*, 87*v*, 90*v*–93*v*; leather-covered boards (both covers detached).

1*r*–8*r*	appropriation deeds, unions of benefices etc. (not in strictly chronological order) Nov. 1357–Jan. 1369
9*r*–87*r*	institutions Apr. 1355–Aug. 1369 (between fos. 60 and 61 there is a section missing, containing entries between June 1362 and July 1364)
88*r*–90*r*	ordination of Wingfield college June 1362

VACANCY 1369–1370

LPL, register of Archbishop William Whittlesey, fos. 75*v*–80*r* *passim*.

Norwich vacancy business Jan.–May 1370 among the general section of Canterbury institutions

Institutions are calendared by Bishop M.N. Trollope (1914) in NNRO, MC. 16/61.

HENRY DISPENSER (1370–1406)

NNRO, Reg/3/6. Parchment register; average $14\frac{1}{2}'' \times 10''$; fos. ii (paper) + 362 (1 loose) + vii (paper), foliated 1–361; blank: fos. 335*v*–337*v*; hide-covered boards.

1*r*–335*r*	institutions July 1370–Aug. 1406
338*r*–361*v*	appropriation deeds, unions of benefices etc. Mar. 1371–June 1398 (last legible date)

VACANCY 1406–1407

1. LPL, register of Archbishop Thomas Arundel, volume I, fos. 521*v*–549*v*.

Norwich vacancy business Aug. 1406–Oct. 1407

2. *ibid.*, fos. 311*r*–316*v passim.*

Norwich vacancy business Nov. 1406–Oct. 1407, among the general section of Canterbury institutions

Institutions are calendared by Bishop M. N. Trollope (1914) in NNRO, MC. 16/61.

ALEXANDER TOTTINGTON (1407–1413)
RICHARD COURTENAY (1413–1415)

NNRO, Reg/4/7. Parchment register; fos. i (paper) + 104 (1–71 $13\frac{1}{2}'' \times 10''$; 72–104 $13\frac{3}{4}'' \times 9\frac{1}{2}''$) + x (paper), foliated 1–104; blank: fos. 94*v*, 100*v*; hide-covered boards.

Register of Bishop Alexander Tottington

1*r*–56*v*	institutions Nov. 1407–Apr. 1413
57*r*–64*v*	grant of pension, manumission etc. Nov. 1410–June 1414
65*r*–71*v*	appropriation deeds, unions of benefices, compositions etc. June 1409–Jan. 1411

Register of Bishop Richard Courtenay

72*r*–94*r*	institutions by vicar-general Sept. 1413–Sept. 1415
95*r*–100*r*	ordinations Sept. 1413–May 1415
101*r*–104*v*	register *extra diocesim* of the bishop (including ordinations) Apr. 1414–July 1415

VACANCY 1413

LPL, register of Archbishop Thomas Arundel, volume II, fos. 187*r*–198*v*.

Norwich vacancy business May–Oct. 1413 (mostly testamentary business)

Institutions are calendared by Bishop M. N. Trollope (1914) in NNRO, MC. 16/61.

VACANCY 1415–1416

1. LPL, register of Archbishop Henry Chichele, volume I, fos. 67*v*–74*r passim.*

Norwich vacancy business Nov. 1415–May 1416, among the general section of Canterbury institutions

Printed, *Register of Henry Chichele* i, pp. 139–46 *passim.*

2. *ibid.*, volume II, fos. 149*r*–179*r*.

Norwich vacancy business Sept. 1415–May 1416

Printed, *Register of Henry Chichele* iii, pp. 347–425.

JOHN WAKERYNG (1416–1425)

NNRO, Reg/4/8. Parchment register; 14″ × 9½″; fos. 161 + x (paper), foliated 1–161; blank: fos. 94*v*, 124*v*; leather binding (both covers detached).

1*r*–4*v*	memoranda (appropriation deeds, unions of benefices, statutes against Lollards, etc., not in strict chronological order) 1416–Nov. 1422
5*r*–94*r*	institutions (including acts of the vicar-general) May 1416–Apr. 1425
95*r*–124*r*	ordinations June 1416–Apr. 1425
125*r*–161*v*	memoranda (as above, but also royal letters, taxation business, wills, ordinations of vicarages, compositions, etc.; this section is not in chronological order and some material, e.g. wills 1418–19, is grouped together. Fo. 147 should follow on fo. 4*v*) Nov. 1416–Dec. 1424

A chronological name index of ordinands 1416–25 (fos. 95*r*–124*r*) by J. F. Williams is in NNRO, MC. 16/5.

VACANCY 1425–1426

1. LPL, register of Archbishop Henry Chichele, volume I, fos. 155*r*–162*r* *passim*.

Norwich vacancy business May 1425–July 1426, among the general section of Canterbury institutions

Printed, *Register of Henry Chichele* i, pp. 225–34 *passim*.

2. *ibid*., volume II, fos. 220*r*–239*r*.

Norwich vacancy business Apr. 1425–May 1426

Printed, *Register of Henry Chichele* iii, pp. 467–85.

See also below.

VACANCY 1425–1426
WILLIAM ALNWICK (1426–1436)

NNRO, Reg/5/9. Parchment register; 14″ × 10″. fos. v (paper) + 146 + viii (paper), foliated 1–146; blank: fos. 7*v*, 106*v*, 113*r*, 115*v*; hide-covered boards. The register is misbound: the correct sequence should be 1–7, 17–27, 8–16, 28–96, 117, 97–116, 118–146.

1*r*–7*r*	*sede vacante* register Apr. 1425–Aug. 1426 (see also above)
17*r*–27*v*, 8*r*–16*v*, 28*r*–90*v*	institutions etc. Feb. 1426–Feb. 1437
91*r*–117*v*	register *extra diocesim* of the bishop (general register: institutions, wills, memoranda, licences, writs, dispensations, etc.) Oct. 1426–Sept. 1436
118*r*–146*v*	ordinations (and suffragan's commission) Aug. 1426–Dec. 1436

THOMAS BROUNS (1436–1445)

NNRO, Reg/5/10. Parchment register; 14¼″ × 11″; fos. v (paper) + 119 + ix (paper), foliated 1–121, [122] (including inserts); blank: fos. 1*r*, 4*r*, 5*v*, 54*r*, 63*v*, 87*v*; hide-covered boards (spine broken).

1*v*	suffragan commission Oct. 1442
2*r*–63*r*	translation of bishop, commissions, institutions etc. Sept. 1436–Dec. 1445

64*r*–87*r* ordinations Mar. 1437–Sept. 1445

88*r*–100*v* general memoranda Jan. 1439–Nov. 1445

101*r*–112*v* similar memoranda section (papal bulls, licences, dispensations, etc. with copies of earlier documents. Fos. 109–12 of this section relate to documents *pro ecclesia cathedrali*. This section is not in chronological order) Oct. 1438–Jan. 1445

113*r*–121*v* documents in a divorce case *temp.* Bishop Alnwick Oct.–Nov. 1436

VACANCY 1445–1446

1. LPL, register of Archbishop John Stafford, fos. 57*r*–72*v*.

Norwich vacancy business Dec. 1445–Mar. 1446

2. *ibid.*, fos. 86*v*–88*r passim.*

Norwich vacancy business Dec. 1445–Feb. 1446, among the general section of Canterbury institutions

Institutions are calendared by Bishop M. N. Trollope (1914) in NNRO, MC. 16/61.

WALTER LYHERT (1446–1472)

NNRO, Reg/6/11. Parchment register; $15\frac{1}{4}'' \times 11\frac{1}{4}''$; fos. iii (paper) + 300 + xix (paper), foliated 1–300; blank: fos. 37*r*–*v*, 43*r*–*v*, 188*v*, 256*r*, 269*v*, 295*v*, 300*v*; hide-covered boards (spine broken).

1*r*–36*v* register heading, and institutions by vicar-general (includes enthronement of bishop etc.) Feb. 1446–Aug. 1455

38*r*–42*r* institutions by bishop *infra diocesim* June 1450–Aug. 1452

44*r*–184*v* institutions by bishop *infra et extra diocesim* (including occasional vicarial acts) Apr. 1446–May 1472
(with isolated exceptions the entries on fos. 38–42 are not repeated in this section)

185*r*–188*r* chantry foundations and augmentation of vicarage Mar.–July 1459

189*r*–255*v* ordinations Mar. 1446–Feb. 1472

256*v*–300*r* general memoranda (not always in chronological order; once had separate foliation) Oct. 1446–Jan. 1472

A chronological name index of ordinands 1446–72 (fos. 189*r*–255*v*) by J. F. Williams is in NNRO, MC. 16/5.

JAMES GOLDWELL (1472–1499)

NNRO, Reg/7/12. Parchment register; $14\frac{1}{2}'' \times 10\frac{1}{2}''$; fos. i + 310 + xxi (paper), foliated [i], 1–87, 89–219, 219[A], 220–309; blank: fos. 20*v*, 23*r*–24*v*, 123*v*, 305*r*; hide-covered boards.

[i*r*] register heading

1*r*–2*v* institutions by vicar-general (begins in mid-entry; these fos. should follow fo. 309) [Aug.]–Dec. 1473

3*r*–11*v* memoranda (*registrum . . . de litteris indulgentiarum, commissionum ac de ceteris munimentis*) Nov. 1473–Feb. 1479

12*r*–20*r* institutions by bishop *extra diocesim* Feb. 1475–Dec. 1479

21*r*–123*r* institutions, mostly by vicar-general July 1472–June 1487

124*r*–205*v* institutions by bishop *infra et extra diocesim* Dec. 1485–Feb. 1499

206*r*–255*v* general memoranda (not in strictly chronological order, and occasionally includes copies of earlier documents; once had separate foliation) Nov. 1472–Jan. 1499

256*r*–304*v*	ordinations Dec. 1472–Dec. 1486
305*v*	memorandum of receipt Oct. 1481
306*r*–309*v*	institutions by vicar-general Dec. 1472–Aug. 1473 (fos. 1–2 should follow straight on fo. 309*v*)

Ordinations, Mar. 1499, are entered in NNRO, Consistory Will Register 'Sayve', fo. [xi*r*–*v*].

VACANCY 1499

LPL, register of Archbishop John Morton, volume II, fos. 2*r*–121*v*.

Norwich vacancy business Feb.–July 1499

Calendared in C. Harper-Bill, 'An edition of the register of John Morton, archbishop of Canterbury, 1486–1500' (London University Ph.D., 1977). *Libri cleri* for the Sudbury archdeaconry in connection with the visitation of the diocese during this vacancy are to be found in LPL, Carte Miscellanee XIII/48. See also C. Harper-Bill, 'A late medieval visitation—the diocese of Norwich in 1499', in *Proceedings of the Suffolk Institute of Archaeology and History* 34, part 1 (1977), 35–47.

VACANCY 1500–1501

CAL, register F, fos. 110*r*–164*v*.

Norwich vacancy business Sept. 1500–Mar. 1501

Institutions are calendared (by place) in *Sede Vacante Institutions*.

RICHARD NYKKE (1501–1535)

VACANCY 1535–1536

WILLIAM REPPS (1536–1550)

1. NNRO, Reg/8/13. Parchment register; $15\frac{3}{4}'' \times 11\frac{3}{4}''$; fos. iv (paper) + 120, foliated 1–17, [18–20], 1–108; blank: fos. 1*v*, [18*r*–20*v*], 2nd series 95*v*, 96*v*; hide-covered boards (both covers detached).

1*r*	register heading	
2*r*–17*v*	institutions (including vicar-general's business) Mar. 1501–Dec. 1503	
(*2nd series*)		
1*r*–85*v*	institutions (including vicar-general's business) Mar. 1501–Sept. 1507	
86*r*–107*r*	institutions by vicar-general (includes episcopal collations)	
	86*r*–95*r*	Norwich archdeaconry Oct. 1507–Oct. 1510
	96*r*	papal dispensation June 1512
	97*r*–107*r*	Norfolk archdeaconry Mar. 1508–Nov. 1511 (some lacunae)
108*r*–*v*	ordinations (begins in mid-entry) May 1502 (only dated entry)	

2. NNRO, Reg/9/14. Paper register; average $12'' \times 8''$; fos. ii + 297 + 2 (loose fos.) + ii, foliated 1, 22, 2–21, 25–60, 60B–60T. [60U–60Y], 61, 61[A], 62–154, 154[A], 155–157, 157[A], 158–228, [229, 230], 1–33; blank: fos. 20*r*–21*v*, 40*v*–42*v*, 51*v*, [60U*r*, 60V*v*–60W*v*], 61[A]*v*, 115*v*–117*r*, [230*v*]; hide-covered boards.

1*r*–60B*r*	accounts (institutions, first fruits, synodals, etc.) Oct. 1503–Sept. 1507 (some occasional misbinding)
60C*r*–62*v*	memoranda (absolutions, bonds, licences, administrative notes, not in chronological sequence) June 1505–July 1528
63*r*–229*v*, (*2nd series*) 1*r*–33*v*	accounts June 1507–Nov. 1535 (later entries are a fuller record of institutions etc.; fos. 1–33 were originally a separate book)

Calendared, and indexed by place, by E. D. Stone (1933), in NNRO, MC. 16/50.

3. NNRO, Reg/9/15. Paper register; average 12″ × 8½″ (some sections 11¼″ × 8″); fos. iii + 162 + iii, foliated 1–116, 118–122, [122A], 123–132, 134–139, 146–168; blank: fos. 11*v*, 79*v*–81*v*, 90*v*–99*v*, 101*v*–106*v*, 108*v*–114*v*, 118*r*–119*v*, 122*r*–*v*, [122A*r*–*v*], 131*v*–134*v*, 136*v*–139*v*, 151*v*, 158*r*–162*v*, 168*v*; hide-covered boards.

1*r*–90*r*	accounts of fees received by the vicar-general (institutions etc.)	
	1*r*–30*v*	Norwich archdeaconry Oct. 1507–Dec. 1516
	31*r*–60*v*	Norfolk archdeaconry Oct. 1507–Jan. 1517
	61*r*–79*r*	Suffolk archdeaconry Oct. 1507–Oct. 1516
	82*r*–90*r*	Sudbury archdeaconry Oct. 1507–Apr. 1516
100*r*–168*r*	accounts of the fees received by the bishop (arranged by archdeaconry at first but then general accounts) Oct. 1507–Aug. 1514	

4. NNRO, Reg/10/16. Paper register: 11½″ × 7¾″; fos. iii + 133 + iii, foliated [i–iii], 1–129, [130]; blank: fos. [i*v*, ii*v*, iii*v*], 26*v*, 27*v*, 36*v*–37*v*, 102*r*, 104*r*, 124*r*, [130*r*–*v*]; hide-covered boards.

1*r*–6*v*	institutions Apr.–Dec. 1535
7*r*–15*v*	*sede vacante* institutions Jan.–May 1536
16*r*–26*r*	institutions June 1536–Apr. 1537
27*r*	*sede vacante* institutions Mar. 1536
28*r*–36*r*	grants of next presentation, visitation business, dispensation, etc. (not in chronological order; some documents registered much later than their dates) Oct. 1535–Mar. 1553
38*r*–103*v*	institutions (including grants of pensions, unions of benefices etc.) Nov. 1516–June 1527
104*v*–129*v*	memoranda (grants of pensions and of next presentation, papal letters, caveats and miscellaneous administrative business—not in any chronological sequence) Apr. 1513–July 1541

5. NNRO, Reg/11/17. Paper register; 15¾″ × 11″; fos. iii + 143 + 16 (11½″ × 8½″) + 101 + iii, foliated [i–ii], 1–76, 78–87, 89–143, 1–10, [11–14], 144, [145], 146–211, [211A], 212–224, 224[A], 224[B], 225–238, [239–243]; blank: fos. [i*v*–ii*v*], 20*v*, 29*r*–30*r*, 2nd series 6*v*, 8*v*, 10*v*–[14*r*], [145*v*], 146*r*–188*v*, 202*r*–212*r*, 213*r*–218*r*, 221*r*, 238*v*–[243*v*]; hide-covered boards (both covers detached).

1*r*–3*v*	memoranda Mar.–Dec. 1537
4*r*–10*v*	institutions (including some memoranda) Jan.–Nov. 1529
10*v*–28*v*	memoranda Nov. 1528–Dec. 1544
30*v*–143*v*	institutions by vicar-general Apr. 1537–Dec. 1549
(*2nd series*)	
1*r*–10*r*	institutions by bishop Feb. 1540–May 1543
144*r*–[145*r*]	consolidation of benefices Apr. 1548
189*r*–201*v*, 218*v*–238*r*	memoranda (in chronological confusion) July 1532–Jan. 1558

VACANCY 1550

LPL, register of Archbishop Thomas Cranmer, fos. 107*v*–115*r*.

Norwich vacancy business Jan.–Apr. 1550

Institutions are calendared in A. J. Edwards, 'The *sede vacante* administration of Archbishop Thomas Cranmer, 1533–53' (London University M.Phil., 1968); also in NNRO, MC. 16/61.

THOMAS THIRLBY (1550–1554)
JOHN HOPTON (1554–1558)
VACANCY 1558–1560

NNRO, Reg/12/18. Paper register; 16½″ × 11¼″; fos. ii + 234 + ii, foliated 1–5, 1–85, 87–227, [228–230]; blank: 2nd series, fos. 81*v*, 82*v*–83*v*, 85*v*, [228*v*, 229*r*, 230*v*]; hide-covered boards (spine broken).

Register of Bishop Thomas Thirlby

1*r*–5*v* commissions, enthronement of bishop, dispensation etc. Apr. 1550–Oct. 1551

(*2nd series*)

1*r*–81*r* institutions etc. Apr. 1550–Sept. 1554

82*r* grant of next presentation Apr. 1551

Register of Bishop John Hopton

84*r*–85*r* commissions etc. Oct.–Nov. 1554

87*r*–88*v* letter of Cardinal Pole Mar. 1555

89*r*–*v* grants of next presentation Jan. 1538–Nov. 1551 (latter registered July 1556)

89*v*–90*v* composition July 1557

91*r*–210*v* institutions Nov. 1554–Dec. 1558

Vacancy Register 1558–1560

211*r*–227*v* *sede vacante* institutions Jan.–July 1559

[228*r*] note of subsequent institutions being registered in the Administrations Book (see below)

[229*v*] note of benefices in the Norwich archdeaconry which pay double fees for institutions

See also below for further vacancy material.

VACANCY 1554

CAL, register N, fos. 111*v*–113*r*.

Norwich vacancy business Sept.–Oct. 1554

Institutions are calendared (by place) in *Sede Vacante Institutions*.

VACANCY 1558–1560

1. CAL, register U2, fos. 20*v*–25*v*.

   Norwich vacancy business Dec. 1558–Sept. 1559

   Institutions are calendared (by place) in *Sede Vacante Institutions*.

2. NNRO, Consistory administrations act book Jan. 1558–Jan. 1560.

   between fos. 1*r*–200*v* institutions *sede vacante* Jan.–Aug. 1559 (duplicate of NNRO, Reg/13/19 below—entered among grants of administration and then discontinued in Aug. 1559)

3. LPL, register of Archbishop Matthew Parker, volume I, fos. 152*r*–155*r*.

   Norwich vacancy business Jan.–Aug. 1560

   Printed, *Registrum Matthei Parker* i, pp. 181–8.

VACANCY 1558–1560
JOHN PARKHURST (1560–1575)
VACANCY 1575
EDMUND FREKE (1575–1584)

NNRO, Reg/13/19. Paper register; 15¼″ × 11″; fos. ii+266, foliated 1–7, 9–45, 47–89, 100–220, 225–229, 232–237, 240–250, 252–257, 259–288; blank: fos. 1*v*, 4*v*, 39*r*, 214*v*–215*v*, 217*v*–253*v*, 254*v*–257*r*, 262*v*, 265*v*, 267*r*, 274*r*, 277*r*, 278*r*, 288*r*; hide-covered boards (spine broken).

1*r*–9*v* dispensations, caveats, commissions etc. Apr. 1555–Aug. 1568

Vacancy Register 1558–1560
10*r*–38*v* *sede vacante* institutions July 1559–Sept. 1560

Register of Bishop John Parkhurst
39*r*–210*v* institutions Oct. 1560–Jan. 1575

Vacancy Register 1575
210*v*–214*r* *sede vacante* institutions June–Nov. 1575

Register of Bishop Edmund Freke
216*r*–217*r* institutions Feb.–Mar. 1576
254*r* list of procurations n.d.

257*v*–288*v* memoranda (royal and archiepiscopal letters, dispensations, accounts, letters of orders, etc.) Sept. 1543–Dec. 1582

VACANCY 1575

1. LPL, register of Archbishop Matthew Parker, volume II, fos. 62*r*–63*v*.

Norwich vacancy business Feb.–May 1575

Printed, *Registrum Matthei Parker* iii, pp. 1017–19.

2. *ibid.*, fos. 128*v*–132*v* (register of the dean and chapter of Canterbury *sede vacante*).

Norwich vacancy business May–Oct. 1575

Printed, *Registrum Matthei Parker* iii, pp. 1185–94.

EDMUND FREKE (1575–1584)
VACANCY 1584–1585
EDMUND SCAMBLER (1585–1594)
VACANCY 1594–1595
WILLIAM REDMAN (1595–1602)
VACANCY 1602–1603

NNRO, Reg/14/20. Paper register; 17″ × 11″; fos. ii + 331 + 11 (12″ × 7¾″) + ii, foliated [i], 1–4, [5], 1–88, 90–298, 300–335, [336–339]; blank: fos. [i*r*–*v*, 5*r*–*v*], 2nd series 88*r*, 118*r*–120*v*, 263*r*, 330*v*, 332*v*, 333*v*, 335*v*–[339*v*]; hide-covered boards.

1*r*–4*v* commissions for vicars-general Dec. 1575–Feb. 1589

Register of Bishop Edmund Freke (2nd series)
1*r*–114*r* institutions Apr. 1576–Nov. 1584

Vacancy Register 1584–1585
114*v*–116*r* *sede vacante* institutions by authority of the archbishop of Canterbury Dec. 1584–Feb. 1585
116*v* *sede vacante* institutions by authority of the dean of Norwich Dec. 1584–Jan. 1585

Register of Bishop Edmund Scambler
117*r* court allegation Apr. 1589
117*v* presentations with bonds n.d.
121*v*–228*v* institutions Apr. 1585–May 1594

Vacancy Register 1594–1595

228*v*–229*v* commission and list of clergy instituted by the archbishop of Canterbury May–July 1594 (not all the entries are dated)

Register of Bishop William Redman

230*r*–231*v* enthronement of bishop Feb. 1595
232*r*–302*r* institutions Mar. 1595–Sept. 1602

Vacancy Register 1602–1603

302*v*–304*v* *sede vacante* business Oct.–Nov. 1602

304*v* letters of orders (bishop of Coventry and Lichfield) June 1596
305*r*–335*r* memoranda (not in strict chronological order) Apr. 1569–Dec. 1610

VACANCY 1584–1585

LPL, register of Archbishop John Whitgift, volume I, fos. 379*v*–380*v*.

Norwich vacancy business Dec. 1584–Jan. 1585

See also above.

VACANCY 1594–1595

LPL, register of Archbishop John Whitgift, volume II, fos. 225*r*–232*v*.

Norwich vacancy business May–Dec. 1594

See also above.

VACANCY 1602–1603

LPL, register of Archbishop John Whitgift, volume III, fos. 231*r*–240*r*

Norwich vacancy business Sept. 1602–Feb. 1603

See also above.

JOHN JEGON (1603–1618)
SAMUEL HARSNETT (1619–1629)

1. NNRO, Reg/15/21. Paper register; $16\frac{1}{4}'' \times 11''$; fos. ii + 175 + vi, foliated [i–ix], 1–45, [46–131], 1–5, [5A], 6–9, [10–12], 13, [14], 15, [16–19], 20, [21–23], 24, [25], 26, [27], 28, [29–34]; blank: fos. [i*v*–ii*v*, iv*v*–v*v*, ix*r*–*v*], 45*v*, plus 86 blank fos., 2nd series 34*r*–*v*; hide-covered boards.

[iii*r*–iv*r*] royal grant July 1553
[vi*r*–viii*v*] enthronement of bishop Mar. 1603
1*r*–10*v* institutions, mostly by vicar-general Mar. 1603–July 1604
11*r*–45*r* institutions by bishop July 1604–June 1608 (incomplete at end)
(*2nd series*)
1*v*–[33*v*] memoranda (consecrations, unions of benefices, faculties, dispensations, etc., not in any chronological order) Sept. 1602–Aug. 1638

Reg. 17/21 is a seventeenth-century index of this register.

2. NNRO, Reg/16/22. Paper register; fos. i + 81 ($11\frac{1}{4}'' \times 7\frac{1}{2}''$) + 6 ($11\frac{3}{4}'' \times 7\frac{3}{4}''$) + 33 ($11\frac{1}{2}'' \times 7\frac{1}{2}''$) + 127 ($12'' \times 8''$) + i, foliated [i–xx], 1–60, 70–75, [76–86], 1–33, [1–127]; blank: fos. [xix*v*, xx*v*], 74*r*–*v*, [76*v*–80*v*, 84*v*–85*v*], 3rd series [1*r*–*v*, 35*r*–38*v*, 74*r*–*v*]; hide-covered boards (front cover detached).

Register of Bishop John Jegon

[i*r*–xx*r*]	place index to Jegon's register
1*r*–73*v*	institutions July 1604–Mar. 1618
75*r*–[76*v*]	copy of an inspeximus by the prior of Norwich of charters of Bishops Thomas, W., and John of Norwich about Sibton church and Peasenhall chapel (registered Mar. 1638)

Register of Bishop Samuel Harsnett

[81*r*–84*r*]	institutions Oct. 1619–Jan. 1627
[86*r*–*v*]	place index to the following section
(*2nd series*)	
1*r*–33*r*	institutions and ordinations Apr. 1624–Jan. 1629
(*3rd series*)	
[2*r*–127*v*]	visitation of the diocese 1627—exhibit book (arranged by rural deanery)

VACANCY 1618

LPL, register of Archbishop George Abbot, volume I, fos. 361*r*–374*r*.

Norwich vacancy business Mar.–Sept. 1618

VACANCY 1619

LPL, register of Archbishop George Abbot, volume II, fos. 241*r*–247*v*.

Norwich vacancy business May–Aug. 1619

VACANCY 1629

LPL, register of Archbishop George Abbot, volume II, fo. 308*r*–*v*.

Norwich vacancy business Jan.–Feb. 1629

FRANCIS WHITE (1629–1631)
RICHARD CORBET (1632–1635)
MATTHEW WREN (1635–1638)

NNRO, Reg/16/23. Paper register; 12″ × 7½″; fos. iii + 125 + iii, paginated [i–ii], 1–55, 57–126, [127–133], foliated 147–185, [186–205]; blank: pp. 4–6, 23, 24, [127–133], fos. 147*v*, 148*v*, 149*v*, 150*v*, 151*v*, 185*v*–[200*v*, 205*r*–*v*]; hide-covered boards.

Register of Bishop Richard Corbet

[i]	register heading
1–126	institutions and ordinations May 1632–Apr. 1635

Register of Bishop Francis White

147*r*–151*r*	institutions Mar.–Dec. 1631

Register of Bishop Matthew Wren

152*r*–185*r*	institutions and ordinations Dec. 1635–Apr. 1638
[201*r*–*v*]	presentation deed and letter of institution Nov. 1634
[202*r*–204*v*]	place index to the volume

VACANCY 1631–1632

LPL, register of Archbishop George Abbot, volume III, fos. 153*r*–159*v*.

Norwich vacancy business Dec. 1631–Jan. 1633

VACANCY 1635

LPL, register of Archbishop William Laud, volume I, fos. 137*v*–140*v*.

record of visitation of the diocese *sede vacante* Aug.–Dec. 1635

Institutions are calendared by E. D. Stone in NNRO, MC. 16/19.

RICHARD MONTAGUE (1638–1641)
JOSEPH HALL (1641–1656)

NNRO, Reg/18/24. Parchment register; fos. iv (paper)+vi (paper index, 13¾″ × 6″)+ii (limp parchment covers)+26 (14″ × 9¼″)+vi (paper index, 14″ × 6″)+75 (14″ × 9¾″)+iv (paper), foliated [i–xi], 1–23, [i–xii], 1–70; blank: fos. [vi*v*, vii*v*–viii*v*, ix*v*–xi*v*], 23*v*, 2nd series [xii*v*], 70*v*; hide-covered boards.

Register of Bishop Richard Montague

[i*r*–vi*r*]	place index to Montague's register
[ix*r*]	register heading
1*r*–23*r*	institutions and ordinations May 1638–Apr. 1641

Register of Bishop Joseph Hall (*2nd series*)

[i*r*–vi*v*]	place index to Hall's register
[vii*r*]	register heading
[vii*v*]	episcopal coat of arms
[viii*r*–xii*r*]	enthronement of bishop Dec. 1641
1*r*–70*r*	institutions and ordinations Dec. 1641–Sept. 1648 (last ordination Sept. 1644)

ORDINATION BOOKS

1. NNRO, ORR/1a. Paper register (damaged by damp, repaired); 11½″ × 8¼″; fos. i+110+i, foliated 1–110; blank: fos. 33*r*, 38*v*, 39*v*, 40*r*, 41*r*, 49*r*, 55*r*, 59*r*, 60*r*, 62*r*, 63*v*; modern binding.

1*r*–110*v*	ordinations Mar. 1532–Dec. 1561

NNRO, MC. 16/6 is a calendar and index of names of this volume.

2. NNRO, ORR/1b. Paper register; average 12″ × 8″; fos. 108, foliated [i–iv], 1–87, [88–104]; blank: fos. [i*v*–iv*v*], 5*r*–*v*, 7*r*–*v*, 15*v*–17*r*, 28*r*–*v*, 29*v*–30*v*, 87*v*–[102*v*, 103*v*–104*v*]; limp parchment covers.

1*r*–27*v*	visitation of the diocese Apr.–June 1556
29*r*	consistory proceedings Aug. 1556
31*r*–86*v*	ordinations June 1563–Sept. 1574, Sept. 1595–Sept. 1609 (including some dispensations copied in)
87*r*	ordinations Dec. 1619
[103*r*]	lists of names and sums of money headed 'The prestes booke' 'Tenantries'

NNRO, MC. 16/6 is a calendar and index of names of fos. 31–87.

OXFORD

Repositories

1. Bodleian Library, Department of Western Manuscripts, Oxford OX1 3BG (Bodl.).
2. Lambeth Palace Library, London SE1 7JU (LPL).
3. Canterbury Cathedral Archives and Library, The Precincts, Canterbury CT1 2EG (CAL).

Area

The diocese of Oxford was established in 1542 when the archdeaconry of Oxford was severed from the huge diocese of Lincoln. The new bishop originally had his cathedral at Osney Abbey but within a few years the see was transferred to Christ Church. The diocese extended over the whole of Oxfordshire, except for isolated peculiar jurisdictions, and there were no further changes in the diocesan boundaries until the nineteenth century.[1]

Bibliographical Note

The Oxford diocesan registers, which are basically records of institutions and ordinations, begin shortly after the establishment of the new bishopric. They are approximately chronological in arrangement and originally some attempt seems to have been made at a division of the volumes by category of business. The first register contains a separate section for caveats for a brief period and ordinations are registered separately until 1608. After that date they are recorded with the institutions and cognate benefice material in one general sequence. A distinctive, but understandable, feature of these early Oxford registers is the considerable number of extracts from the medieval Lincoln episcopal registers copied into them, particularly concerning the ordination of vicarages in Oxfordshire. The Oxford diocese experienced three extensive vacancies in the second half of the sixteenth and the early seventeenth centuries—1557–67, 1568–89 and 1592–1604—and although some vacancy entries are contained in all three Oxford registers, they certainly do not constitute the duplicate *sede vacante* registers occasionally to be found elsewhere. A fuller record of the archbishop of Canterbury's vacancy administration on these occasions is entered in the archiepiscopal registers.

The contents of these Oxford registers have been the subject of detailed treatment by Canon W. J. Oldfield and his resulting two-volume manuscript compilation, *Clerus Dioc. Oxon.*, or to give it its full title, *Index to the Clergy whose Ordination, Institution, Resignation, Licence or Death is recorded in the Diocesan Registers of the Diocese of Oxford from the Foundation of the See in 1542 to the end of July 1908*, was presented to the Bodleian Library in 1915 (MS. Top. Oxon. c. 250). The volumes are arranged alphabetically by surname of clergy and by benefice.[2]

ROBERT KING (1542–1557)

VACANCY 1557–1567

HUGH CUREN (1567–1568)

VACANCY 1568–1589

[1] For an ecclesiastical map of Oxfordshire, see *VCH Oxfordshire* ii (1907), between pp. 58–9; also the frontispiece to E. Marshall, *Diocesan Histories: Oxford* (London, 1882).

[2] Lists of medieval incumbents for parishes in the Oxfordshire hundreds of Banbury, Bullingdon, Dorchester, Lewknor, Ploughley, Pyrton, Thame and Wootton, taken from the Lincoln episcopal registers, are contained in *Lists of medieval incumbents of Oxfordshire parishes compiled for the Oxfordshire Victoria County History* (Bodl., MS. Top. Oxon. d. 460). Further details of the clergy in the diocese in the early years of Elizabeth I's reign are to be found in a series of articles by S. S. Pearce in the *Reports of the Oxfordshire Archaeological Society*, 58 (1912), 89–110; 60 (1914), 180–237; 62 (1916), 15–86; 64 (1918), 127–189; 65 (1919), 198–234; 66 (1920), 242–289.

JOHN UNDERHILL (1589–1592)
VACANCY 1592–1604

Bodl., MS. Oxf. dioc. papers d. 105. Paper register; $11\frac{1}{2}'' \times 8''$; pp. ii + 306 + ii, paginated i–xvi, 1–69, 71–270A, 270B, 271–294; blank: pp. ii, iv–xvi, 22, 67–69, 89, 98, 107, 117, 277, 279–294; rough hide binding.

1–7	caveats Sept. 1543–May 1546
8–21	institutions May 1544–Mar. 1546
23–117	ordinations Sept. 1544–Apr. 1558, Nov. 1567–Aug. 1568 (includes dispensations to take orders outside the statutory time and occasionally other miscellaneous business, e.g. copy of Edward VI's injunctions sent to the bishop after the royal visitation of 1547, administrative proceedings before the diocesan chancellor (institution, resignation, grant of pension), copies of ordinations of vicarages from the medieval Lincoln episcopal registers)
118–255	institutions and resignations etc. Mar. 1546–Mar. 1570 (includes caveats, grants of next presentation, occasional extracts from the medieval Lincoln episcopal registers, the grant of a pension, the lease of a rectory)
256	ordinations June 1597
257–258	copy of medieval ordination of Shipton-under-Wychwood vicarage (from Lincoln episcopal register)
260–270	ordinations June–Oct. 1568, July 1597–Mar. 1602 (includes commission to the bishop of Carlisle to ordain in the diocese *sede vacante*)
271–276	18th-cent. index of places
278	miscellaneous administrative notes

For further material relating to this period, see the vacancy registers and Bodl., MS. Oxf. dioc. papers c. 265 below.

VACANCY 1557–1567

1. LPL, register of Archbishop Reginald Pole, fos. 61*r*–62*r*.[3]

   Oxford vacancy business Dec. 1557–Oct. 1558

2. CAL, register U2, fos. 39*v*–41*r*.

   Oxford vacancy business Dec. 1558–Nov. 1559

   Institutions are calendared (by place) in *Sede Vacante Institutions*.

3. LPL, register of Archbishop Matthew Parker, volume I, fos. 185*r*–191*r*.

   Oxford vacancy business Dec. 1559–Apr. 1567

   Printed, *Registrum Matthei Parker* i, pp. 245–60.

VACANCY 1568–1589

1. LPL, register of Archbishop Matthew Parker, volume II, fos. 49*v*–59*v*.

   Oxford vacancy business Dec. 1568–May 1575

   Printed, *ibid.*, iii, pp. 991–1013.

2. LPL, register of the dean and chapter of Canterbury *sede vacante* (part of Parker II), fos. 118*r*–119*v*.

   Oxford vacancy business June 1575–Mar. 1576

   Printed, *ibid.*, pp. 1160–63.

[3] See under Canterbury for a description of this and subsequent archiepiscopal and capitular registers.

3. LPL, register of Archbishop Edmund Grindal, volume II, fos. 345*r*–378*r*.

   Oxford vacancy business Mar. 1576–June 1583

4. LPL, register of the dean and chapter of Canterbury *sede vacante* (part of Grindal II), fos. 581*r*–582*v*.

   Oxford vacancy business July 1583

5. LPL, register of Archbishop John Whitgift, volume I, fos. 296*r*–306*r*.

   Oxford vacancy business Nov. 1583–Dec. 1589

VACANCY 1592–1604

1. LPL, register of Archbishop John Whitgift, volume II, fos. 188*r*–200*v*.

   Oxford vacancy business May 1592–Nov. 1597

2. LPL, register of Archbishop John Whitgift, volume III, fos. 166*v*–179*v*.

   Oxford vacancy business May 1598–Feb. 1604

For further material relating to the above three vacancies, see the first and third diocesan registers (Bodl., MS. Oxf. dioc. papers d. 105, c. 265).

JOHN BRIDGES (1604–1618)
JOHN HOWSON (1619–1628)
RICHARD CORBET (1628–1632)
VACANCY 1632
JOHN BANCROFT (1632–1641)
VACANCY 1641
ROBERT SKINNER (1641–1663)

Bodl., MS. Oxf. dioc. papers c. 264. Paper register; $11\frac{3}{4}'' \times 7\frac{1}{2}''$; fos. vi + 162 (some misplaced) + iv, foliated i–xii, 1–160; blank: fos. iv–vi*v*, vii*v*–xii*v*, 7*v*–8*v*, 10*v*, 85*v*, 120*v*, 124*r*–*v*, 136*r*–142*v*, 152*v*–154*r*, 156*r*; modern binding.

1*r*–7*r*	miscellaneous business (Privy Council letter, patent of official, surrogation acts) Dec. 1604–Nov. 1607
9*r*–17*v*	ordinations Aug. 1604–June 1606
18*r*–23*v*	institutions and resignations Aug. 1604–Mar. 1607
24*r*–26*v*	ordinations Apr. 1606–Dec. 1607
26*v*–109*r*	institutions, resignations, ordinations (from Feb. 1608) and cognate business Nov. 1607–Mar. 1623
109*v*–135*v*	institutions etc (but excluding ordinations) July 1627–May 1642 [Fos. 147, 149 and 150 should come between fos. 130 and 131; fo. 148 should follow fo. 61. Fo. 119*v* contains one *sede vacante* entry May 1632, and fos. 134*v*–135*v* four similar vacancy entries Feb.–July 1641]
143*r*–146*v*	statutes for King James' school, Henley on Thames
151*r*	note on dispensation of benefices
151*r*–152*r*	18th-cent. place index (A–M only)
154*v*–155*r*	note of payments from benefices (? institution fees) 1612–[1617]
157*r*–158*r*	18th-cent. copy of institution entry for Waterperry Feb. 1608 (on fo. 27*r*)

For 1632 vacancy business, see also below.

The following volume contains entries which overlap chronologically material included in the first two diocesan registers.

Bodl., MS. Oxf. dioc. papers c.265. Parchment register; $12\frac{1}{4}'' \times 8\frac{3}{4}''$; fos. i (paper) + 33 + i (paper), paginated i–iv, 1–48, 51–58, 61–70 (gaps due to misnumbering); blank: pp. i–ii, 57, 58, 61, 64–67, 69, 70; parchment-covered wooden boards.

1–63 general register June 1579–July 1638

This register, which is somewhat miscellaneous in nature and not always in strict chronological sequence, can be divided (by category if not physically) into three distinct sections—the first being a record of institutions, resignations and other benefice matters for the periods June 1579–Dec. 1590 (pp. 1–9), Aug. 1597–July 1601 (pp. 10–13) and Feb. 1604 (p. 18); the second comprising a collection of copies of ordinations of vicarages in the diocese and other medieval material, for the most part extracted from the Lincoln episcopal registers (pp. 14–17, 19–30, 33–38); and finally, a variety of administrative documents dating between June 1613 and July 1638 and dealing with such business as the consecration of college chapels, the consolidation of benefices, the settlement of a parochial dispute and royal letters on diocesan affairs (pp. 30–33, 38–63). No institutions, ordinations and the like are included in this last section.

VACANCY 1618–1619

LPL, register of Archbishop George Abbot, volume I, fos. 374*v*–378*v*.

Oxford vacancy business Mar. 1618–Apr. 1619

VACANCY 1628

LPL, register of Archbishop George Abbot, volume II, fos. 307*r*–308*r*.

Oxford vacancy business Sept.–Oct. 1628

VACANCY 1632

LPL, register of Archbishop George Abbot, volume III, fos. 162*v*–163*v*.

Oxford vacancy business May 1632

See also above (Bodl., MS. Oxf. dioc. papers c. 264) for 1632 vacancy material.

PETERBOROUGH

Repositories

1. Northamptonshire Record Office, Delapre Abbey, Northampton NN4 9AW (NRO).
2. Lambeth Palace Library, London SE1 7JU (LPL).
3. Canterbury Cathedral Archives and Library, The Precincts, Canterbury CT1 2EG (CAL).

Area

The archdeaconry of Northampton, comprising Northamptonshire and Rutland, was removed from the diocese of Lincoln in 1541 to form the new diocese of Peterborough. The boundaries of the bishopric, as originally constituted, remained unaltered until the nineteenth century.[1]

Bibliographical Note

The Peterborough diocesan act books comprise two separate series—institution books and ordination books, the contents of which obviously require no further elucidation. One interesting feature about the institution books is that from 1599 until the end of the period under consideration a subsidiary series of duplicate volumes exists. In one sense they are not exactly duplicates, since although they note the same institutions they constitute a fuller record of the administrative procedure followed in each case and indeed have merited the description 'institutions proceedings books'. Whereas the institution books proper contain a brief summary of the act of institution, these subsidiary volumes detail the proceedings before the bishop in respect of the admission to, and vacation of, benefices, each entry generally being prefaced by a heading such as *negotium institutionis A. ad rectoriam ecclesie parochialis de B.* These volumes also contain occasional licences for curates and non-residence but only the first volume (X957/5) includes other court material relating to testamentary and matrimonial cases and the like. Resignations are not noted in the main series of institution books after 1599 when the fuller record survives in the 'duplicate' volumes. The separate series of ordination books does not survive the fourth volume cited below. Between 1688 and 1719 no ordinations are recorded at all and from the latter date they are entered in the institution books. The Canterbury archiepiscopal registers contain a record of their *sede vacante* administration in the diocese and some material for the vacancies of 1556–7 and 1559–61 is also to be found in the Peterborough institution books. The latter duplicate entries in the Canterbury volumes.

The clergy contained in these diocesan act books have been studied extensively by Rev. Henry Isham Longden and other antiquarians and local historians. Longden's notebooks containing Peterborough institutions 1542–1823 (NRO, HIL. MS. 2109.2) and ordinations 1570–1819 (*ibid.*, HIL MS. 2109.3) were used in his monumental published work, *Northamptonshire and Rutland Clergy from 1500* (16 vols in 6, Northamptonshire Record Society, 1938–52). An annotated copy of this publication is available at the Northamptonshire Record Office. The manuscripts of Rev. E. A. Irons, also in the Northamptonshire Record Office, contain lists of institutions recorded in the first five institution books (IR. MSS. 35–39) and lists of incumbents for the diocese (IR. MSS. 1–30, 34) and also copies of medieval institutions to Northamptonshire benefices contained in the registers of the archbishops of Canterbury *c.* 1420–*c.* 1520 (IR. MS. 33). His manuscripts listing Rutland clergy taken from the Peterborough institution books 1541–1686 and for the period 1220–1540 from the Lincoln episcopal registers (transcribed by Alfred Gibbons) can also be consulted at Delapre Abbey (X962/4). A

[1] For an ecclesiastical map of Northamptonshire, see *VCH Northamptonshire* ii (1906), between pp. 78–9 and for one of Rutland, *VCH Rutland* i (1908), opposite p. 159. See also the frontispiece to G. A. Poole, *Diocesan Histories: Peterborough* (London, 1881).

companion collection (X962/5) contains folders of lists of incumbents for Northamptonshire (*c.* 1220–1928) and Rutland (*c.* 1541–1928), compiled by Mr Dorman.

INSTITUTION BOOKS

NRO, X956/1. Paper register; 12¼″ × 8¼″; fos. 143, foliated [i], 1–130 + 12 unnumbered fos. (the first 10 being a table of contents, place-names only); blank: at the end, the 11th of the unnumbered fos.; modern binding.

1*r*–130*v* institutions and resignations Oct. 1541–Feb. 1574

NRO, X956/2. Paper register; 12¼″ × 8¼″; fos. vi + 71 (1 fo. is inserted), foliated [i–vi], 2–49, 56–78, 80 (some fos. missing); blank: fo. 71*r*; modern binding.

i*r*–vi*v* table of contents (place-names only)
2*r*–80*v* institutions, resignations and cognate business (presentation deeds, dispensations, inhibition etc.) Apr. 1574–Jan. 1585

Because of the missing folios, there are gaps in the entries between Jan. 1581 and Jan. 1582, and between Apr. and Oct. 1584.

NRO, X956/3. Paper register; 11″ × 7¾″; fos. 136, foliated [i], 1–49 (+1 blank), 50 (+2 blank), 51 (+10 blank), 52–76 (+16 blank, except for verso of last fo.), 77–82 (+3 fos., table of contents, place-names only + 21, all but last blank); blank: fos. i*v*, the versos of all fos. from 1–41 inclusive, 49*v*, 50*v*, 51*v*, 57*v*, 58*v*, 76*v*, 81*v*, 82*v* and as indicated above; modern binding.

1*r*–82*r* institutions, resignations etc. June 1585–Jan. 1599 (+1 additional entry, Jan. 1602)

NRO, X956/4. Paper register; 13¼″ × 8½″; fos. ii + 183 (11 fos. inserted) + 6 (table of contents, place-names, fos. 1–127 only, and index of places) + i, foliated [i–ii], 1–183; blank: fos. [i*r*–ii*v*], 103*v*, 144*v*–147*v*, 183*v*, verso of 3rd fo. of table of contents); limp parchment covers.

1*r*–183*r* institutions Jan. 1599–June 1643 (+1 additional entry Apr. 1645), Dec. 1660–June 1685

Four loose folios (unnumbered) are inserted between fos. 124–5 and ten loose unnumbered folios between fos. 134–5. They are fuller copies of entries on fos. 123*v*–124*v* and 135*v*–143*r* respectively. The latter loose gathering contains one additional entry not registered in the institution book.

NRO, X957/5. Paper register; 11″ × 7¼″; fos. 206, foliated 1, 1A, 2–74, 74A, 75–86, 86A (⅔ of fo. torn away), 87–202, [203]; blank: fos. 1*r*–1A*v*, 34*r*–*v*, 37*v*, 47*r*–*v*, 119*v*, 121*v*–122*v*, 177*r*–*v*, 190*v*, 201*v*–[203*v*]; limp parchment covers.

2*r*–201*r* institutions and resignations Jan. 1599–Sept. 1616 (includes some other court material, matrimonial, testamentary)

Fos. 33–4, 56–7, 118–19, 121–2 are bifolia which have been inserted in the volume.

NRO, X957/6. Paper register; 11″ × 7¾″; fos. i + 269 + i, foliated [i–ii], 1–269 (fos. 160–9, 171–2, 176–9, 189–90, 194–203, 205–8, 212–13, 228–9, 231–2, 255–6 are inserted); blank: fos. [i*r*–ii*v*], 160*r*, 161*v*, 164*v*, 167*r*–169*v*, 178*r*–179*v*, 189*v*–190*v*, 193*v*, 194*v*, 195*v*, 196*v*, 198*v*–201*v*, 203*r*–*v*, 207*v*, 211*v*, 212*v*, 213*v*, 227*v*, 229*r*, 231*v*–232*v*, 246*v*, 247*v*, 255*v*–256*v*, 269*r*–*v*; limp parchment covers.

1*r*–268*v* institutions and resignations Nov. 1616–Mar. 1638

NRO, X957/7. Paper register; 11½″ × 7¾″; fos. 270, foliated [i], 1–14, 14A, 15–88 (+16 blank) + 1668 entry (+152 blank) + proxy entry (+1 blank) + 9 (abstracts of leases etc.) (+1 blank); blank: fos. [i*r*–*v*], 87*r*–*v*, 88*v* and as indicated above; limp parchment covers.

1*r*–86*v* institutions and resignations Feb. 1638–Nov. 1648, Aug. 1660–Aug. 1665 (+additional entries Aug. 1668 and undated proxy)
88*r* 2 licences July–Sept. 1676

The nine folios at the end of the volume contain an abstract made in 1647 of leases, patents of officials, etc. recorded 'in the greate booke with the Red leather cover' Oct. 1587–Jan. 1643.

ORDINATION BOOKS

NRO, X959/1. Paper register; 12″ × 8″; fos. 79, foliated 1–61, [62–64], 65–73, [74–79]; blank: fos. 1*r*–*v*, 11*r*–*v*, 14*v*, 19*v*, 21*r*–22*r*, 23*r*–24*v*, 25*v*, 26*v*, 49*r*–*v*, 60*v*–[64*v*], 65*v*, 67*r*–70*v*, [74*v*–79*v*]; limp parchment covers.

2*r*–20*v*	copies of 9 grants, royal letters patent, etc. on miscellaneous administrative matters Feb. 1553–Dec. 1579
25*r*–73*v*	ordinations Dec. 1570–Nov. 1595 (includes occasional miscellaneous entries not connected with ordinations)

NRO, X959/2. Paper register; 12″ × 7¾″; fos. 48, foliated [i], 1–47; blank: fos. [i*r*–*v*], 47*v*; limp parchment covers.

1*r*–47*r* ordinations Jan. 1599–Sept. 1616

NRO, X959/3. Paper register; 12¼″ × 8″; fos. 38, foliated [i], 1–37+i (fo. 25, a loose sheet of paper sewn on to fo. 24); blank: fos. [i*r*–*v*], 25*v*; limp parchment covers.

1*r*–37*v* ordinations Sept. 1616–Mar. 1623

NRO, X959/4. Paper register; 11½″ × 7½″; fos. 163, foliated 1–110 (last 53 fos. unnumbered and blank); blank: fos. 1*r*–3*v*, 90*r*–91*v*, 97*r*, 98*v*–99*r*, 103*v*, 106*r*, 107*r*, 108*v*, 110*v* and all subsequent fos. as indicated above; original covers lost, temporary covers of sugar paper.

4*r*–110*r* ordinations Mar. 1623–Feb. 1643, Sept. 1646, May–Sept. 1648, Sept. 1661–May 1665, Mar. 1669–Jan. 1688

VACANCY ADMINISTRATION

VACANCY 1556–1557

1. CAL, register N, fo. 134A*r*–*v*.[2]

Peterborough vacancy business Feb. 1556

Institutions are calendared (by place) in *Sede Vacante Institutions*.

2. LPL, register of Archbishop Reginald Pole, fos. 37*r*–38*v*.

Peterborough vacancy business Apr. 1556–Aug. 1557

For further material relating to this vacancy see NRO, X956/1, fo. 62*v* (entries July–Aug. 1556).

VACANCY 1559–1561

1. CAL, register U2, fos. 104*v*–105*v*.

Peterborough vacancy business Nov. 1559

Institutions are calendared (by place) in *Sede Vacante Institutions*.

2. LPL, register of Archbishop Matthew Parker, volume I, fos. 160*v*–164*r*.

Peterborough vacancy business Dec. 1559–Mar. 1561

Printed, *Registrum Matthei Parker* i, pp. 198–202. For further material relating to this vacancy see NRO, X956/1, fos. 84*v*–87*r* (entries Aug. 1560–Feb. 1561).

VACANCY 1585

LPL, register of Archbishop John Whitgift, volume I, fo. 384*v*.

Peterborough vacancy business Jan. 1585

[2] See under Canterbury for a description of this and subsequent capitular and archiepiscopal registers.

VACANCY 1600–1601

LPL, register of Archbishop John Whitgift, volume III, fos. 208*r*–212*v*.

Peterborough vacancy business June 1600–Apr. 1601

VACANCY 1630

LPL, register of Archbishop George Abbot, volume III, fo. 148*v* contains a note to the effect that 'nihil omnino expeditum fuit in eadem diocesi dicta vacacione durante'.

VACANCY 1632–1633

LPL, register of Archbishop George Abbot, volume III, fos. 176*v*–179*r*.

Peterborough vacancy business Dec. 1632–Jan. 1633

VACANCY 1634

LPL, register of Archbishop William Laud, volume I, fos. 300*r*–301*v*.

Peterborough vacancy business Mar.–May 1634

ROCHESTER

Repositories

1. Kent County Archives Office, County Hall, Maidstone ME14 1XH (KAO).
2. Lambeth Palace Library, London SE1 7JU (LPL).
3. Canterbury Cathedral Archives and Library, The Precincts, Canterbury CT1 2EG (CAL).

Area

The medieval diocese of Rochester consisted of Kent west of the Medway, and was divided into the rural deaneries of Rochester, Dartford, Malling and Shoreham.[1] There was only one archdeaconry. The deanery of Shoreham was a peculiar jurisdiction of the archbishop of Canterbury, but the bishop had his own peculiar, the deanery of Isleham, comprising the parishes of Isleham (Cambridgeshire) and Freckenham (Suffolk). The bishopric stood in a special relationship to the archbishopric of Canterbury, since the archbishops claimed to be patrons of the see and administered both the spiritualities and temporalities during a vacancy.[2]

Bibliographical Note

The earliest extant Rochester register dates from 1319 but the bishops are known to have kept registers from at least the time of Laurence of St Martin (1251–74), whose register was still in existence in 1347.[3] The series of episcopal registers ceases with the pontificate of John Dolben (1666–83) and is replaced by the so-called muniment book (containing faculties, licences, enthronements of bishops, Convocation business, etc.) and an institution book (institutions, collations and ordinations).[4] The surviving registers 1319–1683 are bound up in six composite volumes (the present binding dates from the first decade of this century), but many of the registers retain evidence of separate foliation. The usual arrangement of these registers is simple, namely, a single, general register in approximate chronological order. Ordination records have not survived for every episcopate; when they do, they are sometimes included in the general register in their proper sequence, and at other times constitute a separate section. The only exception to this general arrangement is the earliest surviving register, that of Hamo Hethe (1319–52), Until 1340, when the keeping of a single general register was adopted, the register was kept in several sections: institutions, ordinations, licences, etc.; royal writs and correspondence with ecclesiastical colleagues and superiors; matters relating to the bishop's Isleham peculiar; and consistory court business.

Only Hethe's register has been published but use has been made of the registers by John Thorpe, *Registrum Roffense* (London, 1769) and by C. H. Fielding in his *Records of Rochester* (Dartford, 1910), the latter volume listing parochial incumbents for the whole diocese.

VACANCY 1317–1319

LPL, register of Archbishop Walter Reynolds, fos. 19*v*–25*r* *passim*.[5]

Rochester vacancy business Mar. 1317–July 1319, among the general section of Canterbury institutions

[1] See *VCH Kent* ii (1926), pp. 110–11, and map facing p. 112. There is also a map of the diocese as a frontispiece to A. J. Pearman, *Diocesan Histories: Rochester* (London, 1897).

[2] For full details of this relationship see I. J. Churchill, 'Relations between the sees of Canterbury and Rochester' in *Canterbury Administration* i (London, 1933), pp. 279–87.

[3] *English Bishops' Chanceries*, p. 148, citing *Registrum Hamonis Hethe* ii, p. 827.

[4] Listed briefly in F. Hull, *Guide to the Kent County Archives Office: first supplement 1957–1968* (Maidstone, 1971), p. 73. Further details are given in a manuscript catalogue compiled by Miss A. M. Oakley in the Kent County Archives Office ('The Archives of the Dean and Chapter of Rochester *c.* 1100–1907', vol. 2, part 1 (1970), pp. 1008–12).

[5] See under Canterbury for a description of this and subsequent archiepiscopal and capitular registers.

HAMO HETHE (1319–1352)
JOHN SHEPPEY (1353–1360)
VACANCY 1360–1362
WILLIAM WHITTLESEY (1362–1364)
THOMAS TRILLEK (1364–1372)

KAO, DRc/R4. Parchment register; 13″ × $9\frac{1}{4}$″ (fos. 238A–B, 10″ × 6″; 309–12, $11\frac{3}{4}$″ × $8\frac{1}{2}$″); fos. iv (paper) + 358 + ii (old covers) + iv (paper), paginated A–F, [G–H], foliated 1–32, 34, 35, 37–84, 86–141, 141A, 142–185, 185A, 186–223, 223A, 224–238, 238A–[B], 239–293, 293A, 294–313, 315–358; blank: p. [H], fos. 72*r*, 148*r*, 179*v*, 180*v*, 185*v*, 296*v*, 307*r*, 311*v*–312*v*; modern binding.

pp. A–F	15th-cent. select alphabetical index of contents	
1*r*–256*v*	register of Bishop Hamo Hethe (see below)	
257*r*–302*v*	register of Bishop John Sheppey	
	257*r*–264*v*, 281*r*–302*r*	general register (including ordinations) Mar. 1353–Oct. 1360
	265*r*–280*v*	*acta iudicialia* (instance act book) *temp.* Hethe Apr. 1347–Oct. 1348
	302*v*	contemporary list of contents (using separate foliation 1–31)
303*r*–308*v*	*sede vacante* register Nov. 1360–Nov. 1361	
309*r*–320*v*	register of Bishop William Whittlesey (this register is misbound, the correct sequence being 314–20, 309–12)	
	309*r*–319*v*	general register Feb. 1362–Nov. 1363
	320*r*–*v*	ordinations Dec. 1362–Feb. 1364
321*r*–355*v*	register of Bishop Thomas Trillek general register (including ordinations) Feb. 1365–Oct. 1372	
356*r*–*v*	portion (incomplete) of a grant of Sunninghill, Broomhall and Ayton to Eton College, n.d.	
357*r*–358*v*	old covers, upon which are inscribed some accounts	

Hethe's register is incomplete, lacking entries for the last two years of the episcopate and some ordinations. As has already been mentioned, there was a change in registrational practice in 1340, when the sectional divisions were superseded by a general, chronological register. The first forty folios of this register contain copies of charters granted to Rochester cathedral and religious houses in the diocese, most of them produced for inspection at the episcopal visitation of 1320.

Hethe's register is printed, *Registrum Hamonis Hethe, diocesis Roffensis, A.D. 1319–1352*, ed. C. Johnson (2 vols, Canterbury and York Society 48–49, 1948).

VACANCY 1360–1362

LPL, register of Archbishop Simon Islip, fos. 222*v*–226*v*.

Rochester vacancy business Oct. 1360–Dec. 1361

A vacancy act of June 1361 is recorded among the general memoranda of Islip's register on fo. 174*v*.

VACANCY 1389

1. LPL, register of Archbishop William Courtenay, fo. 277*r*.

   Rochester vacancy business Aug.-Oct. 1389

2. *ibid.*, fos. 354*r*–361*v*.

   Rochester vacancy business June–Dec. 1389

WILIAM BOTTLESHAM (1389–1400)
JOHN BOTTLESHAM (1400–1404)
VACANCY 1404–1407

KAO, DRc/R5. Parchment register; $13\frac{1}{4}'' \times 10\frac{1}{4}''$; fos. iv (paper) + i (paper) + viii (paper, 11″ × 7″) + 192 + iv (paper), foliated 1–8, 1–91, 91A, 92–192 (including inserts); blank: fo. 8*v* (1st series); modern binding.

1*r*–8*r*	17th-cent. table of contents (*repertorium*)
1*r*–91*v*, 92*r*–143*v*	general register of Bishop William Bottlesham Jan. 1390–Feb. 1400 (the last entry is incomplete)
91A*r*	ordinations May 1429
91A*v*	list of spiritual pensions received by the bishop from churches etc. 1439
144*r*–147*r*	ordinations (incomplete at the beginning) Mar. 1393 (earliest recorded date)–Dec. 1399
147*v*–148*v*	letters of bishop of London to Bishop Young on provincial business July 1416
149*r*–186*v*	general register of Bishop John Bottlesham (including ordinations) July 1400–Apr. 1404
187*r*–191*v*	*sede vacante* register May 1404–Jan. 1407
192*r*	royal letter to bailiff of the liberty of Rochester about Lollards etc. Aug. 1400

A section of Bishop John Bottlesham's register, which should come between fos. 182 and 183 of this volume, is now bound in DRc/R6, fos. 34*r*–41*v* (see below).

VACANCY 1400

1. LPL, register of Archbishop Thomas Arundel, volume I, fos. 463*r*–464*v*.

   Rochester vacancy business Feb.–Apr. 1400

2. *ibid.*, fos. 265*v*–268*v passim.*

   Rochester vacancy business Mar.–May 1400, among the general section of Canterbury institutions

JOHN BOTTLESHAM (1400–1404)
RICHARD YOUNG (1404–1418)[6]
JOHN LANGDON (1422–1434)
THOMAS BROUNS (1435–1436)
WILLIAM WELLS (1437–1444)
JOHN LOW (1444–1467)

KAO, DRc/R6. Parchment register; average $14'' \times 10\frac{1}{4}''$; fos. iv (paper) + i (paper) + 233 + iv (paper), foliated 1–77, 79–100, 111–140, 142–247 (including inserts) (there is also a modern pencil foliation 1–235 which has not been used here); blank: fos. 119*r*, 198*v*, 215*v*; modern binding.

1*r*–6*v*	general register of Bishop Richard Young (last entry incomplete) Dec. 1417–June 1418
7*r*–100*r*	general register of Bishop John Langdon July 1422–Sept. 1434 (this register is now misbound: the correct sequence should be: 7–22, 51–66, 23–30, 43–50, 67–100, 31–33; 42 is a stray which does not fit in the previous sequence, and for fos. 34–41 see below)
100*v*–111*v*	alphabetical contents list of register

[6] Bishop Young, although translated in 1404, did not receive the spiritualities and temporalities until 1407.

34*r*–41*v*	part of the general register of Bishop John Bottlesham Apr.-Nov. 1403
42*r*–*v*	ordinations, and dedication of church June (?1429)–Sept. 1429
112*r*–118*v*	general register of Bishop Thomas Brouns May 1435–Aug. 1436
119*v*	alphabetical contents list of register
120*r*–198*r*	general register of Bishop William Wells Mar. 1437–Feb. 1444
199*r*–247*v*	general register of Bishop John Low June 1444–Dec. 1466

For ordinations, May 1429, see above DRc/R5, fo. 91A*r*, and *ibid.*, fos. 147*v*–148*v* for provincial business addressed to Bishop Young.

VACANCY 1404–1407

1. LPL, register of Archbishop Thomas Arundel, volume I, fos. 465*v*–467*v*.

Rochester vacancy business Apr. 1404–July 1405

2. *ibid.*, fos. 297*r*–313*r passim.*

Rochester vacancy business July 1404–Dec. 1406, among the general section of Canterbury institutions

See also above, DRc/R5 for material for this vacancy.

VACANCY 1418–1419

LPL, register of Archbishop Henry Chichele, volume I, fos. 24*v*–25*v*, 100*v*–101*r*, 113*r*.

Rochester vacancy business Dec. 1418–Aug. 1419, among the general section of Canterbury institutions, and the section concerning appointments of bishops etc.

Printed, *Register of Henry Chichele* i, pp. 60–63, 173, 183–4.

VACANCY 1421–1422

LPL, register of Archbishop Henry Chichele, volume I, fos. 127*v*–131*v passim.*

Rochester vacancy business Aug. 1421–Feb. 1422, among the general section of Canterbury institutions

Printed, *Register of Henry Chichele* i, pp. 201–3 *passim.*

VACANCY 1434–1435

LPL, register of Archbishop Henry Chichele, volume I, fos. 204*v*–206*r passim.*

Rochester vacancy business Oct. 1434–Apr. 1435, among the general section of Canterbury institutions

Printed, *Register of Henry Chichele* i, pp. 285–7 *passim.*

VACANCY 1444

1. LPL, register of Archbishop John Stafford, fos. 43*r*–45*r*.

Rochester vacancy business Feb.–June 1444

2. *ibid.*, fos. 76*r*–78*v passim*

Rochester vacancy business Mar.–June 1444, among the general section of Canterbury institutions

THOMAS SAVAGE (1493–1496)
RICHARD FITZJAMES (1497–1503)
JOHN FISHER (1504–1535)
VACANCY 1535
JOHN HILSEY (1535–1539)
NICHOLAS HEATH (1540–1544)

KAO, DRc/R7. Parchment/paper register; 14″ × 11¼″; fos. iv (paper) + i (paper) + i (parchment) + ii (paper) + 39 (parchment) + i (paper) + 91 (parchment) + 36 (paper) + 2 (parchment) + 14 (paper) + i (paper) + 24 (paper) + 1 (parchment) + 16 (paper) + iv (paper), foliated [i–iv], 1–216, [217–223]; blank: fos. [i*r*, iii*v*–iv*r*], 126*v*, 157*r*–*v*, 208*v*, 216*v*–[223*v*]; modern binding.

[ii*r*–iii*r*]	16th-cent. table of contents of the registers of Savage, FitzJames and Fisher (with later additions)
1*r*–17*v*	general register of Bishop Thomas Savage (in some chronological disorder) Feb. 1493–Nov. 1496
18*r*–36*v*, 39*r*–*v*	general register of Bishop Richard FitzJames (includes ordinations; in some chronological disorder) May 1497–Aug. 1503
37*r*–38*r*	composition concerning the vicarage of St Margaret's, Rochester, Feb. 1489
38*v*	collations Sept. 1493, June 1496
40*r*–182*r*	general register of Bishop John Fisher (includes ordinations, and copies of earlier documents; not always in strict chronological order) Nov. 1504–Dec. 1534
182*r*–*v*	document relating to the election of Bishop Hilsey, and letter dimissory Aug. 1535
183*r*–198*v*	general register of Bishop John Hilsey Sept. 1535–Apr. 1539
199*r*–216*r*	general register of Bishop Nicholas Heath July 1540–Aug. 1542 (for continuation, see below)

VACANCY 1496–1497

LPL, register of Archbishop John Morton, volume I, fos. 159*r*–162*v*.

Rochester vacancy business Nov. 1496

Calendared in C. Harper-Bill, 'An edition of the register of John Morton, archbishop of Canterbury, 1486–1500' (London University Ph.D., 1977).

VACANCY 1503–1504

LPL, register of Archbishop William Warham, volume II, fos. 232*r*–235*v*.

Rochester vacancy business Feb.–Nov. 1504

NICHOLAS HEATH (1540–1544)
HENRY HOLBEACH (1544–1547)
NICHOLAS RIDLEY (1547–1550)
MAURICE GRIFFIN (1554–1558)
EDMUND GHEAST (1560–1571)
EDMUND FREKE (1572–1575)
JOHN PIERS (1576–1577)
JOHN YOUNG (1578–1605)
WILLIAM BARLOW (1605–1608)

RICHARD NEILE (1608–1610)
JOHN BUCKERIDGE (1611–1628)
VACANCY 1628
WALTER CURLE (1628–1629)
JOHN BOWLE (1630–1637)
VACANCY 1637–1638
JOHN WARNER (1638–1666)

KAO, DRc/R8. Paper register; $16\frac{3}{4}'' \times 11\frac{1}{2}''$; fos. iv + 4 (parchment) + 227 + iv, foliated [i], 1–113, 113[A], 114–116, 116A, 117–121, 121A, 122–223, 223[A], 224, 225, [226, 227]; blank: fos. [i*r*], 11*v*, 58*v*, 59*v*, 69*r*–*v*, 70*v*–72*v*, 74*r*–75*v*, 77*v*, 78*v*–81*v*, 85*r*, 87*r*–88*v*, 91*v*, 95*r*–*v*, 99*v*, 131*v*, 157*r*, 186*v*, 203*v*; modern binding.

1*r*–11*r*	general register of Bishop Nicholas Heath (continued) Oct. 1542–Jan. 1544
12*r*–51*r*	general register of Bishop Henry Holbeach June 1544–May 1547
51*v*	caveat June 1549
52*r*–58*r*	general register of Bishop Nicholas Ridley (not in strict chronological order) Sept. 1547–Mar. 1550
59*r*	caveat Sept. 1552
60*r*–84*v*	general register of Bishop Maurice Griffin (not in strict chronological order) Apr. 1554–May 1558
85*v*–120*r*	general register of Bishop Edmund Gheast (not in strict chronological order) Jan. 1560–Dec. 1571
120*r*–140*v*	general register of Bishop Edmund Freke (some institutions on fos. 121*v*–121A*v* are *temp*. Bishop Gheast) Feb. 1572–Aug. 1575
141*r*–155*v*	general register of Bishop John Piers Apr. 1576–Nov. 1577
156*r*–196*r*, 215*r*	general register of Bishop John Young Apr. 1578–Sept. 1604
196*v*–203*v*, 212*v*–213*v*, 215*r*	general register of Bishop William Barlow July 1605–Apr. 1608
203*v*–204*v*, 213*v*–214*v*	general register of Bishop Richard Neile Nov. 1608–Nov. 1610
205*r*–*v*, 208*r*, 209*v*–212*v*, 214*v*–215*v*, 220*v*	general register of Bishop John Buckeridge (in chaotic order) July 1611–June 1628
209*r*	*sede vacante* act 1628 (1 entry)
206*r*–*v*, 207*v*, 209*r*–212*v*	acts of Bishop Walter Curle Sept.–Dec. 1628
206*r*–*v*, 207*r*–209*r*, 215*v*–220*r*	general register of Bishop John Bowle Aug. 1630–May 1637
220*r*–*v*, 221*v*–223*r*	*sede vacante* business Oct.–Nov. 1637
223*r*–225*r*	general register of Bishop John Warner Jan. 1638–May 1640
[226*r*–227*v*]	select table of contents (arranged by folio)

The section from fos. 196 to 220 is in considerable confusion and, as can be seen from the analytical description, the entries for most bishops are widely scattered, without any order, throughout the section and presumably were entered up haphazardly at a date much later than the events they describe. The earlier material among the register of Bishop Freke is included on account of the full copies of annual returns to the Barons of the Exchequer, entered in the register at the beginning of his episcopate.

VACANCY 1544

LPL, register of Archbishop Thomas Cranmer, fos. 391*r*–392*r* *passim*.

Rochester vacancy business Mar.–Apr. 1544, among the general section of Canterbury institutions

Institutions are calendared in A. J. Edwards, 'The *sede vacante* administration of Archbishop Thomas Cranmer, 1533–53' (London University M.Phil., 1968).

VACANCY 1550

LPL, register of Archbishop Thomas Cranmer, fos. 119*r*–120*v*.

Rochester vacancy business Apr. 1550

VACANCY 1551

LPL, register of Archbishop Thomas Cranmer, fo. 121*r*–*v*.

Rochester vacancy business Apr.–May 1551

Institutions are calendared in A. J. Edwards, 'The *sede vacante* administration of Archbishop Thomas Cranmer, 1533–53' (London University M.Phil., 1968).

VACANCY 1552–1554

LPL, register of Archbishop Thomas Cranmer, fos. 134*r*–136*r*.

Rochester vacancy business July 1552–Aug. 1553

Institutions are calendared in A. J. Edwards, *op. cit*.

VACANCY 1558–1560

1. CAL, register U2, fos. 55*v*–70*v*.

   Rochester vacancy business Dec. 1558–Sept. 1559

   Institutions are calendared (by place) in *Sede Vacante Institutions*.

2. LPL, register of Archbishop Matthew Parker, volume I, fos. 151*r*–152*r*.

   Rochester vacancy business Jan.-Mar. 1560

   Printed, *Registrum Matthei Parker* i, pp. 178–81.

VACANCY 1571–1572

LPL, register of Archbishop Matthew Parker, volume II, fo. 49*v*.

Rochester vacancy business Jan.–Feb. 1572

Printed, *Registrum Matthei Parker* iii, pp. 990–1.

VACANCY 1575–1576

LPL, register of the dean and chapter of Canterbury *sede vacante* (part of Parker II), fo. 120*r*.

Rochester vacancy business Dec. 1575–Apr. 1576 (*recte*)

Printed, *Registrum Matthei Parker* iii, pp. 1162–3.

VACANCY 1605

LPL, register of Archbishop Richard Bancroft, fos. 235*r*–236*r*.

Rochester vacancy business Apr. 1605

VACANCY 1608

LPL, register of Archbishop Richard Bancroft, fos. 247*v*–249*r*.

Rochester vacancy business July–Oct. 1608

VACANCY 1610–1611

1. LPL, register of the dean and chapter of Canterbury *sede vacante* (part of Bancroft), fos. 309*v*–310*r*.

   Rochester vacancy business Jan.–Mar. 1611

2. LPL, register of Archbishop George Abbot, volume I, fo. 362*r*.

   Rochester vacancy act Apr. 1611 (1 entry)

VACANCY 1628

LPL, register of Archbishop George Abbot, volume II, fos. 306*v*–307*r*.

Rochester vacancy business July–Sept. 1628

VACANCY 1629–1630

LPL, register of Archbishop George Abbot, volume III, fo. 148*v*.

Rochester vacancy act Dec. 1629 (1 entry)

VACANCY 1637–1638

LPL, register of Archbishop William Laud, volume I, fos. 305*r*–306*v*.

Rochester vacancy business Oct.–Nov. 1637

JOHN WARNER (1638–1666)
JOHN DOLBEN (1666–1683)

KAO, DRc/R9. Paper register; $15\frac{1}{2}'' \times 10\frac{3}{4}''$; fos. iv+135+iv, foliated [i–ii], 1–27, 29–134; blank: fos. [i*r*–ii*v*], 20*v*, 67*v*, 92*r*–*v*, 99*r*, 118*r*, 124*r*, 125*r*–*v*, 127*r*–134*v*; modern binding.

1*r*–91*v*	*Registrum spiritualium* (16th–17th-cent. antiquarian compilation, including copies of early charters, rentals, indentures, memoranda relating to Rochester, *Vita Gundulfi*, etc.)
93*r*–115*r*	general register of Bishop John Warner (includes copies of earlier charters; not always in strict chronological order) Dec. 1637–Apr. 1645, Sept. 1652, May 1660–June 1661
115*r*–126*v*	general register of Bishop John Dolben (not always in strict chronological order) Apr. 1667–Jan. 1672, Mar. 1679

ST ASAPH

Repositories

1. National Library of Wales, Aberystwyth, Dyfed SY23 3BU (NLW).
2. Lambeth Palace Library, London SE1 7JU (LPL).
3. Canterbury Cathedral Archives and Library, The Precincts, Canterbury CT1 2EG (CAL).

Area

The counties of Denbigh and Flint and the greater part of Montgomeryshire came within the boundaries of the diocese of St Asaph, except for enclaves under the jurisdiction of the bishop of Bangor in Denbighshire (Dyffryn Clwyd) and Montgomeryshire (Arwystli), and a few parishes in Flintshire and a single parish in Denbighshire which came within the bishopric of Coventry and Lichfield until 1541 (afterwards in the Chester diocese). The St Asaph bishopric also included eastern Merionethshire and certain Shropshire parishes centred on Oswestry.[1] There were no changes in the diocesan boundaries until the nineteenth century.

Bibliographical Note

The famous 'Llyfr Coch Asaph', now only partially available in transcripts, was not a formal episcopal register as such but a miscellaneous compilation begun in the episcopate of Llywelyn de Bromfield (1293–1314),[2] and the earliest extant bishop's register of St Asaph is that beginning with the appointment of Robert Wharton in 1536.[3] This volume follows the common pattern of a general, usually chronological, register, with a separate section for ordinations. In the sixteenth century a couple of miscellaneous volumes help to supplement the meagre evidence for the administration of the diocese, and abstracts have been published of these two volumes and the earliest register.

VACANCY 1357

1. LPL, register of Archbishop Simon Islip, fos. 218*v*–220*r*.[4]

   St Asaph vacancy business Aug.-Sept. 1357

2. *ibid.*, fos. 275*v*–279*v passim.*

   St Asaph vacancy business May–Oct. 1357, among the general section of Canterbury institutions

3. *ibid.*, fo. 342*v*.

   St Asaph vacancy business Feb. 1357 (a further note about a letter sent in Oct. 1357 is on fo. 342*r*)

[1] A. Hamilton Thompson, 'The Welsh Medieval Dioceses', *Journal of the Historical Society of the Church in Wales* 1 (1947), 91–111, especially 94; D. R. Thomas, *The History of the diocese of St. Asaph* (2nd edn., 3 vols, Oswestry, 1908–13), i, pp. 39–41, 52–6. This work contains parochial histories, with lists of known incumbents. For a map of the diocese see the frontispiece to D. R. Thomas, *Diocesan Histories: St. Asaph* (London, 1888); Ordnance Survey, *Map of Monastic Britain: (south sheet)* (2nd edn., 1954); W. Rees, *An Historical Atlas of Wales from early to modern times* (2nd edn., London, 1972), plate 33.

[2] D. L. Evans, 'Llyfr Coch Asaph' in *Journal of the National Library of Wales* 4 (1945–6), 177–83; R. I. Jack, *Medieval Wales* (The Sources of History, London, 1972), pp. 131–2; see also O. E. Jones, 'Llyfr Coch Asaph: a textual and historical study' (University of Wales M.A., 1968).

[3] There are among the returns to writs of *cerciorari* in the Public Record Office (C269/8/21, 22, 24) references to the registers of Bishops Laurence Child (1382–9) and Alexander Bache (1390–4), both of which are now lost.

[4] See under Canterbury for a description of this and subsequent archiepiscopal and capitular registers.

VACANCY 1389–1390

LPL, register of Archbishop William Courtenay, fo. 275*v*.

St Asaph vacancy act Mar. 1390 (1 entry), among the general section of Canterbury institutions

VACANCY 1406–1407

LPL, register of Archbishop Thomas Arundel, volume I, fos. 310*r*–314*r passim*.

St Asaph vacancy business Sept. 1406–Feb. 1407, among the general section of Canterbury institutions.

VACANCY 1410

LPL register of Archbishop Thomas Arundel, volume II, fos. 57*v*–58*r*.

St Asaph vacancy act Apr. 1410 (1 entry), among the general section of Canterbury institutions.

VACANCY 1433

LPL, register of Archbishop Henry Chichele, volume I, fo. 198*v*.

St Asaph vacancy business May 1433, among the general section of Canterbury institutions.

Printed, *Register of Henry Chichele* i, p. 279.

VACANCY 1513

1. LPL, register of Archbishop William Warham, volume II, fos. 268*r*–269*r*.

   St Asaph vacancy business Feb. 1513 (commission and accounts only)

2. *ibid.*, fos. 348*r–v passim*.

   St Asaph vacancy business Mar.–Apr. 1513, among the general section of Canterbury institutions.

VACANCY 1518

1. LPL, register of Archbishop William Warham, volume II, fos. 269*v*–270*v*.

   St Asaph vacancy business Apr.–July 1518 (commission and accounts only)

2. *ibid.*, fo. 365*v*.

   St Asaph vacancy act July 1518 (1 entry), among the general section of Canterbury institutions.

VACANCY 1535–1536

LPL, register of Archbishop Thomas Cranmer, fo. 358*r–v*.

St Asaph vacancy business Aug. 1535–Feb. 1536

Institutions are calendared in A. J. Edwards, 'The *sede vacante* administration of Archbishop Thomas Cranmer, 1533–53' (London University M.Phil., 1968).

ROBERT WHARTON (1536–1554)
THOMAS GOLDWELL (1555–1559)

NLW, SA/BR/1. Paper register; 15″ × 10¼″; fos. i+86, foliated [i], 1–34, 36–63, 65–76, [76A], 77–86, 87 (fragment)—some loose sheets; blank: fos. 5*v*, 9*r*–10*r*, 22*v*, 30*v*, 33*r*–41*v*, 54*v*–57*v*, 58*v*–59*v*, 65*v*, 73*v*–77*v*, 79*r*; leather-covered pasteboards.

1*r*–58*r*	register of Bishop Robert Wharton June 1536–Nov. 1553 (general acts, including wills and occasional later material. There are some lacunae and the entries are not always in chronological order)
60*r*–65*r*, 84*v*–87*v*	register of Bishop Thomas Goldwell Nov. 1556–July 1558
79*v*–83r	ordinations Sept. 1556–Apr. 1557
66*r*–73r	later material Jan. 1580–Dec. 1639
78*r*–*v*, 83*v*–84*r*	wills, prob. July 1548–Oct. 1549

An abstract of this volume, arranged by type of business, has been published by G. M. Griffiths, 'St. Asaph Episcopal Acts, 1536–1558', in *Journal of the Historical Society of the Church in Wales* 9 (1959), 42–57. See also below, SA/MB.21.

VACANCY 1554–1555

CAL, register N, fos. 120*v*–123*r*.

St Asaph vacancy business Apr. 1554–Sept. 1555

Institutions are calendared (by place) in *Sede Vacante Institutions*.

VACANCY 1559–1560

CAL, register U2, fos. 100*v*–101*r*.

St Asaph vacancy business July–Dec. 1559

Institutions are calendared (by place) in *Sede Vacante Institutions*.

VACANCY 1573

LPL, register of Archbishop Matthew Parker, volume II, fos. 60*r*–61*r*.

St Asaph vacancy business Oct.–Dec. 1573

Printed, *Registrum Matthei Parker* iii, pp. 1014–15.

VACANCY 1600–1601

LPL, register of Archbishop John Whitgift, volume III, fos. 212*v*–223*r*.

St Asaph vacancy business Dec. 1600–July 1601

VACANCY 1604

LPL, register of the dean and chapter of Canterbury *sede vacante* (part of Whitgift III), fos. 286*r*–287*r*.

St Asaph vacancy business Oct. 1604

VACANCY 1623–1624

LPL, register of Archbishop George Abbot, volume II, fos. 271*v*–273*v*.

St Asaph vacancy business Oct. 1623–Jan. 1624

VACANCY 1629

LPL, register of Archbishop George Abbot, volume III, fos. 145*r*–146*v*.

St Asaph vacancy business Aug.–Sept. 1629

JOHN OWEN (1629–1651)
GEORGE GRIFFITH (1660–1666)
HENRY GLEMHAM (1667–1670)

NLW, SA/MB/15. Paper register (repaired); 11½″ × 7¼″; fos. iv+153+iv, foliated 1–153; blank: fos. 1*v*, 2*v*, 7*v*, 22*v*, 27*v*, 67*v*, 77*v*–78*v*, 81*v*, 82*v*, 83*v*, 84*v*–87*r*, 89*v*, 113*v*, 140*v*, 143*v*–145*r*, 151*v*, 152*v*, 153*v*; modern binding.

1*r*–84*r*	acts of Bishop John Owen June 1631–Mar. 1645 (basically institutions and collations, occasionally caveats, arranged in chronological order)
90*r*–148*v*	acts of Bishop George Griffith Dec. 1660–Oct. 1666
149*r*–151*r*	acts of Bishop Henry Glemham [no month discernible] 1667–Jan. 1668 [last legible date]
152*r*	administrative memoranda May 1661–Aug. 1665
153*r*	note about the consecration of Bishop Griffith

This volume gives the appearance of being a contemporary act book, unlike NLW, SA/MB/14 which began as an exhibit book and was then used to record ordinations, institutions and other acts in no particular order (see below).

MISCELLANEOUS VOLUMES

1. NLW, SA/MB/14. Paper register; 12½″ × 8″; fos. iv+63 (last one a fragment)+vii, foliated [i], 1–28, 30, 31, 33–35, [36–63]; blank: fos. 14*r*–*v*, 15*v*, 16*v*, 35*v* and other unnumbered folios; modern binding.

   This is not a register or act book in the accepted sense but originally appears to have been a kind of exhibit book containing copies of letters of orders produced at the episcopal visitation in 1561, and then subsequently used to record ordinations and institutions, and occasionally other administrative business. There is no chronological sequence to the entries, which range from Apr. 1506 to Mar. 1571.

   An abstract of this volume has been published by G. M. Griffiths, 'A St. Asaph "Register" of Episcopal Acts, 1506–1571', in *Journal of the Historical Society of the Church in Wales* 6 (1956), 25–49.

2. NLW, SA/MB/21. This miscellaneous volume contains extracts from the 'Llyfr Coch Asaph', but chiefly records grants of lands, advowsons, tithes, patents of office, etc. The earliest document is dated Nov. 1534, the latest Aug. 1605, but the bulk of the material dates from the episcopates of Robert Wharton (1536–54) and Thomas Goldwell (1555–9).

   An abstract of this volume, arranged by type of business, has been published by G. M. Griffiths, 'St. Asaph Episcopal Acts, 1536–1558', in *Journal of the Historical Society of the Church in Wales* 9 (1959), 58–68.

ST DAVID'S

Repositories

1. National Library of Wales, Aberystwyth, Dyfed SY23 3BU (NLW).
2. Lambeth Palace Library, London SE1 7JU (LPL).
3. Cathedral Library, Hereford HR1 2NG.
4. New College, Oxford OX1 3BN.
5. Canterbury Cathedral Archives and Library, The Precincts, Canterbury CT1 2EG (CAL).

Area

The diocese of St David's covered Pembrokeshire, Cardiganshire, Carmarthenshire, Breconshire, and most of Radnorshire (except for a few parishes in the Hereford diocese). In the north-west it also included the Ceri district in Montgomeryshire and the Ewyas district in the south-west of Herefordshire and Monmouthshire. In the south it encompassed the Gower peninsula and the hinterland in western Glamorgan (a source of dispute with the bishops of Llandaff).[1] It was divided into the four archdeaconries of St David's, Brecon, Cardigan, and Carmarthen.

Bibliographical Note

The St David's registers are the earliest surviving Welsh episcopal registers,[2] although even in this diocese the losses have been considerable. When Edward Yardley, archdeacon of Cardigan (died 1770), was compiling his *Menevia Sacra* he had access to, and made use of, the registers of Bishop Benedict Nicolls (1417–33) and Bishop Thomas Rodburn (1433–42), now both lost, and also additional sections of the registers of Bishop Chichele and his vicar-general, which are no longer to be found in the first St David's volume.[3]

In addition to the fragments at New College, Oxford, and Hereford Cathedral Library, there are a few folios in a manuscript at the Bodleian Library, Oxford, described in the catalogue as 'formulare epistolarum, apparently extracted from the register of Thomas Bek (1280–93)'.[4] While the documents recorded on these folios might indeed have been taken from a register, I can find no internal evidence to confirm that they definitely were. What is certain is that these folios do not constitute a fragment of Bek's register as such.

The surviving registers are simple in arrangement and follow one general, chronological sequence, although of course there are occasions when the order is confused.

[1] A. Hamilton Thompson, 'The Welsh Medieval Dioceses', *Journal of the Historical Society of the Church in Wales* 1 (1947), 91–111, especially 94–5; for a map of the diocese see the frontispiece to W. L. Bevan, *Diocesan Histories: St. David's* (London, 1888); Ordnance Survey, *Map of Monastic Britain* (*south sheet*) (2nd edn., 1954); W. Rees, *An Historical Atlas of Wales from early to modern times* (2nd edn., London, 1972), plates 32–33. For the boundary disputes see J. Conway Davies, *Episcopal Acts and cognate documents relating to Welsh Dioceses 1066–1272* i (Historical Society of the Church in Wales 1, 1946), pp. 147–90.

[2] The registers are described by J. Conway Davies, 'The Records of the Church in Wales' in *Journal of the National Library of Wales* 4 (1945–6), 6; and R. I. Jack, *Medieval Wales* (The Sources of History, London, 1972), pp. 128–30.

[3] *J. Le Neve: Fasti Ecclesiae Anglicanae 1300–1541: xi The Welsh Dioceses*, ed. B. Jones (London, 1965), pp. v, 52; Yardley's work, *Menevia Sacra*, was published by the Cambrian Archaeological Association, ed. F. Green (supplemental volume, 1927). The returns to the writs of *cerciorari* provide references to the register of Bishop Adam Houghton (1362–89), who also mentions the registers 'predecessorum nostrorum' in answer to a writ of Feb. 1375 (Public Record Office, C269/6/18, C269/7/37, see also C269/8/40). Canon David Walker has kindly pointed out that Bishop Guy Mone also refers to the registers of his predecessors in the return to a writ of 1401 (*The Episcopal Registers of the Diocese of St. David's, 1397 to 1518*, i, pp. 220–2).

[4] Oxford, Bodleian Library, MS. Auct. F.5.25, fos. 151*r*–156*r*, described in *A Summary Catalogue of Western Manuscripts in the Bodleian Library at Oxford* ii (2) (Oxford, 1937), pp. 816–17, no. 4056; see also J. Conway Davies, *Episcopal Acts and cognate documents relating to Welsh Dioceses 1066–1272* i, p. 8.

VACANCY 1361–1362

LPL, register of Archbishop Simon Islip, fo. 233*r–v*.[5]

St David's vacancy business June–Nov. 1361 (with acquittances to Sept. 1362)

CAL, register G, fos. 188*r*, 198*r* contains an institution *sede vacante*, July 1374 during the 'false' vacancy of the see. The news of Bishop Houghton's death in that year was erroneous.

VACANCY 1389

1. Hereford Cathedral Library, MS. O.8.ii (14th-cent. manuscript containing a text of Gregory IX's Decretals and Boniface VIII's Sext), second flyleaf at the beginning of the volume.

   St David's vacancy business Feb.–July 1389

   Noted in A. T. Bannister, *A Descriptive Catalogue of the Manuscripts in the Hereford Cathedral Library* (Hereford, 1927), pp. 82–3, and in E. D. Jones, 'St. Davids Episcopal Registers', *National Library of Wales Journal* 6 (1949–50), 391. Printed in H. D. Emanuel, 'Early St. Davids Records', *ibid*., 8 (1953–4), 258–63.

2. LPL, register of Archbishop William Courtenay, fo. 167*r–v*.

   St David's vacancy business Feb. 1389–Apr. 1390

   An institution to a prebend of St David's *sede vacante*, June 1389, is to be found *ibid*., fo. 273*v*, among the general section of Canterbury institutions.

VACANCY 1397

LPL, register of Archbishop Thomas Arundel, volume I, fos. 455*r*–458*v*.

St David's vacancy business Aug.–Oct. 1397

GUY MONE (1397–1407)
VACANCY 1407–1408
HENRY CHICHELE (1408–1414)
RICHARD MARTIN (1482–1483)
HUGH PAVY (1485–1496)
JOHN MORGAN (1496–1504)
EDWARD VAUGHAN (1509–1522)

NLW, SD/BR/1. Parchment register; fos. iv (paper) + 124 + 16 (paper, 15″ × 9″, 19th-cent. contents list) + iv (paper), foliated 11–68, 70–76, 78–109, 111–137 (also numbered in pencil 1–124); fos. 11–68 (15″ × 9¾″), 70–76 (13¾″ × 10″), 78–125 (13¼″ × 9½″), 126–137 (average 14″ × 9½″); modern binding.

This composite volume contains the registers or parts of the registers of six bishops and a record of vacancy administration. Chichele's episcopate is represented only by the register of his vicar-general from Sept. 1408 to Sept. 1410 (for losses see the bibliographical note). In arrangement, the registers are generally chronological, although there is occasional confusion, particularly under the later bishops. Ordinations are included in the main sequence of registered acts. The last entry in Vaughan's register is dated Apr. 1518.

Printed (with translation), *The Episcopal Registers of the Diocese of St. David's, 1397 to 1518*, ed. R. F. Isaacson, with a study of the registers by A. Roberts (3 vols, Cymmrodorion Record Series 6, 1917–20).

[5] See under Canterbury for a description of this and subsequent archiepiscopal and capitular registers.

VACANCY 1407–1408

LPL, register of Archbishop Thomas Arundel, volume I, fos. 319*v*–320*v* *passim*.

St David's vacancy business Apr.–July 1408, among the general section of Canterbury institutions (see also above)

VACANCY 1415

LPL, register of Archbishop Henry Chichele, volume I, fo. 64*r*.

St David's vacancy act May 1415 (1 entry), among the general section of Canterbury institutions

Printed, *Register of Henry Chichele* i, p. 134. The accounts of the bishopric during the vacancy are to be found in LPL, Carte Miscellanee XIII/43.

STEPHEN PATRINGTON (1415–1417)

New College, Oxford, MS. 360, fos. 14–17, Parchment; $11\frac{1}{4}'' \times 8''$; fos. 4. There is a facsimile at the NLW, SD/BR/1A.

14*r*–17*v* fragment of the register June–Nov. 1415

Printed, H. D. Emanuel, 'A Fragment of the register of Stephen Patryngton, Bishop of St. Davids', in *Journal of the Historical Society of the Church in Wales* 2 (1950), 31–45. Also noted by E. D. Jones, 'The Discovery of a St. Davids Episcopal Register', in *National Library of Wales Journal* 5 (1947–8), 68.

VACANCY 1417–1418

LPL, register of Archbishop Henry Chichele, volume I, fo. 94*r*.

St David's vacancy business Jan.–Mar. 1418, among the general section of Canterbury institutions

Printed, *Register of Henry Chichele* i, p. 165.

VACANCY 1433

LPL, register of Archbishop Henry Chichele, volume I, fos. 199*r*–201*r* *passim*.

St David's vacancy business July–Nov. 1433, among the general section of Canterbury institutions

Printed, *Register of Henry Chichele* i, pp. 280–2 *passim*.

VACANCY 1446–1447

LPL, register of Archbishop John Stafford, fos. 90*v*–92*r* *passim*.

St David's vacancy business Nov. 1446–Jan. 1447, among the general section of Canterbury institutions

VACANCY 1447

LPL, register of Archbishop John Stafford, fos. 94*v*–95*r* *passim*.

St David's vacancy business July–Oct. 1447, among the general section of Canterbury institutions

VACANCY 1504–1505

1. LPL, register of Archbishop William Warham, volume II, fos. 222*r*–231*v*.

St David's vacancy business June 1504–Feb. 1505

2. *ibid.*, fo. 322*v*.

St David's vacancy act Jan. 1505 (1 entry), among the general section of Canterbury institutions

VACANCY 1508–1509

1. LPL, register of Archbishop William Warham, volume II, fo. 254*r*–*v*.

St David's vacancy business (accounts only) Nov. 1508–July 1509

2. *ibid.*, fo. 335*r*.

St David's vacancy act June 1509 (1 entry), among the general section of Canterbury institutions

HENRY MORGAN (1554–1559)
THOMAS YOUNG (1560–1561)
RICHARD DAVIES (1561–1581)

NLW, SD/BR/2. Paper register (repaired); $16\frac{1}{4}'' \times 11\frac{1}{4}''$; fos. iv+36+iv, paginated 1–72; blank: pp. 19, 32; modern binding.

1–31 register of Bishop Henry Morgan
institutions Apr. 1554–May 1559 (not always in strict chronological order)

33–37 register of Bishop Thomas Young
institutions Apr.–Dec. 1560 (on p. 37 is a collation of Feb. 1561)

38–72 register of Bishop Richard Davies
institutions and ordinations and other administrative business Nov. 1561–Mar. 1566

Calendared by G. Williams, 'The Second Volume of the St. David's Registers, 1554–64', in *Bulletin of the Board of Celtic Studies* 14 (1950–2), 45–54, 125–38.

VACANCY 1559–1560

1. CAL, register U2, fos. 99*r*–100*r*.

St David's vacancy business Sept.–Nov. 1559

Institutions are calendared (by place) in *Sede Vacante Institutions.*

2. LPL, register of Archbishop Matthew Parker, volume I, fo. 149A*v*.

St David's vacancy business Jan. 1560

Printed, *Registrum Matthei Parker* i, pp. 172–3.

VACANCY 1561

LPL, register of Archbishop Matthew Parker, volume I, fo. 178*r*–*v*.

St David's vacancy business Mar.–May 1561

Printed, *Registrum Matthei Parker* i, pp. 225–6.

VACANCY 1581–1582

LPL, register of Archbishop Edmund Grindal, volume II, fos. 492*r*–501*v*.

St David's vacancy business Nov. 1581–Feb. 1583

SUSPENSION OF BISHOP MARMADUKE MIDDLETON

LPL, register of Archbishop John Whitgift, volume II, fos. 177*r*–182*v*.

acts relating to St David's diocese during the suspension of Bishop Middleton June 1592–Nov. 1593

VACANCY 1593–1594

LPL, register of Archbishop John Whitgift, volume II, fos. 182*v*–186*v*.

St David's vacancy business Dec. 1593–June 1594

VACANCY 1615

LPL, register of Archbishop George Abbot, volume I, fos. 329*r*–331*r*.

St David's vacancy business Mar.–Oct. 1615

VACANCY 1626–1627

LPL, register of Archbishop George Abbot, volume II, 286*r*–288*r*.

St David's vacancy business Sept. 1626–Aug. 1627

VACANCY 1635

LPL, register of Archbishop William Laud, volume I, fo. 303*v*.

St David's vacancy business Dec. 1635

ROGER MAINWARING (1636–1653)
WILLIAM LUCY (1660–1677)
WILLIAM THOMAS (1678–1683)
LAWRENCE WOMACK (1683–1686)
THOMAS WATSON (1687–1699)
SUSPENSION OF BISHOP WATSON AND VACANCY 1694–1705

NLW, SD/BR/3. Parchment register (damaged); $13\frac{1}{4}'' \times 9\frac{3}{4}''$; fos. iii (paper)+i+i (paper)+89+iv (paper), paginated 1–37, 38A, 39A, 38–173, [174]; blank: [p. 174]; modern binding.

1–20	register of Bishop Roger Mainwaring Apr. 1636–July 1638 (institutions and ordinations in one general sequence)
21–157	register of Bishop William Lucy Jan. 1661–Oct. 1677
157–158	acts of Bishop William Thomas Feb.–Apr. 1678
159–160	acts of Bishop Lawrence Womack Dec. 1685–Feb. 1686
161–165	acts of Bishop Thomas Watson May 1691–July 1693 (with Trinity Sunday 1688 ordinations added at the end)
166–168	record of the visitation of the archbishop of Canterbury June 1694–Sept. 1695
169–170	*sede vacante* acts Nov. 1699–May 1705
171–173	miscellaneous acts Feb. 1682–Sept. 1688

NLW, SD/BR/3A is a 19th-cent. index to the volume.

SALISBURY

Repositories

1. Wiltshire County Record Office, County Hall, Trowbridge BA14 8JG (WRO).
2. Lambeth Palace Library, London SE1 7JU (LPL).
3. Canterbury Cathedral Archives and Library, The Precincts, Canterbury CT1 2EG (CAL).

Area

The medieval diocese of Salisbury extended over Wiltshire, Berkshire and Dorset and was divided into four archdeaconries—Wiltshire (covering northern Wiltshire), Salisbury (covering southern Wiltshire), Berkshire and Dorset. In 1542 Dorset was transferred to the newly created diocese of Bristol but there were no further boundary changes until the nineteenth century.[1]

Bibliographical Note

The Salisbury episcopal registers have been described by Miss Stewart in her published guide to the diocesan records.[2] The earliest surviving register is of Bishop Simon de Gandavo (1297–1315) but there is evidence for the existence of registers of Bishop Robert Wickhampton (1271–84), Bishop Nicholas Longespee (1292–7), and of one of the late thirteenth-century bishops named Walter.[3] The arrangement of the extant registers varies in detail but generally the fourteenth-century volumes divide into sections for institutions, diverse letters (miscellaneous memoranda), and licences, commissions and dispensations. From the time of Bishop Martival (1315–30), some episcopal registers include a section of royal writs, and records of ordinations of clergy are found from 1396. In the fifteenth century there are certain modifications in the arrangement of the registers, the chief categories being institutions, ordinations, and a general memoranda section (combining diverse letters and licences, commissions, etc.). From the mid-sixteenth century the registers are basically records of institutions and ordinations.

Only the first two Salisbury registers have been published by the Canterbury and York Society but place indexes have been compiled for the registers from Wyvil (1330–75) to Davenant (1621–41) by the late Rev. N. A. H. Lawrance (died 1973). These indexes are available in the Wiltshire County Record Office, as is also a modern typescript index of wills entered in the episcopal registers from the fourteenth to the sixteenth centuries. Some hundred and fifty years before the Lawrance indexes, Sir Thomas Phillipps had indexed the Wiltshire institutions in the bishops' registers in his publication, *Institutiones clericorum in comitatu Wiltoniae ab anno 1297 ad annum 1810* (2 vols, Middle Hill Press, 1825). The first volume covers the years 1297–1411, 1598–1810, the second 1412–1596. They are arranged chronologically with the name of the benefice, patron and incumbent and the reason for the vacancy if it was noted. A place index to these volumes was published by J. E. Jackson.[4]

[1] For details of the diocesan boundaries, see *VCH Wiltshire* iii (1956), p. 154 (ecclesiastical map of the county); *VCH Berkshire* ii (1907), pp. 47–8 and map facing p. 47; *VCH Dorset* ii (1908), pp. 45–6 and map facing p. 45. There is also a map of the diocese as a frontispiece to W. H. Jones, *Diocesan Histories: Salisbury* (London, 1880).

[2] P. Stewart, *Diocese of Salisbury: guide to the records of the bishop, the archdeacons of Salisbury and Wiltshire, and other archidiaconal and peculiar jurisdictions, and to the records from the bishop of Bristol's sub-registry for Dorset* (Wiltshire County Council, 1973), pp. 2–6.

[3] C. R. Cheney, *English Bishop's Chanceries 1100–1250*, p. 148 and nn. 6–7. Bishop Walter is either de la Wyle (1263–71) or Scammell (1284–6); Public Record Office, C269/3/24 (Longespee).

[4] 'Index to the "Wiltshire Institutions" as printed by Sir Thomas Phillipps', *Wiltshire Archaeological and Natural History Magazine* 28 (1894–6), 210–35.

VACANCY 1286–1287

LPL, register of Archbishop John Pecham, fo. 72*v*.[5]

Salisbury vacancy act n.d. (1 entry)

Printed, *Registrum Johannis Peckham* iii, pp. 933–4.

SIMON OF GHENT (1297–1315)
VACANCY 1315

WRO, no class reference. Parchment register; $10\frac{3}{4}'' \times 7''$; fos. i (limp parchment cover)+410+i (limp parchment cover), foliated A–E, 1–188, E–M, 1–74, 76–167, 160–172, 172*, 173–176, 176*, 177–200 (renumbered since publication to 1–174, 175A, 175B, 176–339, 340A, 340B, 341–349, 350A, 350B, 351–388, 389A, 389B, 390–409 (175B is an insert); modern binding.

The register is divided into four distinct sections: the *registrum de diversis emanentibus de cancellaria domini* (new foliation 6*r*–193*v*), miscellaneous letters and memoranda; the *registrum ... de presentacionibus, inquisicionibus, institucionibus, ecclesiarumque commendis, collacionibus prebendarum et ecclesiarum necnon custodiis hospitalium et rectorum impotencium concessis* ... (fos. 202*r*–357*r*); the *registrum ... de licenciis studendi, absentandi et peregrinandi ac dimissoriis et aliis concessis* ... (fos. 366*r*–407*v*); and finally the *sede vacante* register for 1315 (fos. 358*r*–364*v*). One quire of institutions is misbound and two similar quires have been lost. A detailed description of the register is given on pp. liii–lvii of the first volume of the printed edition.

Printed, *Registrum Simonis de Gandavo, diocesis Saresberiensis, A.D. 1297–1315*, ed. C. T. Flower and M. C. B. Dawes, (2 vols, Canterbury and York Society 40–1, 1934). The first volume contains the *registrum de diversis* section, the second the remaining sections.

ROGER MARTIVAL (1315–1330)

1. WRO, no class reference (vol. I of register). Parchment register; $11'' \times 7\frac{1}{4}''$; fos. ii+408, foliated 1–103 (Roman)+1 unnumbered, 104–120 (Roman), 121–216 (Arabic), 168–188 (Roman)+8 unnumbered, 217–224 (Arabic), 121–142, 143A, 143B, 144–167 (Roman), 225–267, 268A, 268B, 269, 270A, 270B, 271–324 (Arabic)+4 unnumbered; hide-covered boards.
2. WRO, no class reference (vol. 2 of register). Parchment register; $11'' \times 7\frac{1}{4}''$; fos. iii (paper)+i (limp parchment cover)+ii+375+ii (limp parchment cover), foliated (9 unnumbered fos. at beginning, including cover), 1–244, 145, 246–336, 337A, 337B, 338–365+2 unnumbered (including cover); hide-covered boards.

The first volume comprises two sections: the register of presentations and institutions, and the register of royal writs. Several quires of this volume are misbound. The second volume consists of the register *de diversis litteris* and the register of inhibitions at the Court of Canterbury. The registers are described in considerable detail on pp. xliv–lv of the fourth volume of the printed edition.

Printed, *The Registers of Roger Martival, bishop of Salisbury, 1315–1330, vol. I*, ed. K. Edwards (Canterbury and York Society 55–6, 1959–60), containing the register of institutions; *vol. II* and *vol. II bis*, ed. C. R. Elrington (Canterbury and York Society 57–8, 1963-72), containing the register *de diversis litteris; vol. III*, ed. S. Reynolds (Canterbury and York Society 59, 1965), containing the register of royal writs; and *vol. IV*, ed. D. M. Owen (Canterbury and York Society 68, 1975), containing the register of inhibitions and a general introduction by K. Edwards.

VACANCY 1330
ROBERT WYVIL (1330–1375)

1. WRO, no class reference (vol. 1 of register). Parchment register; $13\frac{1}{4}'' \times 8\frac{3}{4}''$; fos. ii (paper)+i (limp parchment cover)+iii+228+ii (paper), foliated 1–217, 218A, 218B, 219–231; blank: fos. 1*r*–4*r*, 21*v*, 22*r*, 32*r*–*v*; modern binding.

5*r*–231*v* general memoranda Oct. 1330–Dec. 1369

[5] See under Canterbury for a description of this and subsequent archiepiscopal and capitular registers.

This memoranda register is unfortunately very confused in arrangement. Several quires were misplaced during binding but this is not the sole reason for the confusion. The register does not appear to have been kept very well at certain periods, unless much material has been lost—for example, little is registered in the late 1340s and the late 1350s, and nothing is registered after 1369. Many entries are misplaced, apparently having been added at a later date when and where possible. Fos. 165*v*–169*r*, 161*v*–162*v* contain a 15th-century calendar of contents of the register (noting marginal captions in each case).

2. WRO, no class reference (vol. 2 of register). Parchment register; $12\frac{3}{4}'' \times 7\frac{3}{4}''$; fos. xi (paper)+i+vii ($11\frac{1}{4}'' \times 7''$)+412+ix (paper), foliated [i–viii], 1–87+14 unnumbered, 1–209, 211, 212, 214–270, 273–315; blank: fos. [i*r*, vi*v*, viii*v*], 8*r*–*v*, 87*v*, 2nd series 12*r*–*v*, 149*r*, 170*r*–*v*, 273*r*–*v*, 294*v*; modern binding.

[ii*r*–viii*r*]	*sede vacante* register	
	[ii*r*]	commissions and mandates Mar. 1330
	[ii*r*–iv*v*]	institutions Mar.–June 1330
	[v*r*–vi*r*]	dispensations and licences Mar.–June 1330
	[vii*r*–viii*r*]	royal writs Apr.–June 1330
1*r*–87*r*	dispensations, licences, etc. (there is a gap in the entries from May 1348 to Feb. 1353. The register includes material issued by the vicar-general in the normal sequence of entries) July 1330–Mar. 1356	
(13 unnumbered fos.)	place index of institutions	
(*2nd series*)		
1*r*–314*r*	institutions etc. (including acts of the vicar-general. Some folios are misbound: 171–82 should come between 158 and 159. There is a gap in the entries between Mar. 1355 and Mar. 1361, and a leaf is missing between 149 and 150) June 1330–June 1366	
314*v*	note of sequestrators	
315*v*	15th-cent. administrative memoranda	

A modern typescript place index to both volumes is available at the Wiltshire Record Office (Lawrance index 1).

RALPH ERGHUM (1375–1388)

WRO, no class reference. Parchment register; $12'' \times 8\frac{1}{2}''$; fos. ii (paper)+204+2 inserted documents+ii (paper), paginated 1–4, then foliated 5–25, 27–209; blank: fos. 31*v*, 208*v*, 209*r*; modern binding.

p. 1–fo. 10*v*	register of dispensations and licences Feb. 1376–Aug. 1378
11*r*–12*v*	dispensations and licences (separate section but similar sort of entries to above) Mar. 1376–July 1378
13*r*–16*r*	register of institutions of the vicar-general Nov. 1375–Mar. 1376
16*v*–102*r*	register of institutions Feb. 1376–Aug. 1388
102*v*–105*v*	late 15th-/early 16th-cent. place index of institutions
106*r*–207*r*	*registrum de litteris emanantibus* (*sic*) *de cancellaria sua* (general memoranda; in some chronological confusion at times) Dec. 1375–Aug. 1388
208–209	2 notarial instruments of 1425 (trimmed) inserted in the register (probably once used in the binding)

A modern typescript place index is available at the Wiltshire Record Office (Lawrance index 2).

JOHN WALTHAM (1388–1395)

WRO, no class reference. Parchment register; $12\frac{1}{2}'' \times 8\frac{1}{2}''$; fos. ii (paper)+i (limp parchment cover)+i+231+i+i (limp parchment cover)+ii (paper), foliated 1–235; blank: fos. 83*v*, 90*r*, 140*v*–141*v*, 179*v*, 209*r*–*v*, 234*r*–235*v*; modern binding.

1*r*–35*v*	*registrum litterarum emanencium de cancellaria* Apr. 1388–Jan. 1391
36*r*–71*v*, 73*r*–83*r*	visitation business Mar.–Apr. 1394
72*r*–*v*	licences and dispensations Sept. 1389–Jan. 1390
84*r*–*v*	licences and dispensations Sept.–Oct. 1388
85*r*–92*v*	institutions Sept.–Nov. 1388
93*r*–98*v*	licences and dispensations (fo. 72 should follow on here) Oct. 1388–Sept. 1389
99*r*–169*r*	institutions (including acts of the vicar-general) Nov. 1388–Sept. 1395
169*v*–171*v*	late 15th-/early 16th-cent. place index of institutions
172*r*–179*v*	licences and dispensations granted by the vicar-general Feb. 1392–Apr. 1395 (including 2 inserted entries May 1389, Sept. 1391)
180*r*–199*v*	institutions by the vicar-general Dec. 1392–Sept. 1395 (see also above)
200*r*–208*v*	*littere diversorum tenorum que emanarunt sub sigillo* of vicar-general, and wills proved before him Jan. 1392–Apr. 1395
210*r*–213*v*	licences and dispensations Mar. 1392–Nov. 1394
214*r*–221*v*	memoranda (dispensations, commissions, election of monastic head, mandates etc.) June–Nov. 1394
222*r*–233*v*	court proceedings (including some probate material, occasionally mandates, commissions for visitation, sequestrations) July 1389–Jan. 1395

A modern typescript place index is available at the Wiltshire Record Office (Lawrance index 2).

VACANCY 1395–1396

LPL, register of Archbishop John Morton, volume II (Courtenay), fo. 231*v*.

Salisbury vacancy act Dec. 1395 (1 entry), among the general section of Canterbury institutions

RICHARD MITFORD (1395–1407)
NICHOLAS BUBWITH (1407)

WRO, no class reference. Parchment register; $13\frac{1}{4}'' \times 9\frac{1}{4}''$, except for fos. 112–17, $11\frac{3}{4}'' \times 8\frac{1}{2}''$; fos. ii (paper)+ii (inserted 15th-cent. notarial document)+v+183+ii (paper), foliated 1–191 (including inserts); blank: fos. 1*v*, 7*v*, 111*v*, 117*v*, 162*v*, 183*v*, 184*r*, 185*v*, 191*v*; modern binding.

Register of Bishop Richard Mitford

3*r*–7*r*	late 15th-/early 16-cent. place index of institutions
8*r*–22*r*	commissions, *et aliis actis et litteris* (commissions, licences, dispensations, letters dimissory, etc. to mid-1396 (continued below, fos. 123*r*–162*r*) and from fo. 16*r* to the end of this section only wills are recorded) Oct. 1395–Mar. 1405
22*v*–24*v*	late 15th-/early 16th-cent. table of contents
25*r*–111*r*	institutions Jan. 1396–Sept. 1406

112*r*–114*v*	institutions Sept.–Oct. 1406 (Although this small quire bears the heading: ... *de et super presentacionibus, inquisicionibus, admissionibus, collacionibus et permutacionibus beneficiorum ecclesiasticorum, testamentis et eorum approbacionibus et commissionibus administracionum et acquietanciis ac super aliis actis et litteris*, it does not in fact contain any probate material. Institutions from Nov. 1406 are entered on fos. 179*r*–181*v* below.)
115*r*	heading of Bishop Bubwith's register (only)
115*v*–116*r*	list of benefices and religious houses etc. in the bishop's patronage, with the value of benefices
116*v*–117*r*	list of bishops of Salisbury (from Richard Poore to John Coldwell)
118*r*–122*v*	royal writs and returns Nov. 1396–Apr. 1407
123*r*–162*r*	commissions, licences, letters dimissory, etc. (continuation of first section of the register) July 1396–Aug. 1402 (fo. 145*r* bears the annual heading: *acta de dimissoriis, dispensacionibus non residencie ac aliis litteris* ...)
163*r*–178*v*	ordinations Apr. 1396–Mar. 1406
179*r*–181*v*	institutions Nov. 1406–Apr. 1407
182*r*–183*r*	commission, licence, etc. Dec. 1406
184*v*–185*r*	ordinations Dec. 1406

Register of Bishop Nicholas Bubwith (for heading see fo. 115*r*)

186*r*–*v*	commissions Oct.–Dec. 1407
187*r*–190*v*	institutions by the vicar-general Oct. 1407–Mar. 1408
191*r*	ordinations Mar. 1408

A modern typescript place index is available at the Wiltshire Record Office (Lawrance index 3).

VACANCY 1407

LPL, register of Archbishop Thomas Arundel, volume II, fos. 73*v*–77*r*.

Salisbury vacancy business July–Sept. 1407

ROBERT HALLUM (1407–1417)

WRO, no class reference. Parchment register: $13\frac{1}{2}'' \times 10\frac{1}{4}''$; fos. ii (paper)+ii (covers)+197+ii (paper), foliated 1–28, 29A, 29B, 30A, 30B, 31–89, 90A, 90B, 91–197 (1 fo. inserted); blank: fos. 1*v*, 8*v*, 23*v*–24*v*, 90A*v*, 133*r*–*v*, 174*v*, 188*v*, 192*v*, 193*r*, 197*v*; modern binding.

3*r*–8*r*	taxation of benefices in the diocese (arranged by rural deanery)
9*r*–18*r*	institutions Apr. 1408–Feb. 1409
18*r*–22*v*	wills July 1408–Mar. 1413
23*r*	modern list of wills in the preceding section
25*r*–90A*r*	institutions (including acts of the vicar-general) Feb. 1409–Aug. 1417
90B*r*–157*v*	general memoranda (this section is in some chronological disorder, caused partly by misbinding and the incorporation of other leaves. However, there also seems to have been an initial attempt to separate certain categories of business, e.g. licences, (which was not adhered to) and this fact compounds the confusion) Mar. 1408–Dec. 1416
158*r*–174*r*	ordinations Apr. 1408–June 1417
175*r*–186*v*	royal writs and returns May 1408–Dec. 1416
187*r*–188*r*	miscellaneous letters (including Hallum's creation as a cardinal) Nov. 1410–Feb. 1417

189*r*–192*r*	judicial *acta* (ecclesiastical court proceedings) May 1408–Sept. 1412
193*v*–194*r*	miscellaneous notes
194*v*	brief place index of institutions
195*r*–196*v*	place index of institutions
197*r*	note about 'halowyng of a churche'

The register has been edited by J. M. Wilkinson (now Mrs J. M. Horn), 'The Register of Robert Hallum, Bishop of Salisbury, 1407–1417' (Oxford University B.Litt., 1960) and Mrs Horn's edition is to be published shortly by the Canterbury and York Society. A modern typescript place index to this register is available at the Wiltshire Record Office (Lawrance index 4).

VACANCY 1417

LPL, register of Archbishop Henry Chichele, volume II, fos. 181*r*–183*r*.

Salisbury vacancy business Oct.-Dec. 1417

Printed, *Register of Henry Chichele* iii, pp. 425–7.

JOHN CHAUNDLER (1417–1426)

WRO, no class reference. Parchment register; 13½″ × 10″; fos. ii (paper) + i (limp parchment cover) + 185 + i (limp parchment cover) + iv (paper), foliated i–xiv, 1–92, 1–81; blank: fos. iii*r*, x*v*, xiv*v*, 2nd series 45*v*, 81*r*–*v*; modern binding.

iii*v*–v*v*	papal confirmation of the composition made Aug. 1392 between Bishop Waltham and the dean and chapter of Salisbury over visitation of the cathedral Apr. 1393
vi*r*–x*r*	documents relating to the election and confirmation of Bishop Chaundler Nov. 1417–July 1418
xi*r*–xiv*r*	15th-cent. place index of institutions
(*1st series*)	
1*r*–92*v*	institutions and commissions Dec. 1417–July 1426
(*2nd series*)	
1*r*–61*v*	general memoranda (in some chronological confusion with a section of wills grouped together. It includes elections of monastic heads and dispensations. The last entry is incomplete) Dec. 1417–May 1426
62*r*–80*v*	ordinations Mar. 1418–Mar. 1426

A modern typescript place index is available at the Wiltshire Record Office (Lawrance index 5). The papal confirmation of the composition over visitation (fos. iii*v*–v*v*) is printed, from another copy, in *Statutes and Customs of the Cathedral Church of the Blessed Virgin Mary of Salisbury*, eds. C. Wordsworth and D. Macleane (London, 1915), pp. 282–306.

VACANCY 1426–1427

LPL, register of Archbishop Henry Chichele, volume I, fos. 162*r*–168*v* *passim*.

Salisbury vacancy business July 1426–June 1427, among the general section of Canterbury institutions

Printed, *Register of Henry Chichele* i, pp. 234–46 *passim*. See Hereford and Worcester Record Office, b716.093–BA.2648/5(iv), pp. 43–4 for ordinations *sede vacante*, July 1427.

ROBERT NEVILL (1427–1438)

WRO, no class reference. Parchment register; 14″ × 11″; fos. iii (paper) + 215 + ii (paper), foliated 1–80, 1–87, 89–136; blank: fos. 1st series 6*v*, 2nd series 5*r*–*v*, 90*r*–*v*, 116*r*–*v*, 136*v*; modern binding.

(1st series)	
1*r*–3*r*	papal bulls relating to Bishop Nevill's provision July 1427
3*v*–6*r*	15th-cent. place index of institutions
7*r*–80*v*	institutions Nov. 1427–Apr. 1438
(2nd series)	
1*r*–115*v*	general memoranda (in chronological confusion, partly because certain similar entries are gathered together in sections—elections of monastic heads (9*r*–27*v*); writs, Convocation and subsidy business (91*r*–103*v*, 113*r*–115*v*); wills (105*r*–107*r*); licences and dispensations (110*r*–112*v*) Nov. 1427–Mar. 1438
117*r*–135*v*	ordinations Mar. 1428–Mar. 1438
136*r*	administrative notes

A modern typescript place index is available at the Wiltshire Record Office (Lawrance index 5).

VACANCY 1438

LPL, register of Archbishop Henry Chichele, volume I, fo. 220*r*–*v passim*.

Salisbury vacancy business May–July 1438, among the general section of Canterbury institutions

Printed, *Register of Henry Chichele* i, pp. 299–300 *passim*. See also below.

WILLIAM AISCOUGH (1438–1450)

WRO, no class reference. Parchment register; 13$\frac{1}{2}$″ × 10$\frac{1}{4}$″; fos. i (paper)+iv+264+ii+i (paper), foliated [i–iv], 1–125, 1–76, 78–80, 82–143; blank: fos. [i*r*–*v*, ii*v*–iii*r*], 2nd series 41*v*–42*v*, 52*r*, 75*v*–76*v*, 102*v*, 141*v*–143*v*; hide-covered boards.

iv*r*–*v*	papal bulls relating to Bishop Aiscough's provision Feb. 1438
(1st series)	
1*r*–125*r*	institutions July 1438–June 1450
125*v*	brief index of contents of memoranda section (below)
(2nd series)	
1*r*–87*v*, 91*r*–102*r*	general memoranda (this memoranda section is further divided into category sections: e.g. elections of monastic heads (1*r*–20*v*); Convocation and subsidy business and mandates (21*r*–44*v*); abjurations of heretics (52*v*–54*v*); unions of benefices and appropriations (55*r*–70*r*); visitations (78*r*–87*v*); licences, dispensations, letters dimissory (91*r*–102*r*). As is to be expected, these category sections are not always rigidly adhered to) July 1438–Apr. 1450
88*r*–90*v*	15th-cent. place index of institutions
103*r*–141*r*	ordinations Sept. 1438–May 1450

A modern typescript place index is available at the Wiltshire Record Office (Lawrance index 6).

VACANCY 1438
VACANCY 1450
RICHARD BEAUCHAMP (1450–1481)

1. WRO, no class reference (vol. 1 of register). Parchment register; 13$\frac{3}{4}$″ × 10″, except for fos. 91–97, 11$\frac{1}{2}$″ × 8″; fos. ii (paper) +vi+397+ii (paper), foliated i–iv, 1–2, 4–33, 35–62, 64–97, 98A, 98B, 99–142, 143A, 143B, 144–188, 1–35, 37–39, 41–55, 58–139, 141–148, 149A, 149B, 149C, 150–153, 154A, 154B, 155–161, 162A, 162B, 163–213; blank: fos. 1st series 4*v*, 143A*v*, 183*v*, 188*r*–*v*, 2nd series 49*v*, 52*v*, 55*v*, 79*v*, 91*r*, 97*v*, 105*v*, 110*v*–111*v*, 126*r*, 127*v*, 141*r*, 148*v*, 149A*r*–149B*v*, 154A*r*–*v*, 183*r*, 208*r*, 211*r*, 212*r*, 213*v* with 1 unnumbered fo.; modern binding.

ii*r*–2*v*	place index of institutions
(*1st series*)	
4*r*	*sede vacante* institutions May 1438 (see also above)
4*r*, 5*r*–181*v*	institutions Oct. 1450–Sept. 1474
181*v*–183*r*	foundation of a chantry at Marlborough Apr. 1475
184*r*–187*v*	*sede vacante* register July–Sept. 1450
(*2nd series*)	
1*r*–148*r*	general memoranda (in some chronological confusion. There is some gathering together of similar material, but not as regularly as in previous registers) Oct. 1450–July 1475
149C*r*–153*v*	licences and letters dimissory June 1451–Mar. 1463
154B*r*–210*v*	ordinations Dec. 1450–June 1474
211*v*, 212*v*, 213*r*	administrative jottings

2. WRO, no class reference (vol. 2 of register). Parchment register; 15″ × 11″; fos. i (paper) + 96 + i (paper), foliated 1–44, 1–52; blank: fos. 1st series 44*v*, 2nd series 12*v*, 24*v*, 25*r*, 41*v*, 52*v*; hide-covered boards.

(*1st series*)	
1*r*–42*r*	institutions Sept. 1475–Oct. 1481
42*v*–43*v*	place index of institutions
43*v*–44*r*	brief index of contents of memoranda section (below)
(*2nd series*)	
1*r*–31*r*	general memoranda (in chronological disorder and overlaps with the memoranda section in the first volume. It includes copies of earlier documents) May 1473–May 1481
31*v*–32*v*	list of pensions from churches in the diocese
33*r*–52*r*	ordinations Dec. 1474–Sept. 1481

A modern typescript place index to both these registers is available at the Wiltshire Record Office (Lawrance index 7).

THOMAS LANGTON (1485–1493)

WRO, no class reference. Parchment register; 16″ × 11″; fos. i (paper) + 137 + i (paper), foliated 1–48, 1–16, 18–44, 47–76, 78–93; blank: fos. 2nd series 17*v*, 44*v*, 81*v*; hide-covered boards.

(*1st series*)	
1*r*–47*v*	appointment of officials and institutions May 1485–June 1493
47*v*–48*v*	place index of institutions
(*2nd series*)	
1*r*–79*v*, 81*r*	general memoranda (This section is in more approximate chronological order than its predecessors—although there are inevitable lapses. There seems to be less deliberate grouping of similar material than before, except for abjurations (35*r*–42*r*) and business relating to Convocation and subsidies (55*r*–64*r*, 65*r*–74*v*), although in these cases the sections do not cover any great span of time) Sept. 1485–June 1493
80*r*–*v*	brief index of contents of memoranda register
82*r*–93*v*	ordinations Feb.–May 1486, June 1489–June 1493

A modern typescript place index is available at the Wiltshire Record Office (Lawrence index 8). A calendar of the register by Mr P. D. Wright is at present in the possession of the Canterbury and York Society.

JOHN BLYTHE (1494–1499)

WRO, no class reference. Parchment register; 14¼″ × 10″; fos. i (paper) + i + 114 + i (paper), foliated [i], 1–7, 10–67, 69–117; blank: fos. [i*r*–*v*], 85*r*, 101*v*; hide-covered boards.

1*r*–7*v*	institutions by the vicar-general Feb. 1494–Aug. 1499
10*r*–34*v*	institutions (by the bishop) Jan. 1494–Aug. 1499
35*r*–43*v*	general memoranda (commissions, licences, appointments, grants, indulgences) Dec. 1493–Aug. 1499
44*r*–45*r*	early 16th-cent. place index of institutions
45*v*–101*r*	general memoranda (continued) (kept in separate category sections: Convocation and subsidy business, mandates, royal writs (46*r*–69*v*); abjurations of heretics (70*r*–79*v*); benefice matters (appropriation, endowment of vicarages) (80*r*–84*v*); elections of monastic heads (86*r*–100*r*); exemplification of letters dimissory and letters of orders (100*v*–101*r*))
102*r*–117*r*	ordinations Mar. 1494–Mar. 1499
117*v*	list of benefices in the patronage of Sir William Herbert (administrative note)

A modern typescript place index is available at the Wiltshire Record Office (Lawrance index 8).

VACANCY 1499–1500

LPL, register of Archbishop John Morton, volume I, fos. 191*r*–197*r*.

Salisbury vacancy business Sept. 1499–Mar. 1500

Calendared in C. Harper-Bill, 'An edition of the register of John Morton, archbishop of Canterbury, 1486–1500' (London University Ph.D., 1977). Clergy lists for a visitation *sede vacante* in 1499 are to be found in Lambeth Palace Library, Carte Miscellanee XVIII/10–12.

EDMUND AUDLEY (1502–1524)

WRO, no class reference. Parchment register; 15″ × 11″; fos. i (paper) + i + 232 + 18 ($13\frac{1}{4}$″ × $10\frac{3}{4}$″) + i + 40 (paper, index, $11\frac{3}{4}$″ × 8″) + i (paper), foliated [i], 1–100, 100[1], 100[2], 101–164 + 18 fos. (first numbered 165, last numbered 167), 164[1]–167[1], 168–183, 1 (also numbered 184)–47; blank: fos. 1st series 100[2]*v*, 142*v*, 2nd series 47*r*–*v*; hide covered boards.

(*1st series*)

[i*r*]	list of bishops of Salisbury (Richard Poore to Seth Ward)
[i*v*]	administrative notes
1*r*	register heading
1*r*–100*v*	appointment of officials Apr. 1502, and institutions May 1502–Aug. 1524
100[1]*r*–100[2]*r*	collation of vicarage and grant of pension Sept. 1520
101*r*–183*v*	general memoranda (very confused in arrangement and date. Apart from a few abjurations (fos. 143*r*–149*v*, 155*v*–163*v*) entered together, no attempt is made to follow the divisions in Blythe's register. This section also contains copies of earlier documents) May 1502–Sept. 1521

(*2nd series*)

1*r*(184*r*)–46*v*	ordinations Dec. 1503–Sept. 1521
unnumbered	16th-cent. place index of institutions

A modern typescript place index is available at the Wiltshire Record Office (Lawrance index 9).

VACANCY 1524

LPL, register of Archbishop William Warham, volume II, fos. 308*r*–310*v*.

Salisbury vacancy business Aug.–Dec. 1524

LORENZO CAMPEGGIO (1524–1534)
VACANCY 1534–1535

WRO, no class reference. Parchment register; 15″ × 11″; fos. ii (paper) + 87 + 19 (paper, index, 12″ × 8″) + i (paper), foliated [i–ii], 1–85; blank: fo. 53*r*; hide-covered boards.

[i*r*–ii*r*]	register heading, and note of installation of Campeggio's proctor and his appointment of a vicar-general and official Jan. 1525
[ii*v*]	copy of absolution granted by Archbishop Warham of Canterbury Sept. 1517
1*r*–48*v*	institutions (by the vicars-general) Feb. 1525–Oct. 1534
49*r*–52*v*	register of the vicar-general appointed by Henry VIII after Campeggio's deprivation institutions Dec. 1534–Apr. 1535
53*v*–54*r*	composition June 1527
54*v*	presentation deed Nov. 1533
55*r*–71*v*	ordinations (including dispensations granted by Cardinal Wolsey and vacancy ordinations) Mar. 1525–Mar. 1535
72*r*–85*v*	memoranda (papal bulls, letters issued by Wolsey, dispensations and benefice matters, including copies of earlier documents) Jan. 1525–Dec. 1535
unnumbered	16th-cent. place index of institutions

A modern typescript place index is available at the Wiltshire Record Office (Lawrance index 9).

NICHOLAS SHAXTON (1535–1539)
JOHN SALCOT or CAPON (1539–1557)
VACANCY 1557–1560
JOHN JEWELL (1560–1571)

WRO, no class reference. Parchment register; 13¼″ × 9¼″; fos. i (paper) + 21 + 4 (paper, 12″ × 8″) + 84 + 10 (paper, 12″ × 8″) + 51 + i (paper), foliated 1–21, 1–77, 78A, 78B, 79–83, [i–ii], 1–34, 1–9, 11–16, paper inserts not numbered; blank: fos. 1st series 21*r*–*v*, 2nd series 78B*r*, 3rd series [i*v*–ii*v*], 28*v*, 30*v*–34*v*; hide-covered boards.

Register of Bishop Nicholas Shaxton (1st series)

1*r*–17*v*	institutions May 1535–June 1539
18*r*–20*v*	ordinations (including occasional dispensations) Jan. 1536–Mar. 1539
unnumbered	16th-cent. place index of institutions

Register of Bishop John Salcot (2nd series)

1*r*–78A*r*	institutions (including institutions performed by the vicar-general in London) Aug. 1539–May 1557
78A*v*	confirmation of the sale of a prebend and rectory Dec. 1547
78B*v*–83*r*	ordinations Dec. 1539–Mar. 1545, Apr. 1547, May 1548
83*r*–*v*	composition over benefice Aug. 1540
unnumbered	16th-cent. place index of institutions

loose leaf inserted here, fragment of sede vacante register 1557–1560

institutions May–June [1558] (the year is confirmed from other dated sources) (see also below)

Register of Bishop John Jewell (3rd series)

[i*r*]	register heading

1*r*–28*r* institutions May 1560–Sept. 1571
29*r*–30*r* 16th-cent. place index of institutions
(*4th series*)
1*r*–11*v* benefice and miscellaneous business (augmentations, unions, compositions, etc., in chronological confusion) Mar. 1560–Mar. 1571
12*r*–16*v* ordinations Apr. 1560–Dec. 1569

A modern typescript place index is available at the Wiltshire Record Office (Lawrance index 10).

VACANCY 1539

LPL, register of Archbishop Thomas Cranmer, fo. 381*v*.

Salisbury vacancy act Aug. 1539 (1 entry), among the general section of Canterbury institutions

Calendared in A. J. Edwards, 'The *sede vacante* administration of Archbishop Thomas Cranmer, 1533–53' (London University M.Phil., 1968).

VACANCY 1557–1560

1. LPL, register of Archbishop Reginald Pole, fos. 49*r*–54*r*.

Salisbury vacancy business Oct. 1557–Nov. 1558

2. CAL, register U2, fos. 71*r*–78*r*.

Salisbury vacancy business Dec. 1558–Dec. 1559

Institutions are calendared (by place) in *Sede Vacante Institutions*.

3. LPL, register of Archbishop Matthew Parker, volume I, fos. 148*r*–149A*v*.

Salisbury vacancy business Dec. 1559–Jan. 1560

Printed, *Registrum Matthei Parker* i, pp. 169–72.

VACANCY 1571

LPL, register of Archbishop Matthew Parker, volume II, fos. 48*r*–49*v*.

Salisbury vacancy business Sept.–Dec. 1571

Printed, *Registrum Matthei Parker* iii, pp. 984–90.

EDMUND GHEAST (1571–1577)
JOHN PIERS (1577–1589)

WRO, no class reference. Fos. ii (paper) + 20 (parchment, $13\frac{3}{4}'' \times 10\frac{1}{4}''$) + 18 (paper, $12'' \times 8''$) + ii (paper), foliated i, 1–15, 1–4, 1–18; blank: fos. 1st series i*v*, 11*v*–14*r*, 2nd series 1*r*, 4*v*, 3rd series 17*r*–18*v*; parchment binding.

(*1st series*)
i*r*–15*r* register of Bishop Edmund Gheast
  i*r* register heading
  1*r*–11*r* institutions and collations Feb. 1572–Feb. 1577
  14*v*–15*r* 16th-cent. place index of institutions
15*v* ordinations *temp*. Bishop Piers May 1582, Sept. 1588
(*2nd series*)
1*v*–4*r* benefice documents (concerning prebend and rectory, union of churches, including copy of earlier document) June 1572–Feb. 1575

(*3rd series*)

1*r*–16*r*	institutions and collations *temp*. Bishop Piers Dec. 1577–Mar. 1585

A typescript place index of Piers's institutions is inserted loose at the back of the register. A modern typescript place index to the whole register is available at the Wiltshire Record Office (Lawrance index 11).

VACANCY 1577

LPL, register of Archbishop Edmund Grindal, volume II, fos. 402*r*–406*v*.

Salisbury vacancy business Mar.–Nov. 1577

VACANCY 1589–1591

LPL, register of Archbishop John Whitgift, volume I, fos. 388*r*–419*r*.

Salisbury vacancy business Feb. 1589–Nov. 1591

JOHN COLDWELL (1591–1596)

WRO, no class reference. Parchment register; $14\frac{1}{2}'' \times 11\frac{1}{4}''$; fos. ii (paper)+24+iii (paper), foliated [i], 1A, 1B, 2–22; blank: fos. [iv], 20*r*, 21*r*–*v*, 22*v*; parchment binding.

[i*r*]	register heading
1A*r*–*v*	appointment of vicar-general and official Dec. 1591
1B*r*–10*r*	institutions and collations Jan. 1592–Sept. 1596
10*v*	note of bishop's death and burial Oct. 1596
11*r*–16*v*	ordinations June 1592–Aug. 1596
17*r*–19*v*	visitation of cathedral June 1593
20*v*	contemporary place index of institutions
22*r*	note of lands exchanged by the bishops of Salisbury from Salcot/Capon to Gheast)

A modern typescript place index is available at the Wiltshire Record Office (Lawrance index 11).

VACANCY 1596–1598

1. LPL, register of Archbishop John Whitgift, volume II, fos. 290*r*–298*v*.

   Salisbury vacancy business Oct. 1596–Nov. 1597

2. *ibid*., volume III, fos. 190*r*–195*r*

   Salisbury vacancy business Dec. 1597–Oct. 1598

HENRY COTTON (1598–1615)

WRO, no class reference. Parchment register; $13'' \times 9\frac{1}{4}''$; fos. ii (paper)+51+ii (paper), foliated i–ii, 1–49; blank: fos. i*r*–*v*, ii*v*, 35*r*, 42*v*–44*r*, 47*v*–49*v*; parchment binding.

ii*r*	register heading
1*r*–34*v*	institutions and collations Nov. 1598–Mar. 1615
35*v*–36*v*	appointment of vicar-general and official Apr. 1615
36*v*–37*r*	note of substitution, Consistory court Dec. 1615 (*temp*. Bishop Abbot)
37*v*	note of bishop's death and burial May 1615
38*r*–42*r*	ordinations Nov. 1599–Mar. 1612
44*v*–47*r*	17th-cent. place index of institutions

A modern typescript place index is available at the Wiltshire Record Office (Lawrance index 12).

VACANCY 1615

LPL, register of Archbishop George Abbot, volume I, fos. 331*r*–334*r*.

Salisbury vacancy business May–Nov. 1615

ROBERT ABBOT (1615–1618)
MARTIN FOTHERBY (1618–1620)

WRO, no class reference. Parchment register; $14\frac{1}{4}'' \times 10\frac{3}{4}''$; fos. ii (paper)+16+ii (paper), foliated 1–4, 1–7 (blanks unnumbered); blank: fos. 1st series 4*v*, 2nd series 1*r*, 5*v*, 7*v* and 4 unnumbered fos.; parchment binding.

(*1st series*)
1*r*–4*r* register of Bishop Robert Abbot (preceded by an unnumbered folio containing the register heading) institutions and collations Dec. 1615–Feb. 1618
(*2nd series*)
1*v*–5*r* register of Bishop Martin Fotherby
- 1*v*–4*v* institutions and collations Apr. 1618–Mar. 1619
- 5*r* ordinations Sept. 1618–Sept. 1619

6*r*–7*r* register of Bishop Abbot (cont.) ordinations Feb. 1616–June 1617.

A modern typescript place index is available at the Wiltshire Record Office (Lawrance index 12).

VACANCY 1618

LPL, register of Archbishop George Abbot, volume I, fos. 359*r*–360*v*.

Salisbury vacancy business Mar.–Apr. 1618

VACANCY 1620

LPL, register of Archbishop George Abbot, volume II, fos. 247*v*–251*v*.

Salisbury vacancy business Mar.–June 1620

ROBERT TOWNSON (1620–1621)
JOHN DAVENANT (1621–1641)

WRO, no class reference. Parchment register; $13\frac{1}{2}'' \times 10\frac{1}{2}''$; fos. ii (paper)+58+ii (paper), foliated [i–ii], 1–7, 12–53, 55–59, 62; blank: fos. [i*v*–ii*v*], 3*v*, 12*v*, 55*r*–*v*, 57*v*, 62*r*–*v*; parchment binding.

1*r*–3*r* register of Bishop Robert Townson
- 1*r*–2*v* institutions and collations July 1620–May 1621
- 3*r* ordinations Sept. 1620–Mar. 1621

4*r*–59*v* register of Bishop John Davenant
- 4*r*–14*r* miscellaneous business, mostly augmentations of benefices, but including Star Chamber decree censuring the recorder of Salisbury for breaking and defacing glass windows in St Edmund's church, Salisbury, and the recorder's submission; consecration of cemetery; rebuilding of parsonage house Apr. 1633–May 1639
- 14*v*–50*r* institutions and collations Nov. 1621–Oct. 1640
- 50*v*–53*r* 17th-cent. place index of institutions in both registers
- 53*v* brief note of institutions Jan.-Apr. 1641

56*r*–57*r* 3 royal letters about the leasing of episcopal and capitular lands June–Oct. 1634
58*r*–59*v* ordinations June 1622–Dec. 1625

A modern typescript place index is available at the Wiltshire Record Office (Lawrance index 12).

VACANCY 1621

LPL, register of Archbishop George Abbot, volume II, fos. 260*r*–264*r*.

Salisbury vacancy business May–Nov. 1621

BRIAN DUPPA (1641–1660)
HUMPHREY HENCHMAN (1660–1663)
JOHN EARLE (1663–1665)
ALEXANDER HYDE (1665–1667)
SETH WARD (1667–1689)

WRO, no class reference. Parchment register; 14″ × 11″; fos. ii (paper) + 72 + ii (paper), foliated 1–7, 9, paginated 11–30, then foliated 1–19, 1–6, 1–4, 1–25; blank: 1st series fos. 5*v*, 6*v*–7*v*, 9*r*–*v*, pp. 11, 15–22, 2nd series fos. 18*v*–19*v*, 5th series 22*r*–*v*, 24*v*–25*r*; parchment binding.

(*1st series*)
1*r* heading of Bishop Ward's register
1*v*–2*v* institutions *temp*. Bishop Duppa Mar. 1645–Aug. 1646
3*r*–5*r* list of institutions by Bishop Duppa (date, benefice, name of clergy instituted) Dec. 1641–Oct. 1645, June–Sept. 1660
6*r* inventory of goods in the residence house of Alexander Hyde, canon residentiary, called Leadenhall in the Close of Salisbury Oct. 1663
pp. 12–14 documents relating to Bishop Ward's complaint about lack of vestry-men in the parishes of St Thomas, St Edmund and St Martin, Salisbury, and the subsequent appointment of vestry-men and their taking of the oath Oct. 1673–Apr. 1678
23–26 appointment of vicar-general and Official Sept. 1671
27–29 agreement between the proprietor and vicar of White Waltham Sept. 1663

(*2nd series*)
1*r*–16*r* institutions and collations *temp*. Bishop Henchman Oct. 1660–Sept. 1663
16*v* contemporary place index to Henchman institutions
17*r*–18*r* ordinations *temp*. Bishop Henchman Dec. 1660–June 1662

(*3rd series*)
1*r*–6*r* institutions and collations *temp*. Bishop Earle Oct. 1663–Sept. 1665
6*r* contemporary place index to Earle institutions
6*v* modern place index to Hyde institutions

(*4th series*)
1*r*–4*v* institutions and collations *temp*. Bishop Hyde Feb. 1666–Aug. 1667

(*5th series*)
1*r*–17*v* institutions and collations *temp*. Bishop Ward Oct. 1667–July 1674
18*r*–*v* ordinations *temp*. Bishop Earle Dec. 1663–Sept. 1665
19*r*–*v* ordinations *temp*. Bishop Hyde Jan. 1666–Mar. 1667
19*v*–21*v* ordinations *temp*. Bishop Ward Sept. 1668–Sept. 1674
23*r* institutions and collations *temp*. Bishop Ward (cont.) Aug.–Oct. 1674
23*v*–24*r* modern place index to Ward institutions
25*v* revocation of marriage Mar. 1661

WESTMINSTER

Repository

Guildhall Library, Aldermanbury, London EC2P 2EJ (GL).

Area

The diocese of Westminster was constituted by letters patent of 17 December 1540 in accordance with the statute 31 Hen. VIII, c. 9, and extended over the county of Middlesex, except for the parish of Fulham.[1] Ten years later, following the resignation of the first bishop, the see, together with several exempt jurisdictions in London, Westminster, Hertfordshire and Essex, was annexed to the bishopric of London.[2]

Bibliographical Note

The solitary episcopal register of Westminster follows the pattern of the London registers of the period, with sections for institutions and general memoranda.

THOMAS THIRLBY (1540–1550)

GL, ms. 9531/12, part 1. Parchment register; 15¾″ × 13″; fos. ii (paper) + i (medieval manuscript paste-down) + 274 + ii (paper), foliated 1–54, 56–97, 170–177, 98–105, 108–111, 106, 107, 112–169, 178–246, 248–257, 257[A], 258–275 (modern binding foliation 1–276, including inserts); blank: fos. 169*r*–*v*, 176*v*–177*v*, 275*v*; modern binding.

242*r*–246*v*	institutions Jan. 1541–Feb. 1550
248*r*–249*r*	royal foundation of the see of Westminster Dec. 1540
249*v*–250*v*	commission, mandates etc. connected with royal visitation Aug. 1547
251*r*–275*r*	general memoranda Jan. 1541–Dec. 1549 (on fo. 273*r* is a note of the dissolution of the see Apr. 1550)

Fos. 1–241 of this volume contain Bishop Bonner's London register (1539–49) and the London vacancy register following his deprivation. This register obviously became part of the London diocesan archives after the merging of the bishoprics in 1550.

[1] *Letters and Papers, Foreign and Domestic, Henry VIII*, xvi, no. 379 (30); see also no. 333.

[2] Letters patent of 1 April 1550 (*Calendar of Patent Rolls 1549–51*, pp. 171–2).

WINCHESTER

Repositories

1. Hampshire Record Office, 20 Southgate Street, Winchester SO23 9EF (HRO).
2. Lambeth Palace Library, London SE1 7JU (LPL).
3. Canterbury Cathedral Archives and Library, The Precincts, Canterbury CT1 2EG (CAL).

Area

The diocese of Winchester consisted of two archdeaconries: that of Winchester, which included all Hampshire and the Isle of Wight, except for peculiar jurisdictions; and Surrey, which likewise extended over the whole of that county save for parishes in the archbishop of Canterbury's peculiar, the deanery of Croydon.[1] The diocese also included the Channel Islands.

Bibliographical Note

The series of Winchester episcopal registers from 1282 to 1684 are described by Canon Deedes in his published report on the diocesan muniments.[2] John of Pontoise's register (1282–1304) is the earliest to survive, although there is evidence that his predecessor, Nicholas of Ely (1268–80) had a register,[3] and Pontoise himself is known to have had an ordinations register which is now lost.[4] In common with other dioceses, as the analytical descriptions show, the fourteenth century was the period of greatest experimentation and variation in the arrangement of the Winchester registers, and by the fifteenth century the registers are normally divided into sections for institutions and collations; general memoranda; elections of heads of religious houses; and ordinations. From the time of Thomas Wolsey (1529–30) onwards, the volumes take the form of a general, chronological register, the only exception being that of Robert Horne (1561–79).

The first four registers are published, as are those for William of Wykeham (1367–1404) and the sixteenth-century bishops from Wolsey to John White (1556–9). In the nineteenth century, W. T. Alchin compiled 'Indexes to the Episcopal Registers of Winchester 1282–1555' and his four manuscript volumes are now in the British Library, Egerton MSS. 2031–4; another copy is in Winchester Cathedral Library, and modern typescripts of the Alchin indexes are amongst the Edwards Papers (19M54) in the Hampshire Record Office. There are also many volumes of abstracts and indexes of registers up to the eighteenth century made by F. J. Baigent in Winchester Cathedral Library and further Baigent Papers are to be found in the British Library, Add. MSS. 39959–39994. Probate material to be found in the episcopal

[1] For the ecclesiastical divisions of the diocese, see *VCH Hampshire* ii (1903), app. i, pp. 101–2 and map facing p. 101; *VCH Surrey* ii (1905), app. ii, pp. 49–53 and map facing p. 50. For further maps of the diocese see the frontispiece to W. Benham, *Diocesan Histories: Winchester* (London, 1884); and Ordnance Survey, *Map of Monastic Britain: (south sheet)* (2nd edn., 1954).

[2] C. Deedes, *Report on the Muniments of the Bishopric of Winchester preserved in the Consistory Court in Winchester Cathedral: including a subject-index to Bishop John de Pontissara's Register* (Winchester, 1912). The registers are listed by A. J. Willis in his *Hand List of the Episcopal Records of the Diocese of Winchester* (typescript, Folkestone, 1964).

[3] C. R. Cheney, *English Bishop's Chanceries*, pp. 148–9, citing *Register of John de Pontissara* i, pp. 9, 12, and also p. 164 for a general reference. It has been suggested that seven folios of Pontoise's register (printed in *Register of John de Pontissara* ii, pp. 739–64) might form part of Nicholas of Ely's register, but I do not incline to that view and agree with the editor that it may have been begun as a cartulary.

[4] *Register of John de Pontissara* i, p. 158; *Register of Henry Woodlock* i, p. 353 (both noted by Cheney, *op. cit.*). Much of Cardinal Beaufort's register has also been lost, and Bishop Waynflete refers to entries in Beaufort's lost institutions register for June 1445 (HRO, A1/13, fo. 5**r*) and his lost ordinations register for March 1440 (*ibid.*, fo. 0**v*).

registers from the time of Henry Woodlock (1305–16) to that of Richard Fox (1501–28) is included in a general probate index available in the Hampshire Record Office.

VACANCY 1280–1282

LPL, register of Archbishop John Pecham, fos. 24*r*, 51*v*–96*v* *passim*, 142*r*, 146*v*, 166*v*, 176*v*, 180*v*, 182*r*.[5]

Winchester vacancy business Feb. 1280–May 1282

Printed, *Register of John Pecham* i, pp. 118–75 *passim*; ii, p. 147; *Registrum Johannis Peckham* i, pp. 98–9, 118, 219, 255–6, 311–12, 362–3.

JOHN OF PONTOISE (1282–1304)

HRO, A1/1. Parchment register; $12\frac{1}{2}'' \times 8\frac{3}{4}''$; fos. ii+220+7 (12″ × 8″), foliated [i–ii], 1–34, 36–202, 202A, 203–226; leather-covered wooden boards.

Pontoise's register, which occasionally is somewhat confused in arrangement, is divided into three sections: firstly, institutions, collations and presentations; a general memoranda section, containing monastic business, commissions, mandates, letters to and from bishops and cardinals, like the *execuciones diversorum mandatorum* section of the later Winchester registers; and, finally, *registrum in temporalibus*, including royal writs and business relating to subsidies, compositions, and the episcopal estates.

Printed, *Registrum Johannis de Pontissara, episcopi Wintoniensis, A.D. MCCLXXXII–MCCCIV*, ed. C. Deedes (2 vols, Canterbury and York Society 19, 30, 1915–24; also Surrey Record Society 1, 4, 6, 9, 12, 14, 16, 19, 20). The first volume of the Canterbury and York Society edition contains the institutions and general memoranda, the second the temporalities register.

HENRY WOODLOCK (1305–1316)

HRO, A1/2. Parchment register; fos. ii+13 ($12\frac{1}{4}'' \times 8\frac{1}{2}''$)+390 ($12\frac{3}{4}'' \times 8\frac{1}{2}''$)+ii ($12\frac{1}{4}'' \times 8\frac{1}{2}''$)+i, foliated [i–ii], A–N, 1–176, 178–216, 216B, 217–278, 278B, 279–304, 304B, 305–339, 1*–28*, 1^{+}–15^{+} (blanks omitted in the numbering); leather-covered wooden boards.

The arrangement of Woodlock's register differs slightly from that to be found in the earliest extant Winchester register. The *quaternus de privatis negociis* (letters, bonds, grants, commissions, etc.) is followed by *quaterni memorandorum* (akin to the memoranda section of Pontoise's register) and subsequently by sections containing royal writs; letters dimissory and ordinations; institutions and collations; and a short, final section of visitation injunctions. Part of Bishop Sandale's register is bound into this volume (see below).

Printed, *Registrum Henrici Woodlock, diocesis Wintoniensis, A.D. 1305–1316*, ed. A. W. Goodman (2 vols, Canterbury and York Society 43, 44, 1940–1), the memoranda register being printed in the first volume, the remainder of the register in the second. See also H. Johnstone in *Church Quarterly Review* 140 (1945), 154–64.

JOHN SANDALE (1316–1319)

1. HRO, A1/3. Parchment register; $13'' \times 9\frac{1}{4}''$; fos. iii (paper)+35+ii (paper)+26+ii (paper), foliated 1–61 (blanks omitted in the numbering); hide binding.

   This volume contains three main sections: *execuciones diversorum mandatorum*; institutions and collations; ordinations and letters dimissory. The first two sections are further divided into sections for acts performed by the bishop as elect and for his acts after consecration. The later institutions section and the ordinations register are incomplete, both now finishing in Sept. 1318.

2. HRO, A1/2, fos. 187*v*–188*r*, $1^{+}r$–$15^{+}v$ (for description see under Woodlock).

   This short section bound into Woodlock's register comprises the 'second quire' of royal writs Sept. 1318–June 1319 (the 'first quire' is now missing), an account of stock on the episcopal manors

[5] See under Canterbury for a description of this and subsequent archiepiscopal and capitular registers.

at the time of Sandale's death, and an account of the livestock belonging to the bishopric delivered to Bishop-elect Assier. Fos. 187*v*–188*r*, containing *cauciones* 1316–18, were written in a section of the Woodlock register which had been left blank by the previous bishop's clerks.

Printed, *The Registers of John de Sandale and Rigaud de Asserio, Bishops of Winchester* (*A.D. 1316–1323*) *with an appendix of contemporaneous and other illustrative documents*, ed. F. J. Baigent (Hampshire Record Society, 1897). A1/3 is printed on pp. 1–212; the sections from Woodlock's register on pp. 213–64.

RIGAUD OF ASSIER (1320–1323)

HRO, A1/4. Parchment register; $13\frac{1}{4}'' \times 9\frac{1}{4}''$; fos. iv (paper)+38+ii (paper), foliated A–E, 1–30 (blanks omitted in numbering); hide binding.

Assier's short register is divided into the following sections: ordinations; *execuciones diversorum mandatorum et licencie*; institutions and collations (a separate section for acts performed by the bishop-elect); and a vicar-general's register.

Printed, *The Registers of Sandale and Asserio*, pp. i–xliv, 385–554.

JOHN STRATFORD (1323–1333)

HRO, A1/5. Parchment register; $14\frac{1}{2}'' \times 10\frac{1}{4}''$; fos. ii (paper)+ii+220+i+ii (paper), foliated [i–ii], 1–133, 133A, 134–219; blank: fos. 159*v*, 167*r*, 168*v*–169*v*, 180*v*–181*v*, 187*r*–189*v*; leather-covered wooden boards.

1*r*–88*v*	*execuciones diversorum mandatorum et licencie concesse* (including acts of the vicar-general) Feb. 1324–Dec. 1333
89*r*–139*v*	institutions, collations and dispensations for study (including acts of the vicar-general) Mar. 1324–Jan. 1334
140*r*–159*r*	ordinations (including commissions to ordain, letters dimissory) Mar. 1324–Dec. 1333
160*r*–168*r*	*quaternus causarum* (proceedings, sentences, judicial *acta*) Mar. 1324–July 1328
170*r*–180*r*	visitation business Feb. 1324–Jan. 1328
182*r*–186*v*	*registrum temporalium* July 1324–Apr. 1332
190*r*–219*v*	royal writs Nov. 1323–Aug. 1331

Alchin's index to this register is British Library, Egerton MS. 2032, and in Winchester Cathedral Library. A modern copy of the index in the Edwards Paper is HRO, 19M54/2–3 and 10 (index of institutions).

ADAM ORLETON (1333–1345)

1. HRO, A1/6. Parchment register; $12\frac{3}{4}'' \times 8\frac{1}{2}''$; fos. i (cover)+i+190+i, foliated 1–29, 29*, 30–57, 57*, 57+, 58–100, 100A–D, 101–183; blank: fo. 183*v*; leather binding, incorporating front cover of earlier hide binding.

1*r*–128*v*	*De commissionibus, dispensacionibus, dimissoriis et brevibus regiis* (also includes licences, elections of monastic heads, appointment of officials, and other memoranda, but few royal writs (see below). Occasionally some material is out of chronological sequence. Fos. 100A–D (containing entries Sept.–Dec. 1337) are inserted.) Mar. 1334–Apr. 1345
129*r*–182*v*	royal writs Apr. 1334–Aug. 1343
183*r*	list of cardinals

2. HRO, A1/7. Parchment register (damaged by damp); $12\frac{1}{2}'' \times 8\frac{1}{2}''$; fos. i (cover)+98, foliated 9–107; blanks: none; leather binding, incorporating front cover of earlier hide binding.

9*r*–42*v* papal bulls and related business (*registrum bullarum*) May 1335–Aug. 1344
43*r*–107*v* institutions and collations Apr. 1334–July 1345

A claim that 10 missing folios from this register are now British Library, MS. Royal appendix 88/60, is, to my mind, open to considerable doubt. Despite the fact that the foliation begins at number 9, there does not appear to be anything missing. Fo. 9*r* bears an initial register heading. Alchin's index to these registers is British Library, Egerton MS. 2032, and also in Winchester Cathedral Library. A modern copy of the index in the Edwards Papers is HRO, 19M54/2–3.

WILLIAM EDENDON (1346–1366)

1. HRO, A1/8. Parchment register; 14¾″ × 10″; fos. i+133+i, foliated [i], 1–90, 92–134; blank; fo. 14*v*; leather binding.
   [i*r*] list of bishops of Winchester
   1*r*–11*v* register as bishop-elect (general register, including ordinations) Dec. 1345–May 1346
   12*r*–13*v* composition between the bishop and the archdeacon of Surrey over jurisdiction 1348
   15*r*–134*v* *De presentationibus, collationibus, institutionibus et inductionibus beneficiorum vacantium, electionum processibus, dispensationibus et licentiis obsequiorum et studii* (including acts of the vicar-general) May 1346–Oct. 1366
2. HRO, A1/9. Parchment register; 14¾″ × 10″; fos. i+124, foliated 1–32, 36–53, 53*, 54–77, A–Z (no J), AA–YY (no JJ); blank: fo. 53**v*; leather binding.
   1*r*–53**r* *De diversis commissionibus, inquisitionibus, procuratoriis, licentiis, oratoriis ac aliis litteris cum earum executionibus* May 1346–Aug. 1366
   54*r*–60*v* *De bullis et aliis litteris apostolicis, processibus et executionibus earundem* (including some bulls addressed to the bishop-elect) Feb. 1346–Feb. 1366
   61*r*–77*v* *De litteris temporalium, brevibus et aliis litteris regiis cum executionibus earundem* May 1346–Aug. 1366
   A*r*–YY*v* ordinations (including letters dimissory and some letters of orders) May 1346–Oct. 1366

Alchin's index to these registers is British Library, Egerton MS. 2033, and also in Winchester Cathedral Library. A modern copy of the index in the Edwards Papers is HRO, 19M54/4–5.

VACANCY 1366–1367

1. CAL, register G, fos. 136*r*–139*r*.
   Winchester vacancy business Oct. 1366
2. LPL, register of Archbishop Simon Langham, fos. 85*v*–89*r*.
   Winchester vacancy business Nov. 1366–May 1367

Printed, *Registrum Simonis Langham*, pp. 244–60. Other vacancy acts on fos. 95*r*–*v*, 97*v* (Dec. 1366–Feb. 1367) are printed *ibid*., pp. 271–2, 281.

WILLIAM OF WYKEHAM (1367–1404)

1. HRO, A1/10. Parchment register; 14¼″ × 10″; fos. ii+421+ii, foliated 1–144, 144*, 145–421; leather binding.
2. HRO, A1/11. Parchment register; 14¼″ × 10″; fos. i+415+i, foliated 1–38, 38*, 39–237, 239–365, 1–3, 3B, 4–47; leather binding.

The first register contains three sections: the acts of the vicar-general at the time Wykeham was administrator of the see; the bishop's institution register; and his ordination register. The second volume comprises the general memoranda register[6] and the register of royal writs.

Printed, *Wykeham's Register*, ed. T. F. Kirby (2 vols, Hampshire Record Society, 1896–9), the first volume containing A1/10, the second A1/11.

VACANCY 1404–1405

1. LPL, register of Archbishop Thomas Arundel, volume I, fos. 499*r*–518*r*.

   Winchester vacancy business Oct. 1404–Mar. 1405 (and an additional entry Dec. 1405)

2. *ibid*., fos. 298*v*–299*v* *passim*.

   Winchester vacancy business Nov.–Dec. 1404, among the general section of Canterbury institutions

HENRY BEAUFORT (1405–1447)

HRO, A1/12. Parchment register; $13\frac{3}{4}'' \times 10\frac{1}{4}''$; fos. i+186+i, foliated 1–15, 1–32, 34–41, 46–68, 76–108, A–O (no J), 1*–6*, 1^{+}–55^{+} : blank; 1st series 15*r*–*v*, 2nd series 23*v*, 34*r*, 88*v*, 107*r*, 108*v*, 6* *v*, 3^{+} *r*, 5^{+} *v*, 37^{+} *v*, 53^{+} *v*, 54^{+} *v*, 55^{+} *r*; leather binding.

(*1st series*)

1*r*–14*v* miscellaneous lists and memoranda (papal bull regarding the assessment of Peter's Pence in English bishoprics; lists of religious houses in the diocese; lists of bishops of Winchester; taxation of benefices in the diocese and of temporal property of religious houses; lists of benefices etc. in the bishop's patronage; taxation of spiritual and temporal possessions of the bishop; list of annual pensions due to the bishop)

(*2nd series*)

1*r*–146*v* institutions Apr. 1405–Mar. 1415

148*r* collations and presentations by the bishop Aug. 1406–Nov. 1414 (not in strict chronological order)

A*r*–O*v* ordinations (including some letters of orders) Mar. 1406–May 1418

1**r*–6**r* royal writs Jan. 1406–Jan. 1418

1^{+}*r*–53^{+}*r* general memoranda (in considerable confusion) Oct. 1405–Mar. 1415.

54^{+}*r* memorandum of papal bull Oct. 1425

Alchin's index to this register is British Library, Egerton MS. 2034, and in Winchester Cathedral Library. A modern copy of the index in the Edwards Papers is HRO, 19M54/6–7.

VACANCY 1447

LPL, register of Archbishop John Stafford, fos. 92*v*–94*r* *passim*.

Winchester vacancy business Apr.–June 1447, among the general section of Canterbury institutions

[6] The heading of this section of Wykeham's register is given as *Incipit tercia pars registri . . . in qua describuntur bulle et litere apostolice, mandata dominorum cardinalium, litere pro convocacione cleri et commissiones et alie litere ac alia memoranda tempore suo executa, et execuciones eorundem, licencie non residendi, et dispensaciones super defectu natalium, cum aliis ibidem particulariter designatis.*

WILLIAM WAYNFLETE (1447–1486)

1. HRO, A1/13. Parchment register; 15″ × 10½″; fos. i+332+ii, foliated 1–148, 150–164, 1*–22*, 24*–87*, 89*–98*, A–Z (no J), A*–Q* (no J*), 1–24, 1*–8*; blank; fos. 89*r, Q*v; leather-covered wooden boards.

1r–164v	institutions and collations (last entry incomplete) Oct. 1447–Aug. 1469
1*r–98*v	general memoranda (last entry incomplete) Jan. 1448–Apr. 1470
Ar–Q*r	ordinations (including letters dimissory) Dec. 1447–Dec. 1470
(2nd series)	
1r–24v	royal writs and subsidy business (last entry incomplete) Oct. 1449–Oct. 1468
1*r–8*v	temporal business (appointment of temporal officials, indentures, homages, etc., last entry incomplete) Oct. 1447–Aug. 1461

2. HRO, A1/14. Parchment register; 15¼″ × 10½″; fos. i+233, foliated 1–69, 80–144, 146–203, 1–41; blank: fos. 128v, 138r; leather-covered wooden boards (front board loose).

1r–126v	institutions and collations (begins in mid-entry) Apr. 1470–Aug. 1486
127r–165v	general memoranda (last entry incomplete; a confused section including a few earlier items) July 1470–Nov. 1473
166r–203v	ordinations (including letters dimissory) Sept. 1470–May 1486
(2nd series)	
1r–24v	royal writs and subsidy business Oct. 1469–June 1485
25r–32v,	temporal business Oct. 1477–Aug. 1486
33r–40r	temporal business Sept. 1461–Feb. 1486 (2 separate quires were used for temporal business and there is much overlapping and chronological confusion)
40v	form of profession of hermit
41v	grant of next presentation Sept. 1460

Alchin's index is British Library, Egerton MS. 2034, and in Winchester Cathedral Library. A modern copy of the index in the Edwards Papers is HRO, 19M54/6–7.

VACANCY 1486–1487

LPL, register of Archbishop John Morton, volume II, fos. 129v–130v *passim*.

Winchester vacancy business Feb.–Mar. 1487, among the general section of Canterbury institutions

Calendared in C. Harper-Bill, 'An edition of the register of John Morton, archbishop of Canterbury, 1486–1500' (London University Ph.D., 1977).

PETER COURTENAY (1487–1492)
VACANCY 1492–1493

HRO, A1/15. Parchment register; 18¼″ × 13½″; fos. i (cover)+46, foliated 1–46; blank: fos. 12v, 20v, 24v, 27v, 46v; modern binding, incorporating front portion of earlier limp parchment cover.

1r–12r	elections of monastic heads Nov. 1487–Apr. 1492
13r–19v	ordinations June 1487 (*recte*)–June 1492
20r	election of abbess of Romsey 1491
21r–36v	general memoranda (not in any chronological order. Several sections of similar material gathered together. In general, a very confused and haphazard section) Mar. 1487–Sept. 1492
37r–45r	institutions and collations Mar. 1487–Sept. 1492
45r	*sede vacante* institutions Oct. 1492

45*v*	abjuration for witchcraft Sept. 1491
45*v*	inhibition for visitation *sede vacante* Oct. 1492
46*r*	augmentation of benefice May 1488

For further vacancy material see below. Alchin's index to this register is British Library, Egerton MS. 2034, and in Winchester Cathedral Library. A modern copy of the index in the Edwards Papers is HRO, 19M54/6–7.

VACANCY 1492–1493

1. LPL, register of Archbishop John Morton, volume I, fos. 78*r*–92*r*.

   Winchester vacancy business Oct. 1492–June 1493

2. *ibid.*, volume II, fos. 154*r*–155*r passim.*

   Winchester vacancy business Feb.–May 1493, among the general section of Canterbury institutions

Calendared in C. Harper-Bill, 'An edition of the register of John Morton, archbishop of Canterbury, 1486–1500' (London University Ph.D., 1977). For the dispute between Morton and the cathedral priory of Winchester over the churches of East Meon and Hambledon during the vacancy, see *ibid.*, volume I, fos. 227*r*–250*v*.

THOMAS LANGTON (1493–1501)

HRO, A1/16. Parchment register; 17¼″ × 12″; fos. ii (paper) + 83 + ii (paper), foliated 1–82, [83]; blank: fos. 25*v*, [83*r*–*v*]; modern binding.

1*r*–*v*	papal bulls of translation etc. Mar. 1493 (with additional bull July 1491)
2*r*–22*v*	institutions and collations (including some commissions, inquisitions, grants of pensions and probate material) July 1493–Jan. 1501
23*r*–36*v*	ordinations (first entry undated) Mar. 1494–Apr. 1500
37*r*–57*v*	elections of monastic heads (also includes other general memoranda) Mar. 1494–Aug. 1500
58*r*–82*v*	general memoranda Aug. 1495–Dec. 1500

The initial impression gained from a consultation of this register is that registration was somewhat careless, and that while the customary subdivisions of the register were observed, quite a lot of material has in fact been misplaced. A 'rough index' of this register compiled by A. W. Goodman is in Winchester Cathedral Library.

VACANCY 1501

CAL, register R, fos. 108*r*–171*v*.

Winchester vacancy business Feb.–June 1501

Institutions are calendared (by place) in *Sede Vacante Institutions.*

RICHARD FOX (1501–1528)

1. HRO, A1/17. Parchment register; 18½″ × 13¾″; fos. i (cover) + 38, foliated 1–36 (ignoring blanks); blank: fos. 8*v*, 34*v* and 2 unnumbered; leather binding, encasing earlier limp parchment front cover.

1*r*–8*r*	institutions and collations Oct. 1501–Feb. 1503
9*r*–32*v*	elections of monastic heads etc. Oct. 1501–Sept. 1504
33*r*–34*r*	Convocation mandate July 1502
35*r*–36*r*	Convocation business Jan.–Mar. 1502
36*r*–*v*	injunctions for Merton priory n.d.
36*v*	institutions and collations July 1503–Dec. 1504

2. HRO, A1/18. Parchment register; 14½″ × 10¾″; fos. i (cover) + i + 154, foliated 1–150 (ignoring blanks); blank: fo. 150*v* and 4 subsequent fos.; leather binding, encasing earlier limp parchment front cover.

1*r*–21*v*	institutions and collations Sept. 1506–Mar. 1511
22*r*–27*v*	ordinations Sept. 1506–Mar. 1511
28*r*–34*v*	wills prob. Apr. 1507–Oct. 1510
35*r*–141*v*	general memoranda (including visitation business) Dec. 1506–June 1510
142*r*–150*r*	mandates and commissions (not always in chronological order) May 1508–Feb. 1511

3. HRO, A1/19. Parchment register; 14¼″ × 11″; fos. 80, foliated 1–78 (ignoring blanks); blank: fos. 23*v*, 29*v*, 56*v*, 68*v* and 2 unnumbered; leather binding.

1*r*–9*v*	institutions and collations Apr. 1511–Nov. 1512
10*r*–36*v*	a confused section containing memoranda, elections of monastic heads, dispensations, licences, Convocation business, and institutions for late 1515
37*r*–50*v*	institutions and collations (some chronological confusion) Dec. 1512–July 1515
51*r*–56*r*	ordinations Sept. 1511–Oct. 1515 (interspersed in this section are mandates, commissions, *littere questuarie*, etc.)
57*r*–68*r*	wills prob. May 1511–Aug. 1516
69*r*–76*v*	abjurations of heretics and related material (several entries undated) Feb. 1513–Sept. 1514
77*r*–78*v*	composition between Godstow abbey and the rector of Faringdon May 1518

4. HRO, A1/20. Parchment register; 18″ × 12½″; fos. i (cover) + iii + 79 + i + i (cover), foliated 1–76, 78–80; blank: fos. 17*v*, 30*v*, 43*v*, 74*v*, 76*v*, 80*v*; leather binding, encasing earlier hide covers.

1*r*–15*v*	institutions and collations (occasionally some chronological confusion) Mar. 1518–June 1522
16*r*–17*r*	exchange of benefices Feb. 1522
18*r*–19*v*	confession and absolution of heretic Nov. 1521
20*r*–43*r*	elections of monastic heads etc. Mar. 1519–Feb. 1521
44*r*–51*v*	grants of pensions from benefices Apr. 1520–Apr. 1522
52*r*–55*v*	visitation of Magdalen College, Oxford Sept.–Dec. 1520
56*r*–60*v*	temporal business Nov. 1518–Oct. 1521
61*r*–69*r*	visitation business Sept. 1520–Oct. 1522
69*v*–73*v*	ordinations Feb. 1518–June 1522
74*r*	commission Oct. 1521
75*r*–76*r*	proceedings concerning God's House, Southampton and their ecclesiastical possessions July 1519
78*r*–80*r*	proceedings concerning churches and chapels pretending to be donatives Apr. 1521
80*r*	disciplinary proceedings, Romsey abbey Jan. 1527

5. HRO, A1/21. Parchment register; 15¼″ × 11¼″; fos. ii (paper) + i + 163 + i, foliated 1–40, 50–172; blanks: none; leather binding.

1*r*–25*v*	institutions and collations (including some Convocation material and commissions; some chronological confusion) June 1522–Nov. 1523
26*r*–29*v*	general memoranda (in confusion) Apr. 1522–Mar. 1524
30*r*–39*r*	ordinations Sept. 1522–Sept. 1528
	(Fo. 35A is an inserted fragment from the ordination register, discovered in the binding, and containing ordinations for Mar. 1525. It fits in between fos. 35 and 36)

39*v*–40*v*	unions of churches Dec. 1526, June 1528, and an institution Feb. 1516
50*r*–87*r*	institutions and collations Dec. 1523–Jan. 1525 (this section follows straight on from fo. 25*v*. Like that section it includes occasional memoranda. There is also an additional entry June 1526)
88*r*–94*v*	Convocation business Apr. 1523–Jan. 1524
95*r*–167*v*	institutions and collations Feb. 1525–Sept. 1528 (including isolated ordinations (Sept. 1525) and abjurations)
169*r*–172*v*	value of benefices in the diocese 1535
168*r*	grant of next presentation July 1527

Alchin's index to these registers is British Library, Egerton MS. 2034, and in Winchester Cathedral Library. A modern copy of the index in the Edwards Papers is HRO, 19M54/6–7.

THOMAS WOLSEY (1529–1530)

HRO, A1/22. Parchment register; 16″ × 12¼″; fos. ii (paper) + 72 + ii (paper), foliated 1–72; modern binding.

This register is approximately chronological in arrangement with no subdivision by category of business.

Printed, *Registrum Thome Wolsey, cardinalis ecclesie Wintoniensis administratoris*, ed. F. T. Madge and H. Chitty (Canterbury and York Society 32, 1926).

STEPHEN GARDINER (1531–1551; 1553–1555)

HRO, A1/23. Parchment register; 15½″ × 12″; fos. ii (paper) + i (Gratian fragment) + 66 + ii (paper), foliated 1–65; modern binding.

Like Wolsey's register, this volume is arranged more or less chronologically and records acts of Gardiner's episcopate from 1531 up until a few months before his deprivation. The acts of Bishop Gardiner after his restoration in 1553 are contained in Ponet's register (see below).

Printed, *Registra Stephani Gardiner et Johannis Poynet, episcoporum Wintoniensium*, ed. H. E. Malden and H. Chitty (Canterbury and York Society 37, 1930), pp. 1–91, 104–33, 136–42 (including acts of the restored bishop).

VACANCY 1551

LPL, register of Archbishop Thomas Cranmer, fos. 120*v*–121*r*.

Winchester vacancy business Feb.–Mar. 1551

Institutions are calendared in A. J. Edwards, 'The *sede vacante* administration of Archbishop Thomas Cranmer, 1533–53' (London University M.Phil., 1968).

JOHN PONET (1551–1553)

HRO, A1/24. Parchment register; 15″ × 11½″; fos. ii (paper) + 15 + xxiv (paper), foliated 1–15; modern binding.

A general, chronological register, containing acts of Bishop Ponet for the first six folios, and from fo. 7*r* recording entries from the time of the restoration of Bishop Gardiner (Aug. 1553) down to Sept. 1554. The four final folios of the register (12–15, formerly numbered A, B, D, C respectively) duplicate, with minor variations, two earlier folios, 2 (A, B) and 8 (D, C). There is one additional institution not recorded in the earlier part of the register.

Printed, *Registra Stephani Gardiner et Johannis Poynet*, pp. 93–103, 133–6. For the acts of the restored Bishop Gardiner, see above.

VACANCY 1555–1556

1. CAL, register N, fos. 124*r*–133*v*.

Winchester vacancy business Dec. 1555–Mar. 1556

Institutions are calendared (by place) in *Sede Vacante Institutions.*

2. LPL, register of Archbishop Reginald Pole, fos. 38*v*–42*r*.

Winchester vacancy business Mar.–Sept. 1556

JOHN WHITE (1556–1559)

HRO, A1/25. Parchment register (repaired); 18″ × 12½″; fos. ii (paper) + 14 + xxvi (paper), foliated 1–14; modern binding.

This register is chronological in arrangement, beginning with a record of the bishop's installation and commissions to diocesan officials, and then followed by institutions and collations.

Printed, *Registrum Johannis Whyte, episcopi Wintoniensis, A.D. MDLVI–MDLIX*, ed. H. Chitty, with preface by W. H. Frere (Canterbury and York Society 16, 1914).

VACANCY 1559–1561

1. CAL, register U2, fos. 90*r*–94*v*.

Winchester vacancy business June–Dec. 1559

Institutions are calendared (by place) in *Sede Vacante Institutions.*

2. LPL, register of Archbishop Matthew Parker, volume I, fos. 164*v*–171*r*.

Winchester vacancy business Dec. 1559–Feb. 1561

Printed, *Registrum Matthei Parker* i, pp. 202–14.

ROBERT HORNE (1561–1579)

HRO, A1/26. Parchment register; 16″ × 11¾″; fos. i (paper) + i + 119 + i, foliated [i], 1–5, [5A], 6–26, 28–119; blank: fos. [5A*r*–*v*], 119*v*; leather-covered wooden boards.

1*r*–2*r*	register heading and installation of bishop Feb.–Mar. 1561
2*r*–11*r*	institutions and collations Mar. 1561–Mar. 1566
11*v*–12*r*	ordinations Feb. 1563–Dec. 1565
12*v*–16*v*	visitation business (not in strict chronological order) June 1561–Sept. 1562
17*r*–19*r*	institutions and collations Apr. 1566–May 1567
19*r*–*v*	ordinations Sept. 1566–Mar. 1567
19*v*–66*v*	visitation business Sept. 1566–Aug. 1567
66*v*–68*r*	appointment of dean and commissary in the Channel Islands, June 1569, and undated injunctions to the clergy and churchwardens in the Islands
68*r*–*v*	ordinations Mar. 1568–Oct. 1569
69*r*–73*r*	institutions and collations July 1567–Nov. 1569
73*r*–78*v*	royal decree relating to Pamber church Feb. 1568
78*v*–79*r*	institutions and collations Dec. 1569–Mar. 1570
79*v*	ordinations Mar. 1570
79*v*–80*r*	institutions and collations Apr.–Sept. 1570
80*r*–89*v*	visitation business Oct. 1570–Aug. 1571
90*r*–*v*	ordinations Aug. 1570–Oct. 1573
91*r*–103*v*	institutions and collations Oct. 1570–Oct. 1575
103*v*–104*v*	ordinations May 1574–Jan. 1576

104*v*–108*v* institutions and collations Oct. 1575–July 1577
109*r*–115*r* visitation business Jan.–Dec. 1576
115r–117*v* institutions and collations Aug. 1577–Apr. 1579
118*r*–119*r* ordinations Feb. 1576–Mar. 1579

This is not strictly a chronological register, as can be seen from the foregoing analysis. Sections (institutions, ordinations, visitations) have been entered up in batches of two- or three-year periods.

VACANCY 1579–1580

LPL, register of Archbishop Edmund Grindal, volume II, fos. 407*r*–426*r*.

Winchester vacancy business June 1579–Oct. 1580

JOHN WATSON (1580–1584)
THOMAS COOPER (1584–1594)

HRO, A1/27. Parchment register; $16\frac{1}{4}'' \times 12''$; fos. ii (paper) + i (cover) + 37 + i (cover) + ii (paper), foliated [i], 1–11, 1–26; blank: 2nd series 26*v*; modern leather binding, encasing earlier limp parchment covers.

(*1st series*)
1*r*–11*v* general register of Bishop John Watson Sept. 1580–Nov. 1583
(*2nd series*)
1*r*–26*r* general register of Bishop Thomas Cooper Mar. 1584–Apr. 1594 (all the business is in approximate chronological order, except for ordinations which are noted together at the end of the entries for each calendar year)

VACANCY 1584

LPL, register of Archbishop John Whitgift, volume I, fos. 368*r*–369*r*.

Winchester vacancy business Jan.–Feb. 1584

VACANCY 1594–1595

LPL, register of Archbishop John Whitgift, volume II, fos. 241*r*–246*v*.

Winchester vacancy business May 1594–Feb. 1595

WILLIAM WICKHAM (1595)
WILLIAM DAY (1596)

HRO, A1/28. Parchment register; $16\frac{1}{2}'' \times 12\frac{1}{2}''$; fos. ii (paper) + 10 + xxii (paper), foliated 1–10; blank: fos. 3*v*, 7*v*–10*v*; modern binding.

1*r*–3*r* general register of Bishop William Wickham Feb.–May 1595
4*r*–7*r* general register of Bishop William Day Feb.–Sept. 1596

VACANCY 1595–1596

LPL, register of Archbishop John Whitgift, volume II, fos. 269*v*—273*v*.

Winchester vacancy business June–Dec. 1595

VACANCY 1596–1597

LPL, register of Archbishop John Whitgift, volume II, fos. 284*r*–289*v*.

Winchester vacancy business Sept. 1596–May 1597

THOMAS BILSON (1597–1616)

HRO, A1/29. Parchment register: 16½″ × 12½″; fos. ii (paper)+i+44+i+ii (paper), foliated 1–44; blanks: none; modern binding.

1*r*–44*v* general register (some chronological confusion at the beginning of the volume) May 1597–Apr. 1616

VACANCY 1618–1619

LPL, register of Archbishop George Abbot, volume I, fos. 378*v*–383*r*.

Winchester vacancy business July 1618–Feb. 1619

VACANCY 1626–1628

LPL, register of Archbishop George Abbot, volume II, fos. 288*r*–296*v*.

Winchester vacancy business Sept. 1626–Jan. 1628

RICHARD NEILE (1628–1632)

HRO, A1/30. Paper register; 13¾″ × 9″; fos. ii (paper)+i (cover)+63+i (cover)+ii (paper), foliated 1–57 (ignoring most blanks); blank: fos. 50*v*, 57*v* and 5 unnumbered; modern leather binding, encasing earlier limp parchment covers.

1*r*–50*r* general register (mostly institutions and collations) Feb. 1628–Mar. 1632

51*r*–57*r* miscellaneous acts (appointments of archdeacon's official and commissary, schools business, settlement of dispute, etc.) Oct. 1630–Feb. 1632

Fos. 51–57*v*, formerly numbered 198–211 (including some blanks), presumably once comprised part of another volume, the rest of which is no longer extant. A modern typescript index of this register, arranged by place but giving details and dates of institutions etc., is available in the Hampshire Record Office.

VACANCY 1632

LPL, register of Archbishop George Abbot, volume III, fos. 159*v*–162*v*.

Winchester vacancy business Mar.–Sept. 1632

WALTER CURLE (1632–1647)

HRO, A1/31. Paper register; 13½″ × 8¾″; fos. ii (paper)+82+i+ii (paper), foliated 1–54, 59–82 (ignoring blanks); blank: fos. 1*v*, 6*v*, 9*v*, 19*r*, 29*v*, 31*v*, 36*v*, 37*v*, 42*v*, 43*v*, 45*v*, 46*v*, 49*v*, 50*v*, 52*r*, 53*v*, 54*v*, 60*v*, 63*v*, 65*v*, 66*v*, 67*v*, 68*v*, 70*v*, 71*v*, 73*v*, 74*v*, 75*v*, 76*v*, 78*v*, 80*v*, 81*v* and 5 unnumbered; modern binding.

1*r*–81*r* general register Dec. 1632–Oct. 1642

82*r* late 17th-/early 18th-cent. table of contents (place names only)

The table of contents indicates that a final folio of institutions is now missing. This register follows its predecessors in being in general, chronological order but it differs from them in registrational arrangement. As a rule, institutions and collations are entered on the right-hand page, records of resignations and inductions on the left-hand page (this explains why there are so many blank versos). Other material is inserted as and when appropriate, generally without regard to this division. Fo. 82 is half a folio torn from a large deposition file.

WORCESTER

Repositories

1. Hereford and Worcester Record Office, St Helen's, Fish Street, Worcester WR1 2HN (HWRO).
2. Cathedral Library, Worcester (WCL).
3. Lambeth Palace Library, London SE1 7JU (LPL).
4. Canterbury Cathedral Archives and Library, The Precincts, Canterbury CT1 2EG (CAL).

Area

The medieval diocese of Worcester comprised Worcestershire, except for a few parishes in the west of the county within the boundaries of the bishopric of Hereford, the southern part of Warwickshire, and Gloucestershire east of the river Severn. It was divided into the two archdeaconries of Worcester and Gloucester. Gloucestershire was removed from the diocese in 1541 with the creation of the bishopric of Gloucester.[1]

Bibliographical Note

The series of Worcester episcopal registers is complete from 1268 and no reference has been found to any earlier volumes. The volumes are described in the Fourteenth Report of the Historical Manuscripts Commission.[2] The earliest register, that of Godfrey Giffard (1268–1302), is basically a general, chronological register, but in the subsequent volumes there is some variation in format. Some, particularly in the fifteenth and sixteenth centuries, remain fairly simple in arrangement: they merely comprise a general register and a separate section for ordinations. Several of the fourteenth-century registers are more elaborate and often the general register is divided up into sections for institutions, memoranda, royal writs and occasionally, dispensations and licences etc. William Lenn's register has a section for wills and testamentary business and Simon Montacute's contains a register of inhibitions from the Court of Canterbury. In the early sixteenth century, when a succession of Italians were provided to the see of Worcester, there is some confusion in the arrangement of their registers.

Several of the medieval registers have been published, all save one by the Worcestershire Historical Society. These calendars and editions use the earlier foliation of the volumes which in recent years has been replaced by pagination. There is a late fifteenth-century 'repertorium' to the registers with the parishes arranged by archdeaconry and deanery (HWRO, b 716.093–BA.2648/20(i)) and also an eighteenth-century table of contents of registers from Maidstone (1313–17) to Lenn (1369–73) (b 716.093–BA.2648/20(ii)). A parochial survey of the diocese (when it was confined to Worcestershire and part of Warwickshire) has been compiled by G. Miller.[3] The first volume, concerning Warwickshire parishes, gives lists of incumbents without dates of their tenure: the second volume, covering Worcestershire, provides dates.

[1] *VCH Worcestershire* ii (1906), app. i, pp. 89–92 and map facing p. 90; *VCH Warwickshire* ii (1908), p. 50 and map facing. R. M. Haines, *The Administration of the Diocese of Worcester in the first half of the fourteenth century* (London, 1965), p. 13 and map facing p. 1. For other maps of the diocese see the frontispieces of *Worcester Sede Vacante Register* and I. G. Smith and P. Onslow, *Diocesan Histories: Worcester* (London, 1883); Ordnance Survey, *Map of Monastic Britain: (south sheet)* (2nd edn., 1954).

[2] *Historical Manuscripts Commission: Fourteenth Report*, part 8 (1895), pp. 165–205.

[3] *The Parishes of the Diocese of Worcester* (2 vols, London, 1889–90). Sir Thomas Phillipps, *Nomina Domorum Religiosarum quarum mentionem faciunt Registra Episcoporum Vigorn.* (1861), lists of patrons of churches in the archdeaconry of Gloucester before the Reformation. T. R. Nash, *Collections for the history of Worcestershire* (2 vols., London, 1781–2, 2nd edn. and supplement, 1799) lists incumbents for the county.

GODFREY GIFFARD (1268–1302)

HWRO, b 716.093–BA.2648/1(i). Parchment register; average $11'' \times 7\frac{3}{4}''$, except for fos. 121–272, $10'' \times 7\frac{1}{4}''$; fos. ii ($12'' \times 7\frac{3}{4}''$)+ii ($11\frac{1}{2}'' \times 8''$)+i+460+12 (paper, $12'' \times 8''$)+ii ($11\frac{1}{2}'' \times 8''$)+ii ($12'' \times 7\frac{3}{4}''$), paginated 1–955 (including inserts); parchment-covered boards.

Initially there appears to have been an attempt to divide the register into archdeaconry sections but this was almost immediately abandoned in favour of a general, chronological register with annual headings, at first using the calendar year and then the pontifical year of the bishop.

Printed, *Episcopal Registers, diocese of Worcester: register of Bishop Godfrey Giffard, September 23rd 1268 to August 15th 1301*, ed. J. W. Willis Bund (2 vols, Worcestershire Historical Society 15, 1898–1902), using earlier foliation.

VACANCY 1302–1303

1. WCL, MS. A.1., fos. 1*r*–34*v*. Parchment register (composite volume, bound in hide-covered wooden boards); $13\frac{3}{4}'' \times 9\frac{3}{4}''$; fos. 34.

   Worcester vacancy business (including later material; the arrangement of this section is at times confused) Feb. 1302–June 1303

   Printed *Worcester Sede Vacante Register*, pp. 1–80.

2. LPL, register of Archbishop Robert Winchelsey, fos. 286*v*–287*v passim*.[4]

   Worcester vacancy business May–July 1302

   Printed, *Registrum Roberti Winchelsey* i, pp. 436–42 *passim*.

WILLIAM GAINSBOROUGH (1303–1307)

HWRO, b 716.093–BA.2648/1(ii). Parchment register; $12\frac{1}{2}'' \times 8''$; fos. ii+i (parchment cover)+57+i (paper, contents table)+i (parchment cover)+ii, paginated 1–121 (including covers); parchment-covered boards.

Gainsborough's register falls into three basic sections, although there is considerable overlapping and occasionally the arrangement is confused. It begins with a short section of general memoranda (commissions, dispensations, mandates, proxies and legal business, papal, royal and archiepiscopal letters, and occasional writs, licences and letters dimissory), followed by a longer section chiefly devoted to institutions, collations, ordinations, licences and letters dimissory but again at times including writs, mandates and other memoranda. This section also includes institutions performed by the bishop's vicar-general in his absence. The register concludes with a section of royal writs.

Printed, *The Register of William de Geynesburgh, Bishop of Worcester, 1302–1307*, ed. J. W. Willis Bund with an introduction by R. A. Wilson (Worcestershire Historical Society 22, 1907–29), using earlier foliation.

VACANCY 1307–1308

WCL, MS. A.1, fos. 35*r*–79*v*. Parchment register (composite volume, bound in hide-covered wooden boards); $13\frac{1}{2}'' \times 9\frac{1}{2}''$; fos. 45.

Worcester vacancy business (including business of the bishop-elect and later entries) Oct. 1307–Aug. 1309

Printed, *Worcester Sede Vacante Register*, pp. 80–134.

WALTER REYNOLDS (1308–1313)

HWRO, b 716.093–BA.2648/1(iii). Parchment register; $13'' \times 8\frac{1}{2}''$ (pp. 3–102, 195–226), $13\frac{1}{4}'' \times 8\frac{3}{4}''$ (pp. 103–94); fos. ii+i (parchment cover)+112+ii (paper, index, $12'' \times 6\frac{1}{4}''$)+i (parchment cover)+ii, paginated 1–233; parchment-covered boards.

[4] See under Canterbury for a description of this and subsequent archiepiscopal and capitular registers.

A general, chronological register, with annual headings, the only separate category subdivision being that devoted to royal writs.

Printed, *The Register of Walter Reynolds, Bishop of Worcester, 1308–1313*, ed. R. A. Wilson (Worcestershire Historical Society 39, 1927, and Dugdale Society 9, 1928), using earlier foliation.

VACANCY 1313

WCL, MS. A.1, fos. 80*r*–97*r*. Parchment register (composite volume, bound in hide-covered wooden boards); 13½″ × 9½″; fos. 18.

Worcester vacancy business (with additional material) Oct. 1313–Feb. 1314

Printed, *Worcester Sede Vacante Register*, pp. 137–77.

WALTER MAIDSTONE (1313–1317)

HWRO, b 716.093–BA.2648/1(iv). Parchment register; 13″ × 9¾″; fos. ii+i (parchment cover)+56+i (paper, index, 12″ × 6½″)+i (parchment cover)+ii, paginated 1–118 (including covers); blank: p. 118; parchment-covered boards.

3–101 general register, including ordinations, arranged chronologically Feb. 1314–Jan. 1317
101–103 acts of the vicar-general Jan.–Mar. 1317
103–104 miscellaneous administrative and legal memoranda (no years given)
105–108 acts of the vicar-general of Bishop Thomas Cobham June–Nov. 1317
109–110 ordination of Kempsey chantry June 1316
111–114 royal writs and related business *temp.* Bishop Cobham July 1317–May 1321
115–116 later table of contents

VACANCY 1317

WCL, MS. A.1, fos. 98*r*–105*v*. Parchment register (composite volume, bound in hide-covered wooden boards); 13½″ × 9¾″; fos. 8.

Worcester vacancy business Apr.–May 1317

Printed, *Worcester Sede Vacante Register*, pp. 177–91

THOMAS COBHAM (1317–1327)

HWRO, b 716.093–BA.2648/2(i). Parchment register; 12½″ × 9″; fos. ii+i (parchment cover)+126+ii (paper, 12″ × 6½″)+i (parchment cover)+ii, paginated 1–265; parchment-covered boards.

The volume takes the form of a general, chronological register with annual headings, although ordinations are grouped together. There is some confusion in the arrangement, and it could be that the clerks intended to keep a separate section for papal letters and important documents, such as agreements and compositions. For the acts of Cobham's vicar-general in 1317, and for royal writs 1317–21, see under Walter Maidstone above.

Printed, *The Register of Thomas de Cobham, Bishop of Worcester, 1317–1327*, ed. E. H. Pearce (Worcestershire Historical Society 40, 1930), using earlier foliation.

VACANCY 1327

WCL, MS. A.1, fo. 105*r* (for description see under 1317 vacancy).

Worcester vacancy act Dec. 1327 (1 entry)

Printed, *Worcester Sede Vacante Register*, p. 190.

ADAM ORLETON (1327–1333)

HWRO, b 716.093–BA.2648/2(ii). Parchment register; $12\frac{1}{2}'' \times 8\frac{1}{2}''$; fos. ii + i (parchment cover) + 44 + i (parchment cover) + i (parchment cover) + 57 + iii (paper, $12'' + 6\frac{3}{4}''$) + 2 + i (parchment cover), paginated 1–32A, 32B, 33–217; parchment-covered boards.

Orleton's register was originally two volumes (pp. 1–89, 90–217), the former containing ordinations 1328–33; institutions 1328–32; letters dimissory and dispensations 1328–34, the last two initially recorded separately and then combined into one section. The second part comprises a section of general memoranda, in which there is some gathering together of similar business, and a section of institutions 1328–34, in part duplicating entries in the similar section of the first volume.

Printed, *Calendar of the Register of Adam de Orleton, Bishop of Worcester, 1327–1333*, ed. R. M. Haines (Worcestershire Historical Society and Historical Manuscripts Commission Joint Publication 27 (1980)).

SIMON MONTACUTE (1334–1337)

HWRO, b 716.093–BA.2648/2(iii). Parchment register; $14\frac{1}{4}'' \times 9\frac{1}{2}''$, except for pp. 221–32, $12\frac{1}{2}'' \times 8\frac{1}{2}''$; fos. ii + i (parchment cover) + 66 + i (parchment cover) + i (parchment cover) + 41 + 6 + iv (paper, $12\frac{1}{2}'' \times 6\frac{1}{2}''$) + ii, paginated 1–241 (including covers); blank: pp. 58, 68, 150, 170, 184, 186, 190, 219, 220, 231, 232; parchment-covered boards.

3–13	general register as bishop-elect Mar.–Apr. 1334
14–57	general register (basically institutions, licences and commissions) May 1334–May 1337
59–60	indentures between the bishop and Worcester cathedral priory 1336
61–62	dispensations July 1334–Feb. 1337
63–67	royal writs Apr. 1335–Apr. 1337 (see also below 195–218)
69–70	material relating to subsidies Aug. 1335–Apr. 1337
71–74	inspeximus of papal privilege for the friars hermit of the order of St Augustine in France and England Jan. 1337
75–111	letters dimissory and ordinations July 1334–Apr. 1337
113–134	*registrum . . . concernens capellam sancti Thome Martiris de Stretford et appropriationem ecclesie de Stretford' dicte capelle appropriate* (with copies of earlier documents) Apr. 1336–Feb. 1337
139–189	*quaternus de emanentibus* (general memoranda) May 1334–Feb. 1337
191–194	*quaternus de inhibitionibus et certificatoriis earundem* (inhibitions etc. from the Court of Canterbury) May 1334–Mar. 1337
195–218	royal writs May 1334–Mar. 1337 (see above 63–67)
221–230	visitation business (including earlier injunctions) Oct. 1335–June 1336
233–235	table of contents to volume 1 (i.e. pp. 1–136)
237–239	table of contents to volume 2 (pp. 137–232)

THOMAS HEMPNALL (1337–1338)

HWRO, b 716.093–BA.2648/2(iv). Parchment register; $12\frac{1}{2}'' \times 8\frac{3}{4}''$; fos. ii + i (parchment cover) + i (inserted document) + 36 + i (paper, $12\frac{1}{2}'' \times 6\frac{1}{2}''$) + i (parchment cover) + ii, paginated 1–81 (including inserts); blank: pp. 2, 64, 79; parchment-covered boards.

3–4 (insert)	copy of decree of papal judges delegate *temp.* Bishop Walter Maidstone
5–32	general register Apr. 1337–Dec. 1338
33–63	ordinations Sept. 1337–Sept. 1338
65–76	royal writs May 1337–June 1338
77–78	late 17th–early 18th-cent. table of contents

VACANCY 1338–1339

WCL, MS. A.1, fos. 145*r*–163*r*. Parchment register (composite volume, bound in hide-covered wooden boards); $12\frac{1}{2}'' \times 8\frac{1}{4}''$; fos. 19.

Worcester vacancy business Dec. 1338–Feb. 1339

Printed, *Worcester Sede Vacante Register*, pp. 256–82.

WULSTAN BRANSFORD (1339–1349)

HWRO, b 716.093–BA.2648/3(i). Parchment register; average $13'' \times 9''$ (varies considerably); fos. iii (paper, $13\frac{1}{2}'' \times 9\frac{1}{2}''$) + i (parchment cover) + 185 + i (fragment of parchment cover) + 18 + vi (paper, index, $12\frac{1}{4}'' \times 6\frac{1}{4}''$) + 36 + i + iii (paper, $13\frac{1}{2}'' \times 9\frac{1}{2}''$), paginated 1–509 (including inserts); modern leather binding.

Bransford's register was originally in two volumes, separately foliated. The first volume is subdivided into four sections: the record of the bishop's consecration and enthronement followed by memoranda such as commissions, licences, letters dimissory; institutions, licences and appropriations (*registrum institucionum, licenciarum, prefeccionum et appropriacionum ecclesiarum*); ordinations; and royal writs. The second volume, for the year 1349, contains sections of memoranda, institutions, ordinations, court of audience proceedings, and royal writs (including some for John Thoresby's episcopate).

Printed, *A Calendar of the Register of Wolstan de Bransford, Bishop of Worcester, 1339–49*, ed. R. M. Haines (Worcestershire Historical Society, new series 4 and Historical Manuscripts Commission Joint Publication 9, 1966), using earlier foliation.

VACANCY 1349–1350

WCL, MS. A.1, fos. 120*r*–144*v*. Parchment register (composite volume, bound in hide-covered wooden boards); $13\frac{1}{4}'' \times 9\frac{1}{2}''$; fos. 25.

Worcester vacancy business Aug. 1349–Mar. 1350

Printed, *Worcester Sede Vacante Register*, pp. 223–56.

JOHN THORESBY (1350–1352)

HWRO, b 716.093–BA.2648/3(ii). Parchment register; $12\frac{3}{4}'' \times 9\frac{3}{4}''$; fos. ii + i (parchment cover) + 54 + i (paper, index, $12\frac{1}{4}'' \times 6\frac{1}{2}''$) + 2 + i (parchment cover) + ii, paginated 1–125 (including covers); blank: pp. 9, 10, 119; parchment-covered boards.

3–8	dispensations, licences Feb. 1350–July 1351
11–18	register heading, and memoranda (commissions, letters dimissory, indulgences, licences, mandates, indentures, etc.) Jan.–Nov. 1350
19–26	memoranda (heading) (the contents as the previous section; some chronological confusion) Mar.–Nov. 1350
27–40	ordinations Feb. 1350–Dec. 1351
41–115	institutions (this section is confused in arrangement and contains material other than institutions, including a record of ordinations, Mar. 1352. The heading indicating that entries concern the Gloucester archdeaconry only is erroneous, since the section covers parishes in the whole diocese) June 1350–Jan. 1353
117–118	later table of contents
123	memoranda Oct.–Nov. 1351

A section containing royal writs Nov. 1350–Dec. 1352 is now bound up in Wulstan Bransford's register above, and is calendared in the printed edition, nos. 1344–64. Some institutions by Thoresby's vicar-general are to be found in Bishop Brian's register (see below).

VACANCY 1352–1353

WCL, MS. A.1, fos. 106*r*–111*r*. Parchment register (composite volume, bound in hide-covered wooden boards); 13″ × 9½″; fos. 6.

Worcester vacancy business Jan.–Apr. 1353

Printed, *Worcester Sede Vacante Register*, pp. 191–202. An exchange of benefices in Worcester and Canterbury dioceses, Mar. 1353, is recorded in Lambeth Palace Library, register of Archbishop Simon Islip, fo. 264*v*.

REGINALD BRIAN (1353–1361)

HWRO, b 716.093–BA.2648/3(iii). Parchment register; 13½″ × 9″; fos. ii + i (fragment of parchment cover) + 1 (10½″ × 7¼″) + 1 (13¼″ × 7¾″) + 119 + 3 (paper, index, 12¼″ × 6¾″) + i (parchment cover) + ii, paginated 1–263 (including inserts); blank: pp. 2, 30, 98, 202, 219, 240; parchment-covered boards.

3–4	institutions of vicar-general *temp.* Bishop John Thoresby Sept. 1350–Oct. 1351
5–6	administrative and legal memoranda [Sept.] 1358–Jan. 1359
7–86	institutions (including some memoranda, and also ordinations Dec. 1353–Mar. 1354) July 1353–Dec. 1361
87–123	ordinations June 1354–Sept. 1361 (see also above)
125–136	*registrum ... de dimissoriis, dispensacionibus et licenciis celebrandi* Oct. 1353–May 1361
137–228	memoranda (not always in chronological order) Sept. 1355–July 1361
229–252	royal writs and related business July 1353–Apr. 1361
253–258	later table of contents

The paper volume, HWRO, b 716.093–BA.2648/3(iv), sometimes known as *Register Brian 2*, is not a register, but a formulary, see R. M. Haines, 'The compilation of a late fourteenth-century precedent book—*Register Brian 2*' in *Studies in Church History* 11 (1975), 173–85; *The Register of Henry Wakefield*, pp. xiii–xiv.

VACANCY 1361–1362

1. WCL, MS. A.1, fos. 111*v*–117*v*. Parchment register (composite volume, bound in hide-covered wooden boards); 13″ × 9½″; fos. 7.

   Worcester vacancy business Dec. 1361–Mar. 1362

   Printed, *Worcester Sede Vacante Register*, pp. 202–16.

2. LPL, register of Archbishop Simon Islip, fo. 240*v*.

   Worcester vacancy business Jan.–Mar. 1362

JOHN BARNET (1362–1363)

HWRO, b 716.093–BA.2648/4(i). Parchment register; average 13″ × 9″; fos. ii + i (parchment cover) + 27 + ii (paper, index, 12¼″ × 6½″) + i (parchment cover) + ii, paginated 1–63 (including covers); blank: pp. 2, 41, 61; parchment-covered boards.

3–8	register of vicar-general (including ordinations) June–Sept. 1362
13–16	register of vicar-general Mar.–Apr. 1362
17–46	general register (including ordinations) May 1362–Feb. 1363
47–52	register of vicar-general Feb.–July 1363
52–55	general register (cont.) July–Aug. 1363
56, 9–12	register of vicar-general Sept. 1363–Mar. 1364
57–59	later table of contents

VACANCY 1363–1364

WCL, MS. A.1, fos. 118*r*–119*v*. Parchment register (composite volume, bound in hide-covered wooden boards); $13'' \times 9\frac{1}{4}''$; fos. 2.

Worcester vacancy business Apr.–June 1364

Printed, *Worcester Sede Vacante Register*, pp. 216–22.

WILLIAM WHITTLESEY (1364–1368)

HWRO, b 716.093–BA.2648/4(ii). Parchment register; average $14'' \times 10''$; fos. ii + i (parchment cover) + 37 + i (paper, $11\frac{3}{4}'' \times 8''$) + i (paper, $11\frac{3}{4}'' \times 9\frac{1}{4}''$) + ii (paper, $12\frac{1}{2}'' \times 6\frac{3}{4}''$) + ii, paginated 1–88 (including inserts); blank: pp. 46, 56, 57, 70, 71, 76, 77, 80, 86–88; parchment-covered boards.

3–4 charter about Westbury collegiate church and Hembury June 1367
5 bull of Pope Urban V to the prior of Worcester about the use of the mitre etc. Feb. 1365
6–34 institutions etc. (mostly by the vicar-general; there is some slight chronological confusion) Apr. 1364–Jan. 1368
35 ordination of the chapel of Henle 1367
36–37 *exhibiciones beneficiorum et expectacionum* (certificates of obtaining, and value of, benefices) Aug.–Oct. 1367
38 miscellaneous administrative business Dec. 1367–[ ]1368
39–45 ordinations June 1365–Sept. 1367
47–55 institutions etc. (cont. from p. 34) Jan. 1368–Jan. 1369
58 will May 1369 (repeated in Bishop Lenn's register)
59 list of names n.d. (? first tonsure)
60–69 memoranda (dispensations, commissions, fincancial business, purgation, composition) Jan.–Dec. 1368
72–74 ordinations (cont. from p. 45) Mar.–Sept. 1368
75 royal writs Nov. 1367–Oct. 1368
78 miscellaneous administrative business Jan.–Sept. 1368
81–83 late 17th-/early 18th-cent. table of contents

A version of Urban V's bull on p. 5 is printed, *Monasticon Anglicanum* i, pp. 618–19.

VACANCY 1368–1369

1. LPL, register of Archbishop William Whittlesey, fo. 132*r–v*.

Worcester vacancy business Jan.–May 1369

2. WCL, MS. A.1, fo. 119*v* (for description see 1363–4 vacancy).

Worcester vacancy act Feb. 1369 (1 entry)

Printed, *Worcester Sede Vacante Register*, p. 222.

WILLIAM LENN (1369–1373)

HWRO, b 716.093–BA.2648/4(iii). Parchment register; average $12\frac{3}{4}'' \times 9''$; fos. ii + i (parchment cover) + 53 + ii (paper, $12\frac{1}{4}'' \times 6\frac{1}{2}''$) + i (parchment cover) + ii, paginated 1–119 (including inserts); blank: pp. 48, 62–64, 74, 84, 92, 96–98, 106, 112, 117, 118; parchment-covered boards.

3–4 institutions by commissaries July–Sept. 1369
5–14 institutions by bishop Sept. 1369–May 1373
15–44 exchanges of benefices Sept. 1369–May 1373
45–47 confirmations and benedictions of heads of religious houses Sept. 1369–Mar. 1372
49–61 ordinations Sept. 1369–Nov. 1372

65–83	memoranda about royal subsidies, papal letters, and mandates May 1371–Dec. 1372
85–91	administrative and legal commissions and mandates July 1369–May 1370
93–95	gaol deliveries and pleas of the Crown Mar. 1364–Mar. 1372
99–105	royal writs Nov. 1369–Feb. 1373
107–111	wills Dec. 1367–Sept. 1371
113–116	late 17th-/early 18th-cent. table of contents

VACANCY 1373–1375

1. WCL, MS. A.1, fos. 164*r*–198*v*. Parchment register (composite volume, bound in hide-covered wooden boards); 13¼″ × 9½″; fos. 35.

Worcester vacancy business Nov. 1373–Oct. 1375

Printed, *Worcester Sede Vacante Register*, pp. 282–353.

2. LPL, register of Archbishop William Whittlesey, fo. 139*r–v*.

Worcester vacancy business Nov. 1373–Apr. 1374

HENRY WAKEFIELD (1375–1395)

HWRO, b 716.093–BA.2648/4(iv). Parchment register; 13″ × 9″; fos. ii + i (leather cover) + 170 + x (paper, 12″ × 7″) + 2 + ii, paginated 1–367 (including inserts); parchment-covered boards.

The register is divided into three sections: institutions and licences etc., followed by a section containing archiepiscopal mandates, royal writs and episcopal letters etc., and finally a section devoted to ordinations. A full description of the register is given in the published edition (see below), pp. ix–xvi.

Printed, *A Calendar of the Register of Henry Wakefield, Bishop of Worcester 1375–95*, ed. W. P. Marett (Worcestershire Historical Society, new series 7, 1972), using earlier foliation.

VACANCY 1395

WCL, MS. A.1, fos. 199*r*–216*v*. Parchment register (composite volume, bound in hide-covered wooden boards); 13¾″ × 10″; fos. 18.

Worcester vacancy business Mar.–Nov. 1395

Printed, *Worcester Sede Vacante Register*, pp. 353–71.

TIDEMAN OF WINCHCOMBE (1395–1401)

HWRO, b 716.093–BA. 2648/4(v). Parchment register; 14″ × 9½″; fos. ii + 69 + iii (paper, 12″ × 7½″) + 1 + ii, paginated 1–147 (including inserts); blank: pp. 40–42, 131, 144–146; parchment-covered boards.

1	register heading
2–8	acts of the vicar-general Sept.–Nov. 1395
9–122	general register (there is occasional chronological confusion; the beginning of the register appears to be missing) Mar. 1396–June 1401
123–137	ordinations (last entry incomplete) Sept. 1395–Dec. 1397
139–143	late 17th-/early 18th-cent. table of contents

VACANCY 1401

WCL, MS. A.1, fos. 217*r*–227*r*. Parchment register (composite volume, bound in hide-covered wooden boards); 13¼″ × 9¼″; fos. 11.

Worcester vacancy business (with some later material) June–Oct. 1401

Printed, *Worcester Sede Vacante Register*, pp. 371–86.

RICHARD CLIFFORD (1401–1407)

HWRO, b 716.093–BA.2648/5(i). Parchment register; fos. ii+i (parchment cover)+24 (13″ × 8½″)+27 (11½″ × 7½″)+48 (13″ + 8½″)+iv (paper, 12″ × 7″)+i (parchment cover)+ii, paginated 1–210 (including inserts); parchment-covered boards.

The register is divided into three sections: *registrum litterarum emanancium de cancellaria* (p.3); *registrum . . . de collacionibus, institucionibus et permutacionibus expeditis* . . . (p. 19); and *registrum . . . de ordinibus celebratis* (p. 51).

Printed, *The register of Richard Clifford, bishop of Worcester, 1401–1407: a calendar*, ed. W. E. L. Smith (Pontificial Institute of Mediaeval Studies, Subsidia Mediaevalia 6, Toronto, 1976), using earlier foliation.

VACANCY 1407

WCL, MS. A.1, fos. 227*v*–228*v*. Parchment register (composite volume, bound in hide-covered wooden boards); 13″ × 9½″; fos. 2.

Worcester vacancy businesss Oct.–Nov. 1407

Printed, *Worcester Sede Vacante Register*, pp. 387–90

THOMAS PEVEREL (1407–1419)

HWRO, b 716.093–BA.2648/5(ii). Parchment register; 13¾″ × 9½″; fos. ii+i (parchment cover)+106+v (paper, 12¼″ × 7½″)+ii, paginated 1–224 (including inserts); blank: pp. 2, 3, 20, 22, 38, 136, 172; parchment-covered boards.

4	register heading
5–166	general register Dec. 1407–Apr. 1417
167–213	ordinations Dec. 1407–June 1417
215–223	late 17th-/early 18th-cent. table of contents.

There is a modern transcript of pp. 4–15 inserted loose in the front of the register.

VACANCY 1419

1. WCL, MS. A.1, fos. 229*r*–243*r*. Parchment register (composite volume, bound in hide-covered wooden boards); 12″ × 8¾″; fos. 16.

   Worcester vacancy business Mar.–Dec. 1419

   Printed, *Worcester Sede Vacante Register*, pp. 390–407.

2. LPL, register of Archbishop Henry Chichele, volume I, fo. 117*v*.

   Worcester vacancy act July 1419 (1 entry), among the general section of Canterbury institutions

   Printed, *Register of Henry Chichele* i, p. 190.

PHILIP MORGAN (1419–1426)

HWRO, b 716.093–BA.2648/5(iii). Parchment register; 14″ × 9″; fos. ii+i (parchment cover)+35+70+ii (paper, 12¼″ × 6½″)+iii (paper, 12″ × 7¼″)+i (parchment cover)+ii, paginated 1–225 (including inserts); blank: pp. 15, 58, 172, 224; parchment-covered boards.

3–57	acts of the vicar-general Sept. 1419–July 1421
59–72	ordinations celebrated by authority of the vicar-general Mar. 1420–Mar. 1421
73	(mounted) register heading (? fragment from old cover)
75	register heading

77–151 general register of bishop May 1420–Apr. 1426
152–188 memoranda (judgments, compositions, appointment of officials, manumissions, abjurations of heretics, etc. in some chronological confusion. This is not a separate memoranda section distinct from the general register, but a collection of documents entered at the end of the register) May 1422–Apr. 1426
189–212 ordinations Sept. 1421–Mar. 1426
213–215 late 17th-/early 18th-cent. table of contents to volume 2 (pp. 3–72)
217–222 similar table of contents to volume 1 (pp. 73–212)

The front limp parchment cover is labelled *Registrum Secundum Philippi Morgan* and it is clear from this and the later contents lists that the register was originally in two separate volumes.

THOMAS POLTON (1426–1433)

HWRO, b 716.093–BA. 2648/5(iv). Parchment register; average 14″ × 10″; fos. ii + i (fragment of parchment cover) + 152 + vi (paper, 12½″ × 6½″) + i (parchment cover) + ii, paginated 1–322 (including inserts); blank: pp. 230, 238; parchment-covered boards.

3–206, 299–308 general register (this section includes some ordinations, Sept. 1427 (pp. 59–60), Dec. 1427 (p. 69), Sept. 1428 (pp. 100–1), Mar. 1429 (pp. 125–6); and also ordinations *vice* Archbishop Chichele, Apr. 1427 (p. 37) and for the Salisbury diocese *sede vacante* July 1427 (pp. 43–4)) Feb. 1426–Jan. 1432
207–237 ordinations (in some confusion) Dec. 1426–Sept. 1433
239–308 general register (cont.) (including some earlier entries at the end. Pp. 299–308 are misplaced, see above) Oct. 1431–Sept. 1433
309–320 late 17th-/early 18th-cent. table of contents

VACANCY 1433–1435

1. WCL, MS. A.1, fos. 244*r*–269*v*. Parchment register (composite volume, bound in hide-covered wooden boards); average 12¼″ × 9¼″; fos. 26.

   Worcester vacancy business Oct. 1433–May 1435

   Printed, *Worcester Sede Vacante Register*, pp. 408–46.

2. LPL, register of Archbishop Henry Chichele, volume I, fo. 203*r*.

   Worcester vacancy act May 1434 (1 entry), among the general section of Canterbury institutions

   Printed, *Register of Henry Chichele* i, p. 284.

THOMAS BOURGCHIER (1435–1443)

HWRO, b 716.093–BA.2648/6(i). Parchment register; 14¼″ × 10″; fos. ii + i (former limp leather cover) + i + 101 + iv (paper, i = 12″ × 6″, ii–iv = 12½″ × 7″) + i + ii, paginated 1–222 (including inserts); blank: pp. 2–4, 6, 36, 48, 196–198, 217, 218, 220–222; parchment-covered binding.

7–195 general register (including acts of the vicars-general. There is occasionally some slight chronological confusion in arrangement. On p. 35 is the formal register heading. This section includes ordinations Dec. 1436–Apr. 1438 (pp. 60–64)) May 1435–Jan. 1444 (1 entry dated Sept. 1444, *recte* 1443)
199–208 ordinations Mar. 1440, Dec. 1442, Mar.–Sept. 1443
209–216 late 17th-/early 18th-cent. table of contents

JOHN CARPENTER (1444–1476)

1. HWRO, b 716.093–BA.2648/6(ii). Parchment register; average 13″ × 9″; fos. ii–i (former limp leather cover) + i + 290 + ii (paper, $12\frac{1}{2}$″ × $6\frac{1}{4}$″) + i + ii, paginated 1–590 (including inserts); blank: pp. 2, 6, 11, 12, 22, 69, 347, 371, 372, 446, 586, 588–590; parchment-covered boards.

7–10	contemporary table of contents
13	register heading
14–496	general register (including acts of the vicars-general. There is some occasional chronological disorder in arrangement) Mar. 1444–Feb. 1470.
497–580	ordinations Dec. 1444–Apr. 1471
581–584	late 17th-/early 18th-cent. table of contents

2. HWRO, b 716.093–BA.2648/6(iii). Parchment register; average 13″ × $9\frac{1}{2}$″; fos. ii + i (fragment of former parchment cover) + 108 + ii (paper, $12\frac{1}{4}$″ × 6″) + ii, paginated 1–19A, 19B, 19C, 20–59A, 59B, 59C, 60–89A, 89B, 89C, 90–220 (including inserts); blank: pp. 2, 119, 218–220; parchment-covered boards.

3–182	general register (some gatherings are missing and others misplaced, e.g. p. 71 should follow straight on p. 48) Apr. 1469–Sept. 1476
183–209	ordinations Sept. 1471–June 1476
210–212	contemporary table of contents
213–215	late 17th-/early 18th-cent. table of contents

JOHN ALCOCK (1476–1486)

HWRO, b 716.093–BA. 2648/7(i). Parchment register; $13\frac{1}{2}$″ × $10\frac{1}{4}$″; fos. ii + i (former parchment cover) + 134 + iii (paper, $12\frac{1}{2}$″ × $6\frac{3}{4}$″) + i (former parchment cover) + ii, paginated 1–286 (including inserts); blank: pp. 2, 19, 20, 244, 282, 284–286; parchment-covered boards.

3–243	general register Feb. 1479–Nov. 1486 (It is evident that there was an earlier section of the register for the years 1476–9, which is now lost. The present first folio is numbered 50 in an older foliation)
245–274	ordinations Apr. 1477–Sept. 1483
275–279	late 17th-/early 18th-cent. table of contents

ROBERT MORTON (1487–1497)
[GERONIMO DE' GHINUCCI (1522–1535)]

HWRO, b 716.093–BA.2648/7(ii). Parchment register; $14\frac{3}{4}$″ × $11\frac{1}{4}$″; fos. ii + 88 + ii (paper, $11\frac{3}{4}$″ × $7\frac{1}{4}$″) + 2 + ii, paginated 1–188 (including inserts); blank: pp. 69, 70, 126, 133, 136, 181–184, 186–188; parchment-covered boards.

1	register heading
2–135	general register of Bishop Robert Morton (some entries at the end are out of chronological sequence) Oct. 1486–Feb. 1497
137–162	ordinations Apr. 1487–May 1494
163–174	ordinations *temp.* Bishop Geronimo de' Ghinucci Mar. 1527–Sept. 1533 (this section should follow on after p. 186 of Ghinucci's register, see below)
175–176	18th-cent. table of contents
177–179	late 17th-/early 18th-cent. table of contents

GIOVANNI DE' GIGLI (1497–1498)

HWRO, b 716.093–BA.2648/7(iii). Parchment register; 15″ × $11\frac{3}{4}$″; fos. ii + i (former parchment cover) + 13 + i (paper, 12″ × $7\frac{1}{2}$″) + 1 + i (former parchment cover) + ii, paginated 1–40 (including inserts); blank: pp. 2, 10, 30, 33–40; parchment-covered boards.

4–24	general register Aug. 1497–Aug. 1498
25–28	ordinations Apr. 1497 (*recte* 1498)–June 1498
29	18th-cent. table of contents
31–32	late 17th-/early 18th-cent. table of contents

VACANCY 1498–1499

LPL, register of Archbishop John Morton, volume I, fos. 167*r*–187*r*.

Worcester vacancy business Sept. 1498–Feb. 1499

Calendared in C. Harper-Bill, 'An edition of the register of John Morton, archbishop of Canterbury, 1486–1500' (London University Ph.D., 1977).

SILVESTRO DE' GIGLI (1499–1521)
[GIULIO DE' MEDICI (1521–1522)]
GERONIMO DE' GHINUCCI (1522–1535)
VACANCY 1535
HUGH LATIMER (1535–1539)

1. HWRO, b 716.093–BA.2648/8(i). Parchment register; $15'' \times 11\frac{3}{4}''$; fos. ii + 191 + ix (paper, index, $11\frac{3}{4}'' \times 8\frac{1}{4}''$) + i (former parchment cover) + ii, paginated 1–425; blank: pp. 20, 285, 286, 336–338, 372, 392–394; parchment-covered boards.

1	register heading
2–284	general register of Bishop Silvestro de' Gigli (some chronological confusion, particularly at the beginning) Dec. 1498–Nov. 1517
287–335	ordinations *temp.* Bishop Gigli [Sept.] 1503–Mar. 1517 (continuation of p. 404 below)
339–391	memoranda, of the sort found in the general register section—confirmations of heads of religious houses, visitation business, appropriation deeds, subsidy material, judicial sentences, etc., not arranged in strict chronological sequence and giving the distinct impression that they were entered after the general register section had been compiled. Sept. 1499–Jan. 1513
395–404	ordinations May 1499–Sept. 1503 (continued above on p. 287)
405–422	late 17th-/early 18th-cent. table of contents

2. HWRO, b 716.093–BA.2648/8(ii). Paper register; $11\frac{1}{2}'' \times 12\frac{1}{2}''$ (some mounted on larger paper sheets, $14\frac{1}{2}'' \times 9\frac{1}{2}''$); fos. i (parchment) + 5 (large paper) + x (19th-cent. index, $14\frac{1}{2}'' \times 9''$) + 43 + 6 (large paper) + i (parchment), paginated 1–108; blank: pp. 1, 20, 21, 24, 55, 97, 102–104, 108 (+9 unnumbered fos.); parchment-covered binding.

2–19	19th-cent. table of contents and separate indexes of places and persons
22–26	fragmentary extracts *temp.* Bishops Gigli and Ghinucci (grant of next presentation, caveats, dispensation, fragment of will) Mar. 1517–Feb. 1529
28–90	general register of Bishop Geronimo de' Ghinucci Mar. 1528–Jan. 1535
90–94	general register of Henry VIII's vicar-general after the deprivation of Bishop Ghinucci Feb.–July 1535
94–101	general register of Bishop Hugh Latimer Dec. 1535–Aug. 1536 (with 1 additional entry *temp.* Bishop Bell May 1541)
105–107	caveats (only three dated 1518–1535)

3. HWRO, b 716.093–BA.2648/9(i). Parchment register; 14¾″ × 11¼″; fos. ii + ii (former parchment covers) + 87 + v (paper, index, 12″ × 8¼″) + ii, paginated 1–186, 188–197 (including covers and inserts); blank: pp. 3–5, 13, 15, 179–181; parchment-covered boards.

14	heading of Ghinucci's register
16–21	general register of Bishop Gigli Oct. 1520–Apr. 1521 (includes some ordinations)
22–25	papal bulls relating to Giulio de' Medici's provision and incomplete copy of Medici's letter of proxy recited by Archbishop Wolsey June 1521 (3 folios are cut out at this point)
26–33	acts of Bishop Ghinucci Feb. 1523–Nov. 1525
34–159	general register of Bishop Ghinucci (some entries are in confusion and there are indications of late registration) Oct. 1522–Jan. 1535 (see also above, preceding volume, pp. 28–90)
159–163	register heading and acts of Henry VIII's vicar-general following Ghinucci's deprivation Feb.–Oct. (*sic*) 1535 (see also above, preceding volume, pp. 90–94)
164–178	miscellaneous section, mostly memoranda, letters from the pope, Archbishop Wolsey and other bishops, including Convocation material. Feb. 1525–July 1535
182–186	ordinations Mar.–May 1523, Sept. 1526–Mar. 1527 (last entry incomplete) (see also continuation in Bishop Morton's register above)
188–197	late 17th-/early 18th-cent. table of contents

4. HWRO, b 716.093–BA.2648/9(ii). Parchment (1st part), paper (2nd part); fos. ii + 11 (parchment, 12½″ × 8¾″) + ii (former covers to 2nd part) + 12 (paper, 12½″ × 8¼″) + ii (paper, 12″ × 7¼″) + ii, paginated 1–55 (including inserts, but ignoring certain blank folios); blank: pp, 19, 43, 47, 51–55 (+ 6 unnumbered pages); parchment-covered boards.

(*part 1*)	
1–8	general register of Bishop Latimer Nov. 1536–Oct. 1537
8–14, 17	record of a case leading to the deprivation of an incumbent Aug.–Sept. 1536
15	note of grants of letters questory Oct. 153[?1]–Mar. 153[?2]
18	table of contents (for pp. 1–8 only, old foliation cited)
(*part 2*)	
20	register heading
20–39	general register of Bishop Latimer (institutions and collations) Aug. 1537–May 1539
40–42	record of 3 institutions to Comberton July 1539, Dec. 1545, Aug. 1550 (inserted)
44	table of contents
48	late 17th-/early 18th-cent. copy of table of contents on p. 18 (with additional reference to deprivation case on pp. 8–14, 17)
50	late 17th-/early 18th-cent. copy of table of contents on p. 44 (same handwriting as on p. 48)

VACANCY 1521

LPL, register of Archbishop William Warham, volume II, fos. 292*r*–294*v*.

Worcester vacancy business Apr.–July 1521 (with vacancy accounts Nov. 1521–May 1523)

VACANCY 1539

LPL, register of Archbishop Thomas Cranmer, fos. 368*r*, 381*r*.

Worcester vacancy business July 1539

Calendared in A. J. Edwards, 'The *sede vacante* administration of Archbishop Thomas Cranmer, 1533–53' (London University M.Phil., 1968).

JOHN BELL (1539–1543)

HWRO, b 716.093–BA.2648/9(iii). Parchment register; $12\frac{1}{2}'' \times 8\frac{3}{4}''$; fos. ii+i (former cover)+40+iii (paper, $12'' \times 7\frac{1}{2}''$)+i (former cover)+ii, paginated 1–90; blank: pp. 38, 78, 82, 88; parchment-covered boards, encasing limp parchment covers (sections of a 14th-cent. papal bull relating to chantries in St Michael's chapel, Breadstone, now pp. 1–2, 89–90).

1	register heading
4–77	general register (including ordinations in chronological sequence) Sept. 1539–Nov. 1543
79–81	18th-cent. place index
83–87	late 17th-/early 18th-cent. table of contents

VACANCY 1543–1544

LPL, register of Archbishop Thomas Cranmer, fo. 391*r*.

Worcester vacancy act Feb. 1544 (1 entry), among the general section of Canterbury institutions

Calendared in A. J. Edwards, 'The *sede vacante* administration of Archbishop Thomas Cranmer, 1533–53' (London University M.Phil., 1968).

NICHOLAS HEATH (1544–1551; 1553–1555)
JOHN HOOPER (1552–1553)
RICHARD PATES (1555–1559)
EDWIN SANDYS (1559–1570)

HWRO, b 716.093–BA.2648/9(iv). Parchment register; $15'' \times 11\frac{3}{4}''$; fos. ii+ii (former covers)+46+ii, paginated i–iv, 1–98, [99–106] (including inserts); blank: pp. i–iv, 2–4, 6, 38, 46, 59, 60, 88–90, 93, 94, 96, [99–106]; parchment-covered boards.

5	caveats Sept. 1533 and one n.d. (? 1551)
6–37	general register of Bishop Nicholas Heath (there are not many entries for the late 1540s and the arrangement is confused in the early 1550s) Apr. 1544–Sept. 1551
39–43	general register of Bishop John Hooper (including some Gloucester entries) June 1552–June 1553
43–45	general register of Bishop Heath (restored) Aug. 1553–Mar. 1554
47–52, 61–78	general register of Bishop Richard Pates Apr. 1556–Feb. 1559 (p. 52 should be followed immediately by p. 61)
53–58	copy (loose insertion $11\frac{1}{4}'' \times 8\frac{1}{4}''$) of Edward VI's foundation charter of Stourbridge grammar school June 1552
79–87	general register of Bishop Edwin Sandys May 1560–Nov. 1563
91–92	copy of royal charter (Augmentations Court) relating to annual pensions formerly paid to Worcester cathedral priory by certain dissolved religious houses Nov. 1538
95	late 17th-/early 18th-cent. index of places (arranged by rural deaneries, Gloucestershire) and significant subjects
97–[99]	18th-cent. copy of p. 95

There are no ordinations recorded in this register.

VACANCY 1551–1552

LPL, register of Archbishop Thomas Cranmer, fos. 128*r*–129*v*.

Worcester vacancy business Oct. 1551–June 1552

Institutions are calendared in A. J. Edwards, 'The *sede vacante* administration of Archbishop Thomas Cranmer, 1533–53' (London University M.Phil., 1968). One entry is erroneously dated Jan. 1555 (*recte* Jan. 1552).

VACANCY 1559

CAL, register U2, fos. 102*v*–103*r*.

Worcester vacancy business June–Nov. 1559

Institutions are calendared (by place) in *Sede Vacante Institutions.*

VACANCY 1570–1571

LPL, register of Archbishop Matthew Parker, volume I, fos. 203*v*–204*r*.

Worcester vacancy business July 1570–Jan. 1571

Printed, *Registrum Matthei Parker* i, pp. 298–301.

NICHOLAS BULLINGHAM (1571–1576)
VACANCY 1576–1577
JOHN WHITGIFT (1577–1583)
VACANCY 1583–1584
EDMUND FREKE (1584–1591)
RICHARD FLETCHER (1593–1595)
THOMAS BILSON (1596–1597)
GERVASE BABINGTON (1597–1610)
VACANCY 1610
HENRY PARRY (1610–1616)
JOHN THORNBOROUGH (1617–1641)

HWRO, b 716.093–BA.2648/10(i). Parchment register; 13″ × $8\frac{3}{4}$″; fos. ii + ii (former parchment covers) + 124 + iv (paper, $11\frac{3}{4}$″ × $7\frac{3}{4}$″) + 1 + ii, paginated 1–261 (including covers and inserts); blank: pp. 2–4, 6, 119, 121, 122, 176–178, 191, 193, 259, 260; parchment-covered boards.

5–26	general register of Bishop Nicholas Bullingham Feb. 1571–Apr. 1576
26–29	*sede vacante* register May 1576–Apr. 1577 (see also below)
29–50	general register of Bishop John Whitgift May 1577–Sept. 1583
50–61	*sede vacante* register Jan.–Nov. 1584
62–70	general register of Bishop Edmund Freke Nov. 1584–Mar. 1587
71–90	dispensations and licences *temp.* Bishop Whitgift Apr. 1579–Dec. 1582
91–93	ordinations *temp.* Bishop Bullingham Sept. 1571–Apr. 1576
94–95	ordinations *temp.* Bishop Whitgift July 1577–June 1583
96–97	ordinations *temp.* Bishop Freke July 1585–Apr. 1590
97	ordinations *temp.* Bishop Fletcher Feb. 1593–Dec. 1594
98–101	ordinations *temp.* Bishop Babington June 1598–May 1602
101–104	18th-cent. copy of judicial sentence concerning the church of Suckley and the chapel of Alfrick Apr. 1585
105–118	dispensations, licences and letters dimissory Dec. 1582–Mar. 1585

120	licence Aug. 1605 (1 entry)
123–138	general register of Bishop Freke (cont.) May 1587–Mar. 1591
138–144	general register of Bishop Richard Fletcher Jan. 1593–Jan. 1595
144–149	general register of Bishop Thomas Bilson Apr. 1596–May 1597
149–190, 192	general register of Bishop Gervase Babington Sept. 1597–Sept. 1609, May 1610
190	*sede vacante* act Sept. 1610 (1 entry)
192	institution Dec. 1612 (1 entry)
194	letter of the Archbishop of Canterbury about prohibitions Feb. 1609
195	assignment of a pew by Bishop Babington July 1610 (*sic*) (Bishop Babington died 17 May 1610)
196–210	general register of Bishop Henry Parry Oct. 1610–Nov. 1616
211–240	general register of Bishop John Thornborough (part 1) Oct. 1617–Dec. 1625
241–243	18th-cent. copy of decision about the tithes of the parish of Burton on the Heath [? Bourton on Dunsmore] Michaelmas 1698
244	miscellanea (appointment of bishop's domestic chaplain, grant of next presentation, presentation deed) June 1597–Feb. 1606
245–252	18th-cent. copy of indentures about Fleet or Chandler's Gift to the city of Worcester Mar.–June 1595
253–258	18th-cent. index of places and table of select contents

VACANCY 1576–1577

LPL, register of Archbishop Edmund Grindal, volume II, fos. 287*r*–288*v*.

Worcester vacancy business May–Sept. 1576

See also above.

VACANCY 1583–1584

LPL, register of Archbishop John Whitgift, volume I, fos. 366*r*–368*r*.

Worcester vacancy business Oct. 1583–July 1584

VACANCY 1591–1593

LPL, register of Archbishop John Whitgift, volume I, fos. 306*v*–308*v*.

Worcester vacancy business Mar. 1591–Dec. 1592 (the last entry on fo. 308*v* is completed on 306*r*)

VACANCY 1595–1596

LPL, register of Archbishop John Whitgift, volume II, fos. 260*v*–264*r*.

Worcester vacancy business Jan. 1595–May 1596

VACANCY 1597

LPL, register of Archbishop John Whitgift, volume II, fos. 302*r*–304*v*.

Worcester vacancy business May–Sept. 1597

VACANCY 1610

LPL, register of Archbishop Richard Bancroft, fos. 263*r*–264*r*.

Worcester vacancy business May–Sept. 1610

VACANCY 1616–1617

LPL, register of Archbishop George Abbot, volume I, fos. 340*r*–342*r*.

Worcester vacancy business Dec. 1616–Feb. 1617

JOHN THORNBOROUGH (1617–1641)
VACANCY 1641
JOHN PRIDEAUX (1641–1650)

HWRO, b 716.093–BA.2648/10(ii). Parchment register; $11\frac{3}{4}'' \times 8''$; fos. ii+i (former parchment cover)+50+i (paper, $11\frac{1}{2}'' \times 8''$)+i (former parchment cover)+ii, paginated 1–106 (including covers); blank: pp. 2, 69, 70, 99–102, 105, 106; parchment-covered boards.

3–46	general register of Bishop Thornborough (part 2) Nov. 1625–July 1641
46–48	*sede vacante* register July–Oct. 1641
49–68	general register of Bishop John Prideaux Nov. 1641–May 1646
71–98	miscellanea (letters and instructions of Charles I about the leasing of church lands, fees, and cognate business, letter from Archbishop Laud, record of the unions of benefices and the consecration of a churchyard, petition to Prince Maurice of the Rhine from the diocesan chancellor) May 1595–May 1645
103–104	18th-cent. index of places and table of select contents

YORK

Repositories

1. Borthwick Institute, University of York, St Anthony's Hall, York YO1 2PW (BI).
2. Minster Muniment Room, Minster Library, Dean's Park, York YO1 2JD (YM).
3. British Library, Department of Manuscripts, London WC1B 3DG (BL).

Area

The medieval diocese of York was divided into five archdeaconries—York (or the West Riding), Cleveland, the East Riding, Nottingham and Richmond; in addition the archbishop possessed personal jurisdictions outside the diocese in Gloucestershire (St Oswald's, Gloucester) and Northumberland (Hexhamshire). The diocesan boundaries and the peculiar jurisdictions have already been the subject of detailed treatment and it is only necessary here to refer to previous studies.[1] In 1541 the Richmond archdeaconry was transferred to the newly-established bishopric of Chester, but this was the only boundary change during the period under consideration.

Bibliographical Note

The series of York archiepiscopal registers has by no means been neglected by historians and archivists. The earliest registers (1225–1317) were printed by the Surtees Society between 1872 and 1940 and in recent times the Canterbury and York Society and the Borthwick Institute at York University have begun the publication of further registers of the fourteenth and fifteenth centuries. A summary list of those registers on deposit at the Borthwick Institute was published in 1973,[2] but long before this date a detailed introduction to the York registers had been provided by Professor Hamilton Thompson.[3] It still remains the best introductory study of diocesan registration at York. A comparative study of the archiepiscopal registers of Canterbury and York was made by Professor E F. Jacob[4] and a survey of the lost medieval York registers has been undertaken recently.[5]

The classification and arrangement of the registers will become apparent from a consultation of the appended descriptive list. Whereas the archbishops' registers were subdivided into sections according to geographical area, jurisdiction, or category of business, the arrangement of the registers of the vicars-general and of the archbishops *extra diocesim* was generally chronological, without any subdivisions, probably because of contemporary uncertainty as to the duration of the vicar-general's commission or the length of the diocesan's absence from his see. During the vacancy of the archbishopric, the dean and chapter of York exercised jurisdiction in the diocese. The resultant *sede vacante* registers of acts performed by the custodians of the spiritualities differ in arrangement and there is evidence (in 1315–17, 1397, 1398, 1423–6, 1464–5, 1480, 1500–1, 1507–8 and 1514) that a duplicate copy of the register was compiled, usually neater in appearance and, in the case of the 1315–17 vacancy, rearranged

[1] See the introduction to the five volumes of the edition of Archbishop Greenfield's register (see descriptive list below, p. 236); D. M. Smith, *A Guide to the archive collections in the Barthwick Institute of Historical Research* (Borthwick Texts and Calendars 1, York, 1973), pp. 86–7, 101–2; *VCH Yorkshire* iii (1913), pp. 80–8; A. Hamilton Thompson, 'The jurisdiction of the archbishops of York in Gloucestershire', *Transactions of the Bristol and Gloucestershire Archaeological Society*, 43 (1921), 85–180. For a map of the diocese see the frontispiece to G. Ornsby, *Diocesan Histories: York* (London, 1882); and also Ordnance Survey, *Map of Monastic Britain: (north and south sheets)* (2nd edn., 1954–5).

[2] Smith, *Borthwick Guide*, pp. 6–18.

[3] 'The registers of the archbishops of York', *Yorkshire Archaeological Journal*, 32 (1936), 245–63.

[4] *The medieval registers of Canterbury and York* (St Anthony's Hall publication 4, York, 1953).

[5] D. M. Smith, 'Lost archiepiscopal registers of York: the evidence of five medieval inventories', *Borthwick Institute Bulletin*, i no. 1 (1975), 31–7.

into sections like the archiepiscopal registers. In shorter vacancies, the duplicate copy was not rearranged in such a manner. It may be conjectured that the making of a later duplicate register was the normal practice in these vacancies and that other duplicates have been lost in the course of time. It is not clear which copy—the 'working' register or the later duplicate—was retained by the cathedral chapter and which was handed over to the new archbishop and his registry officials. In 1480, the neater version (BL, Cotton Galba E x) is marked *pro cancellario* and this may provide the answer.

While the medieval York registers include material for the semi-autonomous Richmond archdeaconry, it should be pointed out that registers of the archdeacons also survive, in a transcript for the period 1361–1442, and in the original for 1442–77. They have both been printed by Professor Hamilton Thompson.[6] Moreover, the register of Bishop John Gynwell of Lincoln contains a folio relating to his activities as vicar-general of the archdeacon of Richmond in 1348.[7]

The supplementary series of institution act books which are extant from 1545—and indeed may have been begun before then—are initially more in the nature of rough working notebooks than a finished, formal record of acts of the archbishops.[8] The early volumes are in some confusion (later entries were recorded where space permitted) with many annotations over fees and other memoranda made by the archbishops' clerks and officials. A check of many entries having the annotation 'R' against them has made it clear that these volumes were registry 'rough books', recording the day-to-day business of the vicars-general and that these selective marked entries were then formally copied into the archbishops' registers. A change of function occurs from the time of Archbishop Sandys (1577–88) when these volumes become the only source for institutions, collations, ordinations and the like and such material is no longer recorded in the main series of registers. As a consequence of this change, the act books assume a tidier and more methodical appearance.

Editions or articles on specific registers have been noted in the descriptive list but there are also certain published collections like *Historical Letters and Papers from the Northern Registers*,[9] the third volume of *Historians of the Church of York and its Archbishops*[10] and *The Records of Northern Convocation*[11] which print extracts from the medieval registers.[12] Lists of incumbents for the Doncaster, Dickering and Craven rural deaneries have been published in the *Fasti Parochiales* series of the Yorkshire Archaeological Society and Nottinghamshire clergy lists have been published by the Thoroton Society.[13] Wills were first registered *in extenso* in 1316 and an index has been published of all wills and other probate

[6] *Yorkshire Archaeological Journal*, 25 (1920), 129–268; 30 (1931), 1–134; 32 (1936), 111–45.

[7] Lincolnshire Archives Office, Episcopal register IX, fo. 415*r*, mentioned in *Yorkshire Archaeological Journal*, 25 (1920), 163. A photocopy is available at the Borthwick Institute, Ph. 35.

[8] For a full discussion of these records, see D. M. Smith, 'The York institution act books: diocesan registration in the sixteenth century', *Archives*, 13 (1977–8), 171–9.

[9] Ed. J. Raine (Rolls Series, 1873).

[10] Ed. J. Raine (Rolls Series, 1894). *Fasti Eboracenses: Lives of the Archbishops of York*, ed. W. H. Dixon and J. Raine, 1 (London, 1863, all published) calendars extracts from the registers.

[11] Ed. G. W. Kitchin (Surtees Society 113, 1907).

[12] It is not of course possible to refer to every isolated printed extract from the registers but attention can be drawn to the larger collections relating to monasteries and other ecclesiastical corporations such as the material abstracted for Hexham Abbey and Ripon and Beverley Minsters (Surtees Society 44, 78, 108, 1864–1903), and J. Raine's lists of licences and dispensations for marriage and vows of chastity taken from the York, Durham and Richmond registers 1374–1531 in *Testamenta Eboracensia* iii (Surtees Society 45, 1865), pp. 311–75.

[13] Ed. A. Hamilton Thompson, C. T. Clay, N. A. H. Lawrance and N. K. M. Gurney (Yorkshire Archaeological Society Record Series 85, 107, 129, 133, 1933–71); ed. K. S. S. Train (Thoroton Society Record Series 15, 20, 1953–61), for clergy of northern and central Nottinghamshire only. There are also typescript fasti lists at the Borthwick Institute compiled by the late Rev. N. A. H. Lawrance for the rural deaneries of Buckrose, Harthill and Holderness to 1660 (Add. MSS. 149, 152–5). James Torre (died 1699) made lists of incumbents for the whole diocese (YM, L1/6–10), as well as transcribing many York records, and these have been used by such local antiquaries as J. Graves, *The History of Cleveland* ... (Carlisle, 1808) and T. D. Whitaker, *History of Richmondshire* (2 vols, London, 1823). Lists of dignitaries and canons of York Minster have also been published to 1857 (*York Minster Fasti, being notes on the dignitaries, archdeacons and prebendaries in the Church of York prior to the year 1307*, ed. C. T. Clay (Yorkshire Archaeological Society Record Series 123–4, 1958–9); see also articles by the same writer on the early dignitaries and archdeacons, *Yorkshire Archaeological Journal*, 34 (1939), 361–78; 35 (1943), 7–34, 116–38; 36 (1947), 269–87, 409–34; for 1300–1857 see the *Le Neve* revision.

documents entered in the archiepiscopal registers for this period.[14] In addition a considerable number of the wills have been printed in the *Testamenta Eboracensia* series of the Surtees Society.[15]

WALTER DE GRAY (1215–1255)

BI, Reg. 1. Two parchment rolls, both slightly damaged at the beginning:

A. *Rotulus major* 26 mems.; 511″ × 8¼″, containing acts of the archbishop Mar. 1225 (first legible entry)—Nov. 1235; loose 16th–17th-cent. paper index, 4 pp.

B. *Rotulus minor* 16 mems. + 3 mems. of 16th–17th-cent. parchment index (every entry on both rolls was numbered at the time these indexes were compiled); 329″ × 8¼″, containing acts Feb. 1236 (first datable entry)—Apr. 1255.

The rolls are divided into pontifical years and within each year there are monthly headings in the left-hand margin. This margin also contains a note against each entry identifying the place or, occasionally, the person or type of business involved. There are spaces left between the monthly sections, presumably for any additional material. The dorse of each roll is reserved mainly for matters pertaining to the temporalities of the see. For reasons never satisfactorily explained, there are fewer entries for the last twenty years of the pontificate than for the preceding ten.

Printed, *The register, or rolls, of Walter Gray, lord archbishop of York: with appendices of illustrative documents*, ed. J. Raine (Surtees Society 56, 1872).

WALTER GIFFARD (1266–1279)

BI, Reg. 2. Parchment register; 11″ × 7″ (fos. 1–109); 11″ × 8″ (fos. 110–140); fos. v (16th–17th-cent. paper index) + ii + 135, foliated i–vii, 1–87, 89–105, 105A, 106–146 (some inserts foliated); the second part of the register (fos. 110–140) was previously foliated 1–30; modern binding, encasing original limp parchment covers.

The roll was abandoned in favour of the book by the clerks of Archbishop Giffard and it is conceivable that the change in methods of registration at York was due to current practice in the Bath and Wells diocese. Two quires (fos. 64–71, 79–86) contain Giffard's register as bishop of Bath and Wells, to which entries relating to the York diocese have been added at a later date. The volume is in considerable confusion but there was clearly some attempt made (albeit unsuccessful) to classify material by the five archdeaconries or by nature of business (*liberationes*, officiality, chapters (cathedral and collegiate), Howdenshire and Allertonshire peculiars, ordinations). The register is by no means a continuous record of the pontificate, only one entry being found between late 1272 and September 1274 (the period during which the archbishop was acting as one of the regents of the kingdom); the second part of the register (fos. 110–140) mainly covers the period 1274–76 and there appears to have been no later material registered.

Printed, *The register of Walter Giffard, lord archbishop of York, 1266–1279*, ed. W. Brown (Surtees Society 109, 1904). Fos. 64*r*–66*r*, 70*r*–71*v*, 79*r*–*v*, 83*r*–*v* of the register contain the Bath and Wells entries and are printed, *The registers of Walter Giffard, bishop of Bath and Wells, 1265–6, and of Henry Bowett, bishop of Bath and Wells, 1401–7*, ed. T. S. Holmes (Somerset Record Society 13, 1899), pp. 1–11.

WILLIAM WICKWANE (1279–1285)

BI, Reg. 3. Parchment register; 11½″ × 7½″; fos. 168, foliated 1–200 (including inserts); the second part of the register (fos. 97–200) was previously foliated 1–87; modern binding, encasing original limp parchment covers.

The register reveals an advance upon that of Giffard. In addition to the sections devoted to the archdeaconries, officiality, Howdenshire, *liberationes*, and cathedral and collegiate chapters (kept separately by

[14] *Index of wills and administrations entered in the registers of the archbishops at York, being Consistory wills, etc., A.D. 1316 to A.D. 1822, known as archbishops' wills*, ed. J. Charlesworth and A. V. Hudson (Yorkshire Archaeological Society Record Series 93, 1937).

[15] Ed. J. Raine senior and J. Raine junior, J. W. Clay (Surtees Society 4, 30, 45, 53, 79, 106, 1836–1902).

institution), Wickwane's clerks included further subdivisions: the peculiar jurisdictions of Hexhamshire, St Oswald's Gloucester, Laneham with Southwell, and the provostship of Beverley; *correctiones claustrales* (arranged by archdeaconry); letters sent to the pope; *intrinseca*; *extrinseca*; licences for study; *obligationes*; vacancy administration of the sees of Carlisle and Durham; and the provincial visitation of Durham and the subsequent dispute. The register survives in duplicate, although the two versions are now bound together. These duplicates are by no means exact copies either in content or arrangement. One register (fos. 1–96) was clearly copied from the other (fos. 97–200) at a later date. The latter contains more entries than the former and from its format was evidently a working register, space being left under the sectional headings for additional entries to be made as they occurred. The later version—which was never completed—seems to have been copied towards the close of the pontificate, perhaps even after the archbishop's death, and could not possibly have been a working record. On fo. 36*v*, for example, the heading and acts of Wickwane's first pontifical year for Howdenshire follow immediately (on the same folio without a gap) the acts of the fourth pontifical year in Hexhamshire. Such examples can be multiplied and indicate that this copy was not a gradual compilation, but was written up as an entity in a relatively short space of time.

Printed, *The register of William Wickwane, lord archbishop of York, 1279–1285*, ed. W. Brown (Surtees Society 114, 1907).

JOHN LE ROMEYN (1286–1296)

BI, Reg. 4. Parchment register; 12¼″ × 8½″; fos. ii + 122 + v (16th–17th-cent. paper index) + ii, foliated i–v, 1–165 (including inserts); modern binding, encasing original limp parchment covers.

With Romeyn's register the sectional divisions underwent further modification and to some extent simplification and became the basic model for later York registers. Material relating to the cathedral and collegiate chapters was brought together in one section; the peculiar jurisdictions of Howdenshire and Allertonshire were linked under one heading; and the personal temporal and spiritual jurisdictions of the archbishop were combined in the section called *ballive cum prepositura Beverlaci*. References to dealings with monasteries, for instance, visitation material, were included in the appropriate archdeaconry or jurisdiction division. Provincial matters were gathered together in a suffragans section and the *intrinseca de camera* division contains general memoranda and financial business. An indulgence section also made its appearance but is not found in later registers.

Printed, *The register of John le Romeyn, lord archbishop of York, 1286–1296, part I*, ed. W. Brown (Surtees Society 123, 1913), containing indulgences, officiality, the five archdeaconries and chapters (1286–91) sections; *The registers of John le Romeyn, lord archbishop of York, 1286–1296, part II, and of Henry of Newark, lord archbishop of York, 1296–1299* (Surtees Society 128, 1917), pp. 1–203, containing chapters (1291–6), Allertonshire and Howdenshire, *ballive*, suffragans, *intrinseca de camera* sections, the calendar of precedents and miscellanea. The small section containing the constitutions of Pope Boniface VIII (fos. 153*r*–154*v*) was not printed.

HENRY NEWARK (1298–1299)

BI, Reg. 5. Parchment register; 12″ × 8¼″; fos. 29, foliated 2–55 (including inserts); inner edge of some folios missing, damaged by damp; modern binding (until 1972 this register was bound up with the *sede vacante* register 1299–1555, now Reg. 5A).

The register is incomplete and contains only the following sections: East Riding, Nottingham and Richmond archdeaconries; chapters; suffragans; *ballive*; Howdenshire and Allertonshire. The *intrinseca* section is divided up into three categories, entitled *acta diversa*, *diverse littere* and letters to the papal curia.

Printed, *Romeyn Register part II*, pp. 205–317.

VACANCY 1299–1300

BI, Reg. 5A. Parchment register; 13″ × 8¾″; fos. 8, foliated 56–68 (including inserts); inner edge of some folios missing, damaged by damp; modern limp parchment covers.

The register is divided into five archdeaconry sections.

Printed, *Romeyn Register part II*, pp. 318–32.

THOMAS CORBRIDGE (1300–1304)

BI, Reg. 6. Parchment register; 12″ × 8½″; fos. vii (16th–17th-cent. paper index) + 106 + i (paper), foliated 1–249, 260–325 (including inserts); modern binding, encasing original limp parchment covers.

Corbridge's register omits the *intrinseca* section (or its alternatives), but adds *homagia et fidelitates*, arranged by place.

Printed, *The register of Thomas of Corbridge, lord archbishop of York, 1300–1304, part I*, ed. W. Brown (Surtees Society 138, 1925), containing the officiality and the five archdeaconries; *part II*, ed. W. Brown & A. Hamilton Thompson (Surtees Society 141, 1928), pp. 1–165, containing chapters, *ballive*, homages, Allertonshire and Howdenshire, suffragans and miscellanea.

VACANCY 1304–1306

BI, Reg. 5A. Parchment register; 12½″ × 8¾″; fos. 13, foliated 69–81; modern limp parchment covers.

The register is divided into the following sections: archdeaconries of York, Cleveland, East Riding and Nottingham; chapters; and Howdenshire.

Printed, *Corbridge Register part II*, pp. 165–80.

WILLIAM GREENFIELD (1306–1315)

1. BI, Reg. 7. Parchment register; 12½″ × 9″; fos. x (16th–17th-cent. paper index) + 205, foliated i–x, 1–349 (including inserts); modern binding.

   Part I of the archbishop's register covering the years 1306–1311.

2. BI, Reg. 8. Parchment register; 12½″ × 9″; fos. i + 250, foliated 1–315 (including inserts); modern binding, encasing original limp parchment covers for vicar-general's register.

   Part II of the archbishop's register covering the years 1311–1315. It also includes some registers of vicars-general. It should be noted however that a great deal of business emanating from successive vicars-general is entered in the archbishop's register under the relevant section.

3. BI, Reg. 5A. Parchment bifolium, foliated 83–84 (bound up with the vacancy register 1304–1306).

   Register of the archbishop's vicar-general 1306 (York and East Riding archdeaconry sections only).

4. BI, Reg. 5A. Parchment register; 12½″ × 9½″; fos. 22, foliated 142–174 (including inserts); modern limp parchment covers.

   Register of business emanating from archiepiscopal visitations, dealing mainly with the examination of evidence for the appropriation of parish churches to religious houses 1308–1309 (+ one additional entry 1310).

5. BI, Reg. 8A & B.
   A. parchment roll; 17 mems.; 468″ × 15″.
   B. parchment roll; 18 mems.; 459″ × 12″.

   Archiepiscopal visitation of the city and cathedral of Durham, the deaneries of Alnwick, Bamburgh, Corbridge, Darlington and Newcastle upon Tyne during the vacancy of the see of Durham 1311. The second roll is a copy of the first, but has one additional membrane at the beginning. Both rolls are imperfect at the beginning, the second roll being particularly damaged.

   Items 1–4 are printed, *The register of William Greenfield, lord archbishop of York, 1306–1315, part I*, ed. W. Brown & A. Hamilton Thompson (Surtees Society 145, 1931), containing the register of the vicar-general 1306, chapters, officiality and *ballive* sections; *part II* (Surtees Society 149, 1934), containing the York archdeaconry; *part III* (Surtees Society 151, 1936), containing the Cleveland and East Riding archdeaconries; *part IV* (Surtees Society 152, 1938), containing the Nottingham and Richmond archdeaconries and *intrinseca camere* 1306–11 sections; *part V* (Surtees Society 153, 1940), containing *intrinseca camere* 1311–15, suffragans, Allertonshire and Howdenshire, homages, the registers of the vicars-general, and the register of business arising out of the 1308–09 visitations.

VACANCY 1315–1317

1. BI, Reg. 5A. Parchment register; 12¾″ × 9¼″; fos. 27, foliated 192–220; modern limp parchment covers.

   'Working' register, arranged chronologically, without any subject or geographical divisions. Against each entry is an abbreviated note, indicating into which section the entry should be placed in the 'final' copy. This volume initiates the practice of registering copies of wills *in extenso* in the registers. A separate section of the register devoted to testamentary business survives from the time of Archbishop Zouche (see below).

2. BI, Reg. 5A. Parchment register; 12½″ × 9″; fos. 34, foliated 119–141, 175–186; modern limp parchment covers.

   'Final' copy of the vacancy register, arranged into five archdeaconries; chapters; Allertonshire and Howdenshire; suffragans.

   Printed from 2 in *Greenfield Register part V*, pp. 243–97. A York ordination celebrated at the Minster during the vacancy in September 1317 by Bishop John Sandale of Winchester is recorded in the latter's register: *The registers of John de Sandale and Rigaud de Asserio, bishops of Winchester* (*A.D. 1316–1323*), ed. F. J. Baigent (Hampshire Record Society 8, 1897), pp. 184–6.

WILLIAM MELTON (1317–1340)

1. BI, Reg. 9. Parchment register; 14½″ × 9½″; fos. vii + 596 + ii (original limp parchment covers for suffragans section), foliated 1–416, 416A, 417–739 (including inserts); blank: fos. 151*v*, 399*v*, 477*v*, 621*v*, 700*v*, 736*v*; modern binding (re-bound as two volumes in 1968).

9A	1*r*	Title
	2*r*–6*v*	16th–17th-cent. index
	7*r*–82*v*	*intrinseca camere* Jan. 1318–Apr. 1340
	83*r*–151*r*	chapters Dec. 1317–Dec. 1339
	152*r*–268*v*	archdeaconry of York Dec. 1317–Mar. 1340
	269*r*–320*v*	archdeaconry of Cleveland Jan. 1318–Jan. 1340
	321*r*–399*r*	archdeaconry of the East Riding Dec. 1317–Mar. 1340
9B	400*r*–477*r*	archdeaconry of Nottingham Dec. 1317–Apr. 1340
	478*r*–554*v*	*ballive* Dec. 1317–Dec. 1339
	555*r*–578*v*	archdeaconry of Richmond Feb. 1318–Oct. 1339
	579*r*–607*v*	suffragans Dec. 1317–Jan. 1340
	608*r*–621*r*	Howdenshire and Allertonshire Feb. 1318–May 1337
	622*r*–688*v*	diverse letters Jan. 1318–Mar. 1340
	689*r*–700*r*	officiality Dec. 1317–Jan. 1338
	701*r*–719*v*	register *extra diocesim* June 1325–Feb. 1327
	720*r*–726*r*	register *extra diocesim* Dec. 1330–Apr. 1331
	726*v*	register of vicar-general Feb.–Apr. 1331
	727*r*–*v*	register of vicar-general Dec. 1326–May 1328
	728*r*–729*v*	register of vicar-general Oct. 1325–July 1326
	730*r*–734*v*	miscellaneous entries (earlier draft) Jan. 1321–July 1329
	735*r*–*v*	register of vicar-general Feb.–Mar. 1331 (see 726*v* above)
	736*r*	notes on fees (15th cent.)
	737*r*–739*v*	homages and fealties (arranged by place) Dec. 1317–Jan. 1340

2. BI, Reg. 5A. Parchment register; 12½″ × 9¼″; fos. 4, foliated 187–191; blank: fos. 189*v*–191*v*; modern limp parchment covers.

   187*r*–189*r* register of vicar-general Nov.–Dec. 1317

Fos. 555*r*–621*r* are printed, *The register of William Melton, archbishop of York, 1317–40, volume I*, ed. R. M. T. Hill (Canterbury and York Society 70, 1977); fos. 269*r*–320*v* are printed *ibid., volume II*, ed. D. B. Robinson (Canterbury and York Society 71, 1978). See also W. Brown, 'A list of benefices in the diocese of York vacant between 1316 and 1319' in *Miscellanea* i (Yorkshire Archaeological Society Record Series 61, 1920), pp. 136–48, which calendars fos. 636*r*–638*r* (except for the Nottinghamshire section). Melton is also known to have kept an ordinations register and a register of judicial acts (Smith, 'Lost archiepiscopal registers', 33–4). Bishop John Kirkby of Carlisle held an ordination on behalf of Melton in Feb. 1336 (Cumbria County Record Office, Carlisle, DRC/1/1, fos. 166*v*–168*r*). A record of a similar ordination celebrated by the bishop of Durham on Melton's authority in Dec. 1336 survives in a fragment of Bury's register (*Registrum Palatinum Dunelmense* iii, pp. 172–83). The two registers of the vicar-general in 1331 (fos. 726*v*, 735*r–v*) are virtual copies with the exception of a couple of entries.

VACANCY 1340–1342

BI, Reg. 5A. Parchment register; $12\frac{3}{4}'' \times 8\frac{1}{4}''$; fos. 33, foliated 85–118 (including inserts); blank: fos. 89*v*–90*v*, 98*r*–99*v*, 101*r*–103*v*, 104*v*, 106*v*–108*v*, 115*r–v*, 118*r–v*; modern limp parchment covers.

85*r*–89*r*	archdeaconry of York May 1340–June 1342
91*r*–97*v*	chapters May 1340–Apr. 1342
100*r–v*	archdeaconry of the East Riding May 1340–Aug. 1342
104*r*	[Allertonshire and Howdenshire] June–Dec. 1341
105*r*–106*r*	archdeaconry of Cleveland May 1340–May 1342
109*r*–113*v*	archdeaconry of Nottingham May 1340–July 1342
114*r–v*	archdeaconry of Richmond Feb. 1341–May 1342
116*r–v*	diverse letters Nov. 1340–May 1341
117*r–v*	*ballive* Apr. 1340–Feb. 1341

A composite register in the YM, known as the *Registrum Antiquum de Testamentis* (M2/4f) contains a small section devoted to this vacancy. On fo. 47*r* and again on fo. 48*r* are vacancy register headings. However, upon examination, this register is not a duplicate, and apart from a few exceptions at the beginning, the entries seem to relate to business normally pertaining to the chapter's jurisdiction transacted during the time of the archiepiscopal vacancy.

WILLIAM ZOUCHE (1342–1352)

1. BI, Reg. 10. Parchment register; $14\frac{1}{4}'' \times 10''$; fos. ii + xii (16th–17th-cent. paper index) + iv ($12\frac{1}{2}'' \times 8''$) + 358 + i, foliated i–xvi, 1–291, 291A, 292–296, 296A, 297–356; blank; i*r–v*, ii*r–v*, xii*v*, xv*r–v*, xvi*r–v*, 64*r–v*, 82*v*, 174*r–v*, 241*v*, 243*v*, 252*v*, 254*v*, 266*r–v*, 273*r–v*, 277*v*, 290*v*, 299*r–v*, 356*v*; hide-covered wooden boards.

iii*r*–xii*r*	16th–17th-cent. index
xiii*r*–xiv*v*	register of vicar-general Aug.–Nov. 1342
1*r*–63*v*	archdeaconry of York Nov. 1342–July 1352
65*r*–86*v*	archdeaconry of Richmond Nov. 1342–Feb. 1352
87*r*–153*v*	archdeaconry of Nottingham Nov. 1342–July 1352
154*r*–173*v*	archdeaconry of Cleveland Nov. 1342–July 1352
175*r*–213*v*	archdeaconry of the East Riding Dec. 1342–July 1352
214*r*–241*r*	chapters Nov. 1342–June 1352
242*r*–252*r*	officiality Nov. 1342–Feb. 1352
253*r*–254*r*	synodal statutes of Archbishop Greenfield 1306
255*r*–265*v*	diverse letters Nov. 1342–Apr. 1352
267*r*–272*v*	*intrinseca* Nov. 1342–July 1352
274*r*–277*r*	Allertonshire and Howdenshire Apr. 1345–Apr. 1352
278*r*–280*v*	admission of friars etc. as penitentiaries or to hear confessions Feb. 1348–Mar. 1352
281*r*–290*r*	suffragans Nov. 1342–June 1352
291*r*–298*v*	*ballive* Nov. 1342–July 1352
300*r–v*	homages and fealties June 1343–Nov. 1351
301*r*–346*v*	testamentary business (confused arrangement) May 1345–June 1352
347*r*–356*r*	criminous clerks (*de condempnationibus*) Dec. 1342–July 1352

2. BI, Reg. 10A. Parchment register; $14'' \times 9''$; fos. 57, foliated 1–57; blank: fos. 56*v*–57*v*; modern binding encasing former limp parchment covers.

1*r*–55*v*	ordinations Dec. 1342–June 1352
56*r*	note of issue of letters dimissory (mostly undated)

A few selected letters have been printed by A. Hamilton Thompson, 'Some letters from the register of William Zouche, archbishop of York' in *Historical Essays in honour of James Tait*, ed. J. G. Edwards, V. H. Galbraith & E. F. Jacob (Manchester, 1933), pp. 327–43. They relate to the Richmond archdeaconry and to Zouche in his capacity as protector of the orders of friars.

VACANCY 1352–1353

No record of this vacancy now survives. A register of 14 folios existed until at least the late 17th century when a brief abstract was made by James Torre (d. 1699), now YM, L1/2, section ii, 3–8. A calendar of this 17th-century abstract is printed with an index in 'A reconstruction of the York *sede vacante* register 1352–1353', ed. D. M. Smith, *Borthwick Institute Bulletin*, i no. 2 (1976), 75–90.

JOHN THORESBY (1353–1373)

1. BI, Reg. 11. Parchment register; 14″ × 9″; fos. iii (paper) + 408 + iii (paper), foliated i–iii, 1–172, 172A, 173–285, 285A, 286–294, 294A–B, 295–307, 307A–D, 308–400; blank: fos. 80*v*–81*v*, 172*v*, 172A*r*–*v*, 193*v*, 233*v*, 279*v*, 285*v*, 285A*r*–*v*, 294*v*, 294A*r*–294B*v*, 307*v*, 307A*r*–307D*v*, 314*v*, 328*r*–*v*, 394*v*–395*v*, 397*v*; hide-covered wooden boards.

1*r*–80*r*	chapters and officiality Aug. 1352–July 1373
82*r*–172*r*	archdeaconry of York May 1354–Oct. 1373
173*r*–193*r*	archdeaconry of Cleveland May 1354–Aug. 1373
194*r*–233*r*	archdeaconry of the East Riding [May 1354]–Oct. 1373
234*r*–279*r*	archdeaconry of Nottingham May 1354–Oct. 1373
280*r*–285*r*	Howdenshire and Allertonshire July 1356–Oct. 1373
286*r*–294*r*	archdeaconry of Richmond Jan. 1356–Oct. 1373
295*r*–298*v*	'Lay folks' catechism'
299*r*–307*r*	*ballive* July 1354–Oct. 1373
308*r*–314*r*	diverse letters Apr. 1356–Nov. 1373
315*r*–327*r*	[*intrinseca de camera*] Feb. 1360–Sept. 1373
329*r*–393*r*	ordinations Dec. 1356–Sept. 1373
393*v*–394*r*	election and benediction of John, abbot of Whitby June 1374
396*r*, 397*r*	admission of friars as penitentiaries etc. and homages
396*v*–397*r*	articles for a rural visitation and a visitation of nuns
398*r*–399*v*	suffragans Mar. 1357–Dec. 1359
400*r*	2 licences and an oath 1366–1369

The heading of the first section is usually *Capitula cum capella et officialitate Ebor*' but on fo. 35*r* the heading also refers to the collegiate church of Howden and isolated entries relating to this church are found in this section as well as in the Howdenshire and Allertonshire section. Fos. 295*r*–298*v* have been printed, *The Lay Folks' Catechism*, ed. T. F. Simmons & H. E. Nolloth (Early English Text Society, original series 118, 1901). The Whitby abbey entry (fos. 393*v*–394*r*) is an addition from the time of Archbishop Neville.

2. Register of vicar-general (missing)

This volume, which was in existence in the late 17th century, covered the years 1353–8 and 1361. It was bound up with the 1352–3 vacancy register and extended from fo. 14 to fo. 95 of the composite volume. Even in the 17th century fos. 18–32, 66–68 were missing. An abstract of the remainder was made by James Torre and is now YM, L1/2, section ii, 8–21.

ALEXANDER NEVILLE (1374–1388)

1. BI, Reg. 12. Parchment register; 17½″ × 12½″; fos. i + vi (paper, 12¼″ × 8″) + 142, foliated i–vi, 1–100, 100A, 101–141; blank: fos. iv*v*–vi*v*, 35*v*, 45*v*, 46*v*, 67*v*, 85*v*; modern binding, encasing former limp parchment covers.

i*r*–iv*r*	17th-cent. index
1*r*–12*v*	chapters June 1374–Sept. 1382
13*r*–35*r*	archdeaconry of York June 1374–June 1384
36*r*–45*r*	archdeaconry of Cleveland June 1374–May 1387
46*r*	1 East Riding archdeaconry entry Apr. 1384
47*r*–67*r*	archdeaconry of the East Riding Oct. 1374–May 1384
68*r*–85*r*	archdeaconry of Nottingham July 1374–Mar. 1387
86*r*–89*r*	archdeaconry of Richmond Nov. 1374–Mar. 1383
90*r*–95*r*	Howdenshire, Allertonshire, Hexhamshire and Snaith Mar. 1375–Feb. 1384
95*r*–99*r*	register of vicar-general (confused arrangement) Dec. 1385–July 1387
100*r*–111*r*	diverse letters Oct. 1374–Jan. 1384 [fo. 100A contains acts of vicar-general Mar.–Nov. 1387 and should have followed fo. 99]
111*r*	homages (brief memoranda) Apr. 1375–Feb. 1380
111*v*	Ripon hospital collation 1382
112*r*	[*liberationes*] Sept. 1374–Dec. 1376
112*v*–117*v*	[suffragans] June 1376–Dec. 1382
118*r*–141*v*	ordinations Dec. 1374–Apr. 1384 [There are folios missing between present fos. 132 and 133, and 138 and 139]

2. BI, Reg. 13. This volume is a York formulary of the 14th–15th centuries, and is only included here insofar as it contains a register of acts relating to Archbishop Neville's conflict with the canons of Beverley.

77*r*–92*v*	register of the archbishop's visitation of Beverley Minster and the quarrel with the canons Mar.–May 1381

The Beverley visitation is printed, *The Chapter Act Book of the collegiate church of S. John of Beverley, A.D. 1286–1347*, ed. A. F. Leach (Surtees Society 108, 1903), pp. 202–65. In 1405 the archbishop's register of acts in Durham diocese *sede vacante* and his visitation of the archdeaconries of Durham and Northumberland [1381] still survived (Smith, 'Lost archiepiscopal registers', 34–5).

VACANCY 1388

This vacancy register was still in existence in 1423 but was not included in the 1464 inventory (Smith, 'Lost archiepiscopal registers', 35).

THOMAS ARUNDEL (1388–1396)

BI, Reg. 14. Parchment register; $14\frac{1}{4}'' \times 9\frac{1}{2}''$ (fos. 1–76), $11'' \times 8\frac{3}{4}''$ (fos. 77–81); fos. i+82, foliated i, 1–3, 3A, 4–81; blank: fos. i*r*–*v*, 74*v*–76*v*; modern binding (bound up with Reg. 15), encasing former limp parchment covers.

1*r*–62*v*	register of vicars-general (including ordinations celebrated by their authority) Sept. 1388–Jan. 1397
63*r*–74*r*	ordinations (celebrated by authority of the archbishop) Sept. 1391–Dec. 1396
77*r*–81*v*	record of the administration of the Carlisle diocese *sede vacante* Dec. 1395–Feb. 1396

Arundel's own register, as opposed to the above register of the vicars-general, was in existence until at least 1464 (Smith, 'Lost archiepiscopal registers', 35).

VACANCY 1397

1. BL, Cotton Galba E x, fos. 121*r*–130*v* ($12'' \times 8\frac{3}{4}''$; blank: fos. 121*v*–122*r*).

121*r*–129*v* general acts Jan.–Mar. 1397
130*r*–*v* ordinations Mar. 1397

2. BI, Reg. 5A. Parchment register; 12¾″ × 9″; fos. 10, foliated 211–230; blank: fos. 221*v*, 230*v*; modern limp parchment covers.

221*r*–229*v* general acts Jan.–Mar. 1397
229*v*–230*r* ordinations Mar. 1397

2 appears to be the 'final' copy of the vacancy register. A microfilm of 1, covering the 1397, 1398, 1480 and 1500 vacancies, is available at the BI, MF.43.

ROBERT WALDBY (1397)

BI, Reg. 15. Parchment register; 14¼″ × 10¼″; fos. i+16+i, foliated 1–16; bound up with Reg. 14.

Printed, *A calendar of the register of Robert Waldby, archbishop of York, 1397*, ed. D. M. Smith (Borthwick Texts and Calendars 2, 1974). Reg. 15 is the register of the vicar-general; there are references to Waldby's own register *extra diocesim* in inventories of 1398 and 1405 (Smith, 'Lost archiepiscopal registers', 35) but it is likely that it never came to York after Waldby's death (it was in London *in scribendo et componendo*) and soon disappeared.

VACANCY 1398

1. BL, Cotton Galba E x, fos. 91–120.

The arrangement of this register is purely chronological (Jan.–June 1398) and the ordinations have not been separated from the other acts.

2. BI, Reg. 5A. Parchment register; 13″ × 9¼″; fos. 28, foliated 231–258; modern limp parchment covers.

231*r*–252*v* general acts Jan.–June 1398
253*r*–256*v* ordinations Mar.–June 1398
257*r*–258*v* general acts May–June 1398

RICHARD SCROPE (1398–1405)

BI, Reg. 16. Parchment register; 14¼″ × 10½″; fos. iv+170+i, foliated i–iv, 1–12, 15–68, 71–102, 105–144, 149–180; blank: fos. iii*r*–iv*v*, 12*v*, 102*v*, 105*r*–*v*, 111*r*–113*v*, 144*v*; modern binding, encasing original limp parchment covers.

i*r*–ii*v* 17th-cent. index
1*r*–12*r* chapters July 1398–Mar. 1405
15*r*–46*v* archdeaconry of York July 1398–May 1405
47*r*–52*v* archdeaconry of Cleveland July 1398–Feb. 1405
55*r*–68*v* archdeaconry of the East Riding June 1398–Apr. 1405
71*r*–99*v* archdeaconry of Nottingham July 1398–Apr. 1405
100*r*–102*r* archdeaconry of Richmond Aug. 1398–Jan. 1402
106*r*–110*v* diverse jurisdictions (a combination of *ballive* and Allertonshire and Howdenshire) July 1398–Mar. 1405
114*r*–132*v* diverse letters July 1398–Apr. 1405
133*r*–144*r* testamentary business Sept. 1398–Jan. 1405
149*r*–151*v* suffragans June 1398–Aug. 1400
152*r*–167*v* ordinations Sept. 1398–Apr. 1405
168*r*–180*v* register of vicars-general (including ordinations celebrated by their authority) June 1398–Apr. 1404

* fos. 47, 48 are transposed

The first part of a calendar of this register (covering fos. 1*r*–110*v*) will be published in the Borthwick Texts and Calendars series in 1980–1.

VACANCY 1405–1408

BI, Reg. 5A. Parchment register; 12¾″ × 9″; fos. 78, foliated 259–338; blank: fo. 316*v*; modern binding.

259*r*–316*r*	general acts June 1405–Apr. 1408
317*r*–326*v*	ordinations June 1405–Mar. 1408
327*r*–338*v*	testamentary business Apr. 1406–Jan. 1408

HENRY BOWET (1407–1423)

1. BI, Reg. 17. Parchment register; 13¼″ × 9½″; fos. i + 46, foliated i, 1–46; blank: fo. i*r*–*v*; modern binding (bound up with Reg. 21), encasing original limp parchment covers.

1*r*–46*v*	acts of the archbishop *extra diocesim* Oct. 1407–June 1416

2. BI, Reg. 18. Parchment register; 14¾″ × 10″; fos. iii + 429, foliated i–iii, 1–39, 39A–39I, 40–76, 80–260, 260A, 261–267, 267A, 268–269, 269A, 270–283, 283A, 284–287, 287A, 288–330, 330A, 331–416; blank: fos. i*r*–*v*, iii*v*, 38*v*, 39I*v*, 65*r*, 202*r*–*v*, 269A*r*–269B*v*, 283A*r*–*v*; modern binding.

ii*v*–iii*r*	list of archbishops from the establishment of the see (added to by later scribes to 1606)
1*r*–38*r*	register of vicars-general Apr. 1408–May 1416
39*r*–39I*r*	ordinations celebrated by authority of the vicars-general June 1408–June 1416
40*r*–76*v*	chapters Dec. 1408–Oct. 1423
80*r*–148*v*	archdeaconry of York Dec. 1408–Oct. 1423
149*r*–164*v*	archdeaconry of Cleveland Jan. 1409–Oct. 1423
165*r*–201*v*	archdeaconry of the East Riding Apr. 1409–Oct. 1423
203*r*–264*v*	archdeaconry of Nottingham Dec. 1408–Oct. 1423
265*r*–269*v*	archdeaconry of Richmond July 1410–Nov. 1420
270*r*–283*v*	diverse jurisdictions Dec. 1408–Aug. 1422
284*r*–287*v*	suffragans Dec. 1408–May 1423
288*r*–342*v*	diverse letters Dec. 1408–Sept. 1423
343*r*–385*r*	testamentary business Jan. 1409–Apr. 1423
385*v*–388*r*	17th-cent. index
388*r*–*v*	17th-cent. index of wills
389*r*–416*v*	ordinations Dec. 1408–Sept. 1423 (1 quire containing ordinations between Dec. 1413 and Apr. 1417 lost)

Fos. 43*r*, 55*r*–56*v*, 82*v*–85*r*, 86*r*–*v*, 150*r*–151*r*, 166*r*–168*r*, 204*v*–205*v*, 206*v*, 270*r*–271*r*, 273*r* are printed by A. Hamilton Thompson, 'Documents relating to the visitations of the diocese and province of York, [1407–1452]' in *Miscellanea* ii (Surtees Society 127, 1916), pp. 152–201.

VACANCY 1423–1426

1. BI, Reg. 5A. Parchment register; 13″ × 9″; fos. 108, foliated 341–449; modern binding (bound up with 2 below and 1464–5 vacancy register).

341*r*–449*v*	general acts (including ordinations in the general sequence) Oct. 1423–Apr. 1426

2. BI, Reg. 5A. For description, see above; fos. 4, foliated 450–453.

450*r*–453*r*	general acts Oct. 1423–Mar. 1424 (unfinished; entries differ from above)

JOHN KEMPE (1426–1452)

BI, Reg. 19. Parchment register; 14¾″ × 10¾″ (fos. 1–488, 501–506); 13¼″ × 9¾″ (fos. 489–500); fos. ix + 489 + i, foliated i–viii, 1–18, 20–45, 47–177, 177A, 178–269, 280–289, 289A, 290–293, 293A, 294–361, 361A, 362–366, 366A, 367–371, 371A, 372–451, 459–468, 471, 474–475, 475A, 476–477, 479–481, 483–

506; blank: fos. *ir–iiv*, *viiiv–ixr*, 45*v*, 166*v*, 177A*r–v*, 199*r*, 205*v*, 226*v*, 304*v*, 451*v*, 468*v*, 488*v*, 494*v*, 495*v*–496*r*, 499*r*, 500*v*, 506*v*; hide-covered wooden boards.

This chaotic register, aptly described by Professor Hamilton Thompson as *indigesta moles*, comprises five main, though not always immediately discernible, sections: the register *extra diocesim* of the archbishop; the register of acts of the archbishop while he was in the diocese; the register of the vicars-general; the register of the administration of the vacant see of Durham; and a record of the archbishop's primary visitation.

iii*r*–viii*r* 17th-cent. index
ix*v* title of register
1*r*–177*v* acts of the archbishop *extra diocesim* May 1426–Oct. 1452

This section of the register, which for the most part is a register *extra diocesim*, is in considerable chronological disorder—even the year of the archbishop's translation is given incorrectly—and clearly some sections have been misbound. However, unlike other York *extra diocesim* registers which are purely chronological in arrangement, there appears to have been a half-hearted attempt to separate certain types of business, even if the bound sequence of some of the gatherings was later confused. For instance, collations and institutions are recorded together and form two distinct sections of the register: fos. 1*r*–6*v* (May 1426–June 1438), 47*r*–77*v* (May 1441–Aug. 1452). Similarly, there are sections of diverse letters (licences, letters testimonial, commissions, indulgences, dispensations, etc.) which are equally fragmented in the bound volume: fos. 25*r*–32*r* (June–Dec. 1426), 167*r*–169*v* (Nov. 1433–Dec. 1435), 21*r*–24*v* (June 1441–Mar. 1442), 81*r*–160*v* (Mar. 1442–July 1452), and a section relating to the appointment of temporal officials of the diocese (stewards, wardens, bailiffs, park-keepers, etc.), fos. 169*v*–177*r* (Dec. 1435–Aug. 1452). It is of course possible that all this material was entered up in batches at a later date. To add to the confusion, certain of the aforesaid business performed by the archbishop *infra diocesim* is also entered up with *extra diocesim* material. The register includes ordinations celebrated by the archbishop at London in Feb. 1434 (fo. 167*v*) and May 1434 (fo. 168*r*).

178*r*–226*r* acts of the archbishop while he was in the diocese
- 178*r*–193*v* archdeaconry of York Aug. 1430–Dec. 1449
- 194*r*–198*v* archdeaconry of the East Riding Aug. 1427–Mar. 1447
- 199*v*–205*r* archdeaconry of Cleveland May 1438–Apr. 1447
- 206*r*–209*v* archdeaconry of Nottingham Aug. 1434–Apr. 1447
- 210*r*–214*v* archdeaconry of Richmond June 1428–Sept. 1446
- 215*r*–226*r* ordinations celebrated by authority of the archbishop Sept. 1426–Apr. 1447

227*r*–304*r* ordinations celebrated by authority of the vicars-general May 1426–Sept. 1452
305*r*–468*r* register of vicars-general Apr. 1426–Sept. 1452
471*r*–488*r* visitation records July 1439–Oct. 1442
489*r*–503*v* record of the administration of the Durham diocese *sede vacante* Nov. 1437–Apr. 1438
504*r*–506*r* copy of the confirmation by the papal commissary of the composition between Archbishop Melton and the dean and chapter of York concerning the manner and form of visitation June–July 1328

Fos. 210*r*–213*r*, 474*r*–488*r*, 491*r*–495*r*, 504*r*–506*r* are printed, *Miscellanea* ii (Surtees Society 127, 1916), pp. 201–90.

WILLIAM BOOTH (1452–1464)

BI, Reg. 20. Parchment register; $15\frac{1}{4}'' \times 11\frac{1}{4}''$; fos. vi+461+ii, foliated 1–60, 62–69, 65A–69A, 70–74, 76–88, 88A, 89–222, 224–256, 258–298, 300–342, 342A, 343–349, 351–365, 367–371, 373–404, 404A, 404B, 405–460; blank: fos. vi*v*, 27*v*, 60*r–v*, 74*v*, 105*v*, 288*v*–289*v*, 326*v*–327*v*, 349*v*, 371*v*, 411*v*, 460*v*; hide-covered wooden boards.

iii*r*–vi*r* 17th-cent. index
1*r*–27*r* archdeaconry of York Sept. 1452–Aug. 1464
28*r*–59*v* chapters Nov. 1452–Aug. 1464
62*r*–74*r* archdeaconry of Cleveland Aug. 1454–Aug. 1464
76*r*–105*r* archdeaconry of Nottingham Oct. 1452–Sept. 1464
106*r*–122*v* archdeaconry of the East Riding Oct. 1452–Aug. 1464
123*r*–146*v* diverse jurisdictions (on this occasion the Richmond archdeaconry is included in this section) Oct. 1452–Aug. 1464
147*r*–222*v* diverse letters Sept. 1452–Sept. 1464
224*r*–256*v* appropriations of churches and endowments of vicarages (and occasionally chantries) Oct. 1453–Aug. 1461
258*r*–288*r* testamentary business Mar. 1453–Aug. 1464
290*r*–326*r* criminous clerks (commissions to deliver, certificates of purgation) Aug. 1453–Feb. 1464
328*r*–349*r* tenths and subsidies (Convocation material, appointments of collectors, some visitatorial material) Oct. 1453–Aug. 1464
351*r*–360*v* registers *sede vacante* for Durham diocese July 1457–Feb. 1459, and for Carlisle diocese Apr. 1462–Dec. 1463
361*r*–366*v* delegated case: St Mary's abbey, York v. vicar of St Lawrence, York 1456–58
367*r*–371*r* suffragans Oct. 1452–Jan. 1464
373*r*–411*r* register of vicars-general Sept. 1452–June 1463
412*r*–460*r* ordinations Dec. 1452–May 1464

VACANCY 1464–1465

1. BI, Reg. 5A. For description see 1423–1426 vacancy register; fos. 26, foliated 453*v*–478*v*.

453*v*–478*v* general acts (including ordinations in the general sequence) Sept. 1464–May 1465

2. BI, Reg. 5A. As above; fos. 30, foliated 479–508; blank: fo. 508*v*.

479*r*–508*r* general acts (including ordinations in the general sequence) Sept. 1464–June 1465

GEORGE NEVILLE (1465–1476)
LAURENCE BOOTH (1476–1480)

1. BI, Reg. 21. Parchment register; 12½″ × 10″; fos. 30, foliated 1–7, 7A, 8–29; blank: fos. 6*r*, 29*v*; modern binding (bound up with Reg. 17), encasing former limp parchment covers.

1*r*–29*r* acts of the archbishop *extra diocesim* Dec. 1474–June 1476

2. BI, Reg. 22. Parchment register; 15″ × 11½″; fos. i+374+i, foliated i–iv, 1–6, 11–16, 18–20, 27–38, 40–70, 75–85, 85A, 86–173, 173A, 174–210, 210A, 211–385; blank: fos. ii*v*, iv*r*–*v*, 18*r*–*v*, 20*v*, 32*v*, 38*v*, 65*v*, 68*v*, 70*r*–*v*, 75*r*–*v*, 173A*r*–*v*, 194*r*–*v*, 240*v*, 248*v*, 250*v*, 253*v*, 261*v*, 267*v*, 275*v*, 361*v*, 385*r*–*v*; modern binding, encasing fragments of former limp parchment covers.

Register of Archbishop George Neville

ii*r*–iii*v* documents concerning Neville's provision Apr.–Sept. 1465
1*r*–6*v* collations July 1465–May 1468
11*r*–16*v* archdeaconry of York Sept. 1465–Apr. 1468
19*r*–20*r* archdeaconry of Cleveland Oct. 1465–Dec. 1469
27*r*–28*v* archdeaconry of the East Riding July 1465–Mar. 1468
29*r*–32*r* 17th-cent. index
33*r*–38*r* archdeaconry of Nottingham Sept. 1465–Sept. 1469

40*r*–47*v*	diverse jurisdictions (including Richmond archdeaconry) July 1465–Mar. 1468
48*r*–65*r*	diverse letters June 1465–Sept. 1469
66*r*–68*r*	testamentary business Jan. 1466–Apr. 1468
69*r*–*v*	proceedings against a crystal-gazer of Wombwell Aug. 1467 (printed, *Archaeological Journal*, 13 (1856), 372–4)
76*r*–178*v*	register of vicars-general June 1465–May 1476
179*r*–240*r*	ordinations Sept. 1465–June 1476

Register of Archbishop Laurence Booth

241*r*–248*r*	chapter of York (and St Mary & Holy Angels) Oct. 1476–Mar. 1480
249*r*–250*r*	chapter of Southwell Nov. 1476–Nov. 1479
251*r*–252*v*	chapter of Beverley Oct. 1476–Mar. 1479
253*r*	chapter of Ripon Apr. 1477–Oct. 1479
254*r*–261*r*	archdeaconry of York Dec. 1476–May 1480
262*r*–263*v*	archdeaconry of Cleveland Oct. 1476–May 1479
264*r*–267*r*	archdeaconry of the East Riding Nov. 1476–Apr. 1480
268*r*–275*r*	archdeaconry of Nottingham Oct. 1476–May 1480
276*r*–277*v*	archdeaconry of Richmond Nov. 1476–Aug. 1477
278*r*–280*v*	diverse jurisdictions Nov. 1476–Apr. 1480
281*r*–361*r*	diverse letters Nov. 1476–May 1480
362*r*–384*v*	ordinations Sept. 1476–Apr. 1480

The heading of the diverse letters section of this register is extremely full and gives a good idea of the contents of this section in York registers: *De diversis litteris, videlicet, dimissoriis, indulgentiis, concessionibus officiorum et eorum custodiis, inquisitionibus de iure patronatus ecclesiarum et earum certificatoriis, procuratoriis sub instrumento publico et aliis, necnon diversis commissionibus, oratoriis, inhibitionibus, sequestrationibus, unacum assignationibus pensionum, ecclesiarum resignationibus et multis aliis litteris.* Booth's register originally had a separate foliation, 1–139.

VACANCY 1476

BI, Reg. 5A. Parchment register; 13″ × 8½″; fos. 6, foliated 509–514; blank: fos. 510*r*–*v*, 514*v*; modern limp parchment covers.

509*r*–514*v*	general acts June–Aug. 1476

Typescript calendar and index at BI, Add. MS. 160.

VACANCY 1480

1. BI, Reg. 5A. Parchment register; 12½″ × 8¾″; fos. 6, foliated 515–520; modern binding (bound up with 1500–1 and 1507–8 vacancy registers).

515*r*–516*r*	ordinations May 1480
516*r*–520*v*	general acts May–July 1480

2. BL, Cotton Galba E x, fos. 133*r*–137*v*.

133*r*–134*r*	ordinations May 1480
134*r*–137*v*	general acts May–July 1480

This copy of the register has a note *pro cancellario* on fo. 133*r*.

THOMAS ROTHERHAM (1480–1500)

1. BI, Reg. 23. Parchment register; 15¼″ × 11¾″; fos. x + 464 + i, foliated i–viii, 1–95, 95A, 96–104, 104A, 105–197, 199–311, 313–317, 322–468, blank: fos. iv, 95A*r*–*v*, 112*v*, 140*v*, 166*v*, 185*v*, 191*v*, 193*v*, 197*v*, 275*v*, 283*v*, 284*r*, 371*v*, 379*v*; modern binding.

ir	title of register
i*ir*–viii*v*	17th-cent. index
1*r*–95*v*	register of vicars-general Sept. 1480–Mar. 1497
96*r*–111*v*	collations Sept. 1481–Feb. 1500
113*r*–140*r*	archdeaconry of York July 1481–Apr. 1500
141*r*–157*v*	archdeaconry of the East Riding July 1481–May 1500
158*r*–166*r*	archdeaconry of Cleveland July 1481–May 1500
167*r*–185*r*	archdeaconry of Nottingham Aug. 1481–May 1500
186*r*–191*r*	diverse jurisdictions July 1482–May 1500
192*r*–197*r*	suffragans Apr. 1484–Apr. 1493
199*r*–268*v*	diverse letters Sept. 1480–May 1500
269*r*–289*v*	appropriations of churches and endowments of vicarages Feb. 1483–Aug. 1499
290*r*–311*v*	tenths and subsidies (Convocation material, appointments of collectors, etc.) Oct. 1481–July 1497
313*r*–317*v*	criminous clerks (commissions to deliver, certificates of purgation) Sept. 1488–Dec. 1499
322*r*–371*r*	testamentary business Oct. 1484–Dec. 1499
372*r*–468*v*	ordinations Sept. 1480–Apr. 1500

2. BI, Reg. 24. Parchment register; 15¾″ × 11″; fos. 87, foliated 1–87; blank: fos. 17*v*, 30*v*, 47*r*, 78*v*, 86*v*–87*v*; modern binding.

This small register, which in all essentials is a duplicate to 1487 of some parts of Reg. 23, was perhaps a registry 'working copy' or at least an earlier version of the archbishop's acts. The collations and archdeaconry sections are identical with the entries in Reg. 23 as far as they go, apart from very occasional rearrangement. The diverse letters section, however, is much fuller than in the later register and contains testamentary material, tenths and subsidies business and entries relating to the appropriation of churches which each have separate sections in Reg. 23. The annotations against these entries in Reg. 24 indicates the earlier compilation of this volume, before further subdivision of the sections was undertaken. Part of the East Riding archdeaconry section was misbound and one bifolium (18–19) should have been folded the opposite way—the correct sequence of folios should be 1–7, 10–17, 19, 8, 9, 18, 20–87.

1*r*–6*v*	collations Sept. 1481–Apr. 1487
7*r*, 10*r*–17*r*	archdeaconry of York July 1481–Aug. 1487
8*r*–9*v*, 18*r*–19*v*	archdeaconry of the East Riding Mar. 1483–Oct. 1487
20*r*–22*v*	archdeaconry of Cleveland July 1481–Aug. 1487
23*r*–28*v*	archdeaconry of Nottingham Aug. 1481–Oct. 1487
29*r*–30*r*	diverse jurisdictions July 1482–Oct. 1487
31*r*–78*r*	diverse letters Sept. 1480–Oct. 1487
79*r*–86*r*	tenths and subsidies Oct. 1481–Oct. 1487

Fos. 1*r*–289*v* of Reg. 23 are printed, *The register of Thomas Rotherham, archbishop of York, 1480–1500, vol. I*, ed. E. E. Barker (Canterbury and York Society 69, 1976).

VACANCY 1500–1501

1. BI, Reg. 5A. For description see 1480 vacancy register; fos. 13, foliated 521–533*r*; blank: fos. 522*v*, 527*r*.

521*r*–526*v*	general acts June 1500–Mar. 1501
527*r*–533*r*	ordinations June 1500–Apr. 1501

2. BL, Cotton Galba E x, fos. 131–132, 138–147 (incomplete); blank: fos. 141*v*, 147*v*.

131*r*–132*v*, 138*r*–141*r*	general acts June 1500–Mar. 1501
142*r*–147*r*	ordinations June 1500–Apr. 1501

From a check made against entries in the first vacancy register, it is evident that the second register lacks a folio between the present fos. 138 and 139.

THOMAS SAVAGE (1501–1507)

BI, Reg. 25. Parchment register; $15\frac{3}{4}'' \times 11\frac{3}{4}''$; fos. ii+173, foliated i–ii, 1–108, 108A–B, 109–171; blank: fos. 19*v*, 50*v*, 70*v*, 108A*v*, 160*v*, 169*r*, 170*r*–171*v*; modern binding, encasing former limp parchment covers.

1*r*–19*r*	register of vicars-general Apr. 1501–Jan. 1504
20*r*–31*v*	collations May 1501–Sept. 1507
32*r*–50*r*	archdeaconry of York Apr. 1502–Aug. 1507
51*r*–61*v*	archdeaconry of the East Riding Oct. 1502–June 1507
62*r*–70*r*	archdeaconry of Cleveland Aug. 1502–June 1507
71*r*–85*v*	archdeaconry of Nottingham Jan. 1503–July 1507
86*r*–87*v*	diverse jurisdictions Oct. 1503–July 1507
88*r*–107*v*	diverse letters Aug. 1502–Aug. 1507
108*r*–108A*r*	17th-cent. index
108B*r*–141*v*	ordinations June 1501–May 1507
142*r*–160*r*	suffragans (Durham vacancy) Oct. 1501–Oct. 1502
161*r*–168*v*	testamentary business Mar. 1505–May 1507
169*v*	copy of undated grant of next presentation and note of its exhibition Mar. 1514

Fos. 142*r*–160*r* are printed, *The injunctions and other ecclesiastical proceedings of Richard Barnes, bishop of Durham, from 1575 to 1587*, ed. J. Raine (Surtees Society 22, 1850), appendix I, pp. i–xl.

VACANCY 1507–1508

1. BI, Reg. 5A. For description see 1480 vacancy register; fos. 79, foliated 533*v*–611; blank: fo. 577*v*.

533*v*–573*v*	general acts Sept. 1507–Nov. 1508
574*r*–577*r*	acts relating to the vacant see of Durham Oct.–Nov. 1507
578*r*–605*v*	ordinations Sept. 1507–Sept. 1508
606*r*–608*v*	acts relating to the vacant see of Carlisle Sept. 1507–Nov. 1508
[609*r*–611*v*	16th-cent. index to composite vacancy register]

2. YM, H3/2. Parchment register; $16'' \times 11\frac{1}{2}''$; fos. 39, foliated 1, 1A, 2–31, 31A, 32–37; blank: fos. 1*r*, 24*v*–25*v*; modern binding (detached limp parchment covers kept with volume).

1*v*–22*r*	general acts Sept. 1507–Nov. 1508
22*v*–24*r*	acts relating to the Durham vacancy Oct.–Nov. 1507
26*r*–36*r*	ordinations Sept. 1507–Sept. 1508
36*v*–37*v*	acts relating to the Carlisle vacancy Sept. 1507–Aug. 1508 (incomplete; lacks one folio)

A ms. calendar and index of 2 is in YM, H3/2a.

CHRISTOPHER BAINBRIDGE (1508–1514)

BI, Reg. 26. Parchment register; $16\frac{1}{4}'' \times 12''$; fos. 134, foliated 1–88, 91–93, 97, 99–115, 118–126, 135–141, 143–151; blank: fos. 50*v*, 151*r*–*v*; modern binding incorporating former parchment covers.

1*r*–50*r*	register of vicars-general Dec. 1508–July 1514
51*r*–62*v*	collations Mar. 1509–Apr. 1514
63*r*–88*v*	diverse letters Dec. 1508–May 1514
91*r*–93*r*	suffragans Dec. 1508–June 1509
93*r*–*v*,	17th-cent. index
97*r*–*v*	
99*r*–126*v*	ordinations Dec. 1508–Dec. 1513

135*r*–141*v*	testamentary business Mar. 1509–Jan. 1514
143*r*–150*v*	vacancy register Aug.–Oct. 1514 (see below)

The ordination list for 14 June 1511 (fos. 113*v*–114*v*) is printed, *Liber pontificalis Chr. Bainbridge archiepiscopi Eboracensis*, ed. W. G. Henderson (Surtees Society 61, 1875), pp. 361–7.

VACANCY 1514

1. BI, Reg. 5A. Parchment register; $13\frac{1}{4}'' \times 9\frac{1}{2}''$; fos. 12, foliated 612–623; modern binding (bound up with 1530–1 and 1544–5 vacancy registers).

612*r*–620*r*	general acts Aug.-Oct. 1514
620*v*–623*v*	ordinations Sept. 1514

2. BI, Reg. 26. For description, see above.

143*r*–148*r*	general acts Aug.–Oct. 1514
148*v*–150*v*	ordinations Sept. 1514

THOMAS WOLSEY (1514–1530)

BI, Reg. 27. Parchment register; $15\frac{1}{4}'' \times 12''$; fos. ii+218+i, foliated i–ii, 1–138, 138A–138C, 139–216; blank: fos. 138C*v*, 216*r*–*v*; modern binding.

1*r*–100*v*	register of vicar-general Nov. 1514–Aug. 1529
101*r*–109*v*	collations May 1515–Oct. 1523
110*r*–133*v*	diverse letters Nov. 1514–Nov. 1528
134*r*–138*v*	[suffragans] June 1521–Apr. 1523
138*v*–138C*r*	17th-cent. index
139*r*–165*r*	testamentary business Dec. 1514–July 1529
165*r*–*v*	17th-cent. index of wills
166*r*–215*v*	ordinations Dec. 1514–Apr. 1528

An edition of the register to be undertaken by Professor Hamilton Thompson and Miss M. P. Howden was mooted in 1935 (BI, DR.C & P. 1935). A calendar of fos. 1*r*–100*v* in Professor Hamilton Thompson's handwriting is now BI, Add. MSS. 115, 116, the latter volume including selected full transcripts. Further transcripts to fo. 98*v* are in the Yorkshire Archaeological Society, Leeds, MS. 1002. A 20th-cent. transcript of the early ordination lists (fos. 166*r*–172*r*) is BI, Add. MS. 165.

VACANCY 1530–1531

BI, Reg. 5A. For description see 1514 vacancy register; fos. 48, foliated 623A–657, 659–671; blank: fos. 626*r*, 656*r*–657*v*, 668*r*–*v*.

623A*r*–667*v*	general acts Dec. 1530–Mar. 1531
669*r*–671*v*	ordinations Mar.–Apr. 1531

EDWARD LEE (1531–1544)

BI, Reg. 28. Parchment register; $15\frac{1}{2}'' \times 12\frac{1}{4}''$; fos. iii+206+v, foliated i–iii, 1A–1C, 2–141, 141A, 142–207; blank: fos. 1A*v*, 1B*r*–*v*, 202*r*, 203*r*–207*v*; modern binding.

i*r*–iii*v*	17th-cent. index
1*r*–1A*r*	papal bulls concerning Lee's appointment and patents for vicar-general and official Sept.–Dec. 1531
1C*r*	benefices in the archbishop's patronage by reason of the exchange with the King.
1C*v*	benefices in the archbishop's collation
2*r*–21*v*	archdeaconry of York Jan. 1532–June 1544

22*r*–37*v*	archdeaconry of the East Riding Jan. 1532–Sept. 1543
38*r*–45*v*	archdeaconry of Cleveland Apr. 1532–Sept. 1543
46*r*–63*v*	archdeaconry of Nottingham Mar. 1532–Jan. 1544
64*r*–77*r*	collations Apr. 1534–June 1544 (confused arrangement)
78*r*–79*v*	Howdenshire and Allertonshire Mar. 1534–Oct. 1543
80*r*–157*v*	miscellaneous section, containing commissions, licences, institutions, injunctions, abjurations, ordination of vicarage, confirmations, appropriation of church, etc., and national affairs such as the divorce of Anne of Cleves (the arrangement is very confused) [ ] 1532–Aug. 1544
158*r*–183*v*	testamentary business Mar. 1532–Aug. 1540
184*r*–201*v*	ordinations Mar. 1531 (*recte* 1532)–Apr. 1541
202*v*	17th-cent. index of wills

For a more detailed study of this register and that of Lee's successor, see J. S. Purvis, 'The registers of Archbishops Lee and Holgate', *Journal of Ecclesiastical History*, 13 (1962), 186–94. Injunctions and other visitation material to be found between fos. 91*v*–99*v* are printed, 'Visitations in the diocese of York, holden by Archbishop Edward Lee (A.D. 1534–5)', *Yorkshire Archaeological Journal*, 16 (1902), 424–58.

VACANCY 1544–1545

BI, Reg. 5A. For description see 1514 vacancy register; fos. 11, foliated 672–682; blank: fo. 682*v*.

672*r*–681*v*	general acts Sept. 1544–Jan. 1545
682*r*	note of 2 caveats 1534, 1543

ROBERT HOLGATE (1545–1554)
NICHOLAS HEATH (1555–1559)

BI, Reg. 29. Parchment register; 15″ × 11¼″; fos. ii (+iv paper, 12″ × 8″, inserted) + 151 + ii, foliated i–vi, 12–14, 16–54, 56–60, 63–74, 74A, 75–87, 89–104, 104A, 105–132, 132A, 133–151, 154–169; blank: fos. i*v*, ii*r*–*v*, v*r*–vi*v*, 16*r*–*v*, 51*v*–52*v*, 60*v*, 63*r*–*v*, 67*v*–68*v*, 71*v*–72*v*, 74A*r*–*v*, 110*r*–*v*, 124*v*, 136*v*–137*v*, 143*v*–144*v*, 151*v*, 162*v*–163*v*, 169*v*; modern binding.

iii*r*–iv*v*	16th–17th-cent. index

Robert Holgate

12*r*–14*v*	Convocation business (incomplete) Sept. 1547–Jan. 1548
17*r*–67*r*	general acts (institutions, collations, commissions, inquisitions, visitation), all archdeaconries Oct. 1545–Oct. 1553
69*r*–71*r*	Convocation business (incomplete) Sept.–Oct. 1553
73*r*–74*v*	testamentary business (incomplete) Sept. 1540–Jan. 1541 [It is possible that these folios should follow fo. 183 of Reg. 28]
75*r*–109*v*	testamentary business Oct. 1545–Oct. 1553 (see also below)

Nicholas Heath

111*r*–114*r*	papal bulls concerning Heath's appointment and patents for diocesan officials June 1555–Jan. 1556
114*r*–122*v*	institutions, all archdeaconries (no collations of prebends and dignities) Oct. 1555–July 1558
123*r*–136*r*	[diverse letters] July 1555–Oct. 1557 (mostly dispensations and material relating to advowsons, including copies of earlier documents)

Holgate/Heath

138*r*–167*v*	testamentary business (This section is in considerable confusion, the probate dates ranging from Mar. 1547 to Mar. 1559, the bulk

	of the material (fos. 145–167) dating from Holgate's pontificate. Some wills have no probate date).
168*r*–169*r*	17th-cent. index of wills

For a description of this register, see the Purvis article (cited above). Holgate's injunctions for York Minster in 1552 (fos. 57*r*–60*r*) are printed, *The Statutes etc., of the Cathedral Church of York* (2nd edn., Leeds, 1900), pp. 67–78. For institutions performed during the Royal Visitation of 1559 see *The Royal Visitation of 1559: act book for the Northern Province*, ed. C. J. Kitching (Surtees Society 187, 1975), pp. 57–61.

VACANCY 1554–1555

BI, Reg. 5A. Parchment register; 12¼″ × 9¾″; fos. 16, foliated 683–698; modern limp parchment cover (part of former parchment cover retained).

683*r*–698*v*	general acts (beginning with royal injunctions) Mar. 1554–May 1555

A calendar of entries on fos. 687*v*–698*v* (old foliation 655*v*–666*v* given) printed, A. G. Dickens, *The Marian Reaction in the diocese of York: part I, The Clergy* (St Anthony's Hall publication 11, York, 1957), appendix B, pp. 32–9.

THOMAS YOUNG (1561–1568)
VACANCY 1568–1570
EDMUND GRINDAL (1570–1576)

BI, Reg. 30. Parchment register; 15″ × 11½″; fos. 163, foliated 1–163; blank: fos. 3*v*, 6*r*–*v*, 9*v*, 12*v*, 13*v*, 19*v*, 34*v*, 38*v*–40*v*, 55*v*, 68*v*, 74*v*, 77*v*, 81*v*, 122*v*; modern binding, encasing former limp parchment covers; inserted inside front cover, fos. iv (paper, 12″ × 8″, 16th–17th-cent. index).

Thomas Young

1*r*–3*r*	archdeaconry of York Mar. 1565–Jan. 1567
4*r*–5*v*	archdeaconry of the East Riding June 1565–Jan. 1568
7*r*–9*r*	archdeaconry of Nottingham Apr. 1565–Mar. 1568
10*r*–*v*	archdeaconry of Cleveland Apr. 1565–Jan. 1568
11*r*–12*r*	collations June 1565–Oct. 1567
13*r*	Allertonshire and Howdenshire Sept. 1565–Jan. 1566
14*r*–19*r*	general business (composition, consecration of suffragan bishop, visitation) June 1564–May 1567
20*r*–34*r*	testamentary business Oct. 1563–May 1568
35*r*–38*r*	ordinations July 1561–Apr. 1568

Vacancy 1568–70

41*r*–61*v*	general acts June 1568–June 1570 (some attempt at division made; fos. 41*r*–50*v* mostly institutions; 51*r*–55*r* commissions and other administrative business; 56*r*–61*v* testamentary business)

Edmund Grindal

62*r*–68*r*	archdeaconry of York July 1570–Jan. 1576
69*r*–74*r*	archdeaconry of the East Riding Aug. 1570–Jan. 1576
75*r*–77*r*	archdeaconry of Cleveland Apr. 1571–Feb. 1576
78*r*–81*r*	archdeaconry of Nottingham July 1570–Dec. 1575
82*r*–84*v*	collations June 1570–Dec. 1575
85*r*–134*v*	general business (commissions, visitation articles and injunctions, wills proved *ratione visitationis*, etc.) June 1570–June 1575
135*r*–157*v*	testamentary business July 1570–Jan. 1576
158*r*–162*r*	ordinations May 1570–Nov. 1575
162*r*–163*r*	17th-cent. index of wills

The injunctions to the archdeacons 1571 (fo. 96*r*) and the injunctions for York Minster 1572 (fos. 123*r*–125*v*) are printed, W. H. Frere and W. M. Kennedy, *Visitation Articles and Injunctions of the period of the Reformation* (Alcuin Club collections 14–16, 1910) iii, appendix lvii, pp. 294–5 and appendix lxvii, pp. 345–54 respectively. The latter is also printed, *Statutes of the Cathedral Church of York*, pp. 79–89. The published version of the injunctions for the province 1571 (fos. 126*r*–131*r*) is printed, Frere and Kennedy, *op. cit.*, appendix lvi, pp. 274–93. In Young's register, the headings note that the entries were made *post introitum et deputacionem magistri Richardi Frankland in artibus magistri notariique publici in registratorem.*

VACANCY 1576–1577
EDWIN SANDYS (1577–1588)
VACANCY 1588–1589
JOHN PIERS (1589–1594)
MATTHEW HUTTON (1595–1606)
TOBIAS MATTHEW (1606–1628)

BI, Reg. 31. Parchment register; 15″ × 12″; fos. iii + 283, foliated i–iii, 1–283; blank: fos. i*r*–iii*v*, 7*r*–*v*, 11*v*, 38*v*–40*v*, 71*v*–73*v*, 151*v*, 156*r*–*v*, 283*v*; modern binding; inserted inside front cover, fos. iv (17th-cent. index).

1*r*–11*r*	vacancy register Feb. 1576–Feb. 1577
12*r*–282*v*	register of Archbishop Sandys (fos. 12*r*–61*v*, 74*r*–106*r*), the vacancy register of 1588–9 (fos. 106*r*–110*v*) and the registers of Archbishops Piers, Hutton and Matthew (62*r*–71*v*, 111*r*–282*v*) June 1589–Feb. 1628
282*v*–283*r*	one entry relating to Archbishop Harsnett Mar. 1630

The arrangement of the register is roughly chronological (some sections are more confused than others), except for one misbound gathering relating to Archbishop Piers (fos. 62–73) which comes between entries of the time of Sandys. The vacancy registers each have headings but otherwise the entries are continuous and no distinction is made between one archbishop's pontificate and the next. From the time of Sandys, no institutions to benefices or collations are recorded in the registers except where the archbishop is performing such activities in another diocese of the province *ratione visitationis*. The bulk of the register contains copies of wills proved in the archbishop's Chancery court and the administrative business is normally restricted to visitation material (including articles and injuctions) and the confirmation of bishops, with occasional commissions and patents. There does not appear to have been any vacancy business entered in the register after the 1588–9 vacancy.

Sandys' articles for York Minster 1578 (fos. 46*v*–47*r*) and the injunctions after the same visitation (fos. 48*r*–50*r*) are printed, W. P. M. Kennedy, *Elizabethan Episcopal Administration: an essay in sociology and politics* (Alcuin Club collections 25–7, 1924) ii, appendices xvi-xvii, pp. 82–9.

SAMUEL HARSNETT (1629–1631)
RICHARD NEILE (1632–1640)
JOHN WILLIAMS (1641–1650)

BI, Reg. 32. Parchment register; 15¼″ × 12″; fos. xi (paper, 12″ × 7½″) + 120, foliated i–xi, 1–120; blank: fos. i*r*–*v*, 10*r*–12*v*, 13*v*, 22*v*, 23*v*–24*v*, 120*r*–*v*; modern binding.

ii*r*–vi*v*	indexes (i–iv probably of the time of Archbishop Richard Sterne (1664–83); v–vi wills (unidentified))
vii*r*–xii*v*	index of wills
1*r*–119*v*	This volume consists primarily of probate material (Chancery court) with some formal business such as visitations (including articles and injunctions) and the confirmation of bishops. The arrangement of the register is confused, the first entries being of the 1639–41 period

and the title page of Neile's register occurring on fo. 13*r*. The earliest entries, from the time of Harsnett, begin on fo. 49*r*. The dates of the material in the volume extend from Apr. 1629 to June 1650.

The articles of enquiry for Neile's visitation of York Minster in 1632 (fos. 18*r*–19*v*) are printed, *The Statutes of the Cathedral Church of York*, pp. 90–4.

INSTITUTION ACT BOOKS

BI, Inst. AB.1. Paper register; 11″ × 8¼″; fos. 218, foliated 1–4, 6, 7, 9–132, 132A, 133–219; blank: fos. 1*v*–4*r*, 6*v*–7*v*, 11*v*, 19*r*–*v*, 21*v*, 28*v*, 34*v*, 56*r*–*v*, 99*v*, 100*r*, 112*v*, 114*v*, 127*v*–128*v*, 131*v*, 132*v*, 147*v*, 180*r*, 210*r*, 211*r*, 216*r*–217*v*; modern binding, encasing limp parchment covers (1582 cause paper sewn inside front cover).

1*r*–211*v* acts and memoranda (including some probate acts, material relating to disputed presentations, and a section on purgations and delivery from the archbishop's prisons) Dec. 1545–Jan. 1554, Oct. 1558–Dec. 1568
212*r*–215*v* 16th–17th-cent. index
218*r*–219*r* warrants for taking bucks from the archbishop's parks June–Sept. 1544

There are occasional entries 1554–8 which seem to have been added later. The missing period is covered by Inst. AB.2, part i (see below), although there does not appear to be any evidence that the latter volume ever formed part of Inst. AB.1. For institutions performed during the royal visitation of 1559, see *The Royal Visitation of 1559: act book of the northern province*, ed. C. J. Kitching (Surtees Society 187, 1975), pp. 57–61.

BI, Inst. AB.2. Paper register in three parts, encased in modern binding.

part i
11¾″ × 8″; fos. i+43+i, foliated 1–43; blank: fos. 41*v*–43*v*; limp parchment covers.

1*r*–40*r* general acts during the vacancy 1554–5 and of the vicars-general *sede plena* Mar. 1554–Sept. 1558
40*r*–41*r* 16th–17th-cent. index

part ii
12¼″ × 8½″; fos. i+70+i, foliated 1–70; blank: fos. 3*r*, 25*r*–*v*, 54*v*; limp parchment covers.

This volume begins primarily as a subscription book, and after the record of a majority of institutions and ordinations, the incumbent's or ordinand's signature is found. In addition, there are notes of sequestrations, resignations, monitions, licences to preach and for readers and occasional marriage licences, and papers relating to the raising and collection of a subsidy.

3*v*–68*r* general acts May 1561–May 1567
68*v*–70*v* 16th-17th-cent. index

A new institution book was begun in Jan. 1567 and continued until Jan. 1568. It was then abandoned and later became a High Commission court book (for institutions, see HC. AB.8, fos. 177*r*–215*v* in reverse).

part iii
11½″ × 8″; fos. 178, foliated 1–179 (insert foliated); blank: fos. 137*r*–*v*, 143*v*, 149*v*, 150*r*; limp parchment covers.

1*r*–179*v* general acts July 1568–Mar. 1572

A typescript index is available at the BI.

BI, Inst. AB.3. Paper register; 12″ × 7½″; fos. ii+479+iv, foliated 1–456, 481–507 (no sections are missing; an error in numbering was made at fo. 56, which was corrected as far as fo. 456); blank: 27*v*, 28*r*, 105*v*, 111*r*, 186*r*, 189*r*–*v*, 211*v*, 212*r*, 504*r*–507*v*; modern binding.

1*r*–503*v* general acts Mar. 1572–Apr. 1619

There is a separate 17th-cent. index.

BI, Inst. AB.4. Paper register; 7¾″ × 6″; fos. i + 422 + i—chaotic arrangement of foliation and pagination, viz. fos. 1–119, pp. 120–174, fos. 175–215, pp. 216–243, fos. 244–302, pp. 303–456, fo. 457, pp. 458–463, fos. 464–543; blank: fos. 487–532; modern binding, incorporating former parchment covers.

1–486	general acts Mar. 1607–Mar. 1628
533–540	17th-cent. index
541–543 (reversed)	miscellaneous licences July 1611–Mar. 1612

BI, Inst. AB.5. Paper register; 11½″ × 7½″; pp. xii + 656, paginated up to 220; one section (pp. 25–32) is lacking; modern binding.

The section 1619–28 is nearly identical with the appropriate section of Inst. AB.4. The arrangement of the entries for Montaigne's and Harsnett's pontificates is somewhat confused.

v–ix	17th-cent. index
1–220	Mar. 1619–Sept. 1630 (+ isolated entry July 1632)

A modern typescript list of institutions and ordinations 1616–27, taken from the subscription books but not included in the institution act books is BI, Add. MS. 167.

BI, Inst. AB.6. paper register; 13½″ × 9″; pp. 450, paginated up to 425; modern binding, incorporating former parchment covers.

1–293	general acts Apr. 1632–Oct. 1640
293–301	general acts June 1642–May 1644
302–425	general acts Oct. 1660–May 1668

17th-cent. index, in pocket at end of volume.

CARLISLE

Repositories

1. Cumbria County Record Office, The Castle, Carlisle CA3 8UR (CRO).
2. Borthwick Institute, University of York, St Anthony's Hall, York YO1 2PW (BI).
3. Minster Muniment Room, Minster Library, Dean's Park, York YO1 2JD (YM).

Area

The diocese of Carlisle comprised a single archdeaconry and covered most of what later became the county of Cumberland (except for the two parishes of Alston and Upper Denton in the Durham diocese and the deanery of Copeland in the archdeaconry of Richmond and diocese of York) and the eastern part of Westmorland. The ecclesiastical divisions of the diocese have been described by Canon Wilson.[1]

Bibliographical Note

The losses among the Carlisle episcopal registers have been considerable. In the period under review, there are three composite volumes extant, covering the years 1293–1347, 1352–92 and 1561–1643. The physical arrangement of the surviving registers is generally chronological, although Bishop Appleby's is more confused than the others. Registration certainly began at Carlisle before Bishop Halton's time (1292–1324), since the register of his predecessor, Ralph Ireton (1280–92), was still in existence in 1566 but had disappeared by 1613.[2] Thanks to the efforts of Canons Wilson, Ferguson and Lowther Bouch, it has been possible to find references to registers of Bishops Strickland (1400–19), Lumley (1429–50), Scrope (1464–8) and Oglethorpe (1556–9), unfortunately all now lost.[3]

The survival of several diocesan account rolls between 1401 and 1529 (CRO, DRC/2/7–25) helps to fill a few gaps caused by the loss of the episcopal registers of this period. Certain accounts include a note of fees paid by individual incumbents on institution and there are also occasional references to synodals, payments for licences, *littere questuarie* and the like, and correction and probate fees.[4]

Vacancy jurisdiction was exercised by the archbishops of York and entries relating to their *sede vacante* administration are to be found in the archiepiscopal registers, and occasionally in a Carlisle register. It should also be remembered that from time to time the York registers will contain acts relating to suffragan sees performed by the archbishops *ratione visitationis*.

The two earliest Carlisle registers were described in the ninth report of the Historical Manuscripts Commission and selected abstracts given.[5] Before this date, the two notable historians of the area, Joseph Nicolson and Richard Burn, had made extensive use of the surviving

[1] *VCH Cumberland* ii (1905), pp. 117–24 and map facing p. 126. C. M. Lowther Bouch, *Prelates and People of the Lake Counties: a history of the diocese of Carlisle 1133–1933* (Kendal, 1948), pp. 15–16, prints a list of medieval parishes in the diocese taken from the 1291 papal taxation. For maps of the diocese see the frontispiece to R. S. Ferguson, *Diocesan Histories: Carlisle* (London, 1889); and Ordnance survey, *Map of Monastic Britain* (*north sheet*) (2nd edn., 1955).

[2] J. Wilson, 'The bishop's lost registers', *Carlisle Patriot*, 15 June 1894, p. 5.

[3] In addition to Canon Wilson's contribution in the preceding footnote, see also his book, *Rose Castle; the residential seat of the bishops of Carlisle* (Carlisle, 1912), p. 165 and app. xv, p. 223; R. S. Ferguson, 'An attempt to trace the missing episcopal registers of the see of Carlisle', *Transactions of the Cumberland and Westmorland Antiquarian and Archaeological Society*, 7 (1884), 295–9; C. M. Lowther Bouch, 'The muniments of the diocese of Carlisle', *ibid.*, new series, 46 (1946), 174–90.

[4] For a description of these account rolls, see C. R. Davey, 'Early diocesan accounts at Carlisle', *Journal of the Society of Archivists*, 3 (1965–9), 424–5.

[5] *Historical Manuscripts Commission: Ninth Report* (1883), app., pp. 178–96.

registers in their history of Cumberland and Westmorland, including the compilation of lists of incumbents.[6] Wills which are entered in the registers between 1353 and 1386 have been edited by Canon Ferguson.[7]

VACANCY 1278–1280

BI, Reg. 3 (register of Archbishop William Wickwane), fos. 49*r–v*, 133*r–v* (partial duplicate but the latter has more entries).[8]

Carlisle vacancy business Nov. 1279–July 1280

Printed, *The register of William Wickwane, lord archbishop of York, 1279–1285*, ed. W. Brown (Surtees Society 114, 1907), nos. 544–6.

VACANCY 1292

BI, Reg. 4 (register of Archbishop John le Romeyn), fo. 135*v*.

Carlisle vacancy business Apr.–June 1292

Printed, *The registers of John le Romeyn, lord archbishop of York, 1286–1296, part II, and of Henry of Newark, lord archbishop of York, 1296–1299*, ed. W. Brown (Surtees Society 128, 1917), nos. 1373–6.

JOHN DE HALTON (1292–1324)
JOHN ROSS (1325–1332)
JOHN KIRKBY (1332–1352)

CRO, DRC/1/1. Parchment register; 12″ × 7½″ (very variable) (fos. 1–121); 12″ × 8½″ (fos. 122–291); fos. ii+269+iv, foliated [i–ii], 1–144, 146–192, 192A, 193, 195, 196, 198–212, 113–118 (*sic*), 219–256, 272, 277–291; blank: fo. 72*v*; leather binding (now loose).

This composite volume contains the registers of Bishops Halton and Kirkby and a fragment of the register of Bishop Ross. The arrangement within each register is approximately chronological, and ordinations are recorded in the general sequence. A noteworthy feature of Halton's register is the practice of recording the presentation deeds to benefices, rather than the more usual letters of institution or memorandum of the act of institution. Occasionally, letters of presentation and institution are found registered together but, in general, presentations predominate for the earlier part of the episcopate and from about 1313 onwards are replaced by letters of institution. The more accepted practice is followed in Ross's and Kirkby's registers. The last entry in Halton's register, a record of ordinations celebrated in June 1324 (fo. 121*v*), is incomplete and presumably there were additional folios containing a note of further episcopal acts until the bishop's death in November. The one surviving quire from Ross's register, covering entries from late 1330 to the beginning of 1332, is bound in after the first quire of Kirkby's. The record of the last years of Kirkby's pontificate, including the period of the Black Death, is missing. From time to time the bishops of Carlisle held ordinations on behalf of other English diocesan bishops, and these ordinations are entered in this register in the regular sequence. They are noted in detail under the appropriate diocese.

1*r*–121*v*	register of Bishop John de Halton general acts Mar. 1293–June 1324
122*r*–129*v*, 141*r*–256*v*	register of Bishop John Kirkby general acts July 1332–May 1347
130*r*–140*r*	register of Bishop John Ross (one quire) general acts Dec. 1330–Jan. 1332
272*r–v*	list of benefices in the diocese, arranged by deanery, with a note of spiritual payments and pensions payable to the bishop

[6] J. Nicolson and R. Burn, *The history and antiquities of Westmorland and Cumberland* (2 vols, London, 1777).

[7] *Testamenta Karleolensia: the series of wills from the prae-Reformation registers of the bishops of Carlisle, 1353–1386*, ed. R. S. Ferguson (Cumberland and Westmorland Antiquarian and Archaeological Society, extra series 9, 1893).

[8] See under York for a description of this and subsequent archiepiscopal and capitular registers.

277*r*–291*v* rentals of episcopal manors, arranged by place (the date referred to throughout is *anno domini etc. xxix*, i.e. 1329, in the time of Bishop Ross)

Halton's register (fos. 1*r*–121*v*) is printed, *The register of John de Halton, bishop of Carlisle A.D. 1292–1324*, ed. W. N. Thompson (2 vols, Canterbury and York Society 12–13, and Cumberland and Westmorland Antiquarian and Archaeological Society, record or chartulary series 2, 1913). A modern transcript of part of Kirkby's register (fos. 122*r*–180*v*) is in the possession of the Canterbury and York Society.

VACANCY 1324–1325

BI, Reg. 9B (register of Archbishop William Melton), fos. 588*r*–591*r*.

Carlisle vacancy business Oct. 1324–Sept. 1325

Printed, *The register of William Melton, archbishop of York, 1317–40, vol. I*, ed. R. M. T. Hill (Canterbury and York Society 70, 1977), nos. 249–67.

VACANCY 1332

BI, Reg. 9B (register of Archbishop William Melton), fos. 596*r*–597*r*.

Carlisle vacancy business May–July 1332

Printed, *ibid.*, nos. 302–11.

[JOHN HORNCASTLE (1352)]
GILBERT WELTON (1353–1362)
THOMAS APPLEBY (1363–1395)

CRO, DRC/1/2. Parchment register; 12½″ × 8½″ (pp. [i–ii]), 13½″ × 9½″ (pp. [iii–xiv], 1–367); fos. ii + 244 + ii, paginated [i–xiv],. 1–187, 189–222, 222(2), 222(3), 223–343, 348–473; no blanks; leather binding.

This is a composite volume and both Welton's and Appleby's registers still retain their previous foliation from the time they were separate volumes. In both cases, the arrangement is approximately chronological (exceptions are noted below), the only development being the separation of ordinations from the general sequence. In Welton's register a start is made with annual headings at the beginning of each year but this practice soon lapses. In spite of the statement in the Historical Manuscripts Commission report (9th Report, p. 191) that pages 105–24 of the register occur where they do because of a binding fault, it has become obvious that this single quire does not fit into the sequence of the general register (1–104) but on the other hand is not a duplicate (I have only noted one identical entry in both). The quire does indeed include a number of royal writs, *littere questuarie* and commissions, but by no means exclusively, and the only immediate conclusion to be drawn (pending more detailed work on this individual register) is that for some reason, either by design or circumstance, two separate registers were kept for a period. Between 1363 and the early 1370s the arrangement of Appleby's register is at times chronologically confused, presumably indicating the late registration of the material, since there is no evidence of misbinding nor of any deliberate division of the register into category sections, with the solitary exception of ordinations. Episcopal and vicarial acts (when they occur) are entered in one general sequence. Two leaves have been cut out between pages 343 and 348, creating lacunae in the entries between Dec. 1382 and June 1384.

[i–ii] register of John Horncastle, bishop-elect
 general acts Feb.–Apr. 1353
[ii] one institution performed by Welton's vicar-general Feb. 1354
[iii–xiv] table of contents of Welton's register (using obsolete foliation)
1–128 register of Bishop Gilbert Welton
 1–104 general acts July 1353–Nov. 1362 (on p. 104 a copy of a document relating to Horncastle church, Lincs., 1344)
 105–124 general acts (see note above) July 1353–Aug. 1357
 125–128 ordinations Mar. 1354–Dec. 1361

129–140 diocesan statutes (attributed to Bishop Robert de Chaury and dated 1258 × 1259) [with the addition on p. 140 of a copy of a final concord, 17 Edward II]

141–367 register of Bishop Thomas Appleby

141–265 general acts Aug. 1363–Sept. 1375

266–283 ordinations Dec. 1363–Sept. 1388

284–367 general acts Oct. 1375–Dec. 1392

Pages 368–473 contain a collection (in a variety of medieval hands and folio sizes) of legal texts, including legatine and provincial canons. As this section does not form an integral part of the preceding episcopal registers, it has not been described in detail.

For the identification of the diocesan statutes (129–40), see *Councils and synods with other documents relating to the English Church, II*, ed. F. M. Powicke and C. R. Cheney (2 vols, Oxford, 1964), *part 1* (*1205–1265*), pp. 626–30. Some of the chapters are printed here and for others almost identical with statutes attributed to Wells and York, see *ibid.*, pp. 586–626.

VACANCY 1395–1396

BI, Reg. 14 (register of Archbishop Thomas Arundel), fos. 77*r*–81*v*.

Carlisle vacancy business Dec. 1395–Feb. 1396

VACANCY 1399–1400

BI, Reg. 16 (register of Archbishop Richard Scrope), fos. 150*v*–151*v*.

Carlisle vacancy business Jan.–Aug. 1400

VACANCY 1462

BI, Reg. 20 (register of Archbishop William Booth), fos. 357*v*–359*r*.

Carlisle vacancy business Apr.–Oct. 1462

VACANCY 1463–1464

BI, Reg. 20 (register of Archbishop William Booth), fos. 359*r*–360*v*.

Carlisle vacancy business Nov.–Dec. 1463

VACANCY 1507–1508

1. BI, Reg. 5A (York vacancy register), fos. 606*r*–608*v*.

   Carlisle vacancy business Sept. 1507–Nov. 1508

2. YM, H3/2 (duplicate of York vacancy register), fos. 36*v*–37*v*.

   Carlisle vacancy business (as above but incomplete, lacking one folio) Sept. 1507–Aug. 1508

VACANCY 1521

BI, Reg. 27 (register of Archbishop Thomas Wolsey), fos. 134*r*–136*v*).

Carlisle vacancy business June–July 1521

VACANCY 1559–1561

BI, Inst. AB. 1 (institution act book 1545–54, 1558–68), fo. 79*r*.

Carlisle vacancy act Dec. 1560 (1 entry)

JOHN BEST (1561–1570)
RICHARD BARNES (1570–1577)
VACANCY 1577
JOHN MAY (1577–1598)
VACANCY 1598
HENRY ROBINSON (1598–1616)
ROBERT SNOWDEN (1616–1621)
RICHARD MILBOURNE (1621–1624)
RICHARD SENHOUSE (1624–1626)
FRANCIS WHITE (1626–1629)
BARNABAS POTTER (1629–1642)
VACANCY 1642
JAMES USSHER (1642–1656)

CRO, DRC/1/3. Paper register; 15½" × 10½"; pp. 332, paginated [i–vi], [1, 2], 3–317, [318–326]; blank: pp. [ii–vi, 1, 2], 90, [318–326]; leather binding.

The contents of this composite volume are in approximate chronological order, the bulk of the entries being institutions, collations and ordinations. There is relatively little material for the episcopates of Francis White and James Ussher. In connection with the exercise of patronage *pro hac vice*, the earlier grants of next presentation are also normally copied into the register. All but two of the episcopal registers (May and Ussher) have individual headings and between 1579 and 1602 the change of year is also noted. BI, Inst. AB. 2, part iii (institution act book 1568–72), fos. 68*v*–69*r*, contains a *sede vacante* institution, May 1570. BI, Inst. AB. 3 (institution act book 1572–1619) contains one institution *sede vacante* for each of the vacancies of 1577 (fo. 110*r*, Aug. 1577) and 1598 (fo. 297*v*, Feb. 1598).

[i]	heading and list of bishops whose acts are contained in the register
3–29	register of Bishop John Best general acts Sept. 1561–Mar. 1570
30	note of the translation of Bishop Barnes
31–86	register of Bishop Richard Barnes general acts Aug. 1570–Apr. 1577
87–88	vacancy institution by the archbishop of York, Aug. 1577 (1 entry)
88–89	2 grants of next presentation and caveats Oct.–Nov. 1577 and a note of Bishop May's election and consecration
91–206	register of Bishop John May general acts Dec. 1577–Feb. 1598
206	vacancy institution by the archbishop of York June 1598 (1 entry)
206–241	register of Bishop Henry Robinson general acts Nov. 1598–Mar. 1615
242–251	register of Bishop Robert Snowden general acts Mar. 1617–June 1620
252–262	register of Bishop Richard Milbourne general acts Dec. 1622–May 1624
262–269	register of Bishop Richard Senhouse general acts Dec. 1624–Mar. 1626
269–271	register of Bishop Francis White general acts Apr.–June 1627

271–307 register of Bishop Barnabas Potter
general acts Sept. 1629–Dec. 1641
308–309 vacancy commission by the vicar-general of the archbishop of York Jan. 1642
309–317 register of Bishop James Ussher
general acts Feb. 1642–Nov. 1643

VACANCY 1616

BI, Inst. AB. 3 (institution act book 1572–1619), fos. 451*r*–454*r* (inserted among York diocesan entries).

Carlisle vacancy business July–Oct. 1616

VACANCY 1621

1. BI, Inst. AB. 5 (institution act book 1619–32), pp. 47–9 (inserted among York diocesan entries).

Carlisle vacancy business May–Sept. 1621

2. BI, Inst. AB. 4 (institution act book 1607–28), fos. 286*v*–292*r* (inserted among York diocesan entries).

Copy of above.

VACANCY 1626

1. BI, Inst. AB. 5, pp. 150, 153.

Carlisle vacancy business June–July 1626

2. BI, Inst. AB. 4, pp. 455–6, 461.

Copy of above.

CHESTER

Repositories

1. Cheshire Record Office, The Castle, Chester CH1 2DN (Ch. RO).
2. Borthwick Institute, University of York, St Anthony's Hall, York YO1 2PW (BI).

Area

The diocese of Chester was created in 1541 by the union of the archdeaconries of Chester and Richmond, severed respectively from the dioceses of Lichfield and York. The area covered by the new diocese was thus Cheshire, Lancashire, Copeland deanery in Cumberland, the western part of Westmorland, Richmondshire in Yorkshire and a few parishes in the counties of Denbigh and Flint.[1] The bishopric was originally placed within the province of Canterbury but by act of Parliament of 1542 (33 Henry VIII, c. 31) was transferred to the province of York.

Bibliographical Note

The first register was begun before the creation of the diocese. As a result of arrangements with the bishops of Lichfield, the pre-1541 archdeacons of Chester had powers in matters of probate, the cognizance of office and instance cases and the exercise of corrective jurisdiction within the archdeaconry.[2] This earliest volume is basically a register of wills and inventories and sentences in matrimonial cases, the expected presentations and institutions being entered in the supplementary act books. The register also contains copies of compositions and of earlier documents, and the foundation deed and statutes of a school. The second register, which begins in 1579, contains in addition to the probate material and matrimonial sentences, consecrations, commissions and orders, patents of office, deeds, agreements, sequestrations, and notes of fees and valuations. The volumes are approximately chronological in arrangement, although there are additional entries here and there.[3] The act books of presentations and institutions begin in 1541 but there is a section containing copies of Lichfield acts relating to benefices in the Chester archdeaconry, 1502–13, sewn into the first volume. Ordinations are recorded in separate registers. All these volumes are also generally arranged in chronological sequence. Some of the probate material in the registers has been published, as is noted below, and lists of incumbents have been abstrated from the act books by several local historians.[4] After 1542, *sede vacante* jurisdiction was exercised by the archbishops of York and the York registers and act books contain some material for most vacancies in this period.

JOHN BIRD (1541–1554)
GEORGE COTES (1554–1555)
CUTHBERT SCOTT (1556–1559)

[1] For a map of the original diocese of 1541, see the frontispiece to R. H. Morris, *Diocesan histories: Chester* (London, 1895).

[2] For details of this jurisdiction, see P. Heath, 'The medieval archdeaconry and Tudor bishopric of Chester', *Journal of Ecclesiastical History* 20 (1969), 243–52.

[3] E.g., the latest entry I have located in the second register, for March 1647, relating to the parliamentary surveyors of the bishopric, is to be found on fo. 226*v*.

[4] G. Ormerod, *The history of the county palatine and city of Chester* . . . (3 vols, 1819); J. P. Earwaker, *East Cheshire: past and present or a history of the hundred of Macclesfield in the county palatine of Chester from original records* (2 vols, London, 1877–80); E. Baines, *The history of the county palatine and duchy of Lancaster* (2 vols, Manchester 1824); T. D. Whitaker, *History of Richmondshire* (2 vols, London, 1823); R. Richards, *Old Cheshire Churches* (London, 1947).

WILLIAM DOWNHAM (1561–1577)

Ch. RO, EDA. 2/1. Paper register; 16″ × 10½″; fos. iv (loose) + 502, foliated 1–3, 7–430, 430A, 431–461 (+12 blank fos.), 462, 463 (+8 blank fos.), 464–485 (412, 415 merely small fragments); blank: fos. 2*v*, 3*v*, 7*v*, 32*r*, 36*v*, 37*r*, 46*v*, 51*r–v*, 59*v*, 455*v*, 456*r*, 462*r*, 464*r*, 467*r–v*, 475*r–v*, 485*r–v*; no covers.

i*r*–iv*v*	18th-cent. index
1*r*–484*v*	general register Mar. 1525–Mar. 1575

Fos. 412–485 are now detached from the rest of the volume and were bound in pasteboard in the 18th century. EDA. 2/1a is a 17th-century table of contents (fos. 15, loose, 12¼″ × 8″). The wills transcribed into this and the second register are indexed in *An index to the wills and inventories now preserved in the court of probate at Chester from A.D. 1545 to 1620*, comp. J. P. Earwaker (Lancashire and Cheshire Record Society 2, 1879), pp. xi–xix. Some of the wills and inventories are also printed in *Lancashire and Cheshire wills and inventories from the ecclesiastical court, Chester*, ed. G. J. Piccope (3 vols, Chetham Society, old series, 33, 51, 54, 1857–61).

VACANCY 1559–1561

BI, Inst. AB. 1 (institution act book 1545–54, 1558–68), fos. 62*v*, 73*v*, 78*r*.[5]

Chester vacancy business Mar.–Nov. 1560

For a few institutions performed during the royal visitation of 1559, see *The Royal Visitation of 1559: act book for the Northern Province*, ed. C. J. Kitching (Surtees Society 187, 1975), pp. 58–61; and for additional vacancy material see below, EDA. 1/1.

VACANCY 1577–1579

1. BI, Reg. 31 (register of Archbishop Edwin Sandys), fos. 49*r*–60*v*.

   Chester vacancy business (including formal record of election and consecration of new bishop) Dec. 1577–Oct. 1579

2. BI, Inst. AB. 3 (institution act book 1572–1619), fos. 114*r*–136*v* (inserted among York diocesan material).

   Chester vacancy business Jan. 1578–Oct. 1579 (for the most part a duplicate of the appropriate section of 1)

WILLIAM CHADERTON (1579–1595)
HUGH BELLOTT (1595–1596)
RICHARD VAUGHAN (1597–1604)
GEORGE LLOYD (1604–1615)
THOMAS MORTON (1616–1619)
JOHN BRIDGEMAN (1619–1652)

Ch. RO, EDA. 2/2. Paper register; 14¾″ × 10½″; fos. vi (18th-cent. index) + 359, foliated i–x, 1–106, 112, 114–129, 131–168, 168[A], 169–191, 191[A], 192–260, then paginated 261–307, then foliated 308–380; blank: fos. i*v*, v*v*, viii*r*–ix*v*, x*v*, 4*v*, 27*r–v*, 32*r–v*, 35*r*, 38*r*–39*v*, 45*r–v*, 51*v*, 81*v*, 86*v*, 91*v*, 100*r*, 106*v*, 112*r–v*, 114*r–v*, 129*v*, 151*v*, 162*v*, 184*v*, 259*r*; leather covers (loose).

i*r*	heading of register
ii*r*–vii*v*	17th-cent. table of contents
1*r*–380*v*	general register Nov. 1579–Mar. 1647

EDA. 2/2a is a 17th-century index (fos. 3, first one missing, loose, 12″ × 7½″). See under the notes to the first register for the printed index of probate material contained in the volume and the published edition of selected wills and inventories. The so-called Bishop Bridgeman's Register or Ledger (Ch. RO, EDA. 3/1) is a compilation of documents relating to the Chester diocese and not a working register.

[5] See under York for a description of this and later act books and registers containing Chester material.

VACANCY 1595

BI, Inst. AB. 3 (institution act book 1572–1619), fo. 174*v*.

Chester vacancy business (1 entry) May 1595

VACANCY 1596–1597

BI, Inst. AB. 3, fos. 286*v*–293*v* (inserted among York diocesan material).

Chester vacancy business Aug. 1596–July 1597

VACANCY 1615–1616

1. BI, Inst. AB. 3 (institution act book 1572–1619), fos. 441*r*–450*v* (inserted among York diocesan entries).

   Chester vacancy business Aug. 1615–July 1616

2. BI, Inst. AB. 4 (institution act book 1606–27), fo. 104*r*–p. 133 (*sic*) (inserted among York diocesan material)

   Chester vacancy business as above, but with one additional entry

VACANCY 1619

1. BI, Inst. AB. 3, fos. 502*v*–503*r*.

   Chester vacancy business (2 entries) Mar. 1619

2. BI, Inst. AB. 5 (institution act book 1619–32), pp. 1–3 (inserted among York diocesan material).

   Chester vacancy business (continuation of above), Mar.–May 1619

3. BI, Inst. AB. 4, pp. 216–232 (inserted among York diocesan material).

   Chester vacancy business as above in 1 and 2

ACT BOOKS AND ORDINATIONS REGISTERS

Ch. RO, EDA, 1/1. Parchment register (except for final section); $16\frac{3}{4}'' \times 12\frac{1}{2}''$ (fos. i–ii, 7–9, 11–52); $14\frac{3}{4}'' \times 5\frac{1}{4}''$ (fos. 1–6); 12″ × 8″ (final section, paper, [i], 1–8). This volume consists of three separate sections, namely: fos. i+47, foliated i–ii, 7–9, 11–52; fos. 6, foliated 1–6; fos. 9 (final section), foliated [i], 1–8 (also referred to as 53–60, [i] being ignored in this numbering); blank: fos. ii*r*–*v*, 17*r*–*v*, 21*r*–*v*, 31*v*, 32*r*–*v*, 34*r*–*v*, 36*r*–*v*, 38*v*, 40*v*, 43*v*, 46*v*, 47*r*, 52*v*, [final section], [i*r*–*v*], 4*v*–5*v*; modern binding (covers loose).

i*r*–*v*	17th-cent. index
1*r*–6*v*	copies of acts of Bishops Arundel and Blyth of Lichfield and the vicar-general *sede vacante* relating to admissions to benefices in the Chester archdeaconry May 1502–Feb. 1513
7*r*–52*r*	general acts, diocese of Chester Dec. 1541–Feb. 1561
1*r*–8*v* (53*r*–60*v*)	general acts July 1569–Dec. 1576

There is a little business for the 1559–61 vacancy, not the same material as in the York act book. For other *sede vacante* material, see above. A partial 19th-century calendar covering entries 1542–76 is among the Fergusson Irvine collection, Ch. RO, DFI/162, pp. 169–76.

Ch. RO, EDA. 1/2. Paper register (extensively repaired); 12″ × 8″; fos. 89, foliated 2, 5, 6, 9–31, 33–95; blank: fos. 10*r*–*v*, 14*v*, 16*r*, 17*v*, 18*v*, 22*r*, 24*r*, 25*v*, 28*r*, 29*r*, 31*r*, 35*v*, 40*r*–*v*, 42*r*, 43*v*, 44*r*, 45*v*, 47*v*, 48*v*, 50*r*, 57*v*, 58*r*, 59*v*, 60*v*, 61*v*, 63*v*, 68*v*, 69*r*, 70*v*, 71*v*, 72*v*, 73*v*, 77*v*, 79*v*, 82*v*, 83*r*–*v*, 86*r*, 87*r*, 93*v*; modern binding (guarded and filed).

2*r*–95*v*	ordinations register [Easter?] 1542–Dec. 1547, Easter 1555–Sept. 1558

Printed, 'The earliest ordination book of the diocese of Chester, 1542–7 and 1555–8', ed. W. F. Irvine in *Miscellanies relating to Lancashire and Cheshire* iv (Lancashire and Cheshire Record Society 43, 1902), pp. 25–126. Since publication, fos. 1, 3 (blank), 4, 7 (blank), 8 (blank), 32, 96, 97, 98, 99, 100, 101 (blank), 102 (blank), 103 (blank), 104 (blank) have been lost. The register originally continued up to Dec. 1558.

Ch. RO, EDA. 1/3. Paper register (damaged by damp); 12¼″ × 8″; fos. 41 (some loose), foliated 1–41; blank: fos. 5*r*, 9*v*, 10*r*, 16*v*; limp parchment covers.

1*r*–41*v*	ordinations register [April] 1562–Mar. 1611

The April 1562 entry is the first datable ordination, although there is a fragment of an earlier ordination. At least one other folio once existed, only a loose fragment of which now survives. There are also occasional loose documents (letters, a list of ordinands) to be found in the volume. EDA. 3/2, known as Bishop Bridgeman's Act Book, is primarily a court book containing a record of office and correction causes and also occasional licences, probate acts, notes of commutations of penance and sequestrations, July 1626–Oct. 1634, July 1661–May 1685. It also contains occasional ordinations.

Ch. RO, EDA. 1/4. Paper register (repaired); 16½″ × 11½″ (fos. 1–87, 137–213, 221–227); 12″ × 8″ (fos. 89–134); 12¼″ × 8″ (fos. 214–220); fos. (first part) 174, numbered (some inserts included in the numbering sequence, others ignored) pp. 1–14, fos. 1–87, 134–165, 167–213, 221–[227] (not numbered after 219); (second part) fos. 50, foliated (some blanks not numbered) 89–91, 91A, 92–97 (+2 blank fos.), 98–101 (+2 blank fos.), 102–111 (+ 1 blank fo.), 112–131, 133; blank (numbered): fos. 22*v*, 23*r*–*v*, 91A*r*–*v*, 92*v*, 97*v*, 118*v*, 122*r*–134*v*, 135*r*–136*v*, 139*v*, 140*r*–*v*, 143*v*, 156*v*, 157*v*, 161*v*–164*r*, 167*v*, 168*v*, 169*v*, 170*v*, 171*v*–188*r*, 203*v*–204*v*, 206*v*–213*v*, 215*r*–*v*, 218*v*, 219*v*–[227*v*]; modern binding.

pp. 1–4	18th-cent. index of places
1*r*–87*r*	general acts Nov 1579–June 1644
89*r*–121*v*	miscellaneous benefices matters (notes, some institutions, copies of certified lists of institutions, etc.) Apr. 1598–Nov. 1634
137*r*–171*r*	general acts Nov. 1660–July 1686
188*v*–203*r*	caveats Aug. 1583–Aug. 1644
205*r*–206*r*	caveats Oct. 1661–Oct. 1676
214*r*–219*r*	miscellaneous benefice matters (mostly caveats, sequestrations) Oct. 1604–Oct. 1678 (much loose material sewn in)

A copy of the certificate of institutions returned to the barons of the Exchequer for Oct. 1638–Apr. 1640 is also to be found among the diocesan archives (Ch. RO, EDA. 1/5—fos. 4, unnumbered, 12″ × 7½″). A partial 19th-century calendar covering entries 1579–1601 is in the Fergusson Irvine collection, Ch. RO, DFI/162, pp. 177–82.

DURHAM

Repositories

1. Department of Palaeography and Diplomatic, University of Durham:
   a) The Prior's Kitchen, The College, Durham DH1 3EQ, Durham dean and chapter muniments (DPK).
   b) South Road, Durham DH1 3LE, Durham diocesan records (DSR).
   It is expected that the diocesan records will be moved to new premises at 5, The College, Durham, in 1981.
2. Dean and Chapter Library, The College, Durham DH1 3EH (DCL).
3. Borthwick Institute, University of York, St Anthony's Hall, York YO1 2PW (BI).
4. Public Record Office, Chancery Lane, London WC2A 1LR (PRO).
5. Minster Muniment Room, Minster Library, Dean's Park, York YO1 2JD (YM).

Area

The medieval diocese of Durham comprised two archdeaconries—Durham and Northumberland[1]—and extended over the counties which eventually gave them their territorial titles. In addition, the diocese included Crayke (an enclave of county Durham surrounded by the North Riding of Yorkshire), part of Girsby in the North Riding itself and the Cumberland parishes of Alston and Upper Denton. Within the diocesan boundaries was the archbishop of York's liberty of Hexhamshire. Outside the counties of Durham and Northumberland, the bishop (and the cathedral priory) possessed the extensive ecclesiastical franchises of Allertonshire and Howdenshire in Yorkshire. The ecclesiastical divisions of Durham and Northumberland have been described by Dr Hadcock,[2] and the Durham peculiars by Professor Barlow.[3]

Bibliographical Note

Of the medieval dioceses of the northern province, only York can boast an impressive survival rate for its registers and although Durham has fared slightly better than Carlisle in this respect, the number of extant episcopal registers is still disappointingly small. Of the pre-Reformation bishops, only the registers of Kellaw, Hatfield, Langley and Fox and fragments of Bury's survive.[4] There are occasional tantalising references to indicate the extent of the losses. Bek (1283–1311) is certainly known to have kept a register[5] and later references confirm that registers once existed for Lewis de Beaumont (1318–33), John Fordham (1382–8) and Walter Skirlaw (1388–1406).[6] Mr Martin Snape of the Prior's Kitchen, Durham, has kindly

[1] For the evolution of these archdeaconries, see H. S. Offler, 'The early archdeacons in the diocese of Durham', *Transactions of the Architectural and Archaeological Society of Durham and Northumberland* 11 (1958–65), 189–207.

[2] R. N. Hadcock, 'Map of mediaeval Northumberland and Durham', *Archaeologia Aeliana*, 4th series, 16 (1939), 148–218. The ecclesiastical divisions of Durham are also described in *VCH Durham* ii (1907), pp. 76–7. For a map of the diocese see the frontispiece to J. L. Low, *Diocesan Histories: Durham* (London, 1881); and also Ordnance Survey, *Map of Monastic Britain: (north and south sheets)* (2nd edn., 1954–5).

[3] F. Barlow, *Durham Jurisdictional Peculiars* (Oxford, 1950), pp. 53–115 (for the Yorkshire franchise). See also K. Emsley, 'The Yorkshire enclaves of the bishops of Durham', *Yorkshire Archaeological Journal*, 47 (1975), 103–8.

[4] A brief list of the Durham registers was produced in typescript by the Department of Palaeography and Diplomatic of Durham University in 1964 (revised in 1977).

[5] The mention of a register of Bishop Hugh (DPK, Reg. Hatfield, fo. 43*r*, *inspecto registro bone memorie Hugonis dudum Dunelmensis episcopi*) must also in fact refer to Bek, since the extract is dated 1294. Presumably Hugh was written in error for Antony. See also Public Record Office, C269/5/19 for a further reference.

[6] DPK, Reg. Hatfield, fo. 40*r* (Beaumont); Registrum III, fos. 234*v*–235*r* (Fordham); Registrum II, fos. 30*r*, 322*v*, 325*r*; and Cartuarium I, fo. 116*r* (Skirlaw). All the Skirlaw references relate to ordinances concerning hospitals and a collegiate church. I am most grateful to Mr Martin Snape for allowing me to consult his notes on lost Durham registers.

drawn my attention to an interesting document (DPK, Miscellaneous charter 6795), a parchment roll of one membrane containing apparently contemporaneous copies of twelve acts of Bishop Robert Stichill (1261–74), the dated material belonging to 1261, some of it issued before his consecration. The entries primarily relate to bonds and receipts and the appointment of proctors, but in addition to secular business it does include some ecclesiastical material, such as an ordination respecting the division of the revenues of a parish church. Whether this membrane can be taken to indicate some scheme of registration for Stichill's episcopate is not at all certain.

The physical arrangement of the surviving registers varies from episcopate to episcopate. The later volumes, for Fox and the sixteenth- and seventeenth-century bishops, are arranged in approximate chronological order without further subdivision. Langley's register, too, adopts a chronological arrangement but the vicars-general's acts are kept separate. This does not seem to have been the case in earlier times (episcopal and vicarial acts are found recorded together), but on the whole the fourteenth-century registers were divided into rudimentary sections, according to the type of business or the tenure of office of certain diocesan officials, and these divisions are described in more detail in the appended handlist. It will be noted that Kellaw's register, for example, includes business concerning the bishop's secular franchise. Nevertheless, the many records in the Public Record Office and at Durham relating exclusively to the administration of the palatinate have been considered to be outside the scope of this descriptive list and are not included here.[7]

The right to administer the vacant diocese of Durham was the source of much friction and legal contention between the northern metropolitan and Durham priory and, in the event of a double vacancy at York and Durham, between the two cathedral chapters. The history of this controversy from the time of the 1286 compromise down to the 1939 vacancy has not been neglected by modern historians and it is only necessary to refer to their work.[8] Of the administrative records at York relating to Durham vacancies there is comparatively little for the thirteenth century. A solitary Durham institution by Archbishop Gray is recorded in the course of the 1237–41 vacancy[9] and two institutions by Archbishop Giffard in 1274,[10] but it is not until the time of Giffard's successor, William Wickwane (1279–85), that a separate *Officialitas Dunelmensis sede vacante* section appears in the York registers. While occasionally there are such separate vacancy divisions, more often than not *sede vacante* business is to be found in the regular suffragan section of the registers, alongside other material for Carlisle and Durham *sede plena* (Convocation business, consecrations of bishops etc.).[11]

Of the extant Durham episcopal registers between 1311 and 1577, Hatfield's alone is unpublished. An index of persons and places named in Kellaw's register was printed as an appendix to the thirtieth annual report of the Deputy Keeper of the Public Records in 1869 and between 1873 and 1878 the register was published in the Rolls Series. In the sixty years from 1910 editions of the later registers have appeared among the Surtees Society's publications.

[7] For the Durham palatinate, see G. T. Lapsley, *The county palatine of Durham: a study in constitutional history* (New York, 1900); J. Scammell, 'The origin and limitations of the liberty of Durham', *English Historical Review* 81 (1966), 449–73, and the appropriate sections of G. V. Scammell, *Hugh du Puiset, bishop of Durham* (Cambridge, 1956); C. M. Fraser, *A History of Antony Bek, bishop of Durham, 1283–1311* (Oxford, 1957); and R. L. Storey, *Thomas Langley and the bishopric of Durham, 1406–1437* (London, 1961). The records in London are described in the *Guide to the contents of the Public Record Office* i (London, 1963), pp. 177–9, and *Lists of records of the palatinates of Chester, Durham and Lancaster, honour of Peveril, and principality of Wales* (Public Record Office lists and indexes xl, 1914), pp. 30–51. The Department of Palaeography and Diplomatic of Durham University has also issued several duplicated lists of palatinate material in its custody.

[8] See R. Brentano, *York metropolitan jurisdiction and papal judges delegate (1279–1296)* (Berkeley, 1959), especially pp. 109–74, and his earlier article, 'Late medieval changes in the administration of vacant suffragan dioceses: province of York', *Yorkshire Archaeological Journal* 38 (1952–5), 496–503; R. B. Dobson, *Durham priory, 1400–1450* (Cambridge, 1973), pp. 218–22. In the fifteenth century a record was compiled noting the procedure followed by the cathedral priory in the vacancies of 1274, 1283, 1311, 1316–18, 1333 and 1381. It has been printed by Professor Brentano, 'The *Jurisdictio Spiritualis*: an example of fifteenth-century English historiography', *Speculum* 32 (1957), 326–32.

[9] *The register, or rolls, of Walter Gray, lord archbishop of York: with appendices of illustrative documents*, ed. J. Raine (Surtees Society 56, 1872), no. cccxxviii.

[10] *The register of Walter Giffard, lord archbishop of York, 1266–1279*, ed. W. Brown (Surtees Society 109, 1904), nos. 890–1.

[11] Photocopies of most of the York-registered vacancy material listed below are available at the Prior's Kitchen. Of course the Howdenshire and Allertonshire sections of the York registers contain relevant Durham material.

Before this time, however, considerable use had been made of the registers by antiquaries. Indeed, the fact that one fragment of Bury's register has come down to us at all, albeit in transcript, is due solely to the work of Dr Christopher Hunter (1675–1757). Later historians of the locality, William Hutchinson, Robert Surtees and James Raine, have all made extensive use of the registers in their publications.[12] Lists of Durham parish clergy continuing up to the Reformation have been printed by Rev. D. S. Boutflower[13] and this volume has been supplemented by R. Donaldson's Edinburgh University Ph.D. thesis (1955), 'Patronage and the church: a study in the social structure of the secular clergy in the diocese of Durham (1311–1540)', in particular the second volume (Durham benefices and their incumbents 1311–1540). There is an annotated copy of this volume in the Prior's Kitchen.

VACANCY 1283

BI, Reg. 3 (register of Archbishop William Wickwane), fos. 49*v*, 145*r* (duplicate).[14]

Durham vacancy business Aug. 1283

Printed, *The register of William Wickwane, lord archbishop of York, 1279–1285*, ed. W. Brown (Surtees Society 114, 1907), nos. 544–6.[15]

ANTONY BEK (1283–1311)

A register of Bishop Bek was still in existence in 1428 when Bishop Langley inspected it in connection with Bek's statutes for the collegiate church of St Andrew, Auckland, issued in 1293 (*The register of Thomas Langley, bishop of Durham, 1406–1437*, ed. R. L. Storey, iii (Surtees Society 169, 1959), no. 782). Dr C. M. Fraser has made a collection of administrative documents emanating from or received by Bek's chancery (*Records of Antony Bek, bishop and patriarch, 1283–1311* (Surtees Society 162, 1953)). Bishop Halton of Carlisle ordained clergy on behalf of Bek in 1294 and the list of ordinands is entered in his register (*The register of John de Halton, bishop of Carlisle, A.D. 1292–1324*, ed. W. N. Thompson, i (Canterbury and York Society 12, 1913), pp. 23–5).

VACANCY 1311

1. BI, Reg. 7 (register of Archbishop William Greenfield), fos. 336*r*–347*r*.

   Durham vacancy business Mar.–[June] 1311

   Printed, *The register of William Greenfield, lord archbishop of York, 1306–1315*, ed. W. Brown and A. Hamilton Thompson, v (Surtees Society 153, 1940), nos. 2513–50.

2. BI, Reg. 8A & B (for description see under York).

   Archiepiscopal visitation of the Durham diocese *sede vacante*

RICHARD KELLAW (1311–1316)

PRO, Durham 3/1. Parchment register; $13\frac{1}{4}'' \times 9\frac{1}{2}''$ (average fos. 1–253), $13\frac{1}{2}'' \times 9\frac{1}{2}''$ (average fos. 254–333), $13\frac{3}{4}'' \times 9\frac{1}{2}''$ (fos. 334–345); fos. ii (paper)+324+12 (19th-cent. index)+ii (paper), foliated 1–345 (this new foliation includes inserts and replaces the foliation used in the printed edition. In the following

[12] W. Hutchinson, *The history and antiquities of the county palatine of Durham* (3 vols, Newcastle, 1785–94); R. Surtees, *The history and antiquities of the county palatine of Durham* (4 vols. London, 1810–40); J. Raine, *The history and antiquities of North Durham* ... (London, 1852) and also his editions, *Wills and inventories* ... (Surtees Society 2, 1835); *Depositions and other ecclesiastical proceedings from the courts of Durham extending from 1311 to the reign of Elizabeth* (Surtees Society 21, 1845). His son and namesake also used the Durham registers in *Historical papers and letters from the northern registers* (Rolls Series, 1873), as does the more recent *A history of Northumberland* (Northumberland County History Committee, 15 vols, Newcastle, 1893–1940).

[13] *Fasti Dunelmenses: a record of the beneficed clergy of the diocese of Durham down to the dissolution of the monastic and collegiate churches* (Surtees Society 139, 1926).

[14] See under York for a description of this, and later registers, containing Durham material.

[15] For Wickwane's attempt to hold a visitation of the Durham diocese *sede plena* and the ensuing conflict, see R. Brentano, *York metropolitan jurisdiction*, pp. 115–47.

descriptive note and in section 3 of Bury's register, the new foliation is placed first and this is followed by the equivalent foliation used in the edition); leather binding.

Kellaw's register takes up the first 253 folios of this volume and can be divided into several distinct sections. The first of these (fos. 1*r*–147*v*/1*r*–171*v*) is a general, chronological register of acts concerning the spiritualities of the see and originally comprised sixteen numbered quires, the second (once obsolete foliation 11–20) and fifth (once obsolete foliation 41–50) of which are now missing. The pontifical year of the bishop is frequently noted at the top of the folio, as also in subsequent parts of the register. This section has been described by a fifteenth-century scribe as *registrum communium litterarum* (fo. 147*v*/171*v*) but this is not a strictly accurate description. Kellaw's register contains institutions, collations, etc. as well as miscellaneous letters and if a comparison is made with Hatfield's register (see below), it will be seen that in reality this first part of Kellaw combines both the *de communibus litteris* and the *de beneficiis* sections of the latter volume. The second part of the Kellaw volume is a register of royal writs, entitled *quaterni brevium* (*regis*) (fos. 148*r*–196*v*/172*r*–219*v*); the third section (fos. 197*r*–230*r*/220*r*–265*r*) *quaterni cartarum*, dealing with palatinate and secular business of the bishop. The next section (fos. 231*r*–248*v*/266*r*–283*v*) is of a very miscellaneous nature and includes copies of earlier documents, chiefly relating to secular matters. The final section of this part of the register is the *antiqua taxatio* of the diocese (fos. 249*r*–253*v*/284*r*–288*v*). The remainder of the volume contains a fragment of Bishop Bury's register (see below) and one leaf (fo. 333*r*/367*r*) with entries concerning the consecration of Alexander Neville as archbishop of York (1374) and the presentation of the pallium.

Printed, *Registrum Palatinum Dunelmense*, ed. T. D. Hardy (4 vols, Rolls Series, 1873–8), i, ii and iii, pp. 1–105. An index of persons and places named in the register was first published in the *30th Annual Report of the Deputy Keeper of the Public Records* (1869), appendix 3, pp. 99–120.

VACANCY 1333

BI, Reg. 9B (register of Archbishop William Melton), fos. 597*v*–601*v*.

Durham vacancy business Sept. 1333–Jan. 1334

Printed, *The register of William Melton, archbishop of York, 1317–40, vol. I*, ed. R. M. T. Hill (Canterbury and York Society 70, 1977). nos. 314–47.

RICHARD BURY (1333–1345)

Two original fragments of Bishop Bury's register survive, together with a late seventeenth- or early eighteenth-century transcript of another short section, now lost. The most substantial fragment is bound up with Richard Kellaw's register, and shows evidence of subdivisions similar to the arrangement found later in Hatfield's register. There are two quires of ordinations 1334–40 (fos. 262*r*–273*r*/297*r*–308*r*) and 1341–5 (fos. 254*r*–261*v*/289*r*–296*v*), and the remainder of the fragment seems to begin as a general register and then approximates to Hatfield's *de communibus litteris* and *de beneficiis* sections, although there is some slight cause for uncertainty here and there is not always a strict adherence to these category divisions. Following the ordinations is a register *tempore* John de Wytcherche, vicar-general, 1338–44 (fos. 274*r*–304*r*/309*r*–339*r*); despite the register heading on fo. 274*r*/309*r*, it is clear that Wytcherche was not Bury's vicar-general for the whole period covered by the register. This part also includes secular estate material in addition to the normal entries relating to the spiritualities. A folio or folios are lacking before fo. 302*r*/337*r*. There is some chronological confusion in the arrangement of this section and up to 1340 it is in the nature of a general chronological register and includes many *de beneficiis* entries (institutions, collations, induction mandates and so on). From 1340 to 1345 there are two separate *quaterni beneficiorum* (fos. 305*r*–324*v*/340*r*–358*v*) which contain later material of such a nature. Another section (fos. 325*r*–331*v*/359*r*–365*v*), less easy to classify, contains many formal documents (appeals, protests, agreements), licences, letters and commissions, covering the period 1340–2. It is most akin to the *de communibus litteris* section but, if so, it is uncertain why these entries were not included in the register *tempore* Wytcherche, as a strict distinction between episcopal and vicarial acts does not appear to have been observed at this time. The Bury fragment bound with Kellaw's register concludes with one folio (fo. 332*r*–*v*/266*r*–*v*) of a register *tempore* William Legat, presumably vicar-general or diocesan chancellor (see below under Hatfield), 1342–3.

1. DPK, bound up at the beginning of Bishop Hatfield's register (no class reference); 13½″ × 9½″; fos. 8, foliated i-viii.

Fragment of a register Sept. 1343–May 1344

Printed, *Richard d'Aungerville of Bury: fragments of his register and other documents*, ed. G. W. Kitchin (Surtees Society 119, 1910), pp. 22–64.

2. DCL, Hunter ms. 132*, fos. 1*r*–11*v*.

Transcripts of entries from lost fragment of a register Jan.–Apr. 1343

Printed, *ibid.*, pp. 10–21.

3. PRO, Durham 3/1, fos. 254*r*–332*v* (for description see Kellaw above).

Fragment of a register July 1338–Apr. 1345 and a record of ordinations Mar. 1334–Mar. 1345.

Printed, *Registrum Palatinum Dunelmense* iii, pp. 106–523. The headings of documents contained in this register are also printed in *Richard d'Aungerville of Bury*, pp. 65–84.

A record of those ordinations performed between 1334 and 1340 by Bishop John Kirkby of Carlisle, acting on behalf of Bishop Bury, is also to be found in his Carlisle register (Cumbria Record Office, Carlisle, DRC/1/1, fos. 148*v*, 157*v*–158*v*, 163*v*, 182*v*–183*r*, 211*r*). The lists are by no means always identical.

VACANCY 1345

1. BI, Reg. 10 (register of Archbishop William Zouche), fos. 282*v*–284*v*.

Durham vacancy business Apr.–June 1345

2. BI, Reg. 10A (ordination register of Archbishop William Zouche), fos. 10*v*–12*v*.

Ordinations of Durham clergy *sede vacante* May 1345 (sections for Durham clergy in regular York ordination)

THOMAS HATFIELD (1345–1381)

DPK (no class reference). Parchment register; 13½″ × 9½″ (fos. i–viii), 13¾″ × 9½″ (average fos. 1–179); fos. i (paper) + viii + 183 + iii (18th-cent. index), foliated i–viii, 1–110, 110A, 111–146, 146*, 147–159, 159*, 160, 160*, 161–179; blank: fos. 6*v*, 50*v*, 110A*v*; modern binding.

Hatfield's register is incomplete as far as a continuous record of administrative acts is concerned, material other than ordinations lacking for his first five years as bishop and there being a further gap between 1355 and 1359. Except for the section recording ordinations of clergy, the rest of Hatfield's register seems to be divided up chronologically by the tenure of office of the diocesan chancellors. For instance, the heading on fo. 7*r* reads: *[R]egistrum domini Thome dei gratia Dunelmensis episcopi de tempore magistri Iohannis Grey cancellarii incipiens xxii die mensis Septembris anno domini millesimo trecentesimo quinquagesimo secundo*. The heading on the first section (fo. 1*r*) is all but illegible and the third section (fo. 39*r*) lacks a heading altogether but I think it is clear that the cancellarial division is being adhered to throughout the four extant sections. Within two of these sections, there is a further subdivision, *de beneficiis* (containing institutions, collations, exchanges, resignations, presentations, various licences, etc.) and *de communibus litteris*, somewhat akin to an expanded diverse letters section of the York archiepiscopal registers, containing general memoranda, commissions, letters testimonial, some probate material, royal writs, appropriations and ordinations of churches, licences for oratories, entries relating to criminous clerks and so on. Occasionally, there is some overlapping of the two categories and the registry clerks were not consistent about the registration of certain business—licences for non-residence, for example, are to be found in both subdivisions.

i*r*–viii*v*	Richard Bury's register (see above)	
1*r*–6*r*	[heading illegible][16]	
	general acts Sept. 1350–Jan. 1352 (some chronological confusion, one additional entry July 1361)	
7*r*–38*v*	Register *tempore* John Grey, chancellor	
	7*r*–26*v*	[*De communibus litteris*] Sept. 1352–May 1355
	27*r*–38*v*	*Quaternus beneficiorum* Sept. 1352–May 1355

[16] William Legat occurs as diocesan chancellor on fo. 2*v* and received a commission to act as vicar-general on fo. 3*v*; perhaps this is his section of the register. For Legat, see also Bury above.

39*r*–79*v*	[no heading, but clearly a new section] 39*r*–50*v* *De communibus litteris* Nov. 1359–Oct. 1373 51*r*–79*v* *De beneficiis* Dec. 1359–Oct. 1375 (The chronological sequence of institutions etc. is interrupted on fo. 68*v* where three later entries have been inserted in the gap left before a lengthy record of court proceedings against William of Beverley, archdeacon of Northumberland, who was accused of killing a man, 1370–1 (fos. 69*r*–75*v*), the latter entry itself being somewhat of an interpolation in this section.)
80*r*–91*v*, 114*r*–179*v*	Register *tempore* John Maundour, chancellor general acts Nov. 1375–May 1380 (A bifolium (85–86) containing acts Oct. 1376–Sept. 1377 is interpolated. The last entry on fo. 84*v* is continued on fo. 87*r*. Likewise the final entry on fo. 91*v* continues on fo. 114*r*, the ordinations section having been erroneously inserted between them.)
92*r*–113*v*	ordinations Sept. 1345–May 1380 (last ordination incomplete)

Abstracts and transcripts from Hatfield's register have been made by Professor A. Hamilton Thompson and are deposited at the Prior's Kitchen.

VACANCY 1381–1382

BI, Reg. 12 (register of Archbishop Alexander Neville), fos. 113*v*–115*r*.

Durham vacancy business May 1381–Jan. 1382

There also seems to have been a separate Durham vacancy register and a roll recording the archiepiscopal visitation of the diocese *sede vacante*, both now lost. The register is last mentioned in 1423, the roll in 1405 (D. M. Smith, 'Lost archiepiscopal registers of York: the evidence of five medieval inventories', *Borthwick Institute Bulletin*, i no. 1 (1975), 34–5).

VACANCY 1406

The see of York was also vacant on this occasion and Durham custodians *sede vacante* were appointed by the cathedral priory of Durham.

1. DPK, Miscellaneous charter 5723. Paper register; 11½″ × 8½″; fos. 7, foliated 1–7; modern binding.

   Durham vacancy business Mar.–Aug. 1406

2. DPK, 1.12. Pont. 6. Paper roll of 3 membranes; 45¾″ × 11½″; no endorsements.

   Durham vacancy record as above but not completely identical with it, only eight entries being registered. From the amount of cancellation and emendation, this would seem to be a draft record.

3. DPK, Cartuarium III, part 2, fos. 145*r*–150*v* (for description, see Davis no. 329).

   Identical copy of 2. There is a gap in the foliation of this section of the volume between 145 and 148, but this is due to misnumbering and not evidence of a missing part.

THOMAS LANGLEY (1406–1437)

1. DPK (no class reference). Parchment register; 13″ × 9¾″; fos. iii (paper) + iv (18th-cent. index) + i (17th-cent. title) + 299 + i + iv + iii (paper), foliated (excluding endpapers, index and title) 1–25, 27–30, 32–47, 49–129, 132–167, 167A, 168–226, 229–304 (some folios missing, other gaps due to misnumbering); leather binding.

The volume can be divided into the bishop's register (fos. 1*r*–257*r*) and the register of Langley's vicars-general (fos. 258*r*–304*v*). The arrangement within both these sections is chronological. The latter register has been bound out of sequence and the editor of the printed edition has provided a revised order for the folios.

Printed, *The register of Thomas Langley, bishop of Durham, 1406–1437*, ed. R. L. Storey (6 vols, Surtees Society 164, 166, 169, 170, 177, 182, 1956–70).

2. The editor of the register also points out a reference to a paper register of the bishop (*The register of Thomas Langley* ii, pp. 76–7). It has not chanced to survive and apart from this solitary reference, its contents are uncertain.

3. DPK, Registrum Parvum II (Prior's letter book 1407–35), fos. 1*r*–7*r*.

These initial folios include acts of the prior of Durham, John Hemingburgh, acting as vicar-general of Bishop Langley, Mar. 1407–Mar. 1408.

VACANCY 1437–1438

BI, Reg. 19 (register of Archbishop John Kempe), fos. 489*r*–503*v*.

Durham vacancy business Nov. 1437–Apr. 1438

Visitation material on fos. 491*r*–495*r* is printed by A. Hamilton Thompson in *Miscellanea* ii (Surtees Society 127, 1916), pp. 221–38.

VACANCY 1457

BI, Reg. 20 (register of Archbishop William Booth), fos. 351*r*–357*v*.

Durham vacancy business July 1457–Feb. 1459 (later material dealing with the goods of the late Bishop Neville)

VACANCY 1483–1485

BI, Reg. 23 (register of Archbishop Thomas Rotherham), fos. 192*r*–193*r*.

Durham vacancy business [Apr. 1484]–Apr. 1485

Printed, *The register of Thomas Rotherham, archbishop of York, 1480–1500, vol. I*, ed. E. E. Barker (Canterbury and York Society 69, 1976), nos. 1485–90.

VACANCY 1493–1494

BI. Reg. 23 (register of Archbishop Thomas Rotherham), fos. 194*r*–197*r*.

Durham vacancy business Feb. 1493–Feb. 1494

Printed, *ibid.*, nos. 1491–1508.

RICHARD FOX (1494–1501)

DSR, I.1. Parchment register (heavily repaired); 15¼″ × 13″; fos. iv (paper) + 41 + i (paper), foliated 1–19, 25–46; cardboard covers, with leather spine.

The register is arranged chronologically and the change of year is noted in the text. The year is also given at the top of the folio. There is a gap in the foliation and indeed the ordination list beginning on fo. 25*r* is incomplete.

Printed, *The register of Richard Fox, lord bishop of Durham, 1494–1501*, ed. M. P. Howden (Surtees Society 147, 1932).

VACANCY 1501–1502

BI, Reg. 25 (register of Archbishop Thomas Savage), fos. 142*v*–160*r*.

Durham vacancy business Oct. 1501–Oct. 1502

Printed, *The injunctions and other ecclesiastical proceedings of Richard Barnes, bishop of Durham from 1575 to 1587*, ed. J. Raine (Surtees Society 22, 1850), app. I, pp. i–xl.

VACANCY 1505–1507

1. DPK, Priory register V, fos. 85*r*–91*v*.

   Durham vacancy business (acts of the prior and convent of Durham) Sept.–Oct. 1507

   The record of the diocesan synod on fos. 88*r*–89*v* is printed, *Historiae Dunelmensis Scriptores Tres*, ed. J. Raine (Surtees Society 9, 1839), app. no. cccxvi, pp. cccciii–ccccvii.

2. BI, Reg. 5A (York vacancy register), fos. 574*r*–577*r*.

   Durham vacancy business Oct.–Nov. 1507

3. YM, H3/2 (another contemporaneous copy of the York vacancy register), fos. 22*v*–24*r*.

   Durham vacancy register (as above, 2)

   A ms. calendar and index of 3 is in YM, H3/2a.

VACANCY 1508–1509

BI, Reg. 26 (register of Archbishop Christopher Bainbridge), fos. 91*r*–93*r*.

Durham vacancy business Dec. 1508–June 1509

VACANCY 1523

BI, Reg. 27 (register of Archbishop Thomas Wolsey), fos. 137*r*–138*v*.

Durham vacancy business Feb.–Apr. 1523

CUTHBERT TUNSTALL (1530–1559)
VACANCY 1559–1561
JAMES PILKINGTON (1561–1576)
VACANCY 1576–1577

DSR, I.2. Parchment register (decayed at lower edge); $15\frac{1}{2}'' \times 12\frac{1}{2}''$; fos. i (paper) + 78 + i (paper), foliated i, 1–77; cardboard covers, with leather spine.

The arrangement of the register is, as to be expected, approximately chronological and the entries of the bishops and vacancies follow on without any gap. There is some occasional misplacing of entries. The bulk of the register relates to Tunstall (fos. 1*r*–54*r*, 56*r*, 74*v*–77*r*) and there are indications that the section devoted to Pilkington's acts (fos. 56*v*–72*v*, 73*v*) was once foliated separately. The vacancy entries for 1559–61 are on fos. 53*v*, 54*v*–55*v*, and three entries relate to the vacancy of 1576–7 (fos. 72*v*–73*r*), but for other *sede vacante* material issued on this latter occasion, see below. There is one isolated entry of Bishop Richard Barnes (fo. 74*r*).

Printed, *The registers of Cuthbert Tunstall, bishop of Durham, 1530–59, and James Pilkington, bishop of Durham, 1561–76*, ed. G. Hinde (Surtees Society 161, 1952), nos. 1–379 (Tunstall), 380–401 (1559–61 vacancy), 402–536, 540 (Pilkington), 537–9 (1576–7 vacancy), 541 (Barnes). One Durham vacancy entry (July 1560) is to be found in BI, Inst. AB. 1 (institution act book 1545–54, 1558–68), fos. 70*v*–71*r*.

VACANCY 1576–1577

1. BI, Reg. 31, fos. 1*v*–2*r* (being part of the York vacancy register, both sees being vacant) and fo. 39*r* (register of Archbishop Edwin Sandys).

   Durham vacancy business of the dean and chapter of York Feb.–Mar. 1576 (fos. 1*v*–2*r*) and one institution by the archbishop Mar. 1577 (fo. 39*r*, repeated in BI, Inst. AB. 3, fo. 106*r*–*v*).

2. DPK, act book *sede vacante* 1576. Paper register (some damp staining); 12″ × 8″; fos. 9, unfoliated; blank: fos. [1*r*–*v*, 6*r*–*v*, 7*v*, 9*r*–*v*]; modern binding.

   Acts of the dean and chapter of Durham *sede vacante*

[2*r*–4*v*]	administrations Mar.–May 1576
[5*r*–*v*]	diocesan synod May 1576
[7*r*, 8*r*]	institutions and induction mandates Mar. 1576
[8*v*]	note of compromise between the churches of Durham and York over vacancy jurisdiction, arranged by Henry, earl of Huntingdon

   For further information on the dispute between the York and Durham cathedral chapters on this occasion, see C. Cross, *The Puritan earl: the life of Henry Hastings, third earl of Huntingdon, 1536–1595* (London, 1966), p. 250.

3. For three vacancy entries Nov. 1576–Feb. 1577, see above, DSR, I.2, fos. 72*v*–73*r*, printed, *The registers of Tunstall and Pilkington*, nos. 537–9.

RICHARD BARNES (1577–1587)

1. DSR, I.3. Parchment register; 15½″ × 11″; fos. 22, foliated 1–22; cardboard covers, with leather spine.

   1*r*–22*v* general acts, arranged chronologically May 1577–June 1587

   Ordinations are noted (usually only the number of ordinands given) in *The injunctions and other ecclesiastical proceedings of Richard Barnes, bishop of Durham, from 1575 to 1587*, ed. J. Raine (Surtees Society 22, 1850), app. ix, pp. xcviii–cii.

2. DPK, act book *coram episcopo* 1581–2. Paper register; 12¼″ × 8¼″; fos. 18, foliated 1–18; blank: fos. 9*v*–18*v*; modern binding.

   Between fos. 2*r* and 9*r* are included institutions and resignations, July 1581–Apr. 1582. Most of these entries are recorded in the bishop's register.

RICHARD NEILE (1617–1628)
JOHN HOWSON (1628–1632)
THOMAS MORTON (1632–1659)
JOHN COSIN (1660–1672)

DSR, I.4. Paper register (decayed at lower edge); 14″ × 9¼″ (fos. 105–108 have been inserted and are smaller in size, 13¼″ × 8½″); pp. viii + 140, numbered pp. [i–viii], 1–102, fos. 103–121; blank: p. [viii], fo. 121*v*; cardboard covers, with leather spine.

The sequence of entries is approximately chronological, although the later folios of this volume are particularly confused in arrangement and the confusion is compounded by the abrupt changeover from pagination to foliation and the probable transposition of folios in binding (fos. 109, 111). Apart from an isolated interpolation of the time of John Howson (pp. 15–17), the first five-sixths of the register record the acts of Bishop Neile. The remainder of the volume includes material relating to the episcopates of Howson, Morton and Cosin, and even two entries belonging to the pontificate of Nathaniel Crewe (1674–1724). Except for a record of Cosin's institutions to benefices 1660–3, inserted in the volume (fos. 105–108), there are only occasional entries for these later bishops.

pp. [i–viii]	index
pp. 1–15, 18–fo. 104*v*	acts of the time of Richard Neile Mar. 1618–Dec. 1627

pp. 15–17. fos. 104*v*, 110*r*–*v*	acts of the time of John Howson June 1629–Mar. 1632
fos. 109*r*–*v*, 111*r*–116*v*, 118*v*, 120*r*–121*r*	acts of the time of Thomas Morton June 1634–Apr. 1652
fos. 105*r*–108*v*, 117*r*–118*r*, 119*r*–*v*	acts of the time of John Cosin Dec. 1660–Oct. 1663
fo. 116*r*	2 acts of the time of Nathaniel Crewe Sept.–Oct. 1683

BI, Inst. AB. 5 (institution act book 1619–32), p. 196, contains a record of one collation performed by the custodian of the spiritualities of York and Durham, both sees being vacant, June 1628. BI, Reg. 32 (register of Archbishop Richard Neile), fo. 55*v*, contains a copy of an archiepiscopal inhibition sent to the dean and chapter of Durham, the see being vacant, and the certificate of its execution, Apr.–May 1632.

SODOR AND MAN

The diocese of Sodor and Man, or the Isles, was placed under the metropolitical authority of the archbishop of Trondheim (Nidaros) in the mid-twelfth century, having apparently recognised the archbishop of York as metropolitan before this time.[1] Two separate successions of bishops, for Sodor and Man, and the Isles, exist from the time of the Great Schism and from a bull of Pope Calixtus III directed to Archbishop William Booth of York in 1458, it is evident that the bishop of Man was considered to be a suffragan of the archbishop of York.[2] By an Act of Parliament of 1542 (33 Henry VIII, c. 31) the see was annexed to the northern ecclesiastical province. No episcopal registers exist for the diocese (the later diocesan records are deposited at the Manx Museum Library, Kingswood Grove, Douglas, Isle of Man), and the only record of York *sede vacante* administration that I have located relates to the vacancy of 1633–4.[3]

[1] For the claims of Trondheim and York in the medieval period, see A. Ashley, *The Church in the Isle of Man* (St Anthony's Hall Publications 13, York, 1958); D. E. R. Watt, *Fasti Ecclesiae Scoticanae Medii Aevi ad annum 1638* (St Andrews, 1968), pp. 197–202.

[2] Borthwick Institute, Reg. 21 (register of Archbishop Booth), fo. 369*r*; *Monumenta de insula Manniae* ..., ed. J. R. Oliver, iii (Manx Society 9, 1862), pp. 20–3.

[3] Borthwick Institute, Inst. AB. 6 (institution act book 1632–68), p. 49 (institution of the archdeacon of Sodor, Jan. 1634).

INDEX

Abbreviations are used for archbishop (archbp.), archdeacon (archdn.) and bishop (bp.). Pre-1974 counties are noted with place-names.